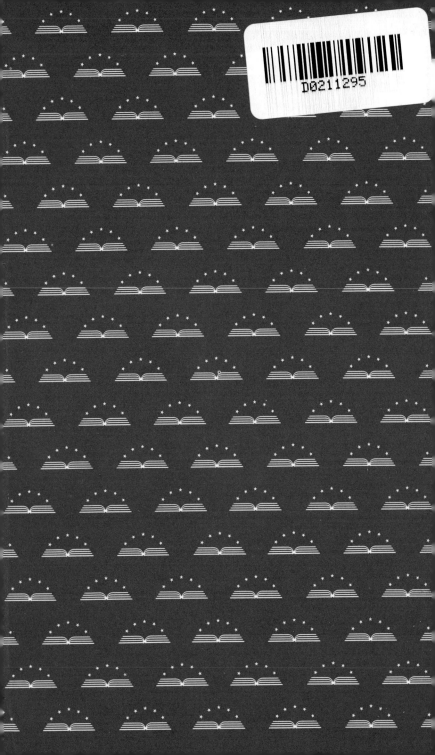

REPORTING WORLD WAR II
PART ONE

REPORTING WORLD WAR II

PART ONE

AMERICAN JOURNALISM 1938–1944

THE LIBRARY OF AMERICA

Some of the material in this volume is reprinted with permission of the
holders of copyright and publications rights. Acknowledgments can be
found on page 869. Cartography on pages 831–47 © Richard Natkiel, 1995.

The paper used in this publication meets the
minimum requirements of the American National Standard for
Information Sciences—Permanence of Paper for Printed
Library Materials, ANSI Z39.48—1984.

Distributed to the trade in the United States
by Penguin Books USA Inc
and in Canada by Penguin Books Canada Ltd.

Library of Congress Catalog Number: 94–45463
For cataloging information, see end of Index.
ISBN: 1–883011–04–3

First Printing
The Library of America–77

Manufactured in the United States of America

Contents

"It's All Over"

by William L. Shirer

MUNICH, *September 30*

It's all over. At twelve thirty this morning—thirty minutes after midnight—Hitler, Mussolini, Chamberlain, and Daladier signed a pact turning over Sudetenland to Germany. The German occupation begins tomorrow, Saturday, October 1, and will be completed by October 10. Thus the two "democracies" even assent to letting Hitler get by with his Sportpalast boast that he would get his Sudetenland by October 1. He gets everything he wanted, except that he has to wait a few days longer for *all* of it. His waiting ten short days has saved the peace of Europe—a curious commentary on this sick, decadent continent.

So far as I've been able to observe during these last, strangely unreal twenty-four hours, Daladier and Chamberlain never pressed for a single concession from Hitler. They never got together alone once and made no effort to present some kind of common "democratic" front to the two Cæsars. Hitler met Mussolini early yesterday morning at Kufstein and they made their plans. Daladier and Chamberlain arrived by separate planes and didn't even deem it useful to lunch together yesterday to map out their strategy, though the two dictators did.

Czechoslovakia, which is asked to make all the sacrifices so that Europe may have peace, was not consulted here at any stage of the talks. Their two representatives, Dr. Mastny, the intelligent and honest Czech Minister in Berlin, and a Dr. Masaryk of the Prague Foreign Office, were told at one thirty a.m. that Czechoslovakia would *have* to accept, told not by Hitler, but by Chamberlain and Daladier! Their protests, we hear, were practically laughed off by the elder statesman. Chamberlain, looking more like some bird—like the black vultures I've seen over the Parsi dead in Bombay—looked particularly pleased with himself when he returned to the Regina Palace Hotel after the signing early this morning, though he was a bit sleepy, *pleasantly* sleepy.

Daladier, on the other hand, looked a completely beaten and broken man. He came over to the Regina to say goodbye to Chamberlain. A bunch of us were waiting as he came down the stairs. Someone asked, or started to ask: "*Monsieur le President*, are you satisfied with the agreement? . . ." He turned as if to say something, but he was too tired and defeated and the words did not come out and he stumbled out the door in silence. The French say he fears to return to Paris, thinks a hostile mob will get him. Can only hope they're right. For France has sacrificed her whole Continental position and lost her main prop in eastern Europe. For France this day has been disastrous.

How different Hitler at two this morning! After being blocked from the Führerhaus all evening, I finally broke in just as he was leaving. Followed by Göring, Ribbentrop, Goebbels, Hess, and Keitel, he brushed past me like the conqueror he is this morning. I noticed his swagger. The tic was gone! As for Mussolini, he pulled out early, cocky as a rooster.

Incidentally, I've been badly scooped this night. Max Jordan of NBC got on the air a full hour ahead of me with the *text* of the agreement—one of the worst beatings I've ever taken. Because of his company's special position in Germany, he was allowed exclusive use of Hitler's radio studio in the Führerhaus, where the conference has been taking place. Wiegand, who also was in the house, tells me Max cornered Sir Horace Wilson of the British delegation as he stepped out of the conference room, procured an English text from him, rushed to the Führer's studio, and in a few moments was on the air. Unable to use this studio on the spot, I stayed close to the only other outlet, the studio of the Munich station, and arranged with several English and American friends to get me the document, if possible immediately after the meeting itself, if not from one of the delegations. Demaree Bess was first to arrive with a copy, but, alas, we were late. New York kindly phoned about two thirty this morning to tell me not to mind—damned decent of them. Actually at eleven thirty p.m.

I had gone on the air announcing that an agreement had been reached. I gave them all the essential details of the accord, stating that the occupation would begin Saturday, that it would be completed in ten days, et cetera. But I should have greatly liked to have had the official text first. Fortunately for CBS, Ed Murrow in London was the first to flash the official news to America that the agreement had been signed thirty minutes after midnight. He picked it up from the Munich radio station in the midst of a talk.

LATER.—Chamberlain, apparently realizing his diplomatic annihilation, has pulled a very clever face-saving stunt. He saw Hitler again this morning before leaving and afterwards a joint communiqué was issued. Essential part: "We regard the agreement signed last night and the Anglo-German naval accord as symbolic of the desire of our two peoples never to go to war with one another again." And a final paragraph saying they will consult about further questions which may concern the two countries and are "determined to continue our efforts to remove possible sources of difference and thus to contribute to the assurance of peace in Europe."

LATER. *On Train, Munich—Berlin.*—Most of the leading German editors on the train and tossing down the champagne and not trying to disguise any more their elation over Hitler's terrific victory over Britain and France. On the diner Halfeld of the *Hamburger Fremdenblatt*, Otto Kriegk of the *Nachtausgabe*, Dr. Boehmer, the foreign press chief of the Propaganda Ministry, gloating over it, buying out all the champagne in the diner, gloating, boasting, bragging. . . . When a German feels big he feels *big*. Shall have two hours in Berlin this evening to get my army passes and a bath and then off by night train to Passau to go into Sudetenland with the German army—a sad assignment for me.

Berlin Diary, 1941

"Peace"—And the Crisis Begins

by Dorothy Thompson

> *'Perhaps the pacifist-humane idea is quite a good one in cases where the man at the top has first thoroughly conquered and subdued the world to the extent of making himself the sole master of it.'*—Adolf Hitler, in 'Mein Kampf.'

WHAT happened on Friday is called 'Peace.' Actually it is an international Fascist *coup d'état*.

The 'Four-Power Accord' is not even a diplomatic document. It is certainly not a normal treaty. It is such a fantastic piece of paper that it is difficult to describe except as a hurriedly concocted armistice made in advance of a war to permit the occupation by German troops of a territory which by sheer threat and demonstration of force they have conquered by 'agreement.'

All of the territory where there are more than fifty per cent of German-speaking peoples will be evacuated by the Czechoslovaks and occupied by the German Army within ten days, although there are hundreds of thousands of people in this territory who are either not German or are anti-Nazi and therefore constitute a racial and political minority.

This document provides no protection whatsoever for their lives, their properties or their existences.

Not a clause indicates that they are to be protected in any manner from this occupation.

Those of us who know and have seen what the Nazi authorities do to political minorities realize that this can only result in a panicky flight into the interior of Czechoslovakia. It means the open establishment of terror.

No consideration is paid anywhere in this fantastic document to the reapportionment of financial and industrial in-

4

terests—banks or industries the ownership of which is not necessarily on the spot—and this in spite of the fact that the British and French governments know that in the occupation of Austria the property of political minorities, and in particular of Jews, was simply confiscated.

There is not the most elementary consideration of justice.

An international commission will determine further territories in which a plebiscite is to be held, and will fix the conditions.

This will give plebiscites in areas containing more than fifty per cent Czechs, although no plebiscites will be held in areas containing more than fifty per cent Germans.

The pressure of the Nazis in contiguous territories occupied by German troops, their immense and cunningly organized propaganda, their house-by-house and name-by-name political organization; the ever-present threat that if the territories go German the political minorities will be exterminated, will assure the outcome of these plebiscites. *One might just as well cede them to Germany in the first place.*

Czechs and political minorities are given the right of option in and out of the ceded territories, but they must move within six months, and the conditions for exercising the option are left to a German-Czechoslovak commission. Which simply means that they are left to the Germans, considering the relative power position.

Compared with this the Treaty of Versailles is a great humane document and a normal and reasonable treaty.

The Treaty of Versailles allowed German nationals incorporated in the then new Czechoslovak state to opt for German nationality. They were given two years in which to make a decision and then twelve months in which to exercise it—three years in all—and the treaty guaranteed their right to retain ownership of their landed property in the territory of the state that they left, guaranteed their right to carry with them movable property of every description and prohibited the imposition of any export or import duties to be made upon them in connection with the removal of such property.

We know that the political minorities in Austria since the Nazi occupation have not been allowed to move anything, and that the property left behind by those who fled was confiscated in the form of an 'emigration tax,' a treatment of property usually described as Bolshevism.

The Treaty of Versailles was made after five months of deliberations, into which scores of experts were called—as experts and not as partisans.

But on Friday Czechoslovakia was disposed of by four men who in four hours made a judgment of the case in which the defendant was not even allowed to present a brief or be heard.

The very basis and spirit of Anglo-Saxon law was violated. What ruled that conference was Nazi law. Not one of the four men who thus arbitrarily disposed of a nation had ever set foot in Czechoslovakia, nor did any of them understand the other's language—except Mussolini. They had a German interpreter. They decided on the primary basis of a report issued by a man who also until two months ago had never spent any time at all in Czechoslovakia.

Furthermore, Lord Runciman's Report, though it recommends the ceding of the territories to Germany, categorically denies that the Germans had ever been 'terrorized,' fixes the blame for the failure of negotiations on the Germans, states that at the time of his arrival many Sudetens still desired to remain in Czechoslovakia and accuses the Sudeten extremists, egged on by Germany, of provoking the demonstrations which, on the German side, were made an excuse for demanding armed occupation.

Even on the basis of what by internal evidence would seem to be a rigged report, Germany is guilty of provoking what was nearly an all-European war. And the punishment for this guilt is that she received everything that she was going to fight the war over.

This 'everything' is more than the Sudeten territories. It is more than a free hand in the east. It is the domination of Europe.

In this whole affair, described as an attempt to keep peace, the democratic process has been completely suspended. In both Britain and France the facts have been suppressed by the exercise of government pressure on the controlled radio and on the newspapers. The people of England and France are confronted with a *fait accompli* without even being able to gain in advance possession of the facts on which it is based.

The Runciman Report was published the day before the *fait accompli!*

Not only is Czechoslovakia dismembered—what is left is destroyed as a democratic republic. *It will be utterly impossible for the new state to exist, under the conditions created, as anything except a military and semi-Fascist dictatorship. There will be no civil liberties. There will be enforced labor. There must be—in order to save the nation at all!*

Let us not call this peace. Peace is not the absence of war. Peace is a positive condition—the rule of law.

This peace has been established on lawlessness, and can only maintain itself by further lawlessness.

This peace has been established by dictatorship, and can only maintain itself by further dictatorship.

This peace has been established on betrayal, and can only maintain itself by further betrayal.

'Peace,' said Spinoza, 'is virtue caused by strength of spirit.' This is not peace without victory, for the victory goes to Mr. Hitler.

This is peace without virtue. Therefore, it is not peace—but the initiation of a terrific world crisis.

October 1, 1938

Let the Record Speak, 1939

Aufenthalt in Rosenheim

by Vincent Sheean

THE CAR broke down not far beyond Siegsdorf on the Reichs-autobahn to Munich—the great Reichsautobahn which is the most beautiful of all German motor roads, since it leads to the home of the Führer. It broke down, precisely, alongside the Chiemsee within sight of the fantastic isle where Ludwig II, another mad South German, built his absurd imitation Versailles. There was no traffic on the road at that hour of the night and four and a half hours passed before a mechanic could be routed out of bed at the nearest town and brought to tow us in.

He towed us in to Rosenheim, a comfortable Bavarian town of something like twenty thousand inhabitants. The car was in a dreadful state, it appeared, all of the teeth having disappeared from its tooth-wheel—I translate literally from the German, with no knowledge of the true English equivalents of such terms—and another could not be obtained nearer than Cologne. So here I sit in Rosenheim, day after day, waiting for a tooth-wheel.

The enforced stay in Rosenheim is not without interest. The place is notable, among other things, for having been the birthplace of the General Field Marshal Hermann Göring, and a place so sanctified cannot be altogether forgotten by Nazi solicitude. As I wander about the streets of the town, over the arcaded footwalks and beneath the tall, narrow oriels which the good Baedeker tells me are characteristic of this region, I observe a variety of edifying phenomena unmentioned in the guidebook. For example, the displays of names, photographs and other material on a glassed-in bulletin board entitled "The Jews Are Our Misfortune" (*Die Juden sind unser Unglück*). Such bulletin boards are at present no less characteristic of the region, I imagine, than arcaded footwalks and tall, narrow oriels.

8

The chief part of the bulletin board is taken up with type-written lists of "racial comrades" (*Volksgenossen*) who have committed the crime of buying something from the Jews. These lists are headed "They bought from Jews." There are two such lists, the one obviously a sort of annex to the first, of slightly more recent date. The lists give full names and addresses of such treacherous "racial comrades," but do not specify what was the object bought from Jews. In one corner of the bulletin board there is a group of eight or nine snapshots of such unfaithful Aryans, labeled also "They bought from Jews," and presumably made just as the guilty purchases were about to be taken home. One of these shows an old woman with a market basket; another shows a young man on a bicycle with a package under his arm.

In the center of the bulletin board there is a list headed "Jewish businesses in Rosenheim." This contains only nine names, four of which have subsequently been crossed out in red crayon. You can imagine for yourself what the crossing out in red crayon signifies.

Every inch of the bulletin board is taken up by material of great interest. For instance, here in the upper right-hand corner is a photograph of three men in evening dress smiling in a group at (obviously) a banquet of some sort. Two of them are shaking hands. The caption on this photograph says: "Jewish Instigators of the Satanic Hatred of Germans" (*Judenhetzer des Satanisches Deutschhass*). Underneath this it specifies the three men: "The physicist Albert Einstein—Rabbi Stephen Wise, a Führer of Zionism—Fiorello LaGuardia, the mayor of the Jewish world-metropolis, New York." Next to this is a peculiarly unesthetic photograph of Mr. LaGuardia, chosen for grotesque effect; he has his mouth wide open and his head thrown back, arms and legs all flailing about in every direction. This picture is entitled: "A Singer of Obscene Couplets? No. The Half-Jew Mayor of the Jewish World Metropolis, New York." Two other photographs show members of the Munich Social Democratic Party of the days just after the War, but are chosen with the utmost skill so as to make these gentlemen look as much as possible like the Nazi idea of a Jewish criminal conspirator.

Press clippings are distributed in any free space there may

be on the board. One clipping narrates the "provocative" deed of a Jewish woman who, on buying some apples in a market, complained of their quality and was then set upon by the Aryan women there present and "taught a lesson." Another discusses the crime of purchasing goods from Jews. A third tells of a Jewish merchant named Hess, who, on being asked what his name really was, replied with criminal impudence, "the same as the Führer's—Stellvertreter" (usurper).

Running across the top of this bulletin board is the text of the decree issued by General Field Marshal Hermann Göring last April, making it a crime punishable by imprisonment and fines to deal with a Jew in business, to represent Jews in the law courts, or to take the place of Jews in running a business.

How, actually, can such things be? The thought torments every hour one spends in Germany. Not that prejudice and cruelty are at all unusual in human nature: we see them everywhere. But how can the German nation, this mighty and splendid nation, have sunk so low as to build a whole system on prejudice, construct a philosophy out of inhumanity? How can the ordinary, friendly, good-natured people one sees in the streets and the beer gardens and shops, the clear-eyed German people, accept such twisted and darkened and hideous nonsense as being a rule of life? Similarly, how do they accept the frightful lies their newspapers and radio gave them every day, a few weeks ago, about Czechoslovakia and "Czech atrocities"? How can they believe, as they do believe, that all non-Fascist countries are controlled by the Jews in a sense of sheer hatred for Germany? How can they join with such alacrity in the whole Nazi rigmarole of salutes and "Heil Hitlers!" and "Sieg Heils!" and the rest of it?

In the restaurants where I eat, while waiting for the toothwheel for the car, I see all the usual types of southern German. They are not physically so beautiful and strong as the types one sees in, say, Saxony, but they have their share of the national gifts in that direction. They come and go with "Heil Hitlers" on their lips, their right hands pawing the air—old men and young, women and children, doing their part in this mad dance which must in the end be a dance of death. They do not seem to be aware that it is a dance of death. "Our

Führer never wanted war, so we knew there would be no war"—that is what several of them have said to me lately, in Rosenheim. "We were not afraid," they say, "because we knew the Führer would not make war." They laugh at the photographs they see of frantic war precautions in London, Paris and Prague; the pictures of Hyde Park dug up to make refuges against air bombing are regarded as particularly humorous.

How was this done? A people like the Germans, heirs to an immense and irreplaceable culture, cannot be all fools. We know that the life of the modern mind would be crippled— would hardly go on at all—in any country if it were not for the contributions made to it by German genius. Then how can the direct heirs and products of this superior culture behave so like gangster children?

We are thrown back on the explanation offered by Prince Bülow, who had had ample opportunities to know his people. He said (it comes somewhere in his memoirs, but I have no copy here in Rosenheim to quote) that God had so enriched the German people with many gifts that he had in the end to take something away from them. The something which he took away, and without which they have floundered so foolishly through epoch after epoch, was a political sense. They have almost everything else, but in everything that has to do with politics they are the prey of tribal instinct, extreme suggestibility, sheeplike obedience and a total lack of humor or imagination. In short, they have no political sense of any kind, and were made not to rule but to be ruled.

Well, there may be something in that theory. I prefer to believe a related but dissimilar explanation of my own—that the political sense is not totally absent from the Germans, but is still extremely immature. Germany came late to political unity and is untrained in the ways of adult thinking. The war of 1914–18 left it with an assortment of grievances and a desperate sense of humiliation. Immature in the one immense department of human activity—immature for the *polis*—the German is, individually and in the aggregate, such a powerful part of the human body that his political adolescence can only be a time of grave danger for all the rest of us. These gentle, kindly, cultivated people, the clear-eyed, loyal, decent people, are the most easily deluded in the world, politically speaking— and, being deluded, are terrible in their strength.

I remember something I saw along the road in Czechoslovakia the other day. It was the day after the Reichswehr had occupied the "third zone" awarded to them by Neville Chamberlain: the zone which extended beyond Carlsbad to Buchau in old Bohemia. We were driving along towards Prague in the car (which then had its tooth-wheel relatively intact) when we passed a Reichswehr staff car drawn up beside the road. Half in and half out of it were two very brave and elegant young fellows in gray. They had a pair of binoculars which they were passing back and forth as they gazed across the valley in the fading day towards the hills beyond— towards the Czechoslovak line of fortifications. They were laughing. Laughing, that is, in their youth and strength and in the power of their great delusion, that the world belongs to them. It would have done no good whatever to stop and tell them what a disastrous delusion that is, and what certain ruin it must bring upon the Germany they love. They believe it: "Heil Hitler!" and "Sieg Heil!" for a while yet.

Well, the tooth-wheel will probably come tomorrow, and I can move on out of Rosenheim and these melancholy reflections. There is some slight, cold comfort in the thought that Germany's value to the human spirit is untouched by these terrifying phenomena of her political adolescence, and that when the torture of the coming years is over their lies and obfuscations will perish too. As the cynical Direktor says in the first speech of Goethe's prologue: "I know how to propitiate the spirit of the people"— *Ich weiss, wie man den Geist des Volks versöhnt.*

The New Republic, December 7, 1938

Hitler Seizes 20,000 Jews

by Sigrid Schultz

BERLIN, Nov. 10.—Systematic destruction of Jewish property, looting, arson, and wholesale arrests of Jews without official charges swept Germany today. It is estimated that 20,000 Jews were arrested in Germany and what was Austria.

The Nazi violence far outdid anything that happened along this line in Germany in the darkest days of the Red revolution. Then hungry mobs stormed food stores. Today the mobs gloated over the smashed stores of Jews. They helped themselves to clothes, furs, and toys, and scattered the goods in the streets for their friends to pick up.

In the days of the revolution the police tried to intervene. Today they walked unconcernedly through the havoc-bent crowds as if everybody was out for an enjoyable afternoon stroll.

This afternoon Dr. Paul Joseph Goebbels, minister of propaganda, issued an appeal to the public to refrain from violence, but it was too late. The Nazis were wreaking vengeance for the death of Ernst von Rath, secretary of the German embassy in Paris. He was shot Monday by Herschel Grynszpan, 17 years old, a Polish Jew.

Two Jews were shot to death during the anti-Semitic riots. One was killed in Polzin, in Pomerania. The other was slain when Nazis clashed with members of a Jewish training camp in Bonndorf.

Twenty synagogues were destroyed in Vienna, either by dynamite or fire. Ten thousand Jews were arrested. Most of them were released. Royston Bryan of Peoria, Ill., correspondent of the London Times, was arrested and released after questioning.

[*Associated Press dispatches said 22 Jews were reported to have committed suicide in Vienna.*]

Nine out of twelve Berlin synagogues were set afire at

dawn. Almost all Jewish temples in Germany were gutted or partly destroyed by fire. Violence was reported in Breslau, Nuremberg, Magdeburg, Stettin, Hamburg, Cologne, Essen, and elsewhere. Many Jews were arrested and carried off to unknown destinations. It was estimated that 10,000 Jews were arrested in Berlin and its suburbs.

In villages, homes of Jews were set afire. Terrified Jews fled into the countryside, hiding in the woods. Nazi manhunts for Jews started near Breslau and Nuremberg. In Munich hundreds of Jews were ordered to leave the city within twenty-four to forty-eight hours with the alternative of being sent to a concentration camp. Since most of them had no passports many were arrested.

The Aufhaeuser, the last remaining Jewish owned bank in Munich, was taken over by a state appointed commissar. One of the partners, named Kraemer, and his wife, committed suicide to escape arrest. Another partner, Martin Aufhaeuser, was seized. The third partner, Siegfried Aufhaeuser, escaped arrest. He is a British citizen.

In Breslau the American consulate was forced to interrupt its duties and close the offices for a few hours until chemical fumes were dissipated. The fumes were blown into the offices as fire brigades sought to prevent flames from burning synagogues from spreading to neighboring buildings.

In Berlin an American walking down the Kurfuersten-damm, one of the city's principal thoroughfares, saw a mob haul a Jew out of a store, knock him down, and trample on him until his shrieks stopped.

In the crowded Leipzigerstrasse six Nazi bicyclists caught sight of two elderly Jews. They chased them until the Jews crumpled on the street. In Fasanenstrasse, near a synagogue, two elderly Jews were dragged out of a house and were seen running with a gang in pursuit. Nazis tried to hit them as they ran by.

A few hours after Goebbels issued his orders to end the "demonstrations and actions of any kind against Jewry," gangs entered houses in the heart of Berlin. They smashed the doors of a number of Jewish homes and dragged the occupants into the streets.

A group of diplomats riding in a diplomatic car attempted

to photograph some of the wreckage, but a mob jumped on them. The police tried to seize the camera of one diplomat. A struggle ensued.

Police officers, who kept looking the other way whenever wrecking gangs were at work, came swarming the minute the word "camera" was called by the Nazis.

An American photographer who possessed official photographic permits was arrested for taking pictures of wreckage. Later, he was released. When German authorities were asked why the taking of pictures suddenly was a crime, they merely shrugged their shoulders and exclaimed: "Orders from higher up."

Mobs broke up all the Jewish stores they could find. Eyewitnesses saw how systematically the "spontaneous demonstrations" had been organized. Young men in lether jackets approached windows of Jewish stores. With a crowbar they gave the plate glass a smart rap and the glass fell on the sidewalks crashing into pieces. Some wreckers were cut.

A few minutes after the windows were smashed a few would sneak up and pull out objects on display. If no Nazi official protested, the gangs broke into stores and helped themselves, while others destroyed the furnishings. Officially, Nazis in uniform forbade the looting. In a number of cases they beat those who were caught stealing, but they explained, "We cannot be everywhere."

Right behind the wreckers came street cleaners with brooms. They swept the broken glass into neat piles.

Gangs attacked the big department store of Israel, which has existed in Berlin since the first years of the nineteenth century. The present owner was born in England, but his father was German. Some tried to restrain the wreckers, because the store was considered English, but cries of "We hit all Jews" ended the argument and the wrecking started.

After the first show windows were smashed, a man armed with a long pole stepped up and fished out a bathrobe and other wearing apparel. A crowd surged into the store. Women started grabbing what they could lay hands on, but stern faced and broad shouldered Nazis in uniforms who had arrived with the wreckers forced them to drop their loot.

A gang quickly started a fire on the first floor, but it was put out. Because fires set in synagogues had endangered a number of buildings, an order was issued to drop arson as an anti-Jewish weapon.

"The spontaneous demonstrations are comprehensible in view of the horrible crime committed by a Jew in Paris," official circles declared.

The wreckings began at 2 a.m. by close knit groups who were well drilled and organized. In Tauenzienstrasse at 6 a.m. wreckers smashed a lether goods store, kicking the trunks and bags into the street.

"We will see that Jews can't fatten on us any more," the Nazis shouted.

They explained they were storekeepers and added: "We shall make sure that the Jews can't continue in business."

Owners of Jewish stores who did not know of the raids and appeared at their places of business this morning were placed "in protective custody."

School children in the poorer sections of Berlin had a great time. The contents of almost all stores in these neighborhoods were scattered in the streets, including goods from candy shops. The youngsters picked up everything and their faces were smeared with chocolate.

Children between the ages of 8 and 10 raided a candy shop in the west end and threw the candy into the sidewalk where friends picked it up. They carried boxes and big bags while adults looked on.

One elderly German who was passing by in his automobile jumped out and turned to the grownups.

"Why do you allow your children to steal?" he cried. "This is nothing but theft, the taking of other people's property."

He nearly was mobbed and was forced to flee.

"Don't you know if you allow this that your children never will again respect private property, just like the red rabbles," he called as his car sped away.

Stores owned by American Jews were not spared by the raiders. One smashed store was decorated with a big American flag. Some neighbors warned the wreckers they should respect foreign property, but the wreckers paid no attention.

In another store the wife of an American merchant who is in the United States was sleeping in a cubby hole behind the store. She heard the store windows being smashed and hid in a closet while the store was being ransacked. The gangs returned later to make certain they had destroyed everything.

A number of American women whose fur coats were being repaired in Jewish stores discovered that their coats were gone. They traveled through the poorer sections of Berlin in hopes they would meet the women who have got their coats.

Berlin Jews were alarmed over the fate of leaders of the Jewish "reich representatives" who represent German Jewry in its dealings with the Nazis. Their headquarters were closed. All visitors in the offices were sent home, while the personnel was detained.

The headquarters of the Zionist organization was raided and wrecked. Newspaper men who had been working on the Jewish newspapers which were prohibited a few days ago were summoned to the GSP [secret police] headquarters, but were released later in the day.

In Berlin's business district, typewriters, adding machines, bales of cloth, cloaks and suits were flung out of the windows of Jewish establishments, endangering passersby.

In the poorest Jewish streets near Alexanderplatz, kitchen cabinets and other furniture of Jewish inhabitants were heaved out of windows, chinaware was spilt all over the street. The furniture was piled together and bonfires were lit.

Shortly after midnight, heavy reinforcements of police and Hitler guards were patrolling Berlin streets to prevent new disturbances.

The wares of some Jewish-owned stores were confiscated by Nazi party officials. Nazi district chiefs said: "We are securing the property of Jewish stores because sooner or later these properties will be nationalized and destruction would constitute a loss to the German people."

The semi-official Neuigkeitsweltblatt, inspired by Joseph Buerckel, Nazi commissioner for Austria, said that in raids on many homes of Jews, "arms, communist agitation pamphlets and illegally possessed foreign currencies were found."

"There is only one path for the Jews if they want to avoid further harsh measures—clear out of Vienna as quickly as possible."

Police at Magdeburg arrested Jews after entering their

homes and saying: "Von Rath died—you know what that means; come with us." It was reported that the entire male Jewish population of Erfurt and Magdeburg were arrested. Nazis in Breslau raided the homes of Jews as well as the homes of their friends in an attempt to find those who had fled.

Goebbels in his appeal to the public to stop violence against Jews said:

"The justifiable and understandable indignation of the German people over the cowardly Jewish murder of a German diplomat in Paris has resulted during the past night in extensive demonstrations.

"In numerous cities and communities of the reich, acts of violence were committed against Jewish buildings and businesses.

"The entire population is now, however, strictly requested to desist immediately from all further demonstrations and actions of whatever nature against Jewdom. The final answer to Jewry will be given in the form of laws or decrees."

The German press added this warning for foreigners: "We warn the foreign friends of Jews not to exploit the developments for an anti-German campaign. This could lead only to the result that in the place of the improvised and spontaneous actions much more stringent actions will be taken by the authorities."

Heinrich Himmler, chief of all German police, issued a decree "forbidding the Jews to own weapons of any kind."

"Offenders will be placed in concentration camps for twenty years," the decree said.

Chicago Tribune, November 10, 1938

"At Dawn This Morning Hitler Moved Against Poland"

by William L. Shirer

BERLIN, *September 1, later*

It's a "counter-attack"! At dawn this morning Hitler moved against Poland. It's a flagrant, inexcusable, unprovoked act of aggression. But Hitler and the High Command call it a "counter-attack." A grey morning with overhanging clouds. The people in the street were apathetic when I drove to the *Rundfunk* for my first broadcast at eight fifteen a.m. Across from the Adlon the morning shift of workers was busy on the new I. G. Farben building just as if nothing had happened. None of the men bought the Extras which the newsboys were shouting. Along the east-west axis the Luftwaffe were mounting five big anti-aircraft guns to protect Hitler when he addresses the Reichstag at ten a.m. Jordan and I had to remain at the radio to handle Hitler's speech for America. Throughout the speech, I thought as I listened, ran a curious strain, as though Hitler himself were dazed at the fix he had got himself into and felt a little desperate about it. Somehow he did not carry conviction and there was much less cheering in the Reichstag than on previous, less important occasions. Jordan must have reacted the same way. As we waited to translate the speech for America, he whispered: "Sounds like his swan song." It really did. He sounded discouraged when he told the Reichstag that Italy would not be coming into the war because "we are unwilling to call in outside help for this struggle. We will fulfil this task by ourselves." And yet Paragraph 3 of the Axis military alliance calls for immediate, automatic Italian support with "all its military resources on land, at sea, and in the air." What about that? He sounded desperate when, referring to Molotov's speech of yesterday at the Russian ratification of the Nazi-Soviet accord, he said: "I can only underline every word of Foreign Commissar Molotov's speech."

Tomorrow Britain and France probably will come in and you have your second World War. The British and French tonight sent an ultimatum to Hitler to withdraw his troops from Poland or their ambassadors will ask for their passports. Presumably they will get their passports.

LATER. *Two thirty a.m.*—Almost through our first black-out. The city is completely darkened. It takes a little getting used to. You grope around the pitch-black streets and pretty soon your eyes get used to it. You can make out the whitewashed curbstones. We had our first air-raid alarm at seven p.m. I was at the radio just beginning my script for a broadcast at eight fifteen. The lights went out, and all the German employees grabbed their gas-masks and, not a little frightened, rushed for the shelter. No one offered me a mask, but the wardens insisted that I go to the cellar. In the darkness and confusion I escaped outside and went down to the studios, where I found a small room in which a candle was burning on a table. There I scribbled out my notes. No planes came over. But with the English and French in, it may be different tomorrow. I shall then be in the by no means pleasant predicament of hoping they bomb the hell out of this town without getting me. The ugly shrill of the sirens, the rushing to a cellar with your gas-mask (if you have one), the utter darkness of the night—how will human nerves stand that for long?

One curious thing about Berlin on this first night of the war: the cafés, restaurants, and beer-halls were packed. The people just a bit apprehensive after the air-raid, I felt. Finished broadcasting at one thirty a.m., stumbled a half-mile down the Kaiserdamm in the dark, and finally found a taxi. But another pedestrian appeared out of the dark and jumped in first. We finally shared it, he very drunk and the driver drunker, and both cursing the darkness and the war.

The isolation from the outside world that you feel on a night like this is increased by a new decree issued tonight prohibiting the listening to foreign broadcasts. Who's afraid of the truth? And no wonder. Curious that not a single Polish bomber got through tonight. But will it be the same with the British and French?

BERLIN, *September 2*

The German attack on Poland has now been going on for two days and Britain and France haven't yet honoured their promises. Can it be that Chamberlain and Bonnet are going to try to sneak out of them? Hitler has cabled Roosevelt he will not bomb open towns if the others don't. No air-raid tonight. Where are the Poles?

BERLIN, *September 3*

Hitler's "counter-attack" on Poland has on this Sabbath day become a world war! To record the date: September 3, 1939. The time: eleven a.m. At nine o'clock this morning Sir Nevile Henderson called on the German Foreign Minister and handed him a note giving Germany until eleven o'clock to accept the British demand that Germany withdraw her troops from Poland. He returned to the Wilhelmstrasse shortly after eleven and was handed the German reply in the form of a memorandum. The extras are out on the streets now. The newsboys are giving them away. The *D.A.Z.* here. Its headlines:

BRITISH ULTIMATUM TURNED DOWN
ENGLAND DECLARES A STATE OF WAR
WITH GERMANY
BRITISH NOTE DEMANDS WITHDRAWAL
OF OUR TROOPS IN THE EAST
THE FÜHRER LEAVING TODAY FOR THE FRONT

A typical headline over the official account:

GERMAN MEMORANDUM PROVES
ENGLAND'S GUILT.

I was standing in the Wilhelmplatz about noon when the loud-speakers suddenly announced that England had declared herself at war with Germany. Some 250 people were standing there in the sun. They listened attentively to the announcement. When it was finished, there was not a murmur. They just stood there as they were before. Stunned. The people cannot realize yet that Hitler has led them into a world war. No issue has been created for them yet, though as this day wears on, it is plain that "Albion's perfidy" will become the

issue as it did in 1914. In *Mein Kampf* Hitler says the greatest
mistake the Kaiser made was to fight England, and Germany
must never repeat that mistake.

It has been a lovely September day, the sun shining, the air
balmy, the sort of day the Berliner loves to spend in the
woods or on the lakes near by. I walked in the streets. On the
faces of the people astonishment, depression. Until today they
have been going about their business pretty much as usual.
There were food cards and soap cards and you couldn't get
any gasoline and at night it was difficult stumbling around in
the black-out. But the war in the east has seemed a bit far
away to them—two moonlight nights and not a single Polish
plane over Berlin to bring destruction—and the papers saying
that German troops have been advancing all along the line,
that the Polish air force has been destroyed. Last night I heard
Germans talking of the "Polish thing" lasting but a few weeks,
or months at the most. Few believed that Britain and France
would move. Ribbentrop was sure they wouldn't and had
told the Führer, who believed him. The British and French
had been accommodating before. Another Munich, why not?
Yesterday, when it seemed that London and Paris were hesitating, everyone, including those in the Wilhelmstrasse, was
optimistic. Why not?

In 1914, I believe, the excitement in Berlin on the first day
of the World War was tremendous. Today, no excitement, no
hurrahs, no cheering, no throwing of flowers, no war fever,
no war hysteria. There is not even any hate for the French and
British—despite Hitler's various proclamations to the people,
the party, the East Army, the West Army, accusing the "English war-mongers and capitalistic Jews" of starting this war.
When I passed the French and British embassies this afternoon, the sidewalk in front of each of them was deserted. A
lone *Schupo* paced up and down before each.

At lunch-time we gathered in the courtyard of the Adlon
for drinks with a dozen members of the British Embassy staff.
They seemed completely unmoved by events. They talked
about *dogs* and such stuff. Some mystery about the French
not acting in concert with the British today, Coulondre's
ultimatum not running out until five p.m., six hours after

Britain was at war. But the French tell us this was due to faulty communications with Paris.

The High Command lets it be known that on the western front the Germans won't fire *first* against the French.

LATER. — Broadcast all afternoon and evening. Third night of the black-out. No bombs, though we rather expected the British and French. The newspapers continue to praise the decree against listening in to foreign broadcasts! What are they afraid of?

Berlin Diary, 1941

Last Warsaw Fort Yields to Germans

by Otto D. Tolischus

WITH THE GERMAN ARMY, Before Warsaw, Poland, Sept. 28
—The German campaign in Poland came to an end today
when the fortress of Modlin followed Warsaw in surrendering
unconditionally at 7 o'clock this morning. At the same time
the bulk of the German Army had returned to the western
side of the German-Russian demarcation line, which army
circles regard as the new Reich border.

With that surrender of the last fort defending the city, Germany has attained her war aims in the East, namely, the partition of Poland, in exactly four weeks. She is already at work
organizing the newly won territory in order to enhance its
agricultural and industrial resources.

Again Chancellor Hitler has proved himself the "Mehrer"
or aggrandizer, of the Reich. To his political triumph he has
added an unprecedented military triumph as well.

But German Army quarters are perfectly well aware that
this new aggrandizement has been obtained at a high price
that is not measured by German casualties, which are comparatively small, but by the fact that, in place of weak Poland,
Germany has again put powerful Russia on her eastern flank.
Army circles are so aware of this new situation that they
frankly declare:

"Germany must now be stronger than ever, not only to win
the conflict with France and Britain but also to prepare for
the inevitable dispute with Soviet Russia that must come
some day."

In fact that is the consolation the German Army offers the
conquered foe remaining on the German side of the demarcation line who still fear National Socialist Germany less than
they do Bolshevist Russia.

The final dramatic scenes of Warsaw's and Modlin's surrender were witnessed by this writer together with a group of

24

other foreign correspondents who arrived at the German front line on the edge of the capital yesterday afternoon to find Warsaw in flames and Modlin still being bombed and shelled to pieces.

We stood at the same spot on the Warsaw-Modlin road where General Werner von Fritsch fell and where a Polish army officer with a white flag had appeared a few hours earlier to offer the surrender of the city.

Around us stood German troops in their first line positions and there also lay the Polish dead. In front of us, some 250 yards away, stood the Polish advance guards in the shelter of a gateway, guns in hands, silently and suspiciously watching every move on their enemy's front.

Where they stood began the sea of houses that was Warsaw. Dense columns of smoke rose high above the Polish capital, which the evening sun painted with a rosy glow that turned blood red.

Behind us, in the background, was Modlin, where fighting still continued and which was just being shelled and bombed by a German air attack. The roar of cannon, the bursting of bombs could be heard plainly to be followed a little later by the roar of the engines of the attacking planes. Appropriately enough, Modlin was overhung by sinister-looking storm clouds into which the evening sun put enough reflected light to convert them into an Autumnal background for the columns of smoke and dust rising from the bursting bombs.

When we arrived at the front line firing had ceased, but the Germans still watched enemy movements as closely as did the Poles. For only today, after the "stop firing order" had been sounded for 9:30 in the morning, some misunderstanding arose as a result of which the Poles resumed fire with rifles, grenades, mine throwers and machine guns about 11 A.M. The Germans replied with artillery until a few more houses went up in flames.

What most interested veterans of former wars in our party, however, was the fact that despite motorization and other mechanical improvements on the war machine, modern warfare had really changed little and that its quintessence as represented by the front line, was still mud holes.

The mud holes of this line, which happily for their occupants were dry, consisted of tiny dugouts about five yards apart manned as a rule by one or two men armed with rifles and hand grenades, while machine guns were posted at strategic points. Behind this first line were deeper trenches manned by larger but still remarkably small troop contingents with rifles, machine guns and mine throwers. After that, for a long distance, came nothing—at least so far as the eye could detect.

In fact, the closer one gets to the front line, the emptier the landscape appears. All outward activity, the mile-long transports and the marching troops, can be seen only far behind the front, usually out of range of artillery fire. But this emptiness behind the front is merely modern camouflage, and any flare-up of serious fighting soon converts innocent-looking woods and peaceful-looking houses into fire-spitting infernos.

The present positions, which will be maintained until all preparations are completed for the German occupation of Warsaw tomorrow, were not established until Sunday. They were so recent and had been under such heavy fire that dead Polish soldiers still lay where they had fallen amid dead horses and abandoned equipment. In the pathetic inertness of their sprawling bodies, they somehow, perhaps because of their surroundings, looked more like inanimate objects than bodies that once were living men, and in the growing darkness their faces began to resemble those of mummies. If war robs death of its majesty, nature compensates by covering up some of the gruesomeness, enabling active men to keep sane.

A weapon more modern even than firearms, propaganda, was also being used right at the front line. A large poster displayed by the Germans announced in Polish:

"Poles! Come to us. We will not hurt you. We will give you bread."

As explained by German staff officers, Warsaw was first treated as an open city and only military objectives were bombed or shelled. Then, however, General Czuma, commander of the defense, restored the old Warsaw forts, such as Modlin, the last to hold out, and established defense lines around the city. Whereupon the German Army command announced it would treat Warsaw as a fortress and shell and bomb it.

But this threat failed to weaken the city's defense. The Germans then offered a truce to evacuate diplomats and the civilian population and called for a Polish representative to appear at a designated point to negotiate.

After this the Germans sent airplanes over Warsaw, throwing millions of leaflets calling on the city to surrender, promising soldiers would be sent home instead of being made war prisoners, and that in view of their brave defense, officers would be permitted to keep their swords. The appeal to the officers was considered especially important because, in the German view, the backbone of the defense consisted of officers who had left their surrendering troops outside and had rallied within Warsaw in regiments consisting for the most part of officers only.

When that failed, two truces were arranged—one for evacuating foreign diplomats, who arrived in Koenigsberg, East Prussia, recently, and another for evacuating sixty-two Soviet diplomats after the Russian occupation of Eastern Poland.

Only then, according to German officers, did the real bombardment start. The forts, and especially the old citadel, were heavily bombed and shelled, as were the barracks, airport and such inferior points as parks where troop concentrations had been observed. As a result, many buildings also were damaged, including, it is understood, the former royal palace. A Polish truce officer, as well as others from Warsaw, asserted that, in fact, a large part of the city is merely "heaps of ruins."

Finally, late Tuesday night a Polish officer bearing a white flag appeared at the German front line and asked for a truce to evacuate the civilian population and the wounded. This was refused and the final unconditional surrender was announced early yesterday morning.

Shortly before midnight last night another Polish officer, a major, appeared at Army Corps Headquarters, where he was cordially received, to arrange for the surrender of Modlin. He carried a letter from General Rommel, commander of the Polish Army around Warsaw, ordering the commander of Modlin to give up.

Accompanied by a group of German officers and announced by a trumpet signal, the Polish major was taken to the Polish front line before Modlin at 1 A.M. A white banner held up on two sticks by two German soldiers was illuminated by a powerful searchlight supplied by a portable dynamo. In conjunction with the bright moonlight, this rather romantic scene was reminiscent of former rather than present-day war practices.

The German demand was surrender by 6 A.M., to be announced by a white flag over the Modlin citadel. When the flag failed to appear promptly the bombing and artillery bombardment of Modlin was resumed and could be heard plainly at our headquarters. Only then the last Polish center of resistance excepting an isolated band on the peninsula of Hela, near Danzig, gave up. The white flag floated over Modlin. The last shot in the German-Polish War had been fired at 7 o'clock this morning.

Today German heavy artillery and munitions trains already are moving westward again, carrying Polish flags and eagles as trophies and bearing on trucks and caissons short inscriptions such as:

"To hell with Poland and England" or "Warsaw-Paris express."

Details of how General von Fritsch was killed in action just before the Polish-German War came to an end were learned here at the front today.

According to this account, General von Fritsch had helped in front-line observation posts throughout the campaign and did so again last Friday in a major reconnoissance attack undertaken with infantry, artillery and bombers to test out the Polish line's strength. Suddenly from a house where no enemy previously was observed, the Poles started a heavy machine-gun fire. A bullet hit General von Fritsch in the thigh and severed an artery. A lieutenant accompanying him tried to bind up the wound but the general merely said:

"Please do not bother!"

These were his last words. Two minutes later he was dead. Despite a heavy fire, the lieutenant carried the body of his commander to the rear.

The New York Times, September 29, 1939

POLAND CAUGHT BETWEEN HITLER AND STALIN:
NOVEMBER 1939

Nazi-Red Animosity Described Along Tense Frontier Border in Poland

by Sonia Tomara

UNGVAR, Hungary, Nov. 19.—In spite of the recent pact linking Germany to the Soviet Union, those two states appear to have no intercourse with each other except through official delegates that usually fly from Berlin to Moscow and vice versa. Definite information to this effect was obtained by this correspondent along the Hungarian frontier during conversations with newly-escaped Polish refugees and with German soldiers stationed at the Russian border.

All the evidence received indicated the same fact. The boundary that has been drawn between German and Soviet territory in Poland is heavily guarded on both sides and no one is allowed to cross it. Many Polish families have been split by the recent partition of their country and now are without news of one another. The Russian and the German soldiers have orders not to communicate across the border; German and Russian sentinels face each other all day long without exchanging a word.

This correspondent happened to witness, however, a meeting between a Russian and a German officer and the meeting was none too friendly. The two had come together on Hungarian ground at the Uzsok Pass to delimit a boundary. The accord partitioning Poland said that the Soviet-German boundary would run to the Hungarian frontier along the River San. Two rivulets with a railroad station between them merge to form the San, and nobody knows which stream is the main one.

Both the Russians and the Germans want the railroad station, and the two officers were to decide which rivulet was the real San. Evidence given by the priest and the school teacher of the nearest village was in favor of Germany.

29

The two officers set out together from the archway, still bearing the Polish eagle, which divides Hungary from Russia. They exchanged brief phrases in German. A German soldier, who was to follow them, said to the correspondent with some bitterness, pointing at the Russian: "It would be better if we fought them and not the French." The correspondent could not stay long enough to learn how the boundary was fixed.

Three Polish refugees I met in a Ruthenian village had crossed the German frontier the night before. They all had come from different parts of Poland and had fled separately. One was a minor official from the region of Pinsk, the other an engineer from Cracow and the third a journalist from Lemberg (Lwow). All three had been in most parts of Poland and they agreed that each of two regimes, Soviet and German, was as bad as the other. One said: "It is like seeking shelter from pouring rain under a running gutter."

On both sides of the new border in Poland there is no merchandise to be found, the refugees said, everything having been taken to Russia or to Germany. There are queues for food and manufactured goods. In German territory Jews are scapegoats number one, and Poles scapegoats number two. Under the Soviet regime the Poles have the worse lot and the Jews are better off. Polish intellectuals are persecuted in both territories, frequently beaten and interned. A distinguished professor of history at Cracow, the refugee engineer reported, was beaten by the Gestapo (German secret police) because he objected to changes in the staff of the University of Cracow.

The Polish official had tried to stay under the Russian regime in his native village near Pinsk, but had to flee when the Russians began to arrest all former Polish officials and deport them into Russia proper. He crossed the Vistula in a rowboat at night, he said, and joined some relatives in German Galicia, but soon found that men were being arrested there, too, and being drafted for forced labor. He fled into Hungary, arriving after walking forty miles through mountains.

The engineer had become separated from his wife and child, who happened to be in Soviet Poland while he remained in Cracow. Having no news of them, he managed to go over to them, walking most of the way and evading German soldiers and Red Guards. He found his family starving, he said, but they refused to follow him into exile. He returned, mostly on foot, to Cracow and then traveled by train to Slovakia and to Hungary. He said he had seen during his trip much evidence of distrust which the Germans had for the Russians.

The Russians, he said, often spoke of the Nazis with contempt. He heard Red soldiers comfort, at Lemberg, a Jewish woman who had been maltreated by the Germans. "Don't weep," they told her. "The Germans could enter Austria, Czecho-Slovakia and Poland, but they will never dare to come to us. We are much stronger than they are."

A continuous thin stream of Polish refugees is pouring into Hungary daily, chiefly over the German border or via Slovakia. The Russian border is more nearly impassable than the other, and probably is better guarded by both Russians and Hungarians, the latter not trusting refugees from Soviet land. Many Poles are still in Hungary, but a number from the first wave of refugees returned to Poland via Vienna and others have gone to France.

New York Herald Tribune, November 20, 1939

Paris Postscript

by A. J. Liebling

I

ON SATURDAY, May 11th, the day after the Germans invaded Holland and Belgium, I had a letter from Jean-Pierre, a corporal in one of the two French armored divisions, which were created after the Polish campaign. They were good divisions, and Jean-Pierre had no way of knowing that the Germans had six times as many. "The real rough-house is about to begin," he wrote. "So much the better! It will be like bursting an abscess." Jean-Pierre, whose parents were my oldest friends in France, was a strong, quiet boy who in civil life had been a draughtsman in an automobile factory. He liked to play ice hockey and collect marine algae. He had not wanted a soft job in a factory during the war because he did not want to be considered a coward.

On the same morning I had a telephone conversation with another friend of mine, Captain de Sombreuil, who had just arrived from Alsace on furlough. Upon reaching the Gare de l'Est, he had learned that all furloughs were cancelled, so he was going back by the next train. He called me up to say that he wouldn't be able to go to the races at Auteuil with me as he had planned. "It's good that it's starting at last," he said. "We can beat the Boches and have it over with by autumn."

In the afternoon I went to Auteuil alone. I watched a horse belonging to Senator Hennessy, the cognac man, win the Prix Wild Monarch for three-year-old hurdlers. The track was crowded with people whose main preoccupations seemed to be the new three-year-olds and the new fashions being worn by the women. That day the Germans were taking Arnhem and Maastricht in Holland and attacking Rotterdam with parachutists. Nobody worried much. Everyone was eager principally to know whether French troops had yet made contact with the enemy. "The Boches have business with somebody their own size now!" they said pugnaciously. "They will see we are not Poles or Norwegians!" It was conceivable, of course, that the Germans would win a few victories, but it would be a long war, like the last one. All France, hypnotized by 1918, still thought in terms of concentrated artillery preparations, followed by short advances and then, probably, by counterattacks. Even if the Allied troops should fail to save Holland, they would join the Belgians in holding the supposedly magnificent fortified line of the Albert Canal. At worst, the armies could fall back to the Franco-Belgian frontier, where, the newspapers had been proclaiming since September, there was a defensive system practically as strong as the Maginot Line. Confidence was a duty. The advertising department of the Magasins du Louvre discovered another duty for France. The store's slogan was "Madame, it is your duty to be elegant!" "They shall not pass" was considered *vieux jeu* and hysterical. The optimistic do-nothingism of the Chamberlain and Daladier regimes was, for millions of people, the new patriotism. Ten days before the war began in May, Alfred Duff Cooper told the Paris American Club, "We have found a new way to make war—without sacrificing human lives."

The news of the break-through at Sedan, which reached Paris on the fifth day of the offensive, was, for a few Parisians who were both pessimistic and analytical, the beginning of fear. But it happened so quickly, so casually, as presented in the communiqués, that the unreflective didn't take it seriously. The Belgian refugees began to arrive in Paris a few days after the fighting started. The great, sleek cars of the de-luxe refugees came first. The bicycle refugees arrived soon after. Slick-haired, sullen young men wearing pullover sweaters shot out of the darkness with terrifying, silent speed. They had the air of conquerors rather than of fugitives. Many of them undoubtedly were German spies. Ordinary destitute refugees arrived later by train and as extra riders on trucks. Nothing else happened at first to change the daily life of the town.

Tuesday evening, May 14th, I climbed the hill of Montmartre to the Rue Gabrielle to visit Jean-Pierre's parents. Henri,

Jean-Pierre's father, had long limbs and sad eyes; he combined the frame of a high jumper and the mustaches of a Napoleonic grenadier. He was a good Catholic, and by birth and training he belonged to the wealthier bourgeoisie. By temperament, which he had never been allowed to indulge, he was a bohemian. A long struggle to succeed in business, which he secretly detested, had ended in a defeat just short of total. When war was declared, he was working for a firm of textile stylists whose customers were chiefly foreign mills. Since September, business had fallen off drastically and Henri had had nothing to do except drop in once in a while to keep up the firm's desultory correspondence. Henri spoke English, German, and Dutch in addition to French, and sometimes sang in a deep voice which sounded like a good but slightly flawed 'cello. He often said that he was happy to be living, at last, high on Montmartre, just under Sacré-Cœur. His wife, Eglée, would never have permitted him to live there for any reason less compelling than poverty. Eglée, before her marriage to Henri, had been a buyer in a department store. Recently she had devised a muslin money belt for soldiers to wear under their shirts. She worked an average of sixteen hours a day, making the belts with a frantic dexterity, but about once a fortnight she got so exhausted that she had to stay in bed for two or three days. She had placed the belts in several of the department stores, but her profit was small. Eglée and Henri were both about sixty years old. For thirty-five years Henri had pretended to like trade in order to hold his wife's respect, and Eglée had pretended to loathe trade in order to hold Henri's affection. Neither had succeeded in deceiving the other. He brooded, she scolded, he drank a little, they quarrelled incessantly, and they loved each other more than any two people I have ever known.

As I came into their apartment Tuesday night, Eglée was saying she felt sure Jean-Pierre was dead. Henri said that was nonsense. She said he was an unfeeling parent. Henri became angry and silent. Then he said that often, when he was at Verdun, Eglée had not heard from him for a week at a time. She said that Henri was always talking about Verdun and belittling "Jean-Pierre's war." "To think that after these years of preparing to avoid the old mistakes," Henri said, "the Germans are now eighty miles from us. If they get to Paris, it's all over." Eglée said he was a defeatist to mention such an eventuality. He said, "I am not a defeatist. I am an old soldier and also an old travelling man, and I know how near they are to Paris." I tried to console him by saying that the Dutch, at any rate, were fighting better than anyone had expected. Henri had cousins in Holland. Eglée said the Dutch were Boches and would before long prove it.

The next morning there was a radio announcement that the Dutch had surrendered in Europe but were going to continue the war in the East Indies. In the afternoon, some of the American correspondents, including myself, went to the Netherlands Legation to meet Mynheer Van Kleffens, the Netherlands Minister for Foreign Affairs, who had arrived from London to explain the Dutch decision. Van Kleffens, accompanied by the Netherlands Minister to France and the Netherlands Minister for National Defence, received us and the journalists of other neutral countries in the Legation garden. While we were talking, sadly and quietly, among the trees, the French were losing the war. On that Wednesday, May 15th, the Germans made the deep incision which a few days later was to split the Allied armies. The Foreign Minister, a blond, long-faced man, had a pet phrase which he repeated many times, as a man does when he is too tired to think of new forms for his thought. "The Germans tried this," he would say, recounting some particular method of the German attack, and then he would add, "It failed." "It failed," he would say, and again, "It failed"—until you thought he was talking of a long, victorious Dutch resistance—and then finally, "But to fight longer was hopeless." "We will fight on" was another recurrent phrase. When we asked him whether the Dutch had any planes left to fight with, he said, "No. We had fifty bombers. The last one flew off and dropped its last bomb and never returned."

Holland, with one-tenth the population of Germany but with several times the wealth per capita, had presented fifty bombers against five thousand. It had been comfortable to believe in neutrality, and cheap. Norway, with the fourth largest merchant marine in the world, had not built the few good light cruisers and destroyers which might have barred the

weak German navy from its ports. France herself had econo-
mized on the Maginot Line, had decided it was too expensive
to extend the fortifications from Luxembourg to the sea. The
democracies had all been comfortable and fond of money.
Thinking of the United States, I was uneasy.

The first panic of the war hit Paris Thursday, May 16th. It
affected, however, only the most highly sensitized layers of
the population: the correspondents, the American and British
war-charity workers, and the French politicians. In Paris, because of censorship, news of disaster always arrived unofficially
and twenty-four hours late. On the evening of the cata-
strophic May 15th, even the neurotic clientele of the Ritz and
Crillon bars had been calm. But on Thursday people began
telling you about Germans at Meaux and south of Soissons,
points the Germans didn't actually reach until over three
weeks later. There was a run on the Paris branch of the Guar-
anty Trust Company by American depositors. I lunched in a
little restaurant I frequently went to on the Rue Ste.-Anne,
and after the meal, M. Bisque, the proprietor, suggested that
we go to the Gare du Nord to see the refugees. M. Bisque
cried easily. Like most fine cooks, he was emotional and a
heavy drinker. He had a long nose like a woodcock and a
mustache which had been steamed over cookpots until it
hung lifeless from his lip. Since my arrival in France in October he had taken me periodically on his buying trips to the
markets so that I could see the Germans weren't starving
Paris. On these trips we would carry a number of baskets and,
as we filled one after another with oysters, artichokes, or
pheasants, we would leave them at a series of bars where we
stopped for a drink of apple brandy. The theory was that
when we had completed our round of the markets we would
circle back on our course, picking up the baskets, and thus
avoid a lot of useless carrying. It worked all right when we
could remember the bars where we had left the various
things, but sometimes we couldn't, and on such occasions M.
Bisque would cry that *restauration* was a cursed *métier*, and
that if the government would permit he would take up his old
rifle and leave for the front. But they would have to let him
wear horizon blue; he could not stand the sight of khaki be-

cause it reminded him of the English. "They say the English are very brave at sea," he would say, winking slowly, "but who knows? We don't see them, eh?"

The trip to the Gare du Nord was solemn. M. Bisque dragged me to see various mothers sitting on rolls of bedding and surrounded by miauling children; his eyes would water, and he would offer a child a two-franc piece, and then haul me to the buffet, where he would fortify himself with a glass of Beaujolais. At the buffet I remember meeting a red-bearded gnome of a colonial soldier who kept referring to himself as "a real porpoise." "Porpoise" was the traditional Army term for a colonial infantryman. "A real porpoise," the soldier repeated dreamily, "an old porpoise, and believe me, Monsieur, the Germans need *somebody* to bust their snouts for them." He had two complete sets of decorations, one from the old war and one from the new. He was going north to rejoin his regiment and he was full of fight and red wine.

Saturday morning I had another note from Jean-Pierre. He enclosed a bit of steel from a Dornier shot down near him. "How I am still alive I have not time to write to you," he said, "but chance sometimes manages things well." The letter produced the same effect on me as news of a great victory. I called up Henri. He and Eglée had had a letter too.

On Saturday, May 18th, I went to a press conference held by the Ministry of Information, which had just organized an Anglo-American press section, with quarters in a vast, rococo ballroom at the Hôtel Continental called the Salle des Fêtes. Pierre Comert, chief of the section, held conferences for the correspondents at six every evening, when he would discuss the day's developments from the government's point of view. This evening he announced that Paul Reynaud had taken over the Ministry of National Defence. He also announced that Reynaud had recalled Marshal Pétain from Spain to advise him. General Weygand had already arrived from Syria and it was understood that he would take over the high command in a few days. The two great names, in conjunction, were expected to raise national morale. The two old men, however, were military opposites. Pétain, cautious at sixty, when he had defended Verdun, was at eighty-four incapable of conceiving any operation bolder than an orderly retreat. Weygand believed in unremitting attack. One staff officer later told me, "Weygand's ideas are so old-fashioned that they have become modern again. He is just what we need." Strategically, the two men cancelled each other, but politically they were a perfect team. Both were clericals, royalists, and anti-parliamentarians. There is something about very old soldiers like Hindenburg and Pétain that makes democrats trust them. But Pétain was to serve Laval's purpose as Hindenburg had served Hitler's. However, we were cheerful on the evening we heard about the appointments. The German advance was apparently slowing down, and all of us thought that Weygand might arrange a counterattack soon. A week earlier we had been expecting victories. Now we were cheered by a slightly slower tempo of disaster.

There was a hot, heavy pause the next few days. I took long walks on the boulevards, and up and down dull, deserted business streets. The wartime population of Paris had slowly increased from late November until April, as evacuated families returned from the provinces, but since the beginning of the offensive the population had again decreased. All the people who remained in town seemed to concentrate on the boulevards. It gave them comfort to look at one another. They were not yet consciously afraid, however. There were long queues in front of the movie houses, especially those that showed double features. You could get a table at a sidewalk café only with difficulty, and the ones that had girl orchestras did particularly well. One girl orchestra, at the Grande Maxeville, was called the Joyous Wings and its bandstand and instruments had been decorated with blue airplanes. There were no young soldiers in the streets, because no furloughs were being issued.

It is simple now to say, "The war on the Continent was lost on May 15th." But as the days in May passed, people in Paris only gradually came to suspect how disastrous that day had been. There was a time lag between every blow and the effect on public morale. I can't remember exactly when I first became frightened, or when I first began to notice that the shapes of people's faces were changing. There was plenty of food in Paris. People got thin worrying. I think I noticed first the thinning faces of the sporting girls in the cafés. Since the same girls came to the same cafés every night, it was easy to keep track. Then I became aware that the cheekbones, the noses, and the jaws of all Paris were becoming more prominent.

There was no immediate danger in Paris unless the Germans bombed it, and when the news was in any degree encouraging I did not think of bombing at all. When the news was bad I thought of bombing with apprehension. It helped me understand why troops in a winning army are frequently brave and on the losing side aren't. We heard anti-aircraft fire every night now, but there were no air-raid alarms, because the planes the guns were firing at were reconnaissance planes. The heaviest shooting would begin in the gray period just before dawn. You wouldn't really settle down to sleep until the morning shooting was over, and you wouldn't wake up until noon.

On the night of May 21st, after Paul Reynaud announced to the Senate that the Germans were at Arras and that France was in danger, I had a *frousse*—a scare—of such extreme character that it amounted to *le trac*, which means a complete funk. It was an oppressively hot night, with thunder as well as anti-aircraft fire, interspersed with noises which sounded like the detonations of bombs in the suburbs. When I lay on my bed face down, I couldn't help thinking of a slave turning his back to the lash, and when I lay on my back I was afraid of seeing the ceiling fall on me. Afterward I talked to dozens of other people about that night and they all said they'd suffered from the same funk. The next morning's papers carried Weygand's opinion that the situation was not hopeless. This cheered everybody. It has since been revealed that May 21st, the day of the great *frousse*, was the day set for the counterattack which might have cracked the Germans. It never came, and by May 22nd, when we were all beginning to feel encouraged, the opportunity had been missed.

Later that day, word got around among the correspondents that negotiations were already on for a separate peace and that if the French didn't sign it the Germans might arrive in Paris in a few days. This counteracted the effect of the

Weygand message. Still later, I felt encouraged again as I watched a city gardener weed a bed of petunias in the Square Louvois, the tiny park under my hotel window. Surely, I thought, if the old man believed the Germans were coming in, he would not be bothering with the petunias.

The greatest encouragement I got during those sad weeks came from Jean-Pierre. Shortly after the Reynaud speech, I went up the hill to Montmartre to take some flowers to Jean-Pierre's mother. For once, Henri and Eglée were smiling at the same time. "You should have been here early this morning for a good surprise!" Henri shouted. "At five there was a knock at our door." "And who do you suppose it was?" his wife cried, taking over the narrative. "Suzette?" I demanded, naming their married daughter, who lived in Grenoble. I was sure that it had been Jean-Pierre, but I wanted to prolong Eglée's pleasure. "No," Eglée announced happily. "It was Jean-Pierre. He was magnificent. He looked like a cowboy." "He came with his *adjudant*," Henri broke in, "to get engine parts they needed for tanks. The boy has no rest, you know," he said proudly. "When the division goes into action he fights. When they are in reserve and the other fellows rest, he is head of a repair section. He is a magician with engines. And his morale is good! He says that the first days were hard, but that now they know they can beat the Boche." "On the first day of the battle, Jean-Pierre's general was arrested," Eglée said, with a sort of pride. "What *canaille*! Jean said it was fantastic what a traitor the general turned out to be. And there were German spies in French officers' uniforms!" "They met a regiment of artillery without officers," Henri said, "but completely! 'So much the better,' the artillerists said. 'They were traitors anyway. But where in the name of God are we supposed to go?' Fifteen German bombers appeared over Jean-Pierre's unit. 'We're in for it,' he said to himself. But the boy was lucky. The Germans had dropped their bombs elsewhere. Then Jean-Pierre's unit met German tanks. He says our fellows rode right over them. 'There may be a great many of them,' he said, 'but we are better than they are. Our guns penetrate them but they do not penetrate us. As for the spy problem, we have solved that. We simply shoot all officers we do not know.' Jean-Pierre and the *adjudant* stayed for break-fast. Then they had to go away."

Although I knew that an individual soldier had no chance to understand a military situation as a whole, Jean-Pierre's optimism raised my spirits considerably. I believe fully the details of the encounter with the German tanks. Jean-Pierre was of that peculiar race of engine-lovers who cannot lie about the performance of a mechanical thing.

When I returned to my hotel, I passed along Jean-Pierre's confident report to Toutou, the hotel's cashier, with whom I often discussed the war. She was a patriot but a congenital pessimist. All the employees slept on the top floor of the hotel, and as soon as Toutou had read of the German parachutists in Holland she had bought a revolver and cartridges. "If one lands on the roof, I'll pop him!" she had said. "Or perhaps as he descends past my window!"

In each week of disaster there was an Indian summer of optimism. On the third Sunday after the offensive started, I had dinner with Henri and Eglée. We teased one another about our forebodings a fortnight earlier. "Do you remember how sure you were that the Germans would be here momentarily?" Eglée said to me. "And how you were certain that Jean-Pierre was no longer alive?" Henri asked Eglée. "It seems a year ago," I said sincerely. "I must admit that the French have their heart well hooked on. Any other people would have caved in after such a blow. I wonder where Weygand will make the counterattack." "In Luxembourg, in my opinion," Henri said. "If he made the counterattack too far to the west he would not catch enough Boches. A good wide turning movement, and you will see—the whole band of them will have to scramble off. They will be on the other side of the Albert Canal again in a week."

We talked and listened to the radio, and, as usual, I stayed for tea, then for supper, and then for the final news bulletin broadcast at eleven-thirty. The bulletins earlier in the day had been dull. But something in the speaker's voice this time warned us, as soon as he commenced, that the news was bad. We began to get sad before he had said anything important. Then he said, "Whatever the result of the battle in Flanders, the high command has made provision that the enemy will not profit strategically by its result." "What can he mean?" Eglée asked. "He means that they are preparing to embark that army for England," Henri said. "Unless the enemy captures the army, his victory is tactical but not strategical." "But why must they embark?" Eglée asked. "I do not know," Henri said almost savagely. That was the day—though none of us knew it—that King Leopold told his Ministers he was going to give up. Eglée began to cry. "Now they are coming to Paris," she said, "now they are coming to Paris."

II

As late as Monday, May 27th, people in Paris still believed that the Allies stood a chance of closing the gap between their southern and northern armies. That evening, Pierre Comert, chief of the Anglo-American section of the Ministry of Information, announced at a press conference I went to that operations in the north were "proceeding normally" and that the high command expected the Battle of Flanders to last at least another two weeks. I slept well that night, awakened only a few times by moderate anti-aircraft fire. In the morning, Toutou, the cashier at my hotel, stopped me as I was going out and said, "Did you hear Reynaud on the radio? The King of the Belgians has surrendered his army." She had been crying.

I walked about the streets stupidly the rest of the morning. I had the map well in mind. The Belgians, by their surrender, had laid bare the left flank of the Franco-British armies in Flanders, and I thought the armies would soon be surrounded. Perhaps the French and British in the north would become demoralized and surrender. If they had been seeking an excuse to quit, they had a good one now. People on the streets were saying to each other, "And that isn't the worst of it. All the refugees probably are spies." They did not seem depressed. A fellow wheeling a pushcart loaded with wood stopped and shouted to a colleague on the other side of the street, "Say, old fellow, did you hear the news? Ain't we just taking it on the potato!" In his voice was a note of pride.

I walked around the Place Vendôme a couple of times; the luxury-shop windows had for me a reassuring association of tourists and normal times. Charvet was showing summer ties. I bought a couple from an elegant and hollow-chested sales-man. I didn't want to talk to him about the war because he looked sad enough already, but he began to talk about it him-self. "We are an indolent people, Monsieur," he said pleas-antly. "We need occurrences like this to wake us up." Paris reminded me of that conversational commonplace you hear when someone has died: "Why, I saw him a couple of days ago and he looked perfectly well." Paris looked perfectly well, but I wondered if it might not be better for a city in such danger to show some agitation. Perhaps Paris was dying.

That night, when the shock of the Belgian surrender had begun to wear off, I had a late dinner with two American friends in a little Marseillais restaurant on the Rue Mont-martre. We were the only customers. We had Mediterranean rouget burned in brandy over twigs of fennel. Although all three of us knew that the war was lost, we could not believe it. The rouget tasted too much as good rouget always had; the black-browed proprietor was too normally solicitous; even in the full bosom and strong legs of the waitress there was the assurance that this life in Paris would never end. Faith in France was now purely a *mystique*; a good dinner was our profane form of communion.

Incredibly, beginning the day after the Belgian surrender, there was a great wave of exhilaration, based on the heroic action of the British and French armies fighting their way out of Flanders. People with relatives in the northern armies had, when they heard of the capitulation, resigned themselves to the capture or death of the trapped men. The German gov-ernment, in radio broadcasts, had threatened that even if the Allies were able to make a stand at Dunkirk the Germans would sink every boat that tried to embark troops. It was one German threat that didn't come off. People in Paris began to receive telegrams from relatives who had safely arrived in En-gland. Several of my acquaintances received such messages, so we assumed that the number of troops saved was very large.

My old friends Henri and Eglée had not worried about their son Jean-Pierre, because, having seen him on leave since the Germans drove the wedge between the Allied armies, they knew he was south of the Somme. But Henri's brother Paul, who at fifty had been called back into service as a lieutenant of artillery, was with the army in Flanders. One evening shortly after the Belgian surrender, I climbed up to the Rue Gabrielle just under the crest of Montmartre, to visit Henri and Eglée, and found them in a happy mood, because Paul had reached England. I tried to talk to Eglée about what she and her husband would do if the Germans turned toward Paris after they finished the Dunkirk job. Her answer was simply that she had an order from the Galeries Lafayette for five dozen of the soldiers' muslin money belts she manufactured at home and that after she completed the order she would have to wait eight days for payment, so how could she think of leaving Paris? As for Henri, he said he now constituted the whole office force of the textile-design company he worked for and couldn't leave without giving a month's notice. Peacetime thought patterns were mercifully persistent.

Everyone now was doing his best to forget that the Allied forces had had too few tanks and guns to begin with, and that now the evacuated armies had lost what little they had. We consoled ourselves with stories of individual heroism and with the thought that the Allies, after all, controlled the sea. Only when the evacuation was completed did the enthusiastic French suddenly take cognizance of the fact that there were no more British troops on their side of the Channel. As if spontaneously, the German gibe, "England will fight to the last Frenchman," swam into the popular consciousness and began to seem like a portent.

Two kinds of person are consoling in a dangerous time: those who are completely courageous, and those who are more frightened than you are. Fernand, the night porter at my hotel, was completely courageous. "Well, what do you know?" he would ask me when I came home at night. Before I answered, he would say, "We will have them yet, the camels. It takes a few defeats to get our blood up. They poison our lives by provoking the anti-aircraft into making a noise at night. A surprise is preparing itself for those cocos!" It was a pleasure to see him during the frequent early-morning *alertes*. Hearing the sirens, he would go out into the small park in front of the hotel and, shielding his eyes with his hands, search the sky for airplanes. Seeing none, he would shake his head disgustedly and shout up to the female guests at the windows of the hotel, "Do not derange yourselves, Mesdames, it is for nothing again!"

The most frightened man I saw in France was a certain well-known French journalist who wrote under various names in a dozen Parisian newspapers of varying political color. He had a broad, paraffin-textured face which, when he was alarmed, appeared to be on the point of melting. Long before the offensive began in May, he had tried to explain to me why Laval, the appeaser, and Paul Faure, the left-of-Blum Socialist, together with Georges Bonnet, representative of the great banking house of Lazard Frères, were all planning a move to get rid of Paul Reynaud in order to liquidate the war as quickly as possible. They wanted to put Daladier back in Reynaud's place because they knew that as long as Daladier headed the government there would be no effectual war— that eventually the war would die of dry rot, which was what ninety per cent of the French politicians and all the French Communists, along with the Germans, wanted. I had asked naïvely why Laval didn't try to become Premier himself. "Because, of course," my journalist friend had said impatiently, "then everybody would *know* he was going to make peace. Then there would be mutiny in the Army." Personally, he used to he was a decided partisan of both Reynaud, who wanted to and of Laval, who wanted to make peace. You were always ning up against things like that in French politics.

When I met my journal st at lunch one day the first week of June, he was in as spectacul a funk as I have ever observed. "What a terrible mistake to hav provoked those people, my dear!" he shrieked. "What madness o concern ourselves with Poland! Laval was so right to have wished to conciliate Mussolini. I am going to give my dog a lethal injection. He could never stand the nervous shock of those bombs that whistle. Working people are so insouciant. They know they have us in their power. I cannot get a man to dig a trench in my garden for me until tomorrow afternoon, and the bombers may be here any minute!" As he stuffed asparagus into his mouth, large tears welled out of his eyes. "Peace, quickly, quickly!" he shouted, after swallowing the asparagus.

Sunday, June 2nd, I visited the country home of a French newspaper publisher who lived with his large, intelligent family near the town of Melun, thirty miles south of Paris. The countryside, hot and rich and somnolent, and the family, sitting on the lawn after a chicken dinner, made me think of Sundays on Long Island. It was as if no war had ever been. We sat around in lawn chairs, fighting against drowsiness, talking unintently, resisting the efforts of one woman to get up a game like charades. We spoke with no originality whatever of all the mistakes all the appeasers in the world had made, beginning with Ethiopia. We repeated to one another how Italy could have been squelched in 1935, how a friendly Spanish government could have been maintained in power in 1936, how the Germans could have been prevented from fortifying the Rhineland in the same year. We talked of the Skoda tanks, built according to French designs in Czecho-Slovakia, that were now ripping the French army apart. The Germans had never known how to build good tanks until Chamberlain and Daladier presented them with the Skoda plant. These matters had become for every European capable of thought a sort of litany, to be recited almost automatically over and over again.

Women in the train which took me back to town that evening were talking about the leaflets German planes had dropped, promising to bombard Paris the next day. The word "bombardment" had a terrible sound, evoking pictures of Warsaw and Rotterdam. The train arrived at the Gare de Lyon after eleven. There were no taxis. In the last month they had become increasingly scarce even in the daytime; the drivers simply refused to risk their necks in the pitch-black streets at night. I could not distinguish one street from another. There was a cluster of dim, moving lights at a distance, like a luminous jellyfish seen by another fish at the bottom of the sea. I started toward the lights and tripped over a plank, skinning my knee. When I reached them, I found they came from the electric lanterns of a group of policemen who were stopping pedestrians and examining their papers. They were polite and quiet. One of them told me how to get to my hotel, which took me almost an hour.

The promised bombardment came at about one o'clock the next afternoon, an anticlimax to its advance notices. It was preceded by a tremendous noise of motors in airplanes too high to be seen, and by the angry hammering of anti-aircraft guns. Technically, I was later given to understand, it was, from the German standpoint, a very good bombardment. Two hundred and fifty planes participated, the largest number that had been assembled for a single operation in this war. The bombing, considering the height at which the planes flew—twenty thousand feet—was commendably accurate. However, the results looked nothing like the photographs of Warsaw and Rotterdam, because Paris was reasonably well defended. "The anti-aircraft fire was well nourished," the French said, "so the bombers stayed high." The pursuit squadrons, although they failed to intercept the bombers on their way to Paris, were on their tails so closely that the Germans dropped their bombs quickly and left. If there had been no defending batteries or planes, as at Rotterdam, the bombers would have loafed along a few hundred feet above the main thoroughfares and dropped their high explosives like roach powder. The bombs hit the huge Citroën factory on the Quai de Javel and knocked down a few scattered apartment houses, but the total effect on public morale was tonic. Forty-eight hours after the bombardment, M. Dautry, the Minister of War Industry, took a group of correspondents through the Citroën plant, which had been the chief German objective. There we found a smell of burnt paint, and a great deal of broken glass on the floor, but no serious damage to the great automobile-assembly lines or the part of the plant where shells were made. The women making shells worked on as calmly as girls in an American candy factory.

The day we visited the factory, June 5th, was also the day the Germans began their second attack, the push southward across the Somme that was to carry them to the Spanish frontier. "It is the beginning of the second round," Pierre Comert announced at the press conference that evening. None of us could admit to ourselves that the war might be a two-round knockout. The French would surely be dislodged from the Somme-Aisne line, we conceded, but it would take weeks to do it. Then they would defend Paris and the line of the Seine, then the line of the Loire. By that time, perhaps, the British would be able to do something. Even the United States might begin to understand what was at stake. But this fight was not to have even a decent second round. The rest after the first round had not been long enough; the French were still out on their feet. Unarmed and outnumbered, they were led by two old men who were at loggerheads. As for Reynaud, he had called into his government Ybarnegaray and Marin, two reactionaries whose only surface virtue was a blustering show of war spirit. Raised to power by Socialist votes, Reynaud had turned toward men whom he trusted because they were of his own Rightist background—Pétain, Mandel, Ybarnegaray, Marin. All his Rightist friends except Mandel joined in smothering him. They felt that by making war against Hitler he was betraying his own class.

When I got back to my hotel that night, tired and discouraged, Fernand the porter, looking radiant, said to me, "What they must be digesting now, the Boches!" He showed me a copy of *Le Temps*, which said the German losses were stupefying. All the attacks had been "contained," but the French Army had executed a slight retreat in good order.

By now there were perceptible changes in the daily life of Paris. There was no telephone service in the hotels, so you had to make a special trip afoot every time you wanted to tell somebody something. Taxis were harder than ever to find. My hotel, which was typical, had six floors. At the beginning of the war in September the proprietor had closed the fourth, fifth, and sixth floors. Now I was the only guest on the second floor, and there were perhaps a half dozen on the first. The staff, naturally, dwindled like the clientele. Every day somebody said goodbye to me. One by one the waiters left, and then it was the headwaiter, who had been kept on after all of his subordinates had been dismissed. The next day it was Toutou, who left the bookkeeping to the housekeeper. A couple of days later, the housekeeper herself left. Finally, there were only a porter and one chambermaid in the daytime, and Fernand at night. "Perhaps, if the line holds, there will be an upturn in business," the proprietor said.

It was at about this time that my restaurateur friend, M. Bisque, with whom I used to make the rounds of the markets, decided to close his restaurant. It was not that the Germans worried him, he explained to me, but there were no more customers, and also his wine dealer was pressing him to pay his bill. M. Bisque, and his wife, who kept the books, and his daughter Yvette, who possessed the *tour de main* for making a soufflé stand up on a flat plate, and his son, who had been an apprentice in the kitchen of the Café de Paris, and Marie-Louise, the waitress, were all leaving the city to run the canteen in a munitions factory south of Fontainebleau. I wished them Godspeed.

For a few days I had lacked the heart to visit Henri and Eglée. Then Henri had come to my hotel to tell me joyfully they had had another letter from Jean-Pierre, who said he had been working twenty-one hours a day repairing tanks for his division. On Sunday, June 9th, which was a warm and drowsy day, I returned Henri's call. On the way I stopped at a florist shop and bought some fine pink roses. The woman in the shop said that shipments from the provinces were irregular, but that fortunately the crisis came at a season when the Paris suburbs were producing plenty of flowers. "We have more goods than purchasers," she said, laughing. When I arrived at the apartment, I found Eglée busy making her muslin money belts. Henri was amusing himself by reading a 1906 edition of the Encyclopaedia Britannica, one of his favorite possessions, and drinking a *vin ordinaire* in which he professed to find a slight resemblance to Ermitage. "This time I think the line will hold," Henri said. "I served under Pétain at Verdun. He will know how to stop them. Only I don't like that talk of infiltration near Forges-les-Eaux."

"Infiltration" was a grim word in this war. The communiqué never admitted that the Germans had pierced the French line, but invariably announced, "Motorized elements have made an infiltration. They have been surrounded and will be destroyed." Two days later the "infiltration" became a salient, from which new infiltrations radiated. When I left the

apartment, Henri walked down as far as the Place des Ab-
besses with me. He wanted to buy a newspaper. As we stood
saying goodbye, we heard a series of reports, too loud and
too widely spaced for anti-aircraft. "Those sound like naval
guns mounted on railroad cars," Henri said. "The Boches
can't be so far away, then." That was the last time I saw
Henri.

At six o'clock that evening, I went to another Anglo-
American press conference at the Hôtel Continental. We were
told that the Ministry of Information was planning to provide
us with safe-conduct passes to use in case we left Paris. That
made us suspect that the government would move very soon.
Then M. Comert told us that Jean Provoust, who had just
been appointed Minister of Information, wanted to talk to all
the American correspondents. M. Provoust, the dynamic publisher of *Paris-Soir*, received us in his office with the factitious
cordiality of a newspaper owner about to ask his staff to take a
pay cut. He said that he didn't want the United States to
think the situation was hopeless. "From a military standpoint," he said, "it is improving steadily. Disregard reports of
the government quitting Paris. We will have many more chats
in this room." John Lloyd, of the Associated Press, who was
president of the Anglo-American Press Association, waited to
see Provoust after the talk and invited him to be guest of
honor at a luncheon the correspondents were having the next
Wednesday. The Minister said he would be charmed, and
then hurried away.

On my way home I saw a number of garbage trucks parked
in the middle of the streets to balk airplane landings. Evidently Paris would be defended. I didn't think, after Provoust's talk, that I would have to leave Paris immediately, but
the situation looked so bad that I decided to begin getting
my passport in order.

Early the next morning, Monday, June 10th, I set out in a
taxi—which the porter had taken two hours to find for
me—to go to the Spanish Consulate General to obtain a
transit visa. This was easy to get if you already had the Portuguese visa, and luckily I already had one which was good for a
year. My taxi-driver came from Lorraine, where, he said,

people knew what patriotism meant. He had fought the other war, four years of it. The country needed men like Poincaré, a Lorrainer, now. "The politicians have sold us out," he said. "And that Leopold," he shouted, "there is a fellow they should have got onto long ago!" Now, he expected, the Germans would come to Paris. But it would be defended, like Madrid. "They will come here, the animals," he said, "but they will leave plenty of feathers! Imagine a tank trying to upset the building of the Crédit Lyonnais! Big buildings are the best defence against those machines." He did not know that the real-estate men would never encourage such an unprofitable use of their property. "Even ten centimes on the franc is something," the rich men were already telling one another, "when one has a great many francs."

From the Spanish Consulate I went to the Prefecture of Police, where I asked for a visa which would permit me to leave France. A woman police official, a sort of chief clerk, said, "Leave your passport and come back for it in not less than four days." "But by that time, Madame," I said, "the Germans may be here and the Prefecture may not exist." Naturally, I didn't leave the passport, but I was foolish to question the permanency of the Prefecture. The French civil servants are the one class unaffected by revolution or conquest. The Germans were to come, as it turned out, but the Prefecture was to stay open, its personnel and routine unchanged. Its great accumulation of information about individual Frenchmen, so useful for the apprehension of patriots and the blackmailing of politicians, was to be at the disposal of the Germans as it had been at Philippe-Egalité's and Napoleon the Little's and Stavisky's. The well-fed young *agents* were to continue on the same beats, unaffected by the end of the war they had never had to fight in. Yesterday the Prefecture had obeyed the orders of M. Mandel, who hated Germans. Now it would obey Herr Abetz, who hated Jews. Change of administration. *Tant pis.*

Afterward I stopped at the Crillon bar, where I met a Canadian general I knew. "The French still have a fine chance," he said. "I am leaving for Tours as soon as I finish this sandwich." I walked over to the Continental to see if M. Comert had any fresh news. As I arrived at the foot of the staircase leading to Comert's office, I met another correspondent on his way out. "If you're going up to the Ministry," he said, "don't bother. The government left Paris this morning." Then he began to chuckle. "You remember when John Lloyd stopped Provoust last night and invited him to the Wednesday luncheon?" he asked. Yes, I remembered. "Well," he said, "Provoust was in a hurry because he was leaving for Tours in a few minutes." I said maybe we had better leave too, and we did.

The New Yorker, August 3 and 10, 1940

The Beginning of the End

by Virginia Cowles

TRY TO THINK in terms of million. Try to think of noise and confusion, of the thick smell of petrol, of the scraping of automobile gears, of shouts, wails, curses, tears. Try to think of a hot sun and underneath it an unbroken stream of humanity flowing southwards from Paris, and you have a picture of the gigantic civilian exodus that presaged the German advance.

I had seen refugees before. I had seen them wending their way along the roads of Spain and Czechoslovakia; straggling across the Polish-Roumanian frontier, trudging down the icy paths of Finland. But I had never seen anything like this. This was the first *mechanized* evacuation in history. There were some people in carts, some on foot and some on bicycles. But for the most part everyone was in a car.

Those cars, lurching, groaning, backfiring, represented a Noah's Ark of vehicles. Anything that had four wheels and an engine was pressed into service, no matter what the state of decrepitude; there were taxi-cabs, ice-trucks, bakery vans, perfume wagons, sports roadsters and Paris buses, all of them packed with human beings. I even saw a hearse loaded with children. They crawled along the roads two and three abreast, sometimes cutting across the fields and straddling the ditches. Tom and I caught up with the stream a mile or so outside Paris on the Paris-Dourdan-Chartres road and in the next three hours covered only nine miles.

We saw terrible sights. All along the way cars that had run out of petrol or broken down, were pushed into the fields. Old people, too tired or ill to walk any farther, were lying on the ground under the merciless glare of the sun. We saw one old woman propped up in the ditch with the family clustered around trying to pour some wine down her throat. Often the stream of traffic was held up by cars that stalled and refused to move again. One car ran out of petrol halfway up a hill. It was a bakery van, driven by a woman. Everyone shouted and honked their horns, while she stood in the middle of the road with her four children around her begging someone to give her some petrol. No one had any to spare. Finally, three men climbed out of a truck and in spite of her agonized protests, shoved the car into the ditch. It fell with a crash. The rear axle broke and the household possessions piled on top sprawled across the field. She screamed out a frenzy of abuse, then flung herself on the ground and sobbed. Once again the procession moved on.

In that world of terror, panic and confusion, it was difficult to believe that these were the citizens of Paris, citizens whose forefathers had fought for their freedom like tigers and stormed the Bastille with their bare hands. For the first time, I began to understand what had happened to France. Morale was a question of faith; faith in your cause, faith in your goal, but above all else, faith in your leaders. How could these people have faith in leaders who had abandoned them? Leaders who had given them no directions, no information, no reassurances; who neither had arranged for their evacuation nor called on them to stay at their places and fight for Paris until the last? If this was an example of French leadership, no wonder France was doomed. Everywhere the machinery seemed to have broken down. The dam had begun to crumble and hysteria, a trickle at first, had grown into a torrent.

Even the military roads were overrun with panic-stricken civilians. Tom was an officially accredited war correspondent, so he swung off on to one of them. Although the entrance was patrolled by gendarmes, who demanded our credentials, there was no one to keep traffic from streaming in at the intersections and a mile or so farther on we once again found civilian cars moving along two or three abreast. At one point an artillery unit on its way up to the new front southeast of Paris was blocked by a furniture truck stalled across the road. The driver, with perspiration pouring down his face was trying to crank the car while the soldiers yelled and cursed at him. One of them paced angrily up and down, saying "Filthy civilians. Filthy, filthy civilians." At last, the truck got started again and the unit moved past. Another time, a procession of ambulances, with gongs clanging frantically, were held up by congestion on the outskirts of a village for over an hour. The drivers swore loudly but it had little effect; I wondered what was happening to the poor devils inside.

The only military units that succeeded in getting a clear berth were the tanks. Once we looked back to see two powerful fifteen-ton monsters thundering up behind us. They were travelling about forty miles an hour and the effect was remarkable. People gave one look and pulled in to the ditches. They went rolling by, the great treads tearing up the earth and throwing pieces of dirt into the air like a fountain. After them came a number of fast-moving lorries and a string of soldiers on motor-cycles with machine-guns attached to the side-cars. They all seemed in excellent spirits: one of the tanks was gaily marked in chalk *"La Petite Marie,"* and the trucks and guns were draped with flowers. Two of the motor-cyclists shouted at us, asking if we had any cigarettes. Tom told me to throw them a couple of packages. They were so pleased they signalled us to follow them, escorted us past the long string of civilian cars to the middle of the convoy and placed us firmly between the two tanks. For the next ten or fifteen minutes we roared along at forty miles an hour. Unfortunately, eight or nine miles down the road they turned off, the motor-cyclists waved good-bye and blew us kisses, and once again we found ourselves caught up in the slow-moving procession of evacuees.

It was nearly nine o'clock now and we had covered little more than twenty miles. "I wonder if we'll make it," said Tom, looking at his watch. When we had left Paris at five o'clock there were already reports that the Germans were circling around on both sides of the capital to cut off the roads in the rear. Tom had a military map and we decided to try the cross-country lanes. Some of them were scarcely more than footpaths but we could at least average ten or twelve miles an hour, which was a great improvement. It was getting so dark it was difficult to see and twice we barely avoided running over people with no lights on their bicycles. Suddenly the sky lit up with a flash and we heard a far-away rumble. It was the first gunfire I had heard all day. "Something's creeping up on us," said Tom. "Still, if we keep on like this, I think we'll be all right."

We drove along the twisting lane for five or six miles. It was a relief to be in the open countryside away from the suffocating smell of petrol, but the road was so black the driving was a strain. Tom had some food in the back of the car and we decided to stop and have something to eat. He was in favour of finding a haystack to lean against, but the next few miles of country were barren and rocky. At last we saw a clump of trees outlined in the darkness. It seemed the best we could do, so we pulled over to the side of the road. The car gave a violent lurch and careened into a six-foot ditch. Only the right wheels were gripping the road. The left side was flat against the earth. We were suspended at such a sharp angle we had difficulty in forcing the upper door, but at last succeeded in climbing out.

The rumble of guns seemed to be louder and the flashes against the sky more frequent. "*Boches* or no *Boches*," said Tom, "it looks as though we're going to linger here a while. Let's pick out a place to eat, then I'll see if I can find someone to give us a hand."

But even here we were frustrated. The field was soaking wet. There was one miserable haystack in the middle of it, damp and soggy. We went back to the road and paced up and down for ten or fifteen minutes, wondering if anyone would pass. It was getting cold and I began to shiver. After having cursed the traffic for hours, it was slightly ironical to find ourselves longing for the sight of a human being.

Tom finally started back to the last village, several miles away, and I climbed back into the car (which was like going down a toboggan slide) to try and get warm. It was a beautiful night. The sky was clear and starry, and the only noise to break the quiet was the drone of crickets and the spasmodic thunder of guns. I wondered how far the Germans had got. Funny to think that people in America probably knew more than we did as to what was going on.

It was nearly midnight when Tom got back again. He had tried a dozen farmhouses but everyone was in bed. At last (with the help of a hundred-franc note) he had extracted a promise from one of the farmers to come at dawn with a team of horses and pull us out.

That was seven precious hours away, but it was the best he could do. As an American citizen, I was in no danger, but if Tom were captured, it meant an internment camp for the rest of the war. He appeared completely unruffled, however, and commented with characteristic English calmness: "Well, there's nothing to be done about it. Now, let's eat. God, I'm hungry."

We sat by the roadside, drinking wine and munching bread and cheese; then we got out all the coats and sweaters we could find, wrapped them round us, and climbed back into the car. The angle was so uncomfortable I slept only by fits and starts, expecting momentarily to be awakened by the noise of German tanks. Luckily, no such startling developments took place. The farmer kept his promise and shortly after five o'clock appeared with two, large, fat, white horses who pulled the car out as easily as though it had been a perambulator. Once again we started on our way.

We stopped at the next village—I can't remember the name of it—to get some coffee. The first sight that greeted us was half a dozen British Tommies lined up on the crooked cobble-stone street, the corporal standing in front of them, bawling them out for some misdemeanour. They were large, beefy-looking men that might have stepped out of a page from *Punch*. When the corporal dismissed them they grinned sheepishly and made a few jokes behind his back. Tom asked one of them where the officers were billeted, and I went into the café to try to get some of the grime off my clothes. In spite of the early hour there was a buzz of activity inside. Several people were sitting around, and a radio was blaring loudly. The announcer was saying something about the "heroic resistance of our troops." An old man made a gesture of disbelief and muttered something I couldn't hear. The woman with him replied angrily, her harsh voice echoing through the café: *"Ne dites pas ça. Il faut espérer."*

I asked the waitress if there was any coffee, but she regarded me in mild surprise and replied that the refugees had gone through the village like a swarm of locusts. "Every-where," she said, "they have stripped the countryside bare."

It took me some time to get clean again, and when I came out I found Tom waiting for me with two officers, wearing the insignia of the Royal Engineers. They offered to give us breakfast and led us down the street to the mess. They seemed to know little more than we did; they told us they had just received orders to move up to a new position. Most of them had been in France for the last five or six months and pressed us eagerly with questions about England. French mo-rale may have been shaky, but there was nothing down-hearted about this group. "You don't think people at home will be discouraged by this setback, do you?" 'Setback!' That was a good one, I thought. When we climbed into the car again they all clustered around and one of them said: "Well, so long. See you in Cologne next Christmas!"

We did the next hundred miles to Tours in about five hours. We had learned the trick now and kept entirely to the country lanes which, rough though they were, were fairly clear of refugees. It was only when we got within ten miles of Tours and were forced back on the main road again that the trickle once again became a mighty stream. Added to this, Tom's radiator began leaking. The water boiled up and clouds of steam began pouring out of the front. It took us nearly an hour to get into the city. The great bridge over the Loire looked like a long thin breadcrust swarming with ants.

Finally at one-thirty, with Tom's car gasping and heaving, we drew up before the Hotel de l'Univers. The first person I saw was Knickerbocker, just coming out of the door.

"My God! How did you get here?"

"You're always asking me that."

"But where've you come from?"

"Paris."

"Paris! But the Germans went into Paris hours ago. When did you leave?"

I told him.

"They were in the Bois de Boulogne last night. You must have rubbed shoulders with them on the way out. Probably you just didn't recognize them," he added with a grin. "All soldiers look grey in the dark."

*   *   *

Tours was bedlam. The French High Command had announced that the River Loire was to be the next line of defence and all sorts of wild rumors were circulating: first, that the German Air Force had threatened to obliterate the town; and, second, that German motor-cycle units had reached Le Mans only thirty miles away, and were likely to come thundering through the streets at any moment now. The Government had already left for Bordeaux and the refugees who had scrambled into Tours in a panic were now trying to scramble out again in still more of a panic. I ran into Eddie Ward of the B.B.C., who told me that *Press Wireless*, the only means of communication with the outside world (all cables to England were sent via America at eightpence a word) was still functioning, and that he and the *Reuter* staff were remaining another day. As it was my only chance to file a story, I decided to stay too. Eddie said *Reuter's* could probably provide me with a bed and he would give me a place in his car to Bordeaux in the morning.

There were a good many speculations about Winston Churchill's conversation with Reynaud and Weygand three days before; he was believed to have urged the French, if the worst came to the worst, to continue the war from North Africa. Although it had been announced in London that complete agreement had been reached, "as to the measures to be taken to meet the developments in the war situation," most of the journalists were pessimistic about the prospects of France's continuation of the fight. French officials seemed in a state of moral collapse; even the censorship appeared to have broken down, but no one complained about that. Up till this time despatches had been censored so rigidly it was impossible to give any indication of the situation. Now, quite suddenly, everyone could say what they liked. I wrote a long piece about the panic and confusion along the road from Paris and not a word was cut. Gordon Waterfield sent a story suggesting that France was threatened with a defeat similar to that of 1870 and the next morning Harold King sent an even more pessimistic cable. Gordon told me later that when these despatches reached London the censors were so surprised they held them up for a considerable time while they found out from higher authorities whether it was really true that France was in such a bad way.

Eddie drove me over to *Reuter's* headquarters, a large, handsome edifice about a mile from the centre of the town. The house had been taken on a six months' lease to the tune of forty thousand francs and, as it turned out, was occupied exactly forty-eight hours. I spent the night there, which seemed an odd interlude. From a world of dirt and discomfort I suddenly found myself plunged into a Hollywood bedroom, decorated with mirrors and chintz, a thick white rug and a pale green telephone. That evening eight of us dined at a table with candles glowing and silver gleaming. We had turtle soup, tournedos with sauce *Bearnaise*, fresh vegetables and a wonderful cherry pie. The world might be turning upside down, but it was difficult to realize it.

The house was run by a charming, middle-aged couple— a caretaker and his wife. The latter, plump and motherly, was also taut and defiant; she refused to let bad news alarm her and clung ferociously to the belief that France would rally in the end. "If there were more people like her," said Eddie, "there wouldn't be an end. But, unfortunately, there aren't."

I spent that afternoon writing my story for the *Sunday Times*. About seven o'clock the wail of sirens hooted through the town and a few minutes later I heard the drone of bombers. I tried to ignore it and went on typing. Suddenly I heard a shriek from the drawing-room. I ran downstairs and found the eight- and nine-year-old children of the caretakers jumping up and down with joy. *"Nous avons vu les Boches!"* Then they both leaned far out of the window, pointing towards the sky. You could just make out a few small specks circling overhead. I wished I could get as enthusiastic over an air raid; in spite of all the talk about sparing children the terrors of bombardment, they seemed to be the only ones who really enjoyed it.

I was surprised that their mother didn't order them into a shelter, but I learned later she was disdainful of people who took cover. The next morning when the German planes came over again, several bombs fell near us, shaking the house violently. Eddie and I went down to the kitchen. She gave us an enquiring look.

"You're not afraid of the *Boches*, are you?"

"Oh, no," said Eddie weakly. "I thought perhaps you might have an extra cup of coffee."

"Oh, certainly." Her face brightened. "I don't like to see people afraid of the *Boches*. They're all filthy bullies and cowards. My husband was in the last war and he said whenever they came up against equal numbers they turned and ran. They're all the same. There's nothing to be afraid of."

"Nothing," I agreed, my heart still pounding uncertainly. Eddie gave me a sour look.

We left shortly after lunch for Bordeaux. There were six of us: Gordon Waterfield, Harold King, Courtenay Young, Joan Slocombe (the pretty nineteen-year-old daughter of George Slocombe of the *Sunday Express*), Eddie and myself. Gordon had a Ford roadster and Eddie a Citroen, with an R.A.F. number plate, which he had picked up somewhere between Brussels and Tours. They had been wise enough to do a good deal of shopping and it took over half an hour to load up the cars with blankets, sleeping-bags, cooking utensils and stores of food—not to mention typewriters, luggage, office files, a camping tent and a collapsible canoe.

Just before we started off, Courtenay Young and I hurried down to the *Press Wireless* office to send a final despatch. On the way back I heard someone call to me and looked around to see the little Egyptian with whom I had travelled to Paris. His hair was streaming round his face, his clothes were caked with mud, and he looked more agitated than ever. He had had a terrible time. He had found his house deserted, and his children gone; he hadn't yet discovered what had happened to them. He had left Paris only twenty-four hours before and had actually seen the Germans entering the city through the Aubervilliers Gate. Motor-cycle units had passed as close as two hundred yards from where he was standing. He said the occupation had come as a shock to many of the people and the scenes of despair were unbelievable. Men and women wept openly in the street. "Some of them went almost crazy," he gasped. "I saw one woman pull out a revolver and shoot her dog, then set fire to her house."

The Egyptian was on his way to Bordeaux. He was in such a rush he couldn't stop to tell me more and I never learned the story of how he had managed to escape from Paris.

Looking for Trouble, 1941

I First Saw the Ruins of Dunkerque

by John Fisher

Berlin (*by cable*)

OUR PARTY was whipped into shape with German precision and we set out from Cologne in seven high-powered Mercedes-Benz staff cars. Along the road to Aachen I saw kids playing soldiers with tin-pipe cannons and little helmets, emulating their fathers at the front. At Maastricht we crossed the Meuse. The Belgians had blown up the bridges but the German *pioniere* [sappers] had slapped up two new iron bridges within 24 hours. Here posters forbade citizens outside their homes after 10 p.m. lest they be shot by patrols.

Along the Meuse Valley we passed long lines of refugees plodding back to their homes after the vain flight, dodging German Army trucks which drove at top speed along the narrow road. In Liège bread was being rationed though food seemed sufficient. We were told to stock up as we were entering an area where food was scarce. On the road to Namur signs of heavy fighting increased. Mine traps, still charged, forced us off the highway. In Namur almost all houses in the northern section of town had been hit or shelled, bridges blown up and guts of houses scattered in the streets. Storekeepers were doing business in shops with their fronts blown out.

This war was fought along the roads. Messerschmitts swept low across the center of a road, machine-gunning Allied truck columns, but bombs were not dropped on the roads. For miles south of Namur I could see holes on either side of the road, about 150 ft. apart, where bombs had been dropped so as to scatter shrapnel over the road surface without tearing up the road itself. German officers informed us: "We would be foolish to demolish the roads since roadside bombings are just as efficient." Unfortunately for the Belgians, they build marvelous roads for the German mechanized army which could speed along unhindered at 30 or 40 miles an hour.

I was amazed to see so few soldiers' graves along the roadside. Only here and there did a cross topped by a steel helmet mark the spot where a man fell. The Germans bury their dead within one hour. This is done to prevent an epidemic and to spare the soldiers the sight of their dead comrades.

Late in the afternoon we drove through the Maginot Line, marked by huge street barricades, barbed wire, deep lines of bunkers strong enough to resist 6-in. shelling. Bunkers were shoved out far ahead of the main fortification, which centered about Maubeuge.

The Germans concentrated strong tank and mechanized infantry forces upon this fortress, shelling and bombing the town itself for three days. On the last day 15 Stukas in 15 minutes gave it the death blow. Inside the town gates I saw with what efficiency Maubeuge had been shelled and bombed, precisely and systematically reducing the homes of 25,000 inhabitants to a heap of rubbish. Yet not one single street was hit or damaged except for refuse which was easily removable. Two old women salvaging bits of furniture from their little shack told me that some 50 civilians had been killed by a shell dropping on the church. Their bewildered expressions and wild gesticulations told adequately of the terrorizing effect of Stuka attacks, with whistling and howling bombs smashing everything within reach. The air was filled with the stench of dead, which German officers called the "perfume of battle."

At Catillon we happened upon 15,000 French and British prisoners taken at La Bassée on May 28. Among them was a platoon of Lancasters, its leader reporting 25% casualties. He said an attack of 300 tanks in combination with heavy trench mortars got them. He said: "It was the fault of our staff in getting orders jumbled. The correct order in the right place would have got us out of that hole." They had been marching for three days in the scorching sun with little food and water, since they had been caught fighting without their complete packs. Frenchmen, he said, had been taken with full equipment including tents.

He further said: "I never saw our own Air Force during all that time." He claimed that for three days straight he never fired a single artillery shot and that when the opportunity arose to lambaste the German tanks a French officer forbade firing, mistrusting the British ability to fire over the French infantry. I asked him about the German Army. He answered: "It looks pretty wonderful and has us absolutely bamboozled. We were no match for it. I'd like to tell this to some officials back home." Grabbing an ax handle tightly and shaking it unmistakably, he said: "Politicians muffed the works!"

The Englishmen's spirits still seemed full of go and ready to fight. "Let me at them again," said the platoon sergeant. But the whole vast camp was a depressing sight. Men were begging for cigarets and asking for bread, since they got only one loaf for four men. They stood along a small river bank washing and shaving or clustered around small wood fires warming up what bits of canned food they had.

We passed through Arras, finding the railway station and the center of town destroyed, and sped on toward the coast at Boulogne. Along the road I saw hundreds of neatly stacked piles of 6-in. Allied shells. Columns of British trucks, now repainted, were carrying German supplies. In between them were motorcycle units with mounted machine guns, a field kitchen cooking on the run or trucks loaded with infantry— magnificent strapping fellows, with the look of conquerors.

Considering the 40-mile clip at which the German columns move, I was amazed at the small number of wrecked trucks. When I asked an officer "How come?" he looked surprised and said: "It is *verboten* to have collisions."

At Boulogne the docks were smashed to bits, warehouses burned to the ground and all around were great piles of Allied war matériel. In the harbor I saw hundreds of wine barrels that the French apparently always carry with them. We passed on up the coast through Calais and St.-Omer to Cassel, a hilltop town bristling with guns and jammed with trucks. Anti-aircraft guns, armored cars, equipment, wine bottles, canned food were lying about in heaps and piles. So well equipped were the British forces that even football shoes, dart-boards and other games were scattered among the rubbish.

Shortly before Bergues, last strong Dunkerque fortification, we had to leave our cars. Picking our way through a swamp, we stopped to watch German Stukas trying to force their way through a barrage of French anti-aircraft fire. We could see the shells exploding close to their tails with little white puffs of smoke but never hitting them.

Along railroad tracks, through a mine-infested wood, we entered Bergues in Indian file. Trucks, tanks, vehicles of all kinds had been hastily pushed together in a futile effort to barricade the road. The town gate was blocked by a huge American caterpillar snow plow, behind which a French machine-gunner had left an unfinished meal. I squeezed past and entered a scene of complete ruin. For four days German Stukas and artillery had rained a shower of steel upon the town leaving no house untouched. Flames were still licking their way among the debris, while charred wood and burning cloth filled the air with stifling smoke. One church had remained untouched while another had its tower completely demolished. German shells were whistling overhead. And underneath these sounds I could hear the rapid staccato bark of German machine guns, answered by the slower *tak tak* of French gunners. To the north we could see the billowing smoke clouds of burning Dunkerque.

As we walked through the streets I noticed people here and there creeping out of their cellars. Two thousand had remained through the six-day bombardment. A French tank car exploded while nearby horses leisurely grazed stray bits of grass surrounding a World War monument. Swallows were flying about the empty street looking for their homes. The war had swept across Bergues and in its wake left nothing but ruins. While the German advance was breaking French resistance barely a mile to the north, soldiers here were already emptying French warehouses. Cigarets, chocolate, millions of rounds of munitions and food supplies for six months were their booty. Allied trucks and motorbikes already were doing their bit for the German Army. Again I saw a litter of abandoned matériel, ping-pong sets and golf clubs among it.

We left Bergues, since the Germans were still pouring shells into Dunkerque, and started down towards Lille, passing an ancient fort which surrendered to a single German tank when the tank appeared in its courtyard. The outskirts of Lille were completely shattered and in ruins, while the center of the town remained intact. The stench of dead horses, some in harness in front of carts, filled the air. Near Ath we passed thousands of French prisoners behind barbed-wire fences, guarded by one German soldier.

Late at night we came into Brussels, undamaged except for blown-up bridges and radio station. Sidewalk cafes were going a booming business as German soldiers tasted good coffee. Food was excellent, trolleys and buses were still running. But German soldiers and foreign correspondents seemed to be getting a corner on the American cigaret supplies, which are getting scarcer every day. Bread has already been rationed but the people of Brussels are not complaining. Although they do not like the Germans commanding the streets, they admit that the conquerors treat them with consideration. They say this is far better than 1918. I noticed that a lot of young Germans had Belgian girl friends. Regarding the capitulation of the Belgian Army, Belgians confide: "To what our King has done our hearts say no but our minds say yes."

Next morning we headed north again and that evening I slept in the hotel at Ostend where the Belgian Government had stopped briefly. A small card on a door said: "Bureau of the Foreign Minister" and beneath was written "Pierlot."

We started back down the Channel coast toward Dunkerque, passing ever-longer returning German supply trains, which told us that the battle of Dunkerque was almost over. We drove along the Moëres Canal, filled with burning barges, and passed a field where hundreds of Allied trucks stretched in lines as far as the eye could see. Equipment, supplies, coats, helmets were lying about in heaps and mounds—an immense booty for the Germans. The attack upon Dunkerque was mainly carried by infantry and artillery, not tanks, as retreating French had flooded the area by opening the sluices of the Moëres Canal. German infantry, I was told, had to advance through water up to their necks. I saw many of them wearing Allied khaki uniforms until their own were dry again.

Before us lay Dunkerque resting at last after seven solid days of the most terrific bombardment by artillery and planes. A few hours after the 40,000 French defenders gave up, I entered this last foothold of the Allied army in Flanders. The city was a pile of rubbish. Every building was destroyed, not a wall intact. Bricks and stones, many feet deep, jammed the streets. Flames were still crackling and smoke swirled through the town as fires spread unchecked. I stumbled through the smoke over twisted iron girders, dodged hanging wires still red hot, jumped across pools of molten tin and piles of glass, walked over boulders weighing hundreds of pounds. I saw a drunk who had blotted out his mind, perhaps to escape the terror of Stuka bombs. I saw a woman completely crazed running to the balcony of her shattered house, shouting an indistinguishable name over and over. I saw men and women with tears running down their dusty faces. But, despite the fact that the town had surrendered only a short time previously, refugees already were returning and people who had remained in their cellars were wandering dazedly about the streets.

André Noël, Assistant Police Commissar of Dunkerque, had lived with his wife in a cellar for two weeks. Oddly enough Noël, onetime German subject, had served in the German Army during the World War in the same regiment of the staff officer leading our party. When the officer said, "Now you can report back for duty," Noël replied unhesitatingly: "I am still a Frenchman after all."

At Dunkerque harbor Frenchmen lay where they fell, their bodies bloated, legs and arms blown off, guts hanging out. Sprawled in groups, they fell behind their machine guns, the gunner still holding the trigger. The horrid stench of the dead was overpoweringly nauseating. Rows of British trucks unable to be loaded aboard ship stood burned on a dock. Piles of bullets and munitions filled the path. At one of the smoldering docks a French tanker named *Salomé* caught fire, its smoke choking us within a few minutes. Distant oil tanks exploded, throwing flames 100 ft. into the air.

One could feel the air filled with plagues so we hastened to get away. Outside of Dunkerque long columns of German soldiers were marching southward. "The war is over up here," said a young infantryman to me. "We are now looking for new battlefields." Some 3,000 French cavalry horses wandered aimlessly in fields along the Moëres Canal, unheedful of their dead comrades that lay about the meadows with broken

backs and shell-torn bodies. Many more were floating in the
Canal. I saw horses standing in water up to their bellies, un-
decided what to do. The Canal waters were rising constantly
as we drove over flooded roads, heading back toward Berlin.

Life, June 24, 1940

French Conceal Despair; Move as Automatons

by Sonia Tomara

BORDEAUX. June 17 (Delayed). Nothing seems outwardly changed in the crowds that fill Bordeaux tonight. Yet it is as if a pall had fallen over the city. Dull hopelessness has overtaken the French people gathered here.

If one looks at them attentively, one notices that they move and act like automatons. Men and women enter restaurants, they fill cafes, for they have no homes where they can go to cry or hide their despair. They talk sometimes, they even laugh, because they have to go on living. But the specter of the future is present in all minds.

I was in a cafe this noon—there is nowhere else to go when one has no room even to sleep in. The papers had announced that Premier Henri Petain headed the government. I knew it meant an armistice, but for the majority of the French the marshal still was the invincible hero of Verdun.

When the radio announced that he would speak, all faces became tense. There was dead silence, and the old voice came clear to all. None moved as he spoke of his own sacrifice, of the heroism of the troops and the plight of the refugees.

Then the marshal said: "It is with a heavy heart that I tell you that we must try to stop the fight."

People looked at one another as if the words had stunned them without quite reaching their conscience. But the old soldier spoke further of "means of putting an end to hostilities." Tears began to fill all eyes.

"It is amistice," a woman said near me. "It is defeat," a man replied in a strange voice. There were no gestures, no words of rebellion.

We all felt it was the inevitable for which we had been prepared by weeks of horror and misery. The military communiques had said openly that the situation on the front was very grave. Tales of men returned from the front had told of the horrible conditions in which French troops had fought against a superior enemy.

A terrific thunderstorm broke over Bordeaux as Petain spoke. Blinding lightning followed by thunder disturbed the radio. People's nerves were so much on edge that women shuddered at the thunder as if bombs were falling.

In the middle of the afternoon, the crowds gathered in the center of the city were frightened by a sudden roaring of a plane, which flew at great speed over the roof-tops. It appeared that the pilot was French. Perhaps he had been made frantic by the idea of the armistice and Adolf Hitler's victory. He roared three times over the town and then vanished.

French aviators seem to feel more acridly than anybody the despair of defeat. They had made super-human efforts to fight by personal valor and skill the German superiority in numbers, and they had succeeded. One of them said to me tonight: "Everything has been useless, as it appears now." And then with a tired gesture: "I have not slept more than ten hours in the last week. If we had even two-thirds of Germany's planes, we should have won the war. Why did America not send them in time?"

New York *Herald Tribune*, June 19, 1940

"Revengeful, Triumphant Hate"

by William L. Shirer

PARIS, *June 21*

On the exact spot in the little clearing in the Forest of Compiègne where at five a.m. on November 11, 1918, the armistice which ended the World War was signed, Adolf Hitler today handed *his* armistice terms to France. To make German revenge complete, the meeting of the German and French plenipotentiaries took place in Marshal Foch's private car, in which Foch laid down the armistice terms to Germany twenty-two years ago. Even the same table in the rickety old *wagon-lit* car was used. And through the windows we saw Hitler occupying the very seat on which Foch had sat at that table when he dictated the other armistice.

The humiliation of France, of the French, was complete. And yet in the preamble to the armistice terms Hitler told the French that he had not chosen this spot at Compiègne out of revenge; merely to right an old wrong. From the demeanour of the French delegates I gathered that they did not appreciate the difference.

The German terms we do not know yet. The preamble says the general basis for them is: (1) to prevent a resumption of the fighting; (2) to offer Germany complete guarantees for her continuation of the war against Britain; (3) to create the foundations for a peace, the basis of which is to be the reparation of an injustice inflicted upon Germany by force. The third point seems to mean: revenge for the defeat of 1918.

Kerker for NBC and I for CBS in a joint half-hour broadcast early this evening described today's amazing scene as best we could. It made, I think, a good broadcast.

The armistice negotiations began at three fifteen p.m. A warm June sun beat down on the great elm and pine trees, and cast pleasant shadows on the wooded avenues as Hitler,

72

with the German plenipotentiaries at his side, appeared. He alighted from his car in front of the French monument to Alsace-Lorraine which stands at the end of an avenue about two hundred yards from the clearing where the armistice car waits on exactly the same spot it occupied twenty-two years ago.

The Alsace-Lorraine statue, I noted, was covered with German war flags so that you could not see its sculptured work nor read its inscription. But I had seen it some years before—the large sword representing the sword of the Allies, and its point sticking into a large, limp eagle, representing the old Empire of the Kaiser. And the inscription underneath in French saying: "TO THE HEROIC SOLDIERS OF FRANCE . . . DEFENDERS OF THE COUNTRY AND OF RIGHT . . . GLORIOUS LIBERATORS OF ALSACE-LORRAINE."

Through my glasses I saw the Führer stop, glance at the monument, observe the Reich flags with their big Swastikas in the centre. Then he strode slowly towards us, towards the little clearing in the woods. I observed his face. It was grave, solemn, yet brimming with revenge. There was also in it, as in his springy step, a note of the triumphant conqueror, the defier of the world. There was something else, difficult to describe, in his expression, a sort of scornful, inner joy at being present at this great reversal of fate—a reversal he himself had wrought.

Now he reaches the little opening in the woods. He pauses and looks slowly around. The clearing is in the form of a circle some two hundred yards in diameter and laid out like a park. Cypress trees line it all round—and behind them, the great elms and oaks of the forest. This has been one of France's national shrines for twenty-two years. From a discreet position on the perimeter of the circle we watch.

Hitler pauses, and gazes slowly around. In a group just behind him are the other German plenipotentiaries: Göring, grasping his field-marshal's baton in one hand. He wears the sky-blue uniform of the air force. All the Germans are in uniform, Hitler in a double-breasted grey uniform, with the Iron Cross hanging from his left breast pocket. Next to Göring are the two German army chiefs—General Keitel, chief of the Supreme Command, and General von Brauchitsch, commander-in-chief of the German army. Both are just approaching sixty, but look younger, especially Keitel, who has a dapper appearance with his cap slightly cocked on one side.

Then there is Erich Raeder, Grand Admiral of the German Fleet, in his blue naval uniform and the invariable upturned collar which German naval officers usually wear. There are two non-military men in Hitler's suite — his Foreign Minister, Joachim von Ribbentrop, in the field-grey uniform of the Foreign Office; and Rudolf Hess, Hitler's deputy, in a grey party uniform.

The time is now three eighteen p.m. Hitler's personal flag is run up on a small standard in the centre of the opening.

Also in the centre is a great granite block which stands some three feet above the ground. Hitler, followed by the others, walks slowly over to it, steps up, and reads the inscription engraved in great high letters on that block. It says: "HERE ON THE ELEVENTH OF NOVEMBER 1918 SUCCUMBED THE CRIMINAL PRIDE OF THE GERMAN EMPIRE . . . VANQUISHED BY THE FREE PEOPLES WHICH IT TRIED TO ENSLAVE."

Hitler reads it and Göring reads it. They all read it, standing there in the June sun and the silence. I look for the expression on Hitler's face. I am but fifty yards from him and see him through my glasses as though he were directly in front of me. I have seen that face many times at the great moments of his life. But today! It is afire with scorn, anger, hate, revenge, triumph. He steps off the monument and contrives to make even this gesture a masterpiece of contempt. He glances back at it, contemptuous, angry — angry, you almost feel, because he cannot wipe out the awful, provoking lettering with one sweep of his high Prussian boot. He glances slowly around the clearing, and now, as his eyes meet ours, you grasp the depth of his hatred. But there is triumph there too — revengeful, triumphant hate. Suddenly, as though his face were not giving quite complete expression to his feelings, he throws his whole body into harmony with his mood. He swiftly snaps his hands on his hips, arches his shoulders, plants his feet wide apart. It is a magnificent gesture of defiance, of burning contempt for this place now and all that it has stood for in the twenty-two years since it witnessed the humbling of the German Empire.

Finally Hitler leads his party over to another granite stone, a smaller one fifty yards to one side. Here it was that the railroad car in which the German plenipotentiaries stayed during the 1918 armistice was placed—from November 8 to 11. Hitler merely glances at the inscription, which reads: "The German Plenipotentiaries." The stone itself, I notice, is set between a pair of rusty old railroad tracks, the ones on which the German car stood twenty-two years ago. Off to one side along the edge of the clearing is a large statue in white stone of Marshal Foch as he looked when he stepped out of the armistice car on the morning of November 11, 1918. Hitler skips it; does not appear to see it.

It is now three twenty-three p.m. and the Germans stride over to the armistice car. For a moment or two they stand in the sunlight outside the car, chatting. Then Hitler steps up into the car, followed by the others. We can see nicely through the car windows. Hitler takes the place occupied by Marshal Foch when the 1918 armistice terms were signed. The others spread themselves around him. Four chairs on the opposite side of the table from Hitler remain empty. The French have not yet appeared. But we do not wait long. Exactly at three thirty p.m. they alight from a car. They have flown up from Bordeaux to a near-by landing field. They too glance at the Alsace-Lorraine memorial, but it's a swift glance. Then they walk down the avenue flanked by three German officers. We see them now as they come into the sunlight of the clearing.

General Huntziger, wearing a bleached khaki uniform, Air General Bergeret and Vice-Admiral Le Luc, both in dark blue uniforms, and then, almost buried in the uniforms, M. Noël, French Ambassador to Poland. The German guard of honour, drawn up at the entrance to the clearing, snaps to attention for the French as they pass, but it does not present arms.

It is a grave hour in the life of France. The Frenchmen keep their eyes straight ahead. Their faces are solemn, drawn. They are the picture of tragic dignity.

They walk stiffly to the car, where they are met by two German officers, Lieutenant-General Tippelskirch, Quartermaster General, and Colonel Thomas, chief of the Führer's headquarters. The Germans salute. The French salute. The atmosphere is what Europeans call "correct." There are salutes, but no handshakes.

Now we get our picture through the dusty windows of that old *wagon-lit* car. Hitler and the other German leaders rise as the French enter the drawing-room. Hitler gives the Nazi salute, the arm raised. Ribbentrop and Hess do the same. I cannot see M. Noël to notice whether he salutes or not.

Hitler, as far as we can see through the windows, does not say a word to the French or to anybody else. He nods to General Keitel at his side. We see General Keitel adjusting his papers. Then he starts to read. He is reading the preamble to the German armistice terms. The French sit there with marble-like faces and listen intently. Hitler and Göring glance at the green table-top.

The reading of the preamble lasts but a few minutes. Hitler, we soon observe, has no intention of remaining very long, of listening to the reading of the armistice terms themselves. At three forty-two p.m., twelve minutes after the French arrive, we see Hitler stand up, salute stiffly, and then stride out of the drawing-room, followed by Göring, Brauchitsch, Raeder, Hess, and Ribbentrop. The French, like figures of stone, remain at the green-topped table. General Keitel remains with them. He starts to read them the detailed conditions of the armistice.

Hitler and his aides stride down the avenue towards the Alsace-Lorraine monument, where their cars are waiting. As they pass the guard of honour, the German band strikes up the two national anthems, *Deutschland, Deutschland über Alles* and the *Horst Wessel* song. The whole ceremony in which Hitler has reached a new pinnacle in his meteoric career and Germany avenged the 1918 defeat is over in a quarter of an hour.

Berlin Diary, 1941

Can They Take It?

by Edward R. Murrow

SEPTEMBER 8, 1940

Yesterday afternoon—it seems days ago now—I drove down to the East End of London, the East India Dock Road, Commercial Road, through Silvertown, down to the mouth of the Thames Estuary. It was a quiet and almost pleasant trip through those streets running between rows of working-class houses, with the cranes, the docks, the ships, and the oil tanks off on the right. We crossed the river and drove up on a little plateau, which gave us a view from the mouth of the Thames to London. And then an air-raid siren, called "Weeping Willie" by the men who tend it, began its uneven screaming. Down on the coast the white puffballs of antiaircraft fire began to appear against a steel-blue sky. The first flight of German bombers was coming up the river to start the twelve-hour attack against London. They were high and not very numerous. The Hurricanes and Spitfires were already in the air, climbing for altitude above the near-by airdrome. The fight moved inland and out of sight. Things were relatively quiet for about half an hour. Then the British fighters returned. And five minutes later the German bombers, flying in V-formation, began pouring in. The antiaircraft fire was good. Sometimes it seemed to burst right on the nose of the leading machine, but still they came on. On the airdrome, ground crews swarmed over those British fighters, fitting ammunition belts and pouring in gasoline. As soon as one fighter was ready, it took the air, and there was no waiting for flight leaders or formation. The Germans were already coming back, down the river, heading for France.

Up toward London we could see billows of smoke fanning out above the river, and over our heads the British fighters, climbing almost straight up, trying to intercept the bombers before they got away. It went on for two hours and then the "all-clear." We went down to a near-by pub for dinner. Children were already organizing a hunt for bits of shrapnel. Under some bushes beside the road there was a baker's cart. Two boys, still sobbing, were trying to get a quivering bay mare back between the shafts. The lady who ran the pub told us that these raids were bad for the chickens, the dogs, and the horses. A toothless old man of nearly seventy came in and asked for a pint of mild and bitters, confided that he had always, all his life, gone to bed at eight o'clock and found now that three pints of beer made him drowsy-like so he could sleep through any air raid.

Before eight, the siren sounded again. We went back to a haystack near the airdrome. The fires up the river had turned the moon blood red. The smoke had drifted down till it formed a canopy over the Thames; the guns were working all around us, the bursts looking like fireflies in a southern summer night. The Germans were sending in two or three planes at a time, sometimes only one, in relays. They would pass overhead. The guns and lights would follow them, and in about five minutes we could hear the hollow grunt of the bombs. Huge pear-shaped bursts of flame would rise up into the smoke and disappear. The world was upside down. Vincent Sheean lay on one side of me and cursed in five languages; he'd talk about the war in Spain. Ben Robertson, of *PM*, lay on the other side and kept saying over and over in that slow South Carolina drawl, "London is burning, London is burning."

It was like a shuttle service, the way the German planes came up the Thames, the fires acting as a flare path. Often they were above the smoke. The searchlights bored into that black roof, but couldn't penetrate it. They looked like long pillars supporting a black canopy. Suddenly all the lights dashed off and a blackness fell right to the ground. It grew cold. We covered ourselves with hay. The shrapnel clicked as it hit the concrete road near by, and still the German bombers came.

Early this morning we went to a hotel. The gunfire rattled the windows. Shortly before noon we rang for coffee. A pale, red-eyed chambermaid brought it and said, "I hope you slept well, sirs." This afternoon we drove back to the East End of

London. It was like an obstacle race — two blocks to the right, then left for four blocks, then straight on for a few blocks, and right again . . . streets roped off, houses and shops smashed . . . a few dirty-faced, tow-headed children standing on a corner, holding their thumbs up, the sign of the men who came back from Dunkerque . . . three red busses drawn up in a line waiting to take the homeless away . . . men with white scarfs around their necks instead of collars and ties, leading dull-eyed, empty-faced women across to the busses. Most of them carried little cheap cardboard suitcases and sometimes bulging paper shopping bags. That was all they had left. There was still fire and smoke along the river, but the fire fighters and the demolition squads have done their work well.

SEPTEMBER 9, 1940

I've spent the day visiting the bombed areas. The King did the same thing. These people may have been putting on a bold front for the King, but I saw them just as they were — men shoveling mounds of broken glass into trucks, hundreds of people being evacuated from the East End, all of them calm and quiet. In one street where eight or ten houses had been smashed a policeman stopped a motorist who had driven through a red light. The policeman's patience was obviously exhausted. As he made out the ticket and lectured the driver, everyone in the street gathered around to listen, paying no attention at all to the damaged houses; they were much more interested in the policeman.

These people are exceedingly brave, tough, and prudent. The East End, where disaster is always just around the corner, seems to take it better than the more fashionable districts in the West End.

The firemen have done magnificent work these last forty-eight hours. Early this morning I watched them fighting a fire which was obviously being used as a beacon by the German bombers. The bombs came down only a few blocks away, but the firemen just kept their hoses playing steadily at the base of the flame.

The Germans dropped some very big stuff last night. One bomb, which fell about a quarter of a mile from where I was standing on a rooftop, made the largest crater I've ever seen, and I thought I'd seen some big ones. The blast traveled down near-by streets, smashing windows five or six blocks away.

The British shot down three of the night bombers last night. I said a moment ago that Londoners were both brave and prudent. Tonight many theaters are closed. The managers decided the crowds just wouldn't come. Tonight the queues were outside the air-raid shelters, not the theaters. In my district, people carrying blankets and mattresses began going to the shelters before the siren sounded.

This night bombing is serious and sensational. It makes headlines, kills people, and smashes property; but it doesn't win wars. It may be safely presumed that the Germans know that, know that several days of terror bombing will not cause this country to collapse. Where then does this new phase of the air war fit? What happens next? The future must be viewed in relation to previous objectives; those objectives were the western ports and convoys, the Midlands, and Welsh industrial areas, and the southern airfields. And now we have the bombing of London. If this is the prelude to invasion, we must expect much heavier raids against London. After all, they only used about a hundred planes last night. And we must expect a sudden renewal of the attacks against fighter dromes near the coast, an effort to drive the fighters farther inland. If the Germans continue to hammer London for a few more nights and then sweep successfully to blasting airdromes with their dive bombers, it will probably be the signal for invasion. And the currently favored date for this invasion—and you will remember there have been others in the past—is sometime about September 18.

SEPTEMBER 10, 1940—6:45 P.M.

These raids against London are, I think, being rather fully and accurately reported in the United States. Sometimes you get the news a bit late. For instance, when I was talking to you last night I knew all about that big fire down near St. Paul's, had been watching it from a rooftop, but couldn't talk about it. The German planes were still overhead and the Ministry of Home Security had no desire that they should be told, by means of a broadcast to the States, just what fires had been started and where they were. And I might add that I had no desire to assist the German bomb aimers who were flying about over my head. When you hear that London has been bombed and hammered for ten to twelve hours during the night, you should remember that this is a huge, sprawling city, that there is nothing like a continuous rain of bombs —at least, there hasn't been so far. Often there is a period of ten or twenty minutes when no sound can be heard, no searchlights seen. Then a few bombs will come whistling down. Then silence again. A hundred planes over London doesn't mean that they were all here at the same time. They generally come singly or in pairs, circle around over the searchlights two or three times, and then you can hear them start their bombing runs, generally a shallow dive, and those bombs take a long time to fall.

After three nights of watching and listening, these night attacks are assuming something of a pattern for me. The Germans come over as soon as it's dark, a few minutes earlier each night. For the first few hours they drop very little heavy stuff, seem to concentrate on incendiaries, hoping to start fires to act as beacons for the high explosives later on. For the last three nights the weight of the attacks developed around midnight. As you know, the damage has been considerable. But London has suffered no more than a serious flesh wound. The attack will probably increase in intensity, but things will have to get much worse before anyone here is likely to consider it too much to bear.

We are told today that the Germans believe Londoners, after a while, will rise up and demand a new government, one that will make peace with Germany. It's more probable that they'll rise up and murder a few German pilots who come down by parachute. The life of a parachutist would not be worth much in the East End of London tonight.

The politicians who called this a "people's war" were right, probably more right than they knew at the time. I've seen some horrible sights in this city during these days and nights, but not once have I heard man, woman, or child suggest that Britain should throw in her hand. These people are angry. How much they can stand, I don't know. The strain is very great. The prospect for the winter, when some way must be found to keep water out of the shelters and a little heat inside, is not pleasant. Nor will it be any more pleasant in Germany, where winters are generally more severe than on this green island. After four days and nights of this air *Blitzkrieg*, I think the people here are rapidly becoming veterans, even as their Army was hardened in the fire of Dunkerque.

Many people have already got over the panicky feeling that hit everyone in the nerve centers when they realized they were being bombed. Those people I talked to in long queues in front of the big public shelters tonight were cheerful and somewhat resigned. They'd been waiting in line for an hour or more, waiting for the shelters to open at the first wail of the sirens. They had no private shelters of their own, but they carried blankets to throw over the chairs in this public underground refuge. Their sleep tonight will be as fitful as you could expect in such quarters without beds. Of course, they don't like the situation, but most of them feel that even this underground existence is preferable to what they'd get under German domination.

All the while strong efforts are being made to remind the British subjects who live underground that RAF bombers are flying in the other direction and that the Germans are having rather a rough time of it, too. For instance, tonight's British news broadcast led off with a long and detailed statement about last night's RAF air raids against Germany—the docks at Wilhelmshaven, Hamburg, Bremen, and Kiel were bombed again, a power station in Brussels wrecked, and a gasworks on the outskirts of Lorraine set afire. Docks and shipping at Calais, Ostend, Flushing, and Boulogne were also bombed.

SEPTEMBER 10, 1940 — 10:30 P.M.

This is London. And the raid which started about seven hours ago is still in progress. Larry LeSueur and I have spent the last three hours driving about the streets of London and visiting air-raid shelters. We found that like everything else in this world the kind of protection you get from the bombs on London tonight depends on how much money you have. On the other hand, the most expensive dwelling places here do not necessarily provide the best shelters, but certainly they are the most comfortable.

We looked in on a renowned Mayfair hotel tonight and found many old dowagers and retired colonels settling back on the overstuffed settees in the lobby. It wasn't the sort of protection I'd seek from a direct hit from a half-ton bomb, but if you were a retired colonel and his lady you might feel that the risk was worth it because you would at least be bombed with the right sort of people, and you could always get a drink if you were a resident of the hotel. If you were the sort of person I saw sunk in the padding of this Mayfair mansion you'd be calling for a drink of Scotch and soda pretty often—enough to keep those fine uniformed waiters on the move.

Only a couple of blocks away we pushed aside the canvas curtain of a trench cut out of a lawn of a London park. Inside were half a hundred people, some of them stretched out on the hard wooden benches. The rest huddled over in their overcoats and blankets. Dimmed electric lights glowed on the whitewashed walls and the cannonade of antiaircraft and reverberation of the big stuff the Germans were dropping rattled the dust boards under foot at intervals. You couldn't buy a drink there. One woman was saying sleepily that it was funny how often you read about people being killed inside a shelter. Nobody seemed to listen. Then over to the famous cellar of a world-famous hotel, two floors underground. On upholstered chairs and lounges there was a cosmopolitan crowd. But there wasn't any sparkling cocktail conversation. They sat, some of them with their mouths open. One of them snored. King Zog was over in a far corner on a chair, the porter told me. The woman sleeping on the only cot in the shelter was one of the many sisters of the former King of Albania.

The number of planes engaged tonight seems to be about the same as last night. Searchlight activity has been constant, but there has been little gunfire in the center of London. The bombs have been coming down at about the same rate as last night. It is impossible to get any estimate of the damage.

Darkness prevents observation of details. The streets have been deserted save for a few clanging fire engines during the last four or five hours. The zooming planes have been high again tonight, so high that the searchlights can't reach them. The bombing sounds as though it was separated pretty evenly over the metropolitan district. In certain areas there are no electric lights.

Once I saw *The Damnation of Faust* presented in the open air at Salzburg. London reminds me of that tonight, only the stage is so much larger. Once tonight an antiaircraft battery opened fire just as I drove past. It lifted me from the seat and a hot wind swept over the car. It was impossible to see. When I drove on, the streets of London reminded me of a ghost town in Nevada—not a soul to be seen. A week ago there would have been people standing on the corner, shouting for taxis. Tonight there were no people and no taxis. Earlier today there were trucks delivering mattresses to many office buildings. People are now sleeping on those mattresses, or at least they are trying to sleep. The coffee stalls, where taxi drivers and truck drivers have their four-in-the-morning tea, are empty.

As I entered this building half an hour ago one man was asking another if he had a good book. He was offered a mystery story, something about a woman who murdered her husband. And as he stumbled sleepily down the corridor, the lender said, "Hope it doesn't keep you awake."

And so London is waiting for dawn. We ought to get the "all-clear" in about another two hours. Then those big German bombers that have been lumbering and mumbling about overhead all night will have to go home.

SEPTEMBER 11, 1940

The air raid is still on. I shall speak rather softly, because three or four people are sleeping on mattresses on the floor of this studio.

The latest official figures for today's air war list at least ninety German planes down, with a loss of seventeen British fighters.

It is now 4:15 in the morning in London. There will be piles of empty shell casings around London's antiaircraft batteries when dawn breaks about an hour from now. All night, for more than eight hours, the guns have been flashing. The blue of an autumn sky has been pockmarked with the small red burst of exploding antiaircraft shells. Never in the long history of this old city beside the Thames has there been such a night as this. But tonight the sound of gunfire has been more constant than the bestial grunt of bombs.

Several hours of observation from a rooftop in central London has convinced me that the bombing of the central and western portion of the city has been less severe than during last night, and tomorrow's official communiqué will confirm that impression. The number of German planes engaged has probably been about the same—something more than a hundred. Most of the bombings have been over near the river. Judging from the height of the shell bursts, the Germans have been bombing from a somewhat lower altitude tonight. They cruise at about the same height, but when they start their bombing runs, the bursts appear lower down. A few fires have been started, but most of them are believed to be under control.

These London gunners, who have spent the better part of a year sitting around doing nothing, are working tonight. There's a battery not far from where I live. They're working in their shirt sleeves, laughing and cursing as they slam the shells into their guns. The spotters and detectors swing slowly around in their reclining carriage. The lens of the night glasses look like the eyes of an overgrown owl in the orange-blue light that belches from the muzzle of the gun. They're working without searchlights tonight. The moon is so bright that the beam of the light is lost a few hundred feet off the ground. Someone should paint the chimney pots and gables of London as they're silhouetted in the flashing flame of the guns, when the world seems upside down.

Walking down the street a few minutes ago, shrapnel stuttered and stammered on the rooftops and from underground came the sound of singing, and the song was *My Blue Heaven.*

Here's a story of a policeman, his whistle, and a time bomb. It's a true story. I saw it. If the story lacks literary merit, put it down to the fact that composition is not easy when your windows are being rattled by gunfire and bombs. In the central district of London a bomb fell. It didn't explode. The area was roped off. People living in the area were evacuated—moved out of the buildings. I happened to be walking in that particular district and talked my way just inside the police cordon. Peering fearfully around the corner of a stout building, I beheld a policeman standing at an intersection, about thirty yards from where that unexploded bomb lay. He was a big policeman—his feet were wide apart, tin hat pushed well back on his head, chin strap between his teeth, left hand hooked in his belt at the back. That policeman's right hand snapped up from the wrist. Something glinted in the sunlight and dropped back into his hand. Again that slow, easy flick of the wrist. And I saw he had taken his whistle off the chain, was tossing it idly in the air and catching it as it fell. It was an effortless, mechanical sort of business. He stood like a statue, just tossing that silver whistle and catching it. I've seen cops at home perform something of the same operation with a night stick on a warm spring day. If that bomb had gone off, the bobby would have been a dead man, the whistle would have fallen to the pavement.

After watching him for perhaps two minutes I withdrew, convinced that it would have been impossible for me to catch that whistle in a washtub. What the policeman was doing there, I don't know. He may be there still.

These delayed-action bombs create special problems. If a bomb explodes in a business district, it may do considerable damage, but demolition and repair work can be started at once. Offices and shops that have escaped damage can carry on. But a delayed-action bomb can paralyze the area for a considerable time. If a bomb explodes on a railway line, only a few hours may be required to effect repairs; but a time bomb on a right of way is more difficult to deal with. Anyone can fill in a bomb crater, but experts are required to handle the ones that don't explode.

I know of a case where there was an unexploded bomb between the rails. The local superintendent organized a volunteer crew to take a freight train over it. But when the freight arrived, the regular crew refused to hand it over to the volunteers. They said the locals could have the bomb, but they'd take the train through. They did and, luckily, the bomb didn't explode.

Military medals are getting rather meaningless in this war. So many acts of heroism are being performed by men who were just doing their daily job. And now at 4:20 in the morning we're just waiting for the "all-clear."

SEPTEMBER 12, 1940

Miss Dorothy Thompson made a broadcast to Britain tonight. Her audience was somewhat reduced, since the air-raid siren sounded just after she started speaking. She informed the British that the poets of the world were lined up on their side. That, she said, was a matter of consequence. I'm not sure that Londoners agreed that the poets would be of much assistance, as they grabbed their blankets and headed for the air-raid shelters. I think these Londoners put more faith in their antiaircraft barrage, which seemed to splash blobs of daylight down the streets tonight. Hitler, said Miss Thompson, wants to destroy the mental and spiritual heritage of free peoples. She promised the British that they would win. She said they had never been so beloved. She predicted that ages from now mothers and fathers would gather their children about their knees and tell them about these days. Well, mothers and fathers have their children about them tonight — underground. They're sustained in part by folklore, the tradition, and the history of Britain; but they're an undemonstrative lot. They don't consider themselves to be heroes. There's a job of work to be done and they're doing it as best they can. They don't know themselves how long they can stand up to it.

I know something about these Londoners. They know that they're out on their own. Most of them expect little help from the poets and no effective defense by word of mouth. These black-faced men with bloodshot eyes who were fighting fires and the girls who cradled the steering wheel of a heavy ambulance in their arms, the policeman who stands guard over that unexploded bomb down at St. Paul's tonight — these people didn't hear Miss Thompson; they're busy, just doing a job of work, and they know that it all depends on them.

SEPTEMBER 13, 1940

This is London at three-thirty in the morning. This has been what might be called a "routine night"—air-raid alarm at about nine o'clock and intermittent bombing ever since. I had the impression that more high explosives and few incendiaries have been used tonight. Only two small fires can be seen on the horizon. Again the Germans have been sending their bombers in singly or in pairs. The antiaircraft barrage has been fierce but sometimes there have been periods of twenty minutes when London has been silent. Then the big red busses would start up and move on till the guns started working again. That silence is almost hard to bear. One becomes accustomed to rattling windows and the distant sound of bombs and then there comes a silence that can be felt. You know the sound will return—you wait, and then it starts again. That waiting is bad. It gives you a chance to imagine things. I have been walking tonight—there is a full moon, and the dirty-gray buildings appear white. The stars, the empty windows, are hidden. It's a beautiful and lonesome city where men and women and children are trying to snatch a few hours' sleep underground.

In the fashionable residential districts I could read the TO LET signs on the front of big houses in the light of the bright moon. Those houses have big basements underneath—good shelters, but they're not being used. Many people think they should be.

The scale of this air war is so great that the reporting of it is not easy. Often we spend hours traveling about this sprawling city, viewing damage, talking with people, and occasionally listening to the bombs come down, and then more hours wondering what you'd like to hear about these people who are citizens of no mean city. We've told you about the bombs, the fires, the smashed houses, and the courage of the people. We've read you the communiqués and tried to give you an honest estimate of the wounds inflicted upon this, the best bombing target in the world. But the business of living and working in this city is very personal—the little incidents, the things the mind retains, are in themselves unimportant, but they somehow weld together to form the hard core of memories that will remain when the last "all-clear" has sounded. That's why I want to talk for just three or four minutes about the things we haven't talked about before; for many of these impressions it is necessary to reach back through only one long week. There was a rainbow bending over the battered and smoking East End of London just when the "all-clear" sounded one afternoon. One night I stood in front of a smashed grocery store and heard a dripping inside. It was the only sound in all London. Two cans of peaches had been drilled clean through by flying glass and the juice was dripping down onto the floor.

There was a flower shop in the East End. Nearly every other building in the block had been smashed. There was a funeral wreath in the window of the shop—price: three shillings and six pence, less than a dollar. In front of Buckingham Palace there's a bed of red and white flowers—untouched—the reddest flowers I've ever seen.

Last night, or rather early this morning, I met a distinguished member of Parliament in a bar. He had been dining with Anthony Eden and had told the Secretary for War that he wouldn't walk through the streets with all that shrapnel falling about and as a good host Eden should send him home in a tank. Another man came in and reported, on good authority, that the Prime Minister had a siren suit, one of those blue woolen coverall affairs with a zipper. Someone said the Prime Minister must resemble a barrage balloon when attired in his siren suit. Things of that sort can still be said in this country. The fact that the noise—just the sound, not the blast—of bombs and guns can cause one to stagger while walking down the street came as a surprise. When I entered my office today, after bombs had fallen two blocks away, and was asked by my English secretary if I'd care for a cup of tea, that didn't come as much of a surprise.

Talking from a studio with a few bodies lying about on the floor, sleeping on mattresses, still produces a strange feeling but we'll probably get used to that. Today I went to buy a hat—my favorite shop had gone, blown to bits. The windows of my shoe store were blown out. I decided to have a haircut;

the windows of the barbershop were gone, but the Italian barber was still doing business. Someday, he said, we smile again, but the food it doesn't taste so good since being bombed. I went on to another shop to buy flashlight batteries. I bought three. The clerk said: "You needn't buy so many. We'll have enough for the whole winter." But I said: "What if you aren't here?" There were buildings down in that street, and he replied: "Of course, we'll be here. We've been in business here for a hundred and fifty years."

But the sundown scene in London can never be forgotten—the time when people pick up their beds and walk to the shelter.

SEPTEMBER 15, 1940

During the last week you have heard much of the bombing of Buckingham Palace and probably seen pictures of the damage. You have been told by certain editors and commentators who sit in New York that the bombing of the Palace, which has one of the best air-raid shelters in England, caused a great surge of determination—a feeling of unity—to sweep this island. The bombing was called a great psychological blunder. I do not find much support for that point of view amongst Londoners with whom I've talked. They don't like the idea of their King and Queen being bombed, but, remember, this is not the last war—people's reactions are different. Minds have become hardened and callused. It didn't require a bombing of Buckingham Palace to convince these people that they are all in this thing together. There is nothing exclusive about being bombed these days. When there are houses down in your street, when friends and relatives have been killed, when you've seen that red glow in the sky night after night, when you're tired and sleepy—there just isn't enough energy left to be outraged about the bombing of a palace.

The King and Queen have earned the respect and admiration of the nation, but so have tens of thousands of humble folk who are much less well protected. If the Palace had been the only place bombed the reaction might have been different. Maybe some of those German bomb aimers are working for Goebbels instead of Goering, but if the purpose of the bombings was to strike terror to the hearts of the Britishers then the bombs have been wasted. That fire bomb on the House of Lords passed almost unnoticed. I heard a parcel of people laughing about it when one man said: "That particular bomb wouldn't seriously have damaged the nation's war effort."

I'm talking about those things not because the bombing of the Palace appears to have affected America more than Britain, but in order that you may understand that this war has no relation with the last one, so far as symbols and civilians are concerned. You must understand that a world is dying, that old values, the old prejudices, and the old bases of power and prestige are going. In an army, if the morale is to be good, there must be equality in the ranks. The private with money must not be allowed to buy himself a shelter of steel and concrete in the front-line trench. One company can't be equipped with pitchforks and another with machine guns. London's civilian army doesn't have that essential equality—I mean equality of shelter. One borough before the war defied the authorities and built deep shelters. Now people arrive at those shelters from all over town and the people who paid for them are in danger of being crowded out. Some of those outsiders arrive in taxis, others by foot. Since it's a public shelter they can't be barred by the people whose money went into the digging. This is just one of the problems in equality that London is now facing.

There are the homeless from the bombed and fire-blackened East End area. They must be cared for, they must be moved, they must be fed, and they must be sheltered. The Lord Mayor's fund, contributions from America, from unofficial agencies, are in the best tradition of Anglo-Saxon generosity and philanthropy, but no general would desire to rely upon such measures for the care and maintenance of injured troops. The people have been told that this is a people's war, that they are in the front lines, and they are. If morale is to be maintained at its present high level, there must be no distinction between the troops living in the various sections of London.

Even for those of us who live on the crest of London, life is dangerous. Some of the old buildings have gone, but the ghosts, sometimes a whole company of ghosts, remain. There is the thunder of gunfire at night. As these lines were written, as the window shook, there was a candle and matches beside the typewriter just in case the light went out. Richard Llewellyn, the man who wrote *How Green Was My Valley*, sat in the corner and talked about the dignity of silence while the guns jarred the apartment house. We went out to dinner and the headwaiter carefully placed us at a table away from the window. "There might be," he said, "one of those blasts." In the West End of London, life follows some kind of pattern. The shops are still full of food; the milk arrives on the doorstep each morning; the papers, too, but sometimes they're a little late. Much of the talk, as you would expect, is about invasion. On that score there is considerable confidence. Everyone is convinced that it will be beaten back if it comes. There are some who fear that it will not come.

SEPTEMBER 18, 1940

   I'd like to say one or two things about the reporting of this air war against London. No one person can see it all. The communiqués are sparing of information because details of damage would assist the Germans. No one can check by personal observation the damage done during a single night or a single week. It would take a lifetime to traverse the streets of this city, but there's a greater problem involved; it's one of language. There are no words to describe the thing that is happening. Today I talked with eight American correspondents in London. Six of them had been forced to move—all had stories of bombs and all agreed that they were unable to convey through print or the spoken word an accurate impression of what's happening in London these days and nights.

   I may tell you that Bond Street has been bombed; that a shop selling handkerchiefs at $40 the dozen has been wrecked; that these words were written on a table of good English oak which sheltered me three times as bombs tore down in the vicinity, but you can have little understanding of the life in London these days—the courage of the people; the flash and roar of the guns rolling down streets where much of the history of the English-speaking world has been made; the stench of air-raid shelters in the poor districts. These things must be experienced to be understood.

A woman inspecting a sweater, taking it to the bright sunlight shining through a smashed skylight for close inspection. A row of automobiles, with stretchers racked on the roofs like skis, standing outside of bombed buildings. A man pinned under wreckage where a broken gas main sears his arm and face. These things must be seen if the whole impact of this war is to be felt.

If we talk at times of the little flashes of humor that appear in this twilight of suffering, you must understand that there is humor in these people, even when disaster and hell come down from heaven. We can only tell you what we see and hear.

The individual's reaction to the sound of falling bombs cannot be described. The moan of stark terror and suspense cannot be encompassed by words, no more can the sense of relief when you realize that you weren't where that one fell. It's pleasant to pick yourself up out of the gutter without the aid of a searcher party.

Between bombing one catches glimpses of the London one knew in the distant days of peace. The big red busses roll through the streets. The tolling of Big Ben can be heard in the intervals of the gunfire. The little French and Italian restaurants in Soho bring out their whitest linens and polish their glass and silver for the two or three guests who brave the blackout, the bombs, and the barrage. There are advertisements in the papers extolling the virtues of little rubber ear plugs which prevent one from hearing the bombs and guns. In many buildings tonight people are sleeping on mattresses on the floor. I've seen dozens of them looking like dolls thrown aside by a tired child. In three or four hours they must get up and go to work just as though they had a full night's rest, free from the rumble of guns and the wonder that comes when they wake and listen in the dead hours of the night.

SEPTEMBER 21, 1940

I'm standing on a rooftop looking out over London. At the moment everything is quiet. For reasons of national as well as personal security, I'm unable to tell you the exact location from which I'm speaking. Off to my left, far away in the distance, I can see just that faint-red, angry snap of antiaircraft bursts against the steel-blue sky, but the guns are so far away that it's impossible to hear them from this location. About five minutes ago the guns in the immediate vicinity were working. I can look across just at a building not far away and see something that looks like a flash of white paint down the side, and I know from daylight observation that about a quarter of that building has disappeared—hit by a bomb the other night. Streets fan out in all directions from here, and down on one street I can see a single red light and just faintly the outline of a sign standing in the middle of the street. And again I know what that sign says, because I saw it this afternoon. It says DANGER—UNEXPLODED BOMB. Off to my left still I can see just that red snap of the anti-aircraft fire.

I was up here earlier this afternoon and looking out over these housetops, looking all the way to the dome of St. Paul's. I saw many flags flying from staffs. No one ordered these people to put out the flag. They simply feel like flying the Union Jack above their roof. No one told them to do it, and no flag up there was white. I can see one or two of them just stirring very faintly in the breeze now. You may be able to hear the sound of guns off in the distance very faintly, like someone kicking a tub. Now they're silent. Four searchlights reach up, disappear in the light of a three-quarter moon. I should say at the moment there are probably three aircraft in the general vicinity of London, as one can tell by the movement of the lights and the flash of the antiaircraft guns. But at the moment in the central area everything is quiet. More searchlights spring up over on my right. I think probably in a minute we shall have the sound of guns in the immediate vicinity. The lights are swinging over in this general direction now. You'll hear two explosions. There they are! That was the explosion overhead, not the guns themselves. I should think in a few minutes there may be a bit of shrapnel around here. Coming in—moving a little closer all the while. The plane's still very high. Earlier this evening we could hear occasional . . . again those were explosions overhead. Earlier this evening we heard a number of bombs go sliding and slither-ing across to fall several blocks away. Just overhead now the burst of the antiaircraft fire. Still the near-by guns are not working. The searchlights now are feeling almost directly overhead. Now you'll hear two bursts a little nearer in a moment. There they are! That hard, stony sound.

SEPTEMBER 22, 1940

I'm standing again tonight on a rooftop looking out over London, feeling rather large and lonesome. In the course of the last fifteen or twenty minutes there's been considerable action up there, but at the moment there's an ominous silence hanging over London. But at the same time a silence that has a great deal of dignity. Just straightaway in front of me the searchlights are working. I can see one or two bursts of antiaircraft fire far in the distance. Just on the roof across the way I can see a man standing wearing a tin hat, with a pair of powerful night glasses to his eyes, scanning the sky. Again looking in the opposite direction there is a building with two windows gone. Out of one window there waves something that looks like a white bed sheet, a window curtain swinging free in this night breeze. It looks as though it were being shaken by a ghost. There are a great many ghosts around these buildings in London. The searchlights straightaway, miles in front of me, are still searching that sky. There's a three-quarter moon riding high. There was one burst of shell-fire almost straight in the Little Dipper. The guns are too far away to be heard.

Down below in the streets I can see just that red and green wink of the traffic lights; one lone taxicab moving slowly down the street. Not a sound to be heard. As I look out across the miles and miles of rooftops and chimney pots, some of those dirty-gray fronts of the buildings look almost snow white in this moonlight here tonight. And the rooftop spotter across the way swings around, looks over in the direction of the searchlights, drops his glasses, and just stands there. There are hundreds and hundreds of men like that standing on rooftops in London tonight watching for fire bombs, waiting to see what comes out of this steel-blue sky. The searchlights now reach up very, very faintly on three sides of me. There is a flash of a gun in the distance, but too far away to be heard.

SEPTEMBER 23, 1940

This is London, about ten minutes to four in the morning. Tonight's raid which started about eight is still in progress. The number of planes engaged is about the same as usual, perhaps a few more than last night. Barring lucky hits, both damage and casualties should be no greater than on previous nights. The next three hours may bring a change, but so far the raid appears to be routine, with the Germans flying perhaps a little lower than they did last night.

Often we wonder what you'd like to hear from London at four in the morning. There's seldom any spot news after midnight, so we just talk about the city and its people. Today I went to our district post office. There was a long line of people waiting for their mail. Their offices or homes had been bombed, and the mailman couldn't find them. There were no complaints. But that's not quite right. One woman said: "They've got to stop this; it can't go on." Her neighbor said: "Have you ever thought what would happen to you if we gave in?" And the lady replied, "Yes, I know, but have you seen what happened to Peter Robinson's?" Others in the queue—those who've been called by Mr. Churchill the more robust elements of the community—silenced the lady with well-modulated laughter.

To me one of the most impressive things about talking with Londoners these days is this—there's no mention of money. No one knows the dollar value of the damage done during these last sixteen days. But nobody talks about it. People who've had their homes or offices bombed will tell you about it, but they never think to tell you what the loss amounted to, whether it was so many tens or hundreds of pounds. The lead of any well-written news story dealing with fire, flood, or hurricane should tell something of the total damage done in terms of dollars, but here it's much more important that the bomb missed you; that there's still plenty of food to eat—and there is.

My own apartment is in one of the most heavily bombed areas of London, but the newspapers are on the doorstep each morning—so is the bottle of milk. When the light switch is pressed, there is light, and the gas stove still works, and they're still building that house across the street, still putting in big windowpanes. Today I saw shopwindows in Oxford Street, covered with plywood. In front of one there was a redheaded girl in a blue smock, painting a sign on the board covering the place where the window used to be. The sign read OPEN AS USUAL. A block away men were working an air hammer, breaking up huge blocks of masonry that had been blown into the streets, cracking those big lumps so that they might be carted away in trucks.

The people who have something to do with their hands are all right. Action seems to drive out fear. Those who have nothing to do would be better off outside London and there are signs that they will be encouraged to go. London comes to resemble a small town. There's something of a frontier atmosphere about the place. The other night I saw half a block evacuated. Time bombs plus incendiaries did it. In half an hour the people who had been turned out of their homes had been absorbed in near-by houses and apartments. Those who arranged for the influx of unexpected guests had, I think, been frightened when those bombs came down, but they were all right when there was something to do. Blankets to get out of closets, tea to be made, and all that sort of thing.

I've talked to firemen fighting a blaze that was being used as a beacon by German bomb aimers. They told me that the waiting about in fire stations was worst of all. They didn't mind the danger when there was something to do. Even my censor when I arrived in the studio tonight was sitting here underground composing music.

A half an hour before the King made his broadcast tonight the air-raid alarm sounded. At that moment a man with a deep voice was telling the children of Britain by radio how the wasps build their nests. He said, "Good night, children everywhere." There was a brief prayer for the children who went down in mid-Atlantic last week. There was a hymn well sung. After that a piano playing some nursery song, I didn't know its name. There was a moment of silence. Then the words, "This is London, His Majesty, the King." The King spoke for half a minute and then the welcome sound of the "all-clear," that high, steady note of the siren, came rolling through the open window. One almost expected His Majesty to pause and let the welcome sound come out through the loudspeaker, but he probably didn't hear it since he was speaking from an air-raid shelter under Buckingham Palace. The only news in the King's speech was the announcement of the two new medals, but his warning of grimmer days ahead must be taken as another indication of government policy—a warning that the full weight of German bombing is yet to be experienced.

Since the disastrous retreat from Norway, the government has been issuing few sunshine statements. Nearly every statement has been couched in subtle language, has contained a warning of worse things to come.

And now the King has added his warning to those of his ministers. He took the advice of his ministers, as he must, in speaking as he did, and his ministers judged, and rightly, that these people can stand up to that sort of warning. There has been much talk of terror bombings, but it is clear that London has not yet experienced anything like the full power of the *Luftwaffe* in these night raids. The atmosphere for full-scale terror bombing is not right. There is as yet no sizable portion of the population prepared to talk terms with the Nazis. You must remember that this war is being fought with political as well as military weapons. If the time comes when the Germans believe that mass night raids will break this government, then we may see German bombers quartering this night sky in an orgy of death and destruction such as no modern city has ever seen. There are no available official figures, but I have watched these planes night after night and do not believe that more than one hundred and fifty have been used in any single night. The Germans have more planes than that. Sometime they may use them. The people had to be warned about that. Therefore, the King spoke as he did.

SEPTEMBER 25, 1940

This is London, 3:45 in the morning. Tonight's attack against the central London area has not been as severe as last night; less noise, fewer bombs, and not so many fires. The night is almost quiet—almost peaceful. The raid is still in progress and it is, of course, possible that we may see a repetition of last night when the weight of the attack developed in the two hours before dawn. Two and sometimes three German planes came boring in through the barrage every five minutes. I spent last night with a bomber pilot who had carried twenty-five loads of bombs over Germany. He talked about a raid over Berlin at this time last night. When we left the studio we'd gone only a few blocks when we heard one coming down. As we lay on the sidewalk waiting for it to thump, he said, "I'd feel better up there than down here." A couple of air-raid wardens standing out in the open were discussing whether the stuff coming down was a flock of incendiaries or high explosives. The bomber pilot said: "These people are too brave. I'll feel better when I get back to my squadron. London is dangerous. I wonder how long it takes to get used to this sort of thing."

Later we went out to see a fire. A block of cheap little working-class houses had been set alight by fire bombs. As we walked toward the blaze, gusts of hot air and sparks charged down the street. We began to meet women. One clutched a blanket, another carried a small baby in her arms, and another carried an aluminum cooking pot in her left hand. They were all looking back over their shoulders at that red glow that had driven them out into the streets. They were frightened. And that bomber pilot who had been over Germany so many times stopped and said: "I've seen enough of this. I hope we haven't been doing the same thing in the Ruhr and Rhineland for the last three months."

We went back to a rooftop and stood watching as the bombers came in. He estimated their height, the speed at which they were traveling, and the point at which they would release their bombs. And he was generally right as to the time when we would hear the bombs start coming down. He was a professional, judging the work of other professionals. But he kept talking of the firemen, the ambulance drivers, and the air-raid wardens who were out there doing their job. He thought them much braver than the boys who'd been flying over Germany every night.

At dawn we saw Londoners come oozing up out of the ground, tired, red-eyed, and sleepy. The fires were dying down. We saw them turn into their own street and look to see if their house was still standing. I shall always wonder what last night did to that twenty-one-year-old boy who had flown so many bombs over Germany but had never heard one come down before last night. Today I walked down a long street. The gutters were full of glass; the big red busses couldn't pull into the curb. There was the harsh, grating sound of glass being shoveled into trucks. In one window—or what used to be a window—was a sign. It read: SHATTERED—BUT NOT SHUTTERED. Near by was another shop displaying a crudely lettered sign reading: KNOCKED BUT NOT LOCKED. They were both doing business in the open air. Halfway down the block there was a desk on the sidewalk; a man sat behind it with a pile of notes at his elbow. He was paying off the staff of the store—the store that stood there yesterday.

I went to my club for lunch. A neatly lettered sign on the door informed me that the club had been temporarily closed, due to enemy action. Returning to my apartment, which is now serving as an office, I found a letter from the China Campaign Committee, informing me that during the last fifteen days they had collected the signatures of individuals and organizations representing more than one and a quarter million people. The signatures were attached to a petition. The petition read as follows: "We demand the immediate and unconditional reopening of the Burma Road." It is necessary to have lived these last fifteen days in Britain to fully appreciate that letter. Collecting signatures to a petition urging the opening of the Burma Road during fifteen days of almost constant air-raid alarms. The petition was started before the *Blitzkrieg*. Therefore, it had to be carried through. These people are stubborn. Often they are insular, but their determination must be recorded.

SEPTEMBER 29, 1940

Tonight I can give you some idea of what it's like to get away from it all, away from the bombs, the guns, and the strained faces. I have spent nearly two days down in West Somerset. That's near the Bristol Channel. The train left from a station that has been burned and bombed by Dr. Goebbels, but I couldn't see any signs of damage. Dinner on the train was as usual. The coffee was still undrinkable, and the cheese is just cheese. It doesn't masquerade under such fancy names as Gorgonzola or Stilton. But they still serve those little red radishes with it. We were only fifteen minutes late at the end of a four-hour trip. Then half an hour by car to a little village tucked away at the end of a finger of salt water. A dozen houses and a tiny little hotel. A row of red geraniums standing guard in front of a whitewashed stone wall. The landlord said, "You'll sleep well tonight." But I didn't. At night a gentle breeze off the Channel nibbled and scratched at the thatched roof outside my window. It sounded like incendiary coming down. The swish of gravel on the beach as each wave retreated resembled that distant sound of falling brick and mortar after a bomb explosion. The clang of ironshod horses' hoofs on stone road was like distant gunfire, but it was only the mounted night patrol riding up to Exmoor, lying brown and wrinkled like a carpet mountain behind the hotel. That's hunting and shooting country down there and they take their night patrol seriously.

At eight in the morning a German bomber crashed on the beach three hundred yards from the hotel. Three members of the crew walked out. The fourth was dead. The three Germans were taken away across the fields in a small car with an armed horseman in front and another behind. It was the first time the war had come to the village. There was great excitement. The bar did a rushing business. The tide came in and covered the twin-engined bomber. The bombing of London, the progress of the war, were forgotten. You must remember there had been only two air-raid alarms in the village during the year. An old lady said she was sorry the Germans had discovered her village. I walked across the moors on grass that seemed to have springs for roots to a little village beside a stream. There was an old Roman footbridge across the stream. The name of the hotel was the Royal Oak. The landlord provided a huge tea, thick cream, and all the rest. He explained that he had enough food to last a year even if nothing came in, offered me a pork sandwich. I said, "I thought you weren't allowed to kill pigs under the new government order." "That's right," he said, "but sometimes they have accidents. This one caught his hind legs in a gate and we had to kill him." His wife wanted to know about London, but the landlord forestalled my answer by saying, "They'll be all right. I was worried about 'em for a couple of days, but they've got their teeth into this thing now, and they'll be all right." And then looking at his snug little hotel and up at the brown slopes of Exmoor, he said a strange thing. He said, "It's too bad some people have to live in terror and fear, being bombed every night, when nothing happens to us. If we could spread it out a bit, all share in it, maybe it wouldn't be so bad." And then I understood what people mean when they say this country is united.

The local paper was already advising people to do their Christmas shopping early, assuring them that large stocks were available, and judging from the appearance of the shop-windows, the paper was right. The paper also reported the meeting of the town council. The session was, I gathered, devoted to a discussion of the street-lighting system installed several years ago. Certain standing charges were still due annually to the public-utility company, in spite of the fact that the lights were, of course, no longer used. One town counselor had said, apparently in all seriousness, that a neighboring town had showed much more foresight, hadn't gone in for this new business of installing street lights.

Everywhere I noticed a change in people's faces. There was no strain. There was color given by sun and wind. They told me how the beech hedges lining the roads that snaked across the moor were cut back every fourteen years and it would soon be time to cut them back again. The harvest was early this year, and now the farmers have a few slack weeks and a chance to attend the autumn sale. And all the time as I listened to those soft voices down in the Lorna Doone country, I kept wondering what was happening in London. So, late in the evening, a train brought me back to London. As we neared the outskirts, the conductor came in, turned out the lights, and said apologetically, "I'm afraid there's an air raid on." Arrived at the station, I found a taxi, gave the aged driver the address, and he said, "Right you are sir. I 'ope it's still there."

It's a strange feeling to ride through dark streets lit by the flash of antiaircraft fire, wondering whether your home is still standing or whether it has become a pile of ruined rubble during your brief absence. All was well. Somehow I thought London would have changed, but it seemed the same. The night raid is still on. The hours away from the city have evaporated. As the man who shared my taxi remarked, "It's like coming back to the front lines after a short leave."

This Is London, 1941

"The Hour Will Come When One of Us Will Break"

by William L. Shirer

BERLIN, *September 1*

I was in my bath at midnight last night and did not hear the sirens sound the alarm. First I knew of the raid was when the guns started to thunder. I dozed off to sleep, still having the flu with me, but was awakened during the night by the thud and shock of two bomb explosions very near the hotel.

Today the High Command announces officially that the British fliers last night were "hindered" from dropping their bombs by the splendid work of the capital's anti-aircraft guns, and that the only bombs dropped therefore fell outside the city limits.

This is strange because the Tiergarten was roped off today and this evening the press admits that several "bomb craters" were discovered in the park after last night's raid. I staggered off to the *Rundfunk* tonight to do an anniversary broadcast. The military censor, a very decent chap, was puzzled about the conflicting German reports of the bombing.

"My instructions are you can't contradict the communiqués of the High Command," he said.

"But the German press contradicts them," I argued. "I heard the bombs fall in the Tiergarten, and the Berlin papers admit that some did."

He was a good sport and let me read the contradictory reports.

The main effect of a week of constant British night bombings has been to spread great disillusionment among the people here and sow doubt in their minds. One said to me today: "I'll never believe another thing they say. If they've lied about the raids in the rest of Germany as they have about the ones on Berlin, then it must have been pretty bad there."

Actually, the British bombings have not been very deadly. The British are using too few planes—fifteen or twenty a night—and they have to come too far to carry really effective, heavy loads of bombs. Main effect is a moral one, and if the British are smart they'll keep them up every night. Tonight another attack began just before I broadcast, but it was not much of a show.

A year ago today the great "counter-attack" against Poland began. In this year German arms have achieved victories never equalled even in the brilliant military history of this aggressive, militaristic nation. And yet the war is not yet over, or won. And it was on this aspect that people's minds were concentrated today, if I am any judge. They long for peace. And they want it before the winter comes.

BERLIN, *September 2*

I learned today that the Germans you see removing time bombs are for the most part prisoners from concentration camps. If they live through the experience, they are promised release. As a matter of fact it probably is an easy choice for them. Even death is a welcome release from the tortures of the Gestapo. And there's always the chance that the bomb won't go off. Some of the bombs that fell in the Tiergarten, it's now revealed, were time bombs.

For some time now our censors have not allowed us to use the word "Nazi" on the air. They say it has a bad sound in America. One must say "National Socialist" or avoid the term altogether, as I do. The word "invasion" in reference to what happened in Scandinavia and the west, and what is planned for England, is also taboo.

Studying the German figures on air losses over Britain, which are manifestly untrue, I find that nearly every day they run 4 to 1 in favour of the Luftwaffe. This ratio must have a magic attraction to someone in the Air Ministry.

BERLIN, *September 4–5 (3 a.m.)*

Hitler made a surprise speech here this afternoon, the occasion being the opening of the *Winterhilfe*—winter relief—campaign. Like the *Volkswagen*, the cheap "people's car" on which German workers are paying millions of marks a month in instalments though the factory which is supposed to make them is actually manufacturing only arms, the *Winterhilfe* is one of the scandals of the Nazi regime, though not one German in a million realizes it. It is obvious that in a country without unemployment not much "winter relief" is necessary. Yet the Nazis go on wringing several hundred million marks each winter out of the people for "winter charity" and actually use most of the money for armaments or party funds.

Hitler's appearance today was kept a secret until the last minute, the Propaganda Ministry rushing off the correspondents from the afternoon press conference to the Sportpalast. What is Himmler afraid of, since British bombers cannot come over during daylight? Is he afraid of an "incident"?

The session was another beautiful example of how Hitler takes advantage of the gullibility of his people. He told them, for instance, that while the German air force attacked Britain by day, the cowardly RAF comes over only at night. He did not explain *why* this is so—that the Germans can get over England by day because it is only twenty-five miles from German bases and they can thus protect their bombers with fighters, whereas Germany is too far from Britain to enable the British to protect their bombers with fighters.

Hitler said with lovely hypocrisy: "I waited three months without answering the British night bombings in the hope they would stop this mischief. But Herr Churchill saw in this a sign of weakness. You will understand that we are now answering, night for night. And when the British air force drops two or three or four thousand kilograms of bombs, then we will in one night drop 150- 230- 300- or 400,000 kilograms."

At this point he had to stop because of the hysterical applause of the audience, which consisted mostly of German women nurses and social workers.

"When they declare," continued Hitler, "that they will increase their attacks on our cities, then we will raze *their* cities to the ground." Here the young nurses and social workers were quite beside themselves and applauded phrenetically. When they had recovered, he said:

"We will stop the handiwork of these air pirates, so help us God." At this the young German women hopped to their feet and, their breasts heaving, screamed their approval.

"The hour will come," Hitler went on, "when one of us will break, and it will not be National Socialist Germany." At this juncture the raving maidens kept their heads sufficiently to break their wild shouts of joy with a chorus of: "Never! Never!"

Though grim and dripping with hate most of the evening, Hitler had his humorous, jaunty moments. His listeners found it very funny when he said: "In England they're filled with curiosity and keep asking: 'Why doesn't he come?' Be calm. Be calm. He's coming! He's coming!" And the man squeezed every ounce of humour and sarcasm out of his voice. The speech was not broadcast direct, but recorded and rebroadcast two hours after he had finished.

LATER.—The British came over again tonight, arriving punctually at fifteen minutes before midnight, which is their usual time. The fact that the searchlights rarely pick up a plane has given rise to whispers among the people of Berlin that the British planes are coated with an invisible paint. Tonight the bombers cruised over the city at intervals for two hours. The *flak* guns thundered away like mad, but without effect. Another bomb dropped in the Tiergarten and killed a policeman.

BERLIN, *September 5*

Very annoyed still that the German radio officials refuse to let me view the nightly air-raids. They come each night when I am at the *Rundfunk*. Nor can we mention them if they occur during our talk. Tonight when I arrived for my broadcast I found that the RRG had installed a lip microphone for us to speak in. In order to make your voice heard you have to hold your lips to it. But the sounds of the anti-aircraft guns firing outside do not register. That is why they installed it. But they have put it in the same building, so that we no longer have to race through a hail of falling shrapnel to get to a microphone.

The United States is to turn over fifty destroyers to the

British in return for naval and air bases in British possessions off our eastern coast. The Germans say it is a breach of neutrality, as it is, but they're not going to do anything about it, not even protest. They're hoping that our isolationists and our Lindberghs will keep us out of the war and they intend to refrain from doing anything to jeopardize their position.

BERLIN, *September 7*

Last night we had the biggest and most effective bombing of the war. The Germans have brought in several more batteries of *flak* during the past few days, and last night they put up a terrific barrage, but failed to hit a single plane.

The British were aiming better last night. When I returned from the *Rundfunk* shortly after three a.m., the sky over the north-central part of Berlin was lit up by two great fires. The biggest was in the freight house of the Lehrter railroad station. Another railroad station at the Schussendorfstrasse also was hit. A rubber factory, I'm told, was set afire.

Despite this the High Command said in its communiqué today: "The enemy again attacked the German capital last night, causing some damage to persons and property as a result of his indiscriminate throwing of bombs on non-military targets in the middle of the city. The German air force, as reprisal, has therefore begun to attack London with strong forces."

Not a hint here—and the German people do not know it—that the Germans have been dropping bombs in the very centre of London for the last two weeks. My censors warned me today not to go into this matter. I apparently have some German listeners, who can pick up my talk from the German transmitter that shortwaves it to New York. Since it's a German transmitter, there is no penalty.

The statement of the High Command, obviously forced upon it by Hitler himself—he often takes a hand in writing the official army communiqués—deliberately perpetrates the lie that Germany has only decided to bomb London as a result of the British *first* bombing Berlin. And the German people will fall for this, as they fall for almost everything they're told nowadays. Certainly never before in modern times —since the press, and later the radio, made it theoretically possible for the mass of mankind to learn what was going on in the world—have a great people been so misled, so unscrupulously lied to, as the Germans under this regime.

And so tonight the High Command, which all good Germans believe tells only the gospel truth, issued a special communiqué saying that as reprisal for the British raids on Berlin, London was attacked with strong forces for the *first* time today. As a result of this reprisal attack, it says, "one great cloud of smoke tonight stretches from the middle of London to the mouth of the Thames."

To give American radio listeners an idea of the kind of propaganda (though I couldn't label it as such) which the German people are being subjected to now, I read in my broadcast tonight the following quotation from today's Berlin newspaper, the *Börsen Zeitung*: "While the attack of the German air force is made on purely military objectives—this fact is recognized by both the British press and radio—the RAF knows nothing better to do than continually to attack nonmilitary objectives in Germany. A perfect example of this was the criminal attack on the middle of Berlin last night. In this attack only lodging-houses were hit; not a single military objective."

The German people have no inkling—because the Nazi press and radio have carefully suppressed the story—that in August alone more than one thousand English civilians were killed by the Luftwaffe's attacks on British "military objectives."

Another type of lying here: The official statement of last night's bombing of Berlin says that the first two waves of British planes were turned back by the capital's defences, and that only a few planes of the third wave were able to slip through. Now, every Berliner knows that from the minute the alarm was sounded last night, British planes were heard overhead. There were several waves and each time you heard the hum of the motors. Yet I fear the majority will believe the official explanation.

The *Börsen Zeitung* even went so far last night as to tell its innocent readers that all military objectives in Germany were so well protected by anti-aircraft guns that it was quite impossible for the British planes to bomb them. Therefore the

British went after unprotected civilian houses. How many Germans will ask then, why, with an admitted concentration of guns in and around Berlin such as no other area in the world has ever seen—why has not a single plane yet been brought down?

And personally I'm getting a little tired of the censorship restrictions on our telling even a modicum of truth about this air war to America. I shall not stand for it much longer.

BERLIN, *September 8*

All Sunday morning papers carry the same headline: "BIG ATTACK ON LONDON AS REPRISAL."

BERLIN, *September 9*

A typical Nazi trick was played on me today. The three censors fought with me so long over the script of my two p.m. broadcast, which they charged was unduly ironic about the "reprisal" bombings of London, which it was, that by the time they had finally okayed it, there was no time for me to go on the air. My five minutes of air time was over.

There was no objection to this, since the censors have a perfect right to hold up a script they don't like, just as I have the right not to talk if I think they've censored the true sense out of my talk. But this evening I learn from Paul White in New York, through channels which permit me to receive cables from him without the Germans knowing their contents, that the short-wave director of the German Broadcasting Company cabled him today an explanation of why I did not broadcast at two p.m. The cable read: "Regret Shirer arrived too late today to broadcast."

The British bombers failed to come over last night or the night before. Official explanation to the German people: The British planes tried to get through both nights to Berlin, but were turned back. Whenever the British choose not to bomb Berlin henceforth, I hear, Goebbels has ordered the people to be told that they tried to but were repulsed by the capital's magnificent defences.

Whenever the British come over Germany now, most of the German radio stations hurriedly go off the air so as not to serve as radio beacons for the British pilots. The German radio announced tonight that its broadcasts, already greatly curtailed in the last fortnight on "military grounds," will be further curtailed. "This is no time," said the announcement, "to explain further the reasons for this."

BERLIN, *September 10*

A light raid last night, though a few houses were demolished. Commenting on the bombing, the *Lokal Anzeiger* says: "The fliers of His Britannic Majesty have given a heavy blow to the laws governing an honourable and manly conduct of war."

At the Propaganda Ministry today we were shown one of Britain's "secret weapons," a new sort of incendiary weapon. It looks like a large calling card—about two inches square—and is made of a celluloid substance. Two celluloid sheets are pasted together and between them is a tablet of phosphorus. The British drop them in a dampened condition. When they dry, after a few minutes of sun, or ten minutes of dry, daytime air, they ignite and cause a small flame that burns for two or three minutes. Actually, they were first used by the Irish Republicans, who dropped them in letter-boxes to burn the mail in England. The Germans admit they have set fire to fields of grain and hay as well as a few forests. Probably the British, who started dropping them in August, hoped to burn up a considerable acreage of grain. Unfortunately, we had a very wet August and few of them got dry enough to ignite.

BERLIN, *September 11*

Last night the severest bombing yet. And the German papers are beside themselves. The *Börsen Zeitung* calls our pilot visitors of last evening "barbarians" and bannerlines: "CRIME OF BRITISH ON BERLIN." According to the Nazis, only five persons were killed, but for the first time the British dropped a considerable number of fire bombs and there were quite a few small fires. Three incendiaries fell in the yard of the Adlon, five in the garden of the Embassy next door, and a half-dozen more in the garden of Dr. Goebbels just behind the Embassy. The office of the Minister of Munitions between the Adlon and the Embassy also was hit. All the incendiaries were put out before they did any damage. Actually the British were aiming at the Potsdamer Bahnhof, and they had bad luck. They took almost a perfect run for it, their first bombs hitting the Reichstag and then falling in a direct line towards the Potsdamer station on the Brandenburger Tor, the Embassy, and in the gardens behind. But the last one was about three hundred yards short of the station.

Today the BBC claims that the Potsdamer station was hit, but this is untrue and at least three Germans today who heard the BBC told me they felt a little disillusioned at the British radio's lack of veracity. The point is that it is bad propaganda for the British to broadcast in German to the people here that a main station has been set on fire when it hasn't been touched.

I almost met a quick end last night. Racing home from the *Rundfunk* after the all-clear at fifty miles an hour in my car, I suddenly skidded into some debris and came to a stop twenty feet from a fresh bomb crater on the East-West Axis about a hundred and fifty yards from the Brandenburger Tor. In the black-out you could not see it, and the air-wardens had not yet discovered it. A splinter from the bomb that made this crater hurtled two hundred yards through the air to the American Embassy and crashed through the double window of the office of Donald Heath, our First Secretary. It cut a neat hole in the two windows, continued directly over Don's desk, and penetrated four inches into the wall on the far side of the room. Don was supposed to have had night duty last night and would have been sitting at his desk at the time, but for some reason Chargé d'Affaires Kirk had told him to go home and himself had done the night trick.

BERLIN, *September 12*

Off to Geneva for a few days so that I can talk some matters over with New York on the telephone without being overheard by the Nazis. The Germans want Hartrich, my assistant, to leave, and I'm against it.

The rumour is that the big invasion hop against England is planned for the night of September 15, when there will be a full moon and the proper tide in the Channel. I'll chance this trip anyway.

GENEVA, *September 16*

The news coming over the near-by border of France is that the Germans have attempted a landing in Britain, but that it has been repulsed with heavy German losses. Must take this report with a grain of salt.

Lunch with John Winant, head of the International Labour Office, who strives valiantly to keep his institution, and what it stands for, from going under after the blow the war has given it. More than any other American in public life whom I know, he understands the social forces and changes that have been at work in the last decade both at home and in Europe, and that are now in new ferment as a result of the war. We talked about the job to be done after the war if Britain wins and if the mistakes of 1919 are not to be repeated. He spoke of his own ideas about reconstruction and how war economy could be replaced by a peace economy without the maladjustment, the great unemployment and deflation and depression that followed the last war. Personally I cannot look that far ahead. I cannot see beyond Hitler's defeat. To accomplish that first is such a gigantic task and so overwhelmingly important that all else seems secondary, though undoubtedly it is a good thing that some are taking a longer view.

Winant is a likable, gaunt, awkward, Lincolnesque sort of man and was a good enough politician and executive to be re-elected Governor of New Hampshire a couple of times. I think he would make a good president to succeed Roosevelt in 1944 if the latter gets his third term.

BERLIN, *September 18*

Somewhere near Frankfurt on the train from Basel last night the porter shouted: *"Flieger-Alarm!"* and there was a distant sound of gun-fire, but nothing hit us. We arrived at the Potsdamer Bahnhof right on time and I observed again that the station had not been hit despite the claims of the BBC. I noticed several lightly wounded soldiers, mostly airmen, getting off a special car which had been attached to our train. From their bandages, their wounds looked like burns. I noticed also the longest Red Cross train I've ever seen. It stretched from the station for half a mile to beyond the bridge over the Landwehr Canal. Orderlies were swabbing it out, the wounded having been unloaded, probably, during the night. The Germans usually unload their hospital trains after dark so that the populace will not be unduly disturbed by one of the grimmer sides of glorious war. I wondered where so many wounded could have come from, as the armies in the west stopped fighting three months ago. As there were only a few porters I had to wait some time on the platform and picked up a conversation with a railway workman. He said most of the men taken from the hospital train were suffering from burns.

Can it be that the tales I heard in Geneva had some truth in them after all? The stories there were that either in attempted German raids with sizable landing-parties on the English coast or in rehearsals with boats and barges off the French coast the British had given the Germans a bad pummelling. The reports reaching Switzerland from France were that many German barges and ships had been destroyed and a considerable number of German troops drowned; also that the British used a new type of wireless-directed torpedo (a Swiss invention, the Swiss said) which spread ignited oil on the water and burned the barges. Those cases of burns at the station this morning bear looking into.

Ribbentrop suddenly went off to Rome tonight. Many guesses as to why. Mine: to break the news to Mussolini that there will be no attempt at invading Britain this fall. This will put Il Duce in a hole, as he has already started an offensive on Egypt and advanced a hundred miles over the desert to Sidi-el-Barrani. But this Italian effort, it seems, was originally planned only to distract attention from the German invasion of Britain. It begins to look now (though I still think Hitler *may* try to attack England) as though the war will shift to the Mediterranean this winter, with the Axis powers trying to deliver the British Empire a knockout blow by capturing Egypt, the Suez Canal, and Palestine. Napoleon did this once, and the blow did not fell the British Empire. (Also, Napoleon planned to attack Britain, gathered his ships and barges just where Hitler has gathered his, but never dared to launch the attack.) But the Axis seizure of Suez might knock out the British Empire now. The reason Franco's handyman, Serrano Suñer, is here in Berlin is that Hitler wants him either to take

Gibraltar himself or to let the German army come in from France to do the job. Much talk here, I find, of Germany and Italy dividing up Africa between themselves, giving Spain a larger slice if Franco plays ball.

Only one air-raid here since I left, and the five million people in Berlin have caught up on their sleep and are full of breezy confidence again. They really think the British planes can't get through. Churchill is making a mistake in not sending more planes over Berlin. A mere half-dozen bombers per night would do the job—that is, would force the people to their cellars in the middle of the night and rob them of their sleep. Morale tumbled noticeably in Berlin when the British visited us almost every evening. I heard many complaints about the drop in efficiency of the armament workers and even government employees because of the loss of sleep and increased nervousness. The British haven't enough planes to devastate Berlin, but they have enough—five or six for Berlin each night—to ruin the morale of the country's most important centre of population. Can it be that the British hope to get the Germans to stop their terrible bombing of London by laying off Berlin? This would be a very silly calculation.

BERLIN, *September 19*

Having saved a little extra gasoline from my ration of thirty-seven gallons a month, I drove out to Siemensstadt with Joe Harsch and Ed Hartrich this afternoon to see if there had been any damage by bombing to the Siemens Electrical Works, one of the most important war industrial plants in Germany. I was also curious to see what mood the workers were in. We drove slowly around the plant, but could find no trace of any damage. The thousands of workers filing out after the afternoon shift seemed well fed and quite contented. Some of them looked downright prosperous and lit up cigars as they came out. During the fortnight that the British came over practically every night, the strain of working a full ten-hour shift after a night without sleep had begun to affect them, several Germans had told me. But today they looked disgustingly fit.

Returning to town somewhat disheartened by our findings,

we noticed a large crowd standing on a bridge which spanned a railroad line. We thought there had been an accident. But we found the people staring silently at a long Red Cross train unloading wounded. This is getting interesting. Only during the fortnight in September when the Poles were being crushed and a month this spring when the west was being annihilated have we seen so many hospital trains in Berlin. A diplomat told me this morning his Legation had checked two other big hospital trains unloading wounded in the Charlottenburg railroad yards yesterday. This makes four long trains of wounded in the last two days that I know have arrived here.

Not since the war started has the German press been so indignant against the British as today. According to it, the British last night bombed the Bodelschwingh hospital for mentally deficient children at Bethel in western Germany, killing nine youngsters, wounding twelve.

The same newspapers which have now begun to chronicle with glee the "reprisal" attacks on the centre of London town and which, to show the success of the "reprisals," published British figures telling of the thousands of civilians, including hundreds of children, killed by German bombs, today are filled with righteous indignation against the British for allegedly doing the same thing to Germans. Some of the headlines tonight: *Nachtausgabe:* "NIGHT CRIME OF BRITISH AGAINST 21 GERMAN CHILDREN—THIS BLOODY ACT CRIES FOR REVENGE." *Deutsche Allgemeine Zeitung:* "MURDER OF CHILDREN AT BETHEL; REVOLTING CRIME." *B.Z. am Mittag:* "ASSASSINS' MURDER IS NO LONGER WAR, HERR WINSTON CHURCHILL!—THE BRITISH ISLAND OF MURDERERS WILL HAVE TO TAKE THE CONSEQUENCES OF ITS MALICIOUS BOMBINGS."

Editorial comment is in a similar vein. The *Börsen Zeitung* writes: "They wished, on the orders of Churchill, simply to murder. . . . Albion has shown herself to be a murder-hungry beast which the German sword will liquidate in the interest not only of the German people but of the whole civilized world. . . . The sadistic threats of the British apostles of hate will end in the smoke of their cities."

This paper in the very same editorial points out how stores

in the west of London as well as a subway station there have been hit by German bombs.

The *Diplo*, written and edited in the Foreign Office, says pontifically tonight: "It is a fact that Germany is waging war with clean weapons and in a chivalrous manner." (And London bombed indiscriminately nearly every night now, the British fighter defence having stopped the Luftwaffe's daytime attacks.)

One must keep in mind that the newspapers here do not reflect public opinion. This hysterical indignation is artificially created from above. No doubt the real reason for it is to justify in the minds of the German people what the Luftwaffe is doing to London.

Censorship of our broadcasts is growing daily more impossible. I had a royal scrap with one Nazi censor tonight. He wouldn't let me read the newspaper headlines quoted above. He said it gave America a "wrong impression." He said I was too ironic, even in my selection of headlines.

BERLIN, *September 20*

Another beautiful example today of Nazi hypocrisy. I wrote in both my broadcasts today that the German press and radio were making the most of a New York report that the British censor had decided to forbid foreign correspondents in London to mention air-raids while they were on. The German Propaganda Ministry jumped on this dispatch and through its short-wave and foreign-press services tried to tell the world that henceforth America was going to be deprived of trustworthy news from London. I pointed out, incidentally, that the Nazis had clamped the same kind of censorship on us some time ago. My censors would not hear of my saying any such thing.

I ask myself why I stay on here. For the first eight months of the war our censorship was fairly reasonable—more so than Sevareid and Grandin had to put up with in Paris. But since the war became grim and serious—since the invasion of Scandinavia—it has become increasingly worse. For the last few months I've been trying to get by on my wits, such as they are; to indicate a truth or an official lie by the tone and inflexion of the voice, by a pause held longer than is natural, by the use of an Americanism which most Germans, who've learned their English in England, will not fully grasp, and by drawing from a word, a phrase, a sentence, a paragraph, or their juxtaposition, all the benefit I can. But the Nazis are on to me. For some time now my two chief censors from the Propaganda Ministry have been gentlemen who understand American as well as I, Professor Lessing, who long held a post in an American university, and Herr Krauss, for twenty years a partner in a Wall Street bank. I cannot fool them very often. Personally, both are decent, intelligent Germans, as is Captain Erich Kunsti, former Program Director of the Austrian Broadcasting System and now my principal military censor. But they must do what they're told. And the Foreign Office and Propaganda Ministry keep receiving reports from the United States—not only from the Embassy at Washington, but from their well-organized intelligence service throughout our country—that I'm getting by with murder (which I'm not) and must be sat upon. Dr. Kurt Sell, the Nazi man in Washington whose duty, among other things, is to report to Berlin on what we send, has several times reported unfavourably on the nature of my broadcasts. I haven't the slightest interest in remaining here unless I can continue to give a fairly accurate report. And each day my broadcasts are forced by the censorship to be less accurate. Tonight I noticed for the first time that one of the young Germans who do my modulating (call New York on the transmitter until time for me to speak) and follow my script to see that I read it as written and censored was *scanning* a copy of my broadcast as I spoke, making funny little lines under the syllables as we used to do in school while learning to scan poetry. He was trying to note down, I take it, which words I emphasized, which I spoke with undue sarcasm, and so on. I was so fascinated by this discovery that I stopped in the middle of my talk to watch him.

BERLIN, *September 21*

  X came up to my room in the Adlon today, and after we had disconnected my telephone and made sure that no one was listening through the crack of the door to the next room, he told me a weird story. He says the Gestapo is now systematically bumping off the mentally deficient people of the Reich. The Nazis call them "mercy deaths." He relates that Pastor Bodelschwingh, who runs a large hospital for various kinds of feeble-minded children at Bethel, was ordered arrested a few days ago because he refused to deliver up some of his more serious mental cases to the secret police. Shortly after this, his hospital is bombed. By the "British." Must look into this story.

BERLIN, *September 22*

We know that Himmler has hanged, without trial, at least one Pole for having had sexual relations with a German woman. We know too that at least half a dozen German women have been given long prison sentences for having bestowed favours upon Polish prisoners or farm labourers. Several Germans have told me of placards prominently displayed in the provincial towns warning Germans not to have anything to do with Polish labourers and to treat them rough. Last week every household in Berlin received a leaflet from the local office of the "Bund of Germans Abroad" warning the people not to fraternize with the Poles now working as labourers or prisoners in Germany. A few choice extracts from this document:

"German people, never forget that the atrocities of the Poles compelled the Führer to protect our German people by armed force! . . . The servility of the Poles to their German employers merely hides their cunning; their friendly behaviour hides their deceit. . . . Remember, there is no community whatever between Germans and Poles! Be careful that no relationship shall result because of the common religious faith! . . . . Our farmers may think each Pole who greets them with a 'Jesus Christ be praised!' is a decent fellow and may answer: 'For ever and ever, amen!'

"Germans! The Pole must never be your comrade! He is inferior to each German comrade on his farm or in his factory. Be just, as Germans have always been, but never forget that you are a member of the master race!"

I note that Poles working in Germany now have been forced to wear an arm-band or an emblem sewn on the front of their coat marked with a large "P" in purple on a yellow background. In German-occupied Poland, Jews wear a similar emblem marked with a "J."

LATER.—Ribbentrop is back from Rome, and the press hints that the "final phase" of the war has been decided upon. Rudolf Kircher, editor of the *Frankfurter Zeitung*, writes from Rome that the military situation is so rosy for the Axis that Ribbentrop and the Duce actually spent most of their time planning the "new order" in Europe and Africa. This may make the German people feel a little better, but most Germans I speak to are beginning for the first time to wonder why the invasion of Britain hasn't come off. They're still confident the war will be over by Christmas. But then, until a fortnight ago they were sure it would be over before winter, which will be on us within a month. I have won all my bets with Nazi officials and newspapermen about the date of the Swastika appearing in Trafalgar Square and shall—or should —receive from them enough champagne to keep me all winter. Today when I suggested to some of them another little bet so they could win back some of their champagne, they did not think it was funny. Neither would they bet.

German correspondents in Rome today reported that Italy is displeased with Greece and that the British are violating the neutrality of Greek waters as they once did those of Norway. This sounds bad. I suppose Greece will be next.

BERLIN, *September 23*

After a week's absence the British bombers came over last night and kept the populace in their cellars for two hours and twenty minutes in the middle of the night. This was a little shock for most people, for they had been told all week that for several nights the British had been trying to get through but had always been turned back by the anti-aircraft defences. The local papers again rage against the "British criminals" for having bombed us last night. The *Nachtausgabe* bannerlines: "NEW NIGHT ACT OF THE PIRATES." The same paper editorializes: "Winston Churchill again yesterday gave British airmen the order to drop their bombs on the German civilian population and thus continue their murder of German men, women, and children." The *Börsen Zeitung* holds that "last night Churchill continued the series of his criminal blows against the German civil population. Frankly, Churchill belongs to that category of criminals who in their stupid brutality are unteachable."

While this line of nonsense is of course dictated to the German press by Goebbels, it does indicate, I think, that the Germans can't take night bombing as the British are taking it. If London was only more on its toes it would realize this. RAF strategy, I gather, is to concentrate on Germany's war industries and supply-depots. But while they've no doubt hit some interesting targets, like the Leuna works, where coal is made into oil (they've hit Leuna, but not knocked it out), it is certain that they have not succeeded in crippling Germany's war industrial production to any appreciable extent, nor have they blown up many stores. What they must do is to keep the German people in their damp, cold cellars at night, prevent them from sleeping, and wear down their nerves. Those nerves already are very thin after seven years of belt-tightening Nazi mobilization for Total War.

Last night an old German acquaintance dropped in on me. He's in the Luftwaffe now and for the last three weeks has been a member of the crew of a night bomber which has been working on London. He had some interesting details.

1. He was impressed by the size of London. He said they've been pounding away on it for three weeks and he is amazed that so much of it is left! He said they were often told before taking off that they would find their target by a whole square mile of the city on fire. When they got there they could find no square mile on fire; only a fire here and there.

2. He relates that they approach London at a height of from 15,000 to 16,000 feet, dive to about 10,000 feet, and release their bombs at this height—too high for accurate night bombing. They don't dare to go below 7,000 feet, he says, on account of the barrage balloons. He describes the anti-aircraft fire over London as "pretty hot."

3. German night bomber crews, he says, are tired. They are being overworked. The Luftwaffe figured that they would destroy the RAF during daylight operations as they had destroyed the Polish, Dutch, Belgian, and French air forces and

neglected to train enough men for night work. Present crews, he divulged, are flying four nights out of seven a week. Unlike Dr. Goebbels, whose propaganda machine drums it into the people that British airmen are cowards when they're not brutes, my friend says quite frankly that the German pilots have the highest admiration for their British adversaries—for their skill and their bravery. They're particularly fond of one British fighter-pilot, he relates, who roars into a fight with a cigarette stuck at a smart angle between his lips. If this man is ever shot down on the German side, the German airmen have sworn to hide him and not to hand him over as a prisoner of war.

4. He confirms that the British bombers are pounding hell out of the French and Belgian coasts at night. And often they swoop down in the night and machine-gun the German bomber bases just as the German planes are taking off or alighting.

5. Göring *did* fly over London, he asserts. This news was given the foreign press here, but withheld from the German papers, which made us suspicious of it.

6. He relates that the British have built a number of dummy airfields and littered them with wooden planes, but the Germans have most of them spotted by now.

7. He confirms that the German bombers usually return from a flight over Britain to different bases, rarely to the one they have taken off from. He says the bombers start from widely scattered fields in France, Belgium, and Holland, but always on a strict time-table so as to avoid collisions in the darkness. The exact course back from London is always prescribed in advance, so that planes entering over the area will not crash into those leaving. He has an interesting explanation of the big beating the Germans took in a daylight attack on London a week ago Sunday when, according to the British, 185 German planes were shot down, mostly bombers. He says that the German time schedule went wrong, that the German fighters which were to protect the bombers arrived at a prearranged rendezvous off the English coast, but found no bombers there. After waiting twenty-five minutes they had to fly home because their gas was getting low. The bombers eventually arrived, coming over the North Sea, but there was

no fighter escort for them, and the British chasers mowed them down.

8. He said the German night bombers go over in squadrons of seven. He also insisted that each Luftwaffe base reports its correct losses and that any doctoring of figures is done either at headquarters or in Berlin.

He confirms that the Luftwaffe has failed so far to gain air supremacy over Britain, though when I was on the Channel five weeks ago the Germans said this would be a matter of but a fortnight.

It's a fact that since about a fortnight the Germans have given up large-scale day attacks on England and have gone over largely to night bombing. This in itself is an admission of defeat.

BERLIN, *September 24*

The British really went to work on Berlin last night. They bombed heavily and with excellent aim for exactly four hours. They hit some important factories in the north of the city, one big gas works, and the railroad yards north of the Stettiner and Lehrter stations.

But we couldn't tell the story. The authorities said no damage of military importance was done and the Propaganda Ministry, suddenly very nervous over last night's destruction, warned all of us correspondents that we could only report what the military said. Goebbels's Ministry even cancelled its usual post-raid conducted tour of the city, giving as an excuse that there was so much to see and so little time to see it in.

The German press and radio have never been made to lie quite so completely about a raid as today. Even the stolid Berliners, judging by their talk, appear to be stirred at the lies of their own newspapers. Said the official account: "In spite of violent anti-aircraft fire a few British bombers succeeded in reaching the northern and eastern suburbs of Berlin last night and dropped a number of bombs. The position of the bombs, far away from all military or industrial objectives, provides fresh evidence of the fact that the British airmen deliberately attack residential quarters. There was no damage of military importance."

Even the High Command, in whose veracity many Germans still believe, repeated the lie later in its daily war communiqué. The hundreds of thousands of commuters from the northern suburbs who had to get off their trains today three times and be conveyed by bus over three stretches of one main railway line where British bombs had blown up the tracks were somewhat surprised by what they read in their papers.

The British just missed twice blowing up the elevated Stadtbahn railroad running east-west through the centre of Berlin. In both places the bomb missed the tracks by a few yards, damaging adjacent houses. This line not only carries the bulk of the suburban electric traffic, but a large number of passenger trains. It's the most important line within the city limits. The debris from buildings which were hit held up traffic last night, but today the line was running.

Serrano Suñer, Franco's brother-in-law and Minister of Interior, returned from a visit to the western front just in time to experience his first British bombing attack. This may have been helpful. We correspondents kept imagining Suñer returning to Madrid, and Franco, who is under tremendous pressure from Berlin and Rome now to hop on the Axis bandwagon, asking him about those British attacks on Berlin, and Suñer replying: "What attacks? I saw no attacks. I was in Berlin ten days. The British couldn't get over even once. The British are finished, generalissimo, and now is the time for Spain to get in on the Axis spoils."

Goebbels and most of the other luminaries of the Nazi Party were dining Suñer at the Adlon last night when the bombing began. The banquet was brought to an abrupt close before the dessert had been served and all present made for the Adlon's spacious air-raid cellar next to the barber-shop. When I returned at four a.m. from the radio, they were just leaving.

I learn Ciano is coming here Thursday. A deal is on between Berlin and Rome to finish the war in Africa this winter and divide up the Dark Continent. But they must be sure of Spain first and are insisting that Franco either take Gibraltar or let the Germans take it.

Berlin pleased tonight that the French, who have practically turned over Indo-China to the Japs without a blow and daily make new concessions to the Axis without a murmur, today opened fire on de Gaulle and the British, who want to have Dakar.

Last night's bombing reminds me that the best air-raid shelter in Berlin belongs to Adolf Hitler. Experts doubt that he could ever be killed in it. It is deep, protected by iron girders and an enormous amount of reinforced concrete, and is provided with its own ventilating and lighting plant, a private movie and an operating room. Were British bombs to blow the Chancellery to smithereens, cutting off all apparent escape from the cellar, the Führer and his associates could emerge safely by simply walking through one of the tunnels that run from his shelter to points several hundred yards away. Hitler's cellar also is fitted out with spacious sleeping-quarters, an important consideration, but one utterly neglected in most shelters, since the loss of sleep is hurting the German people far more than British bombs.

If Hitler has the best air-raid cellar in Berlin, the Jews have the worst. In many cases they have none at all. Where facilities permit, the Jews have their own special *Luftschutzkeller*, usually a small basement room next to the main part of the cellar, where the "Aryans" gather. But in many Berlin cellars there is only one room. It is for the "Aryans." The Jews must take refuge on the ground floor, usually in the hall leading from the door of the flat to the elevator or stairs. This is fairly safe if a bomb hits the roof, since the chances are that it will not penetrate to the ground floor. But experience so far has shown that it is the most dangerous place to be in the entire building if a bomb lands in the street outside. Here where the Jews are hovering, the force of the explosion is felt most; here in the entryway where the Jews are, you get most of the bomb splinters.

BERLIN, *September 25*

Dr. Boehmer, the Propaganda Ministry foreign-press chief, who is a typical Nazi except that he is intelligent and has travelled widely, especially in America, is peeved from time to time over our "lack of appreciation" of such Nazi favours as giving the correspondents extra food. If the way to a

correspondent's heart is through his stomach, then Dr. Goebbels certainly tries hard. In the first place he classifies us as
"heavy labourers," which means we get double rations of
meat, bread, and butter. Every other Thursday, after our press
conference, we line up for a fortnight's extra food cards.
Moreover, Dr. Goebbels not only permits us, but actually en-
courages us to import each week, against a liberal payment in
dollar exchange, a food packet from Denmark. This latter is a
life-saver. It enables me to have bacon and eggs at breakfast
four or five times a week. Ordinarily I do not eat bacon and
eggs for breakfast, but on the short war rations now available,
I find it fortifies one for the entire day. I also got in enough
coffee from Holland before the western campaign to provide
me for the next six months. In a word, we correspondents are
hardly affected by the war-time rationing. We have plenty to
eat. And the Germans see to it that we do have enough, not
because they like us, but because—quite rightly, I suppose—
they think we'll be more kindly disposed to them if we operate on full stomachs, we being human beings after all.

Moreover, the Propaganda Ministry and the Foreign Office, which fight each other over many things, have set up a
fierce rivalry to see which one can establish the best dining
club for the foreign press. Ribbentrop's establishment, the
Ausland Presse Club, off the Kurfürstendamm, is at the moment more sumptuous than Goebbels's Ausland Club on the
Leipzigerplatz. But the *Doktor*, I hear, has just appropriated
several million marks to modernize *his* club and make it more
gaudy than Ribbentrop's. I used to eat a couple of nights a
week at the Ausland Club, it being conveniently located for
me, and the prospect of a real beefsteak and real coffee proving a great temptation. Moreover, it was a place to chew the
rag with the Nazis and see what was in their minds, if anything. Since the wanton aggression against Holland and
Belgium I have not gone there, being unable any more to
stomach Nazi officials with my dinner.

If we eat well, that is not to say that the German people do.
But reports abroad about the people here starving are greatly
exaggerated. They are not starving. After a year of the blockade they are getting enough bread, potatoes, and cabbage to
keep them going for a long time. Adults get a pound of meat

a week and a quarter of a pound of butter. Americans could hardly subsist on this diet. But Germans, whose bodies have become accustomed for a century to large amounts of potatoes, cabbage, and bread, seem to do very well on it. The meat and fat ration, though considerably under what they are used to, is enough to keep them tolerably fit.

The shortage of fruit is acute and last winter's severe cold has ruined the German fruit crop. We saw no oranges or bananas last winter and are not likely to see any this winter. The occupation of Denmark and Holland helped temporarily to augment the stocks of vegetables and dairy products, but Germany's inability to furnish fodder to these countries will shortly make them liabilities in the matter of food. There's no doubt that the Germans looted all the available food in Scandinavia, Holland, Belgium, and France, though it's true they paid for it—in paper marks which cost them nothing. Only Mr. Herbert Hoover's representative here doubts that.

The important thing is that Britain will not win the war, say, in the next two or three years by starving the German people. And Hitler, who is never sentimental about non-Germans, will see to it that every one of the hundred million people in the occupied lands dies of hunger before one German does. Of that the world may be sure.

BERLIN, *September 26*

We had the longest air-raid of the war last night, from eleven p.m. to four o'clock this morning. If you had a job to get to at seven or eight a.m., as hundreds of thousands of people had, you got very little sleep. The British ought to do this every night. No matter if not much is destroyed. The damage last night was not great. But the psychological effect was tremendous.

No one expected the British so early, and thousands were caught in subways, on the Stadtbahn, in buses and street-cars. They hastily made for the nearest public shelter and spent most of the night there. The first result of the early arrival of the British last night—theoretically they can arrive at ten p.m., two hours after dark—is that all the theatres today announce a new opening hour: six p.m., instead of seven thirty or eight p.m. And the Ministry of Education sends out word

128 WILLIAM L. SHIRER

that in case of air-raids lasting after midnight, grade schools will remain closed the following morning in order to allow the children to catch up on their sleep.

It burns me up that I cannot mention a raid that is going on during my broadcast. Last night the anti-aircraft guns protecting the *Rundfunk* made such a roar while I was broadcasting that I couldn't hear my own words. The lip microphone we are now forced to use at night prevented the sound of the guns from accompanying my words to America, which is a pity. Noticed last night too that instead of having someone talk to New York from the studio below to keep our transmitter modulated for the five minutes before I began to talk, the RRG substituted loud band music. This was done to drown out the sound of the guns.

The *B.Z. am Mittag* begins its account of last night's attack: "The greatest war-monger of all times, Winston Churchill, dispatched his murderers to Berlin again last night. . . ."

As soon as I had finished my broadcast at one a.m., the Nazi air-wardens forced me into the air-raid cellar. I tried to read Carl Crow's excellent book *Four Hundred Million Customers*, but the light was poor. I became awfully bored. Finally Lord Haw-Haw and his wife suggested we steal out. We dodged past the guards and found an unfrequented underground tunnel, where we proceeded to dispose of a litre of schnaps which "Lady" Haw-Haw had brought. Haw-Haw can drink as straight as any man, and if you can get over your initial revulsion at his being a traitor, you find him an amusing and even intelligent fellow. When the bottle was finished we felt too free to go back to the cellar. Haw-Haw found a secret stairway and we went up to his room, opened the blinds, and watched the fireworks. To the south of the city the guns were hammering away, lighting up the sky.

Sitting there in the black of the room, I had a long talk with the man. Haw-Haw, whose real name is William Joyce, but who in Germany goes by the name of Froehlich (which in German means "Joyful"), denies that he is a traitor. He argues that he has renounced his British nationality and become a German citizen, and that he is no more a traitor than thousands of British and Americans who renounced their citizenship to become comrades in the Soviet Union, or than those Germans who gave up their nationality after 1848 and fled to the United States. This doesn't satisfy me, but it does him. He kept talking about "we" and "us" and I asked him which people he meant.

"We Germans, of course," he snapped.

He's a heavily built man of about five feet nine inches, with Irish eyes that twinkle and a face scarred not by duelling in a German university but in Fascist brawls on the pavements of English towns. He speaks a fair German. I should say he has two complexes which have landed him in his present notorious position. He has a titanic hatred for Jews and an equally titanic one for capitalists. These two hatreds have been the mainsprings of his adult life. Had it not been for his hysteria about Jews, he might easily have become a successful Communist agitator. Strange as it may seem, he thinks the Nazi movement is a proletarian one which will free the world from the bonds of the "plutocratic capitalists." He sees himself primarily as a liberator of the working class.

(Haw-Haw's colleague, Jack Trevor, an English actor, who also does anti-British broadcasts for Dr. Goebbels, has no interest in the proletariat. His one burning passion is hatred of the Jews. Last winter it used to be a common sight to see him stand in the snow, with a mighty blizzard blowing, and rave to an S.S. guard outside the studio door about the urgent necessity of liquidating all Jews everywhere. The guard, who undoubtedly had no special love for the Jews, but whose only thought was how much longer he must stand guard on an unholy wintry night, would stamp his freezing feet in the snow, turn his head from the biting wind, and mutter: "*Ja. Ja. Ja. Ja,*" probably wondering what freaks Englishmen are.)

Haw-Haw's story, as I've pieced it together from our conversations and from his little booklet, *Twilight over England*, just published in Berlin (and which he gave me after I had presented him with an English book I had smuggled in entitled *The Life and Death of Lord Haw-Haw*), is this:

He was born in New York in 1906 of Irish parents who, he says, lost what money they had in Ireland "by reason of their devotion to the British crown." He studied literature, history, and psychology at the University of London and in 1923, the year of Hitler's ill-fated Munich *Putsch*, joined the British Fascists. He says he earned his living thereafter as a tutor. In 1933 he entered Sir Oswald Mosley's British Union of Fascists and became one of its chief speakers and writers. For three years he was Mosley's propaganda chief. He claims he left Mosley's movement in 1937 "owing to differences on matters pertaining to organization." He teamed up with John Beckett, a former Socialist M.P., and started the National Socialist League, but within a few months Beckett left it because he thought Joyce's methods "too extreme."

Of these days Joyce writes: "We lived National Socialism. . . . We were all poor enough to know the horrors of freedom in democracy. One of our members was driven mad by eighteen months of unemployment and starvation. I lived for months with real friends who loved England and could not get enough to eat from her."

Twice during the year that preceded the war he was arrested on charges of assault and disturbing the peace. Then came the war clouds.

"For me," he writes, "the decision was easy to make. To me it was clear on the morning of August 25 that the greatest struggle in history was doomed to take place. It might have been a very worthy course to stay in England and incessantly work for peace. But I had one traditionally acquired or inherited prejudice. . . . England was going to war. I felt that if, for perfect reasons of conscience, I could not fight for her, I must give her up for ever."

He did. On August 25 he and his wife, "who had to leave without even being able to say farewell to her parents," set out for Germany to take part in what he calls the "sacred struggle to free the world."

Any mind which sees Hitler's cold-blooded tramping down of the free peoples of Europe as a sacred struggle to free the world speaks for itself. Haw-Haw's book is a hodge-podge of Nazi nonsense about England, studded with obvious truths about its blacker and meaner side which the whole world knows.

Haw-Haw's extremely nasal voice was at first considered by Propaganda Ministry officials as wholly unfit for broadcasting. A Nazi radio engineer who had studied in England first saw its possibilities and he was given a trial. On the radio this hard-fisted, scar-faced young Fascist rabble-rouser sounds like a decadent old English blue-blood aristocrat of the type familiar on our stage. Ed Murrow told me last winter that check-ups showed that Haw-Haw commanded at least half of the English radio audience when he was on the air. But that was when the English were bored by the "phony" war and found the war and Joyce amusing. I think he himself realizes that he has lost most of his hold on the English people. Of late he has also begun to chafe at the inane things which Goebbels makes him say.

There is a third English traitor to note here. He is Baillie Stewart, a former captain of the Seaforth Highlanders, who a few years ago was sentenced to imprisonment in the Tower for betraying military secrets to a foreign power. The girl who led him to this was a German siren, and after his release he followed her here. He did some broadcasts at first, but his Scottish nature was too unbending for the Nazi officials of the Propaganda Ministry and the German Broadcasting Company. He is now off the air and working as a translator in the Foreign Office.

While on the subject, I might as well note down the three Americans who are doing Nazi propaganda for the German radio.

Fred Kaltenbach of Waterloo, Iowa, is probably the best of the lot, actually believing in National Socialism with a sincere fanaticism and continually fighting the Nazi Party hacks when they don't agree with him. He is not a bad radio speaker. I avoid all three and have seen Kaltenbach only once. That was at Compiègne when he was having one of his periodic feuds with the Nazi radio authorities. They gave orders that he was not to be taken from Paris to Compiègne, but he stole a ride with some army officers and "gate-crashed" the ceremony. He was continually being arrested by the military and ejected from the grounds, but he came back each time. Most Nazis find him a bit "too American" for their taste, but Kaltenbach would die for Nazism.

The second American speaker is one Edward Leopold Delaney, who goes here by the name of E. D. Ward. He's a disappointed actor who used to have occasional employment with road companies in the United States. He has a diseased hatred for Jews, but otherwise is a mild fellow and broadcasts the cruder type of Nazi propaganda without questioning.

The third person is Miss Constance Drexel, who many years ago wrote for the Philadelphia *Public Ledger*. The Nazis hire her, so far as I can find out, principally because she's the only woman in town who will sell her American accent to them. Bizarre: she constantly pesters me for a job. One American network hired her at the beginning of the war, but dropped her almost at once.

For their other foreign-language broadcasts the Nazis have a strange assortment of hired Balkanites, Dutch, Scandinavians, Spaniards, Arabs, and Hindus. Once in a great while one of these speakers turns out to be "unreliable." Such a one was the Yugoslav speaker who began his broadcast the other night: "Ladies and gentlemen, what you are about to hear from Berlin tonight is a lot of nonsense, a pack of lies, and if you have any sense, you will turn your dials." He got no further, for there are "checkers" sitting listening at the Propaganda Ministry at the other end of town. The last seen of the fellow was when the S.S. guards carted him off to jail.

The Norwegian people were brusquely informed last night in a broadcast by the Nazi Commissar in Oslo, *Gauleiter* Terboven, of the hard row that lies ahead of them. Announced the *Gauleiter*: (1) The Norwegian Royal House has no more political importance and will never return to Norway. (2) The same goes for the Nygaardsvold government which emigrated. (3) Therefore any activity in favour of the Royal House or the government which fled is prohibited. (4) In accordance with a decree of Hitler, a commissarial council is named to take over the business of the government. (5) The old political parties are dissolved immediately. (6) Any combinations for the purpose of political activity of any kind will not be tolerated.

Thus is Norway, all that is decent and democratic in Norway, destroyed—for the time being. And Germany shows so plainly how unfit she is to rule over anybody else. There was a short time, when the Reich first took over Norway—the same is true of Holland—when Germany might have succeeded in winning over the goodwill of the people there, who saw it was hopeless to struggle against the overwhelming military power of Hitler. But the Germans did everything possible to forfeit goodwill, and in a few weeks the sentiment changed. Now in all the occupied countries the German rules are bitterly hated. No decent Norwegian or Dutchman will have anything to do with them.

The *Gauleiter*'s broadcast was a fine example of German tactlessness. He told the Norwegian people that he had tried in vain to negotiate with the old political parties, but they had held out for power and had not "heeded" his warnings; so he had had to liquidate them. In conclusion, he told the Norwegians that it had now become clear that the way of the Quisling movement had always been the only possible one for Norway, and that this party would be the only one tolerated by the Germans in the future. Thus, in effect, he told the Norwegians that a miserable little traitor, detested by ninety-nine and a half per cent of the population, was not only right, but henceforth would have the only say—so far as any Norwegian will have any say, which is little enough—about the future of their country.

You don't have to be profound to conclude that the rule of brute force now exercised by the Germans over the occupied territories can never last very long. For despite complete military and police power, which the Germans admittedly have, you cannot for ever rule over foreign European peoples who hate and detest you. The success of Hitler's "new order" in Europe is therefore doomed even before it is set up. The Nazis, of course, who have never troubled to study European history but are guided by a primitive Germanic tribal urge of conquest with no thought for the possible consequences, think that they are well on their way to installing a European "new order" which will be dominated by Germany for the greater good of Germany for all time. Their long-term plan is not only to keep the subjected European peoples permanently disarmed so that they cannot revolt against their German masters, but to make them so dependent on Germany economically that they cannot exist without Berlin's benevolent will. Thus those heavy and highly technical industries which still function in the slave lands will be concentrated in Germany. The slave peoples will produce the raw materials to feed them, and the food to feed the German masters. They will be largely agricultural and mining communities—much as the Balkan lands fulfil that role for western Europe today. And they will be utterly dependent upon Germany.

The subjected peoples of Europe will be saved, of course, if Britain holds out and ultimately wins this war. But even if Germany should win the war it will lose its struggle to organize Europe. The German, I am profoundly convinced after mingling with him now for many years, is incapable of organizing Europe. His lack of balance, his bullying sadism when he is on top, his constitutional inability to grasp even faintly what is in the minds and hearts of other peoples, his instinctive feeling that relations between two peoples can only be on the basis of master and slave and never on the basis of let-live equality—these characteristics of the German make him and his nation unfit for the leadership in Europe they have always sought and make it certain that, however he may try, he will in the long run fail.

Ciano arrives here tomorrow from Rome. Most people think it is for the announcement that Spain is entering the war on the side of the Axis. Suñer is here for the ceremony, if it comes off.

BERLIN, *September 27*

Hitler and Mussolini have pulled another surprise.

At one p.m. today in the Chancellery, Japan, Germany, and Italy signed a military alliance directed against the United States. I was caught way off base thinking that Ciano had come to pipe Spain into the war. Suñer was not even present at the theatrical performance the fascists of Europe and Asia staged today.

I came to my senses this morning when I noticed the schoolchildren who had been marched to the Wilhelmstrasse to cheer—waving Japanese flags. As I had a broadcast at two p.m. and the correspondents were convoked at the Chancellery for "an important announcement" at one p.m., I asked

Hartrich to cover the actual ceremony. At the *Rundfunk* I followed it by radio.

Core of the pact is Article III. It reads: "Germany, Italy, and Japan undertake to assist one another with all political, economic, and military means when one of the three contracting parties is attacked by a power at present not involved in the European war or in the Sino-Japanese conflict."

There are two great powers not yet involved in either of those wars: Russia and the United States. But Article III does not refer to Russia; Article V refers to Russia. Article V says: "Germany, Italy, and Japan affirm that the aforesaid terms do not in any way affect the political status which exists at present between each of the three contracting parties and Soviet Russia."

The Soviet Union is out. That leaves the U.S.A. in. There was no attempt to disguise this obvious fact in Nazi circles tonight, though, as expected, my censors tried to stop me from saying so and I had to use all my wits in getting the thing across in my broadcasts. Though it would have been more honest and accurate to say bluntly that Nazi circles did not disguise the fact that the alliance was directed against the United States, I had to water it down to this beautiful opening sentence: "There is no attempt in informed circles here tonight to disguise the fact that the military alliance signed in Berlin today . . . *has one great country in mind*. That country is the United States." Then to clinch the argument I had to resort to a nebulous analysis of the text of the treaty and the German interpretation thereof, which the censors, after some sour remarks, finally passed.

Now, why did Hitler, instigator of this alliance, hurriedly rig it up just at this time? My theory is this: Ribbentrop journeyed suddenly to Rome a fortnight ago to break the news to Mussolini that the expected land invasion of Britain, which Hitler in a speech only a few days previously at the Sportpalast had promised the German people would certainly take place soon, could not be carried out as planned. Mussolini had already started an invasion of Egypt to coincide with the attack on Britain and to divide the Empire's forces, but not to do much more than that this fall. We know that Ribbentrop stayed longer in Rome than he planned. The Duce, no doubt, was disturbed at Hitler's abandoning the all-out attack on Britain which he was confident would end the war—and Italy had only entered the war when she did because she thought it was almost over. What was the Axis to do? The obvious thing seemed to devote the winter to attacking the heart of the British Empire in Egypt, conquer that country, take the Suez Canal, then grab Palestine, Iraq, where badly needed oil was at hand, and possibly continue down the Euphrates and take the Persian oil region, or at least its export base at the head of the Persian Gulf. Germany could supply thousands of airplanes and tanks and some complete *Panzer* divisions which had been assembled for the attack on Britain. If necessary, Yugoslavia and Greece could be occupied (Italy to get Dalmatia permanently), and southern Greece used as a starting-place for German planes against Egypt and the British Mediterranean fleet.

To ensure the complete and timely success of the campaign, Spain must be brought in and made to take Gibraltar immediately, thus destroying Britain's position in the western Mediterranean. Serrano Suñer, Franco's brother-in-law, Minister of Interior and leader of the Falangists, was in Berlin. He personally seemed favourable. Only Franco, that ingrate, hesitated. The British, Franco apparently thought, were not yet beaten, and . . .

There was that other factor, the United States.

Until recently, that factor had not been taken much into account in Berlin. Last fall Göring had scoffed to us of the possibility of American aid to the Allies playing a role in this war. All through the summer, as the German army smashed through the west, Berlin was confident that the war would be over by fall, and that therefore American aid, which could only become really effective next spring, was of no concern to Germany. That view seems to have been sincerely held here until very recently. In the last two or three weeks something has gone wrong with the plans to invade Britain. They may or may not be off, but probably are. At any rate it dawned on Berlin a few days ago that Britain might not be defeated after all this fall, might still be fighting next spring, and that then American aid to Britain, especially in planes, would begin to make itself felt rather seriously. Something must be done after all about the United States. What? Something to scare her and to set the American isolationists loose again with a new cry about the danger of war.

In Japan a few weeks ago a new government under Prince Konoye came to power proclaiming a "new life" and a "new order" in eastern Asia. The Prince was a man the Germans could deal with. Herr Stahmer, a confidential man of Ribbentrop's who used to be employed in working on the British appeasers, was dispatched to look over the ground. There follows now a military alliance designed to threaten America and keep her out of the war. If I am any judge of American character, no one at home with the exception of the Wheelers, Nyes, and Lindberghs will be the least bit frightened by this. The effect will be just the opposite from what Hitler and Ribbentrop, who never fail to misjudge Anglo-Saxon character, expect.

Then too, this tripartite pact is a thing the Axis powers and especially Germany can ballyhoo to the skies, thus taking people's minds off the fact that the promised invasion of England isn't coming off and that the war—which every German confidently expected since midsummer would be over in a month or two—isn't going to end before winter comes, after all.

The ballyhoo today has already been terrific, pushing all other news completely off the front page. The German people are told that the pact is of world-shaking importance and will shortly bring final "world peace." The ceremony of signing, as described by Hartrich, who was present, was carried through with typical Axis talent for the theatrical. In the first place, the surprise of the event itself. Then the showy setting. When Ribbentrop, Ciano, and Japanese Ambassador M. Kurusu, a bewildered little man, entered the gala hall of the Chancellery, Klieg lights blazed away as the scene was recorded for history. Brightly coloured uniforms all over the place. The entire staffs of the Italian and Japanese embassies present. (No other diplomats attended. The Russian Ambassador was invited, but replied he would be out of town this noon.) The three men sit themselves at a gilded table. Ribbentrop rises and motions one of his slaves, Dr. Schmidt, to read the text of the pact. Then they sign while the cameras grind away. Then comes the climactic moment, or so the Nazis think. Three loud knocks on the giant door are heard. There is a tense hush in the great hall. The Japanese hold their breath. The door swings slowly open, and in strides Hitler. Ribbentrop bobs up and formally notifies him that the pact has been signed. The Great Kahn nods approvingly, but does not deign to speak. Hitler majestically takes a seat in the middle of the table, while the two foreign ministers and the Japanese Ambassador scramble for chairs. When they have got adjusted, they pop up, one after another, and deliver prepared addresses which the radio broadcasts round the world.

To add: Article I of the pact states that Japan recognizes the leadership of Germany and Italy in the creation of a new order in Europe. Article II says: "Germany and Italy recognize the leadership of Japan in the creation of a new order in the greater east Asiatic territory."

Neither of the two sides can lend the slightest economic or military help to the other so long as they are separated by the British navy. What Japan gets out of it is not clear, since if we should go to war with her neither Germany nor Italy could harm us until they had conquered the British navy. And should we get involved in war with Berlin and Rome, Japan is bound to declare war on us, though her own interests might dictate not doing so. However, she could no doubt find an excuse for forgetting the treaty in that case.

One thing is clear: Hitler would not have promulgated the tripartite pact if he thought the war was coming to an end before winter. There would have been no need of it.

Berlin Diary, 1941

Blitzkrieg Reporting

by Ernest R. Pope

THIRTY American journalists in Berlin, working under handicaps of air raids, blackouts, food cards, tapped telephones and diluted beer, have the ticklish task of trying to tell the United States through a wall of censorship what is going on in Germany.

Theirs is a test of endurance of body and nerves, under which some have cracked, and a greater test of diplomacy, in which a few have failed. The veterans stay on, trying to give the news and yet not be expelled for "abusing the privileges granted by the Reich to foreign correspondents," the standard charge when Berlin wants to get rid of a man too openly hostile. They do not tell all they know or hear, but neither do they write the news the way the Nazis would like it written. Their reports are accurate, assuming that you distinguish between their own observations and that which they carefully tell you was handed out by the Nazis.

Nine-tenths of the war news emanates from Goebbels' Propaganda Ministry or from Ribbentrop's Foreign Ministry, which face each other across the Wilhelmstrasse. The correspondents gather daily at Goebbels' huge and monotonous white building for a conference. Early comers pitch pfennigs in the corridor with blond young Professor Boemer, foreign press chief. Neither his snug army uniform nor his dignity prevents him from being adept at scooping up the coins.

Soon we all troop into Goebbels' private theater, luxurious with red carpets, white and gold walls and polished mahogany furniture, where Goebbels and his friends relax by viewing command performances on stage or screen. We may not smoke. Professor Boemer presides, flanked by advisers on law, transportation, agriculture and so on, ready to answer questions in their fields.

Boemer reads the latest bulletin from the army high command. Then we have a special feature. One day it is Lieut. Prien, straight from his U-boat, who parades his bearded crew into the auditorium to tell how he "foiled the British" and torpedoed the *Royal Oak*. Another day Goebbels is the attraction, staging a dramatic entrance from his adjoining office. Grimly the club-footed little Doctor faces the reporters.

"My colleagues," he shouts, "I have a very serious matter to call to your attention as fellow-journalists. That yellow, lying American writer, Knickerbocker, has accused me and other Nazi ministers of hoarding money in foreign banks. Not one word is true. I call upon you to blot out Knickerbocker's name from your journalistic fraternity."

Or the Reich Minister of Agriculture praises Germany's "strong food reserves" and supplies official figures. Or there is a lecture by a Red Cross officer, a prison camp warden, a labor leader, or some military authority.

Into the conference walks dapper Pete Huss, one of our crowd, accompanied by two army officers. He looks tired, having just come from Templehof Airdrome after a three-day tour of the front in a plane. Pete tells us in German what he saw.

Boemer announces the next press tour; at 4 o'clock tomorrow morning an army bomber will fly ten correspondents to the English Channel. We draw lots or vote among ourselves to pick the lucky ten. "Wear your warmest clothing," the Professor warns us.

On such major press tours we fly in a 50-seater Junkers. A Promi (Propaganda Ministry) camera man goes along. His films are thrown on a screen when we describe what we saw to correspondents left behind. We see ourselves peering at the fighting through field glasses, inspecting blasted French tanks, or drinking beer with Czech girls at Prague. We razz each other on our respective photogenic qualities. Speaking of films, we also preview the regular war newsreels two days before they are shown publicly.

During conferences we may ask Boemer any questions we please. He may answer them, or he may merely smile. The smile is a form of censorship. It means, "I shan't tell you, and I shan't say I won't tell you, and if you find out elsewhere send the story at your own risk."

The conference is about to break up. But not until Boemer announces changes in cable and telegraph facilities, and changes in gasoline rations. We share with diplomats, physicians, the army, the Gestapo and a few high officials the privilege of having cars. A special red check mark on our license plates identifies us. At the start of the war, we were granted 30 to 50 gallons of gas per month, at 75 cents a gallon. But the cylinder capacity of automobiles permitted grew smaller as the war progressed, until we who owned American cars had to lay them up and buy little European models. Almost every day we are entreated to drive only when necessary—not to drive from home to office, or from office to the Ministry, for example.

As we leave the theater Boemer calls out, "Don't forget to pick up your food cards, Meine Herren." The Promi gives us extra butter and meat—several ounces more each week than the average German gets. We are classed as "hard workers" and get the same food allowance as ditch-diggers, construction workers and stevedores. Only one class gets more food, the laborers doing hard work in unpleasant environment—in front of a blast furnace, for example. Dr. Goebbels apparently couldn't quite bring himself to call his theater "unpleasant surroundings."

At the less pretentious conference hall in the German Foreign Office we are permitted to smoke.

What is Germany's attitude toward the nomination of Wilkie? Has the Foreign Office replied to Cordell Hull's note? What is the object of Count Ciano's visit to Berlin? We fire the questions at beefy Dr. Schmidt, Ribbentrop's press chief and, like Boemer, blond and young. His replies, statements and evasions, when carefully examined, worked into a Berlin dispatch or radio script with the censor in mind, and with Schmidt's warning not to quote him, appear in the American news as "It was officially stated at Berlin today that Germany does not intend to . . ." etc.

On special occasions Ribbentrop puts in a ceremonious appearance, in full diplomatic uniform, to "explain and justify" the invasion of Holland, Denmark, or whichever country was latest on the list.

Hitler never sees foreign correspondents. The Reich press

chief, Dr. Otto Dietrich, who follows the Fuehrer around the Reich, occasionally receives reporters. He informs us that "Der Fuehrer eats from the same field kitchen as his soldiers. He is wearing a simple field-gray uniform. He sleeps on an ordinary army cot. Herr Hitler arose at 4 a.m. today. He was in a cheerful mood and his eyes sparkled."

Himmler, Goering, Schacht and Hess are hardly more approachable than the Chancellor himself. Gala banquets for the press are a thing of the past, and the studied informality attempted by the German leaders in dealing with us gave way to grim aloofness and invisibility at the outbreak of war.

When the day's lessons and sermons by official spokesmen are finished, we talk over the gist of them on the sidewalk, then scatter through the blackout to our offices, most of them five minutes' walk distant. Or maybe some of us take our Nazi schoolmasters around the corner to the Adlon bar. This, if it does not yield news, at least reduces friction.

The oiling process is completed later on at the *Taverne*, the only night club in Berlin open after curfew—by special government decree—and only diplomats, journalists, theatrical people and Nazi big shots may frequent it.

Professor Boemer hurries in after his last huddle with the boss and his latest foreign news bulletin for the night. Dr. Schmidt joins the crowd for some rationed food, some of Ribbentrop's *Henkell Trocken* champagne, some ersatz information and some real jokes about "Uncle Hermann" Goering.

The Nazi officials are accompanied by elegant young women who make themselves very agreeable to us. This is the oldest of bait for the unwary. Neutral diplomats, German film stars and Max Schmeling gather around to take advantage of their oversize meat and fat cards and their special police permits to buy drinks after 1 a.m. In the *Taverne* we are supposed to relax and forget there is a war, but, down underneath, the parties are a contest to see who can talk and drink the most and divulge the least. There are always attentive ears on both sides of you, and probably behind you.

The end of a day in the field with the army is quite different. After bumping over air pockets, or lurching over shell holes, ducking shrapnel and machine-gun bullets and eating not much of anything from daylight to dark, we are glad to flop exhausted on a bed as soon as we have sent in our reports by army field telephone.

We were often taken between the lines of fire in France, with German artillery shooting over our heads while army men explained the progress of the fighting and pointed out enemy troops giving way before German advance columns. During a drive through a forest "somewhere in France" a bullet whizzed through our windshield.

All to get the news. Sometimes we'd tell it differently if there were no censors. For example:

American correspondents were driven through several Polish towns to be shown "how German control has improved living conditions." A young Nazi led them to a modern hospital and proudly explained the contrast between Teutonic cleanliness and what he called "Polish housekeeping." One of the correspondents discovered that the Poles themselves had built the hospital just before the German invasion.

The censors work in various ways. Dispatches sent by cable or wireless are taken by the correspondent or his assistant in person to the Haupt Telegrafen Amt; and a long trip it is, in a blackout, when all cats, buildings and streets look alike. The dispatch is not accepted until the bearer has shown his credentials from Promi. An army of experienced censors handles dispatches at the HTA. Another army at the main postoffice handles articles that are mailed. And if we telephone dispatches—to Holland, Denmark or Italy, to be relayed to the United States—a censor listens in and a machine records what we say. If messages thus telephoned do not meet with official approval the correspondent is immediately reprimanded, he is barred from press conferences, his communications are entirely cut off, he may even be expelled.

Radio reporters who broadcast five-minute talks to the United States daily, for NBC, CBS and Mutual, get a thorough going-over by three sets of censors who blue-pencil their script; and a fourth censor listens in, ready to cut them off the air if they deviate from the approved written version.

On their trips with the Nazi armed forces, broadcasters have seen interesting war machines which they would like to describe . . . huge railway guns, new fighter 'planes and other secret weapons. They would also like to tell radio listeners where they have been with the Army, and what sort of troops they saw. Military censors wage blitzkriegs with their blue pencils on such material in the scripts.

The Propaganda Ministry cuts out items such as too vivid descriptions of the bad food Germans are forced to eat. The Foreign Office refuses to let them reveal Ribbentrop's impending diplomatic jumps, about which they have heard from a friend.

Let's follow Bill Shirer of Columbia, veteran of the group, to see how he works. Two hours before the time for his broadcast, he drives to the radio center on Adolf Hitler Platz five miles from the center of town. He writes his broadcast there. It is phoned to Goebbels' and Ribbentrop's ministries, where censors make excisions, while an army censor looks over a copy to be sure Shirer hasn't remarked that "the moon is shining peacefully" or made some other apparently harmless comment that might give a tip to enemy bombers. Goebbels' boys crack down on too vivid descriptions of bad food, Ribbentrop's on any hint of a forthcoming diplomatic move. By the time the three of them are through, the script has been slashed to ribbons. It is standard practice for Shirer to write enough talk to fill ten minutes, hoping five minutes' worth will get through.

His copy ok'd, he is escorted to the short-wave transmitters, each microphone in a booth not much larger than a telephone booth. A German official makes contact with America, and on the split second, Shirer starts to talk. In adjoining booths he can see Lord Haw Haw, a Japanese, an Italian and a renegade Frenchman broadcasting Nazi propaganda.

The Nazis are not too severe in censoring radio talks, adopting the policy that poor propaganda is better than none. If the broadcasters are edited into flabby dullness the American chains will stop taking service. That is the only kind of strike, or threatened strike, that still works in Germany. Incidentally, the government-owned shortwave station pockets an average of $1000 a day, in dollars, for transmitting broadcasts to America. That much foreign exchange is not to be sneezed at.

Neither radio men nor press correspondents tell all they

know—or hear. Discretion is the better part of valor. They know—or hear—that the Czechs have tried to revolt but are being crushed by rough Gestapo methods. They know that the railway system has broken down, that many German families are eating dog-meat, that hospitals have run out of ether, that Goebbels is running around with a new film star, that Goering yesterday had a terrific quarrel with Ribbentrop, that Doctor Sauerbruch has had a rush call to Hitler's bedside, that the Rumanian ambassador became furious during a visit to the Foreign Office. In short, they know or hear many things which are kept secret even from the Fuehrer, so they have no notion that they will be allowed to tell them to millions of Americans.

There are other "dont's." *Don't tell Germans what you know* is one of the first rules. Germans are eager to know what the foreign radio stations are saying, but it is a crime for them to listen, and it is against the law for you to tell them. *Don't air your own opinions* is good common sense if you want to stay in Berlin. *Don't ask embarrassing questions* is another precept. You won't get an answer anyway, and you won't be invited on the next press trip. Finally, *don't discuss news on the telephone*, even with your colleagues. Telephones have extra ears in totalitarian countries.

Every day the blitzkrieg reporter must wrestle with the problem of what not to say, and compromise with his journalistic conscience. Beach Conger of *The New York Herald Tribune* was expelled for smuggling a story out. His successor, Ralph Barnes, was likewise ejected, and Barnes' assistant, Russell Hill. So, too, was Otto Tolischus, veteran and scholarly correspondent of *The New York Times.*

The men from the news agencies (AP, UP, INS) must stick to their posts in Berlin as long as America remains neutral. Consequently, they are the most conservative in their reports. They keep in the good graces of the Nazi authorities by passing on news favorable to the Reich. Nevertheless, they qualify this news, so that the American reader can take it for what it is worth, by specifying "A Nazi spokesman denied the atrocity story that . . .", "foreign correspondents were requested today to deny the story sent by *The Herald Tribune* correspondent in Berlin to the effect that the Czechs have been revolting at Prague . . .", "Official sources stated that Germany's food supplies 'are sufficient for many years of war' . . ."

Despite all this, much unfavorable or critical news is permitted to get through the censorship. The explanation is simple. The Nazis learned a lesson from Stalin and the Soviets. The bombastic self-praise and 100 per cent Communist propaganda from Moscow made the world lose all faith in Russian reports. The Nazis feel that America will be more inclined to believe Berlin dispatches when they contain adverse facts and criticism.

It is the ticklish job of the blitzkrieg reporter to know just how much of this unpleasant material he can salt into his reports, and still not be thrown out as so many of his colleagues have been. His skill accounts for the surprising amount of accurate reporting that has reached America from the most policed, most authoritarian and most belligerent country in the world—the Third Reich.

Current History, September 1940

LONDON ON FIRE:
THE RAID OF DECEMBER 29, 1940

"This Dreadful Masterpiece"

by Ernie Pyle

LONDON (by wireless)—Some day when peace has returned to this odd world I want to come to London again and stand on a certain balcony on a moonlit night and look down upon the peaceful silver curve of the Thames with its dark bridges.

And standing there, I want to tell somebody who has never seen it how London looked on a certain night in the holiday season of the year 1940.

For on that night this old, old city—even though I must bite my tongue in shame for saying it—was the most beautiful sight I have ever seen.

It was a night when London was ringed and stabbed with fire.

* * *

They came just after dark, and somehow I could sense from the quick, bitter firing of the guns that there was to be no monkey business this night.

Shortly after the sirens wailed I could hear the Germans grinding overhead. In my room, with its black curtains drawn across the windows, you could feel the shake from the guns. You could hear the boom, crump, crump, crump, of heavy bombs at their work of tearing buildings apart. They were not too far away.

Half an hour after the firing started I gathered a couple of friends and went to a high, darkened balcony that gave us a view of one-third of the entire circle of London.

As we stepped out onto the balcony a vast inner excitement came over all of us—an excitement that had neither fear nor horror in it, because it was too full of awe.

You have all seen big fires, but I doubt if you have ever seen

147

the whole horizon of a city lined with great fires—scores of them, perhaps hundreds.

There was something inspiring in the savagery of it.

The closest fires were near enough for us to hear the crack-ling flames and the yells of firemen. Little fires grew into big ones even as we watched. Big ones died down under the firemen's valor only to break out again later.

About every two minutes a new wave of planes would be over. The motors seemed to grind rather than roar, and to have an angry pulsation like a bee buzzing in blind fury.

The bombs did not make a constant overwhelming din as in those terrible days of last September. They were intermit-tent—sometimes a few seconds apart, sometimes a minute or more.

Their sound was sharp, nearby, and soft and muffled, far away. They were everywhere over London.

Into the dark, shadowed spaces below us, as we watched, whole batches of incendiary bombs fell. We saw two dozen go off in two seconds. They flashed terrifically, then quickly simmered down to pinpoints of dazzling white, burning ferociously.

These white pinpoints would go out one by one as the un-seen heroes of the moment smothered them with sand. But also, as we watched, other pinpoints would burn on and pretty soon a yellow flame would leap up from the white cen-ter. They had done their work—another building was on fire.

The greatest of all the fires was directly in front of us. Flames seemed to whip hundreds of feet into the air. Pinkish-white smoke ballooned upward in a great cloud, and out of this cloud there gradually took shape—so faintly at first that we weren't sure we saw correctly—the gigantic dome and spires of St. Paul's Cathedral.

St. Paul's was surrounded by fire, but it came through. It stood there in its enormous proportions—growing slowly clearer and clearer, the way objects take shape at dawn. It was like a picture of some miraculous figure that appears before peace-hungry soldiers on a battlefield.

The streets below us were semi-illuminated from the glow.

Immediately above the fires the sky was red and angry, and overhead, making a ceiling in the vast heavens, there was a cloud of smoke all in pink. Up in that pink shrouding there were tiny, brilliant specks of flashing light—anti-aircraft shells bursting. After the flash you could hear the sound.

Up there, too, the barrage balloons were standing out as clearly as if it were daytime, but now they were pink instead of silver. And now and then through a hole in that pink shroud there twinkled incongruously a permanent, genuine star—the old-fashioned kind that has always been there.

Below us the Thames grew lighter, and all around below were the shadows—the dark shadows of buildings and bridges that formed the base of this dreadful masterpiece.

Later on I borrowed a tin hat and went out among the fires. That was exciting too, but the thing I shall always remember above all the other things in my life is the monstrous loveliness of that one single view of London on a holiday night—London stabbed with great fires, shaken by explosions, its dark regions along the Thames sparkling with the pinpoints of white-hot bombs, all of it roofed over with a ceiling of pink that held bursting shells, balloons, flares and the grind of vicious engines. And in yourself the excitement and anticipation and wonder in your soul that this could be happening at all.

These things all went together to make the most hateful, most beautiful single scene I have ever known.

Scripps-Howard wire copy, December 30, 1940

LONDONERS IN THE UNDERGROUND:
JANUARY 1941

"Life Without Redemption"

by Ernie Pyle

LONDON (by wireless)—I got my very first view of an underground shelter crowd at the big Liverpool St. tube station.

It was around 8 o'clock on a raidless night. A policeman in the upper vestibule told us just to go down the escalator and take a look—as though it were a zoo. So we did.

Somehow I must have thought that there'd be nobody down there that night, or that if there were they'd be invisible or something, because I wasn't emotionally ready at all to see people lying around by the thousands on cold concrete.

In my first days in England I had seen terrible bomb damage. I had seen multitudinous preparations for war. I had talked with wounded soldiers. I had gone through London's great night of fire-bombing. I had listened for hours to the crack of guns and the crunch of bombs. And although I didn't especially know it at the time, none of these things went clear down deep inside and made me hurt.

It was not until I went down 70 feet into the bowels of the Liverpool St. tube and saw humanity sprawled there in child-like helplessness that my heart first jumped and my throat caught.

I know I must have stopped suddenly and drawn back.

I know I must have said to myself, "Oh my God!"

*　　*　　*

We hunted up the shelter marshal, and talked to him for a long time. He was immensely proud of his shelter, and I suppose he had a right to be, for they say it is paradise now compared to what it was in the beginning.

He told us to take a walk through the shelter and then meet him at the back entrance.

This is a new section of the tunnel, not yet used by trains. The tube is narrower than most of New York's subway exca-

150

vations, and it is elliptical or egg-shaped. It is walled with steel casing.

We walked to the far end, about an eighth of a mile, through one tube, and then back in the parallel tube, which is just like the other.

On benches on each side, as though sitting and lying on a long street-car seat, were the people, hundreds of them. And as we walked on they stretched into thousands.

In addition, there was a row of sleeping forms on the wooden floor of the tube, stretched crosswise. Their bodies took up the whole space, so we had to watch closely when we put our feet down between the sleepers.

Many of these people were old—wretched and worn old people, people who had never known many of the good things of life and who were now winding up their days on this earth in desperate discomfort.

They were the bundled-up, patched-up people with lined faces that we have seen for years sitting dumbly in waiting lines at our own relief offices at home.

There were children too, some asleep and some playing. There were youngsters in groups, laughing and talking and even singing.

There were smart-alecks and there were quiet ones. There were hard-working people of middle age who had to rise at 5 and go to work.

Some people sat knitting or playing cards or talking. But mostly they just sat. And though it was only 8 o'clock, many of the old people were already asleep.

It was the old people who seemed so tragic. Think of yourself at 70 or 80, full of pain and of the dim memories of a lifetime that has probably all been bleak. And then think of yourself now, traveling at dusk every night to a subway station, wrapping your ragged overcoat about your old shoulders and sitting on a wooden bench with your back against a curved steel wall. Sitting there all night, in nodding and fitful sleep.

Think of that as your destiny—every night, every night from now on.

People looked up as we came along in our nice clothes and our obviously American hats. I had a terrible feeling of guilt as I walked through there—the same feeling that I have had when going through penitentiaries, staring at the prisoners. I felt ashamed to be there staring.

I couldn't look people in the face, consequently I didn't see very much of human visage that night, for I looked mostly at the floor. But I saw all I could bear. I saw enough.

*   *   *

Since that first night I have seen too much of it. I no longer feel that way about the shelterers in mass. Repetition makes the unusual become commonplace. Enough of anything dulls the emotions.

But I still think my first impression was a valid one. I still think it speaks the frightening poverty of character in this world more forcibly than do the bombs that cause it.

A bombed building looks like something you have seen before—it looks as though a hurricane had struck. But the sight of thousands of poor, opportunityless people lying in weird positions against cold steel, with all their clothes on, hunched up in blankets, lights shining in their eyes, breathing fetid air—lying there far underground like rabbits, not fighting, not even mad, just helpless, scourged, weakly, waiting for the release of another dawn—that, I tell you, is life without redemption.

Scripps-Howard wire copy, January 29, 1941

Retreat of Serbs Related by Writer

by C. L. Sulzberger

ATHENS, April 8 — Before attempting to give a description of what has taken place it is necessary to emphasize the Yugoslavs' immediate needs — fighter aircraft, anti-aircraft and effective signal corps equipment that can maintain liaison between various units under any conditions. Lack of this last-named requirement is the chief cause of the confusion that unquestionably prevailed in Yugoslavia when this writer crossed the Greek frontier.

For three days I have been traveling at a time schedule a few hours ahead of the Germans. I left Belgrade at 3 A.M. on Sunday, convinced that war was imminent and determined to join the Yugoslav Army on the Albanian frontier.

At 1:30 A.M., with a car packed with gasoline, tires and food, I called on the United States Minister, Arthur Bliss Lane, and Lieut. Col. Louis Fortier, his military attaché, for a farewell toast. At 3 o'clock I started off with some British diplomatic cars for South Serbia. All the cars of the British Legation and the Consular staffs were massed before the legation for a quick getaway in case the Germans moved on Belgrade from Bela Crkva, one and a half hours away on the Rumanian border.

I had the first news that the war had started at Kraljevo, where I stopped to mend a tire and had luncheon with Pat Page, American manager of Britain's Trepca lead and zinc mines. He told me Belgrade had been bombed for an hour early in the morning. At that moment the air-raid alarm sounded, but no planes appeared.

According to the general in command of the Ibar Division at Mitrovica, Prishtina and Koumanovo were bombed Sunday morning. He also said twenty-seven out of 200 German planes were brought down by the Yugoslavs over Belgrade. He said Skoplje had been heavily bombed.

I started off again for Skoplje, but lost the main road and unknowingly headed in the direction of the Bulgarian frontier east of Prishtina. Fortunately I was warned by Yugoslav and Albanian peasants and was able to turn back toward the highway.

Here I was arrested by a Serbian gendarme, who pointed his automatic at me nervously and shouted orders while I tried to explain my skiing costume and heavily loaded automobile.

After being held two hours I was allowed to proceed until again arrested at Stara Kachanik, where I found my British friends also in the hands of the gendarmes though they had diplomatic passports and their car had diplomatic plates.

It was explained by the commandant that a warning had been issued that a car bearing diplomatic plates and carrying German spies was traveling through South Serbia. We spent several hours there watching the army, with its wagons, horses and guns file past the minareted village in the moonlight. Finally, we were released, but warned that every outpost on the road had been ordered to fire first on any nonmilitary car sighted, so I drove slowly through the pass, followed by the British, who had taken a gendarme to do any necessary explaining.

Having had no sleep for forty-two hours, I lay down in a ditch by the roadside near Skoplje, and after an hour's nap was interrupted by rain and drove to the city in the midst of an air raid. I sheltered a while in the dungeon of an old Roman castle, then was ordered off to the local police station by a gendarme and stayed there during another air raid. I lay in a hastily dug trench with the gendarme commandant and watched the Yugoslav anti-aircraft shoot down a Messerschmitt, while gendarmes pointed rifles at the attacking planes, hoping they would come within range. They didn't.

Then I was conducted through the town to the principal police station, where I waited out another air raid and, after having my papers approved, drove on to divisional headquarters.

During my trips about Skoplje I was able to get a pretty good idea of what the Germans had been able to do from the air. Their bombing had been exceedingly accurate, although most of the bombs were of small caliber. Therefore, the damage was not permanently serious but of a nature to disrupt all regular services.

The power station was out of order. There was neither electric light nor telephone. The radio station had ceased functioning. Army headquarters was knocked about and had been transferred. Telephone cables lay twisted in the road. Glass was piled everywhere and occasional craters testified to the effect of the bombing. Early Monday morning some of the dead, victims of Sunday's bombardment, were still lying about. The British consul told me that in the first raid about thirty persons were killed and more than a hundred wounded.

A divisional general at Skoplje told me the Yugoslavs were holding well at Kriva Palanka and had pushed through toward Juma, Bulgaria. We stood on the porch of his emergency headquarters while we ate a crust of dry bread—no food was available—and looked about for aircraft.

I started off again for Veles, little realizing that in a few hours German parachutists would pave the way to Skoplje's capture. Outside Veles I noticed great columns of smoke through my field glasses and inquired of refugees moving up the road, who told me Veles had just been heavily bombed.

On entering the town I found that both bridges across the Vardar River had been struck. One bridge was in flames and the other damaged by two bomb holes. The latter also was blocked by live wires and rubble, but I managed to get across and drive up the main street, which had been well shaken up and was covered with broken glass.

Fires were burning near the old church and we clearly saw that they were a result of incendiary bombs. A huge bomb crater had ruined the road near the barracks, but it was possible to skirt it.

Civilian refugees dressed in all sorts of clothes, ranging from pajamas to peasant costumes, streamed up the road beside lorries full of troops, apparently evacuating to the south over the Babuna Pass, which should have been impossible to take without a series of stiff assaults. I followed the troop trucks all the way.

Passing through Prilep and entering Bitolj, I noticed that no air raids had yet been staged there and naturally presumed the country was in no serious danger, little aware that before midnight both Skoplje and Veles would be in German hands.

Monday evening after dinner I visited the general in acting command of the Bitolj sector and told him I intended to go on to Albania Tuesday with the Yugoslav Army. He asked me to go to headquarters at 9 A.M. Tuesday so he could visa my papers.

This morning I awoke at 7, intending to go to Ochrida and Struga and thence into Albania around Lake Ochrida. I went to the garage to have my car serviced for the arduous roads. The garage was closed and the owner was not at home. I soon discovered there was neither a mechanic nor a functioning garage in town.

I returned to the hotel for breakfast and there saw some Greek officers of my acquaintance. At 9 I went to army head-quarters and found a few minor officers and some civilians busily packing things in cases. I insisted the general must be there, but they told me he had already evacuated. Finally I returned to the almost empty hotel, convinced that something rotten was going on.

It was only then that I was able to piece the situation together from the tales of various civilian officials, which were confirmed later by officers marching along the road to Greece.

Not more than an hour after midnight the commanding general had ordered the military evacuation of Bitolj. At 8 A.M. civil evacuation—including such bureaus as the National Bank—was ordered. The chief of police was told to remain in the Grand Hotel and surrender the town.

Accompanied by a Bosniak engineer refugee, I drove into Greece around noon. Four German bombers flew overhead, but dropped nothing. There was an air of complete disbelief and bewilderment over the astonishing events.

One cannot yet begin to predict the outcome of this important and complicated campaign. Fighting is going on on so many fronts that it is hard to figure out exactly what is taking place. If the Southern Yugoslav Army can only be co-ordinated and communications restored, it may place the Germans in a very difficult position despite the overwhelming

Nazi air superiority. But at the moment it looks as if Yugoslavia has been encircled by the Axis and she will have to fight
hard to prevent a gloomy future.

The New York Times, April 14, 1941

Under Fire

by Robert St. John

NO ONE agreed about how many people the German bombers killed in Patras, but they surely did a job. A Greek hospital ship with tremendous red crosses painted all over its sides got a direct hit. It was listing badly and before long would go to the bottom. Someone said it was the last hospital ship the Greeks had. The rest were already at the bottom, some of them still weighted down with the bodies of their wounded passengers who hadn't had a chance when the planes came over. The hospital ship in Patras harbor had been full of wounded too. Some said the flimsy wooden boat had been turned into a morgue for at least two hundred soldiers. Others put the casualties lower than that. But the worst job the planes did was on hundreds of refugees.

The people of Patras had had a hunch, like the people of Corfu. Only the Patras hunch came too late. The hunch was that life wasn't going to be pleasant much longer in Patras and they had better get moving. And so they had flocked down to the water front. It had been a well-organized exodus. They were all going away in flat-bottomed barges towed by a large ship. They brought their most precious and their most essential possessions down to the water front with them. They loaded them onto the barges until there was hardly room for the human freight. They were about ready to shove off when the planes came.

Of course it was a stupid mistake. They never should have tried to get away in daylight. Some of them managed to hide between the blocks of concrete on the quay, but most of them just huddled down on the barges, burying their heads in the blankets and mattresses and tin kettles and baby cribs and all the other stuff they wanted so much to save. They tried to play ostrich, but bullets from a machine gun in an airplane can hit people just as well and kill them just as dead even if their heads are buried. That was what happened. The planes dropped some bombs and then they used their machine guns. No one ever counted the bodies exactly. The estimates varied greatly. Anyway at least seventy were killed.

After the planes went away and the dead and the wounded were removed the rest of the people of Patras lost all interest in going places on barges. They fled from the water front. They never wanted to see that water front again. And that was why it was that when we shook hands with the skipper and his crew they weren't paying much attention to us. There was a lot of stuff to look over on those barges. Stuff no one was interested in any more, because most of it belonged to people who were dead now. I saw Shorty's eyes brighten as he stood in the middle of one of the barges holding up a silk dress you could have bought in Klein's, New York, for about ninety-eight cents. He was holding it up at arm's length and admiring it and probably trying to decide whether it would go around his wife's figure. Other members of the crew of the *Spiradon* had their eyes on frying pans and blankets and flash-lights. We thought it was a rather sordid scene, because a lot of that stuff was covered with the blood of the people who had owned it, and it didn't seem right for anyone to be touching it. At least not until the blood was dry.

We went straight from the water front to the office of the *État Major*. Up there we ran onto a Greek lieutenant who had once been in Detroit. He said he thought we would be wise to get out of Patras immediately. The Germans were just across the Gulf of Corinth and they might come over with a landing party any hour now. It was about a hundred and fifty miles along the gulf to Athens, but there wasn't any motor traffic moving along the highway. Too dangerous. Too many planes overhead all the time. However, there was a train leaving at four o'clock in the afternoon. He helped us buy tickets so that we would be sure to have places. It might be, he said, the last train that would ever leave Patras.

We were walking back into town when the sirens went off again. We decided to ignore them, but it was the old story again. The natives started shouting at us and pointing up into the air where the planes were. When we just smiled and tried to keep going, angry gendarmes came running after us.

"This thing is getting damned monotonous," Hill grumbled.

"Yes," I said with some sincere bitterness, "it's like a phonograph when the needle gets stuck in a groove and keeps playing the same bars of music over and over again until you think you'll go crazy unless someone shuts the machine off."

But you can't argue with a gendarme if he's got a rifle in his hand, and we were forced up the street to an air-raid shelter. Over the door it said in English as well as Greek, "Built with funds contributed from America." I grinned when I read that sign. The greatest nation in the world had helped the Greeks. Never let it be said that we hadn't. I had seen the proof with my own eyes. We had gone to their help when they were attacked by all the forces of evil. When vast mechanized armies rolled down from the north, America had stood behind little Greece. We had contributed funds to build an air-raid shelter. And I suppose America would have been hurt if she could have seen the Greeks pouring into that shelter without paying a bit of attention to the sign or giving a thought to the great generosity of the United States.

There were more people trying to get in than the place would hold. Gendarmes barked and cursed. The planes came closer. The gendarmes looked nervously over their shoulders and then put their knees in people's backs and pushed. But there was a wall at the far end of this shelter built in the side of a hill, and the people between the door and the back wall were already packed in there so tightly that it was difficult for any of them to breathe. But the gendarmes kept on pushing, and a woman whose head was inside the shelter but whose broad backside stuck out began to scream her fear of being hit in the rear. It wasn't a pleasant scene, because human beings were acting like terrified animals. The lower the planes came and the more bombs they dropped around the city, the more these people were metamorphized into animals, bent only on self-preservation.

Hill and I finally turned away in disgust and sat down a few yards from the entrance to the shelter. When that raid was over we wandered down into the messed-up city and found a café where we couldn't get any food but where we could set up typewriters on a dirty marble-topped table and pretend

that we were right on a dead line and that a telegraph operator with a wire open to New York was sitting beside us waiting to flash our news to America. It was all make-believe, of
course, because the lieutenant at army headquarters had just
laughed when we asked about communications. The only
communication center left in Greece, as far as he knew, was at
Athens. And there was no way to telephone to Athens. We'd
have to wait until we got there. But since we were going to
take a train at four o'clock for Athens we pounded our typewriters and told about the people who had died like rats on
the quay of Patras and the wounded soldiers who were given
their *coup de grâce* as they lay on the hospital ship.

We talked several times about Mike and White and Atherton. We were worried, because we had asked a lot of people
around town already about them and no one had seen them.
Anything might have happened, but our guess was that they
had fallen into the hands of the Axis when they hit Preveza.

Then Atherton walked into the café. He had blood all over
his shirt. Dark, clotted blood. Almost black. His face had
tragedy written all over it. He was limping badly. He tried to
smile when he saw us. We knew he was glad to see us. And we
were damned glad to see him. But he couldn't smile. He just
said two words, and then we all sat down and didn't say anything else for quite a while. The two words turned something
to stone down inside of me. I guess Hill felt the same way
too.

All Atherton said was, "Mike's dead." Then we knew where
the blood had come from. We didn't ask any questions. We
didn't know yet how Mike had died. But we knew he had
died with his head on Atherton's chest. We knew that because
we knew Atherton and we knew he felt about Mike just like
we did. Mike was sixty years old and he was a tough little
fisherman with big gnarled hands like boxing gloves that
mashed your hand when he grabbed it. And Mike wasn't the
kind of a person you'd invite into your home for a cocktail
party. But Mike was worth most of the people I had ever met
at cocktail parties all thrown in together. We had lived with
Mike for days out there on the Adriatic and we knew that
Mike was a real man, with an honest, open heart. But a heart
that wasn't beating any more now.

"Bombed?" Hill finally asked.

"Yes," Atherton replied. "Killed outright. A Stuka dropped something that got him in the head. Mike never knew what hit him."

We finally got some weak tea by arguing with the café owner. Then the story gradually came out. White and Atherton and Mike had started out from Casopi about the same time we started from Corfu. They had found out about Preveza, and so they went right by it. The trouble began when all the gasoline they had leaked out of the fuel can. They hailed a Greek mine sweeper, which took them aboard and towed the *Makedonka* on behind. But the mine sweeper went so fast that the towline broke, and the *Makedonka* capsized, with everything in it. Then the Greek ship, as it got near Patras, was dive-bombed by those same planes we had been hiding from under the concrete blocks. That was when Mike got it. And at the same time a piece of shrapnel had buried itself in Atherton's right knee, so that it was difficult for him to walk now. White had come through the whole thing without a scratch, and now he was looking around town for communications.

A little before four o'clock we all went down to get on the train that was going to take us to Athens, but the railroad men said it had been canceled. They didn't think there would be any more trains to Athens. Things were getting bad. The Germans were sweeping down from the north. Nobody seemed to be able to stop them. They would probably be here in Patras soon. Thousands of people wanted to get out of Patras. Who were we anyway? Were we any better than the people of Patras? This was their town, their railroad. Even if a train did come along, we couldn't get on it anyway. If a train did run, the people of Patras would be given first chance, but there were thousands of them, and there probably wouldn't be any train anyway.

Of course those railroad men were right. But still, you've got to think of yourself when the sky is always full of planes, and people are being killed all around you. You've got to go Nietzsche and look out for your own skin. We spent all the rest of the afternoon and all evening watching the highway to Athens for some sign of transportation and chasing to different army headquarters trying to get some help.

Late in the night we were ushered into the "Great Presence." I guess he was a general. He had enough gold braid
on his uniform for all the officers at West Point. You never
would have known a war was going on and that right now
Greek soldiers were fleeing like frightened rabbits from the
German motorized army all over the country and leaving the
poor Anzacs to hold what was left of battle lines. We could
tell from the fragments of conversation while he conferred
with his aides and kept us waiting that they were being just as
petty and bureaucratic as ever about a thousand little details
that didn't matter a bit now. Greece was falling, but how
many carbon copies did the general want his orderly to make
of this letter?

Finally he turned to us. So we wanted transportation, did
we? Of course we should have it! An army truck was leaving
for Athens soon. We had his permission to go on it. No, we
didn't need any papers or passes. Just tell the officers out in
the anteroom that the general said we were to go on the truck
to Athens. We went out and told the officers. They looked
puzzled. They talked to other officers. Then they told us the
truck had left two hours ago. They were sorry, but that was
the last truck going to Athens. There wouldn't be any more.
Not tonight or tomorrow either. Maybe later in the week,
if—if nothing happened. We asked to see the general again.
They told us they were sorry, but the general had gone off to
dinner and he wouldn't be back tonight.

Dinner? We decided that we'd like some dinner too, but
the food supply of Patras apparently was reserved for generals
and people like that. We couldn't find any anywhere. Then
Atherton remembered that once when he was down in
Greece before the war he had stopped in Patras and had met
an engineer who lived at the Cecil Hotel, and so we went to
the Cecil. The place had been badly wrecked by bombs, but
we crawled through the debris and got up to the engineer's
quarters.

In some ways going into the engineer's rooms at the Cecil
was just like finding the Monastery of Saint Nicholas on top
of the island of Leukas. As soon as we got inside and shut the
door we were in another world. Outside, most of Patras was
in ruins. There was hardly a building in town with its four

walls still standing. But here in a little room in a bomb-damaged hotel a man who spoke four or five other languages as fluently as he did his own was sitting in front of a fireplace listening to soft orchestra music on a radio and reading, of all things, one of Lamb's essays. He had water boiling on a little alcohol stove and he asked us, with that tone you associate with English parlors, how we would like our tea, with milk or lemon?

I wanted to say, "You don't have a sirloin steak hidden away anywhere, do you?" But I didn't, because the engineer was Atherton's friend, not mine. So we sat and drank tea, and when he brought out some English cookies I guess all of us acted as if we had never seen cookies before and thought the thing to do was to make a sandwich of half a dozen and jam them all in our mouths at one time. But the Greek engineer pretended not to notice. Soon he and Atherton were talking about Lamb and mid-Victorian poetry and then about Nietzsche. And that's how we got around finally to that irrelevant subject of the war, which was being fought almost outside this man's windows.

He said the people of Patras hoped to be occupied by the Germans because they didn't have any feelings about the Germans. They hated the Italians and they'd fight until hell froze over if they were just fighting the Italians. But not many Greeks wanted to fight the Germans. It wasn't that they were any more afraid of the Germans. Not that. It was simply that they had no quarrel with the Germans. Germany was a long way off geographically. Also the Greeks had a great admiration for German thoroughness and German discipline and the German way of life.

"You don't mean the Nazi way of life, do you?" Atherton asked, disgustedly.

The engineer said he did. He talked for an hour about how wise Hitler had been in setting up an economic scheme that wasn't based on gold, and then he expounded a lot of other pro-Nazi arguments.

Atherton answered him, point by point. But he failed to convert the engineer.

I began to understand why Greece was falling so quickly. The country must be lacking in unity of thought and unity of purpose just as much as France and a lot of other countries had been.

While Atherton and the engineer went on talking I looked over the hundreds of books that jammed the little hotel room. The engineer was very catholic in his tastes. He had read everything from Sinclair Lewis to the Koran, but he seemed to specialize in the field dominated by Nietzsche. Perhaps that was the clue to why he thought as he did.

After many hours had been idled away we got down to basic things. We told the engineer we had to find some way to get out of Patras, and quickly. He picked up a telephone and called a friend. It seemed strange to have a telephone operating. It was the first telephone we had seen in use in nearly three weeks. We asked, while he was waiting for his number, "Can we get Athens on your phone?" He shook his head. He asked his friend, who was a railroad executive, about trains, and he found out that at five o'clock in the morning a long train would be loaded at the Patras station and would set out at once with Greek soldiers for Corinth, about a hundred and twenty miles down the gulf and only a short distance from Athens. It was supposed to be a military secret, but if we went down to the station before the train came in there wasn't any reason why we couldn't smuggle ourselves aboard.

We were at the depot at four-thirty. The place was jammed with soldiers and civilians. If the arrival of this train was a strict military secret, the Greek army surely let a lot of people in on its secrets. About five o'clock the train pulled in. Ten coaches, old, dirty, some with broken windows. But it was a train and it had a locomotive that ran, and it was headed toward Athens and communications and maybe safety for a while. We fought just as viciously and as much like hungry animals as all the rest of the people. It was dark, and no one could tell that we were foreigners. The only way not to be mistaken for foreigners there in the dark was to fight for a foothold on that train just the way the Greeks were doing themselves.

We made out rather well, in spite of Atherton's game leg. We found two seats facing each other with only one place taken. White and Hill and I took those three places. Atherton got a seat across the aisle. We sat there in the dark grinning over our good luck and listening to the noise of battle going on out on the platform. The cursing and fighting was being done with a vehemence that might have terrified enemy troops if it had been directed against them. Finally the train got started. There were about seven hundred men aboard, which you'd agree was a lot for ten cars if you knew the size of those Greek coaches.

The sun came up in a burst of red splendor as we were being shunted around the railroad yards. Finally we really got under way. Hill and I spread a map on our legs and studied the route. The tracks followed the very edge of the Gulf of Corinth all the way. We couldn't see the other shore of the gulf at Patras, but we knew that the Germans were in possession over there, just out of sight. The map showed that the farther we went the more the gulf narrowed down, until it ended at Corinth in nothing but a canal. A trainman came through, and we asked him when we would get to Corinth. He said, "With luck, in about fifteen hours." That meant we were going to average exactly eight miles an hour.

The train was full, and we weren't scheduled to make any stops, but every time we hit a town, which was every few miles, we stopped anyway. The engineer couldn't help it. Soldiers, when they saw the train coming, swarmed onto the tracks, waving their arms. Some of them hadn't thrown away their guns yet, so they waved them too. When the engineer put on his brakes rather than mow down a whole Greek regiment, the panicky soldiers clamored to get aboard. Now they were fighting just like the soldiers at Patras. Finally the train started up. Men were hanging onto the steps and some were even sitting on the roofs of the cars. The train looked like a ship covered with barnacles. That same thing happened at each town. Then we began to realize why it was going to take fifteen hours to go a hundred and twenty miles. Fifteen hours would get us into Corinth just after dusk. We would be going along the edge of the gulf all day long. Each hour we would be getting nearer to German territory, because of the way the gulf narrowed down. We thought of all those things as we stared out the window.

That trip in peacetime must be the most delightful, the most scenic in the whole world. The cliffs are high. They drop straight down from the tracks to the sea. A drop of several hundred feet. And at the bottom there's the smooth blue water of the gulf. The map showed that we would never be out of sight of that smooth blue water.

"It's going to be a lovely trip," Hill said.

I knew what he meant, and so did the others. Any minute now German planes might come over from the other shore and pay us a call. After all, our train was a natural for a plane. The men on the roof and the men hanging onto the platforms were living advertisements that this was a troop train. And there was nothing to stop a plane from flying right alongside the train and giving us all guns.

Those were the things we were all thinking, and then I thought, what a hell of a seat I chose! Right next to the window on the gulf side of the car!

"It looks like today's the day," White said.

The rest of us pretended we didn't understand.

"I mean today's the day we'll probably really get it," White went on grimly.

"Well, as long as we can't do anything about it, let's play poker," Hill suggested.

We put a typewriter on our knees, and the three of us tried not to think of what we might soon see out the window. We didn't have any chips or any money, but Hill got out the black notebook in which for more than a year he had been entering material for newspaper stories, magazine articles, and the book that every newspaperman is going to write some day. We didn't play long, but we were playing for high stakes, and Russell had some astronomical figures chalked up in his book. Astronomical if you knew what newspapermen's salaries are. Later we tried to remember who owed whom how much, but those poker winnings were destined never to be paid.

I remember I had just lost a pot and was looking out the window while Hill was making another entry in his notebook. I was facing toward the rear of the train. We were in the next to the last car. The first thing I saw was the wing of the plane. The men in that last car could have reached out and touched it, it was so close. But no one did, because just then the plane's machine gun started to bark out its nasty message.

I never saw men move so quickly. And so instinctively. No

one had ever told us what to do if we were riding in a train and an airplane started machine-gunning us. But we knew without any lessons.

White and Hill were next to the aisle, and they fell onto the floor first. Then a lot of fellows from the other side of the car fell on top of them. I was last man. The plane was just about opposite our window when we all got settled there in the aisle. I kept thinking, what a target I am with my head buried but with my tail sticking right up in the air!

The rattle of the machine gun lasted for about seven seconds. That was long enough for the pilot to go the whole length of the train and give every one of the cars a good dose of lead. Then the plane roared off to make a big circle and come back again.

About that time the train stopped with a jerk. Windows on the far side were thrown open. Hundreds of Greek soldiers dived through them. I saw Atherton go out head first.

White was quite a way under me, but I could hear him hollering, "I've been shot. I've been shot."

By the time the plane had lined up for its next visit there wasn't anyone left in the car but the three of us. Hill and I tried to carry White out before we got a second blasting. But he was heavy. His right thigh was useless. There were three bicycles on the vestibule of the car. We were having our troubles. We were both standing up, with White's arms around our shoulders, when the car got its second dose. Somehow the sprinkle of bullets missed us that time.

While the plane was circling around again we got White under the train. It was impossible to follow the Greek soldiers up into the woods, because the hill leading away from the tracks was so steep and White was so heavy.

By the time the Messerschmitt came back for its third visitation the three of us were hugging the gravel and ties under the car.

White was cursing a blue streak. "Why the God-damned hell doesn't someone fire at him? The son-of-a-bitching bastard! The God-damned Nazi whore!"

But White's other opinions were drowned out by a roar that almost split our heads open. The pilot had dropped a heavy bomb on the right of way a couple of hundred yards behind the train.

Gravel and pieces of ties and rails were flying through the air. There wouldn't be any more trains following us now. There was nothing but a big excavation where the roadbed had been.

I guess we all held our breath for the next second or two. If the pilot dropped a bomb like that on the train, it wouldn't save us to be hiding underneath. I clawed the gravel and gritted my teeth. White was just groaning now. Hill hadn't said a word since the show began.

Now the plane was alongside the train. Now the machine gun began to bark again. Now we could hear the bullets tearing through the windows and the wooden sides of the car. One bullet ripped through a tie just behind us. Another sailed over our heads so close we could feel the heat from it. But the plane was past us now. It was working on the cars up ahead. Now we could breathe again. We could swallow. We could wet our dry lips. We could lift our faces up from the cinders and gravel.

When the plane went off that last time we knew we were safe, because we remembered that a machine-gun belt only has twenty seconds of fire in it, and we surely must have had twenty seconds of punishment by this time.

But just then the engineer got panicky and started off with a roar of steam. Hill and I rolled White out between the wheels just in time.

How many men were killed and how many were wounded inside the cars we never knew, because we never saw that train again.

But the right of way was sprinkled with men who had jumped or been shot off the tops of the cars and with others who had dragged themselves out of the cars and then had collapsed.

Anyway, after the train left we had a problem of what to do with White. He was in great pain. We finally ripped a shutter off a house near the tracks and used that for a stretcher. Then we carried him up the steep hillside to a highway. There wasn't any traffic moving, just as the military people had said.

But Hill and I walked in opposite directions down the road and finally one of us found a broken-down R.A.F. truck. The driver said yes, he'd take us all in to Corinth if we could help him get the truck going. It took about an hour.

Hundreds of Greek soldiers from the train were still up in the woods, some of them in the tops of trees and others hiding under rocks. A lot of them were screaming like mad. We never could figure out why.

A short distance down the road we picked up half a dozen Greeks who had been wounded. Some had shattered legs or arms, and some had machine-gun bullets through their heads or shoulders and were in bad shape, but the worst victim of all was a man nearly fifty years old who kept screaming for his mother. He just lay on top of the truck screaming the word "Mother." When a British ambulance went by we stopped it and asked the driver to look at this man, because his screams were driving us almost crazy. We helped undress the fellow, but the ambulance driver couldn't find a mark on him anywhere. Still, nothing would make him stop screaming. We figured out that he had probably fallen from the top of one of the cars and had had a brain concussion.

On the way into Corinth my right leg felt as if it were asleep and I kept pounding it. Finally I had Hill pull it a few times to loosen the cramped muscles. Since it didn't seem to do any good, I just tried to forget it. Somehow I never thought about being shot. I guess I was too damned tired to think. And besides, things kept happening to keep a man from thinking very much. Like the return visit of that damned Nazi plane. We were about half an hour along the road when someone yelled, "Christ! Here he comes!"

There were no trees along the road, but there was a thicket off in a field. The R.A.F. driver jumped out and started across the field. He yelled at us to follow him. All the Greeks on the truck who could move by themselves went off into the thicket with the driver. But there were two Greek soldiers wounded so badly they couldn't get out of the truck. And then there was White. He was still lying on the shutter. The shutter was on top of a lot of cans of gas. The truck had no top. There was nothing at all between White and the sky. We looked at the plane. It was coming lower and lower. We tried to lift the shutter.

White yelled, "I can't stand the pain, being moved like that. Leave me here."

We didn't like the idea of running off and leaving White lying there on top of the open truck. It didn't seem right. So we buried our heads in some blankets that the other wounded men had left behind and waited. It's crazy how you always want to hide your head. Especially crazy for a newspaperman, who ought to keep his eyes open and see all he can. The plane made a hell of a noise as it came down. Finally it seemed that the landing wheels must be almost touching our backs. As I lay there waiting for something to happen I thought, I wonder whether he'll just drop a bomb or whether he'll play with that God-damned machine gun again. But he didn't do either.

After he disappeared in the clouds the R.A.F. driver and the Greeks came back and we started off again. The driver told me to stand on the running board because he had something he wanted to say. He had to shout so that I could hear him above the noise the truck was making. He said, "Listen, my dear fellow, bravery's a fine thing, but only when there's some sense to it. You and your friends were just sticking your necks out for no good reason. If it happens again you may not be so lucky. Next time you hide with the rest of us. You can't save the wounded men from getting hit just by staying with them. You might as well save yourselves if you can't save them."

Then he told all of us to keep a sharp lookout because he thought the plane would be following us all the way to Corinth. We should hammer on the roof of the cab to warn him if we saw it again. It was only about ten minutes before we did see it. It was coming right down at us again. We all ran into a field. All except White and the poor Greeks who couldn't move either. I saw White pull his coat over his head as we left.

There weren't any trees in the field this time, and we just crouched behind a stone wall. The driver said it was a good safe hide-out. But I didn't feel at all right inside. I could see the truck through a hole in the wall. White and the other wounded men looked as if they were dead already. I was sorry

I had left them in spite of all the driver had said. The driver was right, but I felt mean and selfish. I felt that I'd always be ashamed of running away like that, even though I couldn't have done anybody any good by staying on top of the truck. The R.A.F. driver was right beside me. He pulled out his service pistol and got it ready for use. We were only a few feet from the truck. If the plane skimmed over it again the way it had done last time, a good marksman could plant a bullet where it might hurt. I remembered the automatic that King Peter's bodyguard had given us. I yanked it out of my pocket. I know I couldn't have hit the broad side of a barn then, because I was shaking all over, but it gave me some strength to tighten my fingers around the little gun.

The plane didn't come down so low this time. The pilot seemed to be losing interest in the truck. In a few more minutes we were on our way again.

That R.A.F. driver was really a fine person. He tried so hard not to jostle White around when the road got rough, because every time we did hit a bump Leigh screamed in pain. I guess the driver winced as much as the rest of us did when he heard those screams. We kept giving White drinks of cognac to dull the pain. Halfway to Corinth another truck was waiting for our truck. They switched the gasoline cans, and we transferred all our wounded men. The first truck driver said he had to turn around now and go back to Patras. We shook hands and wished him luck. I had a strange feeling that he was in for trouble. That's why I pumped his hand so hard and said, "Happy sailing! You've probably saved a couple of lives today. We're damned grateful. Hope you can save your own on the way back."

He just grinned and said, "What the hell?" and then he was off. Somehow I felt he was going to get it before he ever reached Patras.

From the Land of Silent People, 1942

"Remoteness from the War Affected Everybody"

by A. J. Liebling

I

WHEN I was getting aboard the Clipper at the mouth of the Tagus to come home I told the radio operator, who was checking off the names on the passenger list, that I had been in France. "Yeah," he said offhandedly, "it looks like we'll have to beat the hell out of those Germans." I began to understand that Hitler would not have us as he had had the Social Democrats, without fighting. It made me feel better. At that time I may have had an exaggerated idea of the boldness of German strategy. I was sure that we had no ground or air forces that could meet a series of quick landings at widely separated parts of our or the Mexican coast. That was a good guess, because when I talked to General Marshall in Washington several weeks later he told me that we had "the possible equivalent of three divisions" of troops ready to fight, and that included the garrisons of the Canal Zone and Hawaii. I was not at all sure that Germany would not offer, and Great Britain accept, terms for a peace that would leave the British Empire temporarily intact and the Reich free to move against the richest, softest, and most inviting target: us. My estimate of Great Britain had been conditioned by ten months in France; like the French, I thought that the British showing had been halfhearted and ineffectual. The British newspapers flown over to Paris even in the last days we were there had been full of racing and cricket. If they were the expression of a nation, England wasn't even interested. It is unnecessary to state that I was wrong about what Great Britain would do, but I had logical reasons for being so, like poor Gamelin. The real wonder of the world, though, is that Japan didn't hop in then. If she had, the nearly disarmed British would have been simply outclassed, no matter how great their determination. Certainly no reasons of conscience deterred the Japanese. The dictatorships were too timid. They had the world on the point of a knockout, but they "lost" it, the way a novice boxer fails to finish another novice after having him groggy.

Getting off the plane and meeting people who had stayed in America was a strange experience, because they hardly seemed to know that anything was wrong. When you started to tell them they said soothingly that probably you had had a lot of painful experiences, and if you just took a few grains of nembutol so you would get one good night's sleep, and then go out to the horse races twice, you would be your old sweet self again. It was like the dream in which you yell at people and they don't hear you. I went down to Washington to do a profile of General Marshall. The War Department took the situation seriously enough, God knows, but when you had got out of the Munitions Building you were in an unconcerned world again. It reminded me of leaving a feverish last rehearsal in a theater and coming out on a sidewalk where few of the passers-by even know there's a show about to open.

After you had been here awhile you began to get stupid too, and more recent arrivals from Europe began to bore you slightly. Dick Boyer came back from Berlin, where he had been as a correspondent for *PM*, and visited me at the *New Yorker* office in October.

It was only the second day after Boyer's return, and he still looked at people with astonishment, because they did not seem worried enough. I, who knew the symptoms, understood the way Boyer felt as soon as I saw him come into the office. We were to have lunch together and talk about Europe and Boyer's experiences as a war correspondent. Boyer was bigger and blonder than ever; he walked with chin and nose pointed upward and talked with wide gestures. He would have a noble and stupid face if it were not for his malicious and intelligent little eyes, which redeem it. Boyer still talked a little too loud, as people do in a foreign country where they assume nobody around understands them. He had arrived by Clipper and so had not had time to change back from his foreign to his domestic personality. When we got into the elevator to go down to lunch, Boyer began talking about the bombings he had been in. "The first time they bombed Berlin," he said, "they didn't do enough damage." The office girls who were jammed into the elevator all about him, some with their shoulder blades against his belly and others with their chins against his shoulder blades, looked up with interest. "The second time they bombed it, they were really getting somewhere," he said. "It made me feel good down in my air-raid shelter. Those bastards in Berlin don't like it." When he said "bastards" the girls looked confused, because he had no right to say that to them, but they had no right to be listening, either.

I said in a perfunctory way, "The only bombardment I was in was at Paris." I had said it so often that it didn't even interest me any longer, and June 3, 1940, seemed as long ago as the Battle of Hastings. All the girls continued looking at Boyer as if I had not said anything at all.

The elevator reached the street floor, and Boyer said, "What I want is a really good meal. With wine. I am used to drinking wine with my meals." We headed toward Fifth Avenue. Boyer suddenly stopped and said, "What are we doing about our defenses? I mean, have we really started or are we still futzing around?" His voice sounded very anxious.

I remembered when I had felt the same way, coming back from Lisbon, but just before meeting Boyer for lunch I had been thinking principally about the heavy overlay against a race horse named Hash, on which I had failed to bet. Understanding Boyer's anxiety, I tried to formulate in my mind what I truly believed about defense, canceling out wishful thinking. "Yeah," I said, "I think we've started."

Boyer began walking again, looking over the heads of the people in the street, who were so unworried and foolish. "Well, maybe we'll be all right then," he said.

We walked uptown without any precise destination, until we came to the sunken roller-skating rink at Rockefeller Plaza. As usual, there were a good many people hanging over the railings, watching the skaters. We joined them. Two professional skaters were putting on an exhibition. The man wore a blue uniform like a moving-picture usher's, and the girl short skirts which showed chunky, chapped legs. They were going through a complicated sort of waltz to music relayed by a loud-speaker. The trouble was, however, that while they skated well, they would have danced badly under any circumstances. Several times the girl threw herself sideways through the air, the man holding onto her wrists, and when she landed on her skates with a clacking, mechanical noise, she looked around for approval. There were restaurant tables at either end of the rink and on a level with it.

"This is a pretty good place to eat," I said. "It's nice outdoors today." Boyer thought the place looked all right, too, so we walked down the steps and a maître d'hôtel showed us to a table.

After we had ordered oysters, lobster Thermidor, and a bottle of Pouilly, I asked whether the Germans seemed much bucked up by their victories. Boyer said the army Germans did but the civilians didn't. "But the civilians have nothing to say anyway," he said. "It's just the Army and the Party. The country will never crack until somebody cracks the Army."

"Who?" said I.

We both knew the only possible answer.

Boyer looked gloomily at the people hanging over the railing above the rink and at the skaters. They didn't seem potentially formidable. "It's a wonderful country," he said, "but I think everybody is crazy."

I tried to be funny. "That's just a European frame of mind," I said, imitating the voice of a normal, unfrightened American, like Harold Ross. "You forget about the three thousand miles of ocean and the time Hitler will need to digest all the countries he has already taken."

"People who talk like that give me a pain in the butt," Boyer said.

"I used to be like you myself, old man," I continued, "but now, after a couple of months in a sane atmosphere compounded of Lindbergh's speeches and editorials in the *New Masses*, I see how things really are."

Boyer said, "When you begin to think that sort of stupidity is even funny, you are beginning to go crazy yourself. The first batch of French prisoners I saw, I cried."

I was not listening very intently, because I had said the same things until I had noticed people didn't like to listen to me. Boyer was right, and nobody cared, I thought, and after a while Boyer would understand that without anybody telling him. A waiter served the oysters and poured two glasses of wine, and we began to eat. The beginning of a meal demands concentration, and while we were appraising the oysters and ranking the wine in the scale of all oysters and wine that had gone down our gullets, a tall girl came out of the little skate room under the stairs and began to move about the rink. There is nothing finer to watch than a graceful animal on legs a bit too long for symmetry—a two-year-old thoroughbred, a kudu, or a heron. The girl was leggy, and I thought she was brave to put on skates at all, because her little scut was such a long way from the ground in case she fell. There didn't seem much risk of that, though, the way she moved around. She seldom lifted her skates far off the surface, and she didn't jump up or squat on her haunches and revolve with one foot in the air like the instructress. She just moved well, and her hands made slight, disarticulated motions from the wrist, as if to call attention to the lovely, slow turns she was making.

Boyer had finished his oysters—he always ate with the speed of a small dog consuming meat in the presence of larger dogs of whose forbearance it is not sure—and was beginning to talk of the gray, tasteless fish in Germany and the gray, tasteless people who endured it when he noticed the girl. He said, "It's funny, but when you're terribly worried you're not interested in food. I didn't mind the taste of the stuff. But I wouldn't eat a piece of it now for a buck." The girl was wearing a black skirt and a thin shirtwaist through which the men could see the white, clean straps of her underwear. Boyer's nostrils flared, as if he could smell the faint aroma of laundry soap and ironing board that such underwear should have. If the girl had spoiled this bouquet with a perfume, as she probably had, nobody at that distance could know it.

"I know," I said. "Then, when you're a little less worried, you take an interest in food again, but not in women. When you take an interest in women, you're not worried."

Boyer said, "I don't feel like a man from Mars but like a man from earth who has landed on another planet. Don't the damn fools know what is happening on earth?" But his voice was milder than before, and he watched the girl's thin hips.

The girl summoned a male instructor with one of her small motions, and the two of them skated hand in hand. She was very blonde, with fine, threadlike hair that wouldn't stay up, and she had dark eyebrows and a small, turned-up nose that gave her a silly, friendly look. Boyer and I followed her with our eyes, and both felt angry when she placed the instructor's arm around her, under her right armpit. We were glad she held his hand firmly in hers, so it did not touch her breast.

"That girl skates as if thousands of other girls weren't cold and hungry, or cowering from bombs," Boyer said with a last, feeble effort to appear outraged. But he was obviously more interested in her than in his talk.

"He's beginning to be comfortable," I thought, "and he's ashamed of it." Just then the waiter arrived with the lobster Thermidor. I said, tactfully, "Oh, what the hell! Why don't you tell me all about Europe some other time?"

Boyer looked relieved. "Sure," he said. "That girl looks like somebody I used to know."

II

That kind of feeling was involuntary. It was due to the mental climate. Even actions directly connected with war had an unreal quality when they took place here; I remember the curious feeling I had when I went to register for compulsory service on October 16, 1940, in a schoolhouse where I had to squeeze 215 pounds of me into a child's seat, behind a child's desk, to fill out a blank. The associations evoked were of learning long division and looking forward to recess, rather than of bombed cities. Yet I had seen bombed cities, which none of the other men registering had. After sitting in the small seat for a couple of minutes I began to be overawed by the schoolteacher who was issuing the registration cards. I hoped she wouldn't ask me anything I did not know. I just got into the draft by two days; on October 18 I was going to be thirty-six years old and officially middle-aged. The psychological benefit was not slight; I have thought of myself ever since as a mere kid. I never was destined to fight, though— just get shot at.

Remoteness from the war affected everybody, but there

were at least two groups in the country that tried consciously to minimize our danger. They were precisely these that had worked to the same end in France—a strong faction of men of wealth and the Communist party. The money people wanted to prove fascism more efficient than democracy, the Communists that democracy offered no protection against fascism. A military victory for the democracies would shatter the pretensions of both.

Pierre-Etienne Flandin, a former premier who has never been rated a revolutionary, gave me last winter a concise account of the way in which the French industrialists arrived at their policy of collaboration. Retrospectively it clarifies for me a great deal of what went on here in 1940–41.

"The great industrialists had never contributed so largely to a national campaign as they did to André Tardieu's group in the general elections of 1932," Flandin said. "Tardieu was badly beaten. So they said, 'What has the Republic come to when you can't even buy an election? Evidently it is time to change the system of government.' Being French, they felt particularly bad because they had wasted so much money. So they began to back the French fascist movements—De la Rocque, Doriot, all that, with Chiappe of course running the show. They mounted the riots of February 1934, expecting to take power by a *coup d'état*. The coup didn't come off. Then they gave up on accomplishing anything from inside France and decided to wait for the arrival of the Germans. The Front Populaire Government, elected in 1936" (of which Flandin had been an active parliamentary opponent), "had nothing to do with their decision. They had made up their minds two years earlier."

The American opposite numbers of the men of the *grands cartels* had been too badly panicked in 1932 to get together then. It was not until after the Roosevelt-Landon campaign of 1936 that they began to despair of democracy and to get vocal about it. The little men in Statler Hotel bars and golf-club locker rooms echoed the official line. What good was a system under which the majority of people voted to protect their own interests? It was damn selfish of working people to vote that way. "As a matter of fact this country was never meant to be a democracy anyway," they would say with the same knowing air with which they knocked a competing line of scrapple when they were out peddling pork products, "it was meant to be a republic. Get it?" And suffrage in a republic could be as limited as it was in a stockholder's meeting of Republic Steel. Money had never articulated its dislike of democracy during the years when it had been possible to elect McKinleys and Hardings and Coolidges and Hoovers.

I do not think that the money men who were to turn isolationists ever backed an American fascist movement on a large scale as the cartels had in France in 1934; they were not so conscious of what they wanted or perhaps so cynical as their European counterparts, and besides they had not completely given up on the ballot box. In 1940 they applied not only money but advertising techniques. When the advertising men failed to elect a President, they had to regretfully inform their clientele that the jig was up. There was no time to mount a nationalist authoritarian movement. The money bypassed that step and went in for isolationism, which was a form of passive aid for the Axis.

I stayed in the United States from July 1940 until July 1941. An important phase of the war was being waged all around me. It went well for the ultimate good of the country, but a trifle slowly. The election in the United States was a defeat for Germany; newspapers there and in Great Britain treated it as such. I had never been worried about it; the confidence expressed up to the last minute by my little friends who were identified with big business showed they lacked all sense of reality. The advertising manager of the *Herald Tribune* took five to four from me on the eve of the election. The beating did Willkie good too; it served as a disinfectant bath to rid him of parasites. He came out of the race minus the most antisocial elements of his support. When I met him for the first time, in the following January, he was still astonished by their desertion. I had imagined him a knave. I found him a naïf.

My most nightmarish memory of the year is of a trip I made to Chicago to interview the leaders of America First for an article I had been engaged to write for *McCall's Magazine* on propaganda in the United States. I was to cover all varieties of propaganda in two thousand words and make the subject as clear as a dress pattern. I hit Chicago during the debate on the Lease-Lend Bill. The Chicago *Tribune* carried on its editorial page the day I arrived a cartoon showing Liberty loaded with chains and being beaten with a spiked club by a sort of ape-man. The ape-man was labeled not "Nazism" or "Fascism" but "New Deal." The president of America First, an ecclesiastical-looking white-haired man rather like Warren Harding or Samuel Seabury, told me in a paternal, authoritative tone that Great Britain was in no danger but that it was no use trying to help her because she was doomed. It would be dangerous to help her while she was still in the war, he continued, but if we permitted her to get knocked out of the war we would be well able to take care of ourselves against any combination of powers that could have whipped her and us combined. I detected a certain confusion, but I was there to report and not to argue, and besides a reedy young man who was publicity-directing for the committee told me that the president knew all about modern war because he had been a Quartermaster General in 1917 and sold several million dollars' worth of sundries by mail catalogue every week. I am not sure yet whether all these people desired an Axis victory consciously, but the irrational stubbornness with which they denied its possibility made you think of certain women who continually and compulsively talk about the impossibility of rape. The subject fascinates them. It was a successful article, the editors of *McCall's* said, except that I had mentioned one America Firster's business connection with the Quaker Oats Company, which was an advertiser. They fixed it to read he was "an official of a cereal company."

Although I believed that in the United States, as in France, the para-Fascists were more dangerous than the Communists, the latter caused me considerably more personal annoyance, because a number of my friends had listened to them. I never expect to see eye to eye with a Ford personnel manager or the vice-president of an advertising agency, and it causes me no anguish at all to find myself in disagreement with a newspaper publisher. But I did hate to drop in on a perfectly good reporter or physician and find myself howling and banging the table because he thought that there was no choice between Churchill and Hitler and demanded who were we to object to the slaughter of a couple of million Jews in Poland when there were resort hotels right here that wouldn't take Jewish guests? Unpeculiarly enough, the two propaganda groups had taken the same line on perfecting the United States before we opposed the Nazis—Robert Maynard Hutchins of the University of Chicago, who was the accredited intellect of the money people, hit exactly the same note on that as *New Masses*.

I think I must say here what I believe myself, because if you are going to see a war through a man's eyes you ought to know what there is behind them. I think democracy a most precious thing, not because any democratic state is perfect, but because it is perfectible. It sounds heartbreakingly banal, but I believe that you cannot even fool most of the people most of the time. They are quite likely to vote in their own interest. I also believe that since a democracy is made up of individual electors, the electors will protect the rights of the individual. A democracy may sometimes grant too little power to its government and at others allow government to infringe on the rights of the individual—Prohibition is example enough—but the vote always offers the means of correcting imbalance, and the repeal of Prohibition is an example of that. Any system that is run by a few, whether they sit in a Fascist Grand Council or at the pinnacle of a pyramid of holding companies, is a damned bad system, and Italy is a fine example of that, but unfortunately we didn't have its finish to point to in 1940–41. And so much for my ideology.

I had thought all along that the Germans would invade Great Britain in the spring or summer of 1941 and that that was the place to be for a *New Yorker* man who wanted to see the war, but I had gotten to fiddle-fluting around with the State Department Passport Bureau about giving me permission to travel on a belligerent ship. I also fiddle-fluted with the British Ministry of Information about getting me a passage either on a freighter in convoy or a bomber, and before I got under way Germany had invaded Russia. That slimmed the prospects of an invasion of England, but I choked back my disappointment and decided to go anyway. June 22, when the news of the invasion of Russia got around in New York, was a hot Sunday. I walked up through Union Square, where the free-style catch-as-catch-can Marxist arguers hang out, and all the boys who two days earlier had been howling for Churchill's blood were now screaming for us to get right into the war. "Well," I thought, "we are on the same side of a question for once, anyway." Somehow, I remembered my old French general who had said to his estranged friend, "I will shake hands, if you have arrived at better sentiments." The reason I had thought all year that we should declare war on the Axis immediately was that I didn't think either the training of our Army or war production could attain even half-speed until the Government had war powers.

The Road Back to Paris, 1944

The Way of Subjects

by Otto D. Tolischus

Early August. According to announcements in the press, the Education Ministry, "after painstaking study of one year," had finally completed an elaborate booklet which was represented as the new Bible of the Japanese people. It was entitled *The Way of Subjects*, and was supposed to contain the new ethical code of the Japanese nation. As such, it was now being distributed to all schools and adult organizations for the education and guidance of all Japanese, and especially their youth.

It was a startling document, which I cabled to New York at considerable length. It contained all that the most rabid jingos had been saying, but it was much more elaborate, and systematized, and dogmatic, and authoritative, and fantastic. Under the general motto "Back to the Japanese Spirit," it proclaimed a war of extermination against "European and American thought," the essence of which was declared to be "individualism, liberalism, utilitarianism, and materialism." These evils, said the booklet, had deeply penetrated various strata of Japan's national life, had subverted the traditional Japanese spirit, had undermined the foundation of the Empire, and had thereby imperiled the great tasks confronting the Empire.

These tasks, it explained, had been imposed on Japan by the gods of creation, and especially by the Sun Goddess, from the beginning of the world, and had been crystallized in concrete form by Emperor Jimmu at the founding of the Empire in the Hakko Ichiu principle, which called for the extension of the "Capital." In conformity with this principle, the booklet declared, Japan had the holy mission to rescue East Asia from the evil influences of Europe and America, and to extend the "Capital" until the "whole universe be

184

placed under one roof," that is, under Japanese Imperial Rule, as again decreed in the recent Imperial Rescript on the Axis alliance.

This divine mission, the booklet continued, had been obstructed by the American and European Powers, especially by the United States, Great Britain, and France, who, by "outrageous acts . . . unpardonable in the eyes of God and man," had spread their dominion over the colored races, had killed and enslaved Asiatics, Negroes, and American Indians, and had plotted to keep Japan down by limiting Japan's armament, which is "absolutely necessary for propelling the development of her national destiny."

However, the leaflet continued, with the outbreak of the "Manchurian Affair," which was a "violent outburst of Japanese national life long suppressed," things began to change, for Japan started the construction of a new world order based on the moral principles laid down by the gods, in which all nations are to be allotted each its own proper place. But in order to achieve this lofty goal, it declared, the Japanese people must construct a "highly geared and centralized defense state" and strengthen "a total national war framework." For "a nation without defense is one that belongs to a visionary world." And in order to create such a defense state, the booklet concluded, the Japanese people must cast out from their midst all that they had learned from the West, return to the ancient Japanese ways, abandon all private and selfish interests, and uniting in loyalty and filial piety around the Imperial Throne, obey the Emperor, who "rules and reigns His state with a solemn mind of serving the gods."

"Japan," said the booklet, "is the fountain source of the Yamato race, Manchukuo is its reservoir, and East Asia is its paddy field." And in line with the Tanaka memorial, it declared that the China conflict was merely a "steppingstone" toward the reconstruction of the world in which the "evils of European and American influences that have led China astray," would be eliminated from East Asia, and the world "united as one" on the basis of the moral principles propounded by Japan, which, in turn, are predicated on Japanese world rule. World history, it said, is ever changing, and nations rise and fall. But Japan, born of the gods and ruled over by a line of Emperors unbroken for ages eternal, had been steadily rising to her present eminence and prosperity "through accretion, heap by heap, particle by particle."

"Japan," the booklet proclaimed, "today is facing the moment to achieve unprecedentedly great enterprises amid the severest and most intense disturbances that have ever been recorded in the annals of the world. The China Affair is a holy task . . . to propagate the ideals of the Empire-founding throughout East Asia and also the world over."

And lest, in their addiction to "European and American thought," the subjects should have forgotten the divine origin of this mission and their duty to obey, the booklet recapitulated as eternal verities the ancient legends of Shinto mythology, from the birth of the gods and the Japanese islands to Jimmu and his Hakko Ichiu principle, illustrating at the same time how this mission and this principle had been observed and propagated in Imperial Rescripts through the ages to the present day.

There was Matsuoka's "peerless polity" and its "holy mission" in a nutshell, expounded in an official document prepared by Japanese scholars and issued by the Government for the education and preparation of the nation. Steeped in darkest obscurantism that was exceeded only by its arrogance, it surpassed even Hitler's *Mein Kampf* in its sweeping program of world conquest.

However, this new "Bible" was merely the official summary and endorsement of a development which had been going on in Japan for the last decade in the name of the "Showa Restoration," through which the old Samurai were wreaking posthumous vengeance for the Meiji Restoration that overthrew their rule. And Meiji's hapless grandson, a Westernized intellectual himself, was forced to forswear all that his grandfather had stood for, except only the expansion policy.

When Meiji came to power, and Japan was opened up to Western thought and progress, and constitutional government and a parliamentary Cabinet system were established, the young Emperor took an Imperial Oath in which he pledged himself, his posterity, and the nation to the following:

Old unworthy ways and customs shall be destroyed and the people shall walk along the highway of Heaven and earth. . . .

Knowledge shall be sought among the nations of the world and the Empire shall be led up to the zenith of prosperity.

Later, he issued the famous Imperial Rescript on Education, which up to now had been the guide and inspiration of Japan's intellectual life, in which he instructed his people, among other things: "Pursue learning and cultivate arts, and thereby develop intellectual faculties and perfect moral powers."

Gradually, and in the face of much remaining Samurai opposition and obstruction, these principles were put into effect. The old ways, and especially the Shinto religion, were not entirely abandoned, but they were gradually modified. The constitution still took cognizance of them by specifying that "the Empire of Japan shall be reigned over and governed by a line of Emperors unbroken for ages eternal," and that "the Emperor is sacred and inviolable." But it went no further. Shinto was disestablished as a state religion, and was on the way to becoming a patriotic sentiment and ceremony. Japan sought knowledge among the nations of the world and quickly became Westernized. She was beginning to develop learning and intellectual faculties, and was on the road to the zenith of prosperity. Up to 1931.

Then came the "Manchuria Incident" and the "turning point of the world," through which the descendants of the Samurai plunged the country into war and hoisted themselves into the saddle. Ever since then, using the "Showa Restoration" as a slogan, they had been putting back the clock, not only in matters economic, but more especially in the matter of intellect, of knowledge, and of learning. The ways of Meiji were decried as "un-Japanese," and the "old unworthy customs" proclaimed to be the true Nipponism to which the nation must return. Liberal statesmen were assassinated, parliamentary rule liquidated, the constitution undermined, liberalism and Westernism castigated, and schools and colleges purged of liberal and Western thought and teachers. Nationalism was paired with obscuranticism, and the old Shinto myths, which had always served as a basis of official Japanese history but which enlightened Japanese had come to regard as of merely historic interest to be subjected to higher criticism, were once again installed as the literal, fundamental, and only truth, which scholars disputed at their peril. "Nipponism" became Shinto and Shinto became "Nipponism," and both became words to conjure with; and the only learning of standing was learning in the art of war. It was, therefore, only fitting that in presenting their new-old doctrines, the authors of the new "Bible" should have falsified the Meiji rescript by suppressing, according to the translation by the *Japan Times Advertiser*, the injunction "to develop intellectual faculties."

August 3. A remarkable Shinto ceremony was staged at Hakone, a hot-springs resort, at dawn today by a group of generals, Cabinet Ministers, college professors, lawyers, writers, and other prominent figures in the military, political, educational, and literary circles of Japan, under the auspices of the I.R.A.A. and the supervision of Prince and Princess Kanin of the Imperial family. After worshiping the ancestral gods, they ran in silence, and naked except for a loincloth around their waists, to a stream, waded in knee-deep, and throwing their arms skyward, began to shout "Ei-oh-ei-oh!" until their shouts echoed and re-echoed through the hills. This, it was explained, was a physical exercise practiced by the gods of old in what is known as the Misogi rite. "Misogi aims to lead people to a stage where nothingness prevails," explained General Kuniaki Koiso, former Overseas Minister, "but I don't believe I have reached there yet." But the purpose of this special observance was far removed from "nothingness," for it was staged to harden the participants in the propagation of the Hakko Ichiu principle.

Likewise, solemn Shinto memorial services were held at the Idzumo Grand Shrine for Joseph Warren Teets Mason, American newspaperman and Shinto expert, whose ashes had been brought back to Japan at his request. A temporary altar, draped with white cloth, had been set up at one end of the shrine, above which hung a photograph of Mason. Underneath the photograph reposed the ashes, also wrapped in white cloth. Two sacred Sakaki trees, presented by the *Nichi Nichi*, stood on either side of the altar, and on the right side were vases filled with flowers. The priests, clad in white robes, with black headdresses, offered silent prayers, whereupon offerings of products of the earth and water were brought in and placed on the altar, including sake, fruit, vegetables, seaweed, and uncooked rice.

Tokyo Record, 1943

"See You in Lisbon"

by Wes Gallagher

OUTSIDE the sun beats down in muggy waves, but inside the six stinking railroad cars, fear—like a blanket of dark cobwebs—lies over the lives of 267 passengers.

Fear that visas may expire before a destination can be reached. Fear that each new border check might bring a gruff order to get off the train and turn back. Fear that scanty funds may not last until a safe place is reached in the New World. Fear that an outbreak of war in a new theater will slam the gates to freedom at the last moment. Fears by the hundreds—by the thousands. . . .

For this is a sooty, slow, uncomfortable refugee train bringing people from the hates of Central Europe to the seaports of Spain and Portugal where they hope to embark for the U.S. or South America. Not all are Jews. There is a sprinkling of Czechs, Belgians, Netherlanders, and French who finally obtained exit permits.

There is an American, too, a young dark-haired girl who sits by herself and alternates between moods of forced gaiety and silent tears. She is engaged to a young Austrian doctor who is a refugee in a neutral country. At the last border station she clung desperately to his coat sleeve until it was wrinkled and damp.

"I'll be along soon," he said, trying to be cheerful.

But it was obvious neither believed it. He can't obtain the necessary visas to cross the countries separating him from Lisbon.

A matronly German woman tries to divert the American girl's attention with offers of chocolates and a stream of small talk frequently interspersed with laughter. Or perhaps she is trying to forget her own plight. Her son has been in New York for five years. Her husband was refused permission to leave at the last moment and she is traveling alone to a South American country where she hopes to stay until she can reach the U.S.

"It may take years," she says.

Slowly the train drags along, stopping for hours at isolated stations. No one is allowed to leave the station even for a short walk. Sometimes one can not even get off the train. There are no sleepers. Pullmans are almost a forgotten luxury. The night passes in an endless succession of shudderings as cars are switched, muffled conversations as misfortunes are swapped, and brief restless dozings in the dim compartments crowded to the doors. Always the crushing, invisible net of fear is there.

Shortly after dawn tension increases as the train approaches a new border. Papers—those scores of papers that refugees must carry—are nervously checked for the one hundredth time to make certain everything is there. Police stroll through picking up passports. The passengers are herded off the train with their luggage, through a series of wooden gates, past long lines of officials who, in tired bored voices, ask scores of questions. Suitcases and trunks are unpacked, poked, probed, and repacked.

In the midst of the confusion an anguished cry is heard. It is from a little middle-aged Czech woman, dressed in black cotton. Somewhere a careless official has failed to fill in her visa properly. Now the customs men say she must wait until a telegraphic check can be made.

"It will not take long," one says. "We may hear in a few days." This brings fresh cries. She is on her way to the U.S. and her visa expires within three weeks. She has waited three years to get a quota number and a delay may mean another wait of months or years. The officials, hardened by months of dealing with refugees, shrug.

"It is the war," they say, "not us."

She is led protesting from the room. None of her friends interfere. They are afraid. The officials might stop them too. At last it is over. Baggage is placed on the train again. It crosses the border and the process is repeated at the next stop.

Here, too, there is a casualty. A fat little man who said he was a professor of economics from an occupied country is approached by two plain clothesmen. This time the action is swift.

"You are Herr ——," they say.

He nods and his shoulders sag under the cheap blue serge suit.

"Come with us. A telegram has come. You must stay here awhile."

He starts to say something, then stops and walks away with the plain clothesmen on either side. His fellow passengers have seen the incident but they keep their eyes averted. They are afraid. He may nod and it would not be good to be considered a friend of the little professor. He is not seen again.

This time the luggage inspection lasts for hours because three inspectors must handle hundreds of pieces. Trains leave without their passengers and refugees frantically try to find transportation. If they stay too long in this country, their visas will expire and that means jail. Police keep the group together and finally arrangements are made for them to proceed in a hot, dusty, half-freight, half-passenger train with wooden seats. The Americans are allowed to shift for themselves and wait for faster trains.

As the refugee train pulls away, the plump woman who tried to comfort the American girl, leans out and cries in a voice meant to be hearty but is cracked with fear:

"I'll see you in Lisbon—I hope—soon."

Free Men Are Fighting, 1942

Tokyo Army Aide Bids Japan Fight
If Parleys Fail

by Otto D. Tolischus

TOKYO, Tuesday, Sept. 2 — Declaring that an American, British, Chinese and Netherland encirclement movement was strangling Japan economically and that Japan must break it without delay, by diplomacy if possible, by force if necessary, Colonel Hayao Mabuchi, chief of the Japanese Army press section of Imperial Headquarters, last night attacked the United States and Britain for their "unpardonable crimes." He urged the Japanese people to prepare to defend the country.

His speech, which was broadcast over a national radio hookup and was supposed to instruct the people on air-raid defense, represents one of the most outspoken attacks on the United States and Britain delivered by an official Japanese personage in recent months. Coming in the midst of the Washington negotiations initiated by Premier Prince Fumimaro Konoye's message to President Roosevelt, it aroused considerable speculation.

The German-Russian conflict, Colonel Mabuchi said, came at a time when the "China affair" appeared to be near a settlement, but as a result of that war the United States and Britain started an encirclement movement against Japan that is as great an obstacle to a settlement of the "China affair" as is Anglo-American aid to Chungking.

Furthermore, he said, America, Britain and other countries hostile to Japan froze Japanese assets, deprived Japan of raw materials and are now forcing their overseas territories, the Netherland Indies, Thailand and other countries to do likewise in order to drive Japan into a corner economically. This, he declared, is "a crime against humanity," and their claim that they are doing so in retaliation against Japan's advance into French Indo-China is a "lie."

Japanese authorities, he said, are doing their utmost to settle the problem by negotiations and if a peaceful way out is found it will be a matter of congratulation not only for Japan but for the world. But he urged that Japan must continue the construction of the "greater East Asia co-prosperity sphere" on a firm basis because, he declared: "If the sources of materials in foreign countries are closed to us the day will come when we will be at the end of our domestic resource."

And he added: "In delaying action to break the encirclement we will be inviting danger to our country."

Therefore, Colonel Mabuchi continued: "If Japan cannot reach a peaceful settlement through diplomatic negotiations Japan must break through the encirclement fronts by force. This means engaging the countries involved in the encirclement movement, notably America and Britain, in a long-drawn-out armed conflict. The situation confronting our country is a crisis in the literal sense of the term.

"But it would be the height of folly to look on with folded arms while the forces bent on defeating this country are at work. The situation will compel us to stake all to save ourselves as a nation. Any course open to us will present us with the question of life or death.

"I say with all emphasis that unless the defense resources that we have are linked with those of the greater East Asia co-prosperity sphere the future of the Japanese Empire is endangered. That is why the firm establishment of that sphere is a vital condition for the continued existence of our empire."

America and Britain, he charged, have already started what amounts to an economic war against Japan, which is exposing her to "slow death" and thereby adding another of their "unpardonable crimes," among which he cited Britain's infringement of Iran's sovereignty and America's "attack upon and occupation of Iceland." Furthermore, he said, Prime Minister Winston Churchill's characterization of Japan as an aggressor is an "inexcusable insult" to Japan's officers and soldiers, who are fighting a "holy war in China."

"These outrageous words cannot be tolerated!" he exclaimed.

If war should come, he said, "the Japanese nation would fight to the last man and defend the glorious national polity and history no matter how protracted the war might be," and he pointed out that Japan's national defense line now stretched from the Manchukuoan-Soviet frontier to French Indo-China, a distance of more than 6,000 miles.

Colonel Mabuchi also urged the people to eliminate individualism and liberalism for the sake of the national defense structure, which is "as strong as iron and with which the nation can overcome whatever difficulty may arise."

Lieut. Gen. Eiki Tojo, War Minister, in a speech to the heads of the Divisional Soldiers' Affairs Bureau, likewise declared:

"Japan's national policy is already fixed."

He urged soldiers, officials and civilians to form a united front for further advance.

At a press conference this morning a German correspondent asked the Japanese spokesman, Ichii Kishi, if Colonel Mabuchi's declaration indicated the trend of Japanese-American negotiations. Mr. Kishi promptly said there was no connection and that it was a mistake to make such inferences.

He indicated, however, that Japan again was drawing the attention of the United States and Soviet Governments to the matter of United States oil shipments to Vladivostok. He said official replies to previous Japanese representations had not been received, but "the expressions of certain opinions were unsatisfactory to Japan."

The press today emphasized the recent shifts in the naval command by which Rear Admiral Selichi Ito was appointed Vice Chief of the Naval General Staff. This appointment, outside the seniority rank, is held to be highly significant and to be aimed at further strengthening the first line forces of the Imperial Navy.

The New York Times, September 3, 1941

Death and Life on the Battlefields

by Margaret Bourke-White

I ALWAYS had interesting little adventures on the evenings that I slipped away from the banquet table. Once the soldiers showed me a big cache of captured German mechanized equipment hidden under the fir trees: some Skoda reconnaissance cars, a huge troop carrier with its caterpillar treads blown partially off, a Mercedes gun hauler, field guns, machine guns, and disabled tanks with swastikas painted on their sides.

Once a tankist returning from a battle where several enemy tanks had been surrounded and captured told me how the enemy tank drivers had filled every available bit of space around their feet, inside the tanks, with women's clothing which they had rifled from Russian villages. One tank, he said, was filled with women's underwear and another was crammed full of peasant embroideries, taken, I suppose, as souvenirs for German soldiers' wives. I was glad they had recaptured that tankload of embroidered scarves and blouses, for Russian peasant handiwork has a richness that is hard to match in any part of the world today. I would not have liked to see it go to the enemy.

Frequently, groups of pilots would return from the fight and show me their captured trophies, for a pilot always saves his enemy's medals if he is able to get them. Each of these pilots had his captured Iron Cross, and one of them had seven of them. "All the Fascist pilots want to get Iron Crosses," he said to me, "but we give them crosses of wood."

I was interested to learn that the Soviet fliers frequently recognized captured German pilots who had parachuted to safety when their planes were shot down. The *Luftwaffe* evidently made full use of the men who had flown passenger planes over the commercial line operating between Berlin and Moscow in peacetime—men who were thoroughly familiar

Margaret Bourke-White, Life Magazine, © Time Warner Inc.

GUARDING THE RUINS OF DOROGOBUZH

On guard at these ruined steps were two Red Army sentries, typical in their heavy boots, wool-wrapped legs, long war coats and raincapes. Red Army soldiers have that healthy, red-blooded look that comes from having plenty of meat to eat. They are well disciplined, and while all soldiers are "Comrade" to each other, they salute their superior officers and address them as Comrade Colonel, or Comrade General, or Comrade Political Commissar, as the case may be.

These Russian soldiers are tough and come from hardy peasant stock. The Russian peasant loves his land, and therefore winning back the land from the invader has a deep and sacred meaning. These men know what they are fighting for, and that is one of the secrets of their strength.

with the route. Sometimes the Russians knew these captives well enough to call them by their first names. The Germans, however, never showed a sign of recognition.

Sometimes I talked with scouts who had penetrated far enough back of the enemy lines to make contact with the guerrillas, for the Red Army maintains connections with partisan troops wherever it can. Wherever possible, the regular army smuggles guns to the partisans. One returned scout told me about a group of villagers who were successful in halting an oncoming munitions train by tossing burning trees across the railroad tracks. When the German soldiers ran up to try to clear the tracks, the villagers shot at them from an embankment with the only two rifles they had, and when those gave out they threw rocks at the Germans. In the end more of the partisans than the German soldiers were killed, but the enemy had been delayed.

Another scout came from a region beyond Smolensk, where a detachment of partisans had hidden in the tall grass along the highway, waited until a group of tanks came opposite, and tossed bottles of flaming gasoline* at them, disabling three tanks. As this scout worked his way back, he passed through a town where a group of partisans had actually fallen on two invading tanks with hammers and axes. Machine-gun fire from the tanks killed several of these villagers, but finally, led by the village blacksmith, they managed to bend the machine guns out of commission and then, beating on the armored walls, they created so much din and dust that the tank crews had to surrender.

One of the scouts had come from a tiny village, nine miles behind the lines, with a report of how when the Germans moved in, the men went back into the woods, believing the Nazis would be less suspicious of the women. The German officers took up their quarters in a log schoolhouse, and at midnight the peasant women set fire to it with gasoline-soaked hay. Then, when the officers rushed half dressed out of the burning building, the women set on them with pitchforks.

*This is the Molotov Cocktail, used so successfully by guerrillas in the Spanish Civil War.

PILOTS IN MESS TENT AT AIRPORT

These pilots were photographed at a small landing field of the Soviet Air Fleet, tucked away in the wooded countryside. A handful of planes had been wheeled under the trees, where they were waiting until nightfall.

The Red pilots are fine-looking men, some of them as handsome as any Hollywood movie pilot. Most of them wore decorations: the Order of Lenin, the Red Star, the Mongolian Star. The pilot second from left, rear, had just shot down his twenty-seventh plane the night before.

The Russian people speak of their pilots with the deepest reverence, and when Berlin received a token bombing they were overjoyed beyond measure.

In the Soviet Union when territory is captured one does not see the swarms of refugees which have clogged the roads of other invaded countries. The government has previously instructed civilians to stay and become partisans. They have been given directions in the art of sniping and in guerrilla warfare, and if their village is captured they know just what they are expected to do. Guerrillas cannot win a war, but they can do a great deal to make the enemy uncomfortable.

The person whom I remember the most vividly among the Russians I came to know at the front was Tanya. Tanya was a nurse, with widely spaced blue eyes, honey-colored curls that spilled down shoulder length, and a strong, chunky little body. We were in the Yartsevo sector when I met her, not far from Smolensk, and Tanya had been born here. She knew every footpath, and at night, as soon as it grew completely dark, she would buckle on her sidearms and go crawling on her hands and knees through the long grass and low shrubbery, across to the German lines. There, behind the lines, she would learn what she could about the movements of the enemy and the location of German guns, and creep back just before daybreak to report on what she had seen. Then she would sleep a few hours, go to the hospital tent to help tend the wounded, and at night if she was needed she would be off again.

The area she was working in had changed hands many times between the Germans and the Russians, so she was much needed. It is a sector that is still changing hands, and as I write this today I believe it is being regained by the Russians. So the experience of scouts like Tanya has great value.

Later, the night that I met her, we were allowed to visit an action point. We were led to the edge of our little wood and told that we could run across an open meadow to another grove of trees about a quarter of a mile away. We were instructed to run single file and keep three meters apart. As we reached the middle of the meadow the whole horizon was ringed with light and there was the sound of thunder above us. It was the Soviet battery firing over our heads, and the Germans began answering toward us with machine-gun fire. We quickened our pace, and as we approached the grove for which we were headed the Germans began sending up star

GHOST TOWN

Yelnya was a silent ruin when the Russians finally snatched it back from the Germans. Many of its families had been divided, half on Soviet soil and half behind the German lines. This was because the Nazis, when they retreated, tried to drive the population back with them to keep it captive. Sometimes we found German proclamations posted on these chimneys ordering civilians back to the rear, on pain of death.

But the Russians who managed to remain in Yelnya, although they had no possessions left—no cattle, no fodder, no crops—still found a great deal of work to be done. They had to start the fall sowing, even though that meant they were cultivating their fields within range of enemy guns. The soldiers helped with the plowing on quiet days in between their job of fighting, for the front was but an easy hour-and-a-half walking distance from the place where this picture was taken.

shells, to light the front lines so as to be able to see scouts who might be slipping across. Even as I ran I could not help but notice what a brilliant glow the star shells threw on the ghost-white birch trunks. I hoped that Tanya, wherever she might be at that moment, was sufficiently hidden. And then, in an instant, we were inside the grove.

The action point was less than a quarter of a mile from the Germans. We had to walk on tiptoe and talk in whispers. Here, of course, I was not able to take pictures, because flash bulbs would have revealed our position. Under cover of the darkness, the battery crew moved like clockwork, loading and operating their big guns.

When we returned and started on to another section of the front, it was a little past midnight, much too early for me to find out if Tanya had made the journey safely. I shall always wonder about her.

The next day, we had left the woods and groves behind. We were approaching the great battlefields of Yelnya, where war had lashed back and forth in all its fury, the land sometimes in enemy hands, sometimes in Russian hands, until at the end of six weeks of some of the most savage fighting that the world has perhaps ever seen, the Russians had reclaimed it again. This was sacred soil, for this was the first land to be won back for the Soviet flag, and we arrived directly on the heels of this victory. Here there were no picnic groves, no little woods of fir and birch. We were entering a man-made desert.

The fields were chewed up with the treads of tanks, and we were passing "scorched-earth" villages, with only patches of ashes darkening the ground to show where homes had stood. On the side of a hill, above a small stream and facing the road, was something that looked like a Zuñi village. Just as our American Indians built their holelike houses, tier above tier, up the sides of the mesa, so as to be able to see and face the enemy as he approached, so the Germans had dug themselves into the hillside of Ustinovo. And they had dug in with them several tanks which they could use as pill boxes. Communication trenches had been dug, joining links with forward positions and command posts. Each little cell-like dugout was banked with sandbags and braced with timber, and inside were metal cartons and wicker baskets which still contained

WHERE THE GERMANS DUG IN

Here at Ustinovo, near Yelnya, the Germans dug in like cave dwellers. They had fitted up their little dugouts so thoroughly that it is evident they expected to spend the winter. On this cliff that occupied a position strategically commanding a stretch of the main road, they built a command and observation post. In the dugouts were telephones and supply dumps. Above on the hilltop were networks of trip wires leading to mines, and heavy cannon camouflaged under woven branches. Tanks, which had been dug into the clay, with the gun turrets projecting to serve as rotating fortresses, had already been salvaged by the Red Army when we arrived.

In this sector, General Field Marshal Fedor von Bock's Second, Fourth, and Ninth Armies concentrated for what they expected to be a victorious march on Moscow.

Wherever they attempted to take a permanent position they put up signposts printed in German and issued a new set of laws to govern the captured people. But the Russian people refused to submit to capture, and partisan bands would steal up in the night to snipe at the enemy.

hand grenades and land mines bedded in straw. The Germans must have been driven from this hill suddenly, for large stores of ammunition had been left behind for the Russians.

I heard Erskine shouting to me from the top of the hill. He was waving a German helmet, so I picked up one of my own. There were plenty to choose from; hundreds of them, savagely gashed and broken or riddled with bullets, were lying around in heaps. The metal they were made of was thin, much lighter than the heavy mushroom-shaped casques that protected Russian heads. I selected one that was fairly intact. The owner's name, Herbst, was lettered in white inside, and a single bullethole over the left ear showed how Herr Herbst had met his end. I have the helmet at home now, in Connecticut.

We went on along the wind-swept road, between bursts of rain and hail, and late in the afternoon we came to Ushakovo, where the great battles of Yelnya had been fought.

There was none of the sylvan character we had seen in our earlier views of the front when we reached the battlefield of Yelnya. Here the Germans had poured across the fields, filling up this area like breath being blown into an expanding balloon. After six weeks of fighting, through August and September, the Russians had managed to snip off the balloon and deal with the captives within the Nazi bulge. And now the place looked like the end of the world.

Here were the ghosts of blasted trees, great trunks split and smashed as though a giant hand had picked them up in bundles and dropped them broken back to earth. As far as the eye could reach was wasteland, pitted with shell holes, channeled with trenches, littered with the remains of war which had swept in concentrated fury back and forth across it during those desperate weeks.

The Russian dead had been buried in a common grave, marked with newly planted firs and surrounded by a fence topped with red-painted tin stars. Field asters still showed touches of lavender and purple where they had been laid on the freshly piled mound of earth. The Germans had been hastily shoveled into their own trenches, unmarked—many thousands had been dug into the ten-mile-square battlefield where they had fallen. Like hundreds of empty turtleshells lay

LAND MINES

"Don't touch anything!" the colonel called out from the top of the hill as he saw me edging closer with my camera to these boxes of land mines. Ammunition, left by the Germans in their hasty retreat, lay all over the place. There were thousands of clips of machine-gun bullets, showing good copper, as though the Germans had plenty of that metal. Strangest sight was the many wicker baskets and metal cases of mortar shells and grenades, neatly packed like Florida oranges laid carefully in straw. Thousands of these baskets had been piled into towers along the road, by Red Army salvage crews.

The Russian officers under Timoshenko's command told us that here along the Central Front, the Germans were losing twice as many men and five times as much equipment as the Russians, and from what we saw it may easily have been true.

the German helmets, some decorated with little swastikas painted in white, many cracked viciously through the top where the metal had given way during battle.

Erskine called me and pointed to a zigzag trench. The bottom was sprinkled unaccountably with dead mice.

Everywhere was the paraphernalia of life—a torn sleeve, the piece of a boot, a tattered raincoat, fragments of rain-soaked German newspaper. Erskine stooped over and pulled out a handle projecting from the ground. It was an officer's broken sword.

We had to be careful where we walked because the ground was full of unexploded mines and shells. Once I stepped on something soft, and a green cloud rose into my face. It was a heap of moldy bread which still retained the shape of loaves, so recently had men been breathing and eating there. Near by was a chased-silver samovar, pierced with a bullethole, which raised an image of Russians drinking tea in what seemed like a bygone age.

When we reached the town of Yelnya, fighting was still going on near by. The front was only a few kilometers away, and the rattle of machine guns and the deep roar of artillery sounded restlessly to the west. Yelnya had had an estimated population of five thousand, and now it was a ghost town. When we drove into its ruined streets I knew that here at last I had the pictures I wanted, pictures that would look like war. It was almost twilight, but the clouds, as though they had heard my prayers at last, began lifting, and the rays of the setting sun poured down on the skeletons that had once been homes.

I jumped out of the car and hastily set up a camera. I had just begun work when one of the reporters, a member of the home faction, dashed past me, notebook in hand. "Hurry up, Peggy," he called. "We're clearing out of here in five minutes and we'll be halfway back to Moscow tonight."

It was too much—all the hopes and disappointments, all the fighting to salvage something through the mud and rain, all the arrivals at the most interesting places after dark, the tearing away in the mornings before I could complete my job. "I can't work this crazy way," I said aloud to the empty road. And I began to cry.

GREAT BATTLEFIELD OF YELNYA

Fifty thousand Germans were killed, wounded, or captured on this ten-mile-square battlefield. Buried under our feet, as we plowed through the rain-soaked earth, lay the German dead, for they had been hastily shoveled into their own trenches and into the big round pits made by the explosion of their own shells. Twenty thousand Russians fell here, and they were buried in common graves marked with the Soviet red star. These fields are at Ushakovo, where the great battle of Yelnya was fought.

The Germans, overconfident, had expanded into a bulge, and the Russians, driving ahead by night, finally met the enemy in hand-to-hand combat here and backed by their tanks, fought for six weeks. Hundreds of tanks entered the combat, and their treads chewed up these rich wheat lands beyond recognition.

When we arrived on this battlefield, immediately after it had been captured back by the Russians, the ground was still littered with mud-caked helmets and still pitted with shell craters which had filled with blood and were filling now with rain.

Crying doesn't do much good, because it interrupts focusing. I knew this, but I only stood there weeping, wasting my time. And then the censor came along and guessed what the trouble was, proving that there is some use for censors after all.

I shall never forget how he gathered a squad of soldiers to help me and instructed the officer in command of the town that I should be given all the help I needed. The plan was to have the correspondents go on to a banquet that was waiting for them sixty miles back on the road toward Moscow. Erskine would stay with me, of course. And the censor put a little pile of chocolates in the back seat of our car, cautioned me not to take too long, because the sound of the guns was rising, and the crowd was off.

Darkness was beginning to fall now, but the soldiers helped me string out my extension cords so we could light up portions of the road with flash bulbs. As it grew darker I brought all three of my flash guns into use, each with extension wires, and the soldiers strung out with them along the road, watching me for signals while I capped and uncapped the lens. It was too late to get instantaneous exposures, but it worked.

I was interested to see that the only building left even partially intact was the cathedral with its coppery-green dome, now being used as a Red Army barracks. But for the most part the town had been reduced to a collection of skeleton fingers, pointed toward the sky. These were the central chimneys, some of them still smooth with the polished tiles that are characteristic of peasant dwellings. Still, wherever two walls came together, or wherever there was a scrap of roof, people were creeping back to their homes, so resilient is the human race. Sometimes they were welcomed back by their cats, which have a way of lingering around the house even after bombing, although dogs turn wild and run away.

It was getting late now, and the garrison commander thought we should be on our way. Erskine was talking with a group of soldiers by the church, and I took one last walk, down a side street, and watched some people cooking food, which the soldiers had given them, over what remained of their brick and plaster ovens. They were setting up housekeeping in the midst of the ruins, and I noticed that they

THE CATHEDRAL OF YELNYA

This war-scarred shell of a cathedral served as a welcome shelter for the Red Army troops who reclaimed Yelnya. It was converted into a soldiers' dormitory, for it was the largest building still standing within a radius of twenty miles. Food and wheat seeds and even some farm tools were kept stored in the old church. The soldiers gave potatoes and flour from their stores to the newly freed civilians of Yelnya.

were using strange cooking utensils. I examined these utensils more closely. They were not mere pots and pans bent out of shape from bombing. They were pieces of wrecked German planes, and portions of metal sheeting from captured enemy tanks. Bent into shallow shapes they serve well enough as baking tins or broiling pans.

The officer and my husband were both calling me now, and their voices were almost drowned out with the rising thunder of guns. The star shells that soared over the front lines to the west were gleaming in a cobalt-blue sky. It was time to go.

But as I walked back to the car I paused to look at a woman borrowing some hot charcoals from the fire of a neighbor. "What is she carrying them in?" I wondered, as I watched her heading homeward. The shape was familiar. She was bringing home hot coals in a Nazi helmet.

Shooting the Russian War, 1942

Valhalla in Transition

by Howard K. Smith

A FRIEND of mine who worked in one told me that when you walk through those big German warehouses the propaganda films used to like to show brimming with food supplies of all kinds, the echo of your footsteps frightens you it is so loud and thundery. They're almost empty now. No caravans of trucks and freight cars unload on their platforms for storage any more. The system of food supplying has become much simpler. It is called the "farmhouse-to-mouth" method. What Germans eat today is what was dug right up from the good earth yesterday, so to speak. It didn't go anywhere to be stored because it couldn't; else markets would sell out mornings in one hour instead of two and Alois Hitler's little restaurant and hundreds like it would have to cut serving time from two hours to one, or not serve at all, which happens sometimes anyhow. Shops are clean and empty, except for a few new bottles of chemical sauces with fancy names nobody has ever seen before. Only the windows outside are full. Full of empty cardboard boxes of *Keks*, which is German for cakes, and wine-bottles filled with water. Willi Loerke's grocery shop next to my house has a big cardboard advertisement for Mumm's champagne in the window, with a pretty girl in a short dress holding up a glass of champagne. Once, before Willie was called up to go East, I asked him why he left that sign in the window when he didn't have any champagne to sell; he said it was because it took up lots of room, the girl was pretty and cheerful, and there wasn't much else to put in windows any more except the sign saying "No more potatoes today," and empty boxes of *Keks*. I like the way Germans try and keep up appearances somehow in spite of everything. It reminds me of the way old, aristocratic, southern families in America used to paint the shabby cuffs of their negro butlers' suits with black ink so the lining would not show over their wrists while serving, when friends from the North came to dinner. The little dairy goods shop around the corner from my house has in its window a row of milk bottles which are seven-eighths full with white salt to look like milk. Inside there is three gallons of milk a day, which sometimes lasts two hours when not too many customers come early. Half-pint to a customer while it lasts, and it is so thin it is blue rather than white. Cigarette shops have good windows too, with all kinds of variegated boxes of "Aristons," "Murattis," "Kemals" named after Camels, and a cigarette that used to be called the "Times," but which for patriotic reasons has been changed, at little printing cost, now to the "Timms." The boxes are empty and a sign in the window says they are only for decorations— *Nus Attrapen*. On the shut front door there is a different sign almost every day of the week. The manager, who is a friend of mine, showed me all the signs he keeps under the counter: closed for repairs, or for taking inventory, or for redecoration, or for lunch, or just plain sold-out which he means by all the others, but uses them from time to time "just for variety's sake." On Tauentzienstrasse, one shop-keeper solved the appearances problem by putting no empty boxes at all in the window, but a big profile photograph of Hitler with a gilt swastika above it and below it, in gold letters, "We Thank Our Fuehrer!" The local Nazi party chief thought it was a crack at the leader and made him change his decoration and put some *Attrapen* in the window. The man didn't really mean it to be a gag, he was just trying to be patriotic. But even appearances are beginning to go now. Berlin is really beginning to look the part of a city-at-war. I should like to stroll down Unter den Linden and beyond with my officer friend now. That, however, is impossible because a Bolshevik shot both his legs off east of Kiev. If they hadn't cut off Bus line number one, due to the petrol shortage, we could ride down, or we could take a taxi, if we could find one. It would be mean, but I would like to point out how buildings are getting grey and dirty, and how the paint is peeling, and lots of things. It would be mean, but it is high time somebody broke the Nazi monopoly of being mean.

Do you know Berlin? If you do, maybe you'd like to know

what that grand old city looks like now that it has become the capital of all Europe, Valhalla on earth, with—as Dr. Goebbels wrote last autumn—the highest standard of living on the continent. The highest except for the only two countries not yet blessed by being Newly Ordered—Sweden and Switzerland. That's really not a fair statement, but unfairness is another Nazi monopoly that's begging to be cracked. Take those big, ornate drinking places on the main drag: Café Unter den Linden and Kranzler's. The stuffing is popping out of the upholstery of their overstuffed chairs now. The cigarette girl in one of them, who has nothing else to do now, told me she spent a week recently just sewing up gaps in the upholstery. She couldn't get any thread, but string from wrapping packages will do until the war is over. Not the string from German packages which is made of paper and snaps when you draw it hard with a needle, but string from packages from Switzerland which you can get sometimes. Food there is not appetizing. It is generally a foul-smelling hunk of fish called *Kabeljau* on the menu, covered with a gummy yellow sauce called *Senftunke*. Frankly, it smells like an open garbage pail on Monday morning. Service also is not what it used to be, mainly because there are only three waiters and all are over seventy. They had been retired but, when the young men were called up in June, they had to be called back to work ten hours a day, lumbago or no lumbago. The Café Unter den Linden had a fine, big awning which could be stretched out like a marquee over tables on the sidewalk, in summer time, but the hinges on it got rusty and nobody could be found to fix them, and so rain water was caught in the folds of the awning and ate holes in it. Café Schoen across the street has no troubles about maintaining front. A couple of British fire-bombs solved that seven months ago. The fire-bombs destroyed the upper floors of the building and scaffolding was set up all around it to repair it, but the Russian war came and all the workers were called up so the scaffolding just stays up and hides the whole front of the building. There is lots of scaffolding along Unter den Linden, hiding the fronts of buildings nobody is any longer working on.

All the embassies on that big street, the Russian, the American, and the French, are empty now and closed up. When the

Nazis closed the Russian embassy, they put a big white streamer fifty yards long across the face of the building with black skulls and cross-bones on either end of the streamer, and in the middle the words: "Beware! This building is Being Fumigated!" People snickered. The Nazis removed the hammer and sickle on the door, but forgot the one on the top of the building in the centre, and it is still there. Most of the big tourists' agencies on Unter den Linden are still open but business is not rushing. Tourists these days wear steel helmets and don't buy tickets. Only the Russian agency, Intourist, and the American Express Company were closed. Intourist was later reopened as an "Anti-Komintern" bookshop and in the window is a magic lantern which shows snapshots of ugly Russian soldiers all day long. Above the screen is a sign saying, "BEASTS are looking at you!" The Russian soldiers are very ugly and might be ugly German soldiers, or ugly British or American soldiers but for their uniforms. Or, did you ever look at your own face in the mirror after you haven't shaved or slept for three days and have just had a fight? In the window of the American Express Company, which has been closed since early autumn, the employees—Germans all— took a last bitter crack at the Nazis for making them lose decent-paying jobs by sticking in a poster saying, "Visit Mediæval Germany." But the Nazis are not subtle, so they didn't get it and left the sign in the otherwise empty window. Even the big florist's shop, Blumen-Schmidt, on the main street, is empty. I went in there once in November to buy some flowers for Jack Fleischer's birthday—a hell of a present for a man to give a man, but there wasn't any schnaps—and when I saw how it was I told the salesgirl, my God, *et tu?* She said, yes, she was sorry, but Udet had just been killed and every time there is a state funeral they clean out not only the shop but also the hothouses. A little later I went back, but it was still empty and the salesgirl was sorry but Moelders had just been killed. I suppose if I had gone back later, she would have said, sorry, but von Reichenau, then sorry, but Todt, and so on. Luck never changes, it continues being good.

Turning off Unter den Linden to the left down the government street, Wilhelmstrasse, you can see the only freshly painted building in Berlin: Ribbentrop's ugly yellow palace, with ugly yellow snakes wrapped symbolically around spheres, that look like the world, on its front pillars. He has just had it remodelled. All the rest of the buildings are getting dirty, even Dr. Goebbels' formerly snow-white propaganda palace. After six o'clock, you can't walk on the side of the street where the Fuehrer's house is located. A cordon of policemen make you cross the street, for they are afraid of bombs after dark, even when the Fuehrer is not at home. The Fuehrer's yellow-brown chancellery is still the same except that the enormous bronze doors on its front have been removed and melted down for the arms industry and replaced with big, brown wooden doors. The last building on the street before you turn is where the New York *Herald-Tribune* office was until the *Tribune*'s correspondent, Ralph Barnes, was kicked out for saying German-Russian relations were not so cordial and might lead to an eventual conflict. Every time I pass the place, I remember that last night I spent with him in his office before he caught the train, drinking cognac because he was very sad about being thrown out; Berlin was a good spot then. Ralph was killed in Greece. He would have liked seeing Berlin as it is now.

Turning down Leipziger Strasse in the direction of Dr. Goebbels' fancy, new press club, you pass a whole block filled with nothing but Wertheims' gigantic department store. There used to be an enormous animated map of Russia in the big central show-window, showing the progress of the Germans each day. After Rostov, it was diplomatically removed and replaced with *Attrapen*. Inside, it looks like a rummage depot. It used to be run by Jews and filled with fine things, but since the Jews were the cause of all Germany's misfortunes, it is now owned by pure Aryans and empty except for trash. Half the big cage-like lifts are out of order until after the war.

At the end of Leipziger Strasse is Potsdamer Platz, a busy, German Piccadilly Circus; second to the Friedrichstrasse railway station it is the best place in Berlin to go to if you just want to look at a lot of people in a big hurry. On Potsdamer Platz is a big building called the Pschorr Haus, whose state I have always kept a close watch on because it is *the* typical, average, big *buergerliche* Berlin restaurant. Inside, it is now dingy and dirty, and so much bad fish has been served on its white wooden tables that the whole place smells like bad fish. People from the Potsdamer railway station next door sit at its tables and sip chemical lemonade and barley coffee between trains, as the Pschorr breweries, which own the big restaurant, are no longer making very much beer. I have a menu from the Pschorr Haus somebody gave me dated November, 1916, and on it are nineteen different meat dishes to choose from. Today, also after two years of war, there are only two meat dishes on the menu, one of which is struck through with a pencil mark along the strategy of the Kaiserhof Hotel. The other is generally two little sausages of uncertain contents, each about the size of a cigar butt. Before the meat they give you a chalky, red, warm liquid called tomato soup, but which a good-natured waiter-friend of mine always called: *Ee-gay Farben Nummer zwei null-eex!* all of which means, "Dye trust formula number 20-X." With the meat you get four or five yellow potatoes with black blotches on them. One of the Pschorr Haus' vast windows on the ground floor was broken up by a bomb recently, but since nobody could be found to fix it, the management simply stuck a flattened out cardboard box in the hole, which exudes the odour of bad fish out on the street.

Potsdamer Strasse, which runs from the Pschorr Haus down past the big Sports Palace where Hitler speaks when he comes to Berlin from the front, used to be a busy shopping centre. It is now a row of derelict shops, all closed for different reasons, and their windows dirty and exhibiting pictures which little boys drew in the dirt on the window with their thumbs. The "Fruit Bar" which used to sell fruit drinks is empty because there is no more fruit, and the wood-block letters that form its name on the front are cracking and falling from their white background, leaving dirty stains where the letters were. Many shops are empty because they no longer have things to sell. Some are, as they say, closed for repairs but no repairs are going on. Some are places which had been run for their middle-aged owners who were called up, by wives and daughters who are now also called up into the munitions factories. Farther down the street are the beginnings of a massive structure, behind a big board fence, which was to be the "German Tourists Centre." All tourist agencies in town were to have offices in it. It was being constructed by Professor Albert Speer, Hitler's little dictator for architecture. But Speer's workers had to be called up when the Russian drain on man-power began, and work had to be stopped. Now Speer, too, has been called to the East to take the job of Dr. Todt who died. Thus Potsdamer Strasse is a long monument to the Russian campaign, dead except for the people trudging in thousands down it. It is too bad that the Tourists' Centre could not be finished, for German Tourists deserve a monument of some sort: they've done thorough work this decade.

To the left of Potsdamer Strasse and parallel with it lie the railway tracks from the Potsdamer station. Across them is a huge, long viaduct for the electric, and from it, evenings, you get the best picture of industry and activity in all Berlin, looking down on a maze of criss-crossing railway tracks and a forest of semaphores with engines and trains puffing up and down. It is very smoky and looks good from that height. The reason I mention it is that the three easternmost lines are always filled with long trains and each coach is clearly marked with a red cross on a white circle; hospital trains unloading maimed Germans from the Eastern front to be taken to hospitals in Berlin. One night late, when I was going home on the electric and the train passed over these coaches, a wizened old *buerger*, drunk as a coot, nudged me and pointed to them and said: "From France we got silk stockings. From Russia we got this. Damn Russians must not have any silk stockings, what?" He was lucky he picked on me to say this to, or he would have had his hangover in Alexander Platz prison the next morning. There are other cynical Berliners who say, however, that the coaches are not unloading anybody; that they're just left there on the sidings to discourage the British from dropping bombs on the Potsdamer station. But I've seen them unloading.

If you turn off Potsdamer Strasse to the right just before you get to the Sports Palace and walk about a mile, you run smack into the *elegante Viertel* of Berlin, the West End. They say the Unter den Linden section lives by day, and the West End lives by night. In peace-time it's a gay, brilliantly lighted neighbourhood speckled with dozens of cinemas, theatres and variety houses, and hundreds of little hole-in-the-wall bars. Its geographical and spiritual centre is Kurfuersten-damm, a long boulevard which extends from the big Memo-rial Church to the Berlin lakes. It is also the Bond Street, with fine shops, of Berlin—in peace-time. In war Kurfuersten-damm reminds me of a beautiful woman who became the mistress of a wealthy man and who, after too much loving and living has now become a jaded, gaudy female who daubs her face with too much artificial colour in order to hide the deep-ening lines in it. Her jewels are the thousand and one bars and night-spots. They were once neat-looking little places, cubist in decoration and with bright-coloured stucco fronts. Now, the paint is peeling, the stucco is cracking and falling off in blobs, like the polish from paste pearls and the gilt from brass rings. Most of them have closed. The rest of them stay open only certain nights a week. This is all since the Russian war began, since the supplies of French Cognac, Dutch Bols gin, and good Polish Vodka have been exhausted. As they no longer have any of the ingredients for staple cocktails, they have struck these off the menu and instituted a "standard" cocktail. It is called by different names, and by names of vary-ing fantasy, in different bars: "razzle-dazzle," "Hollywood" (pronounced Holy-Voot cuck-tell; this was before America became an out-and-out enemy), or "Extase." But the mixture is always the same, when it is there—a shot of some kind of raw, stomach-searing alcohol with a generous dilution of thick, sweet grenadine syrup. Or, if you are lucky, you can get a bottle of this year's Moselle.

Dancing is strictly forbidden by law everywhere for the du-ration of the Russian war. Nevertheless, a few joints maintain "hostesses" who sit and drink with Tired Party Men. As the best of their profession have been drawn off eastward for the entertainment of officers, those who remain are a bit on the seedy side. For one thing, gowns are being worn shorter this season; it is impossible to buy new gowns and so the girls simply had to chop off the worn edges of their old ones and put in new hems, higher up. Physical appearance is not so good for the obvious reason that they are remainders of a flock that was never very promising in Germany. Prostitution, itself, is a moribund profession. They tell me there are still a

few places, one on Kanonier Strasse near the Wilhelmstrasse
and one on Giesebrecht Strasse in the West End, which is said
to be run by the foreign office for the comfort of minor visiting diplomats, especially the Japanese. And you can, they say,
be approached on the streets if you try very hard, but you
must try very hard. But generally, the fact that there are more
than twice as many women as men in Berlin, has made in-
roads into the profession. Regarding the general subject of
pornography, those who like to make facile generalizations
about the immutability of human nature may find a trace of
interesting support in this: one of the first Nazi measures, and
one of their best, was the banning of all pornographic picture
magazines, in 1933. Since the war, under the heading of
"Art," pornographic picture magazines have appeared in le-
gions. Be they called as they may—the "Faith and Beauty"
magazine, "The Dance," "Modern Photography"—they all
contain nothing but photos of naked women and all boil
down to the same old pornographic fare of pre-Nazi days.
Sales, I'm told, are terrific.

War seems to have some causal relation with pornography.
Through it one old portrait painter, who has roomy studios
on Unter den Linden, has gained fame in Berlin. He was once
Kaiser Wilhelm's court-artist, by special appointment, but,
since the war, and Hitler, he had not been doing so well on
sales. So, to make money, he hit on the idea of painting a
series of tantalizing nudes and allowing the public in to see
them for a fee. On his front door today there hangs a sign
advertising for all to see: "Sensation! Vast Canvas of Turkish
Harem including eight beautiful nudes, life-sized. Admission:
fifty pfennigs." Inside you can see, among natural-size por-
traits of Bismarck, Hindenburg and Hitler, the Sensation with
its swarthy, shapely nudes reclining on velvet-covered divans.
The Nazis have never objected, not even on racial grounds.
The cheap "art shops" of Friedrichstrasse, just off Unter den
Linden, have their windows jammed with fine looking maids
in undress and attract a goodly public at all hours of the day.

A handful of truly popular spots are (not my tastes, but
those of Germans):

The Golden Horse-shoe. Main attractions: among the
hostesses is the only negress in Berlin. A ring in the centre of

the floor around which lady customers ride a horse to music and show their legs above the knees in so doing, while male *buerger* shout with glee. The ladies or their men pay fifty pfennigs for a slow trot, seventy-five pfennigs for a good gallop.

St. Pauli's Bar. Here labours a hostess who has lost not only a husband in the war, but two of them! She thinks the war is a personal frame-up against her. The façade of the joint formerly consisted of the porcelain inlaid flags of every nation in the world. One by one the flags had to be painted over for political reasons, and now the façade is a checkerboard half of grey splotches and half of flags.

Walterchen der Seelensorger, which means, Little Walter, the Soul-comforter. This is a small dance-hall near the Stettiner station area in working-class Berlin, where the famous proprietor, "Walterchen," mates middle-aged bachelors and widowers with middle-aged spinsters and widows—a sort of public matrimonial bureau where rheumatic old gentlemen can rejuvenate their chivalry, and women who have forgotten can once again learn to be coy. Very amusing. Walterchen's trademark is a red heart with an arrow through it.

Die Neue Welt; the "New World"—a vast multi-roomed beerhall in the East End of Berlin. Once the most profitable amusement concern in Berlin, the *Neue Welt* is now closed most of the time for lack of beer. It is interesting if you like to see the German proletariat at play; also because the Gestapo keeps close check on the clientele, and you're likely to be arrested if you happen not to have an identification card to show them when they ask you. It is the only place in Berlin where plain-clothes men have ever cornered me and made me show my passport to prove I was not a parachute trooper or a Jew enjoying illegal fun.

The X Bar. This is the liveliest spot in town. That is not its real name, but since I want to tell some of its secrets, I had best not be too specific. It was my favourite spot when the blues got me and I had to go night-lifing or bust, because it has a good orchestra which defies Nazi propriety and plays American music, and also because the manager, who is a friend, still has a secret stock of Scotch whisky. As it is also a favourite spot for big-shot Nazis, the band doesn't play

American jazz bluntly; it sandwiches it in between opening
and closing chords from some German number, salving the
consciences of the Nazi visitors who might otherwise be reminded that what they are listening to was written by a racial
inferior. On a Saturday night, after police hours, the manager
shoos everybody out except a couple of friends and the policeman on the beat, gets his private bottle of Johnnie Walker
from under the kitchen sink, and we take off our coats and
smoke cigars he got from someone in the Foreign Office and
drink and talk until three or four in the morning. After that,
the manager used to wrap up a couple of big bottles of beer
in the morning's *Lokal-Anzeiger* and we would go off to my
apartment to mellow up on beer, have an early morning
breakfast and get the first B.B.C. news. The manager never
admitted it, but I think his bar has some special pull with the
government, by which he gets pretty good liquor stocks for
himself and for friends. The Foreign Office boys often take
their foreign guests there. I first saw P. G. Wodehouse there.
The place needs a coat of paint badly, but it's a good place
when you need a change of atmosphere so much you would
pop without it.

Theatres and show-houses out in the West End are packed
overfull every night. People haven't anything else to spend
their money on, so even the worst show in town is a sell-out
every night. The big variety houses, the Scala and the Winter-
garten, are having a hard time finding enough talent to fill
their bills, as narrowed by a whole sheaf of Nazi decrees since
the beginning of the war. Fortune-tellers, crystal gazers and
all kinds of stage soothsayers used to be popular with German
audiences, but when Hess flew to Scotland, Goebbels banned
them all for ever from German showhouses because it was
said that one of these affected Hess' decision to go. Another
big favourite were funny-men who specialized in shady political jokes, but these too were forbidden by Goebbels after a
while. Favourite music was American jazz and blues songs,
but the dictator of German *Kultur* unofficially informed producers this well also was poisoned. The Scala used to draw
entirely on foreign talent, showing a Spanish bill one month
and an American one the next, and so on, but the war has
rather rigorously limited the nationalities available or desir-

able, from the point of view of the authorities. Just about all that is left is acrobatics and juggling, which become tiresome; but they take people's minds off war, and that is what people pay for.

Cinemas are not as popular, principally for the reason that they do not take people's minds off war. Once the Nazi film dictators made the mistake of affording a very visible measure of what the public think of their propaganda films by opening a second-rate comedy called the "Gas Man" at the Gloria-Palast on Kurfuerstendamm, while fifty yards away at the Ufa-Palast an extra, super-colossal one hundred and fifty per cent war film, "Bomber Wing Luetzov," was playing. The medio-cre comedy played to packed houses at every presentation, while the war film showed to a half-empty theatre. Unfortu-nately, even mediocre comedies have become rarities as war and propaganda films increase in number. The latter can be exhaustively described by a five-letter word. They're lousy. Especially the pure-war films. Take the one called "Stukas." It was a monotonous film about a bunch of obstreperous ado-lescents who dive-bombed things and people. They bombed everything and everybody. That was all the whole film was—just one bombing after another. Finally the hero got bored with bombing and lost interest in life. So they took him off to Bayreuth music festival, where he listened to a few lines of Wagnerian music; his soul began to breathe again, he got vi-sions of the Fuehrer and of guns blazing away, so he impo-litely left right in the middle of the first act and dashed back and started bombing things again, with the old gusto.

News-reels which last almost as long as feature-films, used to be very popular with Germans, until the Russian war. Since then Germans have developed a bad case of nerves and don't like news-reels any more. Too many of them can visualize sons, fathers and cousins whom they have lost, in those dra-matic explosions on the screen. Once they showed a big fat Nazi bomber with white teeth painted on it to make it look like a shark, opening up its belly and issuing a school of bombs, twenty or thirty of them, one after another. All over the audience you could hear women sucking their breath in through their teeth as though cold shivers were running up and down their spines. People began writing letters to the

Propaganda Ministry complaining and begging for a change of fare. The bombardment of complaints finally induced the Ministry to allow a sequence of peaceful shots about the home front—harvesting grain, intimate shots of a cement factory at work, a film interview with Franz Lehar, the composer, etc.—before the war films. Then Goebbels began receiving letters expressing thanks, but asking for more home-front sequences and fewer war ones, especially to leave out the shots of dead-bodies on battlefields.

(The Germans do not allow their people to see American films, but the big shots sneak peeps at most of our best while nobody is looking. I tried to creep unnoticed into a showing of "Gone With the Wind" one afternoon in the Propaganda Ministry, but was promptly ordered out because this was a private "study" presentation for German film actors and producers. Some we were allowed to see in private showings, however, "Ninotchka," "Pinocchio" and others.)

In a word, films are trashy just like everything else. The advertisement posters in the subway stations are attractive and full of colour, just like those empty cigarette boxes in my tobacco shop window, but the films themselves are pure trash. I never thought it was possible for a country to go so universally trashy so quickly.

The only things that are not trash are their guns, which are handsome and horrifying. Of these you see many, many more in Berlin now than you used to, on top of buildings and on open fields in the suburbs. The biggest and handsomest ones are within two hundred yards of the Theatre Centre on Kur-fuerstendamm, in the big Tiergarten. They are anti-aircraft cannon mounted on a tower which, itself, looks like a fantastic monstrosity from a lost world, or another planet. It is huge and positively frightening just to look at (Nazis like to hear it described this way; they are specialists in fright-propaganda. But the world has now advanced beyond the stage of being frightened in any decisive way by anything the Nazi do or create.) It is an enormous, square clod of cement a hundred feet high, about five or six storeys. It is painted green so as not to be too visible among the trees from above. On each of its corners is a long, powerful gun, pointed at the sky. They are fired by remote control from another, similar tower about a hundred yards farther on in the wood, on which there is a big "ear" resembling a fishing net, big as a big bomb crater. You should hear these monsters in action during an air-raid. In my apartment half a mile away it sounds as though all four guns were levelled right at my window. I had never been in an air-raid cellar in Germany until the night last summer when they were first used in an air-raid (it took two years of incessant day and night work to finish the construction of the towers). For the first time, I confess I got the jitters. My windows rattled as though they would shatter and the floor underneath never stopped quaking as all four guns blasted away at the sky in unison for awhile, then began firing in rotation, an endless barrage which a soldier who fought in France told me was more nerve-racking and harder on the ear-drums than anything he had been in at the front. I didn't mind bombs, I accepted each one as a personal favour from the Tommies. But I couldn't take the guns. Also, I found after ten minutes that I couldn't stay in the cellar, for the neighbours had grown bitter against America and Americans, and made it unpleasant. So I stuffed cotton in my ears and sat in my hall.

They are building more towers like these in other parts of Berlin. They have converted the old Reichstag building into one, reinforcing its top corners and mounting guns on them. The Nazis expect lots of fireworks before the show is over; and they know what effect fireworks have on their people, so they are working night and day to prepare Berlin defences.

They have undertaken the most gigantic camouflage scheme ever known, covering up big spots which are conspicuous from the air all over the city. The most conspicuous thing is the "East-West Axis," a five-miles long, hundred-yards broad street which runs from the Brandenburg Gate in the centre of the town out to Adolf Hitler Platz where my office in the radio studio is situated. Last spring, they began covering the whole street with a vast canopy of wire netting mottled with strips of green gauze to make the thoroughfare indistinguishable from the trees of the Tiergarten alongside it. Lamp-posts were covered with green gauze to look like little trees. The big Victory Pillar, a monument to the Franco-Prussian War, in the middle of the Street was covered with netting and the shiny golden angel of Triumph on top which looked like a lighted beacon on a moonlight night was tarnished with dull bronze so that it would not reflect light. At the end of the axis, the radio station was covered in green, too, and straight over the centre of the building a strip of grey netting was laid to look, from the air, like an asphalt street. With Nazi thoroughness they even covered over a whole big lake in West Berlin with green netting and ran another grey, artificial roadway diagonally across it. It was all very nice and very clever. Until the first winds of winter came, straight from the steppes of Russia, like most German misfortunes these days. The first gale ripped yawning holes in the camouflage and blew the false trees off the lamp-posts and hung them, shapeless lumps of gauze and wire, in the branches of the Tiergarten trees. Now the Nazis are having to re-do the whole thing at great expense.

In the past year, Berlin has become probably the best defended city against air-raids in the whole world. I doubt if London can have as many batteries around and in it as Berlin has. I've stood on top of the tall Columbus House on Potsdamer Platz on clear nights and watched the British approaching. As they came closer more and more searchlights fingered the sky, and pin-pricks of light from exploding shells in the air increased from dozens to hundreds. Once, on one small arc of the horizon I counted seventy-five beams of light moving in the sky. Seventy-five searchlights; many, many hundreds of guns on this small sector. There must be many, many thousands of guns all around Berlin. An officer on one of the Flak batteries in the Berlin area once told me that the whole area has been armed far beyond the point of saturation; a real waste of guns has occurred. I asked him the reason for this extravagance, and he said that while the German people were among the worst informed people in the world, the German leadership was certainly the best informed leadership, regarding its own people, in the world. The extravagance is for the sake of morale. The German people simply couldn't take it, and the Nazis were afraid to have them subjected to anything like the London Blitz, he said. I believe him. I have heard it from many Germans, and I've seen enough for myself to confirm it. You can see it in them on the streets today more clearly than ever. They simply could not take it, if it came.

To see Berlin, you take a walk. To see the people you take a subway. You also smell them. There is not enough time nor enough coaches, for coaches to be properly cleaned and ventilated every day, so the odour of stale sweat from bodies that work hard, and have only a cube of soap big as a penny box of matches to wash with for a month, lingers in their interiors and is reinforced quantitatively until it changes for the worse qualitatively as time and war proceed. In summer, it is asphyxiating and this is no figure of speech. Dozens of people, whose stomachs and bodies are not strong anyhow faint in them every day. Sometimes you just have to get out at some station halfway to your destination to take a breath of fresh air between trains.

People's faces are pale, unhealthily white as flour, except for red rings around their tired, lifeless eyes. One would tend to get accustomed to their faces after awhile and think them normal and natural but for the fact that soldiers ride the subway trains too, and one notices the marked contrast between young men who eat food with vitamins in it and live out of doors part of the time, and the ununiformed millions who get no vitamins and work in shops and factories from ten to twelve hours a day. From lack of vitamins in food, teeth are decaying fast and obviously. My dentist said they are decaying all at once almost like cubes of sugar dissolving in water. Dentists are severely overworked as most of them must spend half their time working for the army, and take care of a doubled private practice in the rest of the time. They have raised prices tremendously to discourage the growing number of patients; he said they simply had to do this. This winter there has been the most severe epidemic of colds in Berlin in many winters, and doctors predict it will get worse each year and probably assume dangerous proportions if something cannot be done about food and clothing, especially shoes, which are wearing out fast.

Weary, and not good in health, Berliners are also, and consequently, ill-humoured. That is an understatement; they have become downright "ornery." All lines in faces point downwards. I can recommend no more effective remedy for a chance fit of good humour than a ten-station ride on a Berlin tube train. If the packed train suddenly lurches forward and pushes your elbow against the back of the man standing in front of you, it is the occasion for a violent, ten-minute battle of words, in which the whole coach-load of humanity feels called upon to take part zealously as if their lives hung on the outcome. They never fight; they just threaten (*"Ich zeige dich an, junger Mann!"*—That's the magic phrase these days: "I'll have you arrested, you imprudent young man," that and "I have a friend who's high up in the Party and *he* will tell you a thing or two!" They're like children threatening to call my Dad, who's bigger'n yours). Berliners have always been notorious grousers. They always complained about anything and everything. But it was a good-natured kind of grousing you could laugh at. What has happened in the past year is something new and different. It is not funny; it is downright morbid, the way people with pale, weary, dead-pan faces which a moment ago were in expressionless stupor can flash in an instant into flaming, apoplectic fury, and scream insults at one another over some triviality or an imaginary wrong. You could watch people's natures change as the war proceeded; you could clearly watch bitterness grow as the end of the war appeared to recede from sight just as you watch a weed grow. It has been depressing to watch and it leaves a bad taste in your mouth. Partly it's the jitters and partly it's a national inferiority complex. But mostly, it is because people are sick; just plain sick in body and mind.

It may be just an impression, but it seems to me that the sickness has hit the little middle-classes hardest. Take those little family parties I've been to time and again where middle-class people, bred on middle-class Respectability, used to play *Skat* all evening and maybe open up a bottle or two of cool wine for refreshment. Recently, I've been to several, and the whole atmosphere has changed. They do not play *Skat* any more at all. They round up all the old half-filled bottles of anything alcoholic they can find (this was before the December Drouth set in with a vengeance), and just drink. They do not drink for the mild pleasure of drinking, not to enjoy the flavour of what they drink nor its subtle effects. They drink to get soused, completely and unmitigatedly; to get rollicking, loud and obstreperous, pouring down wine, beer, sweet liqueur and raw *Ersatz* cognac all in an evening. The general

atmosphere is that of a cheap, dock-side dive. I'm not trying
to make a moral judgment, but there are grounds for making
a social one. The atmosphere is one of decay. And that atmosphere seems thickest among just those strata of Germany's
population which have always formed the basis of German
society, the *Kleinbuergertum* (lower middle classes). Any type
or form of society exists because broad sections of the people
have an interest in it existing. In Germany, the petty middle-
classes are the ones who have always had an interest in *Bourgeois* society being maintained. They brought Hitler to power
in the hope of maintaining their society against the air-tight
caste of privilege maintained by the classes above them. Now,
it seems to me that the little middle-classes are losing interest,
and drowning their disappointment in alcoholic lethe, or
lethe of any other sort. Superstition has grown apace. There
has been a wave of morbid interest in all sorts of quack sciences and plain superstitions, phrenology, astrology, all kinds
of fortune-telling. I am sure one reason Goebbels banned all
soothsayers from the German stage was that they were becoming too influential among the people. I am always inevitably reminded by these things of another society where a
man named Rasputin gained influence and power in a higher
circle but for the same reason, shortly before that society collapsed. People who are either unwilling to admit they know
what is wrong with them, or are unable to do anything about
it—i.e. get rid of Hitler—are seeking escape in *Ersatz* directions. That is psychological, but it has its physical complement. People who are suffering from nothing else but the
inevitable effects of bad nourishment, are inventing fancy
names for their ailments and buying the patent-medicine
houses out of wares. Outside the armaments industry, the
only business which is making big money in Germany is the
patent-medicine industry. Every woman carries a full pill-box
of some kind along with her almost empty vanity compact,
and no man's meal is complete without some sort of coloured
lozenge for the belly. A substance known as *Okasa* for sexual
potency has become almost a German national institution.
Young girls welch boxes of *Pervitin* from air-force officers to
reinforce energy that should be natural. The general atmo-

sphere smells strangely like that of an opium dive I once visited in New Orleans many years ago.

If I had to describe Hitler's Reich in one figure, I would
compare it with a fine looking fat apple with a tight, red,
shiny skin, which was rotten in the core. The strong, polished
hull is the army and the Gestapo, which has become the main
constituent of the Nazi Party. It is a strong, very strong cover.
The rotten inside is *the whole fabric of Nazi society.*

This is a serious statement to make. I sincerely believe that
a journalist who consciously misinforms his people and allies
about the state of the enemy in time of war for the sake of
sensation is the second lowest type of criminal (the lowest
type being anyone who makes profits out of arms production). I have always sought to avoid underestimating the
strength of the Nazis. I refer to the internal strength of the
Nazi system, which this book concerns itself with alone, not
the military strength. But, with these self-imposed restrictions
in mind, I am sure of what I say: Nazi society is rotten from
top to bottom and in all its tissues, save the strong hermeti-
cally closed hull. The people are sick of it. The general theory
of society denoted by the name *Fascism*, of which Nazism is a
form, has had its flare of popularity in Europe, and so far as
popular following is concerned, its day is over. It will never
again be an attracting force as it was before the world discovered its meaning.

In Denmark, the Nazis are opposed to parliamentary elections being held because they know that elections would result, as certainly as sunrise, in the Danish people throwing out
the three measly Danish Nazis who are in Parliament. In Norway and Holland, the Nazis do not dare even to support a
planned "plebiscite" for fear of the evidence it would give of
how dead their philosophy truly is. As an idea, Nazism is dead
as a door-nail. As for the German people, they are attached to
the Nazis like the man who unexpectedly found himself holding on to a lion's tail, and kept right on holding on, not
because he enjoyed the lion's proximity, but because he was
scared speechless at what might happen if he let go. Or like
the little boys who were having a fine ride on a toboggan
until it hit a slippery place and started zipping down curves on

one runner; they were scared to jump off and it got more impossible every second. Don't get me wrong. I don't mean only that the German people are afraid of the Gestapo and that all they are waiting for is for someone to weaken the Gestapo, and then they will revolt. Though the Gestapo is certainly a big element in the fear complex, it is not the biggest. The main reason the Germans cling to the lion's tail is that they are terrorized by the nightmare of what will happen to them if they fail to win the war, of what their long-suffering enemies will do to them; of what the tortured people of their enslaved nations, Czechoslovakia, Poland, France, will do when there is no longer a Gestapo to hold them down. The German people are not convinced Nazis, not five per cent of them; they are a people frightened stiff at what fate will befall them if they do not win the mess the Nazis have got them into. Take note of the new tone of Nazi propaganda of late. For two years Goebbels blew the shiny, gilded horn of how beautiful Victory was going to be, in order to urge his people on to battle. Suddenly in autumn, the tone changed to that of what will happen to Germany if Germany *fails* to win. If you read the dispatches from Berlin by American correspondents at that time, you will recall that famous editorial written by Goebbels and published in *Das Reich* entitled, "When, or How?" In that leader, for the first time, Goebbels admitted to Germany and the world that conditions had grown extremely bad inside Germany, and he ended by warning his people that however miserable things might be now, they would pale beside what would happen to Germany if Germany lost the war. This tune is now being played long and much in the German press. In all its forms, the incitement of Fear in the hearts of Germans, is the only strong weapon in Goebbels' armoury since Dr. Dietrich played hell with the others.

People in the outside world who know the Nazi system only from photographs and films; from dramatic shots of its fine military machine and the steely, resolute faces of its leaders, would be amazed at what a queer, creaky makeshift it is behind its handsome, uniform exterior. It is not only that the people who support those stony-faced leaders are timid, frightened and low-spirited. It is also, the government, the administration of those people and their affairs. In *The House that Hitler Built*, Stephen Roberts drew as nearly perfect a picture of that strange complicated mechanism as it was in peace time, as it is possible for a human to draw. But even that capable author would be bluffed by the thousand queer, ill-shaped accretions that have been added illogically to it and the contraptions that have been subtracted illogically from it since the beginning of the war. It looks roughly like a Rube Goldberg invention, inspired by a nightmare, but it is more complicated and less logical. And there are no A, B, C directions under it to show how it works. The men who work it have no idea how it works, themselves. The old, experienced, semi-intelligent bureaucrats who made the old contraption function wheezingly in peace, have been drained off to the war machine where their experience can be used more valuably. The new, screwier contraption is operated haltingly by inexperienced little men who do not like their jobs and know nothing about them. The I.Q. of the personnel in the whole civil administration machine has dropped from an average of a fifteen-year-old to that of a ten-year-old.

For example, it is strictly against the law for any foreigner to remain in Germany more than a month without a stamp in his passport called by the formidable name of *Aufenthaltserlaubnis*, a residence permit. But nowadays, between the time you apply for one and the time you get it, a year generally passes; you break the law for eleven months because nobody knows what to do with your application once you've filled it out. Most foreigners never get one at all. But that is one of the more efficient departments. My charwoman's sister, who worked in a hospital, disappeared once. Together my charwoman and I tried every police and Gestapo agency in town to find out about her, but nobody knew anything, or what to do to find out anything. Thirteen months later, it was discovered she was killed in a motor car accident in central Berlin, and the record of it had simply got stalled in the bureau drawer of some little official who didn't know which of eleven different departments he should have passed it on to. He tried three of six possible departments, but they didn't know what to do with it.

Nobody knows who is *zustaendig* (responsible) for anything. When I complained to the Propaganda Ministry about being refused trips to the war-front, I was told the Ministry had nothing to do with the matter, that I should see the radio people. I went to the radio people who were not *zustaendig* for such matters and who sent me to the censors. The Foreign Office censor knew nothing about it and told me to see the High Command censor who told me to see the Propaganda Ministry censor, who told me to go back to the Propaganda Ministry itself and complain there. Ultimately, Dr. Froelich, in the Ministry, showed an uncommon sense of the state of affairs and shrugged his shoulders and told me neither he, nor anybody else, had the least idea who the responsible official was, or which the responsible department. I was simply banned from trips to the front by nobody for no reason, but no one could do anything about it. When I was finally banned from the air, I went to the American embassy and asked the proper officer to protest to the Nazi authorities. He smiled and said: "It has become hopeless to protest to the Nazis about anything. Not only because of their ill-will towards Americans, but also because they frankly do not know which department any particular protest should be delivered to." He told me the whole Nazi civil government is in a state of un-believable chaos. Hitler no longer pays the slightest attention to the civil side of German life, and his underlings have fol-lowed the transition of his interests to the purely military side of things. Nobody of any consequence has any interest in the government of the German people, and it has become hope-lessly confused and chaotic, and, in its innards, irremediably constipated. It is, in short, going to hell in a hurry.

For a land ridden by laws, Germany has become the most lawless land on earth. Law means nothing; the password to-day is *Beziehungen*, which means good relations with a party big-shot, influence, pull, jerk. You can threaten someone on the subway with getting the law on him, but when you threaten a bureaucrat or a grocer who doesn't give you full rations, you must threaten that you have *Beziehungen* who will fix him. If you have no pull you can get no goods or service, no matter how strong the law is on your side. If you have got *Beziehungen* you can get anything, any commodity which has disappeared from the shops, or any service, no matter how many laws there are against it—and there are hundreds, against everything—written down in the law books. Law has lost all meaning. We know cheap, corrupt, court-house politics in localities in America all too well. But Germany is one great big nation of nothing but cheap, corrupt, court-house politics, ruled by a single party whose leaders are mostly fanatical ascetics, but whose several million underlings are as buyable as postcards. For a half-pound of coffee I have rewrit-ten whole German law books in my favour.

In the field of economics Germany is corrupt and rotten too. The state is allegedly national "Socialist," but for a so-cialist state it maintains the finest, fattest crop of unadulter-ated plutocrats you ever dreamed of. Half of them are the old plutocracy, the old families who grew rich on guns and chemicals; half of them are the new plutocracy of higher up Nazis who had not a pfennig ten years ago, but who got in the elevator of financial success on the ground floor in 1933, after its shaft was greased by Nazi victory, and shot straight up to the top, like Ley the contraceptive king, and Goering the steel king. The German people are not as conscious of their money classes as other people are, for the Nazis shrewdly do not allow their newspapers to publish society pages, which make American and British people conscious of their plutocracies. Dividends are, of course, limited to six per cent. But there is no law against watering stock; against giving two six per cents to a shareholder instead of one six per cent, when business is good, as it is today.

The big red apple is rotten and worm-eaten. If and when it is ever pierced, it will stink to high heaven. But the hull is very red and shiny. And it is very strong. And the worms inside who thrive and grow fat on the fruit, like it that way. And the people of Germany are afraid that no matter how rotten it is inside, it is better than being gobbled up by the birds outside.

Only one element has been left out of the picture. It is one of the most important elements of the German population. It, alone of the civil population is not demoralized; it is enthusi-astic and keeps crying for more of the same. It remains, due to the many favours shown it, the most enthusiastic supporter of Adolf Hitler. I mean the German Youth; the little boys and girls. I neglected it, because one no longer sees much of it in Berlin. Most of the little boys and girls have been shipped off to nice boys' and girls' towns in Eastern Germany to get out of the air-raid areas. Hitler is very particular about them.

They are not disappointed with Nazism. Hitler has done well by them, materially and psychologically. His colourful, shallow civilization appeals to them. They enjoy, as children will, its dramatic brutality. Too little attention has been given to the little boys and girls who are growing to maturity in Germany now. For nine years now, their malleable little minds have been systematically warped. They are growing up in a mental plaster-cast, and they like it with its accompaniment of drums, trumpets and uniforms and flags. They are enthusiastic; the biggest hauls in the Winter Relief collections are always made by the Hitler Youth and the *Bund Deutscher Maedel*, the League of German Girls. I have never seen so completely military a German as the little seven-year-old boy who knocked on my door one day and, when I had opened it, snapped to rigid attention, shot his arm high and shouted at me a falsetto "Heil Hitler!" after which he asked me in the clipped sentences of a military command would I donate twenty pfennings to "support the Fuehrer and the Fatherland in this, our life-and-death struggle."

Of all the Germans, they have been most closely guarded in their camps in Eastern Germany against the effects of the Transition. The Fuehrer is still struggling to keep the other side of war a secret from them. With the exception of the soldiers, if it comes to starving, the Youth will be the last to suffer. For Hitler has plans for them, the *Herrenvolk*-in-being.

The little creatures in their brown shirts and short black trousers could be amusing if they were not so dangerous. They are dangerous; more so than a cholera epidemic. There is, so far as I know, no demoralization in their favoured ranks. They love the whole show, and are just aching to get big enough to get into the fight themselves. Frankly, I am more afraid, more terrorized, at watching a squad of these little boys, their tender faces screwed in frowns to ape their idolized leaders, on the streets of Berlin, than I am at seeing a panzer brigade of grown-up fighters speeding across the city. The grown-ups we only have to fight; but we shall have to live under the children who are being trained for their role. They are being trained every day and every hour of the day in their little barracks in Eastern Germany right now. What children of other nations read about, and thrill at, as a record of the past—feudal knighthood—they are reading about and thrilling at in the communiqués of their own High Command every day, embellished by specially trained authors-for-children. Their toys for seven years before the war have been miniature tanks, aeroplanes and guns that actually shoot, and though latest developments have robbed them of their more realistic toys, the insidious training, with cardboard war-games, has continued. Hitler Youth training, drilling and study used to be something which took place after school, extra curricula activities. Now Hitler has decreed it shall be a part of the curriculum: mornings must be given to studying the Nazi version of history and other subjects, and afternoons to Hitler Youth activity. If a boy is a good Hitler Youth, he passes, no matter what he knows about anything else. If he has not been a good, vigorous Hitler Youth, he cannot even enter a secondary school, regardless of how intelligent he is or what talent he has. That is another degree of that year of progress, 1941.

These are the elements of Germany who have not been affected by the Transition. They bear watching. If Hitler wins, they will become the gods, not only of Valhalla but of the rest of the world. They will be worse than the present gods. Hitler got most of his present Gestapo while it was on the verge of becoming adult, or after it became adult. These he has had from birth. If you think the present Gestapo is brutal, just wait until these little tykes—bred on insolence and on their innate superiority to all else in the world, and inspired by the great deeds of the "War of German Liberation," as it will be called—grow up and become the rulers of Victorious Germany and the World. In a sense, this is a war to stop little twelve-year-old Hans and Fritz. We are fighting not so much for the present as for the future. If they win, woe betide, not us so much as our children!

Last Train from Berlin, 1942

"The Worst News That I Have Encountered in the Last 20 Years"

by Robert Hagy

PITTSBURGH, PA.

The strangest development here involved America Firsters assembled in Soldiers' and Sailors' Memorial Hall in Oakland Civic Center, three miles from downtown Pittsburgh. Senator Gerald P. Nye, tall, dark, handsome North Dakotan, spoke to 2500 rank-and-filers (capacity) from a hall-wide platform above which Lincoln's Gettysburg Address is spread in huge dark letters against a dirty buff background. I was assigned to cover it for the *Post Gazette*, and just a few minutes before leaving the office, flashes and bulletins came over the AP wire on the Hawaii and Manila attacks.

I arrived at the Hall at 3:00 p.m., the time the meeting was scheduled to start, and found Nye in a two-by-four room backstage ready to go on with the local officials of the Firsters. I shoved the pasted-up news at him. Irene Castle McLaughlin, still trim wife of the dancer killed in World War I, another speaker, and Pittsburgh Chairman John B. Gordon, clustered around the Senator to read. It was the first they had heard of the war and Nye's first reaction was: "It sounds terribly fishy to me. Can't we have some details? Is it sabotage or is it open attack? I'm amazed that the President should announce an attack without giving details." Cool as a cucumber, he went on to compare the announcement with the first news of the *Greer* incident, which he termed very misleading.

I asked him what effect the Jap war should have on America First, whether it would disband. He replied: "If Congress were to declare war, I'm sure that every America Firster would be cooperative and support his government in the winning of that war in every possible way . . . but I should not expect them to disband even if Congress declared

236

war." Nye and the others then paraded on to the platform as if nothing had happened.

Although the news had come over the radio, apparently nobody in the audience knew anything, and the meeting went on just like any other America First meeting with emphasis on denouncing Roosevelt as a warmonger. Mrs. McLaughlin expressed concern for America's wives and mothers, her voice catching as she referred to Vernon Castle's not coming back; dabbed a tear from her eye as she sat down.

The next speaker was ruddy, ruralish Charlie Sipes, Pennsylvania State Senator, locally famed as a historian. Routine America First stuff until, in the midst of an attack on Roosevelt for trying "to make everything Russian appealing to the U.S.," he cried: "In fact, the chief warmonger in the U.S., to my way of thinking, is the President of the U.S.!" While the hall, decked in red-white-and-blue balcony bunting and "Defend America First" signs, was still full of roaring approval, a white-haired, heavy-set man stood up from an aisle seat well to the rear. The man, although nobody knew him and he was in mufti, was Colonel Enrique Urrutia Jr., Chief of the Second Military Area (Pittsburgh District of Third Corps Area) of the Organized Reserve. "Can this meeting be called after what has happened in the last few hours?" Colonel Urrutia—an infantryman 31 years in the Army—burst out, livid with incredulity and indignation. "Do you know that Japan has attacked Manila, that Japan has attacked Hawaii?"

Apparently the crowd took him for a plain crackpot heckler. They booed, yelled "Throw him out" and "Warmonger." Several men near Urrutia converged toward him. According to Lieutenant George Pischke, in command of a detail of ten policemen assigned to keep down disturbances which usually mark America First meetings here, the committee's blue-badged ushers "tried to manhandle" the colonel. Cops were in quick though, and Lieutenant Pischke escorted Urrutia out of the hall (through a blizzard of "warmonger" shrieks and reaching women's hands) at the latter's own request. "I came to listen," he told me in the lobby, purple with rage. "I thought this was a patriots' meeting, but this is a traitors' meeting." Inside Sipes, a cool hand, tried to restore calm, said soothingly, "Don't be too hard on this poor bombastic man.

He's only a mouthpiece for F.D.R." Then Sipes went on with his speech.

A couple of other people addressed the crowd. Finally came Nye. Still no word from leaders about the war. Nye started at about 4:45 p.m. For nearly three quarters of an hour he went through his isolationist routine. "Who's war is this?" he demanded at one point (referring to war in Europe). "Roosevelt's," chorused the rank-and-filers. "My friends," said Nye callously, "are betting 20 to 1 that if we don't stop in our tracks now, we'll be in before Great Britain gets in." Howls of laughter. A few minutes after this, I was called to the telephone. The city desk had a bulletin on Japan's declaration of war and asked me to get it to Nye. On a piece of copy paper I printed in pencil: "The Japanese Imperial Government at Tokyo today at 4:00 p.m. announced a state of war with the U.S. and Great Britain." I walked out on the platform and put it on the rostrum before Nye. He glanced at it, read it, never batted an eye, went on with his speech . . .

For 15 minutes more, Nye continued his routine, "I woke up one morning to find that we had 50 ships less, that the President had given them away despite laws forbidding it." "Treason," yelled some. "Impeach him," yelled others. Finally, at 5:45 p.m., more than two and a half hours after the meeting started, Nye paused and said: "I have before me the worst news that I have encountered in the last 20 years. I don't know exactly how to report it to you; but I will report it to you just as a newspaperman gave it to me." Slowly he read the note. An excited murmur swept through the packed hall. Nye continued: "I can't somehow believe this. I can't come to any conclusions until I know what this is all about. I want time to find out what's behind it. Previously I heard about bombings in Hawaii. Somehow, I couldn't quite believe that, but in the light of this later news, I must, although there's been many funny things before. I remember the morning of the attack on the destroyer *Greer*. The President went on the radio and said the attack on the *Greer* was without provocation; but I tell you the *Greer* shot first. That was the incident the President said was unprovoked—and that's cheating."

With that, he disposed of the new war, but more or less upset and flushed in the face, he didn't do much more than flounder through five or six more minutes of stuff about America's prime duty being to preserve democracy lest "victor and vanquished alike fall" and communism "grow in the ruins." Loud applause. "Keep your chins up," said Senator Nye and sat down. Benediction, a couple of announcements and the meeting was over.

Plowing through his fanatical followers, I gave Nye a third piece of intelligence—that Roosevelt had called a 9:00 p.m. meeting of the Cabinet and Congressional leaders. I knew he was scheduled to talk tonight at the First Baptist Church (pastor of which is pacifist) and I asked him if he intended to fly to Washington. Flustered, grim-lipped, rosy-faced, sweating, he muttered, "I must, I must try . . ." and strode quickly out of the hall talking to somebody about plane reservations. . . . Whether he couldn't get a plane or what, he nevertheless ended up keeping the church appointment, announcing he would take the train to Washington later tonight. At church, before 600 people, he was grim, bitter, defeated. "I had hoped for long that at least the involvement of my country in this terrible foreign slaughter would be left more largely to our own determination."

Then he reviewed events leading up to the war, accusing Roosevelt of "doing his utmost to promote trouble with Japan." Inferring that we were already at war with Germany, he declared: "I am not one to say my country is prepared to fight a war on one front, let alone two." When several people laughed at a reference (out of habit?) to "bloody Joe Stalin," Nye said coldly: "I am not making a humorous speech." But on the Jap attack he said: "Here is a challenge. There isn't much America can do but move forward with American lives, American blood and American wealth to the protection of our people and possessions in the Pacific."

Leaving the church, another *Post-Gazette* reporter caught him, asked what course he would prescribe for the nation. Finally he gave in completely, the fight gone out of him except for enough to make one more crack at Roosevelt. "We have been maneuvered into this by the President," he said, "but the only thing now is to declare war and to jump into it with everything we have and bring it to a victorious conclusion."

War Comes to the U.S.—Dec. 7, 1941: The First 30 Hours, 1941

President's War Message

WASHINGTON, *Dec. 8.—Following is the text of President Roosevelt's war message as he delivered it to Congress:*

Mr. Vice-President, Mr. Speaker, members of the Senate and of the House of Representatives:

Yesterday, Dec. 7, 1941—a date which will live in infamy— the United States of America was suddenly and deliberately attacked by naval and air forces of the Empire of Japan.

The United States was at peace with that nation, and at the solicitation of Japan, was still in conversation with its government and its Emperor looking toward the maintenance of peace in the Pacific.

Indeed, one hour after Japanese air squadrons had commenced bombing in the American island of Oahu, the Japanese Ambassador to the United States and his colleague delivered to our Secretary of State a formal reply to a recent American message. While this reply stated that it seemed useless to continue the existing diplomatic negotiations, it contained no threat or hint of war or armed attack.

It will be recorded that the distance of Hawaii from Japan makes it obvious that the attack was deliberately planned many days or even weeks ago. During the intervening time the Japanese government has deliberately sought to deceive the United States by false statements and expressions of hope for continued peace.

The attack yesterday on the Hawaiian Islands has caused severe damage to American naval and military forces. I regret to tell you that many American lives have been lost. In addition, American ships have been reported torpedoed on the high seas between San Francisco and Honolulu.

Yesterday the Japanese government also launched an attack against Malaya.

Last night Japanese forces attacked Hongkong.

Last night Japanese forces attacked Guam.

Last night Japanese forces attacked the Philippine Islands.

Last night the Japanese attacked Wake Island.

And this morning the Japanese attacked Midway Island.

Japan has, therefore, undertaken a surprise offensive extending throughout the Pacific area. The facts of yesterday and today speak for themselves. The people of the United States have already formed their opinions and well understand the implications to the very life and safety of our nation.

As Commander in Chief of the Army and Navy I have directed that all measures be taken for our defense.

Always will our whole nation remember the character of the onslaught against us.

No matter how long it may take us to overcome this premeditated invasion, the American people in their righteous might will win through to absolute victory.

I believe I interpret the will of the Congress and of the people when I assert that we will not only defend ourselves to the uttermost but will make it very certain that this form of treachery shall never again endanger us.

Hostilities exist. There is no blinking at the fact that our people, our territory and our interests are in grave danger.

With confidence in our armed forces—with the unbounding determination of our people—we will gain the inevitable triumph—so help us God.

I ask that the Congress declare that since the unprovoked and dastardly attack by Japan on Sunday, Dec. 7, 1941, a state of war has existed between the United States and the Japanese Empire.

New York *Herald Tribune*, December 9, 1941

"This Is For Keeps"

by Max Hill

WAR had come while I was asleep. I rolled over, only half awake, and dug deeper into the blankets the way a sleepy person does in trying to dodge a disturbing noise. I buried my face in the pillow. The knock on the door had been faint and hesitating at first. It was firm now.

"Donna-san," my patient cook said, "Domei." Kin-san didn't sound surprised. Her voice was drowsy. She was used to telephone calls like this one from Domei, the Japanese News Agency. The jangle of the bell at any hour—midnight, or two in the morning, or at six, the present hour—was part of her routine. There was no escape. I had to answer the call.

"Switch it up here," I grumbled. I huddled on the edge of the bed, shivering in the damp cold of Tokyo on a December morning. I muttered irritably to myself about what sort of message Domei could have so early. The receiver was silent a measured moment, then a voice said:

"This is Domei, the English Translation Department. We have sent the following telegram to New York for you: 'Imperial Headquarters announced at six a.m. that a state of war exists between the Anglo-American powers and Japan in the far Pacific.'"

"Jesus!" The word rasped from my quickly dry throat. The Domei man waited. I kept repeating over to myself, It's come, it's come, it's come. His chill voice interrupted:

"Do you understand?"

"Read that again," I shouted.

He did. There it was, the same phrasing—"state of war"—that Chamberlain had used in declaring England's war on Germany. On that September morning I was waiting in The AP office in Rockefeller Center for Prime Minister Chamberlain to make the radio broadcast in which he would declare war on Germany. The impressive gray bulk of the skyscrapers was turning pink with the rising sun. There were just a few devout souls on the street, hustling along toward St. Patrick's Cathedral on near-by Fifth Avenue for early mass. They didn't know, yet, that war was coming to the world, perhaps were making ready to pray to their God for peace among men of all races and creeds.

There was no gold from the sun in the east to relieve the green and gray gloom of Nagai Compound in Tokyo. The hedges and weathered, twisted trees rustled a little in the cold wind. There was no other sound. Only in my house were the lights on. The others were still calm with sleep. The tenseness flowed out of me as quickly as it had come. We needn't worry now. It had happened.

I thought, suddenly, this can't be right. I'd better check that call with Hagiwara. He runs Domei's cable desk and should know.

"Something very bad has happened," he said soberly.

Yes, the information was correct. Also, he added, Domei had heard Pearl Harbor was being bombed. He wasn't trying any longer to conceal his excitement. Of course, he said, my message had been sent urgent rate, and so would all the others till I got there.

"I'll never make it," I said.

Japanese caution came to the surface.

"Why?" he asked doubtfully. "Are there—er—people waiting outside?" He wouldn't say police.

"Not yet, but it's a cinch they will be damn soon."

I had a cold, lost feeling.

"Joe!" I shouted. No answer. "Joe!" His rumpled bed was empty. Then I remembered. Dynan had gone to a special mass. The police had probably nabbed him at the compound entrance, the only way we had of getting in and out of the place, where there was a police box, or koban. They had a 24-hour watch on our arrivals and departures, and also on our guests, no matter how trivial the visit.

My thoughts couldn't have been more confused if I had made a deliberate effort to spill them out in disorder. Should I go to the office in the Dentsu Building? What good would that do? Communication with the United States certainly was cut off. Yet, I've got to file what's happening in Tokyo to our New York office somehow. How? That's the rub. Well, they must know war is on. Even though the messages Domei sent for me were stopped by the censor.

What about the embassy? Probably double lines of soldiers there already. I might be able to crawl over the back wall. What about staying where I was? No, Domei's the best bet. They have the best chance of shoving copy through. There must be some sort of formal declaration of war, a rescript or edict from Emperor Hirohito, the stiff-legged little chap the Japanese revere. (We always used to call him "Charlie" in private.)

I started pulling on my clothes. My fingers turned clumsy. They wouldn't even do the automatic things right, such as tieing shoe laces or buttoning a shirt.

The devil with it!

Shoelaces didn't need tieing in a time like this. Let them drag. Bob Bellaire [United Press] and Max Stewart [Canadian Legation] lived next door. First of all, talk with them. Stewart had an automobile. We might be able to make the Dentsu Building in that.

I sprinted for their house, burst through the kitchen and past Yai-san, the cook, and the other sleepy, astonished servants just as the telephone started ringing.

"Wake up!" I shouted in the hall.

"Bob—Max!"

I hammered on Bob's door.

"War's been declared!"

Bob's door swung open. Stewart came grumbling out of his bedroom.

"Quit your bloody fooling," he growled.

"It's war," I said, more quietly.

Bellaire knew I wasn't, as Stewart put it, fooling. You don't go around making practical jokes about war.

Stewart, a blond hulk of a man, stood rubbing his hairy chest and arms.

"The bloody bastards," he said. "The bloody—"

"Let's get moving," I broke in. "The embassy's our best

bet, if we can get inside. We can file from there, maybe, or at least keep in touch with Domei. I'll dress and be back in ten minutes."

At home I put in a call for Eugene Dooman, counselor of the embassy, at his residence, after I found the embassy switchboard dead. Kin-san, my cook, was caught up in the swirl of excitement. She chattered away at the operator in Japanese, vigorously demanding Dooman's number. I paced the corridor, drank coffee, did a thorough job of useless fretting.

Something to do, that was what I needed; a job, trivial or not, to keep my hands busy. I took the dark, narrow stairs two at a time, pulled a small suitcase from the bedroom storage closet and flung it open on the bed. It wouldn't hold much, but enough—woolen socks and soap and shirts and my shaving kit were tossed in with nervous abandon. I thought of my telephone call.

"Dooman-san must answer," I called down the stairs. "Make servants get him up. Important. Tell them important. Must get up."

My amah pattered in with more coffee. I gulped it down. Stewart called from the roadway outside.

"Seems to me," he said, "we had bloody well stay put till they come and get us."

Bellaire joined him.

"I've got a call in for Dooman," I said. "Let's see what he says." Stewart nodded.

"Okay," Bob said. "Anyhow, I'm going to have breakfast first. We won't eat again until night, if then."

They went home. Bellaire had a taut spring in his step. Stewart, a husky 220-pounder, swung along beside him with the stout waddle of a bear. He had nothing to worry over, I thought; diplomatic immunity.

Kin-san's sharp arguing with the operator was the only sound. I dug through orderly stacks of clothing in half a dozen drawers without finding anything I wanted, and left the stuff in messy piles.

The doorbell rang, long and loud. It rang again. I bolted downstairs, hurried to the door ahead of the amah. Five solemn Japanese clustered around the entrance.

"Come in, gentlemen," I said, "I've been expecting you."

The leader, an owl-faced little fellow, looked at me suspiciously.

"We are policemen," he announced grandly, in the manner of one who has memorized words but doesn't know exactly what they mean.

I was polite in the best Japanese fashion. I bowed. None of them offered to shake hands.

"I know," I said, "I know. Come in."

They circled me with quiet authority, just to let me know who was boss. I backed into the living room without speaking. They followed me, still with their hats and overcoats on. The leader kept looking at me. I could almost see his brain working to form the words he wanted to speak. They took shape slowly.

"You are under arrest," he said haltingly.

I waited for him to continue. It was obvious they weren't paying a social call.

"Dynan-san?" he continued, in the form of a question.

"Church," I responded briefly; "he's gone to mass."

"So," the leader said.

"Just who are you, anyhow?" I asked.

No answer. They kept on watching me with narrowed brown eyes.

"I have a right to know that, at least."

The leader finally repeated, "Policemen."

I bowed with elaborate politeness, stalling for time.

"Sit down," I said, "and I'll order coffee."

The amah sidled into the room, summoned by the ring, but kept a cautious distance between herself and the officers.

"Katsu-san," I said, "coffee for the gentlemen."

We exchanged glances. She knew who the gentlemen were.

This, I thought, is a strange way to play host. We waited in uneasy silence. The officers were as perplexed as I was. I didn't know what was coming. They did, but they weren't sure how to take the next step. After all, Dynan was supposed to be there and he wasn't. That upset their routine, the detailed orders they had down on paper.

Katsu-san returned with a tray of steaming cups. Japanese express their appreciation of foods and liquids audibly, so the officers sipped the hot liquid in a series of swooshing sounds, polite to the last swish. There was no mistaking their pleasure. Coffee can't be bought in Japan; by law it's mostly browned and ground soybeans from Manchuria, a bitter and black stuff that tastes burnt no matter how expertly it is prepared. Only foreigners, with their small and jealously guarded hoards, had coffee.

"Pardon me," I said, still trying to mark time till Dooman's telephone call came through, "I'll order more."

Before anyone could object, I was out in the corridor. The kitchen door swung open and Kin-san said:

"Dooman-san."

The officer in charge, later identified as Kawasaki-san, was at my elbow. He squeezed past me. I couldn't make a break for the phone. But I could shout. I did.

"I'll have to ask the police if I can talk with him," I answered loudly.

I raised my voice to a bellow.

"War has been declared."

Kawasaki was at the telephone, slight and agile. He grabbed the receiver from Kin-san, slapped one palm over the mouthpiece. He glared at her in perturbed silence. Telephone calls to the embassy weren't on the schedule either. He said sharply in Japanese:

"Tell Dooman-san [he knew quite well, naturally, who Mr. Dooman was] that Hill-san has left the house."

Kin-san understood. She obeyed orders. That whispering cluster of officers around her had more than one unpleasant way of making her pay for any attempt at loyalty to me.

Dooman's voice came back faintly in response to her inadequate explanation:

"I understand perfectly."

Well, I had got my message across to the embassy. They would at least know I was in prison. They might even be able to let my family and The AP know what had happened.

Kawasaki was becoming impatient.

"Eat your breakfast," he ordered.

I heard Joe Dynan's cheerful whistle outside, one of the frivolous French tunes he likes so well. I wondered, desperately, how I could warn him to stay out. Why, in heaven's name, didn't the cook or amah stop him? He bustled in, thinking about nothing more serious than breakfast.

He pulled up short, eyes wide.

"Joe," I said, "we've got visitors."

He rubbed his chin and looked around the room at the five strangers.

"So I notice," he observed dryly.

"War," I whispered.

Kawasaki shoved us apart.

"Must not talk," he warned. He led Dynan into the dining room, waved him to a seat at the far end of the table. One of the detectives was showing a sudden interest in the bookshelf. He had spotted a copy of Jimmy Young's book on Japan— *Behind the Rising Sun*—which was verboten in the empire because of its caustic criticism of the police and their methods.

I had borrowed it from a friend in the embassy—and there the damned thing was to confront me at a time like this. The detective, a squat, shortsighted fellow with thick-lensed glasses, plucked it from the case and promptly settled down to some serious reading about himself and others of his ilk.

Another visitor. Bellaire broke in without pausing to ring or knock.

"Let's get—"

The sentence was never finished.

Three of my visitors scurried to his side. They shunted him off into the sun room. "Stay there," he was ordered.

Minutes later the bell signaled the arrival of another caller, this time Merrell Benninghoff, dispatched by Dooman to get to the bottom of the trouble. Embassy credentials weren't much good that day. All Benninghoff found out was that I was under arrest; that Dynan and Bellaire were being held because they were on the scene of a police investigation.

Benninghoff and I stood beside the small, hot stove which heated the living room, Benninghoff rubbing his hands together close to the welcome warmth. Again I whispered, just as I had to Dynan, "War." His skepticism alarmed me.

"Japan's declared war," I repeated.

Merrell nodded. I knew what he was thinking. All of us had been expecting some sort of break. Relations had been too

strained in the few days before December 8th to go on indefinitely that way. But war was something else. Minister Kurusu
might be recalled. Ambassador Grew might return to Washington. Yes, President Roosevelt had made a desperate plea to
Emperor Hirohito for peace in the Far Pacific. But war—?

Kawasaki interrupted us.

"We must go," he said; "eat your breakfast."

I did. Dynan and I passed fragmentary remarks across the
table. I could hear Benninghoff talking with the officers in
Japanese. They told him nothing, not even their names. It
was, they said, none of his business. They suggested, and not
too politely, that Benninghoff might just as well be on his
way; he wasn't welcome. He appeared in the dining-room
doorway.

"Tell The AP and my family what happened," I said as he
sat down in a chair across the table from me.

"All right," he replied, "but eat a good breakfast. You
won't get another meal like this for a long time."

He said good-bye. The police wouldn't let us shake hands.

I dallied over breakfast as long as I could, making it stretch
to the last minute possible of freedom. The police swilled
more coffee, smoked the one package of American cigarettes
we had in the house. All the while the one chap buried his
snub nose in Young's blunt tale of Japanese legal procedure.

Kawasaki, a model of impatience, hovered about like an inevitable shadow. He permitted me to go to my room for a
sweater and overcoat. While I was upstairs he summoned Bellaire and Dynan into the living room and gave them a glib
explanation of what was happening.

I heard him say I wasn't really under arrest, that he was
merely taking me to the police station so that I could make
arrangements for me and the other correspondents to live
under wartime conditions. This, I thought, is a funny way to
go about it.

I came downstairs. I could feel the muscles in my face taut
against my cheekbones. Bellaire had gone back to the sun
room. He sat there with arms folded hard against his chest,
his legs crossed.

I put on my hat.

"See you sometime," I said.

"You'll be back," he replied.
We looked at each other.
"This is for keeps," I said.

Exchange Ship, 1942

JAPAN ATTACKS THE PHILIPPINES:
DECEMBER 8–28, 1941

War Hits Manila

by Melville Jacoby

10 a.m., December 8

Manila has not yet digested the fact of war. Toy vendors are on the streets with newspaper extras, fully equipped soldiers are appearing, women in hotel lobbies are collecting children at their sides. Taxi drivers comment: "Not serious—not the Japanese Government's doings—only the Japanese military's mistake in Hawaii."

MacArthur's headquarters were the grimmest place at dawn this morning when the staff was aroused to face war and send troops to battle stations. Extra guards arrived at 9 a.m. as officers began donning helmets, grabbing cups of coffee and sandwiches. Newsmen were deluging the army press office with questions. Admiral Hart's headquarters were quiet. Air Force headquarters were the scene of most bustling, with helmeted men poring over maps and occasionally peering out windows to the sky.

There has been no air alarm in Manila, but it is expected by the minute. Rumors are flying everywhere. It is nearly impossible to get an operator for phone calls. High Commissioner Sayre's office is blocked off by military police. The whole thing has burst here like a bombshell, though the military had been alert over the week-end.

There is no censorship as yet: the voluntary basis is adhered to. Attacks and defense have not yet taken a definite pattern. The Davao bombing, however, signalizes the possibility of a blitz landing. The Bangkok's radio silence and lack of reports are leaving Manila cut off from news of action anywhere else in the Far East.

War feeling hit the populace about noon when there were runs on banks, grocery stores, gas stations. All taxis and garage cars were taken by the military, clogging transport systems. Our own planes overhead are drawing thousands of eyes now: they didn't earlier this morning. The High Commissioner's office is still holding hurried meetings while Mrs. Sayre's Emergency Sewing Circle called off this morning's session.

In downtown buildings, basement shelters are being put together. Building managers found an acute shortage of sandbags after Quezon's palace had bought the last remaining 20,000 to reinforce the Malacanang shelter. There was a frantic rush this morning to tape all shop windows.

Philippine Scouts, equipped with new packs and uniforms, riding in special orange busses, rounded up the majority of Jap nationals. In surprise raids they took 500 Nips from the Yokohama Specie Bank. At the Nippon Bazaar in the center of Manila, soldiers found twelve Japs barricaded inside. They broke down the glass doors, captured the twelve, found a thirteenth hiding under the counter.

11 p.m.

Sporadic reports are still making it difficult to analyze the Pacific picture, while the slowness of communications is obscuring even the Philippine situation.

The Japanese blitz strategy of thinning forces, striking simultaneously, is sure evidence of German coaching. So far the Japanese are hitting only strategic points, such as airfields. The Japanese bombing fits in with the fact that they improved accuracy immeasurably during the last three weeks of Chungking's bombing season, either by a new bombsight or tactics.

The fact that the U.S. communique this evening quotes "sanguinary losses on both sides" after the heaviest raids on Clark Field at 1:30 this afternoon, explodes the old myth that you can knock Japanese planes out of the air with toothpicks.

Manila tonight is quiet, blacked out, waiting. The war atmosphere, entirely lacking until noon, is finally setting in.

December 9

The appearance of ack-acks on the parkways, wardens, Red Crossers, brought real live war to Manila. The Filipino and American populace is getting the first taste of war, far behind even the Chinese children in Chungking, who can distinguish bomber and pursuit sounds, and know the difference between the flash of ack-acks and searchlights. In a few more days, however, the locals will become veterans and automatically go to cover instead of watching the "show."

Bleary-eyed Americans are still jovial. It is odd to see horse-drawn carriages with Americans in front of the swank Manila Hotel, while all taxis are requisitioned for military usage. Gas stations are closed temporarily following yesterday's rush. There is a terrific run on groceries and other supplies, especially food concentrates, bandages, iodine, flashlights, kotex. Many stores have bare shelves. All Japanese shops are closed while the Chinese shopkeepers are identifying their stores with home-made labels reading "Chinese."

Optimistic signs of the formerly lax Civilian Emergency Administration are the air wardens helping to direct traffic and to avoid panic, cooperating under "advice" from MacArthur's headquarters. Though people are still numbed by the actual Jap attack, they are slowly coming out with grim determination. The smoothness of the Japanese air tactics is amazing. Obviously the Japanese are planning to cripple our striking power, then invade according to blitz plans.

Although it is foolish to draw over-early conclusions, the continual daily and nightly exchange visits between Hart, Sayre and MacArthur point out the seriousness of Manila's position. Hart and MacArthur are in closest cooperation. When Hart left MacArthur's office this morning, MacArthur escorted him arm in arm to his car. Hart commented on the large passageway under the old wall in MacArthur's office, joked that it is better than anything he has to go to during raids.

December 11

Manila this evening was very tense in the blackout, the city faintly outlined in the glow from smoldering fires started in the noontime raid. It is real war now. The U.S. Army and Navy are meeting the enemy face to face, both in Manila and elsewhere as the Battle of the Philippines begins. It is not a matter of individual heroism, but a life and death struggle quickly drawing cooperation from all.

The hour-long noon raid heralded the first popping of ack-

acks over the city. The Japs are using fast, heavily-armed, two-seater pursuit jobs, attempting to draw off our fighters so that the white-winged droning bombers can come in. The bombers are kept high by ack-ack, but the thudding bombs sent Manilans scampering.

Ambulances and red-and-white flagged Red Cross cars were racing over the city after the raid, carrying casualties. Rescue workers began to show their stuff: the Filipinos were good and spirited. An interesting side-note was talking to already stubbled, bearded, grimy Yank soldiers at undisclosed posts, who saw their own comrades go down and commented: "I'd like another crack at those low-flying bastards. Write my mother I'm a hero. I'll stay here. I'll stick it out."

A grizzled, gangling corporal pulled a small piece of shrapnel from his pocket, remarking: "We sold 'em this stuff and now they're giving it back."

December 18

The same sunrise is glowing and the same sun sets over Manila Bay after a fortnight, but everything else is changed. Blackouts and daylight-saving time are changing routines. People are in bed very early, rise at dawn. Government office hours are seven to one, the most important offices getting their basements ready to work through raids.

Manila no longer looks like a Florida resort, the men in white sharkskin, the women gaily decked. Men are in checked suits, women in slacks with uncoiffured hair. Correspondents have long since shed coats and ties. Uniforms are now commonplace. Many civilian men are organized in a people's army, packing .45's, helmets and gas masks. Some women are appearing in Red Cross uniforms with gas masks on their shoulders. Other civilians are wearing a variety of armbands, such as Press, Air Warden.

The transportation problem is working out with a few taxis released by the military. Hitch-hiking is now popular for the first time in Manila's history. Horse-drawn *calesas* are disappearing, carrying evacuees over the countryside. Cycling is suddenly popular but many shops carry only Jap bikes. Everything in Manila is now on a cash basis, ending the signing of chits, which is a very old custom in the Orient.

Hotels and big buildings are swarming with women and children, moved from their homes. People eat on the hotel's lawn before the blackout, while the Army and Navy Club eats after dark, not seeing their food.

Groceries are now open with well-stocked shelves, while stores and hotels, short-handed at first, now report job hunters. Movies are open but with very small attendance. Downtown eating places are crowded with Filipino men whose womenfolk have gone to the country.

There are pup-tent encampments over the city and military patrols everywhere. Relief workers bring sandwiches and coffee to soldiers at gun stations and camps. The Red Cross has opened eight emergency hospitals with plenty of volunteer doctors. Regular hospitals are on a wartime basis, storing supplies, caring for bomb victims. Blood banks have been set up via donors, ranging from a Spanish priest to Austrian refugees. Filipinos are volunteering the services of 16,000 women for making bandages. Cattle-owners are offering their stock, one rancher having given 10,000 head.

Evacuation is still underway. Blackouts are very complete, and no one is allowed in the street after 7:30. The few bars still open draw a mixed crowd. Blackout life is systemized to early dinners. Afterwards there is usually some group singing. People wind bandages and gossip, then go to bed after laying their clothes where they can be most easily reached.

December 22

The first week of war, red flares were shooting up from all sectors, many near to military objectives. One pilot flying at night remarked that he could almost see his way to certain landing fields by following the rockets. There was frequent gunfire as the authorities rounded up most of the flare-shooters.

Manila nights are now quiet: only rarely does one see flashing lights. It is generally considered that the rockets were used to create fear and panic. Though a few Japanese nationalists shot flares, the majority were touched off by uneducated natives who did not realize what they were doing. One said a Japanese gave him a peso, knew nothing else.

Fifth-column stories are numerous yet very difficult to

check. It is known that fifth columnists snipped air alarm wires and continue to snip telephone wires, but activities to date are minor. Authorities are placing a very strong guard at all vital points. Saboteurs recently trying to fire shots at oil tanks were unsuccessful. A typical wild rumor was last week's search of the High Commissioner's premises, even under the beds, for an asserted but non-existent parachutist.

During the first few days, enemy roundups were routine, as the lists had been previously prepared. Japanese consular officials were confined to their homes under guard. Other Japanese internees include bankers, businessmen, newsmen, fishermen, etc. Their knapsacks, containing tinned goods, money and clothing, showed that they were ready. A considerable number, hearing the war news on the radio, piled into taxis and cars and drove to concentration camps, giving themselves up. The majority of Japanese women insisted on accompanying their husbands and bringing their children.

The internees are deprived of radio and writing materials. All phone lines to the concentration camps are cut and the inmates are not allowed to contact anyone, even the guards keeping their distance. The women are given good treatment and allowed to go marketing under guard. The swank Nippon Club is filled with internees, the tennis courts being covered with their washing, and children at play. Internees get two meals a day: soup with vegetables, a little meat and rice.

December 26

Manila is definitely an open city despite Tokyo's radio claim that it is heavily fortified. There are no uniforms on the streets, no rush of tanks, army trucks, no military police guards at night. The Jap bombers are not meeting a single anti-aircraft burst and are calmly crisscrossing above the city, picking objectives as if in practice flights similar to Chungking.

A glance from any window shows great spirals of black smoke as the destruction of everything of military value, including oils, is completed. Even Cavite Base is finished. Last night there was faint singing by a few Christmas carolers, blending with the sharp explosions. Flames from all sides shot a hundred feet into the air, lighting the city.

Military offices of the nearby barracks are ghostly empty after convoys of cheering soldiers left for the front, waving their arms in the "V" sign. The local Filipinos' morale is still good. They are not showing fear and are holding up better than most Americans, although everyone is on edge.

December 28

The bombings to date are severe but not exactly indiscriminate, as reported. A number of Manila's most historic churches, convents, hospitals and newspaper offices lay in the path of the bombing, which was most unfortunate. It is difficult, however, to say that the Japanese intended to destroy Santo Thomas University and Santo Domingo Church. Should Jap bombers really begin indiscriminate bombing in the future, it will be mass murder. No U.S. planes have neared Manila since it was officially declared an open city.

The bombers were lower in today's bombing than the previous 4,000 feet, sometimes making several passes at targets. You can easily hear the crackle sound of the bombs falling in mid-air and see the sun glint on them. The bombing looked like an air review as the big, silver twin-engined planes were circling in the same direction, crossing the bay, banking off at the piers, coming down in a set line over the piers and the walled city to the Pasig River at regular intervals, occasionally letting off a few rounds of machine-gun fire for intimidation purposes.

Groups of fire-fighters have been working the past 36 hours, sweaty, wet and tired, but chins up. The areas of the Walled City that were damaged were large, partly from direct hits of large bombs but more from the fires swept by the strong winds of the past two days. The damage done to churches created resentment, and it was pitiful to watch firemen take off their hats when entering the churches to fight the blazes which soared 100 feet, crackling around the figures of Christ and Mary. Some of the statuary was removed and carefully placed in the streets, the crowds standing at a distance respectfully, though the figures might be next to a basket of eggs or books. Spanish priests and a few nuns were present. The rest, evacuated previously, were disturbed when unable to remove the sacraments. It is pathetic to see the beginning look of tragedy in the faces of women hauling a few belongings and bedding from homes endangered by fire.

History in the Writing, 1945

THE SINKING OF THE REPULSE AND THE PRINCE
OF WALES: DECEMBER 10, 1941

"Prepare to Abandon Ship"

by Cecil Brown

DECEMBER 11, 5:00:16 a.m.

Here's the eyewitness story of how the *Prince of Wales* and the *Repulse* ended their careers in the South China Sea, fifty miles from the Malaya coast and a hundred and fifty miles north of Singapore.

I was aboard the *Repulse* and with hundreds of others escaped. Then, swimming in thick oil, I saw the *Prince of Wales* lay over on her side like a tired war horse and slide beneath the waters. I kept a diary from the time the first Japanese high level bombing started at 11:15 until 12:31 when Captain William Tennant, skipper of the *Repulse* and Senior British Captain afloat, shouted through the ship's communications system, "All hands on deck, prepare to abandon ship. May God be with you."

I jumped twenty feet to the water from the up end of the side of the *Repulse* and smashed my stop watch at thirty-five and a half minutes after twelve. The sinking of the *Repulse* and the *Prince of Wales* was carried out by a combination of high level bombing and torpedo attacks with consummate skill and the greatest daring. I was standing on the flag deck slightly forward amidships when nine Jap bombers approached at ten thousand feet strung in a line, clearly visible in the brilliant sunlit sky. They flew directly over our ship and our anti-aircraft guns were screaming constantly.

Just when the planes were passing over, one bomb hit the water beside where I was standing, so close to the ship that we were drenched from the water spout. Simultaneously another struck the *Repulse* on the catapult desk, penetrating the ship and exploding below in a marine's mess and hangar. Our planes were subsequently unable to take off. At 11:27 fire is raging below, and most strenuous efforts are under way to control it. All gun crews are replenishing their ammunition and are very cool and cracking jokes. There are a couple of jagged holes in the funnel near where I am standing.

It's obvious the Japs flew over the length of the ship, each dropping three bombs so that twenty-seven bombs fell around us at first in their attack. Brilliant red flashes are spouting from our guns' wells. The *Prince of Wales* is half a mile away. Destroyers are at various distances throwing everything they have into the air. A splash about two miles off our port beam may be anti-aircraft but we are uncertain. At 11:40 the *Prince of Wales* seems to be hit. She's reduced her speed. Now they're coming to attack us. The communications system shouts "stand by for barrage." All our guns are going. We are twisting and snaking violently to avoid torpedoes. The Japs are coming in low, one by one in single waves. They're easy to spot. Amid the roar from the guns aboard the *Repulse* and the pom-poms of anti-aircraft fire, we are signalled, "We've a man overboard."

Two Jap aircraft are approaching us. I see more of them coming with the naked eye. I again count nine. They're torpedo bombers and are circling us about a mile and half or two miles away. 11:45—now there seems to me more bombers but they are circling like vultures at about one thousand feet altitude. The guns are deafening. The smell of cordite is almost suffocating and explosions are ear shattering and the flashes blinding. The officer beside me yells, "Here comes a tin fish."

A Jap torpedo bomber is heading directly for us, two hundred yards above the water. At 11:48 he's less than five hundred distant, plowing onward. A torpedo drops and he banks sharply and his whole side is exposed to our guns but instead of driving away he's making a graceful dive toward the water. He hits and immediately bursts into flame in a gigantic splash of orange against the deep blue sky and the robins-egg blue water. Other planes are coming, sweeping low in an amazing suicide effort to sink the *Repulse*.

Their daring is astonishing, coming so close you can make out the pilot's outline. One coming in at 11:48 to our starboard just dropped a torpedo. A moment later I hear shouts of joy indicating that he was brought down but I didn't see that. We also claim we brought down two high level bombers

previously but I didn't see these crash. At least at the moment
I have no recollection of seeing them.

At 12:01 another wave of torpedo bombers is approaching.
They are being met with everything we've got except our
fourteen inchers. Beside me the signal officer flashes word
from Captain Tennant to the *Prince of Wales*. "We eluded all
torpedos this second attack." It's fascinating to watch our
tracer bullets speeding toward the Jap bombers. 12:03: we've
just shot down another torpedo bomber who is about four
hundred yards away and we shot it out. All of its motors are
afire and disintegrating pieces of the fuselage are flying about.
Now it disappears over the surface of the water into scrap.
The brilliant orange from the fire against this blue sky is so
close it's startling. All the men are cheering at the sight. It's
so close it seems you could almost reach out and touch the
remains of this Jap bomber.

At 12:15 the *Wales* seems to be stopped definitely. I've been
too busy to watch the attacks against her but she seems in
utmost difficulty. Her guns are firing constantly and we are
both twisting. One moment the *Wales* is at our starboard, the
next it's at our port. I'm not watching the destroyers but they
have not been subjected to air attacks. The Japs are throwing
everything recklessly against the two capital ships.

There's fire aboard us, it's not out. I just saw some firemen
and fire control parties. The calmness of the crews is amazing.
I have constantly roved from one side of the flag deck to the
other during the heavy firing and attacks and the cool precision of all hands has seemed unreal and unnatural. Even when
they are handing up shells for the service guns, each shell is
handed over with a joke. I never saw such happiness on men's
faces. This is the first time these gun crews have been in action in this war and they are having the time of their lives.
12:20: I see ten bombers approaching us from a distance. It's
impossible to determine whether this will be a high level attack or another torpedo bomber attack. "Stand by for barrage" comes over the ship's communication system.

One plane is circling around, it's now at three or four hundred yards approaching us from the port side. It's coming
closer, head on, and I see a torpedo drop. It's streaking for
us. A watcher shouts, "Stand by for torpedo" and the tin fish

is streaking directly for us. Some one says: "This one got us." The torpedo struck the side on which I was standing about twenty yards astern of my position. It felt like the ship had crashed into a well-rooted dock. It threw me four feet across the deck but I did not fall and I did not feel any explosion. Just a very great jar. Almost immediately it seemed we began to list and less than a minute later there was another jar of the same kind and the same force, except that it was almost precisely the same spot on the starboard side.

After the first torpedo, the communication system coolly announced: "Blow up your life belts." I was in this process when the second torpedo struck and the settling ship and the crazy angle were so apparent I didn't continue blowing my belt.

That the *Repulse* was doomed was immediately apparent. The communication system announced, "Prepare to abandon ship. May God be with you." Without undue rush we all started streaming down ladders, hurrying but not pushing. It was most difficult to realize I must leave the ship. It seemed so incredible that the *Repulse* could or should go down. But the *Repulse* was fast heeling over to port and walking ceased to become a mode of locomotion. I was forced to clamber and scramble in order to reach the side. Men were lying dead around the guns. Some were half hidden by empty shell cases. There was considerable damage all around the ship. Some of the men had been machine gunned. That had been unquestioned fact.

All around me men were stripping off their clothes and their shoes and tossing aside their steel helmets. Some are running alongside the three quarters exposed hull of the ship to reach a spot where they can slide down the side without injuring themselves in the jagged hole in the ship's side. Others are running to reach a point where they have a shorter dive to the water. I am reluctant to leave my new portable typewriter down in my cabin and unwilling to discard my shoes which I had made just a week before. As I go over the side the *Prince of Wales* half a mile away seems to be afire but her guns are still firing the heaviest. It's most obvious she's stopped dead and out of control due to her previous damage.

The air attack against the *Prince of Wales* carried out the same scheme directed against the *Repulse*. The Japs were able to send two British capital ships to the bottom because of first, a determined air torpedo attack and, second, the skill and the efficiency of the Japanese operations. It's apparent that the best guns and crews in the world will be unable to stem a torpedo bombing attack if the attackers are sufficiently determined.

According to the best estimate obtainable, the Japs used in their operations against both the *Wales* and the *Repulse* eighty-six bombers; eighteen high level bombers and approximately twenty-five torpedo bombers against the *Repulse* and probably an equal number against the *Prince of Wales*. In the case of the *Wales*, however, the Japs started the torpedo bombing instead of initial high level bombing. In the first attack, one torpedo hit the *Wales* in the after-part. Some survivors believe the *Wales* was hit twice in the initial attack, then followed two more torpedo attacks, both successful. The final attack on the *Wales* was made by high level bombers around ten thousand feet. When that attack came, the *Wales* was sinking fast and everyone threw himself down on deck.

Most of the guns were unmanageable as a result of the list and the damage. I jumped into the water from the *Repulse* at 12:35. While I was in the water, the *Wales* continued firing for some time. The *Wales* suffered two direct hits by bombs on the deck. Like the attack on the *Repulse*, the Japs flew across the length of the *Wales* in a single line, each bomber dropping a stick. One officer said a child of six could see some of them were going to hit us. During the entire action Admiral Tom Phillips, Commander in Chief of the Far East Fleet, and Captain Leech, Skipper of the *Prince of Wales*, were on the bridge.

While the torpedo bombers were rushing in toward the *Wales*, dropping tin fish and machine gunning the decks, Phillips clambered up on the roof of the bridge and also atop the gun turrets to see better and to direct all phases of the action.

When it was apparent that the *Wales* was badly hit, the Admiral issued an order to the flag officer for the destroyer then lying alongside close by. "Signal to Singapore to send tugs to tow us." Evidently up to that moment, Phillips was not convinced that the *Wales* was sinking. The last order issued by

Phillips came at approximately 1:15. It said, "Blow up your life belts."

Later the ship was under water. Phillips and Leech were the last from the *Wales* to go over the side and they slid into the water together. It's probable that their reluctance to leave the ship until all possible men had left meant their death, since it's most likely they were drawn down by the suction when the *Wales* was on her side and then settled at her stern with her bow rising into the air.

Swimming about a mile away, lying on top of a small stool, I saw the bow of the *Wales*. When Phillips signalled to ask Singapore to send tugs, the *Wales* already had four torpedoes in her. Like the *Repulse*, the *Wales* gun crews were very cool and although many guns were no longer effective the crew stood beside them. When the final high level bombing attack came, only three guns were capable of firing, except the fourteen-inchers which naturally did not go into action. I did not meet Phillips but last week when I visited the *Wales* at the naval base, I had a long talk with Captain Leech. He's a jovial convivial, smiling officer who gave me the impression of the greatest kindliness and ability. The *Wales* carried a complement of seventeen hundred; the *Repulse* twelve hundred and fifty officers and ratings. When the *Wales* sank, the suction was so great it ripped off the life belt of one officer more than fifty feet away. A fortunate feature of the sinking of both the *Repulse* and the *Wales* was that neither blew up.

Since the tide was strong and there was an extremely powerful suction from both ships, it was extremely difficult to make any progress away from the ship in the thick oil. The gentle, quiet manner in which these shell-belching dreadnaughts went to their last resting place without exploding, was a tribute of gratitude from two fine ships for their fine sailors.

From Pearl Harbor into Tokyo, 1945

"Tanks and Cannons Standing Starkly in the Snow"

by Larry Lesueur

December 16

We divided into two convoys of white-painted Zis limousines. The auto seats were draped with heavy, colorful Bokhara rugs. I was in a car with a censor and two Red Army officers.

A cutting wind arose with the sun as we drove north along the Leningrad Chaussée. The broad snow-covered highway was filled with hundreds of black-coated workers plodding to the trolley lines even at this hour. Their factories were far out on the city's outskirts. Our cars passed through barricade after barricade. They were huge blockhouses of rough-hewn logs with a narrow, easily closed passageway between. They were in no way as ornate as the solid concrete "dragon's teeth" roadblocks the British had set up the year before on the Dover Road during the Battle of Britain. The Russians had just cut down the near-by trees and joined them together in a series of old-fashioned stockades and wooden forts.

As we bounced north along the heavily ice-rutted Leningrad road, we passed scores of stolidly marching peasant women going back to their homes in newly freed settlements. They had their meager belongings piled high on wooden sleds and dragged them along by ropes. Here and there we saw peasants slowly dragging small sleds with only coffins on them.

We were forced to a skidding stop once to make way for a column of rumbling Soviet tanks, white-painted for camouflage against the snow. Then our two cars again took their place in the endless line of wooden sleds loaded down with yellow fodder and ammunition. Their small, sturdy Siberian horses were driven by expressionless Red Army men whose faces were set against the bitter edge of the wind. They were going north, too, toward the front.

266

At the first dynamited bridge we turned off the asphalt onto a snowy wood road. A group of Russian sentries scrutinized our passes and then pulled up a crossbar to allow our cars to pass.

We skidded and spun our wheels through a dark pine forest whose towering trees almost hid the light of the day. Here and there we passed a clearing with battered German tanks and cannons standing starkly in the snow. This was the kind of country the Battle of Moscow had raged in. This was the high-water mark of the German advance. We were about twenty-five miles from the city limits of Moscow. The German failure must have been the greatest disappointment for an invading army in history. Hitler's troops could look down the long, straight road that separated them from the Soviet capital. Emergency bridges had been thrown over the tank traps. Dug to a depth of some fifteen feet by the sweat of the mobilized population during the fall, they were now deep with snow. Ice-glazed barbed wire ran across lakes and fields. It was evident that certain areas had been carefully prepared in advance. The defenses were laid out with mathematical precision in the areas in which invading tanks would have to travel to skirt the thick woods. One of the types of anti-tank obstacles in which the Red Army had placed most faith consisted of six-foot lengths of iron rail bolted together in the shape of a gigantic child's jack. No matter which way a tank approached them, they presented a heavy spike. They were difficult to blow up with artillery fire because they had no flat surfaces to catch the blast.

Then we passed the first burnt-out villages. Their charred ruins marred the fresh whiteness of the snow. The only upright objects were the gaunt and blackened chimneys that stood out forlornly. Some of the wrecked foundations still smoked. I watched peasant women who had dragged their sleds of household goods all the way from Moscow, picking about in the wreckage. They had found they had no place to come home to. The older women were weeping silently.

At the roadside was a small graveyard of neatly lettered crosses. We stopped our cars to examine them. The workmanship of the crosses was excellent. The names and ages of the fallen Germans had been carefully burnt in the fresh wood.

Many had the outline of an iron cross inscribed below their names. It was remarkable how young the men had been. Their recorded ages averaged from nineteen to twenty-three years. The Soviet colonel who rode with us remarked: "We estimated that 85,000 of those young Germans died in their two offensives against Moscow."

On one side where a number of German and Russian tanks were strewn in an open field, like a junk yard, the surrounding forest was devastated as by a hurricane. There were broken branches everywhere and trees lay tumbled like jackstraws on the ground, evidence of the terrific artillery fire and the death struggles of the tanks. The blackened wreckage of the villages was appalling. Here, too, one or two peasant women poked silently in the ruins of their houses, attempting to salvage what they could. There were only charred, smoking embers.

Our small convoy stopped often to give marching troops the right of way. They were marching just as they had in Napoleon's day, slogging through the snow and bitter cold, on foot. Many of the Russian soldiers wore no steel helmets, only their warm sheepskin hats with thick earlaps. Only a few wore white-painted steel helmets over a lighter peaked hat. I could see that the Red Army reserves were short of this equipment, but the Russians seemed to have no shortage of artillery. Gun after gun wheeled past us, the lighter ones pulled by horses, the heavier by tractors. They had been rushed to the front; no time had been lost to paint them white. Still green-painted as they had come from the factory, they jolted past the white-painted broken German guns, shattered at the roadside, their spiked muzzles splayed out like the petals of a flower.

As we proceeded, the gross rumble of artillery became more insistent. We passed an entire brigade of Red Army men who looked as though they had been marching for days. Their faces were black with fatigue. They were dragging their feet in exhaustion. Several times we saw men stumble as they plodded forward and fall unconscious on the snow. The columns never stopped moving, but I saw fellow soldiers pick up their companions and place them, senseless, on passing sleds loaded with hay. I recalled that many of Napoleon's men had frozen to death on the retreat from Moscow and wondered what would be the fate of these exhausted Red Army men, for they had no blankets. I later learned that during the winter the Red Army carried no blankets, but slept in their heavy greatcoats. When they bivouacked for the night at a village which the Germans had leveled by fire, they quickly dug into the fire-softened earth, next to the foundations, and hollowed dugouts of snow and branches. Throwing a tarpaulin over the top and pulling a stove inside with them, they huddled together for warmth and slept like so many Russian bears.

I was surprised to note that even these columns on forced march were clean-shaven. Our escorting colonel said that Soviet officers order their men to shave each day for discipline's sake. I asked how they managed it in sub-zero weather. He explained that they heat snow water and work in pairs, the men shaving one another simultaneously.

I watched the living soldiers pass by the dead at the roadside without a glance, and the dead looked scarcely human. They resembled wax mannequins thrown from a show-window, lying about in grotesque, inhuman postures, arms pointing toward the sky, legs frozen as though they were running. Their faces were bloodless, waxy white. The clean, cold air carried no taint of decomposition. But sometimes the wind brought us a whiff of acrid cordite smoke and the soot of a burnt village.

We finally skidded to a halt in the town of Solnetchnogorsk. We were numb from the cold as we stiffly clambered out of the cars and walked over to watch a group of Russian civilians digging a large hole in the frozen ground of the village square. A pile of stiff bodies lay alongside the hole. They were Red Army men who had died to free the city. Solnetchnogorsk, or Sunnyside Hill, had been the first sizable town to be recaptured from the Germans in the astounding winter offensive that saved the capital. It was here that the hitherto invincible blitzkrieg had finally gone into reverse. As we stood shivering in the street, I listened to the Russian officers say: "The city is virtually unharmed, except for a few houses shattered by gunfire. The Germans were surprised in the middle of the night by a Russian outflanking column and they fled, leaving their belongings, and without time for their destruction squads to set fire to the houses."

We were led into a large, one-story frame house, the home of the village druggist. German officers had been quartered here forty-eight hours before. The druggist's wife, Mrs. Garane Bagranov, was a slender, dark, sweet-faced woman, born in Armenia and married to a Russian. She spoke slowly and without emotion.

"Six German medical orderlies were billeted in my house," she said. "They took all the beds, while my daughters and I slept in the kitchen. They didn't molest us because they were afraid of their officers. They went into our drugstore and ransacked it for all the things they could use, like toothbrushes, soap, and perfume. They couldn't read the labels on the drug bottles because they were in Russian, so they threw the bottles on the floor and smashed them. Everything, children's cough medicines, everything. I told them to stop, but they answered: 'We're the bosses here now,' and the breaking of bottles went on. Finally I complained to their officers. They cautioned the men to stop the breakage, but as soon as the officers left the house, the men went back to the drugstore and began smashing things again. They seemed to be mad at the bottles because the labels were in Russian."

Mrs. Bagranov paused and her dark eyes flashed angrily as she thought of the wreckage.

"I ran into the store again," she said, "and told them they must stop. We wouldn't have any medicines left for the winter. But they brushed me aside and went on looking for perfume and broke the bottles they couldn't identify. I went into the street without my coat on and told their officers. Later one of them came in and tacked up a sign. It said that the drugstore was now the property of the German Army. Then the soldiers stopped breaking things.

"After about a week I knew something was happening in front of Moscow. More German soldiers were coming back from the front than were going forward. Then one day the two young Nazi officers I had complained to came into the house and sat at my kitchen table. One of them began to sob. The other rested his head in his hands and began to cry, too. I knew in my heart what had happened. They were retreating from Moscow. Next night while they were asleep, an officer came bursting in the front door spreading the alarm. The Red Army was coming."

Mrs. Bagranov's voice rose with excitement.

"All of them, officers, soldiers, ran around wildly, throwing their things into bags. Their trucks and motorcycles were making a deafening noise outside. Then a few minutes later all was quiet. I opened the door into the dining-room where they slept. They had all gone. We were free again."

The old grandmother, who had stood silent while her daughter spoke, said in a quaver: "They took all our blankets."

I asked the silver-haired "babushka" what the Germans had done to her.

"Nothing," she said. "They just let me starve. But I had some dried bread hidden under my pillow and I lived on that."

The women went back into the kitchen to prepare supper and I leaned against the warm chimney, trying to get the chill of the long drive out of my bones. We would have given a lot for a drink of vodka, but the censor who had the vodka supply said firmly: "In Russia we never drink vodka unless we eat something with it. You must wait."

Shivering, we waited until the table was set with a hot meal. The food had been requisitioned from the Red Army supplies. There was soup, herring, browned beef, and little Russian cakes. The vodka was served in pitchers. All through the night we toasted the Red Army and Hitler's crushing disappointment. I wisely picked out the bed nearest the chimney, and after I lost count of the toasts in vodka, I threw myself on it and fell asleep. When I awakened next morning, I was still dressed, but someone had kindly thrown a quilt over me. It was still dark when I began to stumble toward the kitchen for water. I heard the sound of weeping. I realized that the arrival of the distinguished guests, the foreign corerspondents, in this war-torn village had once more forced the poor old grandmother to suffer almost as much as she had under the Germans. She had been put out to sleep on the ice-cold porch.

At dawn we left to follow the advance of the Red Army. The road wound through forests of dark pines, their boughs sagging under their fluffy white load. Deep in the forest we could see Russian cavalry troops bivouacked for the day. They moved only at night on their raids into the enemy rear. We turned sharply sometimes at strange noises in the somber forests, caused by pine boughs slipping their load of snow. Looking more closely, we could see white-cowled ski soldiers sitting around tiny fires, brewing endless tea and waiting for darkness to fall. They looked like cowled Ku Klux Klansmen in their hide-out.

Here and there the small steppe horses of Russia cropped their fodder noisily in the dark recesses of the woods. The war was hard on horses. All along the roadside their frozen bodies lay in snow-covered blasted chunks. I saw several uncomplaining beasts limping wounded and frightened in the forest. Some of them were lying down in the snow to freeze and die. There was no time to think of wounded horses in this gigantic battle that was deciding the fate of millions of men and women.

Once we passed an entire wood crowded with monstrous lumps of white tanks in hiding, waiting to move up closer to the front under cover of darkness. Some of the Red Army men, woodsmen all, had thrown up neat-looking walls and roofs of rough hewn logs over dugouts as though they planned to stay in this area for a while.

We pushed our car up hills and out of snowdrifts, and once we had to ask the help of a military tractor to get us up the snow-covered side of a steep, ice-glazed slope. German signs were still nailed to the trees, pointing to command posts and field headquarters.

We passed one village in which only half the houses had been burned down. The Red Army men had left the German signs where they stood, as a reminder to themselves and to the inhabitants. It was interesting to note the difference in the German spelling and the Russian for the same towns. In Latin characters the Germans had placed large signs on the sides of peasants' homes, as guides to their own map-readers.

As the sound of artillery grew heavy, we drew up in a clearing in the midst of a heavy forest where, in a wood-cutters' camp, a squad of Russian nurses had set up a casualty clearing station. The buxom, good-natured-looking girls were glad to see us and collected around our cars. They all carried revolvers slung at their hips. We asked the highest-ranking girl, a cool-eyed blonde with her sheepskin hat thrust back over her forehead, if her girls were warmly enough clothed. She smiled. "Warm?" she mocked. Then she began to unbutton her heavy overcoat and conducted our eyes through layer after layer until she suddenly drew her overcoat together again with a loud laugh. From my rather unfavorable position on the wrong side of the car, I could get only a glimpse of what she was wearing—a heavy overcoat, a fur vest, a heavy army shirt, and what appeared to be pink heavy underwear. I wasn't sure. At any rate, we knew now what made the girls look so plump. It was layer after layer of clothing.

The blonde captain of nurses had already been wounded twice, once in 1939 during the three-month Japanese border war and now in this war by the Germans at Lwow.

The nurses were in high spirits over the advance, and when one of the smiling girls learned we were Americans, she jumped on the running board of our car as we started forward and said with fervor: "I always wanted to go to America. Won't you take me with you?" We all wished we could.

The Red Army telegraph linesmen were busy on every side as we moved forward. The Germans in their retreat had sawed down each telegraph pole near its base. Tangled lines were strewn in a jumble all over the roadside. The linesmen, like the bridge-builders, were felling the trees themselves, trimming them, and putting up new poles with remarkable speed.

The countryside was changing now from flat forests with only occasional rises to heavily wooded hills. It grew warmer and began to snow. The thick flakes muffled everything, even the bellow of the guns up ahead. On the opposite side of the road came the wounded on horse-drawn sleds, often with a nurse sitting alongside, holding down the edges of the wind-blown blanket. I remembered what the nurses had said: "To fall down wounded in the snow in this temperature means death within minutes unless you cover the men with blankets." I understood the meaning of some of the boxes mounted on sleds, like small bungalows, that came creaking by. They were hot-boxes with stoves inside. Lucky men had been placed inside these to make the trip from the front line to the casualty clearing station.

Once a brigade of youngsters passed us by. They were no more than nineteen or twenty and I knew this would be only their first action. Their pink, boyish faces were full of wonder as they looked at the wounded going the other way, at the wrecked trucks and German spiked guns and the snow sifting around the stiff bodies at the roadside.

On either side of this road of death were untrodden fields, fenced in by small boards with death's-heads painted on them. They were mined areas as yet uncleared. The officer told us that the Germans were strewing thousands of mines in their retreat, and their method was both simple and deadly. Almost no work was needed because the snow concealed the explosives from sight and the ever falling, impersonal flakes disguised all traces.

Once we passed half a dozen German trucks loaded with rubber boats and tens of paddles. The rivers were long since frozen and it was evident how long the Germans had been held up at this one position, until the rivers of autumn were winter-locked by ice.

We came to the rendezvous where we were to interview General Vlasov, commanding the area. We knew he was simply taking over the last German headquarters as he advanced. But although the sign on the unpainted frame house said plainly "German Divisional Headquarters," there was no one inside. General Vlasov had moved forward again to keep up with the advance of his troops.

A few miles more through the snow-covered forest and we came to a tiny settlement with the unusual name of "Burnt Village." Strangely enough, it was one of the few villages the Germans had not gutted. Here the work of salvaging German war equipment was going on hurriedly. Red Army men were busy gathering up rifles and tommy guns from behind houses and in barns and attics and depositing them in piles on the village square. The Germans had retreated from here within the space of hours.

One happy-looking Red Army man was put-putting through the snow on a captured German motorcycle. When I asked him why it made so much noise, he said gleefully: "All German equipment makes a lot of noise. They think it will scare us."

The Germans had not stopped to bury their dead in this village. Green-gray bodies lay rigid in the snow.

We entered the warmth of an old farmhouse which was now the Soviet Divisional Headquarters. The Germans had vacated it so hurriedly that their excellent maps of the area still remained on the walls. General Vlasov, commander of the Solnetchnogorsk front, was somewhere around but couldn't be found just now, they told us. Instead we were asked by a member of his staff if we would like to see a German prisoner who had just been captured. In a few moments he was led in—a fine-looking soldier.

He was Corporal Albert Koehler of Aachen. He was undaunted, even in the presence of all these Soviet officers and foreign correspondents. We were permitted to question him ourselves. He said bravely that he had been captured going back to rescue prisoners, and the Russian officers nodded agreement. He wore the field-gray double-breasted overcoat that has been standard for the Germans in all their campaigns. It was really not much more than a heavy topcoat. His natty garrison hat was of cotton cloth and his boots the serviceable German jackboots, but they were not suitable for this land of snow and ice. We asked Corporal Koehler if he had been cold.

"No," he replied reluctantly, "not until just recently."

We asked him what equipment he had been issued for winter.

"All of us got a scarf to wear under our hats and a pair of gloves.

Someone inquired why he was fighting against the Russians. Koehler looked surprised and said: "I'm a soldier. I go where I am sent."

"Why are you fighting?"

"To make Germany bigger."

"What do you think of the entrance of America into the war?"

"I heard talk of this on December 14, but we were too busy retreating to discuss it at length."

We thanked Corporal Koehler. He clicked his heels and turned to leave, the very model of a German NCO. One of the intelligence officers whispered to me: "He must be a Hitler Youth."

A violet gloom was falling over the snow as the sun sank behind the wooded hills. Red Army men were busy up and down the streets of the little village, removing engines from the abandoned German trucks, searching through wrecked staff cars for valuable papers; other details were counting German machine guns, tommy guns, rifles, and bayonets. Mounds of captured war material were growing on the snow. I walked over to examine some of the German trophies, hoping to pick up a tommy gun for myself, but the Russian sentry, although he knew full well that a civilian could be at the front only on special duty, threatened me menacingly with his bayonet. I knew he was under orders to let no one approach the pile.

At another point I watched three Red Army men dismantle the motor from a huge German troop-carrier. The speed with which they worked in the sub-zero temperature amazed me. I studied them as they worked and heard them curse as wrenches slipped on frozen bolts. I had more or less expected to see kindly, patient peasant soldiers going about their work by rote, but these men were as sharp and as full of comment about the difficulties of their job as any mechanics I ever encountered in an American garage. I could see that the cold was just as hard for them to bear as it was for the German troops, in full retreat a few miles away.

Here, I thought, was a small cross-section of the Red Army—hard-looking, muscular, young men who would obviously fight hard for an officer they respected and who had confidence in one whose technical knowledge they trusted. I realized that the idea they were men whom the Russian High Command could afford to use extravagantly was as ill-founded as the legend that Russian soldiers had to have their bayonets welded to their rifles so that they could not ruin them by chopping wood. One of the most impressive sights among the combat troops that still marched through the darkening village was the well-oiled cleanliness of their arms, not an easy accomplishment under these tough conditions. The single-mindedness of these men could not be confused with mere simplicity, I thought. They were elated with the defeat of the Germans at Moscow, but from their talk I gathered that they would have been just as critical of the conduct of the war if they were losing. Their curiosity about the German machines was boundless. They poked about in the inside of tanks and troop-carriers like boys on a treasure-hunt.

I could see that the Red Army was really a melting-pot army like the American Army. It had none of that look of race which belonged to the armies of Britain and France. Here were light-haired Ukranians, dark-skinned Armenians and Georgians, blue-eyed Russians, white-toothed and flashing-eyed Uzbeks, and blond Cossacks from the Don. These were seasoned troops. Their confidence in their own abilities was written on their faces. Their attitude was that the Germans had lost the capacity to surprise or frighten them.

As I watched, the little knots of soldiers suddenly stiffened and I followed their gaze to where two finely dressed officers approached through the snow. They were General Vlasov and General Korol, the Divisional Political Commissar. Dressed in handsomely cut long overcoats that reached the ankles of their white felt boots, they gave the impression of great height, emphasized by their tall gray astrakhan hats. With a smile they approached us, and automatically we walked toward them, followed by a group of obviously admiring Red Army men. The soldiers had no fear of their commanding officers, but seemed drawn to them as an admiring college boy is drawn to a respected professor.

"*Zdrastviti tovarishchi* (Good day, comrades)," shouted General Vlasov in greeting, and their answer, "*Zdrastviti General*," re-echoed in the snowy street. When it appeared that the general wished to talk to the Americans, the Red Army men withdrew quickly to their work again.

We shook hands with General Vlasov, who looked more like a teacher than a soldier, so tall that his high gray astrakhan hat with the crimson and gold crown made him tower. He wore gold-rimmed spectacles at the tip of his nose. His eyes had a look of bright elation as he told us his men would capture Volokolomsk this very night. "I have sent my ski battalion out to surround the city," he said. "Von Strauss is trying to avoid combat with us. The Germans hold only until they find themselves in danger of being outflanked. Then they'll send their destruction brigades around, armed with

gasoline and torches, to fire every house so we'll have no protection when we come in." Pointing to the west where a faint
red glow was lighting the sky, he said: "Look, we've already
outflanked Volokolomsk."

I asked General Vlasov where he expected the Germans to
hold a line for the winter. He replied: "I am not planning my
offensive on the basis that the Germans will hold somewhere.
I intend to drive them as far as I can."

I persisted in my questioning. "Do you think they'll try to
hold at Smolensk?" At the word "Smolensk" General Vlasov
looked away and repeated: "Smolensk—that's a different
story." I knew then that I must not expect too much of
Russia's first winter offensive.

We bundled ourselves into the cars and General Vlasov cautioned us against losing the road and running into a mined
area. We thanked him, and our cars spun their wheels on the
hard snow.

As the sun went down, the cold became intense. We heard
cracks in the forest, sharp as rifle-shots, as the sap froze in the
trees. Until eleven o'clock we pushed our car up and down
the snowy hills, making room time and again for the forward
movement of sleds and marching troops. The night march of
the troops, concealed in daylight, had begun.

Finally, we reached our former sleeping-quarters at Solnetchnogorsk. The druggist's wife and her daughters were
not surprised at our late arrival. No time was too late for them
to prepare a hot supper. The same well-rounded waitress sent
down from Moscow was there to serve us. I gazed around the
dining-room as I ate. This house on Russia's "Sunnyside
Hill" was not so different from homes I had known in Indiana. Above the old shawl-draped piano was a picture I recognized. It was none other than the "Three Little Pigs." I
wondered how these Walt Disney characters had got this far
east. A guitar hung near the fireplace, and on the mantelpiece
was a gilt ikon of St. Nicholas, patron saint of Russia.

With a Russian delight in lavishness, our hostess set the
table with all the Red Army provender of the night before,
including unopened boxes of candy, one for each of us. As
the atmosphere grew more friendly, a correspondent suggested that he and the pretty waitress take a walk outside in

the snow to see the stars. The Russian colonel shook his head earnestly and said: "The last three men who took a walk in the moonlight here never came back. They were blown up by mines." We went to bed.

For breakfast we had the traditional Russian meal of "kasha," or brown whole-grain barley, with a piece of butter melting atop it. On the table again were the same large boxes of candy. I didn't realize that to the Russians candy at breakfast was no novelty. They ate it instead of sugar, putting a piece in their mouths while they sipped their hot tea.

I took a last look at the church of Solnetchnogorsk as our cars pulled away. It was from the bell-tower of that gold and blue tulip dome that the Germans first announced they could see, through spy glasses, the towers of Moscow.

We were tired, silent, and thoughtful as our cars rolled back along the four-lane Leningrad Highway, along the brief span of ice-rutted pavement that had stretched immutable and un-attainable for the conquerors of western Europe.

Twelve Months That Changed the World, 1943

Malay Jungle War

by Cecil Brown

Christmas night, Singapore
By cable

"A BRITISH soldier is equal to ten Japanese, but unfortunately there are eleven Japanese." That remark, made to me by a Tommy wounded at Sungei Patani, synthesizes one reason for the present grave situation in Malaya.

But superiority in numbers is not the only reason. There are others equally important, perhaps more so. Whether Singapore will successfully resist, how well she will stand up under continuous air attacks, whether panicky civilians will impede military operations depends on how well Singapore is prepared, mentally and physically, for war. We can't compare the probabilities here with London's ability to stand and take it. The whites here are less than 1% of the population. Malaya has her back to the wall and the retention of Singapore is a touch-and-go affair due to the incredible and unbelievable unpreparedness right up to the moment when Jap bombs gave Singapore's lethargy the first shock in more than a half-dozen complacent decades.

The atrophying malady of dying-without-death, best known as the "Singapore mentality," largely helped to bring the Japanese more than 125 miles inside Malaya. For civilians this walking death is characterized by an apathy to all affairs except making tin and rubber, money, having stengahs between 5 and 8 p.m., keeping fit, being known as a "good chap" and getting thoroughly "plawstered" on Saturday night. Singapore thus far represents the pinnacle of examples of countries which are unprepared, physically and mentally, for war.

Seeking reasons for military unpreparedness, it would, in part, be unfair to lay the blame on Brooke-Popham and Admiral Layton. It is reasonable to suppose that Brooke-

Popham's requests for additional troops and aircraft were delayed and denied by the exigencies elsewhere. It may well be that the tall, gangling Air Marshal lacked the persuasive power to convince London bigwigs of Far Eastern necessities. Brooke-Popham worked long and hard, struggling uphill against "Singapore mentality."

During the week prior to the outbreak, I talked with several score of officers and was told without exception: "There'll be no war in the Far East. Japan will back down." This mentality was rife throughout the armed forces. This military attitude is partly responsible for Malaya's reeling under the sudden attack. For months American and British war correspondents battled against it hopelessly. They had seen war elsewhere and saw preparations here for chaos. Correspondents were made most unwelcome and Admiral Layton said: "Now we are not going to lay on the war just to give you chaps some news."

One British writer made a flight to the Malay airdromes and wrote: "I bring you good news. I visited 20 airdromes as fine as any in existence in the U.S. and Britain. I saw clouds of bombers and fighters who will shoot down any Japanese attempts to attack this country." The British press chief tried to induce American correspondents to use the story—"That's cracking good stuff. That's the kind of thing we want here." Contrarily I cabled: "Have not seen clouds of bombers and fighters." Ten days later I flew to Kota Bharu. It was a grass runway covered with 3 in. of water and mud.

The first knowledge that war was going on was when the Japs landed at Kota Bharu on Dec. 8. Despite the knowledge that the Japs were on the move for two days, a blackout for Malaya was not ordered. At 4 a.m. I received a telephone call to come to Press Relations for an important announcement. The instant I hung up the phone the first bombs fell on Singapore.

In few places in the world has nature conspired more expertly to make fighting as uncomfortable and difficult as in the jungles, mangrove swamps and rice fields of Malaya. Japanese jungle methods are a curious blend of naïveté, guile and imitation of German tricks, but above all the great knowledge of jungle warfare is aided by an innate contempt for whites, especially the British. Orthodox methods—if there is such a thing as orthodox methods for jungle fighting—are forgotten in order to squeeze out the advantages from the disadvantages of nature. The Japanese are showing a peculiar ability to do this. The effectiveness of their tricks is due to surprise, daring execution, indifference to death and British underestimation of the enemy.

To penetrate the jungle the Japanese are not using concentrated forces but thousands of more or less self-sustaining, independent units made up of two to 200 men. It is a lightning war but related to the European type of blitzkrieg only in the fact that each Jap is his own private blitzer. Their main task is to infiltrate the British; cut off battalions, companies, platoons and individuals; surround them; induce confusion and retreat; and inflict the largest possible casualties. Thus far, when the Japanese encounter strong British resistance or fortified positions, they prefer to go around instead of making a direct assault.

To carry out such operations, Jap troops' equipment is very light, consisting of shorts, singlets, tennis shoes, steel helmets, sometimes a handkerchief with corners knotted on top of the head, a bag of rice, with an ammunition belt around the waist. Many carry tommy guns similar to the British whereas others carry rifles. One of the most effective weapons they use is the 4-in. mortar which is carried on head and shoulders. The Japs creep behind the British, plant the mortar and accomplish what would ordinarily take considerable force.

The Japanese improvise readily. In some instances, after a few days, it was found more effective in some areas to have a singlet-clad Jap run ahead with a tommy gun, followed by a uniformed soldier carrying additional ammunition. For some operations, in order to scatter the British, the Japs are using very light tanks. The most unusual trick of the Japanese is their use of firecrackers, ordinary Fourth of July firecrackers. One, two or three Japs, creeping in the jungle, get in between and behind the British and toss firecrackers in all directions. One Britisher said: "When I heard all those cracks, I thought we were surrounded and said to the others we'd better get the bloody hell out of here." A number of British are shot down by Japanese perched on top of coconut palms and teak trees. Others are known to lie in swamps, with only their faces above the water, for three or four hours. Said one white trooper: "You need a dozen eyes to watch these blokes."

The landing operations at, and quick capture of, Kota Bharu Airdrome was achieved partially in this way: The first man ashore at Kota Bharu from each barge charged forward with a 5-ft.-wide mat made of wooden slats and rolled up. With a single motion, he tossed the mat over the top of the barbed wire, unrolling it. He was usually shot down but others scrambled over the mat and barbed wire instantly and dashed toward the airdrome.

To many Britishers every Oriental looks about the same and the Japanese capitalize on this peculiar blind spot of white men. Walking along the road or across a rice field would be an ordinary-looking coolie wearing a cone-shaped straw hat and shorts or sarong and carrying agricultural tools. When approached by a small group of soldiers, he drops the tools, pulls out a pistol and blazes away.

Another favorite practice of the Japs was to send ahead on the road four or five cyclists and when the suiciders were mowed down by British machine gunners, their positions were revealed and the Japs, likewise concealed in the jungle, let go with mortars. Now the British allow cyclists to pass and attack the other forces coming up.

Lunching two days ago with Major General F. Keith Simmons, commander of the Singapore Fortress and one of the Far East's best military brains, I was told: "The best way to get the Japanese is to go in after them the same as you hunt out gangsters." But that's not simple. The British job here is to transform overnight the sheep-herder from Australia, the Scotsman from the moors and the factory worker from Lancashire into a skulking, skilful jungle guerrilla fighter operating in small bands the same as the Japanese.

Some Britons and Indians immediately adopted the tactics necessary to beat the Japanese. One company commander, who had been fighting a rear-guard action for twelve hours, was heavily outnumbered but he fought on. His last message was: "We're going in. Can't last more than ten minutes. Goodby." And he went into the Jap-infested jungle.

While the British in the Western Desert may follow the dictum "Attack and pursue," here in Malaya the strategy may be only to delay and decimate. For more than two weeks the British have used those tactics fighting rear-guard actions, retreating 125 miles to the Perak River. They are tired after this unrelenting Jap advance under surprising conditions, without time to recover their breath after the initial attack. The Japs have lost the surprise of many of their tricks and have lost at least 10,000 men. There is no want of courage among the British and they have the ability to profit individually, to learn lessons proferred each moment. They have found that the Japs do not relish bayonet fighting, though this does not denote a lack of courage on the part of the Japanese whose courage is praised everywhere as "fanatical bravery." The fact that the Japs do not relish bayonet fighting is a source of grim satisfaction to the Gurkhas. At night the Gurkhas, wearing loincloths, their bodies greased to make themselves slippery, venture toward the enemy armed only with a kukri, a 12-in. curved knife sharp enough for shaving. They creep up to the sentry, slice off his head with a single, silent swipe.

As far as nature is concerned, both the British and Japanese are facing the same hazards. It is a country where the jungle undergrowth is so thick it is almost asphyxiating and after minutes of effort sweat pours down as if you were standing under a hot shower. The untrained ones find breathing difficult and it requires at least two months to acclimatize troops. The unearthly stillness and amazing luxuriance of the greenery hemming in the narrow trails give a frightening impression of the jungle closing in. There are pythons, adders, asps—in fact 132 varieties of snakes. There are the tiger and panther, crocodiles, screaming monkeys and shy gibbon. One of the worst menaces are the leeches and when 20 of them are on your body you feel your strength draining. The creeping cane has three-hooked thorns and like a tri-fanged snake it grabs shirt and skin, rips off clothing. Aerial vines as strong as 6-in. rope threaten to strangle the unwary.

The monsoon rains are now going on and nature is unwittingly carrying on a germ warfare on behalf of the British. This is the 16th day since the war started and the incubation period for malaria extends from twelve to 16 days. Every Japanese wounded thus far has been found to be suffering from malaria. And the Japanese are not using mosquito nets. Moreover shorts and singlet provide a greater skin area for mosquito drilling. The British know it is worth a man's life to sleep in jungle areas without a net and the British twice weekly are given atabrin which is considered more effective than quinine.

The British military in this war has a "scorched earth" policy but thus far its most noteworthy aspect is its non-operation. At Penang vast stocks of rice and rubber were left for the Japanese. Barges and tugs were not sunk, docks not dynamited, usable public service buildings not destroyed. Although the telephone transmitters were wrecked, the Penang radio station was not damaged. The Japanese just walked in, turned on the switch and immediately began blasting propaganda over Malaya. As far as could be determined, nowhere have food stocks been destroyed. Britain's problem was one of indecision—whether it was better to leave the foodstuffs for the natives with the hope that they would get it, or take the chance of having the Japanese appropriate it.

Another problem is how to make the scorched-earth policy effective. The Japs easily live off the land, carry a bag of rice comfortably, subsist on coconuts, cane sugar, tropical fruits and berries. Such a diet enables the Japs to maintain fighting efficiency which white men could not do. It is obviously impossible to carry out a scorched-earth policy with regards to coconuts and fruits, and it is likewise impossible to chop down millions of rubber trees.

A few days after the outbreak of war, Lieutenant General Percival, general officer commanding Malaya, was talking on a most important long-distance call with Brooke-Popham. The operator interrupted: "Your three minutes have expired, sir," and cut off the connection. The telephone company is privately owned and the military had failed to take it over.

Singapore is known as a city of "Chinks, drinks, stinks" and it would take more than war to change that. But war is changing the face of this city and is certain to change its mentality. The No. 1 problem is to win the confidence of the natives to avoid the panics of Penang and elsewhere in northern Malaya. Aside from convincing the natives that British protection means something—with a display of military might such as fighters and bombers in the skies and troops pushing back the Japanese—the main burden of winning over the Asiatics to thwart panic and maintain services and food supplies devolves upon Governor Thomas Shenton Whitelegge Thomas, 62, onetime governor of the Gold Coast Colony, handsome, shiny-faced, gray-haired, urbane-mannered, with easy charm and affability. He is credited with sympathy with the natives but his record of accomplishments is unimpressive. Early in October I spent 50 minutes with the Governor and when I emerged from his sanctum in the white rambling Government House I had the strangest sensation of being immersed in an urbane sea of unreality. My first action was to look at the calendar to see if this was 1941, instead of 1931, and war was going on.

One of the most serious sources of civilian uneasiness is the paucity of information contained in communiques. People are bewildered about the situation with the result that they listen to the most pessimistic, most fantastic rumors and due to jitteriness accept them as the true state of affairs. A typical example of the communiques: "We successfully disengaged the enemy and have taken up positions at the River Muda." This is the first word that the Japs are 75 miles inside Malaya and Alor Star, Sungei Patani are lost. The High Command never announced the military evacuation of Penang.

The playing fields of Singapore where British manhood kept fit are now slashed with slit trenches and littered with rotted groups of benches, neat piles of scrap iron, antiquated steam rollers, filled bullock carts to prevent enemy aircraft landings. Several rows of barbed wire surround the harbor front. Plate glass is pasted up with strips of paper and many shops have boarded up windows and are fast building splinter-blocking walls between front and street. Jewelry shops have emptied show cases and placed stocks in steel vaults in the event of fire and looting. The death penalty has been instituted for looting and treachery. During alerts the search goes on for Fifth Columnists flashing lights skyward. Blackout is most effective and filled with dangers. Chinese and Malay guards, many of whom speak only the English word "Halt!" or use the Malay synonym *"Brenti!"* shriek the words out of the darkness with a roar more frightening than

falling bombs. More important, they all have itchy trigger fingers. Every now and then somebody is shot and killed.

There is a 500% increase in autos offered for sale. Gasoline
rations will be reduced one-half by the first of January. The
statue of Sir Stamford Raffles at the front of the Victoria Theatre remains unsandbagged. The snake charmer still does
business in front of the Raffles Hotel. Europeans are moving
out of the downtown area to the outskirts and native servants
in hotels and stores want to do the same. Many people are
bleary-eyed, not from Singapore dissipation but from all-
night fire-watching and working in canteens. Under orders
from the Passive Defense Services' director, the Sultan of
Johore's zoo has been eliminated. The Sultan's favorite orang-
outan was sent to Sumatra for safekeeping.

Singapore is crowded with evacuees, mostly women and
children from Bangkok, Penang, Alor Star, Kuala Kangsar,
Ipoh, Kuala Lumpur, staying with friends and at hotels,
grimly recounting experiences, joining local defense services
and pushing on toward Australia. Trucks filled with sheets of
rubber rumble through the streets as of old. People are
warned to keep bathtubs full of water in case of interruptions
in the water supply and to fight fires. Authorities are allowed
to requisition liquor anywhere in the Federated States. The
latest war racket concerns sandbags. One dealer charged $30
for 100 bags of sand.

Malay youths fresh from kampongs, Chinese clerks and
bearded Sikhs are joining up in the services. Everyone is urged
to wear an identification disk and all persons of whatever nationality must register in order to weed out Fifth Columnists
and check faulty lists. Every day half a dozen profiteers are
fined. For instance, a Chinese who overcharged a half-cent for
a hen's egg was fined $50 U.S. and another Chinese was fined
$425 for selling salt for 3¢ instead of 1½¢. Penalties for blackout
violations are likewise most severe. An Indian was fined $500
for flashing a torch near a military camp and refusing to heed
the "Halt!"

Soldiers are too busy and civilians too preoccupied at
present to pursue usual entertainments. This city, where there
are about 200 officers for each girl, no longer sees these girls

and Singapore now has the most meager and tamest night spots. The girls are working in canteens, as nurses and in voluntary services. Dancing continues at the Raffles nightly but the dancers are mostly upcountry evacuees. The best restaurant remains French Chef Cyrano's which was declared out of bounds last June because officers tended to drop information toward the ears of attractive girls. Seaside Cocoanut Grove, where Cowan and Bailey sang and played double entendre songs, has closed down because it is located in the military area. The military took over the Pavilion and Capital cinemas mainly to secure their air-conditioning system, leaving only the new grandiose Cathay and the antiquated waterfront Alhambra, both air-conditioned.

Within the present crucible of changes going on in Singapore's life, mores, outlook and future — within Malay kampongs, jampacked Chinese quarters, among coolies working on rubber plantations and in tin mines, even among prostitutes of Lavender Street, Singapore's "Street of Sin" — may be elements for toughening the spirit of Asiatics and Europeans. Perhaps there will be brewed from the spirit of those already ashamed of the headlong evacuation from Penang the will to exceed Hong Kong's resistance and even emulate Malta. That there is civilian fortitude remains to be seen. Among soldiers there is greater probability. An officer expressed to me the feeling which I find prevails among troops: "I am sick and tired of evacuations. I am ready to die in Singapore because it is not worth while to go on living if we must have another evacuation."

Life, January 12, 1942

Juke Joint

by Walter Bernstein

THE PRINCIPAL INDUSTRY of the small town of Phenix City, Alabama, is sex, and its customer is the Army. Located ten miles from Fort Benning, Georgia, the town is at least eighty per cent devoted to the titillation and subsequent pillage of that group it affectionately calls "Uncle Sam's soldier boys."

I became acquainted with Phenix following my initial month of recruit drill, when the selectees were first allowed to leave the post. During those thirty days we had heard approximately ninety-four lectures dealing with various sordid aspects of the town. There were some twenty thousand recruits at Benning for these talks. Our first free Saturday night, not more than ten, or at the most twelve, thousand hit the road to Phenix.

The first place to go in Phenix City is usually Frankie's. That is not the real name, but it will do. It is the name of the woman who owns the place, a determined and ageless female with red hair and a strong pioneer streak, only slightly perverted. Frankie's is reached by cutting off the paved main street after it has passed the town's two blocks of stores and climbed the hill past the new courthouse, and then hiking about a mile up a narrow dirt road. The place itself is like the other sagging frame houses that line the back streets of Phenix City, but it has a sign above the porch that says "Café" and on Saturday night there is a long line of taxicabs out front. Some of the soldiers walk from the Georgia town of Columbus, where the bus from camp stops, but only if they feel healthy. Too many bloody men have been found in Phenix alleys. The taxis only charge a quarter a head and for another quarter they will let you in on a number of other good things, and also include the transportation.

This Saturday night was a week after payday and the place

was jammed. Frankie herself was behind the bar, seeing that the percentage of foam to beer was not more than half. Nothing harder than beer was sold at Frankie's; there was no necessity for anything else. The one square room that comprised the café was ugly and low-ceilinged. Now it was packed with soldiers. They stood five deep at the bar that ran across one side of the room. They filled the small dance floor and swallowed the juke box that stood in a corner. They sat on and around the dirty tables that dotted the rest of the room and spilled into the cubicle that had once been the kitchen, but now held three slot machines and a dice table.

There were about fifteen girls in the room. They were very young; some did not seem any more than sixteen or seventeen. They wore cotton dresses and low-heeled shoes and some did not even wear make-up. A few sat at tables, but most of them walked around, stopping every few feet to speak to one of the soldiers. Every so often one would talk a little longer with a soldier and then the two of them would walk out of the room, through the cubicle, and out a door at the other end. They were usually gone about ten minutes, and then they would return, the soldier grinning or shame-faced or defiant; and the girl would continue to walk around or perhaps sit at a table and have a Coca-Cola.

I finally got a bottle of beer from the bar and took it to a table at the edge of the dance floor, where there were some men from my company. They were drinking rye from a bottle and watching the girls. The juke box was screaming "You Are My Sunshine." It was hot and smoky in the room and I drank my beer quickly. As soon as I had finished, a girl came over and took the bottle. She looked very young and she was wearing a cheap housedress that ended an inch above her knee. "You want another beer?" she asked. I shook my head and one of the other soldiers said, "Sit down, Mary." The girl sat down without comment. She said something to the man next to her, who shook his head. She looked around at the rest of us and we all shook our heads. "Oh, well," Mary said.

"Have a beer," a soldier named Pat said.

"Don't mind if I do," Mary said. Pat got up and went to the bar and Mary reached down to loosen her saddle shoes.

"My feet hurt," she said. She looked like the girls whom I had seen working in the town's textile mill.

"I know you," one of the men said. "You work in the dime store."

"That's Peggy," the girl said. "You boys always take me for Peggy."

"I could swear you were sisters," the man said.

"You're crazy," Mary said. Pat returned with the beers and the girl drank hers thirstily. "Well," she said when she was finished, "I got to get back to work."

"How's business?" Pat asked.

"Not good, not bad," Mary said. She stood up, glancing toward the door. Standing in the doorway were two M.P.'s, their eyes searching the crowd. Frankie waved to them from behind the bar and they waved back, still looking through the crowd. When they were satisfied they turned and went out. Mary jerked her head after them. "That don't hurt my business," she said scornfully. She walked off into the crowd and I stood up to stretch my legs. I said good-by to the other men, who were trying to decide what they could do and not be gypped, and went across the room to the cubicle. At the entrance was a blind man holding a cup. A sign in his hat said "God Bless You One and All." Whenever someone put a coin in his cup he would spill it into his hand, feel it very carefully, and then place it in his pocket.

There was a crowd of soldiers around the dice table that occupied most of the little gambling room. Three soldiers and two civilians in shirtsleeves were shooting craps. One of the civilians was the house man; the other looked like a shill of some sort, but I couldn't be sure. One of the soldiers, a corporal, had a pile of bills before him and his face was flushed and excited. The other two soldiers had some money, but not as much. The civilians kept their money hidden.

The corporal had the dice and was evidently riding a streak. He threw two passes and then made a four. The other two soldiers watched him enviously, but the civilians didn't seem very interested. The corporal threw another seven; he had about a hundred dollars in his pile. He threw a six and the spectators cheered. "He'll make that easy," whispered a soldier next to me. The corporal made his point on the next throw and the soldier nudged me happily. "Smart boy," he said. "Must be using his own dice." The corporal then threw a ten, and in rapid succession an eight, a five and a seven. Everyone sighed except the civilians, but the soldier next to me nodded wisely. "Just making it look good," he said. The dice went to one of the other soldiers and I slipped away from the table. There were no windows in the little room and the smoke made the air like lead. A slight draft blew from the door that kept opening at the other end of the cubicle, but that didn't help much. I watched some of the soldiers lose money in the slot machines, lost a few nickels myself, then returned to the main room.

Standing against a wall was a very fat man in civilian clothes. He wore an old windbreaker, a dirty pair of pants, and a slouch hat, pushed back on his head. He was leaning on a thick cane, watching the crowd. His feet were in carpet slippers. His name was Hancock and he was the bouncer. I had been introduced to him once, so I went over to say hello. He didn't remember me, but took my word that we had met. I asked him why he wore slippers and he pulled up his right trouser leg to show a bandage around his foot. "Got kicked by a G.I. boot," he said. I asked what was new. "Can't complain," he said. "For Saturday it's a quiet night." Just then one of the girls came over and said there was trouble by the juke box. "Excuse me," Hancock said, courteously. He limped across the room, his stomach running interference for the rest of his body. A soldier was drunk at the juke box and did not like the selection being played. He was hammering on the window when Hancock tapped him on the shoulder. He turned around full of fight, but Hancock spoke to him quietly and after a moment took him by the arm and walked him to the door. The soldier turned when they reached the door, but Hancock pushed him gently outside and shut the door after him. Then he limped back and resumed his place against the wall. "Boys that age shouldn't drink liquor," he said, shaking his head.

We stood for a while without talking. The room was still packed tight. Frankie's red head shone through the smoke. The girls still walked around, bored and weary, and the juke box still screamed "You Are My Sunshine." The soldiers stood in little knots or sat back at the tables, eyeing the girls. They were all dressed very carefully, with their insignia shining, but most of them looked as if they had gotten into the wrong place.

I stood against the wall wondering what to do. There was a burst of voices from the gambling room and Mary trotted out. "You better go in there," she said to Hancock. Hancock sighed and limped off. Mary stayed behind, taking his place against the wall. "My feet hurt," she said. She took one foot out of her shoe and wrinkled the toes appreciatively. I asked her how long she had been at Frankie's. "This is my first week," she said. "I used to be at Twin Oak." I asked why she had left. "You make more money here," she said. Twin Oak was a place like Frankie's, about six miles out of town. It was owned by the former chief of police, who also owned another place in town. He used to own them while in office, but quit the police department when asked by the respectable element to choose between business and pleasure.

I asked Mary if she preferred Frankie's and she shrugged. "At the other place we got officers." I admitted the distinction. "And this place you got to walk around all the time. But I like it here," she said. "It's more democratic." I asked if the police ever bothered her and she laughed. "That don't hurt my business," she said loudly. She laughed again. "You know what? I'm a food handler. I got a card to prove it." She dug into the pockets of her dress, but came up empty-handed. "All the girls are food handlers," she said. "Every damned one of us." She seemed very proud of the fact, although all the girls who work in places like Frankie's are classified in Phenix City as food handlers. What this means is not exactly certain, since there were still 1082 new venereal disease cases at Benning in the past eight months. Lately, however, there had been a renewed vice crusade by the city authorities, and the F.B.I. was finally summoned. The Army is vehement in its demands that these places be abolished, but the responsibility is still a civil one. And when the lure of easy money and girls will bring thirty thousand paying customers to a town every night, the merchants who own the town are likely to consider health a peacetime luxury.

By now someone had broken the monopoly on the juke box and it was playing "I'm Walking the Floor Over You." Mary was whistling and tapping the floor to the music. "I'm walking the floor over you," she sang nasally. "Please tell me just what should I do." A soldier walking past told her what she should do, and she aimed a kick at him. The kick missed, but the momentum carried her away from the wall and she started her trip around the room again.

Hancock came out of the cubicle, leading another soldier by the arm. It was one of the soldiers from the dice table and he was very angry. He was gesturing wildly and making attempts to get back into the cubicle, but Hancock led him firmly to the door. He was not so gentle this time and tapped the soldier with his cane as he pushed him out. Then he limped back and leaned against the wall. "What kind of a home do these boys come from?" he asked me. "He says the dice were crooked. Why should they be crooked?"

I told him that the soldier wasn't the only one who felt that way.

"They're not smart," Hancock said. "They don't use their heads. Don't they know the odds against them in an honest game? Why should we make it crooked?"

There was no short answer to this, so I changed the subject and invited Hancock to the bar for a beer. The crowd had thinned there and we found a place at the end. Next to us a soldier with the high boots of a parachutist was arguing unsteadily with one who wore the patch of an armored division on his sleeve. "I wouldn't be seen in a tank for all the money in the world," the parachutist was saying emphatically. "Not for a hundred dollars."

"It's because you're old-fashioned," the other said.

"It's because a tank is uncomfortable," the parachutist explained patiently. "A tank is a messy machine."

"A tank is very useful," the other said.

"Now you take the sky," the parachutist said. "What could be cleaner?"

Frankie came over to serve us and Hancock introduced me. "Howdy," Frankie said, professionally. Her mouth opened and closed in a short smile, showing bad teeth. She had a huge, matronly front and her close-bitten nails were painted blood-red. She looked like a suburban mah jong player who played for keeps. "You being treated all right?" she asked me.

"He's in my hands," Hancock said.

"Good," Frankie said. "Anything I can do for you, let me know." We ordered bottled beer and she had one of the girls behind the bar bring it to us. "Here's to the brave young men in the Army," Hancock said. I had the bottle tilted up when I saw four men in civilian clothes come through the front door. They stood for a moment in the doorway, looking around, and then walked slowly toward the bar. They all wore hats and their jackets were open and I had seen enough movies to know they were the Law.

I started to find the back door, but Hancock pulled me over to his old spot against the wall. Frankie had also seen the men and stood quietly behind the bar, not smiling as she had at the M.P.'s. No one else paid much attention to them. The men reached the bar and stopped and still the crowd did not notice them. Then they began pushing people away from the bar and the hush started there and spread through the room until the juke box was suddenly much louder than usual. All the soldiers stood up and a few made a quick break for the door. The men paid no attention to these. They cleared the crowd from the bar and one of the men took out a notebook and said, "O.K., Frankie." Frankie looked at him and then turned to the girls working behind the bar and said, "Get out the beer."

It was all very smooth and quick, as if it had been done many times before. The crowd settled back when they saw what the men were after, and now made a path for them as they carried the cases of beer outside. I noticed some soldiers slip out the back way, but none of the girls left and I could still hear the slot machines clicking. The man with the note-book took down figures as the beer went outside. Frankie talked to him as he wrote, but he kept shrugging his shoulders as if disclaiming any responsibility. After a few minutes the novelty and fear wore off and the room slid back to normal. The people who had been at the bar waited to resume their places, but the rest of the crowd moved off to other parts of the room. In about ten minutes the men had cleared the bar of beer. The man with the notebook wrote something

on a piece of paper and handed it to Frankie. She said something in a low voice and he laughed. Then he tipped his hat
and went out after the other men.

The crowd surged back against the bar as soon as they left
and the girls served up Coca-Cola and Dr. Pepper. I turned to
Hancock, but before I could speak he assured me that everything was all right. "It's only the State Liquor Control boys,"
he said. "They do this all the time." I said I thought the sale
of beer was allowed in Alabama. "Not without no license,"
Hancock said.

Except for the absence of beer nothing seemed changed.
Hancock went off in response to another girl's call and I
walked around the room trying to find some fresh air. The
juke box was playing "Good-by, Dear, I'll Be Back in a Year,"
and some soldiers stood around the machine giving each lyric
a Bronx cheer. I wandered past the blind man into the little
gambling room. The dice game was still going and there were
five soldiers playing now instead of three. I recognized only
the corporal who had been in the money. Now there were
only a few dollars before him and he looked scared. The
house man had also changed, but the other civilian was still
there, pocketing his money as he won. He seemed to be winning more consistently now. The door at the far end of the
cubicle had been left open and the trickle of cool air felt
good. Occasionally one of the couples going through would
close the door after them, and then the house man would
walk patiently across the room and open it again.

After the dice game I put a few more nickels in the slot
machines, then wandered back into the main room. I
searched for someone I knew, but all the faces were strange in
the familiar way most soldiers have to one another. A soldier
hurried past me toward the front door, his face drawn and
white. A girl came up, but I shook my head and she continued on around the room. There was a bad smell in this part of
the room, so I moved away. The juke box was shrieking
"We'll Have to Slap the Dirty Jap." I looked at my watch and
was surprised to see it was not even midnight. I started to find
Hancock when suddenly there was a loud whistle and I
looked up to see the two M.P.'s standing in the doorway. "At
ease!" one of them shouted. "All men of the 19th Engineers

report to their barracks at once." He banged on the wall for emphasis and repeated the sentence. Then the two of them turned and went out.

This time the noise did not return to the room as quickly as it had when the Liquor Control men left. We had all seen this happen too often before, the same words in the same public places, and the next day an outfit gone from the post. The soldiers looked at each other and a few men stood up around the room and walked slowly to the door. The other soldiers watched them go and as soon as they were out everyone began to talk again and laugh, even more loudly than before. The air was getting more and more foul. I found Hancock and said good-night. He shook my hand warmly and told me to hurry back. As I left the room a soldier was being sick in a corner. The juke box was screaming "Good-by, Mama, I'm Off to Yokohama."

Keep Your Head Down, 1945

"The Unexpected Couldn't Happen"

by Raymond Clapper

As I READ the Roberts report on Pearl Harbor, I kept thinking that would be a hell of a way to run a newspaper.

I don't know anything about military affairs. But I have been around newspaper offices all my life. A newspaper office is organized to be ready for the unexpected. We hire an Army and Navy to protect us from the unexpected. But I never saw a newsroom that was as slack and sloppy as the Roberts report shows the Army and Navy at Hawaii to have been.

Go through any well-run newspaper office and you will find galleys of type, with headlines and art, all ready to be thrown into the paper at an instant's notice. Let a flash come through about the sudden death of any prominent figure and the paper will be ready to roll within a few minutes.

A newspaper office always goes on the assumption that the worst is about to happen the next minute. An incredible amount of planning, labor, and watchfulness goes into this side of a newspaper—much of it in vain. But it is necessary if you are not to be caught asleep when a big story breaks.

I remember when Carl Groat, now editor of *The Cincinnati Post*, was manager of the United Press bureau at Washington. After the Shenandoah dirigible disaster he sent a reporter to camp on a deathwatch at the Navy Department whenever a dirigible made a flight. The man-hours which reporters spend on deathwatches and on chasing down tips which do not materialize, the newless days they put in hovering around prominent figures just so they will be on hand in case something happens, are all part of the routine of being prepared for the unexpected.

Around Scripps-Howard newspaper offices is the old story of the Oklahoma City hanging years ago. The sheriff was all ready. Most of the reporters in town were on hand. But one city editor sent a reporter out to watch the governor, who was opposed to capital punishment. Ten minutes before the hanging was to take place, the governor commuted the sentence. The newspaper which was on the job had its newsboys selling papers to the crowd waiting in the jail yard to see the hanging that had been called off.

Newspapers are prepared always for the unexpected. Hawaii seems to have operated on the conviction that the unexpected couldn't happen.

More than that, the Roberts report shows appalling lack of coordination between the Army and Navy. The Army thought the Navy was patrolling. The Navy thought the Army had its detection service operating. Neither bothered to check with the other—or maybe they were not on speaking terms.

In any newspaper office the first business of the managing editor is to see that his city editor and his telegraph editor clear with each other on space. If the city editor went on his own and the telegraph editor sent wire copy to the composing room to his heart's desire, you would have enough type set to fill three newspapers. If a big local story breaks, the telegraph editor's space is reduced. If a big telegraph story breaks, the city editor takes a cut in space. The two subordinate executives must work together.

I have always thought civilians should be extremely sparing in their advice about military affairs, which seem so simple and yet are so intricate. But the Roberts report shows two glaring situations which come down, in civilian language, to sloppy operation. First, the Army and Navy acted on the assumption that the unexpected would not happen, when they should have assumed the opposite. Second, the two services were totally uncoordinated, and neither knew what the other was doing—or, in this case, not doing. And the air force, so supremely important in the new warfare, apparently was regarded by both as a minor auxiliary.

Watching the World, 1944

"The Newspaper Reader Finds It Very Difficult to Get at the Truth"

by E. B. White

IT SEEMS to me that since the entrance of the United States into the war the newspapers have ceased to present the news unemotionally. They have given the news, all right, but they have sprinkled it with Vitalis. Before Pearl Harbor the American press was doing the finest job imaginable. Since Pearl Harbor it has been a touch on the wishful side.

As I write this, in February, it seems to me that if anyone had followed the events of the past two months solely by reading the headlines across the top of Page One he would now be fairly convinced that the Japanese attempt in the Far East was a failure. Somehow or other, the headline writers have managed to give that impression. MacArthur's fox holes have taken on the aspect of a full military victory, and the Japanese fleet is at the bottom.

In last night's paper, from the UP's Far Eastern man, I read the following dispatch: "Allied warcraft operating in the Netherlands East Indies have sunk a Japanese cruiser and a large transport and have damaged and possibly sunk a second cruiser and a submarine, the Netherlands East Indies high command said in a communiqué to-day. It was admitted that the greater part of Amboina Island . . . was now practically in Japanese hands and that Pontianak, capital of Dutch West Borneo, had now been completely occupied by the enemy."

The headline which this story carried (a very big one) was: "ALLIES SINK JAP CRUISER." You certainly wouldn't know, from looking over your neighbor's shoulder in the subway, that the second largest naval and air force base in the Indies had been taken by Japan. You would simply know that everything was going fine for our side and that the Japanese navy was a goner.

Next morning I read the same story in the *New York Times*. The *Times* too ignored the very grave defeat for the Allies in its headline, and merely said: "DUTCH SINK CRUISER AND TRANSPORT," adding, as though in afterthought, in a sub-head, "But Foe Controls Island."

Now obviously the sinking of a Japanese cruiser is news. It is big news and it is good news. In the long run it may even be as valuable to our side as is Japan's occupation of the naval base to Japan. But when, day after day, you are shaken by the detonations of American success and hear only small puffballs of the enemy's fire, a very definite feeling grows in you that Japan has really accomplished very little. The facts show that the Empire of the Rising Sun is doing very well indeed.

Good news probably sells more papers than bad news, but I doubt if the art of headlining is governed by wholly merce-nary principles. I think it is natural for reporters and headline writers to cry out the glad tidings first and let the headaches alone until maybe the second or third paragraph. Certainly the fall of the Netherlands' Number Two Base rated more prominence than it got.

A day or two before Amboina, the New York *Telegram* car-ried a streamer: "U.S. BAGS SEVEN JAP PLANES, RANGOON RAID SMASHED." Here was good news for fair. The reader could throw his paper in the air and pour himself a drink. But if he hung on to his paper and went doggedly ahead he came to this bit of information: "Military and naval experts asserted to-day that the situation of Allied forces in the western Pacific at the end of the second month was very serious and that still further reverses could be expected."

The *Telegram* even has a standing box head called GOOD NEWS, under which it collects each afternoon a few nosegays, favorable to us, ruinous to the enemy.

The President was forthright about the Pacific when the war began; he told everyone there would be bad news before there was good. This sort of realism should be observed by the newspapers in their own field, but I think if a man were to paper his den with headlines he would find himself living in a hall of triumph.

Quite apart from the emphasis, the newspaper reader finds it very difficult to get at the truth of any situation, through

the great mass of conjecture and rumor and conflicting statements. Often he feels completely baffled and defeated. This is
not the fault of the press—it is just that the war is too big
and moves too fast and the facts are not always available. The
news is the privilege which the customer enjoys, but it is also
the crossword puzzle which he alone must solve. One moment he experiences the full flush of victory, the next moment
the chill of defeat. From two stories on the same page, sometimes from two paragraphs in the same story, he runs the
whole gamut.

In the afternoon papers of Wednesday, February 4th, the
biggest news of the day was Wavell's announcement that reinforcements were on the way to Singapore. "GREAT AID ON
WAY," sang the jubilant headline. Two days later, the Associated Press consulted "military and naval experts" and reported: "While fully recognizing the heroic achievements of
defenders in the Philippines, Singapore, and the Dutch Indies
and allowing for Japanese losses of more than 100 ships and
thousands of men, these authorities declared that only the de-
livery of huge reinforcements—difficult if not impossible at
this time—would turn the tide of battle against the enemy."

There you are: Wavell said they were coming, experts in
Washington said it was doubtful if they ever would make it.
The customer rested—until the next edition.

Harper's Magazine, April 1942

"Everybody Knew When the Planes Were Coming"

by Clark Lee

EVERYBODY called Corregidor the "Rock," and the adjective that seemed to fit it best was "rugged." Corregidor was indeed a mighty fortress. Doubtless it would have been impregnable—if the airplane had never been invented.

But airplanes had been invented, and during January they were over Corregidor for two or three hours almost every day. There was something hideously obscene about those tiny silver planes buzzing around high up against the blue cloudless sky. They were so small, at above 20,000 feet, that they looked as if you could put them in a matchbox.

In the intervals when the noise of the last load of bombs had died away, and the planes were out of range of the antiaircraft and circling for their next run, you could hear the motors plainly. The noise of the motors was deadly and vicious. You thought of being tied down to slimy tree roots in a muddy jungle, and having a rattlesnake weave his ugly head two inches from your throat, waiting and picking his place to strike. You thought of all the evil nightmares you had ever had.

Everybody knew when the planes were coming.

First, about seven-thirty in the morning, when the sun was hidden behind the clouds over the mountains in back of Manila, would come the observation plane. It was either "Photograph Joe" in his high-wing monoplane, or the twin-engined, twin-tailed Lockheed monoplane that used to fly right over the island. Joe would circle over the channel between Corregidor and Bataan and the .30- and .50-caliber machine guns would shoot golden tracers all around him. The 3-inch guns had orders not to open up because Joe had a camera and would photograph their flashes and get their location.

Joe would circle deliberately and then he would release a

silver balloon and watch the wind carry it up in the sky. That was to test the wind currents. It filled us with bitter anger to see the deliberate way he got the stage set for the daily murder.

Joe would putt-putt away, flying straight over the middle of Bataan and up to Clark Field, only thirty miles away.

Then Captain Suzuki would call his pilots together out on Clark Field while mechanics loaded the bombs in the silver-winged planes and checked the motors. Suzuki would show the pilots the photographs Joe had taken and give them the weather data and point out their objectives.

At about eleven-thirty the planes would take off and start circling to gain altitude because they had only a short distance to cover and a long way to climb. "Fine weather. Good hunting," Suzuki-san would tell his pilots.

Then the siren would sound on Corregidor and the red lights flash on in Malinta tunnel and the crews would run to their posts on the 3-inch anti-aircraft guns and the .50-caliber machine guns, and everybody else would get under cover.

Then the planes would come over, twenty-seven of them or maybe fifty-four. They would crisscross Corregidor without dropping, taking their time, deliberately getting their targets lined up. The anti-aircraft would open up and burst in them and around them, but if one was shot out they would reform in their V formation and keep coming.

Having picked their targets out they would come back flying straight in from over the channels, sometimes from the north and sometimes from the south.

Then would come the noise of the bombs falling. The bombs didn't screech or whistle or whine. They sounded like a pile of planks being whirled around in the air by a terrific wind and driven straight down to the ground. The bombs took thirty years to hit. While they were falling they changed the dimensions of the world. The noise stripped the eagles from the colonel's shoulders and left him a little boy, naked and afraid. It drove all the intelligence from the nurse's eyes and left them vacant and staring. It wrapped a steel tourniquet of fear around your head, until your skull felt like bursting. It made you realize why man found he needed a God.

The roar of the explosions was a relief from the noise of the falling bombs. You felt the concussion driving against your ears and heard the clatter of collapsing buildings and saw the dust billowing high in the air.

Then would come the fires, and the heroism. Men and women dashing out and picking up the wounded while the bombs were still falling. They would carry the dead and the wounded to the hospital tunnel. You would hear the cars long before they reached the tunnel. The urgency of their horns, blowing all the way down the hill from Topside and then up the slope from Bottomside, told you they were bringing dead and those about to die and those who would be better off dead. The M.P.'s would make the cars slow down as they drove into the big tunnel and they would stop at the hospital tunnel and blood would be dripping down from the cars or the trucks. Then the stretcher bearers would gently lift out the bloody remnants of what had been an American soldier or a Filipino worker a few minutes before. They would lift out the handsome captain whose legs were bloody stumps. They would lift out carefully the 18-year-old American boy who would never again remember his name, or his mother's name, or anything else, but would just look at you blankly when you spoke to him.

When the bombers had finally done their day's murder and gone away there would come the horror, when you went to see the damage they had done. The horror would come when you helped to dig out the bodies of thirty-five young Americans from the "bomb-proof" that had received a direct hit. The bomb explosion didn't kill them, but it blew their mouths and noses and lungs full of dirt and suffocated them.

Then would come the communiqué: "54 enemy bombers raided Corregidor for three hours today. There was no military damage."

Of course, the communiqués had to be worded that way. You couldn't tell the enemy he was hurting you. The wonder was that the bombs didn't do more damage than they did.

The first big raid on Corregidor, on December 29, was one of the worst. The bombs blasted the big barracks on Topside; they tore into the Red Cross painted on the hospital roof, they wrecked the officers' quarters and the cinema, and they knocked out the anti-aircraft control post at Topside. They almost killed MacArthur who was standing in front of his house and refused to be driven to shelter even when the bombs hit near him, and the planes came low and close.

The planes came back on New Year's Day and for the next nine days thereafter. General MacArthur estimated that, considering its size, a greater concentration of bombs dropped on Corregidor than on any other area on earth.

The bombs wrecked the trolley lines and burned out most of the Bottomside shops; they tore down a water tank and repeatedly punctured the water mains, creating a serious problem in sanitation; they burned up fuel supplies; they sank President Quezon's yacht, the ship on which we had escaped from Manila, a half-dozen other ships anchored in a straight line out in the bay, and nearly all the small boats used for communication with Bataan. They bounced off the roof of the power plant and the cold-storage plant leaving both of them in operation.

When the bombers went away for a while, after the 29th, Corregidor shook itself and found amazingly that it was not too badly wounded. Almost everything above ground had been hit but the damage was quickly patched up, as far as possible, and auxiliary shops were built underground and supplies moved into the tunnels. The trolley line was beyond repair but there were plenty of trucks and gasoline. Not much food had been lost. Only one gun was put out of action and that was quickly repaired. Casualties were relatively low.

The planes came back intermittently until about January 20. Then they moved on south to the airfield which had been prepared on the Island of Jolo, in the southern Philippines, and from which the bombers operated against Borneo and the Dutch East Indies.

Corregidor had had a foretaste of what was to come later. It was obvious to everybody on the Rock that with enough bombs and enough bombers the island could eventually be pounded into submission. Even the underground areas could not escape. The Japanese evidently reached the same conclusion, for when they next came back in force, from the first of April onward, they came with scores of dive bombers and heavy bombers and attack planes. They blasted the barbed wire guarding Corregidor's beaches, they knocked out the anti-aircraft guns and the big coast defense rifles, they killed our Marines in the trenches along the beaches. Finally, after a month of pounding, they captured Corregidor.

They Call It Pacific, 1943

Bataan Nurses

as told to Annalee Jacoby by
Willa L. Hook and Juanita Redmond

CONDITIONS at Hospital No. 1 in Bataan were not too good during the last few weeks we spent there. Patients were flooding in. We increased from 400 to 1,300 cases in two weeks' time. Most were shrapnel wounds for surgery, but nine out of ten patients had malaria or dysentery besides. We were out of quinine. There were hundreds of gas gangrene cases, and all our supply of anti-gas gangrene serum had gone months before. There were no more sulfa drugs.

We were working in wards when bombers came overhead on April 4. We hardly noticed them. Suddenly incendiary bombs dropped. They hit the receiving wards, mess hall, doctors' and officers' quarters, and the steps of the nurses' dormitory, setting fire to all buildings, but luckily not hitting the wards. Several enlisted personnel wandering outside were killed. The patients were terrified, of course, but behaved well. The Japanese prisoners were perhaps the most frightened of all. We were still frightened until two hours later when someone heard the Jap radio in Manila announce that the bombings had been an accident and wouldn't happen again.

The morning of April 7 about 10:30, we were all on duty when another wave of bombers came over. The first bomb hit by the Filipino mess hall and knocked us down before we even knew the planes were overhead. An ammunition truck was passing the hospital entrance. It got a direct hit. The boys on guard at the gate were smothered in the dirt thrown up by the explosion, and shell-shocked.

Convalescent patients picked us up and we began doing dressings for patients hurt by shrapnel. Everything was terror and confusion. Patients, even amputation cases, were falling and rolling out of the triple-decker beds.

Suddenly a chaplain, Father Cummings, came into the ward, threw up his hands for silence, said: "All right, boys, everything's all right. Just stay quietly in bed, or lie still on the floor. Let us pray." The confusion and screams stopped instantly. He began the prayer as a second wave of planes came over. The first bomb hit near the officers' quarters, the next directly in the middle of our hospital ward. The next wave struck the patients' mess just a few yards away. The concussion bounced us 3 ft. off the cement floor and threw us down again. The beds were swaying and tumbling down. Desks were doing a jitterbug. Red flashes of heat burned our eyes. But through it all we could hear Father Cummings' voice in prayer. When the bombs hit the ward everyone had begun to repeat the Lord's Prayer. Father Cummings' clear voice went through to the end. Then he turned quietly and said: "All right, you take over. Put a tourniquet on my arm, would you?" And we saw for the first time that he'd been badly hit by shrapnel.

The next few hours were a nightmare, except for the way everyone behaved. We were afraid to move, but realized we had to get to work. One little Filipino with both legs amputated—he'd never gotten out of bed before by himself—rolled onto the ground and said: "Miss Hook, are you all right, are you all right?" We tried to care first for the patients hurt worst. A great many all over the hospital were bleeding badly. We went to where the bomb had hit the ward and began pulling patients from the crater. I saw Rosemary Hogan, the head ward nurse, and thought for a moment her face had been torn off. She wiped herself with a sheet, smiled and said: "It's nothing, don't bother about me. It's just a nose bleed." But she had three shrapnel wounds.

It would be hard to believe the bravery after that bombing if you hadn't seen it. An enlisted man had risked his life by going directly to the traction wards where patients were tied to beds by ropes fastened to wires through the fractured bones. He thought it was better to hurt the men temporarily than to leave them tied helpless above ground where they'd surely be hit by shrapnel, so he cut all tractions and told the patients: "Get under the bed, Joe." He probably saved a good many lives too.

The triple-decker beds were all tumbled over. We gave first-aid treatments, then baths, and cleaned up the beds until after dark. Afraid the Japanese would be back again the next day, we then moved the patients to another hospital. Even the most serious cases were moved; giving them any chance was better than none. There were only a hundred left the next morning. We worked all the next day making up beds to admit new patients. Suddenly, after dark, we were told we were leaving in 15 minutes—that we should pack only what we could carry in our arms. The Japanese had broken through the line and the Battle of Bataan was over.

The doctors decided collectively to stay with the patients, even doctors who'd been told to come to Corregidor. We left the hospital at 9 that night and got to Corregidor at 3 in the morning. The trip usually took a little over an hour. As we drove down to the docks, the roads were jammed. Soldiers were walking, tired, aimless, frightened. Cars were overturned; there were guns in the road and bodies. Clouds of dust made it hard to breathe. At midnight on the docks we heard they'd burned our hospital to the ground.

Bombers were overhead. We were too tired to care. But as we crossed the water with Corregidor's big guns firing over our heads and shells from somewhere landing close by, the boat suddenly shivered and the whole ocean seemed to rock. We thought a big shell had gone through the water just in front of us—it wasn't until we landed that we found an earthquake had come just as Bataan fell.

We were on a cargo boat. Some went in barges, some helped paddle rafts. But we had an easy trip compared to that of the nurses from hospital No. 2. It was 3 in the morning before they got away—Bataan had begun to fall at 8. They were cut off by a burning ammunition dump and waited for hours with explosions ahead of them and Japs a few kilometers behind.

Corregidor seemed like heaven that night. They fed us and we slept, two to an Army cot. We went to work the following morning. There was constant bombing and shelling—sometimes concussion from a bomb landing outside would knock people down at the opposite end of the tunnel. The Emperor's birthday, April 29, was specially bad. Bombing began at 7:30 in the morning and never stopped. Several men counted over a hundred explosions to a minute. Dive bombers were going after the gun on the hill directly above our heads and the concussion inside was terrific.

The worst night on Corregidor was when a bomb lit outside the tunnel entrance on the China Sea side. A crowd had gone outside for a cigaret and many were sleeping on the ground at the foot of the cliff. When the first shell hit nearby, they all ran for the tunnel, but the iron gate at the entrance was shut and it opened outward. As more shells landed, concussions smashed the men against the gate and twisted off arms and legs. All nurses got up and went back to work— surgery was overflowing until 5:30 in the morning. There were many amputations. Litter bearers worked outside in total darkness, groping about for wounded. One rolled a body onto his litter; when he got inside he saw it had no head.

Through all those weeks on Corregidor everyone was grand. At 6 o'clock one evening after the usual constant bombing and shelling, 21 of us were called into a meeting and told we were leaving Corregidor by plane with 10 lb. of luggage apiece. We don't know how we were selected. The pilot hustled us aboard because we were between Cavite and Corregidor, directly in the range of artillery. On that trip we sometimes almost skimmed the water. There was so much fog over Mindanao that we had to make a forced landing. People on Mindanao were just as courageous as the rest on Corregidor and Bataan. They knew they would be trapped but cheerfully wished us a good trip and happy landings. At dusk we left for Australia.

Life, June 15, 1942

The Fever of Defeat

by Jack Belden

THIS IS probably my last message. I'm staying with General Stilwell and a small command post directing the rear-guard action on approaches to India and northernmost Burma.

The Japanese are driving with incredible speed, swinging wide of both our east and west flanks and somehow we have to get the troops out of this closing-in trap.

The Jap column which seized Lashio is coming up the Burma Road to China, with the possibility that it may swing in toward Bhamo in an attempt to sever all our communications with China. Another column is about to seize Mandalay. A third force has already taken Monywa and the Junction of the Irrawaddy and Chindwin Rivers, threatening to outflank us.

The roads are crowded with thousands of refugees who are under constant aerial strafing, suffering from food and water shortage and wearied from the pace that on the Shan States front carried the Japanese forward 350 miles in two weeks, or 25 miles a day.

It is this terrific Jap pressure, plus food and water scarcity and the noncompletion of roads to India, that makes the task so difficult. The railway line leading to a dead end at Myitkyina has been repeatedly smashed by Jap bombers, interrupted by Burmese saboteurs loosening rails, opening switches and shooting at wrecking crews in the dark. Small, tough jeeps may be able to negotiate the oxcart tracks and are being commandeered to carry out the wounded, but the majority must walk. Whether they escape depends upon whether Alexander and Stilwell can block off roads to stem the Jap advance, and whether the rains come to bog down Jap motor columns.

In the midst of writing these words, I heard a sudden roar,

looked overhead at a transport plane circling in low. I heard cries: "Hurray, Hurray" from American enlisted men as the plane circled and landed. "Don't that plane look good. Go kiss it." Someone sang *God Bless America*.

The list is now being made out of those who will evacuate. At any rate I won't go, and "Uncle Joe" Stilwell will stay to the last to direct his troops. I must write fast now and will set down jumbled impressions of the last days of Burma.

Last night I stood on the Ava bridge beside two Scottish lads, Royal Bombay Sappers and Miners, who were ready to plunge a stick that would set off 2,000 lb. of explosives and wreck the second largest bridge in the Far East across the Irrawaddy River. British 25-pounders, manned by Indians, were hurling shells in the direction of Mandalay, which has been burning since April 4th and is overrun with dacoits and traitors who are shooting at the Chinese garrison in the darkness through the completely flattened ruins of a city of one-time 120,000 population, where now only stand the red-washed, almost encircled walls of the palace of Burma's kings. The last rear guard was hurrying across after holding up the main Jap force with just a handful of men.

This ends a definite stage of the war as now all the rice, salt, oil and tin are in Japanese hands, and what remains of Burma will make it difficult to support large armies and the hordes of helpless refugees streaming northward. The plane is going now.

I continue to write this from Stilwell's Headquarters, hoping that someone will pick it up to take to India before I leave. Everyone but Headquarters' doctor and myself has gone. We will set the houses afire with all diaries, documents and anything of value as soon as it gets dark, and leave early tomorrow morning to try to catch Stilwell. We shall travel through what to us is uncharted area. I cannot reveal even a general route for fear the enemy might get on the trail. We poured gasoline on a scout car and a couple of sedans and shot tommy-gun bullets into them only a few short hours ago. We still have a couple of cars to destroy but are waiting to see if someone trying to get out cannot use them. I have just come from the tank corps with a thousand rounds of machine-gun ammunition and we hope this is enough to last out our small unit on what promises to be a long journey. The doctor and I had a box of food and killed a sheep which we put in a burlap bag, for emergency, but someone has stolen these already and we will have to manage to get along on a can of cheese we discovered in the litter of belongings in this abandoned Headquarters. Our supply of boiled water is very low and unless we soon find Stilwell I am afraid we must drink whatever we can find in the dirty ditches along the way. Everything is happening so quickly that I cannot write a coordinated story.

Briefly, here are the last days of Burma. For the last two months the result of the Burma campaign was almost a foregone conclusion.

In the first place we lacked sound political theory; we had no war aim in Burma. The people, advocating independence, were unfriendly from the beginning and when the Japanese began to succeed, this ripened into open hostility.

The open hostility of the people caused us to fight blindly. Without air support, we scarcely ever knew exactly where the enemy was, where he would appear, or in how much strength. Intelligence broke down almost completely. The Japs were led by Burmese people through country paths, jungle thickets, into the rear of our positions time & again, causing numerous road blocks, clogging our supply lines, disrupting communications and causing an adverse psychological effect on the minds of men and officers.

As the Japanese advanced the lawlessness behind the lines increased. Railroads were wrecked, cars were fired upon in the dark, and even in daylight several Chinese were murdered on the road. Gangs of dacoits, as many as four or five hundred, armed with cruel, butcher-knife-like dahs and with torches in their hands often went through towns completing the work of destruction begun by Japanese incendiary bombs. The Japanese, and the small but active group of Burmese that were their allies, literally and devastatingly burned their way through Burma.

Here are some of the other factors of defeat:

▶ Our lines of communications were uncertain. The railroads

often did not run because the railway personnel ran away or was intimidated by Burmese. Our radio communication between echelons was poor.

▶ Water supply was insufficient in the hot wastelands north of Prome and Toungoo and, with the Japs constantly cutting our rear, we often were cut off from watering holes.

▶ We never received any reinforcements. The British troops had to stay in line and slug it out for three months. Not only were the ranks woefully depleted, but the men were tired beyond telling.

▶ Finally, the Japanese fought total war, backed by political theory and strengthened by powerful propaganda. They made this total war feasible by cornering economic life in conquered areas, utilizing labor power and seizing raw materials to supply continuing war from war itself. It is a type of war thoroughly understood by the Russians and Germans, half adopted by the Chinese, and little understood by Britain and America.

Again I must close and try to rush this off. All about me there is nothing but utmost misery. Roads are lined with belongings abandoned by refugees, 20,000 of whom crossed the Irrawaddy only yesterday, hoping to get to India, but their chance is very slight. Evacuation to Bhamo via the river route is practically useless with the Jap capture of Lashio.

Must go. Goodby.

Time, May 11, 1942

Flight Through the Jungle

by Jack Belden

THE ROAD to India that night was flooded by the ebb-tide of the British Empire. Officials, refugees, soldiers were pushing through the dust in columns and groups, trampling on the grass beside the road, knocking over children, stumbling on wounded, jumping into halted trucks, streaming, swirling, and ebbing westward.

Dark Chin tribal soldiers were marching in single file in long, ragged columns on either side of the road; their rifles were slung any old which way on straps over their shoulders; their faces wore sullen, expressionless looks. Darker Indians, with packs half again as high as themselves balanced on their heads, were marching between them. Women were shuffling along beside them, carrying bundles wrapped in orange cloth. Wives marched with soldiers. Children tottered along after their mothers. Everything was buried in a haze of dust. Human feet shuffled up dust. Mules and horses kicked up dust. Automobiles whirled up great clouds of dust.

Three tiny Indian children were enveloped in a whirlpool of flying sand. They turned their backs to the cruel particles. Little fists wiped at dirty eyes. They opened their eyes, big, black, and round. They stared with hurt, dazed looks at the eddying throngs. One of them, a little girl wearing a white skirt, carried a tiny knapsack over her shoulder. She was prepared for a journey. She took the hands of the two boys and they marched stolidly onward, their heads bent down, looking at the dust raised by their little feet.

On the befouled grass in front of a Buddhist temple, among scattered grains of rice, dirty tin wash-basins, and discarded, blood-stained bandages, Chinese wounded of the 200th Division were wallowing. Chinese convoys were passing and dust was raining down on injured hands, legs, heads.

Swarms of flies were picking at wounds. A Chinese medical officer ran out to Williams.

"Where shall I take them?"

"To India. To Imphal."

But how? How? How is anyone going to get to India?

Gloucesters walking along the road jeered at us: "Where's your trailer, Yank?"

The Americans are sitting in cars on their asses. The British Empire is walking on its feet. On its last feet? . . .

A dirty white pagoda leaned precariously over the road. Filthy British soldiers lay underneath it on the grass, flat on their backs, looking at the sky. Indians wearing white shirts squatted down with purple skirts tucked between their legs. Indians wear no shirts and are bare to their waists. Indians wear pants. Indians wear orange and black checked skirts. Indians are wrapped in green and red blankets. Indians are naked. Indians wear towels around their shoulders. Members of the Burma Rifles wear wide bush hats and are sitting quietly. Chinese soldiers with greasy uniforms move ceaselessly, looking at everything curiously, chattering, chattering, chattering and laughing irreverently.

A woman, squatting, was peeling tomatoes and onions, dropping slices in an iron pot. The pot hung on sticks, suspended over a bonfire. An Indian in a blue striped shirt and dirty yellow shorts, was looking in a mirror under the light of a lantern and squeezing pimples on his face. Americans were digging vigorously with shovels under the wheels of a stuck truck. Sweat came through their thick shirts. They stank.

Bony black skeletons were carrying small iron pots in their hands, begging for water. They begged the Americans for water, the Chin soldiers for water, everyone for water. Everyone had a pot, a canteen, a cup. Everyone was begging every one else for water.

And a little boy sat on the ground, his elbow on his pack, his chin in his hand, staring.

An Indian girl, her Western style skirt flashing out with a swirl from her willowy hips, ran up to the car.

"Please may I ride in your jeep?"

"Jump in."

Her name was Zeli. She was twenty-five. She was married

to an Indian sergeant. She was one of a group of seventy-five refugees to be evacuated by the government. The British officer in charge of their group had disappeared that morning in a car. Everyone was walking.

An Anglo-Indian girl, sensuous and coarse-looking, ran up.

"May I ride in your jeep?"

"Jump in."

She climbed on top of the baggage in the back. Zeli slid down on a blanket and sat between Jones and me.

A nurse of Dr. Seagrave ran up.

"Our truck broke down. Can I . . ."

"Jump in."

The columns of the vanquished halt and lie down. Refugees huddle together sighing audibly. Rude gibes and coarse epithets shoot out of the dark as individual English soldiers plod on. Remarks are tinged with bitter cynicism. Everyone is losing faith in himself. The defeat is producing an enormous impression. Fright, disappointment, apathy flow down over the road. The retreat has turned into a march of escape, of preservation. There are only two thoughts in everybody's mind: Get to India. Keep alive.

Throngs move on.

A British colony is passing away.

The tide of empire recedes on itself and ebbs in the opposite direction.

Shortly after we pitched camp in a small clearing of dank swamp grass at midnight on May 5, a mysterious rumor spread through the soldiers, girls, and servants. It was said that the Americans would take the jeeps—two Americans to each jeep, with appropriate food stocks—and try to break their way through the jungle to the Chindwin River. It was further said that the Indian servants would be paid off and given a bonus. They, the Chinese, and the Seagrave nurses would be given food—not so much as the Americans, for the nurses spoke the Burmese language and could forage for themselves—and would be allowed to find their own trail to India—if that's where they wanted to go—by ox-cart or on foot.

Excited voices. Red, angry faces appearing in the light of jeep lamps. Suggestions. Insinuations. Recriminations.

But shortly after three o'clock, when we rose once more, without water to drink, with only a plate of dry oatmeal to eat, it was seen that we were not separating, that we were all going together. Guilty looks, accusing looks, relaxed into expressions of morose fatigue.

Zeli ran up to my jeep again. "I was kicked off the jeep on which I was riding. Please may I ride with you? I won't take up much room."

"Sure, jump in."

The column came to a halt beside a monastery. A pink haze slowly suffused the grayish-blue sky. Wisps of gray clouds hung suspended over low-lying green hills. Golden mohr and flame trees flashed like brilliant yellow and red lanterns. Ducks cackled. I grew drowsy. My head drooped with fatigue. "Rest on my shoulder," says Zeli. I do so. It is soft, yielding, comforting. I sleep.

At nine thirty in the morning we drew into the small town of Mansi on the edge of the jungle. British civilians as well as soldiers were crowding into it. A tall young Eurasian woman was walking by the side of a fat, middle-aged Englishman. She looked up. Her eyes were full of smoking, passionate fire. I thought: "You are that man's mistress. But he is too old. You don't like him. Why don't you come into the jungle with me?"

Stilwell got out to confer with the town elder. Breedom Case, the missionary, translated. We learned that five thousand refugees had already passed through the town, making for India. The headman was not sure about the road westward to Homalin, on the Chindwin River, but he said it would take four days to get there. After that, eight days down river by raft to Tammu on the India highway.

Stilwell obtained as much information as he could, but it was not much. He grunted now and then as Case translated the elder's words, and every once in a while he said: "Humph!" Finally he looked up, made a beckoning gesture with his arm at the column, shouted: "Turn 'em over," and once more we started, soon entering a forest.

In a little while we came into a clearing. All the jeeps were told to get at the head of the column. We drew up in front of a swaying, bamboo rope bridge. Below it was a deep chasm. We realized that empty jeeps might just barely get across this flimsy bridge; trucks, never. Everyone was ordered to get out of the cars. Dimly we felt that this was the end of the motor journey.

"Everyone come over here into the clearing," called Stilwell. "The Americans on the left. The Seagraves next to them. The Chinese here. British here. Now the Indians."

We formed in a chained circle. American, Englishman, Chinaman, Burman, Indian, Chin, Karen, Kachin, Malaysian, Anglo-Indian, Anglo-Burman, half-breeds from all of Asia. A motley crew.

Generals, colonels, young privates, radioman, mechanic, cook, servant, dishwasher. American preacher, British Quaker, Karen nurse. Men, women, and a dog.

American names: Stilwell, Jones, Gish, Nowakowski, Ferris, McCabe, Laybourn, Lee. From American towns: Winnemucca, Indiana; Thermopolis, Wyoming; Hopbottom, Pennsylvania; Meridian, Oklahoma; Damariscotta, Maine; San Francisco, Detroit, Yonkers, Brooklyn, Honolulu. British names: Davidson-Huston, Dykes, Haight, McDonald, Campbell, Inchboard. From Liverpool; Willaston, Cheshire; Wanstead, London; Little Buckland Nr Broadway Wores. Chinese and Indian names: Chow, Tseng, Singh. Shanghai, Kweilin, Calcutta. Half-breeds: Alexander, Nathan, Phillips. Daughters of Burma: Ruth, Emily, Lucy, Lasi. And a dog named James.

All in a circle.

Zeli and the Anglo-Indian girl stood apart, belonging to no group.

"Who are you?" called the general.

"Refugees."

"All right. Get over there with the Seagrave unit."

Colonel Wyman began to call out the names of the Americans: "Belden. Chesley. Janes. Young. . . ."

General Stilwell stood in the center of the circle glaring at the strange crew surrounding him. He was wearing a light khaki windbreaker, long khaki pants, over a pair of sturdy army boots, the tops of which were wrapped in canvas leggings. On his head was a battered campaign hat. In his mouth an amber cigarette-holder and a burning cigarette. At the same time he was chewing gum. As he glared around, his eyes finally came to rest on the British group.

Two men—Colonel Davidson-Huston and Major Dykes, the members of the British Military Mission who had boarded the last train out of Shwebo only to rejoin us later when the train broke down—were the only ones we recognized. Nine others, all of them filthy, unshaven, emaciated, and tired-looking, none of whom we knew, were also there.

"Where did you come from?" snarled Stilwell. "Just picking up a ride, huh? I don't mind you hopping a ride, if you only come and ask first." He glared at them for a moment, then suddenly shot out a question: "Got any rations?" A few shakes of the head. "All right, stay where you are. Colonel Huston, you will take charge of the British group."

With a quick gesture the General threw away his cigarette, put his hands on his hips, raised his chin in the air, and began to address all of us who were standing around him.

"The bridge ahead can take only jeeps. We will abandon the transport here. We will stay together in one group."

As he said this, a few happy smiles shot around the circle.

"But we must have better discipline," he continued. "We must be careful of the food. We don't know what is ahead. Be careful of what you eat. Eldridge, you will be in charge of the food. Don't use a single can without getting word from me. All food will be pooled. If I catch anyone who has not turned in his food, he will immediately leave the party.

"Keep your weapons and ammunition. When we get to Maingkaing, we plan to build rafts and get to Homalin in eight days. If we do this, we will have to leave some of the food. But if we work the rafts night and day, we should be able to get there in four days. We are going to try to get a radio set up and have food sent down to Homalin from India. Now, I'm not going to monkey with this food business. Eldridge will be in charge of all of it.

"Throw away your baggage right here. Limit yourselves to what you can carry on a four days' march. We can perhaps figure on taking a couple of jeeps to Homalin. But you might as well split up your clothes, and those who have too many give to those who haven't enough. Unfortunately there are no extra shoes, but we'll take it easy and give everyone a chance to get accustomed to walking.

"We may have a few trying days, but we are ahead of the mob and I think we are all set."

When the general finished his speech, the circle soberly broke up. All went to the cars and began sadly to discard those things they couldn't carry.

Out of the medical trucks spill heavy boxes of medicine. They are broken open, small quantities of quinine and emytine taken out.

Up the sides of these trucks clamber the girls. White bodices, yellow sweaters, red skirts, pink brassieres tumble down on the forest floor. Tiny hands hold up rich Mandalay silks. Audible sighs, pathetic glances, a shrug of the shoulders, and the silks join the growing heap.

Quickly the girls discard almost everything they own. What is left is put in small leather cases, wrapped in towels, in sheets. Knots are tied, bundles are formed, feminine arms are placed through cloth loops, the weight of a bundle is tested against a female back.

The men are slower, seek to hold onto more of their things than the girls; for they can carry more. But swiftly the rubbish heap grows. American shaving lotions, tins of powder, underwear, notebooks, overcoats find their way into the grass.

The clearing takes on the appearance of a rummage sale. Everything is a kaleidoscopic, colorful mess. Pink brassieres hang on thorns, Oxford-gray pants lie on top of olive-green car radiators, gray steel helmets tumble in the weeds. Whisky bottles, whose presence heretofore has been unknown, mysteriously appear. Heads are tilted back, the bottles emptied, thrown away. Blankets full of cigarette tins are opened; they are bought and sold, traded for a pair of khaki shorts.

Alexander, Stilwell's Anglo-Indian chauffeur, discards his own clothing, dons a pair of army pants, delicately laces up a pair of puttees, puts on a pair of army boots two sizes too big for him. Everything hangs loose on him. He looks like a vaudeville clown. But he grins proudly at his new outfit.

Soldiers, girls, mechanics rush about with shrill cries, flinging their belongings from the cars, bursting into cases, carrying tin cans of food to the jeeps, picking, choosing, and throwing away what they don't want. The clearing fills up. Bulky belongings thud onto the ground, lighter things rain through the air, catching on the branches of bushes. On the jungle floor, among mattresses and whisky bottles, brown and black girls, white and yellow men wallow. Only the Chinese have nothing to throw away. They begin gathering up discarded clothing, placing it hastily in knapsacks. Someone says we may be able to carry our belongings on the rafts, and a momentary pang of disappointment stirs those who begin to feel they have thrown away things too quickly. John Grindley has laid an expensive camera aside to carry with him. Someone has taken it or it has become lost in the discarded rubbish. There is no need to throw everything away. Blankets are kept. Rolls are made. Those of the Americans appear larger than first thought. Finally people begin to wander off in knots and groups over the bamboo bridge ahead. Food is loaded in the jeeps. Only one man is allowed in a jeep. The last motor ride starts.

Eleven jeeps in all went through the jungle. Ahead of us straggled the other members of our party. I saw two members of the Friends Ambulance Unit walking slowly, half supporting a tiny Burmese nurse. As I drew abreast of them, one called out: "Will you take this girl? She's been sick with malaria. She doesn't weigh much."

"Sure, I'll look after her," I said.

"More likely she'll take care of you," called a voice as I drove off.

I looked at my companion. About her slender waist and legs hung a lavender silk skirt. Around her head was a blue flowered cloth under which two black braids fell down to a brown sweater covering her shoulders. Her skin was dark brown, very smooth and without a blemish. She had a clean, washed, fresh appearance. Her name was Than Shwe.

"It means in English 'a million dollars gold,'" she said simply.

I asked her what she thought of leaving Burma and going to India.

"I like to go very much. I don't mind leaving home."

Her answers were all given in a serious, quiet tone of voice

as if she were replying to very important questions. A funny
girl, I thought, and reached into my pocket and took out a
cigarette. Placing it in my mouth, I tried to light it while at
the same time steering the jeep over the bumpy jungle floor.

I felt her hand brush against my lips; she took the cigarette
out of my mouth, placed it in her own, lit it, and gravely put
it back between my lips.

I was surprised. "I'm sorry," I said, "I didn't know you
smoked. Please have a cigarette."

"Don't smoke. I only do this for others," she replied. "I
like do favors for others."

Suddenly I had a feeling that I was looking at myself in the
movies. A tough sailor, cast up on a foreign shore, wandering
into the jungle and finding a simple native girl who performs
little favors for him that charm him and make him forget all
his civilization. Melodramatic, yes; but a feeling of romantic
melancholy stole over me as we wound slowly through that
dry, dead jungle.

We came to a steep bank hanging over a creek. Here we
learned that we were not to go to our original destination.
Crowds of refugees, we were told, had already poured
through there and taken all the rafts. Eighty of them had left
only the day before. Instead we were to go to a village five
miles distant, and there, away from the crowds, build our own
rafts.

"There is almost no road ahead," said an officer. "It will be
very difficult for the jeeps to get through. Only one man to a
car," he said, looking at me and the girl pointedly.

"She's not a man," I said. "And she doesn't weigh more
than a fly, and besides she's sick."

"Okay. Everybody in compound-low," called the officer,
and we slid down the bank into the stream, crossed it, and
came out into a narrow field. Across this field in parallel lines
were a series of ridges, so high that it seemed as if the jeeps
could not possibly get over them. To attempt to do so, we
began roaring around in a circle, getting as far away from the
first ridge as possible, then, like a football backfield, breaking
formation and rushing in high gear at the ridges at an angle
from the side. The jeeps hit the ridges with terrific force, the
front wheels bucked over them, and the momentum brought

the back wheels onto the top of the ridge, where a quick burst of gas carried them across. This process was repeated several times, and the spectacle of the jeeps roaring in circles and bucking high off the ground, throwing out boxes, and once a driver, looked like a wild West rodeo.

After we had cleared the ridges we headed straight up a bank at a seventy-five-degree angle into a mass of thickets where at first there appeared no path. We broke through the trees and finally came out into a narrow corridor down which our jeeps could go. The roots of innumerable large trees stuck out across the path, making of it a washboard on which we shimmied and shook as in a Coney Island jolt-and-shake car. I saw Than Shwe holding on and biting her lips and I slowed to a pace slower than a walk.

At last we came to a village on the outskirts of which Stilwell had already set up his headquarters in a large house. I picked up Than Shwe and carried her in my arms up the steps and laid her on a shelf which ran around the walls of a room. Then I placed my blanket over her and my water bottle by her side.

"Please come back," she said as I left to go back through the jungle once more and pick up the rest of the food. This time it was not like an adventure; it was plain torture. When I returned, Than Shwe had already gone, having joined the Seagrave unit in a separate camp in the village.

By now we learned that we were not going by raft, but were going to start walking the next day. For Stilwell, having discovered that it would take several days to build rafts, had decided to push straight ahead for Homalin and the Chindwin River.

Because there were no rafts, we had to obtain bearers to carry our food. Although the shutting down of the forestry services and the timber monopolies had thrown a great many casual laborers back into the villages, the hordes of refugees pouring through had temporarily taken an equal number out again, and though the village headman was able to promise us a number of bearers, they were not enough to carry all our food.

We were brooding about this problem when, late that afternoon, a rather unexpected event occurred. Sitting on the grass about the house, we suddenly heard a tinkling of bells and then a herd of twenty mules went clattering down the path, followed by two Chinese drivers, who were beating them with switches and urging them on.

A British forester, who had joined us that day, jumped to his feet, called for some Chinese soldiers and went racing after the mules. A little while later they all were brought back and we simply commandeered them. The Chinese muleteer was on his way to India anyway. He was from Shantung, far away in North China, and we never did fathom what he was doing here at this time and place. But whatever he was doing, his unexpected appearance proved a windfall and immediately cut our transport problem in half.

The general was very pleased. "That's our first stroke of luck," he said.

That night I had a long talk with Stilwell about our position. Briefly, it was this.

Our group consisted of about 115 persons, twenty-one of them women. For purposes of easy handling on the march, the group had been divided into four sections. They were:

1. American—18 officers, 5 enlisted men, and 3 civilians (Lilly, Case, and myself).

2. British—11 officers and men and 2 civilians.

3. Seagrave Unit—2 doctors, 7 British Quaker members of the Friends Ambulance Unit, 19 Kachin, Karen, and Burmese nurses, 2 women refugees, and servants, totaling about 40 persons.

4. Chinese—Brigadier General Tseng and about 15 soldiers.

Furthermore, there were Indian cooks and mechanics, the latter being formed into a pioneer unit with the American group. In addition, there were twenty mules and one dog.

The area we were to traverse was part of a great triangle of jungle, bounded on the east by the Irrawaddy River, on the northwest by the Bramaputra River and the Himalaya Mountains, and on the south by a dry belt tapering off into Shwebo. This area differed in many places. In some sectors there was nothing but an impenetrable forest, a wet jungle, dissected by torrential mountain streams; in other places were plains and a dry dead jungle. In parts of the area were to be found heavy timber such as teak, kanyin, ingyin, and thayet; in other places were palms, giant ferns, banana, mango, and bamboo trees. The level land abounded in elephants. In the whole area were innumerable tribes of monkeys, tailed on one side of the jungle, tailless on the other side. Russel's vipers, hamadryads, and king cobras—all of them poisonous snakes—were also known to be present in fairly large numbers. Villages were scarce and the population sparse.

Our plan was to head west across part of this area to Homalin on the Chindwin River, and to cross the river before the Japanese coming up from the south in gunboats could cut across our path. We originally estimated that it would take us four days to reach the Chindwin, but we were inclined to increase this estimate because we had no certain information concerning the exact distance. Using guides, with Case as an interpreter, we planned to cut across country through the jungle and come out a day's boat ride from Homalin, when we would look over the lay of the land and see if any Japanese were around.

Our chief problem before we started seemed to be food. When our party had originally set out from Shwebo, we had been equipped with thirty days' dry rations for sixty-five people. But during the journey, stray groups fastening on us here and there had increased our numbers to almost double their original total. In addition, in examining the stores that afternoon, Captain Eldridge had discovered that they contained an abnormally large amount of butter and jams, which were useless in the hot jungle. Thus, facing a trip the duration of which was unknown, we appeared to be short on adequate food stocks.

But to make up for this shortcoming, the danger of a direct Japanese move against us seemed to have lessened considerably.

"The chief dangers we now face," Stilwell said to me, "are food, rains, and the clogging of the roads by refugees. If the monsoons don't hold off we may not be able to cross the rivers. And rains will slow us up so that our food may not last us long enough. I suppose that is the chief danger—the combined threat of rain and food shortage. There are also the soldiers behind us who have disintegrated and are shooting up the villages and killing cows and bullocks with machine guns. We may have trouble with them.

"I have no news, but I believe the British may have held the Japs off the Kalewa road to India. As far as we're concerned, the Japs might get on our tails, but I consider that a remote danger.

"If we reach Homalin, we ought to be all right. I'm trying to send a radio asking the British in India to get food down through the hills to Homalin. If they do, why, our troubles will be over."

As he was saying these words, Sergeant Chambers, our radio operator, was trying desperately to contact our headquarters in Chungking. Over and over again the message was repeated: "Get food and bearers to Homalin. . . . Food and bearers to Homalin."

The power was fast failing and still there was no contact. It was our last chance. Tomorrow, before starting the march, we would destroy the radio, for we could not carry it with us.

Chambers sat on the ground, tapping out his message under the light of a jeep lamp. By him stood Lieutenant Colonel Frank Dorn writing out messages in code.

The tap-tapping of the radio instrument went like a refrain through the jungle. "Food and bearers to Homalin. Food and bearers. . . ."

I looked at the general.

"I'm also radioing the British to get police, guides, food, and water on this road. If they don't, there's going to be a catastrophe. Everyone trying to get out and everyone out of hand. Thousands will die."

Retreat With Stilwell, 1943

"Damn the Torpedoes!"

---

by Helen Lawrenson

A GROUP of sailors are drinking beer at a bar called George's in Greenwich Village. The juke box is playing "Deep in the Heart of Texas," and every time it stops someone puts another nickel in and it starts up again. A little man with curly hair and bushy eyebrows turns and glares fiercely at it.

"Can't that machine play nothing else?" he roars. He looks tough enough and mad enough to eat it, record, needle, and all.

"Stop beating your gums, brother," drawls the tall sailor with the black jersey. "I like it. It's catchy."

"I just come back from Texas," adds a third whose face is a complete pink circle, illumined by twinkling blue eyes and a cherubic grin.

"How was it?"

"Oh, dandy!" says Cherub, sarcastically. "Just dandy. Fine trip for your health. A Nazi tin fish chased us for three days. We never seen a patrol boat nor a plane the whole time. Saw one destroyer going hell-bent for election into Charleston one afternoon about dusk, but we all figured she was trying to get safe home before dark when the subs come out.

"We was carrying fifty thousand barrels of Oklahoma crude and fifty thousand of high-test gasoline. It sure gives you a funny feeling. I thought we'd get it any minute. Man, those nights are killers! You sleep with your clothes on. Well, I don't exactly mean sleep. You lie in bed with your clothes on. All of a sudden the old engines slow down and your heart speeds up. Someone knocks on the door, and you rise right up in your bed and seem to lie there in the air. So it turns out it's only the watch. You settle down again and try to light a cigarette if your hand don't shake too much. Not that you're scared of course. Oh, noooh!"

The others laugh. "Who ain't scared?" growls the little man with the bushy brows. "A torpedo connects with one of them tankers and it's just like lighting a match to cellophane. You ain't got a chance. Boom! and you're in the hero department. Just like that. And the next thing, all the guys you used to know are going around saying, 'Well, he wasn't such a bad guy after all. Poor old Joe Bananas! He lowered the boom on me for ten bucks the last time he was in port and he never did get a chance to pay it back. Let's have a beer to his memory.'"

"Well, let's have a beer anyway," says Slim, in the black jersey. "Here, Cherub, it's on you. You just got paid off. How about springing for another round?"

"Okay," says Cherub. "Might as well spend it now. It don't do you no good when you're floating around in a lifeboat. No kidding, a guy's a sucker to go through nights like that. You can't believe it. The next morning you come out on deck, and the sea's blue and beautiful and the sun's shining. The night before—with the zigzagging and the sub alarms and the lying there in your bunk, scared stiff and waiting—it can't be true. That night can't have happened to *me*. Impossible. This is the same sea I've always sailed, the same kind of a wagon, the same watch. Last night just didn't happen." He takes a drink of beer. "But then the darkness comes again. Yeah—night must fall."

What worried him most, he adds, was a remark made during lifeboat drill just before sailing. "We was practicing and everything goes off pretty good. Then the Inspector, he says, 'Now just in case any of you fellows have to *jump*—remember when you go over the side to pull down on your lifebelt as hard as you can. Cause if you don't when you hit the water it's liable to break your neck.' . . . My God, I thought. Now I got to worry about holding on to my papers and my chocolate bar and my cigarettes and at the same time I got to hold on to my lifebelt so my neck don't get broke!"

"So you have your choice," says Slim, "burn to death, drown, be blown to bits when the torpedo hits the engine room, starve to death in a lifeboat, or get your neck broke when you first jump over the side. Any way you look at it, you're a gone sucker. Only a lame-brained sailor would go for that. You gotta be muscle-bound between the ears to do that for a living. And what for?"

"I'll tell you what for," says Bushy-Brows. "If the rising sun and the swastika and that bundle of wheat ain't gonna be flying over the White House we gotta keep 'em sailing. They gotta have oil and ore and stuff to fight this war, ain't they? And how we gonna get it to 'em if guys like us don't keep on sailing the ships? So that's what for!"

II

This scene is typical of those being enacted every night in the waterfront bars of ports all over the land. Every few days you pick up the papers and there is the same gruesome picture painted over and over again of sudden death that strikes in the night, of seas brilliant with burning oil, of men screaming in agony, dying in the flaming water under the dark, implacable skies. And every night, in some bar in every port, there will be a group of seamen talking it over, naming the names of those who were once their shipmates, cursing the Axis—what some of them refer to as "Hitler, and his saddle-lights Mussolini and Hirohito"—and drinking toasts to one another's good luck.

"I was asleep when the torpedoes hit us—" said John Walsh, wiper, survivor of the Cities Service tanker, *Empire*, torpedoed off Fort Pierce, Florida "—three of them. I rushed up on deck and helped get one of the lifeboats over the side. I saw our captain on a life raft. He and some of the other men were on it. The current was sucking them into the burning oil around the tanker. I last saw the captain going into a sheet of orange flame. Some of the fellows said he screamed. . . . Monroe Reynolds was with me for a while. His eyes were burned. He was screaming that he was going blind. The last time I saw him he jumped into the fiery water. That was his finish, I guess. . . ."

In the first four months of this year over a hundred American merchant ships were attacked by enemy U-boats off our own coasts. About 950 seamen were killed. Despite improvements in the patrol system, the ships are still being sunk. The average during April was five or six a week.

It is a hideous way to die. I knew two men who were lost when the *Pan-Massachusetts* was sunk. One was a little thin man with spectacles, who had been a newspaperman. His name was Fred Fitzgerald. The other was Paddy Flynn, an oiler, whose two sons had already lost their lives in the war. I don't know how Fitz and Paddy died. The *Pan-Mass* carried 100,000 barrels of gasoline, oil, and kerosene. (A barrel is 53 gallons.) Many of the men burned to death as they stood on the deck of the ship; others died struggling in the blazing sea which was on fire for a mile around the tanker.

"The bo'sun was in charge," said George Lamb, survivor of the *Pan-Mass*. "He did everything possible to save the lives of all the men. He cut a raft loose after the men said they were ready. It burst into flames as soon as it hit the water. . . . Although I couldn't swim I decided to go overboard. I figured it was better to drown than to be burned alive. I said, 'Let's go, Ingraham.' He was the steward. He was standing there beside me in his shorts, the skin peeling off his back from the flames. We shook hands. He said, 'Remember me, Red!' I said, 'OK. If I make it, I'll remember you. . . .' He was burned to death. . . ."

On his final trip Fitz wrote a letter to a man I know. In it he said: "No fooling though, it's a queasy feeling to be shadowed by those bastards. One of them tried to decoy us off St. Augustine by flashing 'P,' which means show your lights. The Old Man zigzagged to hell-and-gone, and most of us were kidding each other about the false alarm when the *Pan Amoco* reported sighting a sub at 6 A.M. off Jupiter. (Our incident had occurred at 11:30 the previous night, 60 miles away.) We quit kidding then."

He went on to report an incident on his previous trip: "Just as the moon was going down the second mate happened to make the big circle with his binoculars and spotted a sub in perfect silhouette. The first thing I knew about it was the Ordinary on watch giving me the shake. 'There's a Jerry on our tail,' he said. 'All hands get dressed with lifebelts and stand by.' I got up all right but nothing happened. Later that day the same sub got the *India Arrow* and the *China Arrow*, just a few miles from where we were. What burns you up is no guns. You can't fight the bastards back. Luckily this crate is fast, so we can get going; but on some of them there isn't a damn thing you can do except call the U-boat commander an old meanie—or something! Later it comes as something of a jolt to discover that fellows you once knew and were shipmates with are gone for good. Worse yet, without a fighting chance."

Hundreds of other American seamen have had to stand by and watch enemy subs sink their ships from under them without guns to fight back. "You can't fight submarines with potatoes," as Bo'sun Walter Bruce said when rescued from the tanker *Malay*, torpedoed off the North Carolina coast.

The law to arm the merchant marine was signed by President Roosevelt on November 18, 1941, but most of the ships which have been sunk have been unarmed. A few which *were* armed have fought off submarines and either damaged them or frightened them away.

Guns are being put on the ships now as fast as possible, but some of the ships are so old and broken down that a gun is almost more of a liability than an asset. As one sailor says, "That rust-pot I just come off, they must of got her out of the Smithsonian Institute! Sure, we had a gun on her. But Holy Mackerel! if we'd ever of had to fire it the whole ship would have fallen apart."

At the insistence of the National Maritime Union, special fireproof life-saving suits have been approved by the Maritime Commission and are being purchased by all tanker companies. On many of the ships new types of life rafts are being installed, and lifeboats are now being stocked with medical kits, food concentrates, and blankets.

When the *Lahaina* was sunk, 34 survivors spent ten days in a lifeboat with a capacity of 17. Two of them became half-crazed with hunger and thirst, jumped overboard, and were drowned. A third lost his mind completely, had to be lashed to the bottom of the boat, and died the next day. A fourth died from exposure. Dan James, nineteen-year-old wiper, describes the death of the last man: "It was cold the last night out. I was sleeping under a blanket with Herman. He'd been feeling low for some time. I kept saying to him, 'Give me some of that blanket.' But he wouldn't let loose. Finally I grabbed it from him. He just lay still. I touched his hand . . . it was cold . . . he was dead the whole time."

The patrol system is still not adequate, although vastly improved. In a letter to Secretary of the Navy Knox last March, President Joseph Curran of the National Maritime Union suggested that the large fleets of fishing boats, most of which are now laid up, be fitted out as patrol boats for the Atlantic coast, as was done during the last war. The sooner this is done the better.

There is no doubt about it, the merchant seamen took it on the chin during the first half of this year—with no guns, no patrols, antiquated lifebelts, and practically no safety precautions. They were sent out as helpless targets for the subs; but their morale was as magnificent as it was unheralded. That precautions are now being taken to protect them doesn't detract from their courage.

All the seamen know what they are facing when they ship out. Yet they keep on sailing. Remember, they don't have to. They are in the private merchant marine, and they can quit any time they want to. Most of them could get good shore jobs, working in shipyards as riggers and welders and mechanics and what-not, where the chief worry would be the danger of someone dropping a wrench on their feet. It isn't the money that keeps them sailing. On the coastwise run, from New York to Texas, they get a war bonus which works out to around $2.33 a day, hardly worth risking your life for. Also the bonus doesn't apply to the Gulf.

As a matter of fact, former seamen who have been working in shoreside jobs are going back to sea. A few months ago the National Maritime Union issued a call to former seamen. Since then over 2,000 ex-sailors have turned up to ship out again, hundreds of them at the union hall in the port of New York alone, among them men who have been working as furriers, truck drivers, electricians, office workers, actors, construction workers, miners, painters, and bakers.

Those who have been torpedoed and rescued ship right out again as soon as they can get out of the hospital. That takes plenty of nerve, but the merchant seamen have it. They don't get much publicity, and you seldom hear anyone making

speeches about them. They don't get free passes to the theater or the movies, and no one gives dances for them, with
pretty young actresses and debutantes to entertain them. No
one ever thinks much about their "morale" or how to keep it
up. It was only recently that a bill was passed to give them
medals. And because they wear no uniforms they don't even
have the satisfaction of having people in the streets and subways look at them with respect when they go by.

It is not that the seamen, themselves, are asking for any
special credit or honors. When you mention words like heroism or patriotism to them they look embarrassed. "Listen,
brother, there's a war on!" they say. Ashore, they frequently
pretend that they are not brave at all. Not long ago I was
talking to a man called Windy, who had just come off the
Texas run and had been chased by a submarine for three days.
"No more of that for me!" he said. "I tell you, any guy who
keeps on shipping these days has got bubbles in his think-
tank. The only safe run is from St. Louis to Cincinnati. I'm
going to get me a shore job. Why commit suicide at my age?"
We believed him; and not one of us could blame him. . . .
The next day we heard he had shipped out again. He is now
on the high seas, en route to India.

Harper's Magazine, July 1942

The Battle of Midway

by Foster Hailey

WHILE our land-based Midway planes and the squadrons from the carriers were attacking the Japanese striking force, the enemy support group, spearheaded by the Hiryu, was streaking eastward.

Our own three carriers, the Hornet and the Enterprise in the lead and to the southward of the Yorktown, were still speeding westward, closing the gap between the two forces.

On the bridge of the Astoria, which was one of the two cruiser escorts for the Yorktown, we were anxiously awaiting the return of the Yorktown's planes. Shortly after 1 P.M. they began to come back, first the fighters, then the dive bombers, all seventeen of them.

The first one had no more than landed on the Yorktown's deck than Admiral Fletcher sent a message to all the ships within visual range:

"One enemy carrier sunk."

The message was broadcast over our loud-speaker system. The kids around the guns cheered like mad.

Up on the bridge, however, the tension was increasing.

Lieutenant Commander "Dave" Davidson, the communications officer, hurrying past on an errand, told me we had been sighted by an enemy scout plane. It had been shot down, but not before it had gotten away a contact report.

"It won't be long now," said Dave, grimly.

It wasn't.

The Yorktown waved off the last of her returning planes and began to launch her reserve fighters. The flag hoist which means enemy planes approaching shot up to her yardarm.

"Stand by to repel attack" went the command booming over our loud speaker, and a moment later, "action starboard."

First visual evidence from the Astoria's bridge of the approaching attack group of eighteen dive bombers was several big splashes to starboard as the enemy bombers began to jettison their loads as our fighters hit them. Then, following the bombs, flaming enemy planes began to fall. In a matter of seconds five twisting columns of smoke marked the death of as many enemy dive bombers.

"They were in three V's of six planes each at about fifteen thousand feet," said Scott (Go Get 'Em) McCuskey, who was up with the Yorktown fighters to protect his carrier, "Adams," his wing man, "and I went at them from a beam approach. They scattered like a bunch of pigeons and we drove right through them. I knocked one out of one side of the V, then went on across and got one on the other side. Adams got another."

The trailing enemy formations, diving under or zooming over the first section, which was the target of the American fighters, continued on toward the Yorktown.

From the Astoria's bridge we saw the end of one Japanese plane. He came diving down out of the fleecy white overcast with a Grumman Wildcat on his tail. He pulled out close to the water and started radical evasive maneuvers.

"Don't let him get away," the marines on the antiaircraft battery just under the bridge were pleading. "Shoot him down."

The Wildcat fighter pilot, as if answering the pleas he couldn't hear, swooped twice at the fleeing enemy plane. After the second pass, it plunged into the sea to explode in a mass of flames.

Say this for the Japanese fliers, though. They kept on coming. Eleven were shot out of the air before they reached dropping distance, but the other seven won their way over the carrier and peeled off.

Every gun in the force was yammering away at the enemy planes as they plummeted, black as hate, out of the white clouds. The whole starboard side of the Yorktown seemed to burst into flame as her gunners poured out red-hot shells at the enemy bombers.

Standing in the port wing of the Astoria's bridge, watching the carrier two thousand yards away, Captain Frank Scanland saw her begin an evasive turn and called to Lieutenant Commander Bill Eaton, the navigator, who always takes the deck during action:

"Better give her twenty-five right, Bill."

The casualness of his tone was so striking I stared in amazement.

The enemy planes were coming down now, one a second, out of the twelve-thousand-foot overcast. I don't know how it is with others, but for me it was like watching a slow-motion picture. It seemed to take minutes for the planes to come down from first sighting to bomb-dropping distance.

The first one down, making a beautiful dive at an angle of about seventy-five degrees, put his bomb on one side of the flight deck, not far from the midships island structure. There was a great flash of fire when it landed. The next one missed, his bomb falling alongside the carrier, throwing a great column of spray in the air. He never pulled out of his dive but flew flaming into the sea.

The air was full of black antiaircraft bursts, through which the first two planes dived unscathed. The third man, however, was hit while still some five thousand feet above the carrier's deck. His plane seemed to hang in the air a moment, then turned a complete somersault. As it straightened out again, the bomb looking almost half as big as the plane, broke loose and started falling. As though running on a wire, it fell straight for the carrier's smokestack. It hit a quarter of the way down the big pipe, penetrating almost to the fireroom before it exploded. Thick black smoke poured out.

Four more made their dives and dropped their bombs, but only one more hit was scored, with an armor-piercing bomb that penetrated the flight deck forward and exploded four decks down.

The Japanese bombers were paying little attention to the cruisers or destroyers. One, however, after dropping his bomb, turned toward the Astoria and gave us one squirt from his machine gun. It was his last one. As he flew past the cruiser at bridge level, the 20-millimeter guns went to work on him. His gunner already was slumped over as he flew past the ship and as he passed the bridge, only fifty feet above the water, he too was hit and sagged down against the side of his cockpit. His plane never came out of its shallow glide, but plunged into the water astern.

The Japanese dive bombers were identified by our gunnery officer as Baugeki '97s. They had long, tapering wings, and long slim fuselages. Red circles were painted on the wing tops. There were two red bands around the fuselage about halfway back. They were painted a mottled brown.

After the bomb went down her stack, the Yorktown slowed to five knots. A great column of black smoke was pouring up amidships, and thinner wisps of smoke could be seen around the forepeak, seeping up from the fire deep in her forward compartments.

Soon her signal searchlight began blinking and to the Astoria came the message: "Send small boat for admiral and staff."

The bombing had knocked out the ship's radio, and the admiral had to be where he could communicate with the other ships and shore stations.

Captain Scanland turned the Astoria to send her across the bow of the slowly moving carrier, and one of our motor sailers was launched, with Lieutenant Willie Isham at the helm, to bring Admiral Fletcher to us.

Pulling under the side of the burning Yorktown, the little boat took a line from the carrier down which the admiral and eight of his staff clambered, including Captain Spencer Lewis, his chief of staff, Commanders Gerry Galpin and Harry Guthrie, Lieutenant Commander Sam Latimer and Lieutenant Harry Smith.

They came aboard dressed in smoke-begrimed coveralls, looking like refugees from a chain gang. Admiral Fletcher moved in with Admiral Smith. His staff set up housekeeping in Captain Scanland's outer cabin, which they dubbed "Boy's Town."

Just as our boat was completing the final trip, two of the Yorktown's dive bombers that had been circling the formation ran out of gas. Seeing the Astoria stopped, they came in and landed alongside. Both pilots set their planes down beautifully in the roughening sea and were out of the cockpits and in their rubber boats without even getting their feet wet. Our small boat picked them up. One of them was Lieutenant

Commander Leslie, who had led the dive-bombing attack on the Akagi.

As the boat was picking up the pilot and radioman gunner of the second plane, a lookout reported a torpedo approaching the ship from dead ahead.

Looking down from the bridge, fifty feet above the water, Lieutenant Commander Davidson said he saw what he also believed was a torpedo passing parallel to the ship and not more than fifteen feet away. It may have been a fish, he said later, since there were no more torpedoes seen, and the destroyers patrolling around the stricken Yorktown made no contacts. If so, it was the biggest, fastest moving one he ever saw. It was running deep, at an estimated speed of forty-five or fifty knots, and leaving a clearly defined wake.

Anxious to get his boat under way, if there were enemy submarines about, Captain Scanland at that moment saw our small boat going back to take aboard the rubber boats the pilots had used.

"Get that damn boat aboard," he roared. "What in hell do they think they are, a salvage crew?"

Aboard the Yorktown, meanwhile, the fire was being brought under control. The smoke from the fire forward had thinned out to only a few small white wisps. Amidships, the black column of smoke pouring up out of the damaged stack had turned from black to brown. The holes in her deck had been repaired. She was picking up speed.

There was a cheer from our cruiser as a new ensign, bright as the morning, was hoisted to the yardarm to replace the smoke-blackened one that had been flying since dawn.

Knowing that the first attack probably would not be the last, Admiral Fletcher had asked for help to protect the stricken carrier, and two cruisers and two destroyers came boiling over the horizon.

The force was now back in cruising formation, the carrier flanked on either side by two cruisers. Ahead and on either side the destroyers patrolled.

"My speed is fifteen knots," the carrier signaled. Then it was seventeen, then eighteen.

There was a momentary scare as a large formation of planes was reported approaching from the southwest. Then they were identified as friendly. Flying high and fast, they passed overhead on a northerly course. Vengeance for the attack on the Yorktown was soon to be had. One of the Yorktown's scout planes finally had located the one undamaged Japanese carrier, the Hiryu, and Admiral Spruance had sent a striking force from the Enterprise to attack.

The American striking group hardly was out of sight when the ominous report, "many bogies bearing 350 degrees" came up from the flag plot. ("Bogies" was the voice code for un-identified aircraft.) That could mean but one thing, another attack. It was 5 o'clock. It had been three hours since the first attack.

Up to flank speed went the destroyers and cruisers, driving to place themselves between the carrier and the incoming enemy planes. The Yorktown, too, could be seen picking up speed. White water was curling away from her bow.

"She's launching fighters," someone on our bridge yelled. Off the patched flight deck the little Wildcats were roaring out to the attack. There was no preliminary circling this time. Straight for the enemy they flew, throttles full out.

Far to the north we saw the first evidence of the attack— the flash of exploding planes. At the same time came the re-port from the attacking fighters that the enemy planes were torpedo bombers, the Kogekiki '97s.

As they came in visual range, flying about five hundred feet off the water and in a fast, downward glide, every gun that could be brought to bear opened fire. One of the cruisers nearest to the approach was using her main batteries, firing into the water to raise the splashes that could be as deadly for an approaching plane as a direct hit.

The northern sky was black with AA shellbursts, forming a deadly curtain of steel in front of the approaching Japanese formation.

One group of five enemy bombers zoomed up and over the shellbursts, and then spread to attack the cruisers and destroy-ers. One of our 5-inch guns, firing point-blank at the enemy pilot that had picked the Astoria as his victim, got a direct hit. The enemy bomber blew up in a great flash of flame. Another skidded into the sea, leaving a flaming trail of burning gaso-line a quarter of a mile in length.

Two of the Japanese pilots were very brave men. Right
through the curtain of antiaircraft fire they flew, straight for
the Yorktown. Captain Elliott Buckmaster, on the Yorktown's
bridge, saw them and started an evasive turn. The "Mighty
Y," lacking her usual speed, couldn't quite make it. The two
enemy bombers, flying within a hundred yards of each other,
made their drops not over five hundred yards out from their
target. The big two-thousand-pound torpedoes, slanting
down to the water, porpoised once or twice, then ran straight
and true for the American carrier.

A great column of water splashed over the Yorktown's deck
at the first explosion, and she shuddered as though she had
hit a stone wall. The other hit within seconds, apparently entering through the hole torn by the first explosion, and exploding deep in the ship.

"I can't bear to watch it," said a young ensign who himself
was to die two months later in the Solomons, and he turned
away, his face set, tears in his eyes.

As the smoke and spray of the two explosions fell away we
could see the big carrier heeling ominously to port.

"My God, she's going to capsize," Captain Scanland whispered, incredulously.

She went over fifteen degrees, twenty, twenty-five, thirty.
Waves were lapping at the port edge of the thwartship pas-
sageways, through which the setting sun was shining.

"What's that signal?" the captain called to a signalman on
the deck below as two colored flags could be seen going up to
the Yorktown's yardarm. But it was unnecessary to ask again.
They could be plainly seen, whipping in the wind. They were
HP (hypo love, to use the phonetics of the fleet). They
meant, "I'm abandoning ship."

From below decks blue-clad and khaki-clad figures could
be seen climbing topside. Soon they were sliding down the
lines to the water.

The "Mighty Y" was fighting hard to save herself. As she
rocked on the long Pacific swells, she would seem, at times, to
regain some of her trim. Then she would lean over again, as
though tired of the struggle. The water rushing through the
hole in her side apparently had smothered whatever fires the
torpedo explosions had set.

All vessels in the area had their small boats over the side, while the destroyers nosed in as close as they could without endangering the swimming men, and started pulling survivors up onto their low decks.

The oil-covered sea was alive with bobbing heads, small rafts and 5-inch shell casings that had slid off the decks, or had been blown off by the force of the torpedo explosions. Unless you looked closely to see they were not leaving a wake, it was difficult to distinguish them from a submarine periscope.

For over an hour the work of rescue went on. Then, convinced there were no more survivors to be picked up, the escort vessels took up their small boats and the force formed up and headed east. One destroyer was left on guard.

As we headed toward the darkening eastern sky the Yorktown was silhouetted against the setting sun. Viewed from broadside her steep list did not show and she looked as battle-worthy as she had that morning.

Pacific Battle Line, 1944

X, B, and Chiefly A

by Brendan Gill

TUESDAY AFTERNOON last week, I saw one of the country's eight thousand ration boards at work. This particular board, which has jurisdiction over sugar, gas, new tires, and the re-capping of old ones, is in White Plains, but it is unquestion-ably a good deal like the board in Rye or Greenwich or New Rochelle. Last week it was occupied almost entirely with lis-tening to gas-rationing appeals. Its behavior struck me as pe-culiarly American, and somehow cheering, and perhaps worth telling about. The White Plains ration board occupies two dusty rooms on the second floor of an old high-school build-ing on Main Street. According to a sign tacked on a door at the head of the stairs, the board meets every afternoon from two to four, Monday through Friday. It was shortly before two when I arrived, and the door was locked. I rapped, and a good-looking young woman opened it. It seemed to me that she glanced rather apprehensively up and down the empty corridor. When I introduced myself she smiled in relief. "Come along in," she said. "I'm Mrs. Christenson. I guess you'd call me a sort of secretary to the board. When I heard your knock I was afraid the rush was beginning already. Yes-terday we had to handle a couple of hundred people. In two hours!"

I told Mrs. Christenson I was sorry to bother her, but she invited me to sit down. Shoving the white stacks of paper covering her desk to one side, she said, "Say, I'm glad to forget about this for a while. I never did any bookkeeping before in my life—just legal typing—and it isn't so easy to keep things straight. You see, some of our reports have to be sent to county headquarters, some to Albany, others to Wash-ington. All reports have to be typed in duplicate, triplicate, or quadruplicate, and they all have to be kept on file here. That's the catch. So far we've only got two little files for the whole job. Two files, one typewriter, and one telephone."

I asked her how she had happened to take on the job.

"I volunteered," she answered. "I hadn't worked since I got married, but I wanted to help."

"You mean you're handling this job without pay?" I asked.

"Of course," she said. "Just like the members of the board. Lately we've been allowed one salaried clerk to help us, but he's only paid about twenty-five a week."

Mrs. Christenson typed a few reports while I wandered about waiting for the board to convene. In the first room there were only Mrs. Christenson's desk and chair, a long table and three chairs for the board, and two long wooden benches against the walls. There was nothing in the other room but some loosely piled pamphlets, sugar-ration books, and gas-ration cards. It wasn't long before the members of the board began to arrive, and Mrs. Christenson introduced me as they came in. The chairman is Mr. Chauncey Griffen, a prominent real-estate man and a former mayor of White Plains. Mr. Griffen is white-haired and handsome and talks with a pleasant, country-club accent. The two other members of the board are Edward Schirmer, a director of several banks, and Thomas Holden, a lawyer. At two o'clock sharp, the board clerk, a former bakery salesman named Mr. Miller, arrived and Mrs. Christenson opened the hall door. As a queue of men and women moved timidly forward, I assured Mr. Griffen that I would not mention the names of all those appearing before the board.

The three members of the board, who sat only a couple of feet apart at the same table, heard cases individually, so there was a certain amount of confusion. The first appeal to which I listened was that of a middle-aged man who was in a state of great excitement. He appeared before Mr. Griffen. "My God," he said, leaning over Mr. Griffen's desk, "it would buy two bonds! It would help win the war! And I got to give it to the railroad." He spread his hands, palms up. "Where's the sense in that?"

"Now, now," Mr. Griffen said. "What would buy two bonds?"

"The price of the railroad tickets. My wife and I, if we want to go down to Maine to see her family, we always hop in the car. It costs five dollars, maybe, to get there by car. Now they give us an A card and say, 'Listen, you go by train.' But by train it costs us up to forty dollars. Thirty-five dollars wasted. That's practically two bonds!"

Mr. Griffen shook his head and said, "I'm sorry, but you go by train." The man began to argue, and Mr. Griffen, looking beyond him, said, "You might just remember that it takes fifty gallons of gas to warm up a bomber. And we need a lot of bombers. Next, please."

The next petitioner was a White Plains man who had come up by train from Florida, where he had found a war job for himself, in order to sell his house in White Plains and drive his car back to Florida. His car, however, had not yet been registered for 1942. Mr. Griffen pointed out to him that he would have to register his car before a gas-ration card could be issued to him. Then he would be given a B-3 card entitling him to fifty-seven gallons of gas, which would be enough, probably, to carry him over halfway to Florida. He would have to stop in some town along the route when his gas ran low and apply to the ration board there for another B-3 card to carry him the rest of the way.

The man thanked Mr. Griffen, and a woman took his place before the desk. She said, rather archly, "My dear Mr. Griffen, is this where you ration everything?"

"Everything but the ladies, Madam," Mr. Griffen said gallantly. "The government hasn't let us do that yet."

The woman fluttered her eyelids. Evidently everything was going to be just as she had hoped it would be. "Well, I've an A card," she said, "but I think I deserve better. You see, my dear mother's eighty, and she's had a stroke. The only real pleasure she gets out of life is a little ride every evening in the fine summer weather. And I'm afraid we won't be able to take our little rides unless you give me a B-3 card, or perhaps an X."

His air of gallantry still intact, Mr. Griffen said, "I happen to have a mother, too, who's over eighty and has had a stroke. She likes to go out riding whenever she can, too. But she'll have to make a certain number of sacrifices, just like the rest of us. She'll have to manage on an A card."

The woman stopped smiling. "But, of course, an A card

isn't enough," she said. "It may be the death of my poor mother."

"All right," Mr. Griffen said, standing up as a hint that the interview was about over. "You go out and get an affidavit from your mother's physician swearing that unless she can ride a minimum of forty or fifty miles a week, every week, she'll die. Then you can come back here and get more gas."

I walked over to Mr. Schirmer's place at the table. He was apparently having some difficulty with an Italian workman. Behind me I could hear Mrs. Christenson dealing with an old man who was asking for thirty-three pounds of sugar for a church supper, and in another part of the room the clerk, who wandered around because he had no place to sit down, was filling out an application for a set of recaps for a man who scraped floors. The room was filled with people by now, most of them looking amiable enough but a few staring at one another in mutual suspicion. I overheard one man ask, of no one in particular, "Well, did you think we'd ever come to this in the good old U.S.A.?"

Mr. Schirmer was saying to the Italian, "Take it easy. One step at a time. You say you work for the New York Central?"

"That's it. That's right."

"You make repairs along the tracks from White Plains to Crestwood? That means you spend the day riding back and forth on the different trains, doesn't it? You just get off wherever there's a length of track that needs repairing?"

"Sure. But at night, after midnight, is no trains. And suppose it rains, suppose I got to get up, emergency, I got to fix the tracks. Then I need a gas for my car."

"But you told me you lived a mile from the White Plains Station. You can't drive your car up and down the tracks. An A card ought to get you back and forth to work as often as you like." The two men had begun to sweat. Mr. Schirmer called to a well-dressed man he evidently knew, who was seated, waiting his turn, on one of the long wooden benches against the wall. The man came up and asked the workman one or two questions in Italian, then exploded into what sounded like a series of unforgivable insults. The workman's head lowered and his hands dropped to his sides. Then he got up and walked quietly out of the room.

"What was that about?" Mr. Schirmer asked the man who had helped him out.

"He was just trying to get away with murder," the man said. "He'd heard about somebody else on the road who got a B-3, so he wanted one. I asked him what kind of a country he thought this was. I asked how he'd like it back in Posilipo."

Just then a short, thin man with a waxed mustache — a dentist, it turned out — hurried into the room and threw down a salmon-pink card on Mr. Schirmer's desk. "I never asked for that X card," the man said, almost fiercely. "I don't want it. I won't touch it. For God's sake, tear it up."

Mr. Schirmer wiped his forehead and said, "Take it easy. One step at a time. How did you happen to get this card?"

"I went over to the nearest school the night they started handing them out. And one of the teachers said to me, 'Why, you deserve an X card, Doctor, if anybody does.' And she made me take it. I tell you, she forced it on me."

Mr. Schirmer smiled. "Cheer up," he said. "You're not the only one. A lot of dentists and a lot of nurses and a whole pack of cops and other city employees got X cards they weren't entitled to." He patted a thick envelope on the table. "We've been calling them in, and over fifty have been turned back voluntarily so far. What kind of a card do you think you ought to have?"

The dentist hesitated. Mr. Schirmer said, "I guess we'd better make it an A card, hadn't we?"

"Yes, sir," the dentist said. "I guess maybe we had."

Mr. Schirmer picked up an A card. "Say, Shine," he called over to Mr. Griffen, who was obviously known to his colleagues as Shine, "what the devil have you done with my pen?"

Mr. Griffen raised his eyebrows. "Why, Eddie, I don't know what you mean," he said, in a tone of mock injury. "I wouldn't borrow that cheap little pen on a bet."

Apparently this was an old and familiar argument, for Mrs. Christenson walked over and searched the drifts of paper on Mr. Griffen's desk until she found a pen under a corner of the blotter. In a stage whisper, she said to me, "Imagine, only one pen among the three of them! They're just like three kids."

Leaving Mr. Schirmer shaking his head in self-pity and filling out an A card for the dentist, I moved over to Mr. Holden. A small, middle-aged woman wearing silver-framed pince-nez was speaking rapidly and, I thought, a trifle desperately into Mr. Holden's ear. Mr. Holden was nodding, his eyes nearly closed. "In the first place, you see," I heard the woman say, "my two children and I have just driven North to spend the summer in Rhode Island. Yesterday I left the children with some relatives out in Quogue, Long Island, while I did some necessary business here in White Plains. Now I have to drive back to Quogue, pick up the children, and drive on to Rhode Island. That'll be over three hundred and fifty miles in two days, and all I have is an A card. My tank has about half a gallon left in it now. At least, the needle's been shivering over zero for miles and miles."

Mr. Holden nodded gently. "There's nothing to worry about, young lady," he said. "We'll see that you get what gas you need." Mr. Holden made this sound like a sort of divine benefaction. "Won't we, Eddie?" Mr. Holden asked, turning to the other members of the board. "Won't we, Shine?" Mr. Schirmer and Mr. Griffen nodded. "You'll just have to sign a statement explaining why you need the gas," Mr. Holden went on. "When you reach Rhode Island we'd like you to mail back to us the supplemental B-3 card I'm going to give you." He fingered the pocket of his coat. "I seem to have left my pen at home. Eddie, would it be too much trouble—"

The woman took off her pince-nez and smiled. She opened her purse. "I think I have a pen," she said. "You can use mine if you like."

When I returned to Mr. Griffen, he had just called up a young man who had been nervously pacing the room. "I'm a manufacturer's salesman," the young man said. "My territory's Connecticut, eastern New York, and New Jersey. I've built up a pretty good business in the last four or five years. I'm married. I got two kids."

Mr. Griffen played with a paper clip. "No reason you can't get as much gas as you need to carry on your business," he said. "I suppose you've used up most of your first B-3 card with a territory as big as that."

"Yes, sir. A boy and a girl," the young man answered excitedly. "We've just bought a house. On the FHA. We have to pay for it by the month."

Mr. Griffen looked as if he thought the young man might break down. "Listen!" he said. "There's nothing for you to worry about. Our ruling, straight from the OPA, is that all you have to do to get another B-3 card is to get your boss to write us a letter. Have him sign his name to what you've told me and you're all set."

"Yes, sir," the young man said. "That's what I told my boss, but he won't listen to me. He's made a ruling of his own that we must sell our stuff by phone or not at all. That's not so bad for the other salesmen, because I'm the only one working outside New York City. My boss says he won't ask any favors for me. He says he loves his country. He says I ought to learn to be a patriot."

Mr. Griffen said, "Well, we have a ruling and we're supposed to stick to it. No letter, no gas." He threw the paper clip on the floor and picked up Mr. Schirmer's pen. "By God," he said, "you just give me your boss's name, and I'll write him a letter! I may not be acting altogether according to Hoyle, but I think you can stop worrying."

As the young man, having given the name, grinned and left, I said to Mr. Griffen, "Isn't it odd that no commuters have bothered you today? I expected them to make more trouble than anyone else."

"Commuters aren't so bad," Mr. Griffen said. "You see, most of them fought it out with the teachers when they got their cards. They're reconciled by now to buses and walking and doubling up. They grouse, but they don't ask the impossible. That's been our experience and the experience of all the other boards in the county, though we've heard of a couple of odd cases. There's a lawyer who practices not only in New York but also in the town where he has his country home. He's elderly, a widower, and has no one to take care of him but his staff of servants. He claims he needs his car to drive himself and the staff back and forth from town every week, that he'd go bankrupt if he had to send the servants by train. At his age it's obvious that he can't just picnic out. And he's working in both places, you see. It's a risky decision, but I guess he deserves a B-3 card. I heard of a case, too, where a man managed to get B-3 cards for three of his cars and only A cards for the remaining two. And he practically tore his ration board apart!" Mr. Griffen tossed me a letter. "We get a few of these every day, but not as many as you might think."

I glanced at the letter. It began:

DEAR MR. GRIFFEN:

I am delighted to know that a man of your integrity and high standing in this community should be chairman of our ration board. It is certainly a lucky thing for all of us that a man of your calibre is willing to serve. I am writing to explain that I'm afraid our A card isn't quite suitable for us. I must take Evangeline to school each morning . . .

Mr. Griffen made a face. Handing me another letter, he said, "And we also get a few like this." It read:

DEAR MR. GRIFFEN:

I hope you will check up on all drivers. While our boys are fighting and dying all over the world, I can't see why anyone should knowingly waste a fraction of an inch of rubber or a single gallon of gas.

The letter was signed: "Brokenhearted."

Mr. Griffen looked apologetic as I finished reading the letter: "Sort of emotional, of course," he said. "Some soldier's mother, I suppose."

He leaned forward over his desk toward the remaining petitioners on the benches. "Next complaint," he said, a bit severely.

The New Yorker, June 13, 1942

THE INTERNMENT OF JAPANESE-AMERICANS:
1942

Concentration Camp: U.S. Style

by Ted Nakashima

UNFORTUNATELY in this land of liberty, I was born of Japanese parents; born in Seattle of a mother and father who have been in this country since 1901. Fine parents, who brought up their children in the best American way of life. My mother served with the Volunteer Red Cross Service in the last war—my father, an editor, has spoken and written Americanism for forty years.

Our family is almost typical of the other unfortunates here at the camp. The oldest son, a licensed architect, was educated at the University of Washington, has a master's degree from the Massachusetts Institute of Technology and is a scholarship graduate of the American School of Fine Arts in Fontainebleau, France. He is now in camp in Oregon with his wife and three-months-old child. He had just completed designing a much needed defense housing project at Vancouver, Washington.

The second son is an M.D. He served his internship in a New York hospital, is married and has two fine sons. The folks banked on him, because he was the smartest of us three boys. The army took him a month after he opened his office. He is now a lieutenant in the Medical Corps, somewhere in the South.

I am the third son, the dumbest of the lot, but still smart enough to hold down a job as an architectural draftsman. I have just finished building a new home and had lived in it three weeks. My desk was just cleared of work done for the Army Engineers, another stack of 391 defense houses was waiting (a rush job), when the order came to pack up and leave for this resettlement center called "Camp Harmony."

Mary, the only girl in the family, and her year-old son,

"Butch," are with our parents—interned in the stables of the Livestock Exposition Buildings in Portland.

Now that you can picture our thoroughly American background, let me describe our new home.

The resettlement center is actually a penitentiary—armed guards in towers with spotlights and deadly tommy guns, fifteen feet of barbed-wire fences, everyone confined to quarters at nine, lights out at ten o'clock. The guards are ordered to shoot anyone who approaches within twenty feet of the fences. No one is allowed to take the two-block-long hike to the latrines after nine, under any circumstances.

The apartments, as the army calls them, are two-block-long stables, with windows on one side. Floors are shiplaps on two-by-fours laid directly on the mud, which is everywhere. The stalls are about eighteen by twenty-one feet; some contain families of six or seven persons. Partitions are seven feet high, leaving a four-foot opening above. The rooms aren't too bad, almost fit to live in for a short while.

The food and sanitation problems are the worst. We have had absolutely no fresh meat, vegetables or butter since we came here. Mealtime queues extend for blocks; standing in a rainswept line, feet in the mud, waiting for the scant portions of canned wieners and boiled potatoes, hash for breakfast or canned wieners and beans for dinner. Milk only for the kids. Coffee or tea dosed with saltpeter and stale bread are the adults' staples. Dirty, unwiped dishes, greasy silver, a starchy diet, no butter, no milk, bawling kids, mud, wet mud that stinks when it dries, no vegetables—a sad thing for the people who raised them in such abundance. Memories of a crisp head of lettuce with our special olive oil, vinegar, garlic and cheese dressing.

Today one of the surface sewage-disposal pipes broke and the sewage flowed down the streets. Kids play in the water. Shower baths without hot water. Stinking mud and slops everywhere.

Can this be the same America we left a few weeks ago?

As I write, I can remember our little bathroom—light coral walls. My wife painting them, and the spilled paint in her hair. The open towel shelving and the pretty shower curtains which we put up the day before we left. How sanitary and clean we left it for the airlines pilot and his young wife who are now enjoying the fruits of our labor.

It all seems so futile, struggling, trying to live our old lives under this useless, regimented life. The senselessness of all the inactive manpower. Electricians, plumbers, draftsmen, mechanics, carpenters, painters, farmers—every trade—men who are able and willing to do all they can to lick the Axis. Thousands of men and women in these camps, energetic, quick, alert, eager for hard, constructive work, waiting for the army to do something for us, an army that won't give us butter.

I can't take it! I have 391 defense houses to be drawn. I left a fine American home which we built with our own hands. I left a life, highballs with our American friends on week-ends, a carpenter, laundry-truck driver, architect, airlines pilot—good friends, friends who would swear by us. I don't have enough of that Japanese heritage *"ga-man"*—a code of silent suffering and ability to stand pain.

Oddly enough I still have a bit of faith in army promises of good treatment and Mrs. Roosevelt's pledge of a future worthy of good American citizens. I'm banking another $67 of income tax on the future. Sometimes I want to spend the money I have set aside for income tax on a bit of butter or ice cream or something good that I might have smuggled through the gates, but I can't do it when I think that every dollar I can put into "the fight to lick the Japs," the sooner I will be home again. I must forget my stomach.

What really hurts most is the constant reference to us evacués as "Japs." "Japs" are the guys we are fighting. We're on this side and we want to help.

Why won't America let us?

The New Republic, June 15, 1942

"A Vast Slaughterhouse"

1,000,000 Jews Slain By Nazis, Report Says

LONDON, June 29 (U.P.)—The Germans have massacred more than 1,000,000 Jews since the war began in carrying out Adolf Hitler's proclaimed policy of exterminating the people, spokesmen for the World Jewish Congress charged today.

They said the Nazis had established a "vast slaughterhouse for Jews" in Eastern Europe and that reliable reports showed that 700,000 Jews already had been murdered in Lithuania and Poland, 125,000 in Rumania, 200,000 in Nazi-occupied parts of Russia and 100,000 in the rest of Europe. Thus about one-sixth of the pre-war Jewish population in Europe, estimated at 6,000,000 to 7,000,000 persons, had been wiped out in less than three years.

A report to the congress said that Jews, deported en masse to Central Poland from Germany, Austria, Czechoslovakia and the Netherlands, were being shot by firing squads at the rate of 1,000 daily.

Information received by the Polish Government in London confirmed that the Nazis had executed "several hundred thousand" Jews in Poland and that almost another million were imprisoned in ghettos.

A spokesman said 10,232 persons died in the Warsaw ghetto from hunger, disease, and other causes between April and June last year and that 4,000 children between the ages of 12 and 15 recently were removed from there by the Gestapo to work on slave-labor farms.

The pre-Nazi Jewish population of Germany, totaling about 600,000 persons, was said to have been reduced to a little more than 100,000.

The New York Times, June 30, 1942

Allies Are Urged to Execute Nazis

LONDON, July 1—The Polish Government in London has been urged in a report on the slaughter of 700,000 Jews in German-occupied territories to call on the Allied governments to adopt a policy of retaliation that will force the Germans to cease their killings.

"We believe," the report says, "that Hitler's Germany in time will be punished for all its horrors, crimes and brutality but this is no comfort for the millions menaced with death. We implore the Polish Government, the guardian representative of all the peoples of Poland, to protect them against complete annihilation, to influence the Allied governments to apply similar treatment against Germans and fifth columnists living at present in Allied countries.

"Let all Germans know this, know that punishment will be meted out to Germans in the United States and other countries.

"We realize we ask the Polish Government to do something most difficult and unusual but this is the only way to save millions of Jews from certain destruction."

The report, describing the Jews' ordeal in occupied Poland and German attempts to exterminate the Jewish population, reached London through underground channels. Szmul Zygelbojm, Jewish Socialist leader and member of the Polish National Council in London, received it and vouched for its trustworthiness. He said the sources were absolutely reliable, although the story seemed too terrible and the atrocities too inhuman to be true.

The report is supported by information received by other Jewish circles here and also by the Polish Government. Its figure of 700,000 Jews slain by the Germans since the occupation—one-fifth of the entire Jewish population of Poland—probably includes many who died of maltreatment in concentration camps, of starvation in ghettos or of unbearable conditions of forced labor.

Here are the main items in the report:

From the first day of the German-Soviet occupation of East Poland the Germans began the extermination of Jews. They started in East Galicia last Summer. Males between 14 and 60

were herded into public squares and cemeteries, forced to dig
their own graves and then were machine-gunned and hand-
grenaded.

Children in orphanages, old persons in almshouses, the sick
in hospitals and women were slain in the streets. In many
places Jews were rounded up and deported to unrevealed destinations or massacred in near-by woods.

At Lwow 35,000 were slain, at Stanislawow, 15,000; at Tar-
nopol, 5,000; at Zloctrow, 2000; at Brzezany only 1,700 were
left of 18,000. The massacre still continues in Lwow.

Last Fall the slaughter of Jews was extended to the Vilna
and Kovno districts. By November 50,000 had been murdered in Vilna and only 12,000 were left. In the two districts
the victims of the German slaughter numbered 300,000.

Simultaneously a massacre started in the Slonim district in
Eastern Poland. Nine thousand were killed in the town of
Slonim, 6,000 in Baranowicze. In Volhynia the killing began
in November and in three days 15,000 had been massacred in
Rovny County.

In the early Winter the Germans were methodically proceeding with their campaign to exterminate all Jews. They
sent special gas chambers on wheels to Western Poland, territories incorporated in the Reich. In the village of Chelmno
near Kolo ninety persons at a time were put in the gas chambers. The victims were buried in graves dug by them in
near-by Lubarski forest.

About 1,000 gassed daily from the townships of Kolo,
Dable, Izbica and others between November, 1941, and
March, 1942, as well as 35,000 Jews in Lodz between Jan. 2
and Jan. 9. Two thousand "gypsies" were gassed. They probably were Yugoslav prisoners and terrorists.

In February the murder wave reached the Gouvernement
General area in Central Poland, Tarnow, Radom and Lublin.
Twenty-five thousand were taken to an unrevealed destination
from Lublin. Nothing has been heard of them since. A few
were detained in the suburb of Majdanek; the others disappeared. No Jews were left in Lublin.

In Warsaw a "blood bath" was arranged in the ghetto on
the night of April 17. Homes were visited by the Gestapo and
Jews of all classes were dragged out and killed.

"This shows," the report concludes, "that the criminal German Government is fulfilling Hitler's threat that, whoever wins, all Jews will be murdered."

The New York Times, July 2, 1942

Bond Rally

by E. B. White

DOROTHY LAMOUR left Portland, Maine, at 7:20 on the morning of September 17th, passed through Woodfords at 7:25, Cumberland Center 7:39, Yarmouth Junction 7:49, and two hours later arrived in Augusta, where she parted with one of her handkerchiefs to a gentleman who bought an unusually large war bond. She left Augusta at 1:38 P.M., passed through Waterville at 2:04, Burnham Junction 2:35, Pittsfield 2:49, Newport Junction 3:01, and arrived in Bangor at 3:40, at the top of the afternoon.

Like most river towns, Bangor is a metropolis loved by the heat, and it was hot there under the train shed that afternoon, where a few dozen rubbernecks like myself were waiting to see a screen star in the flesh. The Penobscot flowed white and glassy, past the wharves and warehouses. On a siding a locomotive sighed its great sultry sighs. The reception committee wiped its forehead nervously with its handkerchief and paced up and down at the side of the waiting Buick roadster— which the daily *News*, in an excess of emotion, described as "blood-red." The guard of honor—a handful of soldiers from the air field—lounged informally, and a sergeant with a flash camera arranged himself on top of a baggage truck. In the waiting room a family of three sat in some embarrassment on a bench.

"I feel so silly," said the woman.

"What d'you care?" replied her husband, obviously the ringleader in this strange daylight debauchery. "What d'you care? I like to come down here to the station and see how things act once in a while." The teen-age daughter agreed with her father and backed him to the hilt, against her mother's deep-seated suspicion of the male errant.

Miss Lamour's train pulled in cautiously, stopped, and she

stepped out. There was no pool, no waterfall, no long dark hair falling across the incomparable shoulders, no shadow cast by the moon. Dorothy the saleswoman strode forward in red duvetyn, with a brown fuzzy bow in her upswept hair. She shook hands, posed for a picture, and drove off through the cheering crowd in the blood-red car, up Exchange Street, where that morning I had seen a motley little contingent of inductees shuffling off, almost unnoticed, to the blood-red war.

While Miss Lamour was receiving the press in her rooms at the Penobscot Exchange Hotel I went down to the men's room to get a shine.

"See her?" I asked the porter.

"Yeah, I was standing right next to her at the curb." Then he added, studiously: "I'd say she was about thirty. A nice-looking woman."

"I suppose they're giving her the works, here at the hotel," I said.

"I'll say they are. Took the furniture right out of Cratty's room. Hell, she's got chairs in there that wide."

Having assured myself that Dorothy was being properly cared for, and having brightened my own appearance to some extent, I went out to the Fair Grounds at the other end of town, where a stamp rally was scheduled to take place. The grandstand alongside the race track was already bulging with children, each of whom had bought a dollar's worth of stamps for the privilege of seeing Lamour. The sale of stamps had been brisk during the week. A booth had been maintained in the square, and Madame Zelaine, the local seeress, had personally handed out stamps and taken in the money for the Treasury. And now the grandstand was a lively place, with much yelling and chewing and anticipation. The Boys' Band of the American Legion, on the platform in the infield, was flashy in blue and yellow silks. In the still air, under the hard sun, gleamed the flags and the banners and the drum majorette's knees. When the car bearing the beloved actress appeared at the infield gate and swept to the bandstand the children hollered and whooped in their delight and little boys threw things at one another in the pure pleasure of a bought-and-paid-for outing.

The meeting got down to business with an abruptness which almost caused it to founder. Miss Lamour was introduced, stepped up, shaded her eyes with an orchid, made a short appeal, and before the little girls in the audience had figured out whether her hair was brown or green, she asked everyone to step along to the booth and buy some stamps. This was an unlooked-for development. Presumably most pockets were empty. Nobody made a move and the silence was oppressive. I have an idea that Miss Lamour herself didn't know quite what she was getting into and perhaps hadn't been told, or hadn't taken it in, that the children were already paid-up supporters of the war and that their presence there, inside the gates, was evidence that they had shelled out. It was simply one of those situations—a situation in the hard, uncompromising sunlight.

Miss Lamour, obviously a sincere and diligent patriot, saw that she was in a spot, and the chairman was visibly embarrassed. He and she hurriedly went into a huddle, shameless in the glaring sun. Then she grasped the mike. "Don't tell me business is *this* slow," she said, rather desperately.

Two or three little millionaires, in sheer anguish at seeing a dream person in distress, got up and moved toward the booth. Miss Lamour seized the moment. "Listen," she said, "I've come a long way to see you—don't let me down." (The bothersome question arose in all minds, the question who had come to see whom in this show.)

"Sing something!" hollered a youngster.

But there was undoubtedly something in her contract which prevented that. After another hurried conference the bandleader handed over his baton.

"I've never done this before," said Dorothy, "but I'm willing to try anything." She stepped up in front of the band, the leader got them started, and then gave over. Miss Lamour beat her way doggedly through a rather heavy number. In a long grueling bond-selling tour this was obviously one of the low moments for her. Low for the children too, some of whom, I am sure, had gone into hock up to their ears. It was just poor showmanship. Disillusion in the afternoon. The music ended and the star took a bow.

A couple of Fortresses flew overhead. This was a break.

Miss Lamour pointed up excitedly. "If you think it doesn't cost money to build those things, look at them. That's what you're buying!"

"Sing something!" shouted the tiny heckler.

Some more customers filed awkwardly down to the booth and in a few minutes the meeting was adjourned.

"I figured her hair was going to be down," said a little girl next me, coming out of a trance. Miss Lamour left in the Buick, respectfully encircled by the Army and the Navy, one man from each.

The big meeting was in the evening, after supper, in the Auditorium; and if Bangor had muffed its afternoon show it made up for it by a curiously happy night performance. It is no secret that enormous sums of money have been raised in America through the generous efforts of motion picture stars, and I was eager to be present at such an occasion. This particular brand of rally is a rather odd American phenomenon — that is, the spectacle of a people with homes and future at stake, their own lives threatened and the lives of their sons hanging by a thread, having to goad themselves to meet the challenge by indulging in a fit of actor worship and the veneration of the Hollywood gods. Everywhere in the country people have shown a peculiar willingness to buy bonds under the ægis of a star of the silver screen. Every race of people has of course its national and religious forms and ecstasies, its own way of doing business, its own system of getting results. The Japanese have their Emperor, an idol who is the same as God; the Germans have the State, closely identified with the Führer. Americans warm to a more diffuse allegiance — they have their Abe Lincoln and their Concord Bridge and their Bill of Rights, but these are somewhat intellectual appurtenances. For pure idolatry and the necessary hysteria which must accompany the separation of the individual from his money, they turn to Dorothy Lamour, or Beauty-at-a-Distance. At first glance this might appear to be a rather shabby sort of patriotic expression, but when you think about it, it improves. It may easily be a high form of national ardor after all, since the Hollywood glamour ideal is an ideal which each individual constructs for himself in the darkness and privacy of a motion picture house, after toil. The spell of

Lamour, the sarong, the jungle code, the water lily in the pool — these tell the frustration of the civilized male, who yearns in the midst of the vast turmoil and complexities of his amazing little life, with its details and its fussiness, to chuck his desperate ways for a girl and an island moon — a dream of amorous felicity and carelessness. To bring this dream into line, for a national emergency, and adapt it to the exigencies of federal finance is an American miracle of imposing and rather jovial proportions. Miss Lamour was introduced as the "Bond Bombshell"; the water lily had become an orchid from a florist's shop, symbol of wealth and extravagance.

The Bangor people, about twenty-five hundred of them, assembled in the hall, which was a sort of overgrown grange hall. Admission was by bond only, plus the Annie Oakleys. The big buyers were in the front seats, the small fellows in the balcony. The notables and the Bombshell and the Dow Field military band and WLBZ assembled on the platform, a mixed group of civil and military servants, variously arrayed. Almost the first thing that happened was the arrival of a contingent of Navy recruits (about fifty of them) who were to submit to a public induction under the combined sponsorship of Uncle Sam and the motion picture industry. They filed down the center aisle and climbed sheepishly to the platform, a rag-tag-and-bobtail company in their ready-to-shed citizens' clothes, sober as bridegrooms and terribly real. This was it, and the people cheered. Miss Lamour, sensing the arrival of actors who could not fail to give an authentic performance and who would never get a retake, stepped deferentially into the wings. A Navy lieutenant lined up his charges and prepared to give the oath. On their faces, bothered by the sudden confusion of lights and the convergence of their personal fates, was a hang-dog look, a little tearful, a little frightened, a little resolved. They were just a bunch of gangling boys in a moderately uncomfortable public position, but they seemed like precious stones. The dust of glamour had shifted imperceptibly from Miss Lamour and settled on their heads. After they were sworn in she glided back on to the stage, shook hands, and gave each her blessing as he shuffled out to gather up his cap and his change of underwear and disappear into the theater of war.

The program continued. A Negro quartet sang. Two heroes were produced—a pint-sized radioman who had been wounded in the Coral Sea, a big lumbering Tiger who had flown for Chennault. They were the "had been" contingent. The radioman told, in masterly understatements, about Pearl Harbor on that Sunday morning. The Tiger, a laconic man in shirtsleeves, was interviewed by a small dapper announcer for WLBZ, and when he was asked how it felt to be an American on foreign shores, he choked up, the strength went out of him, and he couldn't answer. He just walked away. After the band had performed, a young Jewish soldier stepped forward and played a violin solo. For him there could be nothing obscure about war aims. It was a war for the right to continue living and the privilege of choosing his own composer when he played his fiddle. He played solidly and well, with a strength which the Army had given his hands and his spirit. The music seemed to advance boldly toward the enemy's lines.

Here, for a Nazi, was assembled in one hall all that was contemptible and stupid—a patriotic gathering without strict control from a central leader, a formless group negligently dressed (even Dottie had neglected to change into evening dress, thereby breaking the hearts of the women in the audience), a group shamelessly lured there by a pretty girl for bait, a Jew in an honored position as artist, Negroes singing through their rich non-Aryan throats, and the whole affair lacking the official seal of the Ministry of Propaganda—a sprawling, goofy American occasion, shapeless as an old hat.

It made me feel very glad to be there. And somewhere during the evening I picked up a strong conviction that our side was going to win. Anyway, the quota was heavily oversubscribed in this vicinity. I would have bargained for a handkerchief if Miss Lamour had had any to spare. It's the ape-man in me probably.

Harper's Magazine, December 1942

GUADALCANAL: SEPTEMBER 7–24, 1942

Battle of the Ridge

by Richard Tregaskis

MONDAY, *September 7*

This morning Col. Edson told me that he is planning to make an attack on the Jap positions in the Taivu Point area tomorrow. If I wanted to go along, I was to be at a certain embarkation point at 3:45 this afternoon.

It was pelting rain when I arrived. But the Raiders, who seem to love a fight, were in high spirits. I had been assigned by Col. Edson to go with Col. Griffith aboard a tiny Diesel-engined ship which was acting as an auxiliary transport for the occasion. As we stepped aboard, one happy marine said, "This is the battleship *Oregon*, I presume?"

The captain of the little craft was a jovial Portuguese who had formerly been a Tuna captain on the American West Coast. His name, Joaquin S. Theodore. He still spoke in interesting Portuguese constructions, despite his rank as captain of a naval ship.

"We'll have it coffee for everybody in the morning," he said. Kindly, he warned against smoking on deck. "Tal your men I don't like to smoke it on deck," he said.

He wanted to clear away a space in the small ship so that the tight-packed marines might have a little more room. He pointed to a clothes line and said to his first officer, "Whoever this clothes belongs to I want it out of the lines."

The ship was a tiny thing, with only limited supplies of stores. But Capt. Theodore passed out grub and all available cigarettes to the Raiders, and shared his little cabin with Col. Griffith.

As we put out onto a rough sea, the pink-cheeked, hearty Portuguese told me proudly about his two "'lil kids" back home and about the exploits of his ship.

Col. Griffith later went over the plans for our expedition: we are to land our troops to the east of a small village called

365

Tasimboko, in the Taivu Point area, and advance from that direction on the town. Tasimboko is supposed to be the bivouac of a large group of Jap troops—estimated to number from 1,000 to 3,000. But the Japs are supposed to be lightly armed.

A bombing and strafing attack on Tasimboko, and shelling from the sea, will be timed to fit in with our attack.

Getting to sleep was a terrible job. The ship's steaming hold, full of the noise of the engines, was crammed with marines; no room to sprawl there. Every nook about deck seemed to be filled as well.

Finally I found a spot on the deck, which was partially shielded by a hatchway, and curled around it. But the ship rolled heavily and rain began to fall. I found another spot on the forecastle deck and pulled the edge of a tarpaulin over me. The rain fell more heavily, and the wind grew cold. I stumbled along to the captain's cabin and lay down on the floor in the stuffy room. It was better than sleeping in the rain.

TUESDAY, *September 8*

Despite the hardships of sleeping aboard Capt. Theodore's tiny tub, the Raiders were fresh and ready to go this morning when the time came for us to climb into our boats and shove off for shore.

Just as we were starting, there came a fortunate happenstance: a small convoy of American cargo ships, escorted by warships, passed very close to our own transports. They had no connection with us, and were bound for a different part of Guadalcanal; but the Japs, seeing our ships and the others together, evidently got the impression that a mass assault was coming. And so, fortunately, many of them ran.

But we naturally had no way of knowing this as we dashed for shore in our landing boats. We were ready for a real struggle, and a bit puzzled when there were no shots from shore.

We were more mystified, when, a few minutes after landing, as we were pushing along the trail toward Tasimboko, we found a fine, serviceable 37 mm. field piece, with the latest split-trail, rubber-tired carriage, sitting at the edge of the beach. It was complete with ammunition, and surrounded by Japanese packs, life-preservers, intrenching tools, new shoes, strewn in disorder on the ground.

As we moved along, we found more packs, more shoes, and life-preservers, and fresh-dug slit-trenches and foxholes in the underbrush. We also found another fine 37 mm. gun, which like the other was unmanned. This second gun was pointed toward the west, indicating we had possibly, as we had hoped, surprised the Japs by circumventing their positions and attacking from the east.

Or perhaps this was only the entrance to a trap. The Japs are supposed to excel at such tactics. We moved on cautiously, circled a small pond and crossed a ford in a river, wading in water up to our waists.

Beyond the ford, we passed a pile of clam shells, evidently freshly opened. "I'm thinking they've gone up for breakfast and knocked things off," snapped Col. Edson with his humorless grin. But he did not relax. He moved his troops ahead fast, barked at them when they failed to take proper cover.

We heard the sound of approaching plane motors, then saw our dive-bombers come out of the sky and slant westward. A few seconds later we heard the thud of bombs falling.

There were strafing planes, too, the long-nosed Pursuits flashing overhead, and we could hear their guns rattling as they dived.

We moved along the shore through an overgrown cocoanut grove and in the brakes of underbrush; we found more foxholes, carefully camouflaged with palm leaves, and caches of food and ammunition.

Shortly after eight o'clock, we made our first contact with the Japs. I saw our people running in numerous directions at once, and knew that something had happened. I ran to the beach and saw what the others had seen: a row of Jap landing boats lying on the sand some distance away, and amidst the boats, a small group of men in brown uniforms, looking our way—Japs.

The colonel called "Nick," quietly, and Maj. Nickerson (Floyd W. Nickerson of Spokane, Wash.) anticipated the order. "Open fire?" he said hopefully.

The colonel nodded his head.

"Nick," who is as lean and hard as the colonel, called, "Machine-gun runner." And when the man came up, which was almost immediately, he gave him the order. Within two minutes our machine guns were firing.

"Red Mike" (as the Raiders call their colonel for the obvious reason that he has red hair) is most taciturn. I asked him, at this juncture, what was happening.

"I think we might have caught a few," he snapped. And that was all he said.

Now the Japs were answering our fire. I heard the familiar flat crack of the .25 rifle, and the repetition of sound in long bursts of light machine-gun fire. Others of our men joined in the firing, and it swelled in volume. In the midst of the outburst, we heard the crash of a heavy explosion. I was lying on the ground under a bush, near Red Mike, taking thorough cover.

"Sounds like mortar fire," he said, concisely.

The burst of firing stopped, and there was a lull for a few moments. Red Mike was on his feet immediately, moving ahead. He sent a message up to Maj. Nickerson, who was leading the advance elements of our troops.

"Nick's got to push right on up," he said, low-voiced. Then he was gone, tending to some military business in the rear. A few moments later he was back again, still moving fast. I had found the colonel to be one of the quickest human beings I had ever known.

Rifle and machine-gun fire burst out again, the Jap guns standing out in the chorus like a tenor in a quartet. The bullets were closer this time. I crawled under a wet bush and kept my head down.

A man was hit over to our left. I heard the cry, "Pass the word back for a corpsman," felt the sickening excitement of the moment in the air. Our first casualty.

Then there came another loud crash from ahead, close and loud enough so that the earth shook under us. I was lying next to a private. "Sounds like a 90 mm. mortar," he said.

Now the blasting concussion of the explosion was repeated, and we heard the furry whistle of a shell passing over our heads, heard it explode well to the rear. Was it a mortar or a field piece ahead of us? There was more than a possibility, it seemed, that we had run into a heavy Jap force, equipped with batteries of artillery.

I was more certain of it when the explosion was repeated. Again we heard a second crash a fraction of a moment later, well behind us. Now it seemed evident that these were artillery pieces firing, probably several of them.

The Jap artillery was answered by the lighter-toned firing of our own mortars, and another chorus of rifles and machine guns. The Jap guns crashed again, and then the firing stopped.

A runner came to Col. Red Mike, who was sitting for a brief second in a clump of underbrush. "Nick says to tell you there are people across the stream," he said. A small stream ran parallel to the beach at this point, and that stream marked off our left flank. The Japs apparently were moving through the jungle on the inland side of the stream, planning to cut off our rear. "We can't see 'em yet, but we can hear 'em," said the runner.

The Colonel called Capt. Antonelli. "Tony," he said, "Nick says there's somebody working back across the stream. Take a patrol. Flank 'em if you possibly can."

There was other business for Red Mike: he wanted to check on the exact location of our companies; he got the "walky-talky" into action, sent runners out. He checked on the wounded by making a personal tour. Then he was back in time to get a report from Col. Griffith that a Jap field piece had been captured, unmanned.

"Shall I go with Tony or get the gun?" asked Col. Griffith.

"Go get it, take it down to the water and shoot it," said Red Mike.

Next, Red Mike disappeared into the foliage ahead. Now we were out of the cocoanuts, getting into thicker growth. But the colonel still moved like the wind. I followed and after a struggle found him at our foremost position, talking to Maj. Nickerson.

"I'm trying to locate that firing up ahead," said Nick.

Our planes came in again, and dived and strafed the Jap village ahead of us. The Japs were not firing. We moved ahead.

We passed through a jungle brake which looked just like any other from the outside, but inside we found stacks of cases filled with medical supplies. "Opium," said a marine, but I made note of the labels on some of the boxes and checked later. Most of the boxes contained "Sapo Medicatus," which is a blood-coagulating agent.

The foxholes were growing more numerous as we progressed. They were everywhere, carefully camouflaged with leaves. And caches of supplies were also more numerous; crates of canned meat, sacks of crackers; there were more groups of new field knapsacks, with shoes strapped to them, and scores of gray life-preservers, indicating the Jap troops who had been here were probably freshly landed from boats.

Something moved in the bush ahead and to our left. "There are troops going through there," said the colonel. "Find out who they are."

Seven minutes later, firing burst out again. I flopped into thick cover, and none too soon. A bullet snapped into the underbrush very close behind me. I picked out the sounds of Jap .25's, our automatic rifles and our machine guns. There was a torrent of Jap .25 machine-gun firing from the left.

"The boys got on the other side of us," said the colonel, with one of his wry smiles.

Now came a terrific blast from only a few yards ahead. It was so loud it made my ears ring, and the concussion shook chips of wood on my head from the trees above. We heard the shell whiz just over our heads and burst a few hundred yards to the rear. We knew then that we must be right smack up against the muzzle of a Jap field piece.

The piece fired again, and again, and then there was another outburst of machine-gun fire, ours heavy-toned against the Jap's cracking .25's. Then silence.

Maj. Nickerson came back to tell the colonel that our men had "killed the gunners on a Jap 75. It's only 150 yards ahead," said Nick. "It was covered by machine-gun fire. We got the gun."

But the Japs had more guns. We advanced only a slight distance, and another opened on us, as close as the last had been. At the time I was squatting in a thick jungle brake, a tangle of vines and dwarf trees, but the crash of the firing so close was scary, despite the good cover. Each time the gun went off, one felt the blast of hot air from the muzzle, and twigs rattled down from the trees above. But we knew we were safer here than back where the shells were falling. We could hear the explosions of the shells well behind us.

There was quite a cluster of us in this jungle grove: marines, squatting or sprawling unhappily in the green wet underbrush. Then it began to rain, and the rain came in sheets and torrents. The firing kept on. There were Jap riflemen around us too. (I later found that there had been one not more than fifty feet from us. We found his body. Why he did not fire at us I don't know.)

Nick shouted at the little group in the jungle brake. "Spread out," he said, with the proper blistering expletives. "We lost one squad of the second platoon with one shell. One of those might come in here."

I moved off to the right, to try to get a look ahead, and then moved back to the rear to see what damage the Jap shells were doing. I passed a marine who was lying on his back in a foxhole, his face very gray. His upper torso was wrapped in bandage, and I could see there was no arm where his left arm had been, not even a stump. A 75 shell had done the work.

A runner came back to report to Col. Red Mike, at 10:45, that a second Jap 75 had been put out of action and the crew killed.

It began to look as if we might have tackled a bigger Jap force than we could handle. The colonel was concerned about the Japs who might, he thought, be sneaking around our flank, cutting us off from the beach where we had landed. The colonel called for naval gunfire support.

A group of destroyers which had come down with us swung in close to shore and began to shell Tasimboko. I went out to the beach to watch the yellow flashes and the geysers of smoke and debris rising where the shells hit.

Then I went forward to look for Nick. Firing broke out again, torrents of it; but there were no more of the heavy crashes of artillery fire this time, only rifles and machine guns firing, and most of them, according to the sound, ours.

It had stopped raining. When the firing stopped a great quiet fell on the jungle. And in the quiet, we heard the desperate shouting of a man who was evidently in great trouble. He was shouting something like "Yama, Yama!" as if his life depended on it. Then the voice was smothered up in a fusillade of machine-gun and rifle fire. It was a Jap. But we never found out what he was shouting about.

The tide of our action seemed to be turning. We heard no more artillery and a runner came back from Capt. Antonelli's troops with the happy word, "We solved the problem, took the village." Nick's men sent back word that more Jap 75's had been captured, unmanned.

Appropriately, the clouds were clearing and the sun was coming out. Fresh reinforcements for our troops were landing. But now we did not need them.

We marched on into Tasimboko without any further resistance. We found many more cases of Japanese food and sacks of rice, and ammunition for Jap machine guns, rifles and artillery pieces, totaling more than 500,000 rounds, Col. Griffith estimated. We burned the ammunition and destroyed the village of Tasimboko, including a radio station which the Japs had established there.

Looking over the bodies of the Japs who had been killed (about thirty), we found some interesting items: pictures of Javanese women, American ammunition with labels printed in Dutch. And we found that the gun-sights with the 75's were of English manufacture, and that some of the Japs had been armed with tommy guns. It seemed that some of these soldiers who had run so fast had been veterans of the Jap campaigns in the East Indies, and possibly Malaya too. Perhaps this was the first time they had been surprised. Or perhaps they had heard too much about what happened to the Japs who tried to cross the Tenaru.

Most of the loot we had captured was destroyed. But we transported the medical supplies back to headquarters, and our men helped themselves to large stocks of British cigarettes, bearing a Netherlands East Indies tax stamp.

The sun had set and there was only a faint reddish glow on the clouds over the horizon to light the darkening sky, when, in our transport ships, we reached a point offshore from the Tenaru River. We were heading toward home.

But the day's excitement was not yet over. We got word

that twelve Jap aircraft had been spotted. Our fighter planes were rising into the twilight sky.

The transport went into evasive maneuvers, and, fortunately, the sky grew quickly darker, and was black, except for high streaks of silver gray, when the Japs arrived.

They did not come to Guadalcanal. For once, they picked Tulagi as their target, and we saw cup-shaped bursts of bright white light rising from the direction of the island, just over the horizon rim. We heard the distant thudding of the bombs a few seconds later, and wondered if the Japs would spot our wakes in the dark. But they did not.

WEDNESDAY, *September 9*

Shortly after 12:30 this morning, I heard the others in my tent dashing for the shelter. Maj. Phipps shouted to me to come along, and I heard cannonading coming from the north, but I was too tired to move.

At breakfast this morning, I heard that a small group of Jap destroyers or light cruisers had shelled Tulagi—and hit Capt. Theodore's little ship and set it afire.

Later in the day, I heard that Capt. Theodore had been wounded through the chest in the course of the engagement. But he had beached his little craft, and saved it from sinking, despite his wounds. I am glad to hear that he is expected to live.

This is the second time that I have left a ship in the evening and it has been attacked and lost before morning. This fact gives rise to the thought that my luck has been good, so far.

There were two air-raid alarms today. But the Japs never appeared. It was a quiet afternoon. We sat in Col. Hunt's CP after lunch, talking of the reunion we will have ten years hence, and the tales we'll tell about Guadalcanal, then, and how by that time our imaginations will have magnified our deeds immeasurably, and we will all be heroes.

Col. Hunt told us about some of his narrow escapes in the World War, when he commanded the Sixth Marines. Our casualties were very high, then, he said, and gave the figures. But the fighting at the Tenaru Battle, he said, was about as concentrated and intense as in any engagement of the World War.

Tonight we were awakened, just before midnight, by the sound of heavy firing in the jungles. There were machine guns, rifles and, occasionally, the crash of a mortar.

We lay awake and listened. And then cannonading started, to the north. We went to the dugout, and I sat on the sand-bagged entrance with Maj. Phipps. The guns, we knew, were big ones, because of their heavy tone and the brightness of the flashes against the sky. But Bill Phipps was sure they were firing in the Tulagi area, not off our shore. He had measured the interval between the time of the flash and the time the related boom of the gun reached us. That interval, he said, was ninety seconds. Multiply the 90 by 1,100, the number of feet sound travel in a second, and you get 99,000 feet, or about twenty miles. Tulagi is twenty miles north of us.

Star shells glowed in the sky. The Japs were illuminating the Tulagi shore. One of our observation posts phoned in the report that there were three Jap ships, probably cruisers, and that they were firing salvos.

THURSDAY, *September 10*

This morning we heard that the Japs had shelled Tulagi harbor last night and again hit Capt. Theodore's ship, which was still beached.

I went to the CP of Maj. Nickerson (the Raider officer) and talked to some of the men who did outstanding work on the excursion to Tasimboko, day before yesterday. Among them, two young corpsmen, Pharmacist's Mate Alfred W. Cleveland (of South Dartmouth, Mass.) and Pharmacist's Mate, second class, Karl B. Coleman (of McAndrews, Ky.). They told me how they had used a penknife to amputate the ragged stump of one Raider's arm after it had been shattered by a 75 explosion; the wounded man had been the one whom I had seen, lying in a foxhole, just after he had been treated and bandaged. These two lads, Nick told me, had saved the wounded man's life by amputating the remnants of his arm; the medicos themselves had said that the man would have died if the two lads had not done such a good and quick job in the field.

Pvt. Andrew J. Klejnot (of Fort Wayne, Ind.) told me how he had picked off one of the crew of one of the Jap 75's.

"There were only two men on the gun," he said. "I picked off one, and the other went and hid behind some boxes in a little ammunition dump. I fired into the dump and set it afire."

I moved my worldly possessions from Col. Hunt's CP out to Gen. Vandegrift's headquarters today. The general has moved into the "boon-docks," as the marines call the jungles; and the new spot is too much of a trek from Col. Hunt's headquarters.

A tent has been put up for us correspondents, near the general's headquarters. The members of our "press club" now are Bob Miller, Till Durdin, Tom Yarbrough, and there is a new arrival, Carlton Kent.

The Japs air-raided us at about noontime; twenty-seven of the usual silver-colored, two-engine type, flying lower than usual today. But the sticks of bombs fell a long distance from our location at the time.

The general's new CP is located in the thick of the jungle. Sui, pet dog of the Commissioner, Martin Clemens, proved it tonight by dragging an iguana, a small dragon-like lizard, into plain view as we sat at dinner over the crude board table tonight. Sui had unearthed the iguana at the jungle edge, which stands up straight and dense as a wall only a few feet from our mess table.

The tent which has been put up for correspondents is one of a number located at the foot of a ridge, facing the jungle. The general's tent is atop the ridge. Tonight we were told to be on the alert, since the Japs had been reported infiltrating the jungle which we faced. We were told that if an attack came, we should retire up the ridge to the crest, where a stand would be made.

"I wish I had a pistol," said Yarbrough, as we correspondents lay in our bunks, after dark. And the rest of us were nervous, and not anxious to go to sleep. We kept up a clatter of conversation to help our spirits.

The situation was not without an element of humor. For, as we lay awake, the mackaws sat overhead in the trees and bombed our tent. The plopping of their missiles was loud and frequent. The birds seemed to have singled out our tent for the heaviest bombardment. Maj. Jim Murray, the general's adjutant, chided us about the fact. "Those birds have got the correspondents' number, all right," he said.

FRIDAY, *September 11*

The Japs who were supposed to be investing the jungle in front of our tent did not put in an appearance last night. There was not even any firing out in the "boon-docks."

In today's air raid—by twenty-six Jap two-engined bombers—I had my closest escape from a bomb explosion. When the air-raid alert came in, Miller, Durdin and I went to the top of the ridge and walked down it, looking for a good high spot from which we could watch the bombers.

We found three or four men at work building a shelter at a spot several hundred yards away, where the ridge was bare of any foliage except grass, and one had a wonderful view of the sky. The incipient shelter, now only a pit, was just what we wanted in the way of a box seat for the show. It was deep and wide. We could sit on the edge until the bombers were just overhead, then still have plenty of time to dive for cover.

We did just that. The planes came as usual in a wide line that was a very shallow V, stretching across the sky. As usual, the anti-aircraft guns put up bursts in the vicinity, and as usual the bombers plowed on steadily, holding their formation and course.

Then the bombs came. When we heard them rattling down, we piled into the pit, layer upon layer of humanity, and waited. The bombs made a slightly different sound this time, perhaps because they were closer than before. Their sound was louder and more of a whistle. And the explosions were deafening. You could hear fragments skittering through the air over the top of the pit, and in that second all of us must have known that if we had been lying on the bare ridge we would have been hit and hurt.

Till Durdin said, "Hot." I saw that he was touching the sole of his shoe. He pulled a piece of metal out of the leather and held it gingerly between two fingers. It was a bomb fragment, still warm from the explosion.

Miller and I were anxious to see how close the craters had been this time. We spotted a small crater about forty yards from our pit. It was this missile, probably, that had thrown the fragments over our heads.

Beyond the small crater were other, larger holes. One of them must have been thirty feet across. That one lay about three hundred yards from our pit, fortunately beyond effective range. It was one of an irregularly spaced line of craters that led into the jungle beyond the grass.

Now, from the jungle, we heard excited shouting and cries for a corpsman. We knew that meant that there had been some people hurt down there. We saw several being brought out on stretchers.

Our fighter planes were already avenging the casualties. We heard the sounds of a dogfight in the sky, and later came word that they had knocked down six of the bombers and one Zero.

Later this afternoon, our dive-bombers came in from a trip to Gizo. This time they had found a small ship, a patrol-boat type of craft, lying off the base, and had sunk it. They had also bombed the buildings of the base again.

At air-operations headquarters I found a box which had been sent by plane, from my shipmates on a former task-force excursion. It included cans of beans, brown bread, salmon, peaches. Miller, Pvt. Frank Schultz, who drives our jeep, Jim Hurlbut (the Marine Corps correspondent) and I went down to the Lunga, taking the box along, and had a swim in the swift, clear water. Then we opened the cans and had a feast.

SATURDAY, *September 12*

This morning, as an urgent air alert was flashed, we of the Press Club decided to go down to Lunga Point to watch the show for today. So we piled into a jeep and our driver turned out one of the fastest cross-country records such a vehicle has ever achieved. He was not inclined to be caught on the road when the bombers arrived.

At the Point, Miller put on the headphones of the radio set and began calling out the interplane conversations of our fighters, who were by that time rising to search for the foe.

At 11:42 Maj. Smith called: "Control from Smith. They're coming in from the south—a big squadron of 'em." And then we saw them, the usual impressive span of two-motored silver bombers, Mitsubishi 96's, moving like a slender white line of cloud across the blue sky.

This time the planes were set against an almost cloudless sky, and had a long course of blue to traverse before they reached dropping point over the airport. That gave the anti-aircraft an unusually good opportunity to range on them.

At first, the puffs of ackack fire were too high and ahead of the Japs. We saw the silver bodied planes pass under the spotty cloud formed as the bursts spread out and merged. And then the AA began to come on the range. The flashes of the bursts came just in front of the silver-bodied planes; the one bomber in the left side of the formation was hit. We saw the orange flash of the explosion just under his wing, under the starboard motor nacelle, and then the motor began to trail a pennant of white smoke and the plane pulled off and downward, and left the formation.

Just as the plane pulled clear of the formation, another anti-aircraft shell burst directly under the belly of one of the planes at the center of the formation. A tongue of flame spread across the middle of the plane, then receded and was swallowed in a torrent of black smoke, and, in an instant, the plane was nosing straight down toward the ground. Now I saw one wing sheer off as if it were paper, and flutter after the more swiftly falling fuselage. Then the plane simply disintegrated, chunks fluttering away and falling, while the center part of the plane plunged at ever-accelerating speed toward the ground.

By this time the remainder of the Jap bomber formation had passed on out to sea. But one of the planes, possibly crippled by anti-aircraft fire, had become separated from the rest. One of our fighters was quick to pounce on him.

There was quite a group of us on the Point this day, watching the "show." Now they were cheering like a crowd at a football game. "Whoooo-ee," shouted someone, "look at that fighter. He's got him."

The tiny speck of the fighter, looking like a bumblebee in comparison to the bigger, clumsier bomber, was diving now. And we heard the rattlesnake sound of his guns. The bomber slewed, came up in a whipstall, and fell off in a steep dive toward the ocean.

The other bombers had disappeared somewhere in the blue, but we could hear our fighters going after them.

In the beautiful amphitheatre of the sky, the kill of the isolated bomber by the fighter was continuing. We saw the bomber diving straight toward the sea, vertically, but the fighter, like a malevolent mosquito, hovered about the larger object, watching for signs of life.

The bomber dived a few thousand feet, and then, suddenly, pulled out of the dive and climbed straight up into the sky, up and up, like an animal gasping for air in its death struggle.

Quickly, the fighter closed and its machine guns rattled again, for seconds on end, in a long burst. And then the bomber paused, fell off on one wing and with spinning wings fluttered vertically toward Tulagi Bay.

A few seconds later the spinning plane hit the water, and from the spot where it struck came a great backfire of ruddy flame and black smoke. And the watchers on the shore cheered madly, as if our side had made a touchdown.

Back at the airport, we found that the final score for the day was ten bombers and three Zeros; another goodly addition to a total that is mounting much too fast to please the Japs.

Capt. Smith came in to report that he had downed his fourteenth and fifteenth planes today; he did not say so, but it was told at the airport that he has been promoted to the rank of major, an award richly deserved.

We found that Lieut. Ken Frazier (Kenneth D. Frazier of Burlington, N.J.) was the pilot who had destroyed the crippled bomber so spectacularly while we watched from Lunga Point. He had shot down another plane as well.

"The first one went down in flames," he said. "The straggler was simple. I dived on him, saw the tracers falling a little short, pulled up a little, and then watched the chunks fly off the plane."

On one edge of the airfield, we found pieces of the Jap bomber which had disintegrated while we watched. There was quite a large section of the fuselage. The metal seemed much more fragile than the skin of the American bombers I have seen.

The cocoanut grove at one edge of the airfield had been

struck by a stick of large bombs. The craters were huge. But the bombs had hit nothing of value. A 100-pound bomb had smashed directly into a shack, killing one man, destroying some radio equipment. That was the only visible damage of the bombing.

When somebody came into our tent, at about 9:00 o'clock, and shouted, "Get up, fellas, we're moving up the ridge," we did not waste any time, but grabbed helmets and shoes and left. Only a few minutes later, from the ridge-top, we saw a pinpoint of bright green light appear in the sky to the north. The light spread into the glow of a flare, and then we heard the mosquito-like "double-hummer" tone of a Jap float plane. It was "Louie the Louse"—a generic name for any one of the Jap float planes which come to annoy us at night.

"Louie" flew leisurely, as he always does, over the island, dropping more flares, and then we saw the distinctive flashes of naval gunfire coming from the direction of Kukum.

Just as we heard the boom of the gun, the shell whizzed over our heads and crashed a few hundred yards around. There was a second's pause, and then more flashes followed, so continuously that the sky seemed to be flickering constantly, and shells whined overhead almost in column. They kept coming for minutes on end, fortunately hitting the jungle several hundred yards beyond us, skimming over the trees under which we were lying. We simply lay there clutching the side of the ridge and hoping the Japs would continue to fire too high.

The barrage kept up for about twenty minutes, then halted. And we waited in silence—the general and the rest of us lying on the ground, waiting to see if the firing would begin again.

We had just got to our feet when an outburst of rifle and machine-gun fire came from the south, apparently only a few hundred yards away. We wondered then if another big Jap effort to break through our lines had begun.

The firing continued, and the noise was augmented by mortar explosions. Then there came the flash of naval gunfire again, this time from the direction of Tenaru. We hit the deck pronto, but the shells were not coming in our direction. The sound of the explosions indicated they were falling along shore.

Our observation posts reported that four Jap warships—cruisers and destroyers in the usual force—were swinging along the beach, bombarding the shoreline at their leisure, then turning back and making the run in the opposite direction to repeat their performance.

Then the shelling stopped, and gradually, the small arms and mortar fire coming from the south dwindled in volume. But we did not go back into the valley to sleep this night. I slipped my poncho over my head, put on my mosquito head-net and my helmet, and lay down on the top of the hard ridge to sleep.

SUNDAY, *September 13*

We heard this morning that a Jap patrol nipped off one end of our outpost line, last night, a few hundred yards south of the general's CP, on the ridge. That was the firing we heard. The Raiders, who hold the line, are falling back to a better position today, in case a big Jap push develops today or to-night. Last night's fighting was only a minor sort of engagement.

Miller and I went to Kukum this morning to watch the daily air raid, which came in at about noon, on schedule. Interception was good. The bombers got frightened and jettisoned their loads. And Zeros and our Grummans had a terrific dogfight. From Kukum, we could see them dodging in and out of the towering cumulus clouds, occasionally diving down over the water. We saw one Wildcat (Grumman) come diving down like a comet from the clouds, with two Zeros on his tail. He was moving faster than they, and as he pulled out of his dive and streaked across the water, he left them behind. They gave up the chase and pulled sharply back up into the sky. We had a good view of their long, square-tipped wings, and the round red ball of the rising sun insignia, as they turned. They appeared, as the pilots had told me, to be very maneuverable planes.

Many planes were dogfighting in and about the masses of cumulus clouds. I watched two planes, one chasing the other, pop out of the tower of cloud, describe a small, precise semicircle, and go back in again.

A few moments later they made another circle, like two

beads on the same wire. Other planes popped in and out of their levels in the cloud structure, and the whole area of the sky resounded with the rattling of machine guns. With so many guns firing at once, there was a cumulative effect as loud and magnificent as thunder.

Back at air headquarters, we waited for the tally of today's score. It was four bombers, four Zeros.

We went to bed in our tents tonight, but were shortly told to move out and up the ridge-top. This time I had enough foresight to take along a blanket, and my satchel full of notes.

We could hear rifle fire coming from our front lines a few hundred yards to the south. Then machine guns. Flares went up occasionally and shed a glow over the sky.

I spread out my poncho and blanket and tried to sleep. I was awakened by the blasting of our own artillery batteries, to the north of us. The shells were whirring just over our position in the ridge-top, skimming over the trees, then hitting and exploding a few hundred yards to the south, apparently in the area where the fighting was going on.

MONDAY, *September 14*

Shortly after midnight this morning the din of firing grew so tremendous that there was no longer any hope of sleeping. Our batteries were banging incessantly, the rifle and machine-gun fire from the direction of the Raider lines had swelled into a cascade of sound, Louie the Louse was flying about, and flares were dropping north, south, east and west.

We were drawing up a strong skirmish line on the ridge-top. Reinforcements were on their way up. We knew that the Raiders, Col. Edson's people, out on the ridge, had their hands full. We knew then that a major Japanese effort to break through our lines and seize the airport had begun.

Another storm of rifle, machine-gun and mortar fire came now from the direction of Tenaru. Was this another attempt to break through? For the present there was no way to find out.

Naval gunfire began to boom from the north. But it was not coming near us.

The general said to Col. Thomas: "Say, Jerry, ask air headquarters is it feasible to send a plane to see if there are any transports—just to see." The general was as calm and cheery as usual.

Some "shorts" from our own artillery fell in the valley where our tents are located. The flashes were as bright as day. One man standing near where I sprawled on the ground was knocked down by the concussion. We thought at first that the shells were Jap projectiles from their ships, ranging on the CP.

The sounds of firing had now become a din. A gray mist began to drift in among the trees on the ridge. It was thicker in the valley. Was it smoke from our artillery? It might be gas. (It was smoke, released by the Japs to create a gas scare.)

An artillery observer came into our communication dugout and reported to Col. Thomas, who was busy with phone calls, checking on the latest information from all outposts, giving orders. The observer said his telephone line, reaching farther toward the front, had been blown out. He had come back to relay firing instructions to our artillery batteries. He said the Japs were trying to advance down the ridge, but that our artillery fire, coupled with determined resistance from the Raiders on one of the knolls of the ridge, was holding up the enemy.

The observer found a line open from this point back to our batteries. "Drop it five zero and walk it back and forth across the ridge," he said. Then we heard the loud voice of the officer directing the battery: "Load . . . fire!" Then the bang of the cannon, the shells whizzing overhead.

The barrage continued. And after a few minutes, a runner came back from Col. Edson's lines. "Col. Edson says the range is perfect in there," he said, breathlessly. "It's right on. It's knocking the hell out of 'em."

Snipers were moving in on us. They had filtered along the flanks of the ridge, and taken up positions all around our CP. Now they began to fire. It was easy to distinguish the sounds of their rifles. There were light machine guns, too, of the same caliber. Ricocheting bullets skidded amongst the trees. We plastered ourselves flat on the ground.

I went to the communication dugout to see if there might be any room inside. But the shack was filled. I picked a spot amidst some sparse bushes at the foot of a tree. A bullet whirred over my head. I moved to another tree.

A stream of tracer bullets arched through the trees from behind us. We heard Jap .25's opening up from several new directions. It seemed now that they were all around.

The whispered word went round that the Japs were landing parachute troops (later proved false). More reinforcements came through our position on the ridge, while the Japs were firing. But we wondered if we could hold our place. If the Japs drove down the ridge in force, and broke through Col. Edson's lines, they would be able to take the CP. If they had already cut in behind our position, as we suspected they had, they would box us in, and perhaps capture the general and his staff.

But the general remained calm. He sat on the ground beside the operations tent. "Well," he said cheerfully, "it's only a few more hours till dawn. Then we'll see where we stand."

Occasionally, he passed along a short, cogent suggestion to Col. Thomas. He was amused at my efforts to take notes in the dark.

The telephone line to Col. Edson's front had been connected again. The colonel called Col. Thomas to say that the Raiders' ammunition was running low; he needed a certain number of rounds of belted machine-gun bullets—and some hand grenades. Col. Thomas located some of the desired items by phone after a quick canvass. They would be sent over soon, he told Col. Edson.

But at about 3:00 o'clock Col. Edson called again to say that he was "almost out." The ammunition had not arrived.

We were wondering if the Raider line was going to cave in when more Jap planes came over. There were probably two of them. They dropped more flares.

The sounds of heavy firing to our left rear had broken out again. Col. Thomas checked by phone. "It's in McKelvy's area," he said. "The Japs got into his wire."

Snipers were still popping at us from all sides. We had our hands full. But then Col. Edson called back to say that ammunition and grenades had arrived, and the news had a good effect on morale.

At about 4:00 o'clock the snipers were still shooting into our camp, but they had not attacked our skirmish lines on the ridge. Our artillery fire had slackened a little. And the sounds of firing in the Raider area were sporadic. I rolled myself in blanket and poncho (for the early mornings on Guadalcanal are always chill) and lay down in some underbrush on the slope of the ridge. I was able to sleep for about an hour.

As the first light of dawn came, the general was sitting on the side of the ridge, talking to some of his aides. A Jap machine gun opened up, and they high-tailed for the top of the ridge, with me right behind. We were heading for a tent, where we would at least have psychological shelter. Just as we reached the tent, a bullet clanged against a steel plate only two or three feet from us. It was amusing to see the rear ends of the dignified gentlemen disappearing under the edge of the tent. I made an equally undignified entrance.

It was not safe to walk about the camp this morning. Snipers had worked their way into camouflaged positions in trees through the area, and there were some machine gunners, with small, light .25 caliber guns. One had to watch one's cover everywhere he moved.

There were large groups of Japs on the left or east side of the ridge, in the jungles. There was a lot of firing in that area. We had a firing line of men extending south from the CP, out along the ridge, facing those groups of Japs. The men lay along the edge of a road that ran down the exposed top of the ridge, protected only by grass. The Japs were firing at them from the cover of the jungle.

Beyond that firing line, the ridge curved and dipped. It rose like the back of a hog into a knoll, beyond the dip. It was on this knoll that the Raiders had been doing their fiercest fighting.

I worked my way out along the ridge to the firing line, to get a look at the knoll where the Raiders had been fighting. I lay flat next to a machine gunner while the Japs fired at us with a .25 light gun. A man to our right, farther out on the ridge, was wounded. We saw him crawling back toward us, a pitiful sight, like a dog with only three serviceable legs. He had been shot in the thigh. Beyond the bend in the ridge, the machine gunner told me, there were several more wounded. A group of six or seven of our men had been hit by machine-gun fire. Two of them were dead.

In the jungle at the foot of the ridge we heard our own

guns firing as well as the Japs'. Some of our troops were pushing through there, mopping up the groups of Japs.

It was evident that the main Jap attempt, down the top of the ridge, had failed. I moved out a little farther along the ridge, nearly to the bend in the road where the wounded lay, and I could see the knoll where the fighting had been going on. It was peopled with marines, but they were not fighting now.

We heard the characteristic whine of pursuit planes coming. Then we saw them diving on the knoll, and heard their machine guns pop and rattle as they dived. "They've got a bunch of Japs on the other side of the hill," said a haggard marine next to me. "That's the best way to get at 'em."

I worked my way back to the CP and got some coffee. I was cleaning my mess cup when I heard a loud blubbering shout, like a turkey gobbler's cry, followed by a burst of shooting. I hit the deck immediately, for the sound was close by. When the excitement of the moment had stopped, and there was no more shooting, I walked to the spot, at the entrance to the CP on top of the ridge, and found two bodies of Japs there—and one dead marine. Gunner Banta told me that three Japs had made a suicide charge with bayonets. One of them had spitted the marine and had been shot. A second had been tackled and shot, and the third had run away. These three had been hiding in a bush at the edge of the ridge road, evidently for some time. I had passed within a few feet of that bush on my way out to the firing line and back. The animal-like cry I had heard had been the Jap "Banzai" shout.

Col. Edson and Col. Griffith, the guiding powers of the Raiders, came in to our CP this morning to make a report to Gen. Vandegrift and shape further plans. The mere fact that they had come in was a good sign. It meant that the fighting was at least slackening and perhaps ending, for they would not have left their front lines if there had been any considerable activity.

Maj. Ken Bailey, one of the Raider officers and a hero of the Tulagi campaign, also appeared, dirty and rumpled but beaming like a kid on the night before Christmas. Bailey loved a fight. He showed us his helmet, which had been pierced front and back by a Jap bullet. The slug had grazed his scalp without injuring him.

The Raider officers' conversations with the general and Col. Thomas were held in the general's secret sanctum. But I talked to Col. Edson as he left the shack. He said that the large main body of Japs, who had been trying to drive down the ridge, had fallen back.

He said that a force of between 1,000 and 2,000 Japs had tried to storm the ridge, with lesser forces infiltrating along the base. His estimate of the Jap casualties, at that time, was between 600 and 700 in the ridge area alone. Our artillery fire, he said, had smacked into the midst of a large group of Japs and wiped out probably 200 of them. Our own casualties had been heavy, for the fighting was furious.

The colonel gave the impression that the big battle of the ridge had ended; that the only fighting in the area now was the mopping up of small, isolated Japanese groups by our patrols.

But snipers were scattered through the trees of the area. I had a brush with one of them during today's first air raid.

I was sitting on the side of the ridge that looks over the valley where our tents are located. A throng of Zeros were dogfighting with our Grummans in the clouds and I was trying to spot the planes.

Suddenly I saw the foliage move in a tree across the valley. I looked again and was astonished to see the figure of a man in the crotch of the tree. He seemed to be moving his arms and upper body. I was so amazed at seeing him so clearly that I might have sat there and reflected on the matter if my reflexes had not been functioning—which they fortunately were. I flopped flat on the ground just as I heard the sniper's gun go off and the bullet whirred over my head. I then knew that his movement had been the raising of his gun.

But there was no time to reflect on that fact either. I retreated behind a tent. And then anger caught up with me. Again the war had suddenly become a personal matter. I wanted to get a rifle and fire at the sniper. Correspondents, in theory at least, are non-combatants. Several of our men, however, fired into the crotch of the tree where the sniper was located.

Miller had come in from Kukum, where he spent last night. He and I went out on the ridge, later in the day, to have a look at the battleground. We climbed the steep knoll where our troops had made their stand and turned back the main Jap drive.

The hill was quiet now. Small fires smoldered in the grass. There were black, burned patches where Jap grenades had burst. Everywhere on the hill were strewn hand-grenade cartons, empty rifle shells, ammunition boxes with ragged, hasty rips in their metal tops.

The marines along the slope of the hill sat and watched us quietly as we passed. They looked dirty and worn. Along the flank of the hill, where a path led, we passed strewn bodies of marines and Japs, sometimes tangled as they had fallen in a death struggle. At the top of the knoll, the dead marines lay close together. Here they had been most exposed to Jap rifle and machine-gun fire, and grenades.

At the crest of the knoll we looked down the steep south slope where the ridge descended into a low saddle. On this steep slope there were about 200 Jap bodies, many of them torn and shattered by grenades or artillery bursts, some ripped, a marine told us, by the strafing planes which we had seen this morning. It was up this slope that the Japs had sent their heaviest assaults many times during the night, and each time they tried they had been repulsed.

Beyond the saddle of the ridge rose another knoll, and there we could see more bodies, and the pockmarks of shelling. The whole top of this knoll had been burned off and wisps of smoke still rose from the smoldering grass.

Miller and I still stood on the open crest of the knoll. "Better watch it," a marine said. "There's a sniper in the jungle over there."

We moved away from the hill crest and had walked about fifty feet when we heard a shout behind us. A man had been hit at the spot where we had been standing. He had a bad wound in the leg. Our luck was holding.

We went to Kukum to watch for further air raids. But no more planes appeared until late in the afternoon. In the meantime, we heard heavy artillery pounding into the jungle near Matanikau, and saw smoke rising in great clouds above the trees. We heard that a large body of Japs were trying to make a break-through in that area. The first reports had it that casualties were heavy, but later we found that the fighting here had been only a protracted skirmish and our casualties were few.

It was dusk when Jap seaplanes made a low-altitude attack. Three of them, monoplane float aircraft, passed back and forth over Kukum, drawing streams of anti-aircraft fire. Others swung over the beach farther to the east, and the island became alive with ackack; the sky was trellised with the bright lines of tracer.

Again the Japs dropped many flares, and once we saw an extremely bright white light flaming over the Tenaru, which we thought was a flare—and found out later that it was caused by two Jap planes burning simultaneously.

The Jap planes, we learned at air operations headquarters, had tried to make a bombing attack on the airport. A group of fifteen to twenty Jap seaplanes, slow, ancient biplanes, had sneaked over the mountains in southern Guadalcanal, and tried to make a low-altitude attack. But they had been caught by our Grummans, and nine of them shot down. Four Zero float planes had also been shot down. And in the earlier raid of the day, two Zeros and one bomber had been downed— and the bombers had been turned back long before they reached Guadalcanal. The Jap air attacks of the day, like their land effort of last night, had been a failure.

Tonight the general and his staff had moved from the old CP on the ridge to a slightly safer spot, and of course there had been no time during the day to erect tents, cots or the other elementary comforts of Guadalcanal living. So for the third successive night I slept on the bare ground. The senior surgeon of all Gen. Vandegrift's medical troops lay down near by; he, too, had only a poncho for a mattress, and took the discomfort without complaint. "I'm afraid I'm going to have my joints oiled up a bit if this keeps on," he said. And that was his only comment.

TUESDAY, *September 15*

Yarbrough and Kent have shoved off. They sailed aboard a small ship which came in today and made for a rendezvous with a larger craft. Durdin seems to be somewhat pessimistic about the general situation. Miller and I, being somewhat punch-drunk, are more inclined to view the future cheerfully.

This morning we corraled Col. Thomas and asked him to give us a quick outline of the big battle which has been going on for the last two days. He gave us a lucid summary.

The Japs had assembled three large units of troops, by a process of slow accumulation, said the colonel. Two of these large units, totaling 3,000 to 4,000 and possibly more (the figures were estimates based on the observations of our patrols) were massed to the east of the airport; the third, a smaller group, to the west.

"We couldn't get at them because of the terrain," said the colonel, "although we did raid the landing area of the two eastern detachments." (That was the raid which Col. Edson's troops had made on Tasimboko.)

The three groups made three separate attacks, said the colonel. The principal of these was a drive toward the airfield from the south along the top of Lunga Ridge. It was here that the Raiders had had their tough fight.

Two other, much lighter, attacks were made: one from the west, from the Matanikau area; and the second from the east, which was apparently intended to flank our positions along the Tenaru.

Our patrols discovered several days ago that the two eastern groups were moving in, one on our flank, one swinging around to make an attack from the south, our rear.

"On the night of the 12th and 13th," said the colonel, "the Japs came up from the rear (the south) and infiltrated our lines, but did no damage.

"Then, our outpost line being too long, it was withdrawn several hundred yards. One hour after dark on the night of the 13th–14th, groups of 50 to 100 men each broke through the line and attacked the ridge. Col. Edson moved his men 300 to 400 yards to the rear and took up a position on a rugged hill (the step knoll we had visited on the ridge). At about 11:00 o'clock in the evening, the Japs charged in large numbers. Edson had a few hundred men, the Japs about 2,000. Our artillery fire was laid down, causing many casualties.

From then on until 6 A.M. the Japs made many assaults on the hill, including bayonet charges. They lost 500 men."

On the same night the Japs attacked our eastern flank, but ran into barbed-wire entanglements and retired, leaving about thirty dead Japs in the wire, said the colonel. The attack from the west did not come until yesterday, and, thanks to our artillery and stubborn resistance by our troops, that attempt was also pushed back.

Miller, Durdin and I made another swift survey of the high knoll where Edson's men had fought, and decided that since it had no other name, it should be called "Edson Hill" in our stories.

Later in the day we went to Col. Edson's headquarters to get his story of the battle. He told us about the individual exploits of his men and their collective bravery, but did not mention the fact that he himself had spent the night on the very front line of the knoll, under the heaviest fire.

He did not mention it, but the fact was that two bullets had actually ripped through his blouse, without touching him. Another Raider officer whispered that information to me and I nodded absently, then was startled to see that the colonel was still wearing the garment. Bullet holes marred the collar and waist.

The Raiders told us some good stories of valor; about a sergeant named John R. Morrill (of Greenville, Tenn.), who with two buddies had been cut off from the rest of the marines by a Jap advance. And how Sgt. Morrill had walked with impunity through the Jap positions during the darkness.

Then there was a private, first class, named Ray Herndon (of Walterboro, S.C.), whose squad occupied a very exposed position on the south side of Edson Hill at the time the Japs made their heaviest attacks. The Jap firing hit right into the squad and left only four of them alive, three unwounded, and Ray, hit mortally through the stomach. And then Ray, knowing he was hit badly, had asked one of his buddies to give him a .45 automatic, and said: "You guys better move out. I'm done for anyhow. With that automatic, I can get three or four of the bastards before I kick off."

Then there was a young, round-faced lad from Greensburg, Pa., named Corp. Walter J. Burak, the colonel's runner, who had twice during the night traversed the exposed crest of the ridge the whole distance from the knoll to the general's CP, under the heaviest fire. He had made the first trip with a telephone wire, when the line had been blown out. And the second trip, toting a forty-pound case of hand grenades, when in the early hours of the morning, the shortage of that item became pressing.

But the outstanding story was Lewis E. Johnson's (of De Beque, Col.). Lewis was wounded three times in the leg by fragments of a grenade, and at daybreak placed in the rear of a truck with about a dozen other wounded, for evacuation. But as the truck moved down the ridge road, a Jap machine gunner opened up and wounded the driver severely. The truck stopped. Then Johnson painfully crawled from the rear of the vehicle, dragged himself to the cab, got into the driver's seat, and tried to start the motor. When it would not start, he put the car in gear, and, using the starter for traction, pulled the truck a distance of about 300 yards over the crest of the ridge. Then he got the engine going and drove to the hospital. By that time, he was feeling so refreshed, that he drove the truck back to the front and got another load of wounded.

To get the story of the attacks on the other two fronts, we went first to Col. Cates' headquarters, to cover the attack that had come from the east, and then to Col. Hunt's for news on the attack which had come from the west, the direction of Matanikau.

Col. Cates referred us to Lieut. McKelvy (William N. McKelvy of Washington, D.C.), the immediate commander of the troops who had held back the Japs attacking from the east.

"The entire attack was delivered against a road called the Overland Trial," he began.

"On the night of the 13th–14th, and about 10:15, I heard shooting. At 10:30 Capt. Putnam (Robert J. Putnam of Denver, Col.) called to say that one of his listening posts had been jumped. He said that a man came in to his CP, and as he arrived he said, 'They got 'em all,' and fainted.

"At about 11:00 o'clock, Capt. Putnam called and said the Japs had put out a few bands of fire—a few rifle shots, but that there was nothing serious yet.

"Then everything opened up. There was a terrific outburst

of firing, and Capt. Putnam said, 'They're inside the wire. They're being bayoneted.' We found twenty-seven bodies on the wire in the morning.

"We were putting down our big mortars and all the rest. All the activity was on that one flank. The Japs were trying hard to take the road."

The colonel stopped to get a large map and point out the road, a trail which led from the east into our lines, toward the airport.

"At 5:30 the attack stopped and the Japs withdrew. They didn't want to be caught in daylight.

"That morning—that was the 14th—we were given a reserve of six tanks. There was high grass across from our positions and we were afraid the Japs were lying doggo in there. While the tanks were in, one of our own lieutenants jumped on one of the tanks. He was a Lieut. Turzai (Joseph A. Turzai of Great Neck, L.I.), who had been wounded by shrapnel, and stayed surrounded by the Japs all night.

"Lieut. Turzai told us there were Jap machine guns in a shack in the high grass. Later in the day we sent the tanks after them. They accomplished their mission with some losses. (We lost three tanks when the Japs opened fire at point blank range with anti-tank guns.)

"At 11:00 o'clock last night, the Japs hit us again. It was a minor attack. They shelled us with light mortars.

"Just at daybreak this morning we spotted about 300 Japs in a group. We had our artillery batteries laid for a concentration in that area; the fire fell right on them. They undoubtedly lost a lot of people there."

At Col. Hunt's CP, Lieut. Wilson gave us an outline of the fighting in the Matanikau vicinity. That, too, had been of a minor character compared to the finish fight that had raged along the ridge.

"Yesterday morning, just at daybreak, there was mortar and machine-gun fire into our left flank positions," he said. "Col. Biebush (Lieut. Col. Fred C. Biebush of Detroit, Mich.) was commanding our troops.

"At about 8:30 A.M. there came a bayonet charge. But it was repelled with heavy losses for the Japs. The Japs tried it again at 10:30.

"The Japs tried a break-through between two groups of troops on our left flank. They were trying to see how far our wire extended. They were beaten back.

"At about noontime, a patrol went out to reconnoiter the enemy position. Maj. Hardy (former Capt. Bert W. Hardy), who led the patrol, sent back a message, saying, 'The woods are infested with snipers and automatic riflemen. I am pushing forward.'

"Information gathered by our reconnaissance enabled us to put down a heavy concentration of mortar and artillery fire which stopped the attack."

I slept in a shack at Kukum tonight, on the bare board floor. I came awake, once in the night, to hear people shouting. I asked a man next to me what was happening. He grunted. "Those silly sailors don't secure their boats," he said, "so when Oscar goes by, they all bust loose when his wake hits 'em." But he was wrong. It was not Oscar who had gone by, but a couple of Jap destroyer-type warships, apparently paying us a visit after landing troops at Cape Esperance, to the east.

WEDNESDAY, *September 16*
We had some copy to get to Gen. Vandegrift's headquarters for censorship this morning, and were about to start out for the CP, when an air alert came in. But there was no raid, and we reached our destination with our stories and got them off. Till Durdin feared they would be our last.

Today our dive-bombers and torpedo planes from Henderson Field went north on an attack mission. We checked at the airport later in the day and found that they had been after some Jap cruisers and destroyers located between Bougainville and Choiseul. It was believed they got one torpedo hit on a cruiser and got a bomb hit on a second.

THURSDAY, *September 17*
Till Durdin's worry that our story on the Jap attack might be our last, fortunately is not being substantiated. Things seem to be calming down on Guadalcanal. Our patrols on all our fronts contacted no Japs today, and to the east and south, it seems, they have withdrawn a goodly distance. Along Col.

McKelvy's front, we heard, our troops have found abandoned mortars and machine guns, some of them in brand-new condition, indicating the Japs fled in some haste.

Nor was there any air raid today, although our fighters, Pursuits and Grummans, went down to Cape Esperance on a strafing mission. Again they had found Jap landing boats on the shore there but no Japs visible. Evidently they had landed at night on the regular schedule and had time to take good cover.

The dust is getting thick on Guadalcanal. If you move on the roads now, you stir up a cloud of the dirty gray stuff. Planes and trucks moving across the airport trail huge triangular black clouds. You put on clean clothes at nine o'clock and walk down the road and at 9:30 you look like a chimney sweep. When you ride in a car the dust of passing vehicles chokes your lungs and blots out your vision. We now ride about with our helmets held over our faces in an attempt to keep them relatively clean. Schultz has dug up a pair of fancy polaroid goggles somewhere. Also, incidentally, a cowboy-effect belt set with large paste-stones, ruby and emerald-colored. Where he collects such items on Guadalcanal is a mystery. He has also adopted the glamorous sun-helmet which Yarbrough left behind. Schultz' ambition is to be a state cop in Illinois (he's from Chicago) or a border patrol trooper, after the war.

At air headquarters today we saw a complete tabulation of the number of planes shot down by our fighters to date. The total is 131; of these, our marine fighters (Grummans) have knocked down 109; the Army Pursuits, four; our Navy fighters (also Grummans), who have been here only a short time, seventeen; and one of our dive-bombers got a Zero. Our anti-aircraft batteries, in addition, credited with five.

Of the 131 enemy planes destroyed, about half were fighters or other single-engine planes, and about half the fast, two-motored Mitsubishi 97's.

Today I talked to a Coast Guard seaman named Thomas J. Canavan (of Chicago, Ill.), who had just got back after recuperating from a terrible adventure. That adventure happened about a month ago, when Canavan was out on anti-submarine patrol; there were three small boats in the patrol, and they were surprised by three Jap cruisers and sunk. Canavan was the only survivor. He saved his life by floating in the water, playing dead while one of the cruisers came close by and looked over his "body." Then he swam for seventeen hours, trying to get to Florida Island. He finally made the shore.

Canavan, who still looked and talked as if he could feel a ghost looking over his shoulder, said he had only a cocoanut for nourishment during two days on Florida. This he promptly upchucked. He saw fierce-looking natives with spines of bones stuck through their noses and ran from them, but he found later they had been cordially inclined. For when he woke up after falling asleep exhausted on the beach, he found someone had covered him with palm fronds to protect him from the rain and nightly cold. He tried twice to swim to Tulagi Island, and the first time was thwarted by tides. The second time he succeeded.

Our dive-bombers and torpedo planes laden with bombs went out today to target the buildings of the Cape Esperance area where the Japs have been landing. They reported they set the buildings afire.

There are two persistent reports on the "scuttlebutt" circuit today: one is that reinforcements are coming to Guadalcanal—and, on that count, estimates of numbers vary; and the other is that our aircraft carrier *Wasp* has been sunk.

FRIDAY, *September 18*

The rumor that reinforcements were en route to Guadalcanal was substantiated today, when they arrived. Early this morning, a certain colonel told me: "I can't say anything more about it, but I'd recommend that you go for a walk on the beach." I went to the beach and saw cargo and warships and transports steaming into sight.

Miller and I went to the landing point to watch the ships unload. All along the beach our weary veterans stood and watched the process, passively. We had been talking about reinforcements, and waiting for a long time.

They were marines, these new troops, thousands of them, boatload after boatload; they wore clean utility suits and new helmets, and talked tough and loud as they came ashore.

One of our veterans told me he had been talking to some of the new arrivals. "Chees," he said, "these guys want to tell *us* about the war." And we knew then that it would take some time with these men, as it had with us, to get rid of that loud surface toughness and develop the cool, quiet fortitude that comes with battle experience.

Two correspondents came in with the shiploads of re-inforcements. They are Jack Dowling and Frank McCarthy, who is relieving Miller. Miller was delighted and made much noise about the fact that when he hit the deck of the ship that would take him out of here, he was going to shave off his beard. We all cheered, for Miller's beard is one of the true horrors of Guadalcanal. It is almost as raggedy as my mustache.

A very reputable source told me today that the report of the *Wasp*'s having been sunk is true. He said she took two torpedoes in an isolated attack by a submarine (actually she took three), and was abandoned by her personnel.

Another persistent rumor these days is that our naval forces and the bulk of the Jap Navy in this area have fought a great battle somewhere to the north. But there is no confirmation from any official, or even informed direction. The truth seems to be that there has been no major naval action by surface forces since the battle of Savo Island.

Durdin and I sat on the beach most of the afternoon, waiting for the Jap air raid which we thought was inevitable. Our fleet of cargo and transport ships would make excellent targets. But the Japs, fortunately, did not come this after-noon.

They did come tonight, a force of ships estimated to range from two to six. They were too late, for our ships had gone. But Louie the Louse flew over for some time, dropping flares, looking for our ships, and the Jap ships, probably cruisers, lay well offshore and lobbed shells into our coastline.

SATURDAY, *September 19*

At the airport operations building this morning, we watched our dive-bombers taking off for some mission to the north. Probably bombing Gizo, or Rekata Bay, or one of the other Jap bases in the Solomons. Our people have been attacking some such objective frequently during the last few days, but have not had much luck in catching the Japanese ships, although they have damaged shore installations.

I checked over our records in an attempt to find out just how many ships our dive-bombers are credited with sinking since the first group of planes arrived here nearly a month ago. The total of ships sunk, I found, is three destroyers, one cruiser, and two transports. Probably a dozen other ships, mostly cruisers and destroyers, have been damaged by hits or near misses; altogether a good score, considering the fact that poor weather conditions and night operations generally make the location of the enemy difficult.

Still the enemy landings at Guadalcanal go on. Bit by bit, they are building up their forces—even now, so soon after their second big attack to break through our lines and take the airport has failed. Last night the group of ships which came in and shelled us probably also landed their daily load of troops.

This afternoon we talked with some of the Raiders about the Battle of the Ridge, and heard some interesting stories about the Japs, how, for instance, they often ask to be killed when they are captured, but seem relieved when we do not oblige. Then they feel they have complied with their part of the death-before-dishonor formula, and make no further attempt to deprive themselves of life.

Several of the Jap prisoners captured on the ridge it seems, said "Knife" when they were captured, and made hara-kiri motions in the region of the belly. But when no knife was forthcoming, they seemed relieved, and after that made no attempt to kill themselves.

Later this afternoon we heard that a large body of our troops is going out tomorrow to conduct a reconnaissance in force to the south of the airport, to try to find out how far the Japs have fallen back. Durdin, McCarthy, Dowling and I decided to go along.

SUNDAY, *September 20*

Our reconnaissance started at about 5:00 o'clock this morning and after that, for thirteen solid hours, we plowed through jungle and slipped and slid up and down the steepest ridges I have every climbed. It was a lesson in the geography of Guadalcanal which I will not forget.

Much of the time we were hiking was spent in traversing the sides of ridges. The trails were muddy and slippery from rain which fell early this morning, and I found that a tripod posture, the three supports being formed by two legs and one arm, was the best way to stay on your feet.

We also spent considerable time in the thickest and most unpleasant jungles I have seen. We followed trails most of the time, but even these were covered with tangles of brambly vines, prickly leaves and tree branches protected by long spines.

But our group of troops, led by Col. Edson, at least did not run into any Japs. Other groups which joined in our reconnaissance found a few snipers. A group of our new reinforcements fired continuously, as we had done when we first came to Guadalcanal; they were as chary of shadows and as "trigger-happy" as we had been.

We found evidences that the Japs had moved away in a great hurry and in great disorganization. We found bivouac areas where they had left packs, shoes, flags behind. And I spotted a pile of canvas cases by the side of one trail and found they were filled with parts of a serviceable 75 mm. pack howitzer. And others found rifles and ammunition. We found the shattered remains of a few Japs who had been hit by our artillery and others who had evidently died of their wounds.

Today our dive-bombers and torpedo planes had gone out to bomb Rekata Bay, we found on getting back to camp. They had bombed and strafed the base, and uncovered a cruiser near by and got a hit which damaged, but did not sink it.

MONDAY, *September 21*

The ships which brought us reinforcements, also brought supplies, including clothes. I went to the quartermaster depot this morning, got some clothes that smelled delightfully like the dry-goods department in a store, and went up to the Lunga and had a good bath before putting on the new things. Then to Juan Morrera's mess, which the marines call the Book-Cadillac, and afterward felt like a new man.

We sat about at Col. Hunt's CP and talked about the reason for the slackening in the Jap air raids. The optimists said the Japs had taken such a drubbing from our fighters that they had no planes left. The pessimists said the foe were simply consolidating their forces for another and bigger effort; perhaps they would send over more planes less frequently, instead of twenty-five or twenty-seven every day.

TUESDAY, *September 22*

At Kukum this afternoon, I saw Dick Mangrum (now a lieutenant colonel) and Lieut. Turner Caldwell, who led, respectively, the original marine and naval dive-bomber groups which came to this island to work out of Henderson Field. Both Turner's and Dick's original squadrons have been largely supplanted by new fresh groups, but the two leaders continued to fly until recently.

They had both grown thin as scarecrows, since I last saw them, and their faces were haggard. They told me they were exhausted from the night-and-day stint of work they had been doing.

"When the medicos used to tell us about pilot fatigue," said Turner, "I used to think they were old fuds. But now I know what they meant. There's a point where you just get to be no good; you're shot to the devil—and there's nothing you can do about it."

I heard tonight that both Turner and Dick are going to be sent out of Guadal soon for a rest in some peaceful region.

WEDNESDAY, *September 23*

"Signs of civilization are coming to Guadalcanal," said Gen. Vandegrift this morning. He told me how an engineer had come into his quarters and asked where he wanted the light. The general said he was surprised to find that the engineer was actually towing an electric wire behind him. The Jap power house which we had captured was in working order, and they had extended a line to the general's camp.

The general said that he felt our situation on Guadalcanal was brightening a bit. The reinforcements had been a great help, he said, and he seemed assured that the naval protection of our shores would improve. I found out later in the day that a group of motor torpedo boats are on their way to help protect our coastline from the continued Japanese landings.

There is much "scuttlebutt" about more reinforcements coming into Guadalcanal. But the general feeling seems to be that if Army troops are brought in, they will only reinforce, not supplant, the marines, at least for the time being. The old dream of being home for Christmas is fading.

Many of our officers, however, are being sent home, to rest, and to train new groups of troops. That is another sign that we have reached at least a "breather." And the Japs have confirmed the impression by abstaining from air-raiding us for another day, and failing even to send in the usual landing force of troop-carrying warships this evening.

THURSDAY, *September 24*

We went to the Raiders' CP for breakfast this morning, and had a good time yarning over pancakes. We talked about some of the close escapes we have had during this campaign, and Maj. Ken Bailey, one of the heroes of Tulagi and the battle on the ridge, said something touching about taking chances.

"You get to know these kids so well when you're working with 'em," he said, "and they're such swell kids that when it comes to a job that's pretty rugged, you'd rather go yourself than send them."

(Maj. Bailey was killed three days later during a patrol action.)

Guadalcanal Diary, 1943

The Battle of the River

by John Hersey

THE Third Battle of the Matanikau River on Guadalcanal was a laboratory sample of the thousands of skirmishes our men are going to have to fight before the war is won. In terms of Stalingrad or Changsha or El Alamein, it was not a great clash. It flatters the action a little even to call it a battle. But it affords an example of how battle feels to men everywhere.

Few Americans have ever heard of the Matanikau River, to say nothing of its Third Battle. The river is a light brown stream winding through a jungle valley about five miles west of Henderson Field. When I arrived on Guadalcanal, our forces did not hold positions out to the Matanikau. The Japs were moving up in some strength, evidently to try to establish their bridgehead—the first in their series of heavy moves against our camp. It became imperative for our troops to push to the river and force the enemy back beyond it, before it was too late.

The first two battles of the Matanikau River had been earlier attempts to do just that. In the first one, the Marines tried to do the job frontally; but their force was too small. In the second, they tried a tactic of encirclement, but again not enough men were thrown into action. This third time, with the enemy constantly growing in strength, there could be no question of failing. . . .

"Awright! Reveille! It's 6 o'clock. Come on, fellas, all out. Reveille!"

Although it was 6 o'clock and just barely light, it did not take much persuasion to start the men in Col. Amor Leroy Sims's camp stirring, wandering out to brush their teeth, shave, start cramming things into their packs, polish their already polished rifles.

Word was passed up through the encampment: "Mass at

6:30 for those who want it. Six-thirty mass." Attendance was pretty good that morning. While that religious rite was being carried out, there was also a pagan touch. Four buzzards flew over the camp. "To the right hand," said a young Marine, like a Roman sage; "Our fortunes will be good."

One of the last orders we had heard Col. Sims give the evening before was to the officer of the mess: "Breakfast in the morning must be a good, solid, hot meal. And if we get back from starving ourselves for two or three days out there and find that you fellows who stay behind have been gourmandizing, some one'll be shot at dawn."

Breakfast was solid, all right—our last square meal for three days. On the table there were huge pans full of sliced pineapples, beans, creamed chipped beef, a rice-and-raisin stew, crackers, canned butter, jam, and coffee.

As the units began lining up to move out, the first artillery barrage broke out—75's and 105's coughing deeply, and then a minute later the answering coughs, far out. At 8:30 the column started to move. We had a good long hike ahead of us. Col. Sims's encampment was about eight miles from the Matanikau, but terrain would force the column to move at least 15 miles before contact.

Gradually the column fell into silence. The walking, which had been casual and purposely out of step, began to get stiffer and more formal, and finally much of the column was in step. On the engineers' crudely bull-dozed roadway, there began to be a regular *crunch-crunch-crunch* that reminded me of all the newsreels I had seen of feet parading on asphalt, to a background of cheering and band music. As a matter of fact we had a band with us, but the bandsmen were equipped with first-aid equipment, stretchers and rifles.

For a time the column wound through thick jungle, then emerged on a grassy plain edged by a kind of Great Wall of steep, bare ridges. Just before we reached the first of the ridges, Col. Sims turned in his position at the head of the column and said: "Ten minute break. Get off the road, spread right out."

Lieut. Col. Frisbie, Col. Sims's hulking executive officer, sat cross-legged in the grass and thundered at me: "Would you like to hear about our plan of operation?"

"It is a very simple scheme," he explained. "We know that the Japs have moved up into positions on the other side of the mouth of the Matanikau. Perhaps some of them have already crossed to this side. Our aim is to cut off and kill or capture as many as we can. Those which we don't pocket we must drive back.

"Edson—that's Col. Merritt Edson, who trained the first Marine raiders—will push a holding attack to the river right at the mouth, and try to make the Japs think that we intend to force a crossing there. Whaling actually will force a crossing quite a little higher up, and then will wheel downstream beside the river. Hanneken will lead part of our force through behind Whaling, will go deeper than Whaling, and then cut right. If necessary another force will go around by sea and land behind the Japs to close the trap.

"This is very much like a plan Lee used at the Chickahominy, when he had Magruder make a demonstration south of the river, and sent D. H. Hill, A. P. Hill and Longstreet across at successive bridges, with Jackson closing the trap at the rear. We aren't sending the units in with quite the same pattern, but it's the same general idea. The advantage of our scheme is that Whaling goes in, and if he finds the going impossible, we haven't yet committed Hanneken and Puller, and we can revise our tactics.

"I think it'll work."

"All up! Let's go!"

The column started sluggishly up again. As it wound up over the ridges, past a battery of 75's, through a gap in the double-apron barbed-wire barrier, and out into the beginnings of No Man's Land, it looked less like a drill-ground army than like a band of Western pioneers, or some gold prospectors, wary of Indians. Each man was armed to his own taste and heart's content. Most carried rugged old 1903 bolt-action Springfields. A few had Browning automatic rifles. Almost all carried knives, slung from their belts, fastened to their packs, or strapped to their legs. Several had field shovels. Many carried pistols. Pockets bulged with grenades. Some were not satisfied with one bayonet, but carried two. There were even a couple of Jap swords. But probably the greatest refinement was an ugly weapon I spotted in the tunic pocket of Corporal Joseph Gagney, of Augusta, Me.—a 12-in. screw-driver.

I asked him how he happened to bring that along.

"Oh," he said, "just found it on my person."

"When do you expect to use it?"

"Never can tell, might lose my bayonet with some Japs in the neighborhood."

After we came out on the last and highest ridge, Col. Sims and I walked by a shortcut down to a coastwise road. We commandeered a jeep and rode forward as far as we could. This coast sector was where Col. Edson, past master of the bush, was staging his holding attack. We asked our way to his command post.

Col. Edson is not a fierce marine. In fact, he appears almost shy. Yet Col. Edson is probably among the five finest combat commanders in all the U.S. armed forces. "I hope the Japs will have some respect for American fighting men after this campaign," he says so quietly you have to lean forward to catch it all. "I certainly have learned respect for the Japs. What they have done is to take Indian warfare and apply it to the 20th Century. They use all the Indian tricks to demoralize their enemy. They're good, all right, but"—Col. Edson's voice trails off into an embarrassed whisper—"I think we're better."

Edson's forward command post stood in the last of the palm trees, and consisted of a foxhole and a field telephone slung on a coconut tree. As we came up, he was sitting on the ground, cross-legged, talking to one of his units on the phone.

When he was through phoning, Sims asked him what his situation was. "Only slight contact so far," he said. "We've met about a company of Japs on this side of the river, and they seem to be pretty well placed."

"I hope the muzzlers aren't pulling back," Sims said.

"Don't think so. They seem to have some mortars on the other side of the river, and I think they're pretty solid over there."

Here at Edson's C. P. I heard for the first time close at hand the tight-woven noise of war. The constant fabric of the noise is rifle fire. Like a knife tearing into the fabric, every once in a while, there would be a short burst of machine-gun fire. Forward we could hear bombs fumbling into the jungle, and the laughter of strafing P-39's. A mortar battery directly in front of us was doubly noisy, for its commander was an old-fashioned hollering marine. But weirdest of all was the sound of our artillery shells passing overhead. At this angle, probably just about under the zenith of their trajectory, they gave off a soft, fluttery sound, like a man blowing through a keyhole.

I inquired about the doubly noisy mortar battery. It belonged, I was told, to a character such as you would find only in the Marine Corps. This was Master Gunner Sergeant Lou Diamond, who is said to be approximately 200 years old. I saw him presently—a giant with a full gray beard, an admirable paunch, and the bearing of a man daring you to insult him. Lou is so old that there was some question whether to take him along on such a hazardous job as the Solomons campaign. He was getting too unwieldy to clamber up and down cargo nets. On one of the last days before embarking, Lou found out that they were debating about his antiquity, so he went out and directed loading operations with such violence that for a time he lost his voice entirely; the next morning he was told he could go along.

Now here he was, proving that even if he out-Methuselahed Methuselah, he would still be the best damn mortar man in the Marines. As we went by he was, as usual, out of patience. He wanted to keep on firing, and had been told to hold back. "Wait and wait and wait and wait," he roared. "God, some people around here'll fall on their ass from waiting . . ."

For the next two hours and more we were to witness some waiting which was nearly as disastrous. This was the watering of our force. The men had hiked more than ten miles under a broiling sun, and most had emptied their canteens. No one was certain when there would be another chance to get water —and water is the most precious commodity in human endurance. Therefore it was extremely important for the men to fill up.

The disaster was the way they filled up. The water source

was a big trailer tank, which had been towed out from the camp by a truck. The tank had only one faucet, and each man had to file by, turn the faucet on, hold his canteen under it, and turn it off again. This took time, far too much time.

We turned off the beach road and cut up through a jungle defile parallel to the Matanikau. Now we were really moving into position, and word was passed that we must be on the lookout for snipers. The trail led us constantly upward. Occasionally we would break out onto a grassy knoll, then plunge back into the jungle. The jungle seemed alien, an almost poisonous place. It closed in tightly on either side of the trail, a tangle of nameless trees and vines.

By midafternoon our column had emerged on the crest of a broad and fairly high ridge which looked down over the whole area of battle. It was there that I came to understand the expression "the fog of war." We thought we knew where we were, then found we didn't then found it wasn't too easy to locate ourselves. The Matanikau was hidden from our view by intervening ridges, so that we were not very sure of its course.

Fortunately we were high enough to see the coastline; we could figure out where we were by triangulation. One of the men took a bearing with a little field compass on Point Cruz, off to our left. Then he took a bearing on Lunga Point, back where the camp lay. He drew the two lines of bearing on the map, tangent to the tips of the points—and where the lines crossed was our position.

Lieut. Col. Puller's men were following us up the trail. When Col. Sims found where we were, he told Col. Puller that we would have to push on, even though darkness might shut down before we got to the prearranged bivouac. Now Col. Puller is one of the hardest Marine officers to restrain, once he gets started. He is as proud of his men as they are of him. And so when Col. Sims told him to move on, he threw out his chest, blew out his cheeks, and said: "That's fine. Couldn't be better. My men are prepared to spend the night right on the trail. And that's the best place to be if you want to move anywhere."

Col. Frisbie overheard this and couldn't resist giving The

Puller a rib. "Gwan," he said, "we know your men are tough. The trouble with the trails along these ridges is that there's not enough horse dung for your men to use as pillows."

As we moved forward, the high flat snap of Jap snipers' rifles became more and more frequent. Once in a while, from nowhere, a lone bullet would sing over our heads like a super-charged bee, and hundreds of men would involuntarily duck, even though the bullet was long past. The worst seemed to come from a valley ahead and to the left of us. Down there Whaling was trying to force his way through to the river, and his men were meeting not only sniper fire but occasional machine-gun and mortar fire. When I looked at the faces of a handful of Col. Sims's young men, who by now were already friends of mine—C. B., Bill, Ralph, Irving, Ted—I saw that they were no longer boastful joking lads. The music in that valley made them almost elderly.

Our bivouac for the night was on a ridge right above that valley, and we had hardly had time to set up our radio equipment and to get the field telephone working when the walking wounded began to dribble up the awful incline out of the valley: young fellows with bandages wrapped scarf-like around their necks or with arms in slings, or with shirts off and a huge red and white patch on the chest. They struggled silently up that 60° slope, absolutely silent about what they had seen and how they felt, most with a cigaret dangling lifelessly, perhaps unlit, out of one corner of the mouth, their eyes varnished over with pain.

Near the equator, the sun rises at about 6 and sets at about 6 all year round. By a quarter past 6 that night, it was nearly dark. An overcast was settling down; it looked like rain.

Breakfast had been huge, but we had done quite a bit of work in twelve hours. We were famished. There were no niceties out here: no please-pass-the-salt and no sir-may-I-please-be-excused. We just flopped down wherever we happened to be and opened our rations and gulped them down. The main course was Ration C—15 oz. of meat and vegetable hash, straight from the can, cold but delicious. For dessert we had a bar of Ration D. At home this would have seemed most distastefully healthy: it sounded like a convalescent's formula: 4 oz. (equal to 600 calories) of chocolate, sugar, skim-milk powder, cocoa fat, oat flour, vanillin, and 250 International Units of *thiamin hydrochloride* (vitamin B$_1$). But out there it was mighty good.

Gradually our bivouac settled down for the night. The men snuggled down into whatever comfortable spots they could find. They couldn't find many, because Guadal's ridges came up, once upon a time, out of the sea, and their composition is nine-tenths crumbled coral—not the stuff of beauty-rest.

C. B. had had the sense, as I had not, to look for a comfortable bed before it got pitch dark. The spot he picked was at the military crest: not on top of the ridge, but a little down the side—so that we would not be silhouetted at dawn, and so that sniper fire from the opposite side of the ridge could not reach us. Somehow he had found a place about 12 ft. wide and 6 ft. long where the coral was quite finely crumbled. When he heard me stumbling around and cursing coral, he called me over. I took off my pack and my canteen, folded my poncho double, and settled down. There was nothing to serve as pillow except either my pack, which was full of ration cans, or my steel helmet. I finally found that the most comfortable arrangement was to put my helmet on, and let it contend with the coral.

"Well, what do you think of the Marines?" C. B. asked.

I told him I was sold.

"They're a pretty fine bunch," he said. "Lots of this particular gang are pretty green, but they're willing and bright. There's no bitching among the privates in the Marine Corps for two reasons. The first is that they're all volunteers. If one of them starts talking back, the officer says: 'Nobody drafted you, Mac,' and every time, the squawker stops squawking. The other thing is that these men are a really high type. In peacetime the Corps only accepted about 20 percent of the applicants. In fact, the only difference between our officers and our privates is luck. One fellow got a break that the other didn't happen to get, and so he has the advantage of position."

And suddenly, like a child falling off in the middle of a bedtime story, C. B. was breathing hard and regularly. From then on, the night was in my hands, and I didn't like it.

My bedroom was the hollow empty sky, and every once in

a while a 105-mm. shell would scream in one window and out
the other. There was nothing soft and fluffy about the noise
here. We lay within 200 yd. of where the shells were landing,
and we heard the peculiar drilling sound you get only on the
receiving end of artillery fire. All through the night snipers
took pot shots at our ridges.

It was 5 in the morning before I dropped off. At 5:30 it
started raining, and I waked up again. So did all the marines.
The poncho helped, but rain infiltrates better than the Japs.
Soon a spot here, a patch there, got wet. With the damp
came chills, and before long there was a lot of miserable marines. The only consolation was that across the way there were
undoubtedly a lot of miserable Japs.

War is nine-tenths waiting — waiting in line for chow, waiting for promotion, waiting for mail, for an air raid, for dawn,
for reinforcements, for orders, for the men in front to move,
for relief. All that morning, while time seemed so important
to a layman, we waited. The plan was for Whaling to force his
crossing, after which Sims's men, under Hanneken and Puller,
would follow through.

The artillery and plane barrage that morning was a real
show from our grandstand ridge. The climax of the show was
when two TBF's, the Navy's most graceful planes, came over
and dropped two strings of twelve 100-lb. bombs. From our
ridge we could see the bombs leave their bays, describe their
parabola, and fall, terribly, exactly where they were intended
to fall. All along our ridge and the next marines stood up and
cheered.

When the barrage subsided, huge white birds circled in terror over the jungle across the way and we had visions of the
Japs circling in terror underneath. Bill, evidently thinking of
them, said quietly: "War is nice, but peace is nicer."

We settled down to wait for Whaling to have success. A few
of us crept out on a knoll which towered above the river itself;
we could look down on the area where Whaling's men were
doing their bitter work, and we could hear the chatter of their
guns, but we could see no movement, so dense was the
growth. In midmorning we did see seven Japs running away
up a burnt-off ridge across from us. A machine gun about 20
ft. from us snapped at their heels, and they dove for cover.

"How do you like the sound of that gun?" crowed one of the gunners. "That's the best damn gun in the regiment—in the Corps, for that matter."

At 11:40 a.m. the first of Whaling's men appeared on the ridges across the river. A signalman semaphored back the identification of the unit, so that we would not fire on them. At 11:45 a.m. Whaling sent a message back that the crossing had been secured. Col. Hanneken's men began to move. It was time for me to join a unit and go down.

Captain Charles Alfred Rigaud, standing there in the drizzle about to lead his heavy machine-gun company forward, looked like anything except a killer who took no prisoners. He had a boy's face. There were large, dark circles of weariness and worry under his eyes. His mustache was not quite convincing.

We stood on a high grassy ridge above a 300-ft. cliff. In the valley below was a little stream, which ran into the Matanikau River. Captain Rigaud's mission was to clear the valley of snipers, push to the river, and force a crossing.

The crossing was supposed to be made easy by the fact that Whaling's force was working around behind the Japs on the other side of the river, so that the enemy would be trapped. But Whaling had run into trouble and been delayed. Therefore Captain Rigaud's mission was doomed before it started—but he had no way of knowing.

I asked Captain Rigaud if I could go along with him. "You may go if you want to," he said, as if any one who would want to was crazy. My valor was certainly of ignorance: if I had had any understanding of what Company H might meet, I never would have gone along.

This was a company of veterans. They had been in every battle so far, and except perhaps for Edson's Raiders had been in all the toughest spots. The company had already lost 22 dead. They were tired. In the last war, men seldom stayed in the front lines more than two weeks. These men had been on Guadal two months. They were veterans, sure of themselves but surfeited with fighting.

We went down into the valley in single file. My position in line was immediately behind Captain Rigaud. About half the company was ahead of us, about half behind. The company's proper weapons were heavy machine guns, which the men carried broken down. Quite a few of the men carried ammunition boxes in both hands—a terrible load in such country. Some had rifles. Captain Rigaud and some of his platoon leaders had Browning automatic rifles.

After we had forded the stream once, the jungle suddenly became stiflingly thick. This was enemy territory in earnest. Our column moved in absolute silence. Captain Rigaud whispered to the man in front of him and to me that we should pass the word along for men to keep five paces apart, so as not to give snipers bunched targets. The message hissed forward and backward along the line in a whisper: "Keep five paces . . . keep five paces . . . keep five paces. . . ."

It is impossible to describe the creepy sensation of walking through that empty-looking but crowded-seeming jungle. Parakeets and cockatoos screeched from nowhere. There was one bird with an altogether unmusical call which sounded exactly like a man whistling shrilly through his fingers three times—and then another, far off in Jap territory, would answer.

As we sneaked forward, the feeling of tenseness steadily increased. The next word to be passed back from the head of the line came slowly, in whispers, for it was a long message: "Keep sharp lookout to right and to left . . . keep sharp lookout to right and to left . . . keep sharp lookout to right and to left. . . ."

As if we had to be told! After this word, another kind of message came back along the line: the tiny clicks of bullets being slipped into the chambers of weapons.

It was probably because I was a bad soldier, and looked at the ground rather than up in the trees, that I stumbled on my first really tangible evidence of the enemy. To the left of the trail, at the foot of a huge tree, I found a green headnet. It was small, and was made like some little minnow net. I picked it up, touched Captain Rigaud on the arm, and showed it to him.

Without changing his expression, he nodded, and shaped the soundless word "Jap" with his lips. Belatedly, it occurred to me to look up in the tree. There was nothing there.

A little farther along, I noticed a rifle lying in the stream. It had a very short stock and a very long barrel—not like any U.S. type I had seen. Again I touched Captain Rigaud's arm and pointed. He nodded again, and shaped the same word: "Jap."

We were moving very slowly now. It seemed strange to me to be walking erect. I had had visions of men in the jungle slithering along on their bellies, or at least creeping on all fours, like animals. But we didn't even stoop.

Up ahead, suddenly, three or four rifle shots—the high-pitched Jap kind—broke the silence. Almost at once a message came cantering back along the line: "Hold it up . . . hold it up . . . hold it up. . . ."

A strange little conversation followed. Several of us were bunched together waiting to move—Captain Rigaud, Peppard, Calder, Brizard. Suddenly one of them whispered: "Jesu, what I'd give for a piece of blueberry pie!"

Another whispered: "Personally I prefer mince."

A third whispered: "Make mine apple with a few raisins in it and lots of cinnamon: you know, Southern style."

The line started moving again without any more shots having been fired and without the passing of an order. Now we knew definitely that there were snipers ahead, and all along the line there were anxious upturned faces.

About a hundred yards farther along, I got a real shock. I had been looking upward along with the rest when suddenly right by my feet to the left of the trail I saw a dead marine. Captain Rigaud glanced back at me. His lips did not shape any word this time, but his bitter young face said, as plainly as if he had shouted it: "The Japs are bastards."

We kept on moving, crossing and recrossing the stream, which got wider and more sluggish. We were apparently nearing the Matanikau. Up ahead, as a matter of fact, some of the men had already crossed the river. There seemed to be no opposition; we had reason to hope that Whaling had already cleaned out whatever had been on the other side, and that our job would be a pushover. Just a sniper or two to hunt down and kill.

The captain and I were about 75 ft. from the river when we found out how wrong our hope was.

The signal was a single shot from a sniper. A couple of

seconds after it, snipers all around opened up on us. Machine guns from across the river opened up. But the terrible thing was that Jap mortars over there opened up, too.

The Japs had made their calculations perfectly. There were only three or four natural crossings of the river. This was one of them. And so they had set their trap. They had machine guns all set up ready to pour stuff into the jungle bottleneck at the stream's junction with the river. They had snipers scattered on both sides of the river. And they had their mortars all set to lob deadly explosions into the same area. Their plan was to hold their fire and let the enemy get well into the trap before snapping it, and this they had done with too much success.

Had we been infantry, the trap might not have worked. Brave men with rifles and grenades could have wiped out the enemy nests. Captain Rigaud's helplessness was that he could not bring his weapons to bear. Heavy machine guns take some time to be assembled and mounted. In that narrow defile his men, as brave as any, never succeeded in getting more than two guns firing.

The mortar fire was what was terrifying. Beside it, the Japs' sniper fire and even machine-gun fire, with its high, small-sounding report, seemed a mere botheration. But each explosion of mortar fire was a visitation of death.

When the first bolts of this awful thunder began to fall among Rigaud's men, we hit the ground. We were like earthy insects with some great foot being set down in our midst, and we scurried for little crannies—cavities under the roots of huge trees, little gullies, dead logs. Explosions were about ten seconds apart, and all around us, now 50 yd. away, now 20 ft. And all the while snipers and machine gunners wrote in their nasty punctuation. Our own guns answered from time to time with good, deep, rich sound, but not enough.

Individually the marines in that outfit were as brave as any fighters in any army in the world. But when fear began to be epidemic in that closed-in place, no one could resist it. The marines had been deeply enough indoctrinated so that even flight did not wipe out the formulas, and soon the word came whispering back along the line: "Withdraw . . . withdraw

. . . withdraw. . . ." Then they started moving back, slowly at first, then running wildly.

It was then that Charles Alfred Rigaud, the boy with tired circles under his eyes, showed himself to be a good officer and grown man. Despite the snipers all around us, despite the machine guns and the mortar fire, he stood right up on his feet and shouted out: "Who in Christ's name gave that order?"

This was enough to freeze the men in their tracks.

Next, by a combination of blistering sarcasm, orders and cajolery, he not only got the men back into position; he got them in a mood to fight again. I am certain that all along, Captain Rigaud was just as terrified as I was (i.e., plenty), for he was eminently human. And yet his rallying those men was as cool a performance as you can imagine.

When he had put them back into position, he immediately made preparations to get them out in an orderly fashion. He could see that the position was untenable; staying there would merely mean losing dozens of men who could live to fight successfully another day. He could not get his weapons into play; obviously Whaling's force had not unsettled the enemy across the river. Therefore he beckoned to a runner, filled out a request for permission to withdraw on his yellow message pad, sent the runner off to the rear C. P., and then set about passing whispered orders for the withdrawal.

Now the heroism of the medical corpsmen and bandsmen showed itself. They went into the worst places and began moving the wounded. I joined them because, I guess, I just thought that was the fastest way to get the hell out of there.

I attached myself to a group who were wounded in a dreadful way. They had no open wounds; they shed no blood; they seemed merely to have been attacked by some mysterious germ of war that made them groan, hold their sides, limp, and stagger. They were shock and blast victims.

There were not enough corpsmen to assist more than the unconscious and leg-wounded men, so they had set these men to helping each other. It was like the blind leading the blind. I commandeered three unhurt privates, and we began to half-carry, half-drag the worst of these strange casualties.

The rain and trampling had made the trail so bad now that

a sound man walking alone would occasionally fall, and in some steep places would have to crawl on hands and knees, pulling himself by exposed roots and leaning bamboo trunks. We slid, crept, walked, wallowed, waded and staggered, like drunken men. One man kept striking the sides of his befuddled skull with his fists. Another kept his hands over his ears. Several had badly battered legs, and behaved like football players with excruciating Charley horses.

The worst blast victim, who kept himself conscious only by his guts, was a boy whom I shall call John Smith, though that is not his name. Part of the time we had to carry him, part of the time he could drag his feet along while I supported him. Before we went very far, a corpsman, who saw what pain he was in, injected some morphine in his arm. Smith had a caved-in chest, and one of his legs was blasted almost out of use.

As we struggled along the trail he kept asking for his sergeant, whose name I shall change to Bill Johnson. "Don't leave Johnson," the wounded boy pleaded.

Gradually I pieced together what had happened. Smith and several of these others had been the crew of one of the machine guns which did get into action. Sergeant Johnson was in command of the gun. While they were approach-firing, a mortar-grenade went off near them, knocking the crew all over the place. Most of the men took cover. But Johnson crawled back to the gun just in time for another grenade to come much closer yet.

We asked around in the group to see if Johnson was with us, but he was not. "They got him sure," one said.

"He shouldn't have gone back," Smith said. "Why in hell did he have to go back?"

And all the way out of that valley of the shadow, John Smith mumbled about his friend Sergeant Johnson.

The farther we went, the harder the going seemed to be. We all became tired, and the hurt men slowed down considerably. There were some steep places where we had to sit Smith down in the mud, and slide him down 10 ft. to the stream. In other places, uphill, we had to form a chain of hands and work him up very slowly. It was almost dark when we got out of the jungle, and by the time we had negotiated the last steep ridge, it was hard to tell the difference between the wounded men and the bearers. We turned the wounded over to Doc New, the Navy surgeon, who had an emergency dressing station set up on the crest of that last ridge.

While I talked with Captain Rigaud, who had led his men out by a shorter way and beaten us in, corpsmen and bandsmen hurried down for Johnson. It was pitch dark when those heroic boys found him. They were in territory, remember, where snipers had been all around, and where, if they betrayed themselves by the slightest sound, they would have mortar fire pouring down on them. They asked Johnson: "How you feel, Mac?" He said: "I think I can make it." They fashioned a stretcher out of two rifles and a poncho, and started out. Johnson was in bad shape. He was conscious, but that was about all.

The only way they could find their path was to follow, hand over hand, a telephone wire which some wire stringer had carried down into that hot valley. In the darkness they had great difficulty making progress, and had to halt for long rests.

Men who are wounded do not talk rhetorically; famous last words are usually edited after the fact. Johnson's sentences to Sgt. Lewis W. Isaak and Private Clinton Logan Prater were simple requests: "Help me sit up, will you please, oh God my stomach." . . . Soon he said very softly: "I wish I could sleep." The wish was fulfilled: he dropped off in apparent peace. He gave a few short breaths and then just stopped breathing.

I never did find out exactly how many men were killed, and how many wounded in that valley. But I do know that one less died than would have otherwise, if Doc New hadn't been mighty handy in an emergency.

A dying officer was brought to him. He was in absolute shock. He was gray as ashes in the face. His hands were cold. You could not feel his pulse. He had suffered a bad wound from mortar shrapnel in his left knee, and he had another shrapnel wound in his right hand. Doc New realized that plasma, and lots of it, was all that could save this man.

He had to maintain blackout. He had also to try to keep the man warm. To serve both these ends, most of his corpsmen gave up their ponchos. Working feverishly, interposing such expressions as "Dadgummitdingwhiz," he covered first the wounded man, then his own head and shoulders, with ponchos. Before the first unit of 250 cc. was all in, the patient came out of his coma. By the time the second was in, he was able to speak. By morning he was able to talk to his C. P. on a field phone, stand the ride on a stretcher down to the beach road, and sit up in a jeep on the way back to the hospital.

The sunrise next morning, after the slop and terror of the day before, was one of the most beautiful things a lot of marines had ever seen. Bill said: "Any one who can't see beauty in that doesn't deserve to live. My mother would like to see that. 'Dear Mom: You should've seen the sunrise this morning.' . . ."

Operations now proceeded according to plan—the formal way of saying "with moderate but unspectacular success." By 10:20 a.m. the leading troops of the flanking units had reached the beach. They found that most of the Japs had withdrawn during the night, taking their wounded with them. Evidently they had pulled out in quite a hurry, for they left packs and other equipment behind. They left 200 dead on the field. The Marines lost 60 dead—their worst casualties in any single operation on Guadal up to that time.

Probably the bitterest clash of the whole battle occurred at the mouth of the Matanikau. For two whole days, Edson had been unable to root out that entrenched company of Japs on the east side of the river. Finally, on the second night, he called on his Raiders, the men who do or die in the true jams on Guadal. He put them between the Japs and the spit, their only avenue of escape.

In the pitch-black night the Japs made a desperate break. They put on a shrieking attack into the Raiders' positions. Some of them leaped silently into foxholes beside the Marines, who had no way of knowing whether their guests were retreating comrades or advancing enemy. In the knife-work that followed, the Marines came out better than the Japs, to judge by the number of dead Japs in the foxholes. The Raiders lost eleven dead. There were 60 Japanese bodies in the area.

And so, in three days, I had seen the Marines have a partial success. They had driven the Japs back, but they had not killed or captured as many as they hoped to. They had lost too many. They had learned some bitter lessons: they must not delay over such things as watering; they must perfect communications in the field.

But they had fought bravely and better than the enemy. They had shown themselves to be men, with the strengths and the weaknesses of men. That had given me, an unprofessional onlooker, a new faith in U.S. chances of winning the war in the visible future.

Life, November 23, 1942

The Battle for Scoops

by Walter Graebner

EVERY DAY some 25 American and British correspondents in Moscow try to scoop one another on the war in Russia. The task is difficult because 99 per cent of all the news cabled from the Soviet Union comes out of four, four-page newspapers which are available to everyone at the same time every day, and because Soviet censors are naturally reluctant to pass news secured from non-official sources.

The daily struggle for a scoop begins around 8 a.m. when the *Red Star* (top military newspaper), *Pravda* (official mouthpiece of the Communist Party), *Izvestia* and *Komsomol Pravda* are issued. At that hour correspondents sit down with their interpreter-secretaries (only a few correspondents can read Russian) and listen to the war news being unfolded. Most of it is inconsequential from the correspondents' point of view but here and there is a snippet which can be worked into a story. When two or three paragraphs are written, copy is rushed to the censor, then to the cable office. Shortly after noon, all newspapers have been culled, so there is little to do except wait until the following morning's issue arrives.

Competition both for scoops and to get news out quickly is particularly keen among agency men. Consequently, all of them work in a tiny press room at the Foreign Office where they can observe their rivals. If the din from typewriters were not so great, it would be possible for one correspondent to know what the others were getting simply by listening to their secretaries translate.

Various means are employed to get news first to the telegraph company which is about three-quarters of a mile from the Foreign Office. For a time, Harold King of Reuters held the advantage over the others by using a motorcyclist whom he hired from the Turkish Embassay while the ambassador

was away. He was known among correspondents as the
"King's Messenger." The Associated Press and the United
Press have 14-year-old girl runners named Zena and Venus
who are fast as fawns. When the agencies managed to have
their motorcars sent up from Kuibyshev a few days ago, there
arose a new problem which is now in the process of being
solved. For the time being, each agency is rushing its copy to
the telegraph office by car, but this system can't continue
long owing to slim gasoline rations. There is talk of all agencies using one car for a week at a time, but this system has the
obvious disadvantage of enabling no one to be first with the
copy.

The "special" (as distinct from agency) correspondents
work in their hotel rooms. Their secretaries (mostly women)
arrive around 9 a.m. with papers and translate until 12, while
the correspondents make notes from which they write stories
during the next two hours. If the papers were published in
English, newsmen could probably finish their day's work in
two or three hours, but as yet no secretary has been able to
school herself in how to search for the essential facts. Most of
them subject the correspondent to a monotonous literal
translation of every word in the story unless the correspondent calls a stern halt. But if the secretaries are particularly
fascinated by the story, they sometimes ignore the interrup-
tion and drone on to a tiring end.

The Mother Superior of the secretaries is a buxom, middle-
aged woman known only as Sophiana. Easily the most accomplished interpreter of the lot, she has worked at one time or
another for Art Steele, Erskine Caldwell, Margaret Bourke-
White, Negley Farson and Quentin Reynolds. Currently she is
secretary to Paul Winterton of BBC and the London *News
Chronicle*. One of the few male secretaries is a person named
Oscar, who could easily pass for the cousin of Anthony Eden.
No sooner had the British correspondent of the London
Daily Herald arrived from India when he decided to marry
the secretary he had just hired.

My secretary is Lydia Kleingal, a Latvian woman of 30 who
was born in Chicago and moved to the Soviet Union when
she was 10. She is considered the best looking of all the secretaries, but whatever pleasure my eyes derive from her beauty

is offset by the pain her garbled English gives to my ear-drums. The following is typical: "Yesterday I saw in train a man with small apparatus at his right ear. He looked like ar-tillerist officer. From that black apparatus ran down behind his collar a wire. I asked him what has he got there inside. He opened his leather coat and said that in many pockets he has an instrument at the same time he took one out: it had the size of a pocket watch black and several holes. He told me also that the apparatus costs 12,000 rubles. It's the first one and he got it presented from People's Commissariat of De-fense. I was speaking with him in a normal voice."

At 2 p.m. the correspondents lunch together in a private dining room at the Metropole Hotel. They spend a consider-able part of the meal trying to discover how others covered the day's news. Rarely does anyone ask another the straight-forward question: "What did you send today?" Instead, an indirect approach is used, such as, "Did you see the story in *Pravda* this morning on Stalingrad?" Occasionally, when someone discovers he has missed an important story, he will bolt his food and race off to file a report, figuring it's better to be late with news than not to send it at all.

The dining room is a favorite place to plant phony stories for the dessert of those who are overly eager to get scoops. Recently a rumor was whispered that President Roosevelt was due to arrive in Russia. On the strength of it, one correspon-dent actually made a special trip by air to Kuibyshev where he figured the President would most likely stop first.

The most bitter rivalry occurred over the story of Churchill's visit to Moscow. The time set for its release was 8 p.m. on the Monday after his departure. In the afternoon the British correspondents, fearing they would miss the Tuesday morning papers in London (British time is five hours later than New York's) persuaded their ambassador to move the release forward to 3 p.m. This was fine for the British but disastrous for the Americans who would thus be scooped by the foreign press when London picked up the story there and filed it to America. So a delegation of American correspon-dents called on their Ambassador Standley, who telephoned the British Ambassador Kerr, who arranged a joint parley be-tween the American and British correspondents. Everything, however, was settled before the correspondents ever reached the British Embassy. They agreed on the 3 o'clock release time for everyone. In the end, BBC scooped the world by spilling the news long before any copy sent from Moscow could appear in print.

Fear of being scooped again spread among correspondents when Wendell Willkie was in town. Arrangements were made for him to hold a final press conference over cocktails in Eddie Gilmour's (Associated Press) room at the Metropole. Though it was agreed that no one would leave the room until the party was over, several correspondents, doubting the word of others, kept their eyes on the door. To make their day miserable, other correspondents started the rumor that King of Reuters had crawled out the bedroom window the moment Willkie's statement had been read.

The intense preoccupation of the correspondents with affairs of business is partly explained by the fact that they lead practically identical lives, which in wartime Russia are not exactly full of well-rounded pleasures. All are quartered at the big gloomy Metropole Hotel in rooms that look exactly alike. Most of them eat breakfast alone in their rooms but the management discourages room service for other meals so these are taken in the private dining room. All eat about the same food (soup, meat, potatoes, cake and tea with certain variations) and most of them have formed the habit of occupying the same seats for every meal. After the correspondents have discussed the day's news, the conversation often lags into silence which lasts for the rest of the meal. When it is over the correspondents try to carry, silently, their uneaten bread and sugar to their rooms for between-meal snacks.

New faces are not received with the interest one might expect in a land to which foreigners seldom come. Not long ago Mrs. Blakeslee, a correspondent for *Collier's*, arrived after the usual arduous air journey from America. Expecting a jolly welcome, she skipped gaily into the dining room and said, "Well, here I am, boys and girls!" The correspondents merely lifted their heads from the soup, grunted a sour "hullo," and went on with their eating. Mrs. Blakeslee still talks about her chilly reception.

Correspondents buy most of their vodka (the price has

doubled in the last few days), brandy, wine and cigarettes from the Diplomatic Store which the Soviet maintains for the benefit of the foreign diplomatic corps. (The Russians draw no distinction between diplomats and correspondents unless the correspondents receive more facilities for seeing the country.) At the store, too, they can purchase eggs, vegetables, nuts, chocolates in limited quantities to supplement the hotel fare. Since all correspondents thus eat and drink the same things, they are usually in about the same state of health. Most of the time they complain either of constipation from the lack of fruits and vegetables or of mild dysentery from eating too many fresh foods. Few have learned that the sure way to keep healthy in Russia is to eat Russia's black bread. Actually, the food served to correspondents is superior to anything that was available in England when I was there.

Correspondents arrange their cultural lives through two pretty twins of the Intourist organization. The office, located in the hotel, handles tickets for the ballet, the theater, concerts and all other forms of entertainment open to the public. Before the new restrictions were placed on gasoline, cars were also occasionally available through the Intourist. Now correspondents are obliged to walk or travel on public conveyances unless they're bound for the airport or the railway stations.

When anyone has a date with a girl, it's almost an item of news worthy of cable. Except for three correspondents, there are no American or English girls in Moscow and most of the Russian girls are either at the front, in factories, or unavailable. Many evenings are therefore spent playing poker or chess. There's almost nothing to read: books, magazines and newspapers make a complete round of the correspondents' rooms. Right now (October 16) they're reading August and September issues of London and New York newspapers.

Several months ago, when the correspondents were feeling exceptionally matey, they formed an Anglo-American association. First president was Henry Shapiro of UP who has lived in Russia so long that he might easily be mistaken for Russian. A formal constitution was drawn up which the Soviet Government recognized in due course and at the meetings, strict adherence is paid to parliamentary procedure.

The only important meeting to date was exclusively devoted to a lengthy discussion about food. The need for a meeting arose after President Shapiro, acting on what he thought was a majority opinion of the correspondents, arranged with the hotel manager for the secretaries to be segregated at meals. This caused a terrific furor: 1) because Shapiro hadn't raised the matter at a formal meeting of the association; 2) because some of the correspondents feared they would lose the loyalty of their secretaries; and 3) because it turned out that in their new dining quarters the secretaries didn't get the special food served the correspondents.

Leland Stowe made a long impassioned speech in which he claimed the whole question of the "Second Front" was also involved. The others said the secretaries were happy to be away from the correspondents at meal times and really didn't want special food. President Shapiro, taking the blame on himself, seemed on the point of resigning—but he didn't. In the end, a committee was appointed to study the question. The association hasn't met since Churchill's visit. But the daily battle for scoops still continues.

History in the Writing, 1945

A Negro Looks at This War

by J. Saunders Redding

I WAS listening sleeplessly to an all-night program of music interspersed with war news, bad news. The bad news of the war had not seemed bad news to me. Indeed, on this night, it was again giving me a kind of grim, perverted satisfaction. Some non-white men were killing some white men and it might be that the non-whites would win. This gratified me in a way difficult to explain. Perhaps, in a world conquered and ruled by yellow men, there would be no onus attached to being black and I, a Negro. . . . Then a peculiar thing happened. Something seemed to burst and I knew suddenly that I believed in this war we Americans are fighting. I think I said aloud, and with a kind of wonder: "I, a Negro, believe in this war we Americans are fighting." The thought or revelation gave rise to an emotion—keen, purging, astringent.

The thought and the conviction amazed me, for I had thought that I could never believe in war again, or that any war in which I might believe would be truly a race war; and then, naturally, I would believe as I had been taught by innumerable circumstances to believe. I would believe in the side of the darker peoples. But I could envision no such war even in the remote future, for I had been trained in the principles called Christian. I had been trained to believe in the brotherhood of man and that we were approaching that glorious state—slowly, but before complete catastrophe could overtake us.

War had no heroic traditions for me. Wars were white folks'. All wars in historical memory. The last war, and the Spanish-American War before that, and the Civil War. I had been brought up in a way that admitted of no heroics. I think my parents were right. Life for them was a fierce, bitter, soul-searing war of spiritual and economic attrition; they fought it

426

without heroics, but with stubborn heroism. Their heroism was screwed up to a pitch of idealism so intense that it found a safety valve in cynicism about the heroics of white folks' war. This cynicism went back at least as far as my paternal grandmother, whose fierce eyes used to lash the faces of her five grandchildren as she said, "An' he done som'pin big an' brave away down dere to Chickymorgy an' dey made a iron image of him 'cause he got his head blowed off an' his stomick blowed out fightin' to keep his slaves." I cannot convey the scorn and the cynicism she put into her picture of that hero-son of her slave-master, but I have never forgotten.

I was nearly ten when we entered the last war in 1917. The European fighting, and the sinking of the *Lusitania*, had seemed as remote, as distantly meaningless to us, as the Battle of Hastings. Then we went in and suddenly the city was flag-draped, slogan-plastered, and as riotously gay as on circus half-holidays. I remember one fine Sunday we came upon an immense new billboard with a new slogan: GIVE! TO MAKE THE WORLD SAFE FOR DEMOCRACY. My brother, who was the oldest of us, asked what making the world safe for democracy meant. My father frowned, but before he could answer, my mother broke in.

"It's just something to say, like . . ."—and then she was stuck until she hit upon one of the family's old jokes—"like 'Let's make a million dollars.'" We all laughed, but the bitter core of her meaning lay revealed, even for the youngest of us, like the stone in a halved peach.

Even then the war was only as relevant and as close as the powder plant across the river. Explosions at the plant often rattled the windows and shook the crockery in our house. But Negroes were making big money. The river steamers carried three shifts of them a day. They were a reckless and a profane lot, full of swagger and talk on seventy-five dollars a week and double time for overtime. They did not mind having their skins turn nicotine-yellow from the powder they were making for white men to kill each other. "They're white, ain't they? Well, let 'em fight. We hates peace!"

For it was thought at first that the war was more exclusively than ever a white folks' war. Long before the first contingent of draftees left the city, there was a mess about drafting. It

seems that President Wilson, or someone, did not want colored soldiers. Later, the someone changed his mind and some
colored men went away. By this time, trainloads of soldiers
were rolling through our station every day. The Red Cross
ladies were always at the station, giving away chocolates and
cigarettes, doughnuts and coffee. "Nothing's too good for
our soldier boys." But we heard that whenever a colored
troop train rolled in, the ladies retired to the stationmaster's
office until it was gone again.

But someone really had changed his mind completely and
colored boys were not merely staying in the camps to clean up
after the white boys. Somebody said the Ninth and Tenth
Cavalry units had gone across. Somebody said they would not
let Colonel Young go, however. They said that they did not
want to make him a Brigadier-General and that he was somewhere, Cuba or Haiti or down on the Mexican border, dying
of a broken heart. Whoever in the world ever heard of a
nigger general!

Then somebody said that colored boys were really getting
killed. And finally, we learned that in Washington they had
called out a Negro detachment to guard government property. We even saw pictures in a colored paper. White soldiers
could not always be trusted, the article said. A white soldier
might be an Austrian or a German, anything, dressed up in a
soldier's suit. But a "nigger" (I remember the word was in
quotes) in khaki was Uncle Sam himself. You knew what he
was the moment you looked at him. "Yes," I remember my
father saying in a weary, strangely bitter voice, "that's the
trouble. You take him for granted."

There was an excited, theatrical, patriotic glamor. Every
Saturday evening during that summer, under the vast façade
of the Court House and County Building, there was a community sing. The city band played. The words were flashed
from a magic lantern onto a huge screen and everyone sang
his heart out. *Over There, Long, Long Trail, Keep the Home
Fires Burning*, and *Tipperary*. By the time we came to the
close and the throat-caught singing of the Star-Spangled Banner, a great many men and women were crying openingly,
unashamedly. But my Uncle Silas, who was with us in those

days, always broke into a ribald parody of the national anthem as we went down the hill toward home.

After she discovered that Negro soldiers really were dying, my mother did Red Cross work in the small segregated unit. Her youngest brother, who won a commission in the segregated officers' training camp in Iowa, was killed. My father worked in the segregated unit to subscribe the Liberty Loans. But both my parents laughed at the little wizened white man who came to our door selling a cheap lithograph. It represented a colored soldier and a colored sailor, one on each side of crossed American flags. Below them was a legend:

> You fought and died at San Juan Hill;
> Now go and get old Kaiser Bill.

There were several opinions. Negroes were not fighting. They were dying of influenza and dysentery behind the lines, where they served as flunkies. Negroes were fighting. They were holding positions white soldiers could not hold in the most dangerous salients. When they died, they were being dumped into graves without markers of any kind. The positions they were fighting had no medical detachments, no Red Cross units, no hospital facilities. But they died. In any event, quite a few of them died before the war was over.

I remember that first, false, mad Armistice. Everyone seemed crazy drunk and everywhere there was a spontaneous and unabashed breakdown of lines. Banker and butcher, coal-heaver and clerk, black and white, men and women went worming and screaming joyously through the streets. I also remember the real Armistice, and that there was a block party which Negroes could not attend, and that the police would not give them a permit to hold one of their own in the narrow, factory-flanked streets where most of them lived. When the lynchings and the riots started again—in East St. Louis, Chicago, Chester, even in Washington—we knew that, so far as the Negro was concerned, the war had been a failure, and "making the world safe for democracy" a good phrase bandied about by weak or blind or unprincipled men.

And so, since I have reached maturity and thought a man's thoughts and had a man's—a Negro man's—experiences, I

have thought that I could never believe in war again. Yet I
believe in this one.

II

There are many things about this war that I do not like,
just as there are many things about "practical" Christianity
that I do not like. But I believe in Christianity, and if I accept
the shoddy and unfulfilling in the conduct of this war, I do it
as voluntarily and as purposefully as I accept the trash in the
workings of "practical" Christianity. I do not like the odor of
political pandering that arises from some groups. I do not like
these "race incidents" in the camps. I do not like the world's
not knowing officially that there were Negro soldiers on
Bataan with General Wainwright. I do not like the constant
references to the Japs as "yellow bastards," "yellow bellies,"
and "yellow monkeys," as if color had something to do with
treachery, as if color were the issue and the thing we are fighting rather than oppression, slavery, and a way of life hateful
and nauseating. These and other things I do not like, yet I
believe in the war.

The issue is plain. The issue, simply, is freedom. Freedom is
a precious thing. Proof of its preciousness is that so many
men wait patiently for its fulfillment, accept defilement and
insult in the hope of it, die in the attainment of it. It used to
seem shamefully silly to me to hear Negroes talk about freedom. But now I know that we Negroes here in America know
a lot about freedom and love it more than a great many
people who have long had it. It is because we have so little of
it, really, that it used to seem silly to me to hear talk about
preserving it. Giving me a penny, my father would remark in a
satirical way, "That's not enough money, son, to do you any
good. You might as well throw it away." I did not see that
there was enough freedom to do me much good. It's a stage
most public-schooled Negroes go through.

We go through a stage of blind, willful delusion. Later, we
come to see that in the logic of a system based on freedom
and the dignity of man we have a chance. We see that now
and again there are advances. And this new seeing kindles the
hope that Americans are really not proud of their silly preju-

dices, their thick-skinned discriminations, their expensive seg-
regations. And now, I think, we know that whatever the mad
logic of the New Order, there is no hope for us under it. The
ethnic theories of the Hitler "master folk" admit of no chance
of freedom, but rather glory in its expungement.

This is a war to keep men free. The struggle to broaden
and lengthen the road of freedom—our own private and important war to enlarge freedom here in America—will come
later. That this private, intra-American war will be carried on
and won is the only real reason we Negroes have to fight. We
must keep the road open. Did we not believe in a victory in
that intra-American war, we could not believe in nor stomach
the compulsion of this. If we could not believe in the realization of democratic freedom for ourselves, certainly no one
could ask us to die for the preservation of that ideal for others. But to broaden and lengthen the road of freedom is different from preserving it. And our first duty is to keep the
road of freedom open. It must be done continuously. It is the
duty of the whole people to do this. Our next duty (and this,
too, is the whole people's) is to broaden that road so that
more people can travel it without snarling traffic. To die in
these duties is to die for something.

There are men who do not like the road of freedom, men
who would block it, who would destroy it, and that is what
the war is about. What we on our side fight for now has nothing to do with color, nor political forms. It has everything to
do with the estimation in which we hold ourselves and in
which, therefore, others hold us. There are these men, these
"master folk," who hold that all other peoples are of less
worth than they. It is an article of faith with them: not a thing
of intellection, but an emotional thing, and it is hard to be rid
of. Where these men find human dignity and aspiration, they
set about to degrade and quench it. This is an insult and an
injury that has at last to be avenged in blood. Nine-tenths of
the world's people have been insulted. And certainly, since
this insult is so patently the issue, once we Negroes have
fought to avenge it to other men (and ourselves, also) our
brothers in blood-revenge will not return that insult to us
again, as, I say it softly, they have so long done. Certainly
now, over the stink of blood, the holocaust, they will know

that this war for their freedom will be a dead end, unless the road of freedom is made a broad, through highway for all peoples forever.

This, of course, is hope. But you cannot fight wars without hope. This is also belief. And you cannot fight a victorious war without a belief in the thing you fight for. Here in America we believe, however falteringly, in the individual worth and dignity of man. Human dignity counts here.

III

But if the satanic destinies of the New Order fulfill themselves? I, a Negro, would not count. The "master folk" plainly say I will not count if their will prevails. There are people already who do not count: they are in ghettos and concentration camps. There are Jews and Poles and Chinese who do not count. And we Negroes would be done in purposefully, coldly, "according to plan." None of the precious techniques of survival which we learned in slavery would avail. They are smart and they are zealous, those master folk. They are zealous enough in pursuit of their racial purity to brook no interference, and smart enough to know that the lips and thighs of black women have been found sweet before. None of our skills, none of our will to live would count. We would die; and it would be better to die because we are a menace to what we hate than to live in safety in support of it.

I believe in this war, finally, because I believe in the ultimate vindication of the wisdom of the brotherhood of man. This is not foggy idealism. I think that the growing manifestations of the interdependence of all men is an argument for the wisdom of brotherhood. I think that the shrunk compass of the world is an argument. I think that the talk of united nations and of planned interdependence is an argument. I do not know what social forms these arguments will be molded into to achieve the final vindication of wisdom, but I believe that these arguments are themselves so wise and strong that they will push men up, not to a final victory over baseness and fear and selfishness, but to the height from which they can look wisdom in the eye and know that there is only the choice between brotherhood and anarchy.

More immediately, I believe in this war because I believe in America. I believe in what America professes to stand for. Nor is this, I think, whistling in the dark. There are a great many things wrong here. There are only a few men of good will. I do not lose sight of that. I know the inequalities, the outraged hopes and faith, the inbred hate; and I know that there are people who wish merely to lay these by in the closet of the national mind until the crisis is over. But it would be equally foolish for me to lose sight of the advances that are made, the barriers that are leveled, the privileges that grow. Foolish, too, to remain blind to the distinction that exists between simple race prejudice, already growing moribund under the impact of this war, and theories of racial superiority as a basic tenet of a societal system—theories that at bottom are the avowed justification for suppression, defilement and murder.

I will take this that I have here. I will take the democratic theory. The bit of road of freedom that stretches through America is worth fighting to preserve. The very fact that I, a Negro in America, can fight against the evils in America is worth fighting for. This open fighting against the wrongs one hates is the mark and the hope of democratic freedom. I do not underestimate the struggle. I know the learning that must take place, the evils that must be broken, the depths that must be climbed. But I am free to help in doing these things. I count. I am free (though only a little as yet) to pound blows at the huge body of my American world until, like a chastened mother, she gives me nurture with the rest.

American Mercury, November 1942

Negroes Are Saying . . .

by Roi Ottley

*If I were a Negro I would live in constant fury and prob-
ably would batter myself to death against the bars inclos-
ing my condition.*—Westbrook Pegler

LISTEN to the way Negroes are talking these days!

Gone are the Negroes of the old banjo and singin' roun' the cabin doors. Old Man Mose is dead! Instead, black men have become noisy, aggressive, and sometimes defiant. Actually, this attitude is a reflection of a cold enthusiasm toward the war brought on by what the Pittsburgh *Courier* calls 'The War Against Negroes.' The fact is, there still is considerable doubt and apathy in the minds of the Negro civilian and military populations, which seriously hampers the war effort, particularly among those who are unable to lift their eyes to the hills. This is not the idle speculation of irresponsible observers, but an implacable fact that is revealed by the casual remarks dropped daily by the Negro man-in-the-street, and by his overt acts as well.

Recently a Harlem physician was summoned to court for driving about with a large sign tied to the rear of his automobile. It read:

IS THERE A DIFFERENCE?

JAPS BRUTALLY BEAT
AMERICAN REPORTER

———

GERMANS BRUTALLY BEAT
SEVERAL JEWS

———

AMERICAN CRACKERS
BRUTALLY BEAT
ROLAND HAYES & NEGRO SOLDIERS

———

JOIN THE AUTO CLUB PLACARD BRIGADE

A picture of this inflammatory display was reproduced on the entire front page of Harlem's *People's Voice*, with a story applauding the doctor's daring and denouncing his arrest by the police. Such attitudes are by no means sectional. During a quarrel with her white employer in Raleigh, North Carolina, an unnamed Negro woman retorted, 'I hope Hitler does come, because if he does he will get you first!' She was sent to prison for three years. Charles Steptoe, a Negro, twenty-four years of age, was sentenced to ten days in the workhouse because he refused to stand while 'The Star-Spangled Banner' was played in a Harlem theater. When, in another instance, a young Georgia-born Negro, Samuel Bayfield, came before the federal court for sentencing on an admitted attempt to evade the draft, he was asked where he was born. Bayfield told the court, 'I was born in this country against my will!' A Philadelphia Negro truck driver, Harry Carpenter, was held on charges of treason. He was accused of having told a Negro soldier: 'You're a crazy nigger wearing that uniform—you're only out fighting for white trash. This is a white man's government and war and it's no damned good.'

A story is going the rounds in Washington's Negro circles of an old Negro woman who boarded a streetcar and sat in the only available seat—one next to a white sailor. He instantly jumped to his feet and angrily stalked off. The Negro woman calmly spread into the vacancy, and, in mock humility, said, 'Thanks, son, for the whole seat.' Then she slowly appraised the white-clad figure. 'Nice suit you're wearing that Joe Louis bought!'

Sterling Brown, a Negro poet and gifted reporter of Southern life, heard a Negro bragging at a gas station: 'I done regist. Expect to be called soon. That Hitler. Think he can whup anybody. I'm gonna capture Hitler. I'm gonna deliver him to President Roosevelt. At the front door of the White

House.' The white bystanders applauded—but froze when he added, 'Then I'm gonna fight for some rights over here.'

A reporter for Harlem's *Amsterdam-Star News* interviewed James Miller, a Negro aged sixty-two, who had served thirty years in the Navy, concerning Negroes enlisting in the Navy—'a branch of our military service where they are apparently not wanted,' so one question ran. 'Unless they get the same opportunity as white men,' he said, 'I don't think it fair to mislead them.' A veteran of both the Spanish-American War and the first World War, he was bitter because he recalled how two of his uncles had served the Navy with distinction. It was not until 1922, he recalled, that the Navy set up a Jim Crow policy restricting Negroes to certain branches of the service. The Negro seaman added: 'We're the most loyal race in the world. We're supposed to be citizens of this country and our integrity as soldiers remains unquestioned, but they still don't want us.'

A fairly typical attitude is that of the Negro soldier who said, 'Sometimes I feel very proud of being a member of this big, huge army, until I pick up a paper and see where a Negro soldier was lynched and it makes me feel like, "What am I doin' here!"' Other soldiers are disappointed with their own treatment by the Army. One stationed at a camp deep in the South complained in a letter to a Harlem friend that the post restaurant—where he was stationed—was divided with one side marked 'Colored' and the other 'White.' According to his report, two Negro soldiers went into the 'Colored' section and, finding it crowded, went across into the 'White' one. A white officer was called and ordered them to leave, and when they refused, he had them arrested. 'This,' the letter concluded, 'is just one of the milder insults that we go through down here. It will not be long before the [Negro] boys here will resent these un-American practices. . . .'

This sort of attitude is heard in other quarters. A group of rural Negroes living outside Richmond, Virginia, were having a heated argument over what difference there was between the *old* and *new* Negro. 'Well, as I sees it,' drawled an octogenarian finally, 'when the old Negro was insulted he shed a tear; today, when these young ones is insulted they sheds blood.'

This extravagant talk is perhaps wishful thinking on the

old man's part. What is a fact, though, is that events since Pearl Harbor have stirred a sorely driven people. While Nazi spies and saboteurs went to trial one after another in an atmosphere of judicial fairness and public calm—six Negroes were lynched! One of these, Cleo Wright, was burned, his body mutilated and tied to an automobile, and dragged through the streets of Sikeston, Missouri. Right on the heels of this, a Negro sharecropper, Odell Waller, was executed in Pittsylvania County, Virginia, for the killing of his white landlord, though the liberal opinion of the country, acknowledging extenuating circumstances, clamored for clemency. Yet a week or so later a white man, Eugene Ekland, who vowed to exterminate the Negro race and in the process murdered five Negroes in the nation's capital, was sentenced only to fifteen years in prison! A sort of melancholy footnote was the discovery of two fourteen-year-old Negro boys hanging from a bridge in the town of Meridian, Mississippi. They had been taken from a jail, where they had been confined for reportedly confessing to an attempted rape.

When Southern gentlemen take the law in their own hands, Negro women too are victims. An Army nurse, Lieutenant Nora Green, stationed at the Tuskegee Army Air Corps School, received orders to prepare for overseas service. Before sailing, she went on a shopping tour in Montgomery, Alabama. On her return trip to Tuskegee she boarded a bus, and the white driver pummeled her into unconsciousness following a dispute over the denial of a seat she had reserved in advance. Afterward a Negro editor was heard to say, 'Something like that makes you wonder if Montgomery isn't still the capital of the Confederacy.'

Even before the United States entered the war, disturbing reports were tumbling out of the Army camps. There were race riots at Fort Oswego. Fighting between races at Camp Davis. Discrimination against Negroes at Fort Devens. Jim Crow conditions were prevalent at Camps Blanding and Lee. Stabbings occurred at Fort Huachuca, killings at Fort Bragg, and the edict 'not to shake a nigger's hand' at Camp Upton. Nearly every day reports were heard of Negroes going A.W.O.L. So moved was Harlem's *Amsterdam-Star News* that it described the situation with this headline:

TERROR REIGN SWEEPS
NATION'S ARMY CAMPS
NEGROES GO A.W.O.L.

One morning in the summer of 1941, the New York *Times*
calmly reported that following friction with the white population near Little Rock, Arkansas, forty-three Negroes of the
Ninety-Fourth Engineers (labor) battalion, stationed at Camp
Custer, had departed from the maneuver area. Actually, they
had run off to seek safety from violence of the white citizens
and state police. 'As we were walking along the highway,' one
of the soldiers said afterward, 'we saw a gang of white men
with guns and sticks, and white state troopers were with
them. They told us to get the hell off the road and walk in the
mud at the side of the highway. One of our white lieutenants
walked up to a state trooper and said something. I don't
know what. Anyway, the trooper told him to get them blacks
off the highway "before I leave 'em laying there." Then out
of a clear blue sky the state trooper slapped the white lieutenant. . . . Some of our men began to talk about returning to
Camp Custer for protection. That night they left by bus,
train, and walking. Three of us hopped freight trains after
walking forty-two miles to avoid white people, who we felt
would attack us because of our uniforms.'

A Negro who has lived in the freer atmosphere of the
North and has become aware of his rights will not relinquish
them or put up with abuse because he happens to be in the
South. That he wears the uniform of the United States Army
increases his self-respect. To some Southerners such a man is a
dangerous 'nigger' who must be made to 'know his place' —
with violence and terror, if necessary. The prejudiced Southerner refuses to accord even the ordinary decencies to the
Negro and is not impressed by the statements of the federal
government about this being a war for democracy. In his
view, democracy is not a way of life for all, but a luxury for
better-class white people only.

'Make way for that *white* Lord God Jehovah!'

Senator John D. Bankhead of Alabama expressed the
Southern viewpoint in a letter to General George C. Marshall,
Army Chief of Staff. He suggested that Northern Negroes be

quartered in Northern states only. 'Our people feel,' he said, 'that the government is doing a disservice to the war effort by locating Negro troops in the South in immediate contact with white troops at a time when race feeling among the Negroes has been aroused and when all the energies of both the whites and blacks should be devoted to the war effort.' If Negro soldiers must be trained in the South, he said finally, 'as a result of social and political pressure, can't you place Southern Negro soldiers there and place the Northern Negro soldiers in the North, where their presence is not likely to lead to race wars?'

The South proposes to be unbending in extending even the simple dignities to an Army uniform—if a Negro wears one. Negroes are equally insistent that, if they must die as equals, then they must be treated as equals. These sharply differing views met head-on in a flare-up at Fort Bragg, North Carolina, the result of an affray in which a Negro soldier and a white military policeman were killed. In this instance, however, the killing of the white man was the act of a Southern Negro whose resentments against injustice mounted to a desperate thrust for human dignity. The soldier, Ned Turman, had voiced objections to an attack on a fellow Negro soldier and, for his pains, was clubbed over the head by two white M.P.'s. In wrestling to protect himself, the Negro managed to snatch the gun of one of his assailants. Brandishing it, he stepped back and cried, 'I'm gonna break up you M.P.'s beating us colored soldiers!' And with that he fired the fatal shot. The other white M.P., standing near-by, shot the Negro to death. After the shooting, whole companies at Fort Bragg not involved in the affair—their Negro officers included—were forced to stand all night with their hands above their heads while armed military policemen patrolled the camp.

This affair occurred before the war. Today, with national unity desperately needed, racial tensions have increased rather than abated. The N.A.A.C.P. urged the War Department to include in its military instructions courses on the racial implications in the war, believing that such instructions were greatly needed to counteract racial bigotry. The suggestion was courteously but firmly turned down. Meanwhile, friction between white and Negro troops reached a critical stage at

Fort Dix, in New Jersey, which certainly suggests that the
problem is not sectional. Three soldiers were killed and five
wounded in a fifteen-minute gun battle. According to the official Army version, the trouble started when a soldier stepped
out of a telephone booth in the Waldron Sports Palace, an
amusement center across a highway from a Negro barracks,
and two other soldiers in the waiting line outside the booth
made a simultaneous rush for it. A scuffle ensued, the military
police were called, and they attempted to separate the participants. A Negro lunged for the M.P.'s pistol, but only ripped
the holster and then ran out of the tavern.

The M.P. ran after him, commanding him to halt, and
fired a warning shot into the air. This was the signal for a
fusillade of rifle shots from the Negro barracks across the
road. One of the M.P.'s fell mortally wounded at almost the
first volley. White and Negro soldiers began pouring out of
the tavern and the barracks. The military police were called
out, and a battle began from opposite sides of the highway.
The M.P.'s were armed with pistols and the colored soldiers
with rifles. At the height of the battle, two white officers
came running up the highway, yelling the order to cease firing, and both sides obeyed. By then about fifty shots had
been fired. Fifteen Negroes were involved and fifty white
military policemen.

There was more to this affair than met the eye. Under-
scored by smoldering resentments, the gunplay had climaxed
a series of Negro-white clashes, caused mainly by an influx of
a detachment of Southern M.P.'s. Until that time relations
between Negro and white troops were on the whole good,
and were steadily getting better. A Negro officer told a *PM*
reporter that soon after the arrival of the M.P.'s, 'they immediately started kicking the Negro troops around. They'd flare
up at the drop of a hat. Things were especially bad on buses
to and from camp. If the bus was filled and Negro soldiers
had seats, those Southern M.P.'s would order them to stand
up and surrender their places to whites.' Fights became frequent. Race friction increased. Morale declined noticeably.
The Negro regiment, it should be mentioned, was the same
unit whose commanding officer, Colonel Riley E. McGarragh,

posted a particularly offensive notice at temporary regimental headquarters at Marcus Hook, Pennsylvania:

Any cases between white and colored males and females, whether voluntary or not, is considered rape and during time of war the penalty is death.

This order was later rescinded following protests from Negro organizations. 'I've been at Fort Bragg, where things were bad enough,' said the Negro officer. 'But this is worse. Hell may break loose unless something's done quick.' He felt the situation could be improved by removing the Southern M.P.'s because 'the colored man gets on well with Northern soldiers, and even with many Southerners who've learned that we've got to fight against a common enemy, not against each other.' Evidently the authorities paid him no mind. A few months later, Fort Dix was the scene of another fatal brawl in which a Negro soldier was killed.

'It is all right to be loyal if it is encouraged,' ran a letter to the editor of Harlem's *Amsterdam-Star News*. 'But I fail to see where America is doing anything to encourage the loyalty of black men. . . . Remember, that which you [Negroes] fail to get now you won't get after the war.' That comment appeared one week after Pearl Harbor. The issue of the paper that published this comment contained twenty articles by staff writers which dealt critically with the treatment of Negroes. Two weeks later, sixty prominent Negroes met in New York City in a conference called by the N.A.A.C.P. and the National Urban League to consider the Negro's part in the war effort. The group passed with only five dissenting votes a resolution introduced by Judge William H. Hastie, then civilian aide to the Secretary of War, that 'the colored people are not wholeheartedly and unreservedly all out in support of the present war effort.' Walter White, executive secretary of the N.A.A.C.P., attributed this country-wide apathy of Negroes to discrimination in the Army, Navy, and Air Corps, and especially in the war industries.

This situation has its roots in the very immediate past. In the first World War Negroes at once sought to participate as soldiers. With full consciousness of their duties as citizens and with the desire to act the rôles of men, they gladly bore their share of the war effort. W. E. B. Du Bois, then the acknowledged leader of the Negro community, articulated the race's view toward the conflict in his now famous 'Close Ranks' statement to the nation as well as to certain skeptical Negroes:

> We of the colored race have no ordinary interest in the outcome. That which the German power represents spells death to the aspirations of Negroes and all dark races for equality, freedom, and democracy. Let us not hesitate. Let us, while this war lasts, forget our special grievances and close ranks shoulder to shoulder with our own white fellow-citizens and the allied nations who are fighting for democracy. We make no ordinary sacrifice, but we make it gladly and willingly with our eyes lifted to the hills.

This stirred Negroes in 1918. The conditions facing Negroes did not cause any lag when the call for volunteers was heard. Also, more than two million Negroes were registered under the Selective Service Law, and more than three hundred thousand were called. To the number drafted throughout the country were added 37,723, representing the Negro regulars and National Guard members. About two hundred thousand saw service in France, fifty thousand in actual combat. The fighting units constituted the 92d and 93d Divisions. To the 92d was attached the 367th United States Infantry, popularly known as the 'Buffaloes,' while the 15th Regiment (the New York National Guard) was part of the 93d. Two Negroes, Henry Johnson and Needham Roberts, were the first American privates to receive the *Croix de Guerre*, the French award for bravery.

Not until the war was over did the full measure of ill-treatment meted out to the Negro troops come to light and then only after Du Bois had visited Europe in 1919 to attend the Pan-African Congress. Documentary evidence of the discriminatory conditions faced by Negro troops was published by *The Crisis* magazine. One section alone will illustrate the attitude of the American high command, a memorandum called 'Secret Information Concerning Black American Troops.' It began with this statement:

> It is important for French officers who have been called upon to

exercise command over black American troops, or to live in close contact with them, to have an exact idea of the position occupied by Negroes in the United States. The information set forth in the following communication ought to be given to these officers and it is to their interest to have these matters known and widely disseminated. It will devolve likewise on the French Military Authorities, through the medium of Civil Authorities, to give information on this subject to the French population residing in the cantonments occupied by American colored troops.

Here are a few typical passages:

We must prevent the rise of any pronounced degree of intimacy between French officers and black officers. We may be courteous and amiable with these last, but we cannot deal with them on the same plane as with the white American officers without deeply wounding the latter. We must not eat with them, must not shake hands or seek to talk or meet with them outside of the requirements of military service. . . .

Make a point of keeping the native cantonment population from 'spoiling' the Negroes. [White] Americans become greatly incensed at any public expression of intimacy between white women and black men. . . .

The increasing number of Negroes in the United States (about 15,000,000) would create for the white race in the Republic a menace of degeneracy were it not that an impassable gulf has been made between them . . .

This indulgence and this familiarity are matters of grievous concern to the Americans. They consider them an affront to their national policy. They are afraid that contact with the French will inspire in black Americans aspirations which to them [the whites] appear intolerable. . . .

It developed that the Negro soldiers had themselves found a way of showing resentment. In a field near Metz on Thanksgiving evening in 1918, the regiment whose bravery in combat in the great offensive at Champagne had only a month before earned it the *Croix de Guerre* (their casualties were eleven hundred) was ordered to sing 'My Country, 'Tis of Thee.' The music boomed and the soldiers, the black warriors from America, some three thousand of them, stood silent with grim and sober faces. From all that great assemblage rose only the voices of the regiment's six white officers!

While these were the conditions abroad, the Negro civil population was the victim of some of the bloodiest race riots in American history. Even regiments in training in the United States were forced to undergo indignities and violence. One regiment was sent to Spartanburg, South Carolina, and at once the men were beset by Jim Crowism. The white population was no less considerate. The proprietor of a local hotel ordered a Negro officer named Noble Sissle, today a well-known band leader, to remove his hat when he entered the lobby—contrary to Army regulations—and kicked him into the street when he refused. A riot was averted only by the restraining influence of Lieutenant 'Jim' Europe, the regiment's popular band leader. On another occasion fifty Negroes marched on the city to 'avenge' two missing buddies and only the efforts of a sympathetic white colonel prevented bloodshed.

At the close of the war, administration leaders began a campaign to convince Negroes that no great change in their traditional position in America could be expected. With such a government policy, Negroes became the victims of new outrages throughout the country. Even the Ku Klux Klan was revived. In view of these events, Du Bois was forced to confess that he was less sure today than then of the soundness of his war attitude. 'I did not realize the full horror of war and its wide impotence as a method of social reform,' he wrote sadly. 'I doubt if the triumph of Germany in 1918 could have had worse results than the triumph of the Allies. Possibly passive resistance by my twelve millions to war activity might have saved the world for black and white. . . .'

Today, the prejudice shown by Army officials seems very little different from that of yesterday. Reports have trickled back from England—to illustrate—that the American high command is attempting to impose various forms of segregation and discrimination on the Negro troops. The British liberal *New Statesman and Nation* reports examples of discrimination and even assault against Negro soldiers. A British soldier wrote to complain that in a certain English port, Negroes were barred from a well-known restaurant. He said English soldiers were instructed not to eat and drink with Negroes, and restaurant employees were told to bar them. 'I have met [white] Southerners,' an English writer said, 'who seemed rational enough until the Negro problem was mentioned, and who would then show a terrified, lynching spirit, which was about the ugliest thing imaginable.' He also noticed that they 'took it for granted that it is their duty to interfere if they see black troops with white girls.' A most recent episode involves a Southern white soldier who was invited to an English home, and created a scene when he discovered that a fellow guest was an American Negro soldier. He attacked the Negro in the presence of the guests, ruining the evening for everybody.

The *New Statesman and Nation* made this significant comment:

What is to be done? The American government must face the problem itself. It must use every device of persuasion and authority to let white Southern troops know that it is against discipline to treat Negro soldiers in the way to which their training and education has accustomed them. . . . If things are left to drift, unhappy incidents will occur . . . and the British will instinctively take the side of the Negroes against their white assailants.

One interesting fact about these reports is that they were passed by the British censor, which may suggest the emergence of a new British policy on race. Even the conservative elements in the House of Lords have been stirred. The Lord Chancellor, Viscount Simon, is quoted as attacking a proposal to accept the American segregation pattern with the indignant retort: 'I do not suppose Lord Shaftesbury is proposing that any distinction should be drawn between white and colored soldiers. That is the last thing the British Parliament would tolerate for a moment.'

From all reports, Negro troops are very popular with the English people, who have arranged many entertainments for them—much to the disgust and indignation of some white Americans. This very spirit in certain unrelaxing whites is what caused a bloody race riot in the United States, when two thousand whites engaged in pitched battle with five hundred Negroes to prevent them from occupying the Sojourner Truth Homes, a Detroit housing project built with public funds for Negro war workers. Immediately, this occurrence was seized upon by Axis agents to stir up racial strife and disrupt war production. Mob rule gripped one of the country's principal arteries of war industry, and demonstrated the federal government's weakness on the race issue.

A firm stand by the government on racial questions, would be translated into acts by the humblest white citizen in America—not to mention the white troops abroad. More important, though, is the fact that native Fascists, prodded by Axis agents, defied the government in Detroit. This riot was perhaps one of the most successful acts of sabotage during this war. At secret meetings, Ku Kluxers received orders to keep the Negro workers from entering their new homes. The F.B.I. investigation revealed surprising scope to Ku Klux Klan activities in Detroit, even to boring from within labor's ranks, and to links with Axis agents. The National Workers' League, a pro-Nazi group whose officials were later indicted, cooperated with the Klan in preparing and staging the subsequent riot in which scores of people were injured.

Today, however, the importance of millions of Negroes is being increasingly recognized in administration circles—to wage total war, a total population must be set in motion. The President wrote the N.A.A.C.P. convention in the summer of 1942: 'I note with satisfaction that the theme of your significant gathering read, "Victory Is Vital to Minorities." This theme might well be reversed and given to the nation as a slogan. For today, as never before, "Minorities Are Vital to Victory."' The status of the Negro in 1942 is considerably different from that of 1917. For one thing, his opportunities are definitely broadening, but only under public pressure. For example, an aviation unit was established at Tuskegee, though there is provision to train only a dozen Negro pilots a year. With few exceptions, the officer personnel is Negro. The ranking administrative officer is Lieutenant Colonel Benjamin O. Davis, Jr., a graduate of West Point in 1936, son of Brigadier General Benjamin O. Davis, first and only Negro general. This fact, incidentally, reminds me that in the last war, to prevent the promotion that was rightfully due him, the ranking Negro officer, Colonel Charles Young, was retired on the pretext that he suffered from high blood pressure. To prove that he could withstand the rigors of a military campaign, he rode horseback from Chillicothe, Ohio, to Washington, D.C.!

Decidedly on the credit side of the ledger has been the partial removal of a long-standing discrimination in the Navy. It recently agreed to enlist Negro 'reservists,' a step forward, since it hitherto admitted Negroes only in the most menial capacities. Unfortunately, this development was marred by official Jim Crow, Negroes having been placed in distinct units separate from the whites. At the outbreak of the war abroad, there were about fourteen thousand Negro soldiers in the Regular Army, whereas only about four thousand of some hundred and forty thousand enlisted men in the Navy were Negroes. The draft brought many hundreds of thousands into the Army. The War Department has announced that at full strength there will be three hundred and seventy-five thousand Negro soldiers in the Army. However, the Army's more liberal policy toward Negroes has not been duplicated by the Navy— This is, however, somewhat like a choice between the frying pan and the fire. The Army is training several thousand Negro officers, but the Navy has made no provision for training officer material. A high degree of morale has been attained at the Army's Officer-Candidate Infantry School at Fort Benning. Here—on Talmadge's Georgia soil—white and Negro candidates attend the same classes, eat in the same mess hall, sleep in the same barracks, and generally fraternize together. There have been no racial incidents. Encouraging too was the launching of the merchant ship *Booker T. Washington*, with a mixed crew of Chinese, Filipinos, Negroes, and whites, and with a Negro captain, Hugh Mulzac, in full charge of operations. Incidentally, a former British seaman, he sailed his first ship in the United States under the colors of Marcus Garvey's Black Star Line.

These things represent progress. Witness the acts of Negroes. During a drive in Austin, Texas, three Negro brothers—Arthur, Felix, and Osle Jackson—each bought twenty thousand dollars' worth of war bonds. Eddie Anderson, the Negro comedian known as 'Rochester,' invested his earnings in a San Diego parachute factory—and significantly enough, employs Negro, Mexican, and white workers. Two song writers, Andy Razaf and Eubie Blake, turned out a patriotic song called 'We Are Americans Too,' which is currently popular in Negro communities. While pro-Axis agitators shout, the masses of Harlem seek to be included in the war program and confidently carry out the tasks assigned them. For instance, the Negro community has shown better discipline during the city-wide blackout tests than any other area, according to the city officials. Said Newbold Morris, President of the City Council, 'If you give Harlem a chance, the people will respond.'

Listen to the simple faith of a Negro youngster. Alice Godwin, a Harlem high-school student, wrote the following composition in her French class:

I am a member of a race without a chance to do what it wants to do and without liberty in the whole world. I have been told that this war is a war for liberty for everybody. That is the reason this war is important to me. . . . It is with great fear that I consider my future under the heel of Hitler. He has said, hasn't he, that I am only half of a human creature? . . . I shall be glad to wear old shoes not in style. These things are very little compared with the suffering in a world under Hitler. Each little sacrifice I make, I make joyously. It is for a new world, tomorrow, isn't it?

Hope among Negroes rides high. But a minority of vocal whites are determined that the Negro shall not advance. When white liberals and the federal administration appease such elements, the Negro's thinking is confused and his morale lowered. The almost insurmountable prejudice of employers and backward labor unions is no abstraction — but a solid fact the Negro faces day after day. He well knows there are white men in America who would rather lose the war — even their own freedom — than see any change in the racial *status quo*. This attitude has received provocative encouragement from Axis sources.

One of the curious paradoxes of this war, despite its notorious ballyhoo of racism is the fact that Nazi agents have attempted to capitalize on the dissatisfaction of Negroes as well as whites. Adolf Hitler himself seems to have set the pattern. Back in the spring of 1932, he entertained a Georgia-born Negro, Milton S. J. Wright, in a dinner party at the Europäisch Hof, a fashionable hotel in Heidelberg. The Nazi leader had invited Wright, then a student at Heidelberg University, to talk with him about life in the United States. 'As I recall,' says Wright, today a professor at Wilberforce University, 'he mentioned the names of Booker T. Washington, Paul Robeson, Jack Johnson, Florence Mills, W. C. Handy, Josephine Baker, and the Scottsboro boys.' He spoke loudly, long, and with air of authority on American affairs, but stung his Negro guest with this:

'Negroes must be definitely third-class people,' Hitler said slyly, 'to allow the whites to lynch them, beat them, segregate them, without rising against their oppressors!'

A report of this incident was printed in the Negro press. Obviously handicapped by loud pronouncements of 'Aryan' racial superiority, the Nazi agents—Negro and white—have made some amazing détours. Both in the French colonies and the United States, they have tried to rouse the black man against the Jew. Sometimes they have baldly tried to convince Negroes that the Nazis are not anti-Negro. Mercer Cook, a Negro professor at Atlanta University, tells the story of a German professor in a Negro college who invited Jesse Owens to his class to counteract what he called 'the charges of the Jew-financed American press.' He informed his students that the Nazis had treated the colored athletes with every consideration during the 1936 Olympic Games, and that Hitler had not refused to shake the hands of the 'black auxiliaries.'

The Berlin incident once came up in my conversations with Jesse Owens. When he arrived in New York from abroad, I was one of several hundred newspapermen—Nazi and Japanese correspondents included—who met the boat on his return. The American reporters showered him with questions as to how the Nazis had treated the Negro athletes. He was evasive—at least so I felt. After this mass interview, Owens and I, along with two other Negro Olympic competitors, rode up to Harlem in a taxi and I again put the question to him point-blank. He told me candidly—as one Negro to another—that the Nazis bent backward in making things comfortable for them, even to inviting them to the smartest hotels and restaurants. If the Nazis disapproved of the American Negro athletes' associations with the German girls, the athletes said, nothing in what they said or did suggested it. But we know now that that was a shrewd bit of propaganda by the

Nazi leaders, for the story was widely if naïvely told in Negro circles!

Negroes in America have even received reports that the Nazis have cleverly postponed the application of Hitler's anti-Negro dictums in France—perhaps because of the increasing importance of Africa in the war. Mercer Cook, a student of French life, received a report of a Negro soldier from Guadeloupe, demobilized in June, 1940, and about to return to his native land, who was convinced that he had nothing to fear from the Nazis and was persuaded to continue his work on the *agrégation* at the Sorbonne. Even Negroes married to 'Aryans' have been permitted to remain in business in the Paris area. The French Negro author, René Maran, whose *Batouala* won the Goncourt Prize in 1921 and was widely read by American Negroes, was forced to go into hiding in 1940. Yet, after a year of ominous silence, he was again published. Today he is believed to have returned to his apartment in the rue Bonaparte, and in the summer of 1942 received the Grand Prix Broquette-Gonin, awarded by the French Academy. Perhaps to offset the acts of the Negro Governor Félix Eboué, who brought French Equatorial Africa to the side of democracy and gave the Free French movement a territorial base, Hitler allowed Marshal Pétain to name a Martinique Negro, Senator Henry Lémery, as Minister of Colonies! Actually, though an admitted descendant of slaves, he espoused the Rightist cause and openly admired Léon Daudet. Last reports have dispelled this short-lived illusion. In a reshuffle of the Pétain cabinet, Lémery disappeared on Hitler's order.

Negroes today boldly look beyond the horizon of the Negro community, even beyond the borders of the United States, and are concerned with the condition and future of colored peoples elsewhere in the world. Harlem's *People's Voice*, in a long editorial, observed that 'The United Nations must immediately rethink the entire Colonial Problem,' and concluded with the remark, 'The Axis can only be beaten by a free world.' The recent outbreak of rioting at Nassau in the Bahamas, which assumed the proportions of a labor revolt, was not lost on American Negroes. Native despair and unrest in Jamaica, in the face of increasingly serious food shortages, which are being felt throughout the Caribbean, have brought Negroes to voice their indignation to the British and American governments.

Negroes sometimes suspect that there is a tacit understanding among English and American leaders to limit democracy to white men only. Observations of this character are suggested by the demand of the British government that the United States send no American Negroes to work on the West Indian bases; and, what is more important, the fact that the American administration quietly acquiesced. Nor are such feelings dispelled by revelations of wage differentials. Congressman Vito Marcantonio called attention to conditions existing at Borinquen Field, Puerto Rico, where skilled white workers received a dollar and fifty cents per hour and native skilled workers only forty cents per hour.

Negroes are keenly conscious of the ironic fate which has thrown Africa into the vortex of struggling empires. The war's objectives of freedom and democracy are ardently desired by American Negroes for the Africans, who are playing no small part in the contribution of men and resources for the defense of democracy. Du Bois, in a recent lecture at Yale University, expressed the general attitude of American Negroes. He stressed the fact that the white world had millions of dollars invested in Africa, which obviously makes that continent an important part of the world economy. Yet in current plans and discussions, nothing is said about its future. If white America is little concerned, certainly such groups as the African Students' Association in the United States are keeping the issue alive among American Negroes.

These issues are of undoubted propaganda value to the Axis. The unyielding attitude of Britain in India, with the American government's tacit support of this policy, has been the subject of much discussion in Negro circles. To Negroes, these issues are tied to the ultimate objectives of the war! Said the *Courier* editorially, 'The rule of India, like that of other colonies, is based on military force, and when that force remains in the hands of alien rulers there can be no real independence nor successful defense against foreign invaders, as recently demonstrated in Malaya, Burma, and Java.' Pearl

Buck, very much admired by Negroes, has expressed the view
that the progressive character of the war changed when Indian freedom was rejected.

What all this adds up to in the minds of Negroes is a pattern of continued white domination of colored peoples.
Therefore conflicts between the races are regarded as inevitable—that is, without cooperation and desire by whites to
see that freedom is the desire and right of all peoples. These,
and manufactured issues, are daily dinned into the ears of
black men by the Axis. From Berlin, of all places, a broadcast
was heard commenting upon the announcement of a new all-
Negro United States infantry division. Said the announcer:
'President Roosevelt stated recently that he was against race
discrimination. One might ask the President why he was seg-
regating Negroes in a special troop.'

'New World A-Coming,' 1943

"A Horror Beyond What Imagination Can Grasp"

by Edward R. Murrow

December 13, 1942

One of the nice things about talking from London on Sunday night is that one can sit down, review the events of the week, study the reports coming in from all over the world, and then talk about whatever seems interesting. Sometimes it's like putting letters in a hollow log or talking to yourself in a dark room. But tonight it's a little different. One is almost stunned into silence by some of the information reaching London. Some of it is months old, but it's eye-witness stuff supported by a wealth of detail and vouched for by responsible governments. What is happening is this: Millions of human beings, most of them Jews, are being gathered up with ruthless efficiency and murdered.

Some of you will remember the days when we used to bring you broadcasts from Vienna, from Warsaw and from all the other capitals of Europe. Now from that continent there is only silence, but still the information gets out. And when you piece it all together—from Holland and Norway, from Poland—you have a picture of mass murder and moral depravity unequaled in the history of the world. It is a horror beyond what imagination can grasp.

Let me tell you a little about what's happened in the Warsaw ghetto. It was never a pleasant place even in peacetime. The business started in the middle of July. Ten thousand people were rounded up and shipped off. After that, thousands more went each day. The infirm, the old and the crippled were killed in their homes. Some of them were driven to the Jewish cemetery, and they killed them there. The others were put in freight cars; the floors were covered with quicklime and chlorine. Those who survived the journey were dumped out at one of three camps, where they were killed. At a place called Treblinka a huge bulldozer is used to bury the bodies. Since the middle of July these deportations from the Warsaw ghetto have been going on. For the month of September 120,000 ration cards were printed for the ghetto; for October only 40,000. The Jews are being systematically exterminated throughout all Poland. Nobody knows how many have committed suicide; nor does anyone know how many have gone mad. Some of the victims ask their guards to shoot them, and sometimes the guards demand a special fee for doing so. All this information and much more is contained in an official report issued by the Polish government. And few people who have talked as I have with people who have escaped from Poland will doubt its accuracy. The phrase "concentration camps" is obsolete, as out of date as "economic sanctions" or "non-recognition." It is now possible to speak only of extermination camps.

Information coming out of Holland proves that each week four thousand Dutchmen are being sent to Poland, and that is no guess. It is based upon one of the best secret service organizations in Europe. Do you remember the "state of emergency" declared in the Trondheim area of Norway in October? Detailed and documented information about it has now reached the Norwegian government in London. At noon on October 6, the German dictator of Norway and his Gestapo chief drove through the town of Trondheim, together with police on motorcycles with mounted machine guns. At eight o'clock that night the local radio announced that ten hostages had been shot. The ten men heard of their own death over the radio, for they were not in fact shot until the following morning. At Falstad concentration camp, Russian prisoners of war were made to dig an open grave. No one knew who was to be killed. Then at eight o'clock in the morning a group of fifteen men were brought out and ordered to stand at attention. They stood there for eleven and a half hours until 7:30 in the evening. Then they were invited to listen to the announcement of their deaths. The following day they were taken to the edge of the big grave, stripped naked and shot.

It seems that the Germans hope to escape retribution by the sheer magnitude of their crimes. They are exterminating the Jews and the potential leaders of the subject people with ruthless efficiency. That is why newspapers, individuals and spokesmen of the Church in this country are demanding that the government make a solemn statement that retribution will be dealt out to those responsible for the cold-blooded massacre of Jews in Poland. The Archbishop of York insists that there shall be punishment, not only for those who gave the orders, but also for the underlings who seem to be gladly carrying them out.

CBS Radio Broadcast, December 13, 1942

TORPEDOED AND RESCUED AT SEA:
DECEMBER 22, 1942

Women in Lifeboats

by Margaret Bourke-White

THE TORPEDO did not make as loud a crash as I had expected, nor did the ship list as much as it does in the movies. But somehow everyone on the sleeping transport knew almost instantly that this was the end of her.

Tossed out of my upper bunk, I snapped on the light switch. The power had gone. I managed to find my flashlight and began a race into my clothes. I remember deciding whether I should take time to put on a belt and tie. I decided in favor of the belt and against the tie. Should I wear my greatcoat or trenchcoat? The trenchcoat was waterproof but the greatcoat was warmer. I decided on the greatcoat.

My two Scottish roommates were nursing sisters, so-called not from any religious convictions but because they belonged to Queen Alexandria's Military Nursing Reserve Service. Sister Ismay Cooper scrabbled through the bureau drawers for her money and Sister Violet MacMillan pulled on her trousers and tore the curlers out of her hair. Even in the faint flashlight beam I was impressed by the trousers. We had joked about them during the convoy voyage because the nursing sisters, operating under "Old Battle-axe," their strict Scottish matron, had been forbidden to wear slacks except for a torpedoing.

When it came to choosing which of my six cameras I should save I didn't hesitate a second, for I had worked that out carefully in advance. Instead of packing my musette bag with extra clothing as instructed, I had stored in it my Rolleiflex and an emergency film supply, together with one other camera, my favorite Linhof, and the five most valuable of its 22 lenses. I put on my greatcoat, crammed my field cap into my pocket, slipped my lifebelt over my shoulders, my helmet on my head, and started up the companionway.

Although it was less than three minutes before we were out of our cabin, everything seemed to be happening in slow motion. Up from the hold of the transport came two orderly lines of troops, one filing toward the starboard side, the other toward port. Instead of going to my boat station, No. 12 on B deck, I raced up to a spot under the bridge which I had also selected beforehand. In case of enemy action I had arranged with the commanding officer to stay on deck and take pictures. As I reached the top flight of steps I was hoping that dawn had come so I would be able to use a camera, but I came out under a night sky gleaming with moon and stars. "Just like Jerry to do this at night," I said to myself. One of the ship's crew came running over to send me down to my boat station. But when I explained "I am the LIFE photographer and I have permission to be here," he went on.

The ship's deck tilted like a silver tea tray to port side. The gun stations on their pedestals looked like giant mushrooms silhouetted against the sky.

As long as there had been a possibility of working, I had felt no great need for haste, but now that I had decided there was not enough light for pictures, my boat station suddenly became the most desirable place in the world. I was sure that lifeboat No. 12 must have pulled out by now, and it was with grateful surprise that I found my group of American nurses and British sisters just beginning to climb over the rail into the boat under the calm direction of "Old Battle-axe." I just had time to fall into my regular place in line, which I had occupied so many times during daily drill.

In the lifeboat I was astonished to find myself in water up to my hips. The torpedo splash had flooded the lifeboats on the port side aft. I hugged my cameras to my chest to keep them dry but as we made our quivering descent columns of water began pouring down on us from lifeboat No. 11, which was swinging over our heads. Its crew was pulling out plugs to empty the hull before lowering away. On our interminable descent I looked up to see the ship's hulk rising against cloud banks of pure silver. "If that were the sun instead of the moonlight on those clouds," I thought, "this would be a perfect K2 sky!" Just then the attention of all of us was caught by a heavy, dangling chain which swung cruelly back and forth while we ducked and twisted our heads out of the way.

We were in the water at last. The sea, which from above had looked so calm, rose up against us wave after wave and began beating us back against the side of the ship. Our crew strained at the oars. There was so little space left in our crowded boat that we started singing, bending our bodies in rhythm to give the rowers room to move their arms. Just as we had created a small margin between ourselves and the big ship, down came lifeboat No. 11 with its load of British sisters. Its crew had been unable to replace the plugs properly and it filled to the gunwales. A couple of dozen sisters were washed over the side. Some of them were carried immediately back into their flooded boat on the next wave. Others started swimming toward rafts which were tossed from the upper deck.

We tried to force our way toward the swimmers but our rudder broke and we found ourselves being drawn magnetically toward lifeboat No. 14. Getting clear of No. 14 was as long a job as I have ever known. Our ten oarsmen were Goanese from the Portuguese colony of Goa, India. They had made excellent dining-room stewards on the troopship, but this was a different kind of a job. We were not swaying our bodies now just to give them elbow room. All of us who were close enough to reach them were helping with the oars.

"Start bailing!" shouted our skipper, and those of us who were wearing helmets took them off and began to dip and pour. I emptied the batteries out of my synchronizing gun and took the cup-like case off my telephoto lens. They made two more small vessels for bailing.

The two nurses opposite me began trembling in a peculiar way. At first I thought it was fright. In less than five minutes 40 nurses in that boat were as seasick as only human beings in a tossing lifeboat can be. I admired the two American nurses opposite me who kept on bailing between spasms of sea-sickness.

Toward the stern of the big ship a lifeboat was still trying to free itself. Its crew pushed and struggled until one of the Tommies dived under the lifeboat to disengage its ropes from the propeller. The big ship settled down a little lower now, its great bulk listing more sharply to port. In the moonlight I could see that her side was a network of rope ladders, and clinging to the one nearest us was a cluster of nursing sisters. The nurse on the lowest rung was being dipped into and raised out of the sea time after time and the end of the ladder was whirling her about dizzily. A raft drifted close enough so that we could pull a girl into our boat. She had a broken leg and the sisters sitting behind me held her tight to keep her from bouncing back and forth with each swell.

We were bobbing farther away from the big ship but were still too close to lifeboat No. 14, which was also maneuvering a rescue from a raft. Just as a soldier let go of the raft to reach for a rope from the lifeboat, a wave flung the raft against him and cracked his skull. The skipper of No. 14 dived overboard, caught hold of the soldier and the two were dragged back into the lifeboat. Before the night was over the soldier had died. During all this we heard a voice from a distant raft shriek out, "I am all alone! I am all alone!" over and over. We tried to steer our rudderless craft toward the cry but it drifted farther and farther away until it was lost in distant silence. Now the swell was carrying us toward one of two destroyers which stayed behind as the convoy plowed on without us. "Keep away from us! We're dropping depth charges!" There was little we could do to guide our crippled boat but the deep roar of those depth charges was music to us.

Late the afternoon before we had scored a "probable" on a submarine. I knew that we had been pursued for three days, and the talk among the few passengers in the know had been that a pack of subs was after us. The chase followed the most savage and relentless storm that the troopship's captain had experienced in 45 years at sea. For five days we had battled our way through waves sometimes 60 ft. high. The furniture was roped back in the lounge after several passengers had been injured by flying sofas. One afternoon the piano broke loose and rushed back and forth like a great mad beast until it crashed against the wall with its legs broken.

That all seemed like ancient history now. Three whole hours ago we had left the big boat for the little one. Our steering problems were under better control. The Indian rowers in their white turbans had succumbed to dizziness and a few of us who seemed seasick-proof were dragging at the oars under the direction of the little quartermaster who was acting as our skipper. A splendid big Scottish girl, Elspeth Duncan, one of General Eisenhower's clerical staff, made the best rower of all. Rafts with soldiers clinging to them were still drifting by and we managed to intercept three, picking up a total of nine soldiers. Some joked as we dragged them over the gun-wales, but some had a glazed look in their eyes from shock and exposure which I have never seen before and hope never to see again. We peeled off our sweaters for them and our diminutive skipper wrapped them in yellow-hooded oil-skins. "You're all right now, mate," he would say as he tied the capes around each one. "You look just like the donkey in the Christmas play."

We had the boat pretty well bailed out by now. The nurses made the girl with the broken leg as comfortable as they could on the floor boards. I saw that she had no socks and, remembering that I had wrapped one of my lenses in a spare pair, I dug them out of my camera case. The nurses drew them on her feet as gently as they could.

Near us a lifeboat had roped together and was towing three heavily loaded rafts. The sisters in the boat were passing lighted cigarets back to the men on them. From the rafts came snatches of a song: "You are my sunshine, my only sunshine." Sunshine, I thought. That was all I needed to record this drama in pictures instead of words. I felt in my pocket for my notebook and discovered with joy that my fountain pen was still stuck in the cover, so I started jotting down notes in the moonlight.

People began joking now. The irrepressible Kay Summersby, Eisenhower's pretty Irish driver, announced her breakfast order. She wanted her eggs sunny-side up and no yolks broken. One soldier said he'd take his brandy with a dash of hot milk in it. Alfred Yorke, our little skipper, confided to me the story of his life—how he had been a baby photographer before he went to sea.

The moon was sinking, incredibly large and golden. As it lost itself in the sea, the night seemed to darken and the stars blazed brighter than ever. We had drifted away from our little community of boats but could still see dimly the shapes of the mother ship and a destroyer. From the destroyer we could just barely hear a voice through the megaphone say something about towing the ship away, then something we couldn't quite catch about "survivors." A new loneliness came upon us while we watched the fading outline of our mother ship.

"Survivors," I thought. This was the first time I had thought of myself as a survivor. I made a resolution not to allow myself to become impatient until the end of the sixth day. We had each been given a can labelled "emergency ration," about the size of a tin of sardines. It was stamped: "Purpose of contents: to be consumed only when no other rations of any kind are procurable." I resolved not to let myself think again about that can until the morning of the 14th day.

It was growing light now. "Let's tidy up the ship," Skipper Yorke said, and began throwing odd lengths of rope and bits of planks overboard. "Toss out those helmets to save weight," he ordered. But no one would part with a helmet because too many nurses were still getting seasick into them. Around the complete circumference of the horizon, bands of tumbled clouds were picking up the light of dawn—a photographer's dawn!

The skipper, an enthusiast about photography, as any baby photographer would be, helped hold me up on the gunwales of the bobbing lifeboat to get as favorable a viewpoint as possible for snapping my fellow passengers. One of the American nurses had unaccountably saved an orange which she passed out generously, section by section, as far as it would go. Then there was a hum in the sky and a British flying boat dipped over us while we waved back wildly.

After a few more hours we could make out the shape of our destroyer appearing over the horizon and by her interrupted course we guessed that she was picking up other survivors. She reached us after we had been eight hours in our lifeboats and as soon as we were dragged aboard her we were given cups of steaming Ovaltine. I climbed up to the gun station and photographed the last of our family of lifeboats as their occupants were helped to the deck. The man who had died from a cracked skull was handed up strapped to a pair of oars.

Another boat yielded a soldier who had died from shock and exposure. Several nurses were brought up, suffering from sprained ankles, twisted arms and broken legs, and one Scottish sister was moaning about her back, crushed when she had to jump from the ship's ladder into a lifeboat. But the soldier who took all our hearts was sitting alone in the middle of his raft and when we drew close he raised his thumb toward our destroyer and shouted, "Hi, taxi!"

When the last survivor had been transferred, the destroyer pulled away, leaving behind us the deserted lifeboats which swept down our wake like empty walnut shells. I came back to the teeming deck where friends were greeting each other with cries of joy. I was delighted to find my two roommates, Sister Violet with a few curlers still stuck in her hair. I was happy too to find our ship's charming young radio officer, Lord David Herbert III, son of the Earl of Pembrook. He was groping through his pockets for a little box which luckily he had not left behind. In it was a pair of red-enameled cuff-links set with gold crowns which had belonged to his great friend, the Duke of Kent, and had been given to him as a keepsake by the Princess Marina.

Then everyone began fishing in his pockets. The beauteous Kay still had two precious possessions, her lipstick and her French-English "soldier's speak-easy." Lieutenant Ethel Westermann of Englewood, N.J., on her way to be chief nurse of the General Dispensary Headquarters, still had her rosary, and blonde, petite Jeanne Dixon of Washington, D.C., secretary to General Eisenhower, had saved her prayer book.

I found I still had my Short-Snorter bill. Anyone who has flown across an ocean is entitled to carry a signed dollar bill indicating membership in the Short-Snorters. When a Short-Snorter can catch another member without his bill he is entitled to collect a dollar fine. In the six months since my initiation, my bill had been signed by Generals Spaatz, Clark and Doolittle, Prince Bernhard and Eddie Rickenbacker. I looked up to see Waac Ruth Briggs from Westerly, R.I., one of the first five Waacs sent on overseas service. I knew these five Waacs were members, having been sent over by Clipper. "Do you have your Short-Snorter bill?" I shouted. "Bet your sweet life," said Lieutenant (now Captain) Briggs. So on the deck of the destroyer we signed each other's bills.

Most of us carried the special currency issued on board the troopship by the British military authorities, to be used in North Africa where regular British and American currency is kept out of circulation so it can't find its way into enemy hands. We decided that a new organization, even more exclusive than the Short-Snorters, should be formed — the Torpedo Club. Membership bills would consist of 10-shilling notes of the military currency. Only people who had been torpedoed would be permitted to join. One of the Waacs started my bill by lettering on the top, "Property of Torpedo Peggy," meaning me, and we went around the destroyer exchanging signatures.

The nursing sisters were comparing experiences and white-haired Helen Freckleman from Edinburgh turned out to be the sister I had seen clinging to the bottom ladder-rung with the waves over her. "How long were you on that ladder?" I asked. "Half an hour," she replied. "I kept telling myself: 'I must concentrate on holding on with both hands. I must think about nothing else but holding on with both hands.'" I glanced down at those hands which had nursed the wounded of two wars. They were not young enough for such a stern assignment. But they had held.

I hunted up the girls who had managed to stay in flooded lifeboat No. 11. It had stopped sinking just as its gunwales were even with the water. Its buoyancy chambers had held it up, but until the girls were picked up seven hours later they had been in water up to their chests.

Two other boatloads of British nurses had been so far away from the destroyer and so tired from rowing that they dubbed themselves Oxford and Cambridge to keep up their spirits. Cambridge reached the destroyer half a length ahead of Oxford.

I climbed again to the gun station. Far over on the horizon our mother ship was still afloat. She was listing much lower to port now and destroyers were taking off all the troops that were left. The hundreds of survivors on our destroyer watched the mother ship disappear in the distance. She had meant something very special to all of us. She had stood by us through 60-ft. waves and 70-mile-an-hour gales. When wounded she had held up until the last living man was removed from her decks. Our destroyer picked up speed now and before the day was over we sighted the purple hills of Africa.

Life, February 22, 1943

The U.S. and Vichy in North Africa

---

by Ernie Pyle

"Our Policy Is Still Appeasement"

ORAN, Algeria—(By Wireless)—Men who bring our convoys from America, some of whom have just recently arrived, tell me the people at home don't have a correct impression of things over here.

Merchant Marine officers who have been here a couple of days are astonished by the difference between what they thought the situation was and what it actually is. They say people at home think the North African campaign is a walkaway and will be over quickly; that our losses have been practically nil; that the French here love us to death, and that all German influence has been cleaned out.

If you think that, it is because we newspapermen here have failed at getting the finer points over to you.

Because this campaign at first was as much diplomatic as military, the powers that be didn't permit our itchy typewriter fingers to delve into things internationally, which were ticklish enough without that. I believe misconceptions at home must have grown out of some missing part of the picture.

It would be very bad for another wave of extreme optimism to sweep over the United States. So maybe I can explain a little bit about why things over here, though all right for the long run, are not all strawberries and cream right now.

In Tunisia, for instance, we seem to be stalemated for the moment. The reasons are two. Our Army is a green army, and most of our Tunisian troops are in actual battle for the first time against seasoned troops and commanders. It will take us months of fighting to gain the experience our enemies start with.

In the second place, nobody knew exactly how much resistance the French would put up here, so we had to be set for

465

full resistance. That meant, when the French capitulated in three days, we had to move eastward at once, or leave the Germans unhampered to build a big force in Tunisia.

So we moved several hundred miles and, with the British, began fighting. But we simply didn't have enough stuff on hand to knock the Germans out instantly. Nobody is to blame for this. I think our Army is doing wonderfully—both in fighting with what we have and in getting more here—but we are fighting an army as tough in spirit as ours, vastly more experienced, and more easily supplied.

So you must expect to wait a while before Tunisia is cleared and Rommel jumps into the sea.

*   *   *

Our losses in men so far are not appalling, by any means, but we are losing men. The other day an American ship brought the first newspaper from home I had seen since the occupation, and it said only 12 men were lost in taking Oran.

The losses, in fact, were not great, but they were a good many twelves times 12.

Most of our convalescent wounded have been sent to England. Some newly arrived Americans feel that, if more of the wounded were sent home, it would put new grim vigor into the American people. We aren't the sort of people from whom wounded men have to be concealed.

*   *   *

The biggest puzzle to us who are on the scene is our policy of dealing with Axis agents and sympathizers in North Africa. We have taken into custody only the most out-and-out Axis agents, such as the German armistice missions and a few others. That done, we have turned the authority of arrest back to the French.

The procedure is that we investigate, and they arrest. As it winds up, we investigate period.

Our policy is still appeasement. It stems from what might be called the national hodgepodge of French emotions. Frenchmen today think and feel in lots of different directions. We moved softly at first, in order to capture as many French hearts as French square miles. Now that phase is over. We are here in full swing. We occupy countries and pretend not to.

We are tender in order to avoid offending our friends, the French, in line with the policy of interfering as little as possible with French municipal life.

We have left in office most of the small-fry officials put there by the Germans before we came. We are permitting fascist societies to continue to exist. Actual sniping has been stopped, but there is still sabotage.

The loyal French see this and wonder what manner of people we are. They are used to force, and expect us to use it against the common enemy, which includes the French Nazis. Our enemies see it, laugh, and call us soft.

Both sides are puzzled by a country at war which still lets enemies run loose to work against it.

*   *   *

There are an astonishing number of Axis sympathizers among the French in North Africa. Not a majority, of course, but more than you would imagine. This in itself is a great puzzle to me. I can't fathom the thought processes of a Frenchman who prefers German victory and perpetual domination rather than a temporary occupation resulting in eventual French freedom.

But there are such people, and they are hindering us, and we over here think you folks at home should know three things:

That the going will be tough and probably long before we have cleaned up Africa and are ready to move to bigger fronts. That the French are fundamentally behind us, but that a strange, illogical stratum is against us. And that our fundamental policy still is one of soft-gloving snakes in our midst.

Scripps-Howard wire copy, January 4, 1943

"I Gather New Respect for Americans"

WITH THE AMERICAN FORCES IN ALGERIA—(by wireless)—I have been delving further into this strange business of Axis sympathies among the people of French North Africa. It is very involved.

The population is all mixed up—Arabs, Jews, Spanish and French. And there doesn't seem to be much national loyalty. It looks as if the people, being without any deep love of the country, favor whichever side appears most likely to feather their nest.

Outside the big cities, Algeria hadn't fared badly under the Germans. The cities were actually starving, because the Germans bought produce direct from the farms, and the cities couldn't get it.

America has already contributed shiploads of food to the Algerian people, but for some reason little of it has showed up in the public markets. City housewives find the stalls bare as usual, and mutter about "les Americains."

The Germans paid high prices to the farmers for their crops, and paid in French money. They didn't levy the terrific indemnities here that they did in France. Hence the farm population actually prospered, and had almost nothing to kick about.

Now this year Algeria has the biggest orange crop since the war started. In distant sections oranges are actually rotting on the trees for lack of transportation. The farmers blame the Americans for this, and I suppose with some justice. True, we have already arranged to ship vast cargoes of oranges to England in returning convoys, but we can't spare enough transportation to get the whole crop to the docks.

As far as I can see, the only way to get the Arab, French and Spanish farmers on our side would be to buy the whole orange crop, even at the high prices the Germans paid.

*   *   *

When the Germans took control they demobilized the French North African army. That suited the people fine. They didn't want to fight anyway. But now the army is being mobilized again, and people are saying:

"Under the Germans we didn't have to fight. Under the Americans our leaders make us go into the army again."

They are passive about it, but many of them are not happy.

There was a deep Fascist tinge among some of the officers of the regular army. I've tried to find out the reason. And as far as I can learn, it was mostly a seeking for an ordered world to live in.

The people and the army alike were disillusioned and shattered by the foul mess into which Paris had fallen—the mess that resulted in catastrophe to France. They were, and are, bitter against the politicians and the general slovenliness in high places. They want no more of it.

They want things to run smoothly. They want security—and they visualize it as guaranteed by the methodical rule of the Axis.

*   *   *

The German propaganda here has been expert. The people have been convinced that Germany will win. Lacking any great nationalistic feeling, the people jump onto whatever seems to be the leading bandwagon, and they think it's Germany.

Propaganda also has made them think America is very weak. Literally, they believe we don't have enough steel to run our factories nor enough oil for our motors.

German propaganda has drilled into them the glories of the New Order. These people believe that life for them under German control would be milk and honey, perpetual security and prosperity. They really believe it.

*   *   *

Also, our troops have made a poor impression, in contrast to the few Germans they've seen.

We admittedly are not rigid-minded people. Our Army doesn't have the strict and snappy discipline of the Germans. Our boys sing in the streets, unbutton their shirt collars, laugh and shout, and forget to salute. A lot of Algerians misinterpret this as inefficiency. They think such a carefree army can't possibly whip the grim Germans.

Most of the minor peoples of the world expect discipline. They admire strict rulers because to them strictness is synonymous with strength. They can't conceive of the fact that our strength lies in our freedom.

Out of it all I gather a new respect for Americans, sloppy though we may be. They may call us Uncle Shylock, but I know of no country on earth that actually is less grabby. In all my traveling both before and during the war I have been revolted by the nasty, shrivelled, greediness of soul that inhabits so much of the world. The more I see of the Americans and the British, the more I like us. And although Germany is our bitter enemy, at least the Germans have the character to be wholly loyal to their own country.

Once more I want to say that this stratum about which I

am writing is not a majority of the people of North Africa. Much of the population is just as fervent for Allied victory as we are. But there is this Axis tinge, and I wanted to try to explain why it existed. Personally, I don't feel that it can do us any grave harm.

Scripps-Howard wire copy, January 5, 1943

The Girls of Elkton, Maryland

by Mary Heaton Vorse

IT WAS pay day at the munitions plant. There seemed to be a run on the bank at Elkton. The queue extended a half block down the street. There were girls in slacks and coats, bright kerchiefs on their heads, girls in navy reefers, even a few girls in fur coats. They came out of the bank smiling. They felt rich. "I've got as much money as Carter's got Little Liver Pills," said one girl. A pay check of around sixty dollars every two weeks looks good. More girls were packing into the Greyhound bus to spend their money in Wilmington. "Looks like the Black Hole of Calcutta," a woman commented. "It's worse'n the subway rush."

The Elkton post office was almost as crowded as the bus, and a queue like a serpent wound around the lobby of the new gray-stone building. The girls were sending off packages. The little town was crammed to bursting with girls. Houses were full, restaurants were full, stores were full of war workers. The population of 3,800 has doubled. The conversion of a local factory to a munitions plant was followed by further expansions and additions until the plant now employs many thousands. Another munitions company nearby added nearly 2,000 more; 80 per cent of both are women. Girls between eighteen and twenty-five are what both companies prefer.

These girls are part of the vast migration that's going on all over the country. They are the pioneers in the mobilization of the great army of women workers. Many of them are on their first jobs.

Ask a group of girls why they came and you get answers like this: "I wanted to help." "My husband's in the Navy. I felt nearer to him, working like this." "My brother enlisted. I wanted to enlist too."

They have come for service but they have come for adventure also. Their one discipline is that of the munitions plant.

471

They are accountable to no one. They are the recruits of industry and like the boys in the armed forces they are eager for life, eager for fun. They want to dance. There is a massed vitality in these girls that is formidable, and their coming has changed the life, not only of Elkton, but of the whole county.

Before the war the most restful spot between Wilmington and Washington was lovely Cecil County, Maryland. Elkton is the county seat. Its citizens are conservative and have deep-seated convictions which came from the past. It is largely a dairy-farming community and its pleasant people were free from the problems of an industrial age. They were modestly prosperous, even during the depression.

Off the great highways flowing north and south, nothing disturbed the somnolence of Cecil County except the wedding shouts of Elkton's many marriages. Elkton is the great American Gretna Green. There are large blue signs with foot-high letters — MARRIAGES · MINISTER — on all the roads leading to town. The nuptial glee of its elopements (6,000 last year) resounds through the hotels until far into the night.

War shocked the contented community into a reluctant awakening. Not only Elkton, but the other nearby communities, had small munitions factories, each employing a few hundred workers. To the south there was a Naval Training Station, and ten thousand construction workers spilled over the countryside seeking rooms as they prepared the quarters for the naval trainees. The population of the county doubled even before the Naval Training Station added its thousands more.

The draft and the munitions plants between them took the workers from every other enterprise. People sold their dairy farms because there was no one left to milk the cows. By June, 1941, half the stores and all the restaurants displayed "Help Wanted" signs. Household help had practically vanished.

The local children felt the stir of change. Families were upset and family life disrupted because parents in war jobs worked on different schedules. Delicate as a seismograph, the Office of Child Welfare recorded the upset state of Cecil County. Little girls ran away in unprecedented numbers. Boys took to pilfering and "borrowing" cars. The load of juvenile delinquency bounced up. This occurred even in families where parents had not gone away. The less stable of the children felt the impact of war.

The very appearance of the Elkton streets changed. At night girl war workers who had no other place to go strolled up and down. Car prowlers from Wilmington swooped by, agog for a pickup. It go so that nice Elkton girls would not go uptown for a walk or to have a soda at Lyons' drug store. Sailors from the Naval Station jostled soldiers from Aberdeen, and it was necessary to clap on an eleven o'clock curfew. "Be whoopin' it up all night with the twelve o'clock shift, else," people said.

Married couples coming to work could not find a place to stay, and they doubled in with other people. Quickly there was overcrowding. Promising little slums sprang up here and there. Three families lived where one had been before. While there was neither the crowding nor the profiteering that there had been in some boom towns, there was not an empty room in Elkton.

One man even moved out of his home and rented the rooms to twenty-two girls at three dollars and fifty cents apiece. Four girls sleep in the living room, two in the kitchen. There is only one bathroom for the whole lot and the sun porch is the only place not occupied by beds. But there is never a vacancy in this crowded house. The girls say of the hostess: "She treats us like a mother. She comes to see us every day."

The presence of many Negro workers made another problem. Elkton has a Negro population of five hundred. Their houses are small, their families are large. There was no place to put the more than doubled colored population which flowed into town. Colored workers sat up all night in kitchens and sitting rooms, since their hosts had no beds for them; girls who came in jitneys and jalopies in the first rush sometimes worked by day and slept cramped in the cars.

Their pastor, The Reverend D. M. Collins, is the only one to look out for their interests, and he meets almost as many emergencies as there are days. Over Thanksgiving he housed fifteen stranded people—men, women, and children, migratory workers from Florida who had just finished digging potatoes in New Jersey. They had heard Elkton described in glowing terms by someone they believed was connected with the plant; so there they were.

The company does not assume any responsibility for the Negro girls that come looking for work, nor for finding them places to live, as it does for the white girls. The theory is that the Negroes employed shall all commute, and if they come to Elkton they come at their own risk. There is one small Negro restaurant, and unless the girls have kitchen privileges they eat bakery stuff and sardines in their rooms. In the plant they mostly work in separate departments from the white girls, though there are some white foremen who direct the Negroes. Of course numerous local people expected "trouble," but there hasn't been any. The only ripple has been caused by some Northern white girls who twit the Southern girls about their attitude toward the Negroes.

In the end one problem piled on another created a situation too difficult for a small community to meet. There wasn't enough of anything—rooms, food, or restaurants. There was no place for sick people and not a single place of amusement, except a couple of small movie houses, for the crowds of boys and girls adrift on the streets. Even the water system was overtaxed. Moreover the town sulked at what were euphemistically referred to as "certain elements" in the plant, and certain elements in the plant feuded with the town. In the newspaper office, courthouse, and stores people were saying, "They can't cram those girls down our throats." Elkton practiced an almost Gandhi-like non-co-operation with anything which altered its way of life.

Stores were slow to enlarge their stocks to cater to the girls' needs, though seven thousand girls wanting shoes and clothes streamed through the town daily with money to spend. Instead of new restaurants opening, the difficulties of getting equipment, help, and even food were so great that restaurants closed or opened under new management. Only one new shop opened. The Housing Director of the company, Mrs. Margaret Cronin, always looking as if she had stepped from the pages of *Vogue*, sponsored the Victory Shop, which had a full assortment of what the well-dressed war-worker should wear.

Shock followed shock for Elkton's inhabitants. On October 12, 1942, people noticed that the Navy, complete with soup kitchen, was encamped down by the primary school. At first they thought this was only a maneuver. Consternation spread through the town when it was found that the Navy was taking over the plant, and that the Vice President and Manager of the plant was in the hands of the F.B.I. under charges of bribery.

From then until the end of December, 1942, Commander A. B. McCrary was the head of the plant.

Shock No. 2 was the letter in the newspaper which the Commander addressed to the town, in which he raked Elkton over the coals. If he did not call them a generation of vipers, he implied that they hadn't done right by our Nell, and that they were holding out on rooms for the girls employed in the plant. He asked for a recount of Elkton's housing facilities.

A delegation of indignant citizens waited upon him. They pointed to the fact they had a Housing Committee and a Nutrition Committee, and that dances for the girls had been given in the Armory, and that everyone had rented rooms to the girls. A recanvass of the town revealed less than a dozen empty rooms. Elkton was chock-a-block, and the people felt vindicated.

The Commander wrote another letter to the paper, to the people of Elkton, explaining that he had received his information from sources animated with too great zeal for the girls' welfare. The explosion cleared the air. Then the U.S.O. moved into Elkton. The organization proved to be the catalyst that precipitated the latent good will of the town.

What had ailed Elkton has ailed almost every new munitions town. There have been few such towns where the obvious needs—food, shelter, doctors, and recreation—have been handled efficiently. The old residents always feel put upon by the new arrivals. Food for workers is treated as an afterthought and recreation as a luxury, instead of being provided as a matter of course just as motor fuel and oil are provided for the machines.

For a lack of these things the plant was plagued with a fairly high turnover, absenteeism, and rejects, while Elkton was the target of so much criticism from various sources for conditions which it did not make, and which it felt it could not control, that it became as sensitive as an old-fashioned Singer sewing machine.

II

During the last six months of 1942 Cecil County, though set in its ways, began to adjust itself. Surprising things were happening in Elkton. Before that families had been shivering in unheated houses on the edge of the Chesapeake. A few lived in trailers, while for months three hundred and fifty government houses waited for some essential furnace parts and about twenty-five feet of pipe to connect them up with the town water. In Newark, Delaware, six miles away, eighty more houses awaited completion.

Now Grafton Brown of the War Manpower Commission, friendly as a next-door neighbor, handsome as Paul McNutt, sat in the U.S. Employment Service office, in the cellar of the courthouse. Unlike many of the other government officials who had streamed through Elkton, he stayed a while, whereas others "made a sourpuss at us and went away."

With him appeared an expediter from the Federal Public Housing Administration, and it began to look as if the houses might some day be finished. Mr. Brown, the wonder man, took up his telephone and spoke into it. Furnace parts appeared; pipes appeared; plumbers and carpenters appeared. Meantime he stirred around and got acquainted, listened to people's difficulties, and poured oil on troubled waters. Seeing him work was like watching a prestidigitator.

Even the *Whig* published Mr. Brown's release, which announced that the houses were now ready for occupancy. Mrs. Cronin got ready to hang Christmas wreaths on the houses over in Newark, though skeptics were heard to remark, "If those houses are ready to live in, then I'm a desert camel."

Now there are several more dormitories almost finished, and they are going to open progressively. There are to be eleven dormitories for white occupants, complete with a community house which will have a grill, a sandwich bar, and an infirmary. Ground will soon be broken for the four much-needed Negro dormitories, which are also to have a community house. A seventy-five-room addition to the hospital has had its specifications signed, and Elkton is to have a new sewer system.

Until these dormitories are completed the girls must find lodging where they can. Mrs. Cronin's housing canvass included not only Elkton but other towns within a radius of thirty-five miles. Many girls can get a room and two meals for $9.00 a week. The Ross Transportation Co., which was organized to haul them to work, charges from $1.20 to $3.60 a week for transportation.

Those of the girls who board in private homes like the homes and the people with whom they live, though of course there are instances where the twain do not meet successfully.

The Sandy Cove summer hotel is an example and the Kitty Knight House is another. Sandy Cove was formerly a club for professional women who paid $50.00 a week for accommodations. The ladies who run the place have turned the club over to the girls—$9.00 a week for room and two meals—as a war contribution. In the summer there are swimming, tennis, and water sports; there are free indoor games and a fine dance floor. But some girls hate the place. They must walk four miles through woods to get to the State highway and they can't stand being so far away. No strolling up and down Main Street, no picking up drives from boys from Wilmington; callers sternly discouraged.

As for the Kitty Knight House, this famous Colonial mansion, with thirty-two rooms and two cottages, can house over a hundred girls. Mrs. Tomlinson, the owner, has opened her place to them as a contribution to the war, but some of her young charges upset and bewilder her. Even the excellent meals and the Simmons beds don't make up for the fact that it is miles from a movie. The girls don't care whether George Washington slept here or not. Accustomed to evaporated milk from a can, some don't appreciate the lumpy cream from Kitty Knight's pure-bred cows.

Meantime the atmosphere in the office of James Flannery, the head of the Federal Public Housing Administration, is electric. The telephone rings all day. A young man arrives and announces darkly, "Navy's got our dormitory sheets. They've sent blankets like horse blankets that'll take the hides off them gals instead of what we specified." It seems the Navy is always getting everything which by rights belongs to Federal Housing. No. 4 Dormitory 'phones to find out where the janitor is—the furnace is going out. A young lady of the office force comes in and says with the quiet triumphant voice of one announcing the crack of doom, "Eighteen NYA girls have come from South Carolina and want to know where they go from here."

III

Over in the new dormitories the new manager, Mrs. Edith Alexander, is also leaping from crisis to crisis. The dormitories are T-shaped, and the long tight corridors make one think of the corridors on a ship with staterooms on each side. Here the girls get a comfortable room and maid service for $3.50 a week. There are both double and single rooms, shower and baths and tubs and clean towels every day. The lounge is larger than in the old dormitories and there is a room with three ironing boards.

Although Mrs. Alexander is employed by the government as manager of the eleven new dormitories, the girls have adopted her as a new mother. Every problem a girl can have, complicated by sickness and homesickness, is brought to her door. They come to her for everything.

The new North Carolina girls are full of complaints. They had been told that they could get room and board at the dormitory for $12.00 a week, and one of them has quinsy sore throat. Edith, one of the colored maids, comes in to announce with gloomy self-importance, "Mis' Alexander, some of them new girls done stuff up th' toilet! Water's a runnin' all ovah the washrooms just lak th' flood." Dora is sick and wants her husband 'phoned for.

A group of girls chatter excitedly about the U.S.O., whose opening on Christmas changed the whole outlook for hundreds of the girls.

For the first time the girls have a place of their own besides a beer parlor or juke joint where they can dance, play games, write a letter, or receive friends. The clubhouse is theirs. It was made over from a fine old three-storey house and has assembly rooms, game rooms, a writing room, and spare bedrooms for stranded girls.

The girls and the town have been brought together through the U.S.O. There was plenty of good will in Elkton but no channel through which it could flow. Now a gradual welding is going on between the war production workers and townspeople.

The second night the clubhouse was open the U.S.O. were hosts to the town after the community carol singing. It was sleeting, so the singers had to crowd inside the doors of the courthouse. But it was very gay and Christmaslike with the girls handing out the carol sheets to the community members. Afterward the various church choirs and community chorus groups were invited to the new clubhouse for cocoa and cookies. The girls were the hostesses of the evening, they greeted the townspeople at the door, they acted as guides round the house. They showed everyone the way to the coatroom and helped with serving, so that from the very beginning there was the feeling that the house belonged to the girls.

There was a continuous series of parties through the Christmas season. Open house was held on Christmas Day and there was a buffet supper. So many came that the people ate in three shifts. Word went round like wildfire that there was a grand new U.S.O. It spread among the soldiers at Aberdeen and the sailors at the Naval Training Station. On New Year's Eve alone there were five hundred boys and girls in and out, dancing, playing games, or just sitting about chatting. After the soldiers and sailors left at midnight—the curfew had been extended an hour for them—another party was held for the girls who had been working from four to twelve. They came there from work and stayed until half-past three in the morning. Every week-end the place fairly swarmed with soldiers and sailors, and more and more of the men war production workers filtered in.

Mrs. Rhoda Sutton and Miss Archambault are the U.S.O. workers, and Mrs. Sutton is responsible for every detail of the clubhouse. It seems like a dream come true to them when they listen to the comments of the boys and girls.

"This is just like home! This is the friendliest place we've been in since we have been in the Army! We never dreamed there was a place like this in Elkton! We'd rather come here than anywhere! This is the swellest thing that could have happened!"

The boys and girls are allowed to cook. They are encouraged to keep the place clean. Committees of soldiers and sailors and girls are appointed every night to keep track of things. They come to Mrs. Sutton and Miss Archambault and beg to wear a U.S.O. armband, which is the badge of the House Committee. The boys keep one another in line and the same is true of the girls. Every night except Sunday there is continuous dancing until eleven o'clock. The U.S.O. clubhouse with its open fires and its ready welcome has given heart to the lonely boys and girls.

Changes for the better are going on also at the plant. When the rest house for newcomers is under operation, the big turnover which occurs the first two weeks will shrink.

Almost every day busses, each holding forty girls, drive up to the personnel office. They have been on the road anywhere from twelve to eighteen hours. The girls have been recruited from the mining regions of West Virginia, the anthracite coal regions of Pennsylvania, and some of the steel areas, though now North Carolina, Tennessee, and Kentucky are being tapped.

The girls are interrogated, photographed, fingerprinted, blood-typed, and undergo a physical examination. You may see them any day slumped on the wooden benches outside the room marked "Investigation," or leaning against the wall or waiting in the busses, their heads in their hands.

There are young little mammas' girls with their hair curling in page-boy bobs over their shoulders. Fluttery high-school girls on the great adventure of their first jobs. The handsome, well-dressed girl was a doctor's assistant until two days ago.

"Two days ago I didn't know anything about this. I saw the advertisement in the paper and now I don't know what it's all about," one girl told me.

"We don't any of us know what it's all about. We're dead

on our feet. We've been traveling all night. We got here at seven this morning—and it's now after three."

By the time the ordeal is over many girls have made up their minds they are not going to stay. When the white farmhouse is made over into a place where the girls can wash and lie down and have something to eat things will be better.

There is no one thing that has caused more complaint among the girls than food—they complain it is poor, dear, and far off. Although there is now a cafeteria with good food near the dormitories, the girls complain that the food is dear—and it is more expensive than the Savarin or Childs'. Many girls go through the day on a cup of coffee and a piece of toast, or munch doughnuts on the way to work. They have a sandwich and a cup of coffee for lunch and only one good meal a day. The girls get so fat eating starches that their clothes burst the seams and they ultimately lose their pep and bounce, and absenteeism grows.

It's so hard to find a place open on Sunday that asking girls to Sunday dinner is becoming an Elkton custom. Most eating places close at nine o'clock at night, so the girls coming off the twelve o'clock shift who want something to eat are out of luck. Few places in Elkton board girls and such places as afford kitchen privileges are at a premium. Neither the plant nor private enterprise nor the government has as yet made plans for industrial feeding.

IV

It is in the dormitories that one gets to know the girls. A feeling of adventure streams through them. Take the case of Ellen Dearson. One Sunday morning she was a solitary girl standing near the bus station. There was never anyone as lonely and forsaken-looking as she. Her skirt flapped about her ankles, her hair fell lank about her ears. Everything about her spoke of some remote Southern hill town.

She had started on her journey from West Virginia in a company bus full of newly recruited girls, and had got separated from them and had been sent on by the regular bus, but her suitcase hadn't come with her. She didn't know what company she was working for. She didn't remember the name of the man who had hired her and she hadn't a penny in her pocket. She had had nothing to eat since the day before, but would accept only a cup of coffee. "I don't feel hungry—you mustn't spend all this money on me," she protested. She was frightened but she was self-contained and kept her fierce reticence. She was going to let no "foreigner" see her disturbance, but you could feel her all aquiver like a taut violin string.

Two months later she had on a wine-colored corduroy skirt, a pretty shirtwaist, and some costume jewelry, little red flowers that went with her dress. Her dark hair was swept back from her eyes, which had been so guarded and lackluster before, but now shone with pride as though to say, "You wouldn't know me." There was a discreet touch of rouge on her thin face. I'd see her running in and out of the dormitory, always with a group of girls, her face alight. She was rich. She made more money than she had ever thought possible. The dormitory was luxury. The clothes were something she had not even dreamed of. Here all at once was companionship, adventure, a different status.

There are girls from all over and women of all ages, but they all share in the spirit of adventure. The woman in the corner room, for instance, is over sixty. She had left a well-paying job in which she had worked for years because she wanted to be part of the war effort. She wore jodhpurs the first few days. The inspectors are supposed to wear skirts and this earned her the nickname of "Hi-yo Silver."

Next door is a bride. She's the daughter of a steel worker from Johnstown. A very little girl with tiny hands as pretty as a picture, she makes more than anyone else in the dormitory. Her soldier husband is in Aberdeen. The two girls next door are sisters—college girls. Clausine is line leader and makes $74.00 every two weeks. Like many college girls, she came to work during her vacation, and felt that the work being done there was more important than school, and stayed on.

There were two little girls, shy as wood creatures, from a tiny mining town in West Virginia. They had been here less than two weeks, and it seemed wonderful to them that they could live on the pay of one girl and send the whole of the other's pay home. Their father's a crippled miner and there are younger brothers and sisters. There are many women working here whose husbands and whose fathers have been hurt in the mines.

Life in the dormitory has a definite beat and rhythm. By listening you can tell what time it is by the noises in the corridor. Long before light there's a stir and shuffling. Doors bang. The girls are getting ready for the eight o'clock morning shift. In midwinter these girls walk a mile in darkness, up a road swarming with cars and busses. From then on to about ten—until the night shift girls have gone to bed—there's a stir around the place. Then there's a quiet interval until noon, when the girls of the 4 P.M. shift begin to get up. From then on girls wash clothes, visit about, go out to meals. Almost all the girls wear neat zippered housecoats and their hair is done carefully. The movies and the women's magazines don't live in vain. A girl with hair on end, untidy slippers, and a sleazy negligée stands out like a blackbird in snow. There is always a girl ironing clothes. The coming and going never stops until late at night when the girls through working at midnight come in, one by one.

This is a new dormitory and has not yet begun to have a life of its own. It's very largely a West Virginia crowd and they have the reticent ways of a mountain people. At night the girls go out in ones and twos, some of them as beautiful as movie stars. You can hardly recognize them as the same girls who went plowing through the snow in the dark, looking like a flock of refugees in long coats and slacks and kerchiefs over their heads.

Over in the old dormitory there is the feeling of an established community. Around six the lobby fills up. The girls iron and press their clothes. One of the girls, who was formerly in a beauty shop, is doing some handsome hairdressing. The girls are waiting in their coats for their beaus to pick them up.

Outside is a line of cars which beep softly and urgently from time to time like sea monsters calling to their mates. Until recently a large sign reading "ABSOLUTELY NO MEN ALLOWED ON THESE PREMISES" barred the way to the dormitory grounds. This sign has been taken down. Men are allowed to come in only if they have a pass from the main office and then just to call for a girl. So they beep their horns or flash the headlights on and off.

At each new beep Jinny, a little girl with electric red hair and a face like a Toulouse-Lautrec drawing, goes to the door and shouts "What do you want?" The boy shouts back and Jinny rushes off to tell Celia or Mamie that her date has come. Jinny is eighteen, but her mother, who works here too, won't let her go out, and she is getting a vicarious excitement being master of ceremonies. One after another the girls file out, perhaps to go dancing in Wilmington or maybe to the movies or to sit in a beer parlor.

Uncle Sam gives orders that strict morality is to be observed on his premises. But what the girls do after they leave government-owned territory is none of anyone's business. The girls come and go at their will. There are no hours to be kept. The doors of the dormitories are always open, and they must be to the three shifts.

One single soldier has come to get his date. He is an older fellow and sits stolidly while the girls chat. One girl, as pretty as a Christmas card, makes discreet eyes at him, and the others kid him. There's a sense of excitement and of adventure, something just a little forbidden in the beeping cars, but there's good nature and chaff, and above all there's youth. As I go out a sailor looms up. He says "Scuse me, ma'am, is Myrt there?"

"What does she look like?" I ask.

"Did you ever see a dream walking?" he counters.

Romance is on the rampage in Elkton. The streets are full of soldiers and sailors and there are always cars waiting for a pickup. As the girls walk down to go to the cafeteria at night cars follow them and open their doors invitingly. The girls stick their heads in the air or advise the drivers to go about their business.

"They must think we're nitwits to get into a strange car," they comment.

The very danger in which the girls work intensifies the tempo of life. They feel the importance of their jobs. When the lounge, with its green leather chairs, is full of girls having their morning cigarettes the talk crackles with danger.

"Did you hear how Rose got burned?"

"Oh, she wasn't burnt bad. She went right off to First Aid and she was right back to work again."

"I thought I'd die when that new girl come in our department. 'I can't work on this machine,' she says, 'it makes my stomach hop up and down like they do.' You know our machines hop up and down awful fast. You have to look out."

It's amazing how the girls stand up to the danger of their occupation. "Those who can take it stay, and those who can't take it clear out, and the sooner the better for the rest of us. If the boys can take what they do I guess we can," the girls say. The danger of the work identifies them with the men of their family who are overseas.

They never talk about the war and seem to have no curiosity about it. They seldom listen to news broadcasts and rarely look at a newspaper. In this they follow a pattern that is common throughout the munitions towns of the country. Though there are more miners' daughters than anything else, if they have a yearning for a union they never mention it. Nor has any attempt been made to organize them.

The girls like their jobs and complaints about working conditions in the plant are rare. There are a few inevitable clashes of personality between girls and foremen but they're not conspicuous.

There is a feeling among them that is electric and vital. They have shown such a pioneering and adventurous spirit in coming at all that one feels they are waiting for something, perhaps for a way to be found to fill their minds and to bring them closer to the great currents of thought sweeping through the world. They are so near to the war, and are playing so important a part, and their clever fingers are so necessary—yet there is lacking here, as elsewhere, a final urgency which war demands. These girls are waiting for some voice to speak a message which will release all their energy for total war.

Harper's Magazine, March 1943

The Foamy Fields

by A. J. Liebling

I

IF THERE is any way you can get colder than you do when you sleep in a bedding roll on the ground in a tent in southern Tunisia two hours before dawn, I don't know about it. The particular tent I remember was at an airfield in a Tunisian valley. The surface of the terrain was mostly limestone. If you put all the blankets on top of you and just slept on the canvas cover of the roll, you ached all over, and if you divided the blankets and put some of them under you, you froze on top. The tent was a large, circular one with a French stencil on the outside saying it had been rented from a firm in Marseilles and not to fold it wet, but it belonged to the United States Army now. It had been set up over a pit four feet deep, so men sleeping in it were safe from flying bomb fragments. The tall tent pole, even if severed, would probably straddle the pit and not hit anybody. It was too wide a hole to be good during a strafing, but then strafings come in the daytime and in the daytime nobody lived in it. I had thrown my roll into the tent because I thought it was vacant and it seemed as good a spot as any other when I arrived at the field as a war correspondent. I later discovered that I was sharing it with two enlisted men.

I never saw my tentmates clearly, because they were always in the tent by the time I turned in at night, when we were not allowed to have lights on, and they got up a few minutes before I did in the morning, when it was still dark. I used to hear them moving around, however, and sometimes talk to them. One was from Mississippi and the other from North Carolina, and both were airplane mechanics. The first night I stumbled through the darkness into the tent, they heard me and one of them said, "I hope you don't mind, but the tent we were sleeping in got all tore to pieces with shrapnel last night, so we just moved our stuff in here." I had been hearing about the events of the previous evening from everybody I met on the field. "You can thank God you wasn't here last night," the other man said earnestly. The field is so skillfully hidden in the mountains that it is hard to find by night, and usually the Germans just wander around overhead, dropping their stuff on the wrong hillsides, but for once they had found the right place and some of the light anti-aircraft on the field had started shooting tracers. "It was these guns that gave away where we was," the first soldier said. "Only for that they would have gone away and never knowed the first bomb had hit the field. But after that they knew they was on the beam and they came back and the next bomb set some gasoline on fire and then they really did go to town. Ruined a P-38 that tore herself up in a belly landing a week ago and I had just got her about fixed up again, and now she's got shrapnel holes just about everywhere and she's hopeless. All that work wasted. Killed three fellows that was sleeping in a B-26 on the field and woke up and thought that was no safe place, so they started to run across the field to a slit trench and a bomb got them. Never got the B-26 at all. If they'd stayed there, they'd been alive today, but who the hell would have stayed there?"

"That shrapnel has a lot of force behind it," the other voice in the tent said. "There was a three-quarter-ton truck down on the field and a jaggedy piece of shrapnel went right through one of the tires and spang through the chassix. You could see the holes both sides where she went in and come out. We was in our tent when the shooting started, but not for long. We run up into the hills so far in fifteen minutes it took us four hours to walk back next morning. When we got back we found we didn't have no tent." There was a pause, and then the first soldier said, "Good night, sir," and I fell asleep.

When the cold woke me up, I put my flashlight under the blankets so I could look at my watch. It was five o'clock. Some Arab dogs, or perhaps jackals, were barking in the hills, and I lay uncomfortably dozing until I heard one of the soldiers blowing his nose. He blew a few times and said, "It's funny that as cold as it gets up here nobody seems to get a real cold. My nose runs like a spring branch, but it don't never develop."

When the night turned gray in the entrance to the tent, I woke again, looked at my watch, and saw that it was seven. I got up and found that the soldiers had already gone. Like everyone else at the field, I had been sleeping in my clothes. The only water obtainable was so cold that I did not bother to wash my face. I got my mess kit and walked toward the place, next to the kitchen, where they were starting fires under two great caldrons to heat dish water. One contained soapy water and the other rinsing water. The fires shot up from a deep hole underneath them, and a group of soldiers had gathered around and were holding the palms of their hands toward the flames, trying to get warm. The men belonged to a maintenance detachment of mechanics picked from a number of service squadrons that had been sent to new advanced airdromes, where planes have to be repaired practically without equipment for the job. That morning most of the men seemed pretty cheerful because nothing had happened during the night, but one fellow with a lot of beard on his face was critical. "This location was all right as long as we had all the planes on one side of us, so we was sort of off the runway," he said, "but now that they moved in those planes on the other side of us, we're just like a piece of meat between two slices of bread. A fine ham sandwich for Jerry. If he misses either side, he hits us. I guess that is how you get to be an officer, thinking up a location for a camp like this. I never washed out of Yale so I could be an officer, but I got more sense than that."

"Cheer up, pal," another soldier said. "All you got to do is dig. I got my dugout down so deep already it reminds me of the Borough Hall station. Some night I'll give myself a shave and climb on board a Woodlawn express." Most of the men in camp, I had already noticed, were taking up excavation as a hobby and some of them had worked up elaborate private trench systems. "You couldn't get any guy in camp to dig three days ago," the Brooklyn soldier said, "and now you can't lay down a shovel for a minute without somebody sucks it up."

Another soldier, who wore a white silk scarf loosely knotted around his extremely dirty neck, a style generally affected by fliers, said, "What kills me is my girl's brother is in the horse cavalry, probably deep in the heart of Texas, and he used to razz me because I wasn't a combat soldier."

The Brooklyn man said to him, "Ah, here's Mac with a parachute tied around his neck just like a dashing pilot. Mac, you look like a page out of *Esquire*."

When my hands began to feel warm, I joined the line which had formed in front of the mess tent. As we passed through, we got bacon, rice, apple butter, margarine, and hard biscuits in our mess tins and tea in our canteen cups. The outfit was on partly British rations, but it was a fairly good breakfast anyway, except for the tea, which came to the cooks with sugar and powdered milk already mixed in it. "I guess that's why they're rationing coffee at home, so we can have tea all the time," the soldier ahead of me said. I recognized the bacon as the fat kind the English get from America. By some miracle of lend-lease they had now succeeded in delivering it back to us; the background of bookkeeping staggered the imagination. After we had got our food, we collected a pile of empty gasoline cans to use for chairs and tables. The five-gallon can, known as a flimsy, is one of the two most protean articles in the Army. You can build houses out of it, use it as furniture, or, with slight structural alterations, make a stove or a locker out of it. Its only rival for versatility is the metal shell of the Army helmet, which can be used as an entrenching tool, a shaving bowl, a wash basin, or a cooking utensil, at the discretion of the owner. The flimsy may also serve on occasion as a bathtub. The bather fills it with water, stands in it, removes one article of clothing at a time, rubs the water hastily over the surface thus exposed, and replaces the garment before taking off another one.

There was no officers' mess. I had noticed Major George Lehmann, the commanding officer of the base, and First Lieutenant McCreedy, the chaplain, in the line not far behind me. Major Lehmann is a tall, fair, stolid man who told me that he had lived in Pittsfield, Massachusetts, where he had a job with the General Electric Company. When I had reported, on my arrival at the field, at his dugout the evening before, he had hospitably suggested that I stow my blanket roll wherever I could find a hole in the ground, eat at the general mess shack, and stay as long as I pleased. "There are fighter squadrons and some bombers and some engineers and anti-aircraft here, and you can wander around and talk to anybody that interests you," he had said.

Father McCreedy is a short, chubby priest who came from Bethlehem, Pennsylvania, and had been assigned to a parish in Philadelphia. He always referred to the pastor of this parish, a Father McGinley, as "my boss," and asked me several times if I knew George Jean Nathan, who he said was a friend of Father McGinley. Father McCreedy had been officiating at the interment of the fellows killed in the raid the evening before, and that was all he would talk about during breakfast. He had induced a mechanic to engrave the men's names on metal plates with an electric needle. These plates would serve as enduring grave markers. It is part of a chaplain's duty to see that the dead are buried and to dispose of their effects. Father McCreedy was also special-services officer of the camp, in charge of recreation and the issue of athletic equipment. "So what with one thing and another, they keep me busy here," he said. He told me he did not like New York. "Outside of Madison Square Garden and the Yankee Stadium, you can have it." He wore an outsize tin hat all the time. "I know a chaplain is not supposed to be a combatant," he said, "but if parachute troops came to my tent by night, they'd shoot at me because they wouldn't know I was a chaplain, and I want something solid on my head." He had had a deep hole dug in front of his tent and sometimes, toward dusk, when German planes were expected, he would stand in it waiting and smoking a cigar, with the glowing end of it just clearing the hole.

When I had finished breakfast and scrubbed up my mess kit, I strolled around the post to see what it was like. As the sun rose higher, the air grew warm and the great, reddish mountains looked friendly. Some of them had table tops, and the landscape reminded me of Western movies in Technicolor. I got talking to a soldier named Bill Phelps, who came from the town of Twenty-nine Palms, California. He was working on a bomber that had something the matter with its insides. He confirmed my notion that the country looked like the American West. "This is exactly the way it is around home," he said, "only we got no Ayrabs." A French writer has described the valley bottoms in southern Tunisia as foamy seas of white sand and green alfa grass. They are good, natural airfields, wide and level and fast-drying, but there is always plenty of dust in the air. I walked to a part of the field where there were a lot of P-38's, those double-bodied planes that look so very futuristic, and started to talk to a couple of sergeants who were working on one. "This is Lieutenant Hoelle's plane," one of them said, "and we just finished putting a new wing on it. That counts as just a little repair job out here. Holy God, at home, if a plane was hurt like that, they would send it back to the factory or take it apart for salvage. All we do here is drive a two-and-a-half-ton truck up under the damaged wing and lift it off, and then we put the new wing on the truck and run it alongside the plane again and fix up that eighty-thousand-dollar airplane like we was sticking together a radio set. We think nothing of it. It's a great ship, the 38. Rugged. You know how this one got hurt? Lieutenant Hoelle was strafing some trucks and he come in to attack so low he hit his right wing against a telephone pole. Any other plane, that wing would have come off right there. Hitting the pole that way flipped him over on his back, and he was flying upside down ten feet off the ground. He gripped that stick so hard the inside of his hand was black and blue for a week afterward, and she come right side up and he flew her home. Any one-engine plane would have slipped and crashed into the ground, but those two counter-rotating props eliminate torque." I tried to look as though I understood. "Lieutenant Hoelle is a real man," the sergeant said.

I asked him where Hoelle and the other P-38 pilots were, and he directed me to the P-38 squadron's operations room, a rectangular structure mostly below ground, with walls made out of the sides of gasoline cans and a canvas roof camouflaged with earth. A length of stovepipe stuck out through the roof, making it definitely the most ambitious structure on the field.

*   *   *

Hoelle was the nearest man to the door when I stepped down into the operations shack. He was a big, square-shouldered youngster with heavy eyebrows and a slightly aquiline nose. I explained who I was and asked him who was in charge, and he said, "I am. I'm the squadron C.O. My name's Hoelle." He pronounced it "Holly." There was a fire in a stove, and the shack was warm. Two tiny black puppies lay on a pilot's red scarf in a helmet in the middle of the dirt floor, and they seemed to be the centre of attention. Six or eight lieutenants, in flying togs that ranged from overalls to British Army battle dress, were sitting on gasoline cans or sprawled on a couple of cots. They were all looking at the puppies and talking either to them or their mother, a small Irish setter over in one corner, whom they addressed as Red. "One of the boys brought Red along with him from England," Hoelle said. "We think that the dog that got her in trouble is a big, long-legged black one at the airport we were quartered at there."

"These are going to be real beautiful dogs, just like Irish setters, only with black hair," one of the pilots said in a defensive tone. He was obviously Red's master.

"This is a correspondent," Hoelle said to the group, and one of the boys on a cot moved over and made room for me. I sat down, and the fellow who had moved over said his name was Larry Adler but he wasn't the harmonica player and when he was home he lived on Ocean Parkway in Brooklyn. "I wouldn't mind being there right now," he added.

There was not much in the shack except the cots, the tin cans, a packing case, the stove, a phonograph, a portable typewriter, a telephone, and a sort of bulletin board that showed which pilots were on mission, which were due to go on patrol, and which were on alert call, but it was a cheerful place. It reminded me of one of those secret-society shacks that small boys are always building out of pickup materials in vacant lots. Adler got up and said he would have to go on patrol. "It's pretty monotonous," he said, "like driving a fast car thirty miles an hour along a big, smooth road where there's no traffic. We just stooge around near the field and at this time of day nothing ever happens."

Another lieutenant came over and said he was the intelligence officer of the squadron. Intelligence and armament officers, who do not fly, take a more aggressive pride in their squadron's accomplishments than the pilots, who don't like to be suspected of bragging. "We've been out here for a month," the intelligence officer said, "and we have been do-ing everything—escorting bombers over places like Sfax and Sousse, shooting up vehicles and puncturing tanks, going on fighter sweeps to scare up a fight, and flying high looking for a target and then plunging straight down on it and shooting hell out of it. We've got twenty-nine German planes, includ-ing bombers and transports with troops in them and fighters, and the boys have flown an average of forty combat missions apiece. That's more than one a day. Maybe you'd like to see some of the boys' own reports on what they have been doing."

I said that this sounded fine, and he handed me a sheaf of the simple statements pilots write out when they put in a claim for shooting down a German plane. I copied part of a report by a pilot named Earnhart, who I thought showed a sense of literary style. He had had, according to the intelli-gence officer, about the same kind of experience as everybody else in the squadron. Earnhart had shot down a Junkers 52, which is a troop-carrier, in the episode he was describing, and then he had been attacked by several enemy fighters. "As I was climbing away from them," he wrote, "a 20-millimetre explosive shell hit the windshield and deflected through the top of the canopy and down on the instrument panel. Three pieces of shell hit me, in the left chest, left arm, and left knee. I dropped my belly tank and, having the ship under control, headed for my home base. On the way I applied a tourniquet to my leg, administered a hypodermic, and took sulfanilamide tablets. I landed the ship at my own base one hour after I had been hit by the shell. The plane was repaired. Claim, one Ju 52 destroyed." The intelligence officer introduced Earnhart to me. He was a calm, slender, dark-haired boy and he per-sisted in addressing me as sir. He said he came from Lebanon, Ohio, and had gone to Ohio State.

Still another lieutenant I met was named Gustke. He came from Detroit. Gustke had been shot down behind the Ger-man lines and had made his way back to the field. He was a tall, gangling type, with a long nose and a prominent Adam's apple. "I crash-landed the plane and stepped out of it wearing my parachute," he told me, "and the first thing I met was some Arabs who looked hostile to me, and as luck would have it I had forgotten to bring along my .45, so I tripped my parachute and threw it to them, and you know how crazy Arabs are about cloth or anything like that. They all got fighting among themselves for the parachute, and while they were doing that I ran like the dickens and got away from them. I got to a place where there were some Frenchmen, and they hid me overnight and the next day put me on a horse and gave me a guide, who brought me back over some mountains to inside the French lines. I had a pretty sore tail from riding the horse."

A pilot from Texas named Ribb, who stood nearby as Gustke and I talked, broke in to tell me that they had a fine bunch of fellows and that when they were in the air they took care of each other and did not leave anybody alone at the end of the formation to be picked off by the enemy. "In this gang we have no butt-end Charlies," he said feelingly.

I asked Lieutenant Hoelle what was in the cards for the afternoon, and he said that eight of the boys, including himself, were going out to strafe some German tanks that had been reported working up into French territory. "We carry a cannon, which the P-40's don't, so we can really puncture a tank the size they use around here," he said. "We expect to meet some P-40's over the target, and they will stay up high and give us cover against any German fighters while we do a job on the tanks. Maybe I had better call the boys together and talk it over."

A couple of pilots had begun a game of blackjack on the top of the packing case, and he told them to quit, so he could spread a map on it. At that moment an enlisted man came in with a lot of mail and some Christmas packages that had been deposited by a courier plane. It was long after Christmas, but that made the things even more welcome, and all the pilots made a rush for their packages and started tearing them open. Earnhart, one of the men who were going on the strafe job, got some National Biscuit crackers and some butterscotch candy and a couple of tubes of shaving cream that he said he couldn't use because he had an electric razor, and the operations officer, a lieutenant named Lusk, got some very rich home-made cookies that an aunt and uncle had sent him from Denver. We were all gobbling butterscotch and cookies as we gathered round the map Hoelle had spread. It was about as formal an affair as looking at a road map to find your way to Washington, Connecticut, from New Milford. "We used to make more fuss over briefings in England," the intelligence officer said, "but when you're flying two or three times a day, what the hell?" He pointed out the place on the map where the tanks were supposed to be, and all the fellows said they knew where it was, having been there before. Hoelle said they would take off at noon. After a while he and the seven other boys went out onto the field to get ready, and I went with them. On the way there was more talk about P-38's and how some Italian prisoners had told their captors that the Italian army could win the war easy if it wasn't for those fork-tailed airplanes coming over and shooting them up, a notion that seemed particularly to amuse the pilots. Then I went to the P-38 squadron mess with Adler, who had just returned from patrol duty and wasn't going out on the strafe job, and Gustke, who was also remaining behind. This mess was relatively luxurious. They had tables with plates and knives and forks on them, so they had no mess tins to wash after every meal. "We live well here," Adler said. "Everything high-class."

"The place the planes are going is not very far away," Gustke said, "so they ought to be back around half past two."

When we had finished lunch, I took another stroll around the post. I was walking toward the P-38 squadron's operations shack when I saw the planes begin to return from the mission. The first one that came in had only the nose wheel of its landing gear down. There was evidently something the matter with the two other wheels. The plane slid in on its belly and stopped in a cloud of dust. Another plane was hovering over the field. I noticed, just after I spotted this one, that a little ambulance was tearing out onto the field. Only one of the two propellers of this plane was turning, but it landed all right, and then I counted one, two, three others, which landed in good shape. Five out of eight. I broke into a jog toward the operations shack. Gustke was standing before the door looking across the field with binoculars. I asked him if he knew whose plane had belly-landed, and he said it was a Lieutenant Moffat's and that a big, rough Texas pilot whom the other fellows called Wolf had been in the plane that had come in with one engine out. "I see Earnhart and Keith and Carlton, too," he said, "but Hoelle and the other two are missing."

A jeep was coming from the field toward the operations shack, and when it got nearer we could see Wolf in it. He looked excited. He was holding his right forearm with his left hand, and when the jeep got up to the shack he jumped out, still holding his arm.

"Is it a bullet hole?" Gustke asked.

"You're a sonofabitch it's a bullet hole!" Wolf shouted. "The sonofabitching P-40's sonofabitching around! As we came in, we saw four fighters coming in the opposite direction and Moffat and I went up to look at them and they were P-40's, coming away. The other fellows was on the deck and we started to get down nearer them, to about five thousand, and these sonofabitching 190's came out of the sun and hit Moffat and me the first burst and then went down after the others. There was ground fire coming up at us, too, and the sonofabitches said we was going to be over friendly territory. I'm goddam lucky not to be killed."

"Did we get any of them?" Gustke asked.

"I know I didn't get any," Wolf said, "but I saw at least four planes burning on the ground. I don't know who the hell they were."

By that time another jeep had arrived with Earnhart, looking utterly calm, and one of the mechanics from the field. "My plane is all right," Earnhart told Gustke. "All gassed up and ready to go. They can use that for patrol."

The telephone inside the shack rang. It was the post first-aid station calling to say that Moffat was badly cut up by glass from his windshield but would be all right. The mechanic said that the cockpit of Moffat's plane was knee-deep in hydraulic fluid and oil and gas. "No wonder the hydraulic system wouldn't work when he tried to get the wheels down," the mechanic said. The phone rang again. This time it was group operations, calling for Earnhart, Keith, and Carlton, all three of them unwounded, to go over there and tell them what had happened. The three pilots went away, and a couple of the men got Wolf back into a jeep and took him off to the first-aid station. Hoelle and the two other pilots were still missing. That left only Gustke and me, and he said in a sad young voice, like a boy whose chum has moved to another city, "Now we have lost our buddies."

A couple of days later I learned that Hoelle had bailed out in disputed territory and made his way back to our lines, but the two other boys are either dead or prisoners.

II

Not many Mondays ago I was standing in a chow line with my mess tins at an airfield in southern Tunisia, waiting to get into a dugout where some mess attendants were ladling out a breakfast of stew and coffee. The field is enormous, a naturally flat airdrome of white sand and alfa grass that doesn't hold rainwater long enough to spoil the runways—terrain of the kind a French writer once said looked like foamy seas. All around the field there are bulky, reddish mountains. To the east, the sun was just coming up over one of them, and the air was very cold. The mess shack was covered on top and three sides by a mound of earth. It served officers and men of a squadron of P-40 fighters, and on that particular Monday morning I stood between a corporal named Jake Goldstein, who in civilian life had been a Broadway songwriter, and a private named John Smith, of New Hope, Pennsylvania, who used to help his father, a contractor, build houses. Goldstein told me about a lyric he had just written for a song to be called "Bombs." "The music that I think of when it goes through my head now," he said, "is kind of a little like the old tune called 'Smiles,' but maybe I can change it around later. The lyric goes:

> There are bombs that sound so snappy,
> There are bombs that leave folks sad,
> There are bombs that fell on dear old Dover,
> But those bombs are not so bad.

The idea is that the real bad bomb is when this girl quit me and blew up my heart."

"It sounds great," I told the Corporal.

"It will be even bigger than a number I wrote called 'What Do You Hear from Your Heart?'" Goldstein said. "Probably you remember it. Bing Crosby sang it once on the Kraft Cheese Hour. If you happen to give me a little writeup, remember that my name in the songwriting business is Jack Gould." Private Smith started to tell me that he had once installed some plumbing for a friend of mine, Sam Spewack, the writer, in New Hope. "His wife, Bella, couldn't make up her mind where she wanted one of the bathroom fixtures," Smith said, "so I said—"

I never heard any more about Bella Spewack's plumbing, because Major Robert Christman, the commanding officer of the squadron, came up to me and said, "Well, it's a nice, quiet morning." He had his back to the east. I didn't get a chance to answer him, because I started to run like hell to get to the west side of the mound. A number of soldiers who had been scattered about eating their breakfasts off the tops of empty gasoline cans had already started running and dropping their mess things. They always faced eastward while they ate in the morning so that they could see the Messerschmitts come over the mountains in the sunrise. This morning there were nine Messerschmitts. By the time I hit the ground on the lee side of the mound, slender airplanes were twisting above us in a sky crisscrossed by tracer bullets—a whole planetarium of angry worlds and meteors. Behind our shelter we watched and sweated it out. It is nearly impossible to tell Messerschmitts from P-40's when they are maneuvering in a fight, except when one plane breaks off action and leaves its opponent hopelessly behind. Then you know that the one which is distanced is a P-40. You can't help yelling encouragement as you watch a fight, even though no one can hear you and you cannot tell the combatants apart. The Messerschmitts, which were there to strafe us, flew right over the mess shack and began giving the runways and the planes on the field a going-over.

We had sent up four planes on patrol that morning and they tried to engage the strafing planes, but other Germans,

William L. Shirer in August 1942. *(AP/Wide World Photos.)*

William L. Shirer at French surrender at Compiègne, June 21, 1940. *(AP/Wide World Photos.)*

Dorothy Thompson
with Czech Foreign
Minister Jan Masaryk
(l.) and Czech General
Miroslav in England,
1941. *(UPI/Bettmann
Newsphotos.)*

Dorothy Thompson at
Bund rally, Madison
Square Garden,
New York City, 1939.
(UPI/Bettmann.)

Sigrid Schultz with U.S.
Ambassador William Dodd (l.)
and Nazi propaganda chief
Joseph Goebbels in Berlin, 1932.
*(The State Historical Society of
Wisconsin WHi(x3)47222.)*

Sigrid Schultz in 1944.
(AP/Wide World Photos.)

War correspondents in London, June 1944, writing the first accounts of the Allied invasion of France. *(UPI/Bettmann.)*

A. J. Liebling. *(Photo courtesy of John Jay Stonehill.)*

Virginia Cowles broadcasting
on the BBC Home Service,
March 1943. *(UPI/Bettmann.)*

Edward R. Murrow
in London during
World War II.
(Bettmann Film Archive.)

Edward R. Murrow in London. *(AP/Wide World Photos.)*

Ernie Pyle (c.) and another correspondent with Lt. Gen. George S. Patton Jr. (l.) in Sicily, July 1943. *(UPI/Bettmann.)*

Ernie Pyle in Europe, 1944. *(UPI/Bettmann Newsphotos.)*

Robert St. John (l.) escaping from Yugoslavia, April 1941.
(Robert St. John Collection, Department of Special Collections,
Boston University. Copyright NBC.)

Robert St. John broadcasting for NBC, August 1945. *(AP/ Wide World Photos.)*

Wes Gallagher (l.) after announcement of sentences in Nuremberg trials, October 1946. *(AP/Wide World Photos.)*

Margaret Bourke-White
in 1931. *(UPI/Bettmann
Newsphotos.)*

Margaret Bourke-White
in New York City,
October 1939,
about to sail to Europe
to cover the war.
(AP/Wide World Photos.)

Melville and Annalee Jacoby at the Yangtse River airport in Chungking, fall 1941. *(AP/Wide World Photos.)*

Annalee Jacoby in Cebu, the Philippines, during escape from Bataan, March 1942. *(Courtesy Annalee Jacoby Fadiman.)*

Clark Lee (second from r.) with another correspondent and soldiers on New Caledonia, summer 1942. *(AP/Wide World Photos.)*

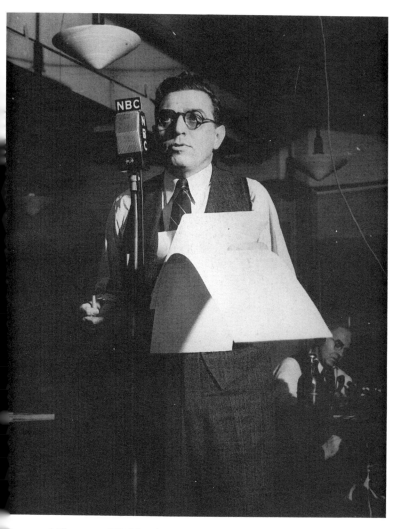

Raymond Clapper at NBC headquarters in New York City, November 1938.
(AP/Wide World Photos.)

Edward R. Murrow (c.) with William L. Shirer (r.) in Paris café.
(The Bettmann Archive.)

Howard K. Smith.
(AP/Wide World Photos.)

Walter Bernstein.
(AP/Wide World Photos.)

Jack Belden in Sicily, August 1943. *(AP/Wide World Photos.)*

Richard Tregaskis (l.) interviewing Lt. Gen. Mark Clark in Italy, October 1943. *(UPI/Bettmann.)*

Richard Tregaskis, 1943. *(UPI/Bettmann.)*

Roi Ottley. *(Schomburg Center for Research in Black Culture.)*

Robert Sherrod in 1944. *(AP/Wide World Photos.)*

Martha Gellhorn with Gurkha soldiers at the Cassino front in Italy, March 1944. *(AP/Wide World Photos.)*

Edward Kennedy watching shelling at Anzio, Italy, 1944. *(UPI/Bettmann.)*

George S. Schuyler, 1941. *(Photo courtesy of the Carl Van Vechten Estate, Joseph Solomon, Executor.)*

Homer Bigart in Italy, January 1944. *(Photo by Bert Brandt. UPI/Bettmann.)*

Vincent Tubbs (c.) in the South Pacific, 1943. *(Copyright, Afro-American Newspapers Archives and Research Center, Inc., 1991. Reprinted with permission.)*

Vincent Tubbs in the South Pacific. *(Copyright, Afro-American Newspapers Archives and Research Center, Inc., 1991. Reprinted with permission.)*

Gertrude Stein with mayor of Culoz, France, 1944. *(UPI/Bettmann.)*

flying high to protect the strafers, engaged the patrol. Some "alert" planes that we had in readiness on the perimeter of the field took off in the middle of the scrap, and that was a pretty thing to watch. I saw one of our patrol planes come in and belly-land on the field, smoking. Then I saw another plane twisting out of the sky in a spin that had the soldiers yelling. We all felt that the spinning plane was a Messerschmitt, and it looked like a sure thing to crash into one of the mountains north of us. When the plane pulled out and disappeared over the summit, the yell died like the howl at Ebbets Field when the ball looks as if it's going into the bleachers and then is snagged by a visiting outfielder. It was a Messerschmitt, all right. A couple of minutes later every one of the German planes had disappeared, with our ships after them like a squad of heavy-footed comedy cops chasing small boys.

The fellows who had ducked for cover hoisted themselves off the ground and looked around for the mess things they had dropped. They were excited and sheepish, as they always are after a strafe party. It is humiliating to have someone run you away, so you make a joke about it. One soldier yelled to another, "When you said 'Flop!' I was there already!" Another, who spoke with a Brooklyn accent, shouted, "Jeez, those tracers looked just like Luna Park!"

We formed the chow line again and one fellow yelled to a friend, "What would you recommend as a good, safe place to eat?"

"Lindy's, at Fifty-first Street," the other soldier answered.

"The way the guys ran, it was like a Christmas rush at Macy's," somebody else said.

Everybody tried hard to be casual. Our appetites were even better than they had been before, the excitement having joggled up our internal secretions. There were arguments about whether the plane that had escaped over the mountain would crash before reaching the German lines. I was scraping the last bits of stew from my mess tin with a sliver of hard biscuit when a soldier came up and told me that Major ——, whom I had never met, had been killed on the field, that five men had been wounded, and that one A-20 bomber had been ruined on the ground.

*   *   *

After I had washed up my tins, I walked over to the P-40 squadron operations shack, because I wanted to talk to a pilot familiarly known as Horse about a fight he had been in two days before. The day it had happened I had been visiting a P-38 squadron's headquarters on the field. I had seen eight P-38's go out to attack some German tanks and only five come back, two of them badly damaged. A lot of Focke-Wulf 190's had attacked the P-38's over the target, and Horse and three other P-40 pilots, who were protecting the 38's, had been up above the 190's. Horse was a big fellow with a square, tan face and a blond beard. He came from a town called Quanah, in Texas, and he was always showing his friends a tinted picture of his girl, who was in the Waves. Horse was twenty-five, which made him practically a patriarch in that squadron, and everybody knew that he was being groomed to command a squadron of his own when he got his captaincy. He was something of a wit. Once I heard one of the other boys say that now that the field had been in operation for six weeks, he thought it was time the men should build a shower bath. "The next thing we know," Horse said, "you'll be wanting to send home for your wife."

I found Horse and asked him about the fight. He said he was sorry that the 38's had had such a bad knock. "I guess maybe it was partly our fault," he said. "Four of our ships had been sent out to be high cover for the 38's. They didn't see any 38's or Jerries either, so when their gas was beginning to run low they started for home. Myself and three other fellows had started out to relieve them and we passed them as they came back. The 38's must have arrived over the tanks just then, and the 190's must have been hiding at the base of a cloud bank above the 38's but far below us. When we got directly over the area, we could see tracers flying way down on the deck. The 190's had dived from the cloud and bounced the 38's, who never had a chance, and the 38's were streaking for home. We started down toward the 190's, but it takes a P-40 a long time to get anywhere and we couldn't help. Then four more 190's dived from way up top and bounced us. I looped up behind one of them as he dived. My two wing men were right with me. I put a good burst into the sonofabitch and he started to burn, and I followed him down. I must have fired a hundred and twenty-five rounds from each gun. It was more fun than a county fair. Gray, my fourth man, put a lot of lead into another 190, and I doubt if it ever got home. The other two Jerries just kept on going."

The P-40 operations shack was set deep in the ground and had a double tier of bunks along three of its walls. Sand and grass were heaped over the top of the shack, and the pilots said that even when they flew right over it, it was hard to see, which cheered them considerably. The pilots were flying at least two missions a day and spent most of the rest of the time lying in the bunks in their flying clothes, under as many coats and blankets as they could find. The atmosphere in the shack was a thick porridge of dust diluted by thin trickles of cold air. Major Christman, the squadron leader, once said in a pleased tone, "This joint always reminds me of a scene in 'Journey's End.'" The pilots, most of whom were in their earliest twenties, took a certain perverse satisfaction in their surroundings. "Here we know we're at war," one of them said to me. "Not that I wouldn't change for a room and bath at a good hotel."

During most of my stay at the field I lived not in the Journey's End shack but in one known as the Hotel Léon because technically it belonged to a French lieutenant named Léon, a liaison officer between the French forces and our fliers. It was the newest and finest dugout on the field, with wooden walls and a wooden floor and a partition dividing it down the middle, and the floor was sunk about five feet below ground level. When I arrived at the field, there were plans to cover the part of the shack that projected above ground with sand, in which Léon intended to plant alfa. I was travelling with an Associated Press correspondent named Norgaard, and soon after our arrival Léon, a slender man with a thin, intelligent face and round, brown eyes, welcomed us to his palace. We put our stuff into the shack and emerged to find Léon throwing a modest shovelful of sand against one of the walls. Norgaard offered to help him. "There is only one shovel," Léon said with relief, pressing it into Norgaard's hands. "It is highly interesting for our comfort and safety that the house be covered entirely with sand. I am very occupied."

Then he walked rapidly away, and Norgaard and I took turns piling sand around the Hotel Léon for endless hours afterward. Léon always referred to a telephone switchboard as a switching board, oil paper as oily paper, a pup tent as a puppy tent, and a bedding roll as a rolling bed.

After my talk with Horse, I walked over to the Hotel Léon and found it crowded, as it usually was. Only Léon and Norgaard and I, together with Major Philip Cochran and Captain Robert Wylie, lived in the hotel, but during the day Cochran and Léon used it as an office, and that was why it was crowded. When I had first come to the field, it had been operating for six weeks practically as an outpost, for there was just a unit of American infantry, fifty miles to the southeast, between it and the region occupied by Rommel's army. Cochran, though only a major, had run the field for almost the entire period, but by the time I arrived he had reverted to the status of operations officer. The shack had telephone lines to detachments of French troops scattered thinly through the hills to our east, and they called up at all hours to tell Léon where German tanks were moving or to ask our people to do some air reconnaissance or drop bags of food to a platoon somewhere on a mountain. The French had no trucks to transport food. Sometimes Cochran flew with American transport planes to tell them where to drop parachute troops and sometimes he flew with bombers to tell them where to drop bombs. Because of Cochran's and Léon's range of activities, they always had a lot of visitors.

Attached to the partition in the shack were two field telephones, one of which answered you in French and the other in English. Two soldier clerks, who were usually pounding typewriters, sat on a bench in front of a shelf along one wall. One of them was Corporal Goldstein, the songwriter. The other was a private first class named Otto, who wore metal-rimmed spectacles with round lenses and belonged to the Pentecostal brethren, an evangelical sect which is against fighting and profanity. Otto owned some barber tools, and he cut officers' hair during office hours and enlisted men's at night. That morning he was cutting the hair of Kostia Rozanoff, the commandant of the Lafayette Escadrille, a French P-40 outfit that was stationed at the field. Rozanoff was a blond, round-headed Parisian whose great-grandfather was Russian. Otto, perhaps taking a cue from the shape of Rozanoff's skull, had clipped him until he looked like Erich Von Stroheim, but there was no mirror, so Rozanoff was happy anyway. Cochran, dressed in a dirty old leather flying jacket, had just come back from a mission in the course of which he thought he had destroyed a 190, and was trying to tell about that while nearly everybody else in the shack was trying to tell him about the morning's strafing. Also in the shack was Colonel Edson D. Raff, the well-known parachutist, who had once unexpectedly found himself in command of all the American ground forces in southern Tunisia and for weeks had successfully bluffed enemy forces many times larger. He had flown in from his post in Gafsa in a small plane which he used as his personal transport. He was crowded in behind Otto's barbering elbow and was trying to talk to Cochran over Rozanoff's head. Raff is short and always wears a short carbine slung over his left shoulder, even indoors. He invariably flies very low in his plane to minimize the risk of being potted by a Messerschmitt. "I have one foot trailing on the ground," he says.

Lieutenant Colonel William Momyer, the commanding officer of the field, was sitting between Rozanoff and Corporal Goldstein, telling about a mission he had been on himself that morning, escorting a lot of A-20's over Kebili, a town where the Italians had begun to repair a dynamited causeway across the Chott Djerid. "I bet the wops will never get any workmen to go back to that place," Momyer said. "We scared hell out of them." Momyer had shot down a Junkers 88 and Messerschmitt within a week. He was hot.

Among the others in the shack that morning were Norgaard, the Associated Press man, and a tall P-40 pilot named Harris, who kept asking Léon whether any French unit had telephoned to report finding the Messerschmitt he had been shooting at during the strafing episode, because he was sure it must have crashed. It was the Messerschmitt we had seen pull out of the spin over the mountain. The English-speaking telephone rang and Captain Wylie answered it. He has the kind of telephone voice that goes with a large, expensive office, which he probably had in civilian life. It was somebody up the line asking for Major ——, the officer who had just been machine-gunned in the strafing. "Major —— has been killed," Wylie said. "Is there anything I can do for you?"

There was a variety of stuff on the field when I was there. In addition to Christman's P-40 squadron and the Lafayette Escadrille, there was a second American P-40 squadron commanded by a Major Hubbard, which had a full set of pilots but only five ships. This was because the powers that be had taken away the other ships and given them to the Lafayettes in the interest of international good will. Hubbard's pilots were not sore at the Lafayettes, but they didn't think much of the powers that be. There was also a bomber squadron. The people on our field were not by any means sitting targets. They constantly annoyed the Germans, and that is why the Germans were so keen on "neutralizing" the field. But they didn't come back that day, and neither lunch nor dinner was disturbed.

The guests of the Hotel Léon often didn't go to the mess shack for dinner, because Léon would prepare dinner for them on the premises. He was a talented cook who needed the stimulation of a public, which was, that Monday evening, us. He also needed Wylie to keep the fire in the stove going, Cochran to wash dishes, and me and Norgaard to perform assorted chores. He got eggs from the Arabs and wine from a nearby French engineer unit, and he had gathered a choice assortment of canned goods from the quartermaster's stores. He also bought sheep and pigs from farmers. Léon's idea of a campaign supper was a *soufflé de poisson*, a *gigot*, and an *omelette brûlée à l'armagnac*. He made the *soufflé* out of canned salmon. The only trouble with dining at Léon's was that dinner was seldom ready before half past eight and it took until nearly midnight to clean up afterward.

During that Monday dinner we speculated on what the enemy would do next day. Norgaard said it was hell to have to get up early to catch the Germans' morning performance, but Cochran, the airfield's official prophet, and a successful one, said, "They'll want to make this one a big one tomorrow, so you can sleep late. They won't be over until two-thirty in the afternoon." Momyer, who was having dinner at the hotel that night, agreed that there would be something doing, but he didn't predict the time of day. Léon said, "I think also that there is something cooking in." Momyer decided to maintain a patrol of eight planes over the field all day. "Of course, maybe that's just what they want us to do, use our planes defensively, so we will fly less missions," he said, "but I think this time we ought to do it."

I had such faith in Cochran that it never occurred to me that the Germans would attack us before the hour he had named, and they didn't. The only enemy over the field the following morning was Photo Freddie, a German reconnaissance pilot who had become a local character. He came every morning at about forty thousand feet, flying a special Junkers 86 job so lightened that it could outclimb any fighter. The anti-aircraft guns would fire, putting a row of neat, white smoke puffs a couple of miles below the seat of Freddie's pants, the patrol planes would lift languidly in his direction, like the hand of a fat man waving away a fly, and Photo Freddie would scoot off toward Sicily, or wherever he came from, to develop his pictures, thus discovering where all the planes on the field were placed. The planes were always moved around after he left, and we used to wonder what the general of the Luftwaffe said to poor Freddie when the bombers failed to find the planes where he had photographed them. Now and then some pilot tried to catch Photo Freddie by getting an early start, climbing high above the field, and then stooging around until he appeared. Freddie, however, varied the hour of his matutinal visits, and since a P-40 cannot fly indefinitely, the pilot would get disgusted and come down. I do not think anybody really wanted to hurt Freddie anyway. He was part of the local fauna, like the pet hens that wandered about the field and popped into slit trenches when bombs began to fall.

At about twenty minutes past two that afternoon Norgaard and I returned to the Hotel Léon to do some writing. An Alsatian corporal in the French army was working in front of the shack, making a door for the entrance. The corporal had been assigned by the French command to build Léon's house, and he was a hard worker. He always kept his rifle by him while he was working. He had a long brown beard, which he said he was going to let grow until the Germans were driven out of Tunisia. Only Goldstein and Otto were inside the hut this time. I said to Goldstein, "Why don't you write a new number called 'One-Ninety, I Love You'?" Otto, who had been reading the *Pentecostal Herald*, said, "I do not think that would be a good title. It would not be popular." At that precise moment all of us heard the deep woomp of heavy ack-ack. It came from one of the British batteries in the mountains around the field. We grabbed our tin hats and started for the doorway. By the time we got there, the usual anti-aircraft show was on. In the din we could easily distinguish the sound of our Bofors guns, which were making their peculiar seasick noises—not so much a succession of reports as one continuous retch. The floor of the shack, as I have said, was five feet below ground level and the Alsatian had not yet got around to building steps down to the entrance, so we had a nice, rectangular hole just outside from which to watch developments. The Germans were bombing now, and every time a bomb exploded, some of the sand heaped against the wooden walls was driven into the shack through the knot-holes. The only trouble was that whenever a bomb went off we pulled in our heads and stopped observing. Then we looked out again until the next thump. After several of these thumps there was a straight row of columns of black smoke a couple of hundred yards to our right. I poked my head above ground level and discovered the Alsatian corporal kneeling and firing his rifle, presumably at an airplane which I could not see. The smoke began to clear and we hoisted ourselves out of the hole to try and find out what had happened. "I do not think I touched," the Alsatian said. A number of dog-fights were still going on over the mountains. Scattered about the field, men, dragging themselves out of slit trenches, were pointing to the side of a mountain to the north, where there was smoke above a downed plane.

Léon had a little and old Citroën car, which he said had become, through constant association with the United States Army, "one naturalized small jeeps." He had left it parked behind the shack, and as Norgaard and I stood gawping about, Léon came running and shouted that he was going out to the fallen plane. We climbed into the naturalized jeeps and started across the field toward the mountainside. At one of the runways, we met a group of P-40 pilots, including Horse, and I yelled to them, "Was it theirs or ours?" "Ours, I think," Horse said. We kept on going. When we reached the other side of the field, we cut across country, and Léon could not make much speed. A couple of soldiers with rifles thumbed a ride and jumped on the running boards. As we went out across plowed fields and up the mountain toward the plane, we passed dozens of soldiers hurrying in the same direction.

When we arrived where the plane had fallen, we found three trucks and at least fifty men already there. The plane had been a Messerschmitt 109 belonging to the bombers' fighter escort. Flames were roaring above the portion deepest in the earth, which I judged was the engine. Screws, bolts, rings, and unidentifiable bits of metal were scattered over an area at least seventy-five yards square. Intermingled with all this were widely scattered red threads, like the bits left in a butcher's grinder when he has finished preparing an order of chopped steak. "He never even tried to pull out," a soldier said. "He must have been shot through the brain. I seen the whole thing. The plane fell five thousand feet like a hunk of lead." There was a sour smell over everything—not intolerable, just sour. "Where is the pilot?" Norgaard asked. The soldier waved his hand with a gesture that included the whole area. Norgaard, apparently for the first time, noticed the red threads. Most of the soldiers were rummaging amid the wreckage, searching for souvenirs. Somebody said that the pilot's automatic pistol, always the keepsake most eagerly sought, had already been found and appropriated. Another soldier had picked up some French and Italian money. How these things had survived the pilot's disintegration I do not know. While the soldiers walked about, turning over bits of the plane with their feet, looking for some object which could serve as a memento, an American plane came over and everybody began to run before someone recognized it for what it was. Just as we came back, a soldier started kicking at something on the ground and screaming. He was one of the fellows who had ridden out on our running boards. He yelled, "There's the sonofabitch's God-damn guts! He wanted my guts! He nearly had my guts, God damn him!" Another soldier went up to him and bellowed, "Shut up! It ain't nice to talk that way!" A lot of other men began to gather around. For a minute or so the soldier who had screamed stood there silently, his shoulders pumping up and down, and then he began to blubber.

Léon picked up a large swatch of the Messerschmitt's tail fabric as a trophy, and as the soldiers walked away from the wreck most of them carried either similar fragments or pieces of metal. After a while Norgaard and I climbed into Léon's car and the three of us started back toward the field. When we arrived, we learned that a lieutenant named Walter Scholl, who had never been in a fight before, had shot down the Messerschmitt. He was the fellow who, in the Cornell-Dartmouth football game of 1940, threw the famous fifth-down touchdown pass for Cornell, the one that was completed for what was considered a Cornell victory until movies of the game showed that it shouldn't have been Cornell's ball at all and the decision had to be reversed. Two other pilots had shot down two Junkers 88 bombers. One of our planes on the ground had been destroyed, and a slit trench had caved in on two fellows, nearly frightening them to death before they could be dug out.

III

Norgaard, the Associated Press correspondent who was with me during a small war that took place at an airfield in southern Tunisia a while ago, often said that the country reminded him of New Mexico, and with plenty of reason. Both are desert countries of mountains and mesas, and in both there are sunsets that owe their beauty to the dust in the air. The white, rectangular Arab houses, with their blue doors, are like the houses certain Indians build in New Mexico, and the Arabs' saddle blankets and pottery and even the women's silver bracelets are like Navajo things. The horses, which look like famished mustangs, have the same lope and are similarly bridle-wise; burros are all over the place, and so is cactus. These resemblances are something less than a coincidence, because the Moors carried their ways of house-building and their handicraft patterns and even their breed of horses and method of breaking them to Spain, and the Spaniards carried them to New Mexico eight hundred years later. All these things go to make up a culture that belongs to a high plateau country where there are sheep to furnish wool for blankets and where people have too little cash to buy dishes in a store, where the soil is so poor that people have no use for heavy plow horses but want a breed that they can ride for long distances and that will live on nearly nothing.

"This horse is young," an Arab once said to Norgaard and me as he showed us a runty bay colt tied in front of a combined general store and barbershop in a village about a mile from the airfield. "If I had had a little barley to feed him, he would be bigger, but what barley we had we have ourselves eaten. It is a poor country."

We used to go down to this village to get eggs when we were too lazy to make the chow line for breakfast or when we felt hungry at any time of day. We'd take them back to the shack a bunch of us were living in and cook them. Solitary Arabs squat along the roadsides all over North Africa, waiting for military vehicles. When one comes into sight, the Arab pulls an egg out from under his rags and holds it up between thumb and forefinger like a magician at a night club. The price of eggs—always high, of course—varies in inverse ratio to the distance from a military post. Near big towns that are a long way from any post the Arabs get only five francs (ten cents at the new rate of exchange) for an egg, but in villages close to garrisons eggs are sometimes hard to find at any price. Norgaard and I followed a standard protocol to get them. First we went into the general store and barbershop, which was just a couple of almost empty rooms that were part of a mud house, and shook hands with all the male members of the establishment. Naturally, we never saw any of the females. Then we presented a box of matches to the head of the house, an ex-soldier who spoke French, and he invited us to drink coffee. The Arabs have better coffee and more sugar than the Europeans in North Africa. While we drank the coffee, we sat with the patriarch of the family on a white iron bed of European manufacture. The patriarch had a white beard and was always knitting socks; he stopped only to scratch himself. Once, as we were drinking coffee, we watched our

French-speaking friend shave a customer's head. He simply started each stroke at the top of the cranium and scraped downward. He used no lather; the customer moistened his own poll with spittle after each stroke of the razor. Once, when the customer made a particularly awful face, all the other Arabs sitting around the room laughed. During the coffee-drinking stage of the negotiations we presented the Arabs with a can of fifty English cigarettes. After that they presented us with ten to fifteen eggs. Soldiers who were not such good friends of theirs usually got twenty eggs for fifty cigarettes, but it always costs something to maintain one's social life. One day I asked the barber why the old man scratched himself, and he said, laughing, "Because of the black spots. We all have them, and they itch." With much hilarity the Arabs showed us the hard, black spots, apparently under their skins, from which they were suffering. I judged the trouble to be a degenerate form of the Black Death, tamed during the centuries by the rugged constitutions of our hosts. Norgaard thought that the spots were just chiggers.

The Germans had come over our airfield on a Monday morning and strafed it and they had come back on Tuesday afternoon and bombed the place. They were going to start an offensive in southern Tunisia, we later learned, so they wanted to knock out this, the most advanced American field. On Wednesday morning the Germans made no attack. That afternoon Norgaard and I decided that we needed some eggs, so we walked down to the Arab village. I carried the eggs home in my field hat, a visored cap which has long flaps to cover your neck and ears when it is cold and which makes a good egg bag. We got back to our shack, which we preferred to call the Hotel Léon, between five and six o'clock. Major Philip Cochran, the airfield's operations officer, who lived in our shack and also used it as an office, was out flying, and Léon, the French liaison officer at the airfield and the titular proprietor of our premises, was out foraging. Jake and Otto, two soldier clerks who worked there during the day, had gone to chow. There was less than an hour of daylight left.

Cochran, who had a fine instinct for divining what the Germans were likely to do, had been sure that they would come over for the third day in succession, and Lieutenant Colonel William Momyer, the commanding officer of the field, had maintained a patrol of P-40's over the field all day. Cochran was among those taking their turns on patrol duty now. In forty minutes more all the planes would have to come down, because the field had no landing lights. And nothing had happened yet.

The walk had made Norgaard and me hungry and we decided to have our eggs immediately. We threw some kindling wood in the stove to stir the fire up and I put some olive oil in the mess tin in which I was going to scramble the eggs. The olive oil belonged to Léon, who went in for *haute cuisine* whenever he could assemble a quorum of majors and lieutenant colonels to act as scullions for him. I took the lid off the hole in the top of the stove, put the mess tin over the hole, and broke all the eggs into the oil. I think there were eleven of them. They floated around half submerged, and although I stirred them with a fork, they didn't scramble. We decided that I had used too much oil, so we added some cheese to act as a cement. Before the cheese had had time to take effect, we heard a loud explosion outside—plainly a bomb—and felt the shack rock. Norgaard grabbed his tin hat and ran out the door to look, and I was just going to follow him when I reflected that if I left this horrible brew on the stove hole a spark might ignite the oil and thus set fire to the shack. I carefully put the mess on a bench and replaced the lid on the stove. I put on my helmet and followed Norgaard out into a kind of foxhole outside our door. More bombs exploded and then all we could hear was the racket of the Bofors cannon and .50 calibre machine guns defending the field. I went back inside, removed the stove lid, and put the eggs on again. Just as some warmth began to return to the chill mess, another stick of bombs went off. In the course of the next minute or so, I repeated my entire routine. Before I finished cooking dinner, I had to repeat it three times more. Finally the eggs and the cheese stuck together after a fashion and I drained the oil off. Then, since no bombs had dropped for a couple of minutes, I poured half the concoction into Norgaard's canteen cup, I put what was left in my mess tin, and we ate.

After we had eaten, we left the shack and started toward

the large, round pit, some fifty yards away, which served as a control room for the field. Night had closed in. There had been no firing now for ten minutes, but as we approached the pit, our anti-aircraft opened up again, firing from all around the field simultaneously. The Bofors tracer shells, which look like roseate Roman candles, reminded me of the fireworks on the lagoon at the World's Fair in Flushing. The burst ended as abruptly as it had begun, except that one battery of .50's kept on for an extra second or two and then stopped in an embarrassed manner.

We saw a lot of our pilots clustered around the pit. A corporal named Dick usually stood in the pit talking to our planes in the air by radio telephone, but a major named Robert Christman, the C.O. of one of the post's fighter squadrons, was in Dick's place. I recognized Christman's voice as he spoke into the telephone, asking, "Did you see the gunfire? Did you see the gunfire?" You wouldn't ask a Jerry that if you were shooting at him, so I knew they were firing the anti-aircraft guns to light one or more of our planes home. Christman asked again, "Did you see the gunfire? Did you see the gunfire?" Then he said to somebody else in the pit, probably Dick, "Hold this a minute." He stuck his head up over the side of the pit and shouted in the direction of a nearby dugout, "They say they saw the fire! Cochran's going to lead in and land to show the other ship the way! Lord, how that Cochran swears when he's excited! Tell the ack-ack to hold everything!" The switchboard through which the control room communicated with all the ack-ack batteries was in the dugout. Nothing was convenient on that field. It sometimes seemed that one of the pilots had scratched the whole thing out of the ground with a broken propeller blade after a forced landing.

We could see a plane showing red and green lights slowly circling over the field, descending gradually in long, deliberate spirals, as if the pilot wanted somebody to follow him. Then there was a blast of machine-gun fire and a fountain of tracers sprayed up from a distant edge of the field. "God damn them!" Christman yelled. "Tell them to hold that fire! What do they want to do—shoot Phil down?" The plane coasted slowly, imperturbably lower. It was Cochran's firm belief, I knew, that the ack-ack on the field had never hit anything, so he probably wasn't worried. The plane skimmed over the surface of the field. There was one pitiful red light on the field for it to land by, like the lantern one hangs on the tail of a hobbled donkey to keep him from being hit by a pushcart. "He'll never make it that way," a pilot near me said. "What the hell is he doing? He'll overshoot. No, there he goes up again."

In a minute Christman, back at the phone once more, said, "Cochran went up because the other fellow couldn't see him. The other ship says he saw the gunfire, though. Now he wants a burst on the southern edge of the field only." Somebody in the switchboard dugout yelled, "Come on now! Battery C only, Battery C only! Everybody else *hold* it!" All the guns on the field immediately fired together. I could hear Momyer's voice yelling in the dugout, "God damn it, I'll have them all court-martialled!" Christman shouted, "He says he saw it and now he can see Cochran! He's coming in!" Cochran was again circling in the blackness above the field. The pilot next to me said, "This is sure sweating it out." I recognized him, partly by his voice and partly by the height of his shoulders, as a fellow the other boys called Horse, a big Texan who wore a square beard.

"Did we get any of theirs?" I asked Horse.

"Yes, sir," Horse said. "Bent got one for sure. He's in already. And a French post has telephoned that another one is down near there in flames and that pilot out there with Cochran had one smoking. He must have chased it so far he couldn't get back before dark. Must have forgot himself. I don't rightly know who he is."

The ack-ack batteries fired again. They apparently did what was wanted this time, because nobody cursed. Christman called up from the pit, "They want one more burst, all together, and then they're coming in!" The message was relayed and the ack-ack fired another salvo. Now there were two planes, both showing lights, moving in the sky above the field, one high and one low. "Cochran's coming in," Horse said. "Look at him. Just like it was day and he could see everything." The lower pair of lights drifted downward, straightened out and ran forward along the field, and stopped. The other lights slowly followed them down, seemed to hesitate a moment, then slanted toward the ground, and coasted into a horizontal. "Good landing," Horse said. "We sure sweated that one." The second pilot to land turned out to be a lieutenant named Thomas, who had become too absorbed in the pursuit of a Junkers 88 to turn back until he had shot it down. That made three Junkers for us, each carrying a crew of four men. I learned that the German bombs had spoiled, to use the airmen's term, two of our planes on the field. A couple of minutes later a jeep that had gone out to meet Cochran's plane brought him to where the rest of us were standing. He is a short, box-chested man, and the two or three flying jackets he was wearing made him look shorter and stockier than he really is. He was feeling good. "I'm sorry I cursed you out, Bob! I was excited!" he yelled down into the control pit to Christman. Momyer, who had come out of the dugout, made as if to grab Cochran and hug him, but stopped in astonishment when he heard Cochran being so polite. It seemed to remind him of something. Looking rather thoughtful, he went back into the dugout and called up the lieutenant colonel in command of the ack-ack, which he had been abusing. "Thank you very much, Colonel," I heard him say. "Your boys certainly saved the day."

That evening was a happy one. Léon's shack was crowded with pilots talking about the successful fight and scrambling eggs and eating them out of mess tins. Cochran felt so good that he decided to have his first haircut since he had left New York three months before, so he sent over to the enlisted men's quarters for Otto, who was a barber as well as a clerk, to do the job. Otto is a young man with reddish hair and white eyebrows and a long nose, and he had a habit of getting interested in a conversation between two senior officers and breaking into it. Once, hearing Colonel Edson D. Raff, the parachute-troop commander, telling Lieutenant Colonel Momyer that he could take Tunis with no more than four hundred and fifty men, Otto blurted out, "How can you be so sure?" Aside from this failing he is a good soldier and when he gives a haircut he really cuts off hair, so nobody can say he is looking for a return engagement in the near future.

It was well after dark when Léon came in from his foraging, which had been a success too. "I have bought three small peegs," he announced triumphantly, "and when they are theek enough we shall eat them." He had left them in the care of a *hôtelier* in a town a few miles away. They were sub-sequently taken, and presumably eaten, by the Germans. At the time, however, Léon thought it a safe *logement* for the pigs. "I have also talked with the aide of General Koeltz," Léon said to Cochran and Momyer, "and he says that in the case any pilot sees any trucks moving on the road of which we have spoken yesterday, he is allowed to shoot without permis-sion." While Otto cut Cochran's hair, we added up the box score of the three-day German attack on the field. The home team felt that it had done pretty well. During the Monday strafing the Germans had spoiled one of our planes on the field and another in the air and had killed one officer, a major, with machine-gun bullets. We had merely damaged one of their fighters. On Tuesday, while they had spoiled two more of our planes on the ground with bombs, we had shot down a Messerschmitt 109 and two Junkers 88's. That meant that we had lost a total of three planes but only one life while they had lost three planes and nine lives. One of our missions had also destroyed a Focke-Wulf 190 on Monday morning and a Messerschmitt had been badly damaged in the dogfight that had accompanied the strafing of our field. Wednesday evening we had destroyed three more planes and twelve men, and the Germans had succeeded only in damaging two planes on the ground, which gave us an imposing lead. "They won't be over tomorrow morning," Cochran said. "Maybe not all day. They'll want to think things over and try something big to make up for their losses and get the lead back. They'll be like a guy doubling his bet in a crap game."

That field had been fought over many times before in the course of history and a corner of it had been the site of a Carthaginian city. Bent, a pilot who talked with a British ac-cent and had once done some digging among old ruins in England, said that every time he flew over that corner he could plainly see the gridiron pattern of the ancient streets on the ground. Horse, the bearded pilot, was irreverent about Bent's claims. "Maybe a couple of thousand years from now," he said, "people will dig around this same field and find a lot of C-ration cans that we've left and attribute them to archeology. They'll say, 'Those Americans must surely have been a pygmy race to wear such small helmets. It scarcely seems possible they had much brains. No wonder they rode around in such funny airplanes as the P-40.'"

Another officer who turned up in Léon's shack that evening was Major (afterward Lieutenant Colonel) Vincent Sheean, who always points out these days that he was once a correspondent himself. He said he had been driving in a jeep on a road near the field when the bombing started, so he had stopped and jumped into a ditch. Sheean had come down from the second highest headquarters of the African Air Forces to see that the French pilots of the Lafayette Escadrille, which had recently arrived at our field, received understanding and kind treatment from their American comrades. A couple of the Lafayette pilots happened to be in the shack when he arrived; they had received so much kind treatment that they could hardly remember the words of "Auprès de Ma Blonde," which they were trying to teach to Momyer on a purely phonetic basis.

The next day, Thursday, was as quiet as Cochran had said it would be. The Germans left us completely alone. In the morning the Lafayette Escadrille fellows went on their first mission, covering a French local offensive in a mountain pass, and returned without meeting any enemy aircraft.

The exposed position of our mess shack had begun to worry Major Christman's men after the strafing we had received the Monday before, and he had ordered the chow line transferred to a place called the Ravine, a deep, winding gulch on the other side of the high road along one end of the field. Most of the men lived in the Ravine and felt safe there. They had scooped out caves in its sides and used their shelter halves to make doors. One stretch of the gully was marked by a sign that said "Park Avenue." Sheean and I stood in the chow line for lunch and then took an afternoon stroll along Park Avenue. Afterward I went back to Léon's shack to write a letter and found it crowded, as usual. An engineer officer who had been at the field a couple of days was asking Cochran how he could be expected to get on with the construction job he had been sent there to do if new bomb holes appeared on the field every day and his detachment had to fill them up. "We've been filling up bomb holes ever since we been here, and it looks like we won't get a chance to do anything else," the engineer said. "My colonel sent me down here to build revetments for airplanes and he's going to expect me back soon." Another visitor, a captain in the Royal Engineers, asked him if there were any unexploded bombs on the runways. Men on the field always referred to this British captain as the booby-trap man, the planting of fiendish traps for the enemy being his specialty, and added with respect, "Even the parachute troops say he's crazy." He had made several jumps with Colonel Raff's parachutists to install his humorous devices in places where he thought German soldiers would later get involved with them. The American officer told him that there were several unexploded bombs on the runways and that he had marked off their positions with empty oil drums.

"But haven't you removed the fuses?" the booby-trap man asked with obvious astonishment.

"To hell with that!" his American colleague said with feeling. "They won't do any harm if they do go off. It's a big field."

"Oh, but they'll make quite a lot of noise," the booby-trap man said, still vaguely unhappy.

The American officer looked at the booby-trap man and Cochran as if they were both lunatics and went out of the hut without saying anything more. "How *extraordinary!*" the booby-trap man said. "He didn't even seem interested." He sounded hurt, like a young mother who has just learned that a visitor does not care for babies.

The booby-trap man looked like a conventional sort of Englishman, with a fair, boyish face and a shy smile. He spoke with the careful accent of the north countryman who has been to a university and he did not himself use the term "booby trap." He preferred to call his darlings, variously, trip mechanisms, push mechanisms, pull mechanisms, and anti-personnel switches. Trip mechanisms, for instance, are the ones soldiers inadvertently set off by stumbling over a concealed wire, and pull mechanisms are those they explode by picking up some innocent-seeming object like a corned-beef tin. The captain was an amateur botanist and seldom went out without a couple of pocketfuls of small devices to set about the countryside in likely spots as he ambled along collecting specimens of Tunisian grasses. I asked him that afternoon how he had started on what was to become his military career, and he said with his shy smile, "I expect it was at public school, when I used to put hedgehogs in the other boys' beds. After a while the hedgehogs began to pall and I invented a system for detuning the school piano, so that when the music master sat down to play 'God Save the King' it sounded god-awful."

"I sometimes try to imagine what your married life will be like, Captain," Cochran said. "Someday the baby will be in the crib and your wife will go to pick it up and the whole house will blow up because you've wired the baby to a booby trap."

"I trust I shall be able to restrain my professional instincts to fit the circumstances of domestic life," the booby-trap man said rather stiffly. He was a man who really took his branch of warfare seriously.

IV

Sleep in the Hotel Léon, which was the colloquial name of a shack on a Tunisian airfield in which I lived for a while not so long ago, was usually interrupted in the gray hour before dawn by the jangle of a field telephone that spoke French. Then Léon, the French liaison officer at our post, who had had the shack built according to his specifications and whom the rest of us residents called *Monsieur le patron*, would sit up and pull the telephone from the holster in which it hung at the foot of his bed. He slept wearing all the clothes he possessed, which included several sweaters, a long military overcoat, and a muffler. When he grabbed the phone, he would say, *"Allo! Oui?"* (The rest of us sometimes would sing "Sweet Allo, Oui" to the tune of "Sweet Eloise.") The French voice at the other end of the phone was almost always audible, and, so that the half-awake American officers in the shack would get the idea of what was going on, Léon would reply in a hybrid jargon. He would say, for example, "One *ennemi apparait* flying sousewest over point 106? *Merci, mon capitaine.*" Then he would hang up and fall back into bed, muttering, "*Imbécile,* why he don't fly west? He will be losted."

A partition divided Léon's shack into a bedroom, in which four of us slept side by side, and an office, in which only two slept. In the bedroom were Léon, Major Philip Cochran, an Associated Press correspondent named Norgaard, and myself. A captain named Robert Wylie and Major (later Lieutenant Colonel) Vincent Sheean slept in the office. We would try to ignore Léon's first morning call, but before long there would be another; Cochran, the operations officer at the field, would be asking what was going on, and we would hear the roar of the motors down on the field being warmed up for the dawn patrol and the morning missions. Then we would hear Wylie clattering around our stove in his G.I. shoes and there would be a glow in the shack when he put the match to the paper with which he started the fire. Wylie, who wasn't a flying officer, always tried to have the shack warm by the time Cochran got up, and he wanted the Major to stay in bed until the last minute. He was as solicitous as a trainer with a favorite colt, and the rest of us benefited from the care he took of Cochran, because we didn't get up early, either. Wylie is a wiry man with a high forehead and a pepper-and-salt mustache. He wears glasses and looks like an advertising artist's conception of an executive who is in good humor because he has had an excellent night's sleep owing to Sanka. He is a highly adaptable man. After Wylie had puttered around for a while, we would sit up one by one and stretch and complain about being disturbed or about the cold and then go outside to wash. Mornings on which the anti-aircraft opened up against early visitors, the tempo was accelerated. Cochran undressed at night by loosening the knot in his tie and drew it tight again in the morning as a sign that he was dressed. These were symbolic gestures he never omitted.

On the morning of the fifth and last day of a small private war during which the Germans had been trying hard to knock out our field, it was the anti-aircraft that brought us out of bed. We scrambled for the door, lugging our tin hats, our

toothbrushes, and our canteens. The Germans were already
almost over our field, but they were quite high, since our
patrol planes had engaged them on the way in and they could
not break off the fight to strafe us. The German planes were
single-engined fighters, which sometimes carry wing or belly
bombs, but this time they were not bombing. Some of the
defending planes were marked with the tricolor *cocarde* of the
French Army. It was, I suppose, a historic combat, because
the pilots of the Lafayette Escadrille, which was stationed at
the field, were making the first French air fight against the
Germans since the armistice of 1940. The Escadrille, which
had been equipped with a number of our Curtiss P-40's in
Morocco, had been with us only a few days.

As we watched, a plane fell, apparently far on the other side
of a ridge of mountains near the field, and we yelled happily,
thinking it was a Messerschmitt. After the fight we were to
learn that it had been a P-40 with a French sergeant pilot.
Cochran kept up an expert running commentary on what all
the pilots were trying to do, but he frequently didn't know
which were French and which Germans. During the battle we
simultaneously watched and brushed our teeth. A couple of
the French planes landed on the field while the others were
still fighting, so we knew that they must have been shot up.
Finally, one group of planes above the field started away and
the others chased them, but the first planes simply outclimbed
their pursuers and left them behind; then there was no longer
any doubt about which were Messerschmitts and which were
Curtisses. One German plane remained over the field, at perhaps thirty thousand feet, even after the rest of the invaders
had disappeared. "That's what kills me," Cochran said, pointing to the lone plane. "There's that sucker stooging around
and casing the joint for a future job and he's so high nobody
can bother him." Finally the stooge, evidently having found
out all he wanted to know, took his leisurely departure.

A group of P-40's from one of the two American P-40
squadrons at the field rose to relieve the Lafayettes, and the
French planes came buzzing in like bees settling on a sugared
stick. In a few minutes Kostia Rozanoff, commandant of the
Escadrille, and his pilots had gathered in Léon's shack to discuss the fight. All of them had had combat experience in 1939

and 1940, but the engagement this morning had been the *rentrée*, and they were as excited as if they had never seen a Messerschmitt before. Despite the fact that they were old hands, Cochran said, they had fought recklessly, climbing up to meet the Messerschmitts instead of waiting until the Germans dived. "If they don't dive," Cochran had frequently warned his own pilots, "you just don't fight." The French pilots' ardor had got them a beating, for besides the pilot whom we had seen fall and who, Rozanoff said, had not bailed out and was quite certainly killed, the two planes that had landed during the combat were riddled and would be of no use except for salvage, and one of their pilots had been wounded. The Germans apparently had suffered no damage at all. Rozanoff, a chunky, blond man who gets his name, as well as his coloring and his high cheekbones, from his Russian ancestry, is thirty-seven and has a deep voice, like Chaliapin's. He said that the pilot who had been killed was his wing man and he could not understand how he had failed to see the Messerschmitt that had attacked him from the rear. "I cry him turn," Rozanoff kept saying. "I turn. He turns not. Poor little one."

It was extremely sad that the first Escadrille combat had not been a victory; it would have been such a fine story to bolster French morale all over the world. I remembered the sergeant pilot, who had been a likable fellow. An officer of the district gendarmerie brought the sergeant's wedding ring back to the field later in the morning.

My friend Norgaard and I had chosen that Friday for our departure from the field. We were going in to the big city, where the censors and the cable offices were, to write some stuff and get it off. There was air transportation between our field and the more settled places to the west, where staff officers and diplomats lived, but the service did not run on a formal schedule. Big Douglas transports skimmed in over the mountains once and sometimes twice a day, carrying mail and supplies, and they usually had room for passengers going back. They came at a different hour each day to make it as hard as possible for the Germans to waylay them. When they came, they stayed merely as long as was necessary, and the only way to be sure of a ride was to have your bedding roll made up and to stay near the landing field waiting for the transports to appear. When they did, an officer would drive you and your luggage out to them in a jeep and you would get your stuff aboard. Norgaard and I hung around in front of our shack that morning, waiting. As the day wore on, a strong wind came up and blew great clouds of sand. At about eleven o'clock two transports arrived, escorted by some Spitfires. Cochran had planned to drive us down to the transports, but he was called to the telephone, and Major Robert Christman, the C.O. of one P-40 squadron, said that he would drive us instead.

When we arrived where the transports were standing on the runway, the transport captain, whose name, I noted from the leather strip on the breast of his flying jacket, was Lively, came over to the jeep and asked where his Spits could get gas. His ship was named the Scarlett O'Hara. He and Christman started discussing what was the quickest way to get the gas. Christman and Norgaard and I stayed in the jeep. Dust was blowing over the field a mile a minute. Suddenly Christman looked over his shoulder, called on God, and vanished. Within a moment Lively was also gone. I turned around to speak to Norgaard, and discovered that he too had evaporated. I hate to sit in an empty jeep when I don't know why the other passengers have jumped. I do not remember actually getting out myself, but I know that I was already running when I heard somebody yell, "Hit the dirt!" Under the circumstances, this sounded so sensible that I bellyflopped to the ground, and I landed so hard that I skinned my knees and elbows. No surface in the world offers less cover than a runway. I regretted that my body, which is thick, was not thinner. I could guess what had happened: German strafers had ridden in on the dust storm and nobody had seen them until they opened fire. I knew that the very nasty noises above me were being made by airplane cannon and that the even nastier ones close to me came from the detonation of the small explosive shells they fire. The strafers, I figured, were heading for the transports—large, expensive, unarmored jobs that you could punch holes in with a beer-can opener. I was therefore in line with the target and was very sorry to be where I was.

As soon as there was a lull in the noises overhead, I got up and ran toward the edge of the runway to get away from the transports, but more noises came before I made it, so I flopped again. After they had passed, I got up and ran off the runway. I saw a soldier in a fine, large hole nearly six feet deep. He shouted, "Come right in, sir!" You can have Oscar of the Waldorf any time; I will always remember that soldier as my favorite host. I jumped in and squeezed up against him. Almost immediately the noises came a third time and two transport pilots jumped down on my back. I was astonished that I had been able to outrun such relatively young men.

By this time all of our machine guns along the edges of the field were firing away, and there was a fourth pass, as the fliers say, and a loud crash, as if one of the Germans had dropped a bomb. A minute or two later the noise began to die down. Looking up from the bottom of the hole, we could see a man descending in a parachute. The big, white chute was swaying this way and that in the wind. The man had an awful time landing. We could see that even from a distance. The chute dragged him and bounced hell out of him after he landed. Afterward, word got around the field that he was an American. I didn't find out until a couple of days later, though, that the man with the chute had been a fellow called Horse, a big, square-bearded, twenty-five-year-old Texan pilot I had come to know well. In landing, he hit his head against the ground and suffered a concussion of the brain. They put him in an ambulance and started for the nearest hospital, which was forty miles by road, but he had bad luck. The Germans had been strafing that road, too, that morning, and when the ambulance got within five miles of the hospital, it was blocked by two burning ammunition trucks. The shells on the trucks were exploding. The squadron surgeon and the ambulance-driver put Horse on a stretcher and carried him around the trucks to a safe point on the other side, and an ambulance from the hospital came out to pick him up, but by the time it got there he was dead.

When the shooting at the field was over, the pilots and the soldier and I got out of the hole and walked back toward the transports, which were still there. Norgaard climbed out of another hole not far away. He said that when he had jumped

out of the jeep he had crawled under it, and there he had
found a transport lieutenant who had had the same idea.
They had given up the jeep after the first pass and run for it,
just as I had already done. We stared at the parallel furrows
the Messerschmitt cannon had plowed down the runway, as if
they had been the teeth of a rake, and ourselves the field mice
between them. The transport boys borrowed our jeep to get
gas for the Spits, which had been immobilized during the raid
because their tanks were empty. When the boys came back,
we climbed into one of the transports. The big planes took
off almost immediately. "Leave them laughing," Norgaard
said to me when he recovered sufficient breath to say anything.

We learned later that the strafing had been done by eight
Messerschmitts flying in four loose pairs, and that was why
there had been four passes. Another Messerschmitt, making a
run by itself, had dropped one bomb, ineffectually. There had
also been a high cover of Messerschmitts; one of them had
accounted for Horse. We were told that Cochran had said,
with a hint of admiration in his voice, "It is getting so that
the Germans patrol our field for us." A lot of Air Forces generals who were on a tour of inspection visited the field shortly
after we left, said that the situation was very grave, and left,
too. This point in the war over the field may be compared to
the one in a Western movie at which the villain has kicked hell
out of the heroine and just about wrestled her to the brink of
ruin in a locked room.

At about two-thirty that same afternoon the Lafayette Escadrille was patrolling the field, in the company of two pilots
from the American P-40 squadron that was commanded by a
Major Hubbard. This squadron had its full complement of
pilots but only five planes. The pilots took turns flying the
five ships, so they were not getting a great deal of practice.
Nevertheless, Hubbard's squadron had already scored two
victories that week. The two American pilots in the air were
Hubbard and a man named Beggs. Two of their mates,
Boone and Smith, were on the ground on alert call, sitting in
their planes ready to reinforce the patrol if they were called.

This field didn't have one of those elaborate radio airplane-detectors that warn swank airdromes of the approach of enemy aircraft. It had to rely on its patrol system and on tips that watchers telephoned in. The tipsters were not infallible, as Norgaard and I had noticed that morning, and in the afternoon they slipped up again. Ten Junkers 88 bombers unexpectedly appeared, flying toward the field at three thousand feet. There was an escort of four fighters, unusually small for so many bombers, flying high above them and, as someone described it to me, acting oddly uninterested. The Frenchmen on patrol, also flying high, made one swipe at the escort and it disappeared, not to be seen again. Nine of the bombers were flying in three loose V's and one ship was trailing the third V. Hubbard took the bomber on the right of the first V and shot it down. Beggs got the middle one and a Frenchman knocked down the one on the left. The other Junkers had begun to drop their bombs. Boone and Smith came up off the field through the falling bombs to join the battle. Hubbard shot down another plane, and Boone, who had never fired a shot at a man or a plane before, came up behind one Junkers and blasted it out of the sky; it caromed against another Junkers on the way down, which gave Boone two planes with one burst of fire. He went on to destroy two more. Smith, opening fire at extreme range for fear that he would be shut out, blew the rudder off another Junkers, which also crashed. The tenth Junkers headed for home, but it never got there; the French picked off that one. It was the jack pot, ten out of ten. It was also the end of the five-day war over our airfield. No producer of Westerns ever wound up a film more satisfactorily. The Germans stayed away, in fact, for nineteen days and then came back only once, for a quick sneak raid.

Of the ten German bomber crews, only four men came out of the fight alive and two of these died in the hospital. The two others said that the ten bombers had been escorted by four Italian Macchi C. 202 fighters, which had deserted them. Why the Luftwaffe should have entrusted four Macchis with the protection of ten Junkers 88's is harder to explain than the result. The Germans, fortunately for our side, sometimes vary their extreme guile with extreme stupidity.

*   *   *

I didn't have a chance to return to the airfield for about ten days, and then I stopped in on my way down to Gafsa, where the Americans were supposed to be launching a ground offensive. Captain Wylie, who told me about the big day at the field, said that Boone had come into the operations shack looking rather incredulous himself. "Probably I'm crazy," he had said to Wylie, "but I think I just shot down four planes." The Frenchmen thought up a gag. They said it was a victory for three nations—"The Americans shot down seven planes, we shot down two, and the Italians shot down the tenth so the crew couldn't tell on them."

The Americans left the field undefeated, for the two P-40 squadrons were relieved not long afterward by other outfits and sent back from the fighting zone to rest. Christman's squadron had been fighting there steadily for two months. I met the fellows from Christman's bunch again while I was trying to get a ride into civilization from another airfield, a bit west of the one where they had been stationed. A lot of trucks drove up and deposited the officers and men of the squadron on the field, with their weapons, their barracks bags, and their bedding rolls. Christman was there, and Private Otto, the squadron barber, and Corporal Jake Goldstein, the reformed songwriter. I renewed my acquaintance with a pilot named Fackler, whom I remembered especially because he had once, finding himself flying formation with two Messerschmitts who thought he was another Messerschmitt, shot one of them down, and I again met Thomas, the Oklahoma boy who had been lost in the air one night and had been lighted home by the fire of the field's anti-aircraft guns, and a non-flying lieutenant named Lamb, who used to practice law in New York, and a dozen others. I felt as if I had known them all for a long time.

Eleven transports came in to take the squadron west, and I arranged to travel in one of them. I was in the lead ship of the flight, and the transport major who commanded it told me that his orders were to drop the squadron at a field only about an hour's flight away. Then the transports would go on to their base, taking me along with them. It was pleasant to see the faces of the P-40 boys aboard my transport when it took off. They didn't know anything about the field they were going to, but they knew that they were going for a rest, so they expected that there would at least be huts and showers there. They looked somewhat astonished when the transports settled down in a vast field of stubble without a sign of a building anywhere around it. There were a few B-25 bombers on the field and in the distance some tents. A transport sergeant came out of the pilot's compartment forward in our plane and worked his way toward the tail of our ship, climbing over the barracks bags heaped in the space between the seats. "I guess this is where you get out," he told the P-40 fellows.

A couple of soldiers jumped out and the rest began passing out bags and rifles to them. Pretty soon all the stuff was piled outside the plane and the soldiers were standing on the field, turning their backs to a sharp wind and audibly wondering where the hell the barracks were. A jeep with an officer in it drove out from among the tents and made its way among the transports until it arrived at our ship. The transport major talked to the officer in the jeep, and then they both drove over to the transport Christman was travelling in and picked him up, and the three of them drove back to the tents. Some soldiers who had been near the jeep had heard the field's officer say that nobody there had been notified that they were coming. The transport major had replied that all he knew was that he had orders to leave them there. The soldiers who had heard the conversation communicated the news to the others by Army telegraphy. "Situation normal!" one soldier called out, and everybody laughed. Soldiers are fatalistic about such situations.

Some time before a report had circulated among the men that the squadron was to go back to the United States. Now I heard one soldier say, "This don't look like no United States to me."

Another one said, "When we get back there, Freddie Bartholomew will be running for President." He didn't seem sore.

Somebody said, "I hear they're going to start us here and let us hack our way through to South Africa."

Somebody else began a descant on a favorite Army fantasy: what civilian life will be like after the war. "I bet if my wife gives me a piece of steak," he said, "I'll say to her, 'What the hell is this? Give me stew.'"

Another one said, "I bet she'll be surprised when you jump into bed with all your clothes on."

The delicacy of their speculations diminished from there on.

After a while the jeep came back. The transport major got out and said, "There seems to be some mistake. You'd better put your stuff back in the ship." We all got back into the planes, and the major told me that this obviously wasn't the place to leave the men but that he would have to wait until base operations could get headquarters on the telephone and find out their destination. We sat in the planes for an hour; then another officer came out in a jeep and said that nobody at headquarters knew anything about the squadron, so the major had better not take it any place else. The major told his sergeant to instruct the men to take their luggage off the planes. "We enjoy doing this. It's no trouble at all," one of the soldiers in my plane said. The transports took off and left them standing there. I learned later that they eventually got straightened out. After two or three days someone at headquarters remembered them; the pilots were sent to western Morocco and the ground echelon was moved to another field.

All this happened what seems now to be long ago, in the pioneer days of the American Army in Tunisia. The old field, from which I had watched the five-day war, was never knocked out from the air, but it was taken by German ground troops with tanks, and then the Americans took it back and went on. The Hotel Léon, if the Germans hadn't burned it, was certainly full of booby traps for the Americans when they got there. I shouldn't like to have slept in it. Léon is now in a large Algerian city, where he has been assigned to a calmer liaison job. Cochran has been promoted and decorated and posted to a new command. A lot of very fine fellows are dead, and I like to think that the best possible use was made of them.

The New Yorker, March 20, April 3, 10, 17, 1943

The War in Tunisia

by Ernie Pyle

"Now It Is Killing That Animates Them"

A FORWARD AIRDROME IN FRENCH NORTH AFRICA—(by wireless)—It is hard for a layman to understand the fine points of aerial combat as practiced at the moment in North Africa. It is hard even for the pilots themselves to keep up, for there are changes in tactics from week to week.

We will have some new idea and surprise Germans with it. Then they'll come across with a surprise maneuver, and we will have to change everything to counteract it.

But basically, at the moment, you can say that everything depends on teamwork. The lone dashing hero in this war is certain to be a dead hero within a week. Sticking with the team and playing it all together is the only guarantee of safety for everybody.

Our fighters go in groups with the bombers, ranging the sky above them, flying back and forth, watching for anything that may appear. But if they see some Germans in the distance nobody goes after them. That would be playing into the Germans' hands. So they stick to their formation above the bombers, making an umbrella.

The German has two choices—to dive down through them, or to wait until somebody is hit by flak and has to drop back. Then they are on him in a flash.

When that happens the fighters attack, but still in formation. Keeping that formation always and forever tight is what the flight leaders constantly drill into the boys' heads. It is a great temptation to dash out and take a shot at some fellow, but by now they've seen too many cases of the tragedy of such action.

The result is that this war doesn't have many individual air heroes. A team may be a composite hero, but not an individual.

One group leader told me: "If everything went according to schedule we'd never shoot down a German plane. We'd cover our bombers and keep ourselves covered and everybody would come home safe."

*   *   *

The fighter pilots seem a little different from the bomber men. Usually they are younger. Many of them were still in school when they joined up. Ordinarily they might be inclined to be more harum-scarum, but their work is so deadly, and the sobering dark cloud of personal tragedy is over them so constantly, that it seems to have humbled them. In fact I think it makes them nicer people than if they were cocky.

They have to get up early. Often I've gone to the room of my special friends at 9:30 in the evening and found them all asleep.

They fly so frequently they can't do much drinking. One night recently when one of the most popular fighter pilots was killed right on the home field, in an accident, some of them assuaged their grief with gin.

"Somehow you feel it more when it happens right here than when a fellow just doesn't come back," they said.

When they first came over here, you'd frequently hear pilots say they didn't hate the Germans, but you don't hear that any more. They have lost too many friends, too many roommates.

*   *   *

Now it is killing that animates them.

The highest spirits I've seen in that room were displayed one evening after they came back from a strafing mission. That's what they like to do best, but they get little of it. It's a great holiday from escorting bombers, which they hate. Going out free-lancing to shoot up whatever they see, and going in enough force to be pretty sure they'll be superior to the enemy—that's Utopia.

That's what they had done that day. And they really had a field day. They ran onto a German truck convoy and blew it to pieces. They'd laugh and get excited as they told about it.

The trucks were all full of men, and "they'd fly out like fire-crackers." Motorcyclists would get hit and dive 40 feet before they stopped skidding.

Two Messerschmitt 109s made the mistake of coming after our planes. They never had a chance. After firing a couple of wild bursts they went down smoking, and one of them seemed to blow up.

The boys were full of laughter when they told about it as they sat there on their cots in the dimly lighted room. I couldn't help having a funny feeling about them. They were all so young, so genuine, so enthusiastic. And they were so casual about everything—not casual in a hard, knowing way, but they talked about their flights and killing and being killed exactly as they would discuss girls or their school lessons.

Maybe they won't talk at all when they finally get home. If they don't it will be because they know this is a world apart and nobody else could ever understand.

Scripps-Howard wire copy, February 9, 1943

"Moving at Night in Total Blackness"

AT THE FRONT IN TUNISIA—(by wireless)—A big military convoy moving at night across the mountains and deserts of Tunisia is something that nobody who has been in one can ever forget.

Recently I have been living with a front-line outfit. Late one afternoon it received sudden orders to move that night, bag and baggage. It had to pull out of its battle positions, time the departures of its various units to fit into the flow of traffic at the first control point on the highway, and then drive all night and go into action on another front.

All the big convoys in the war area move at night. German planes would spot a daytime convoy and play havoc with it.

It is extremely difficult and dangerous, this moving at night in total blackness over strange and rough roads. But it has to be done.

Our convoy was an immense one. There were hundreds of vehicles and thousands of men. It took seven and a half hours to pass one point.

The convoy started moving at 5:30 in the evening, just before dusk. The last vehicle didn't clear till 1 o'clock the next morning.

*   *   *

I rode in a jeep with Capt. Pat Riddleberger, of Woodstock, Va., and Pvt. John Coughlin, Manchester, N.H. Ahead of us was a small covered truck which belonged to Riddleberger's tank-destroyer section. We were a little two-vehicle convoy within ourselves.

We were to fall in near the tail end, so we had half the night to kill before starting. We stood around the truck, parked in a barnlot, for an hour or two, just talking in the dark. Then we went into the kitchen of the farmhouse which had been used as a command post and which was empty now.

There was an electric light, and we built a fire in the kitchen fireplace out of boxes. But the chimney wouldn't draw, and we almost choked from the smoke.

Some officers had left a stack of copies of the *New York Times* for October and November lying on the floor, so we read those for an hour or so. We looked at the book sections and the movie ads. None of us had ever heard of the new books or the current movies. It made us feel keenly how long we had been away and how cut off we were from home.

"They could make money just showing all the movies over again for a year after we get back," one of the boys said.

We finished the papers and there were still three hours to kill, so we got blankets out of the truck and lay down on the concrete floor. We were sleeping soundly when Captain Riddleberger awakened us at 1 a.m. and said we were off.

The moon was just coming out. The sky was crystal-clear, and the night bitter cold. The jeep's top was down.

We all put on all the clothes we had. In addition to my usual polar-bear wardrobe, which includes heavy underwear and two sweaters, I wore that night a pair of coveralls, a heavy combat suit that a tank man lent me, a pair of overshoes, two caps—one on top of the other—and over them a pair of goggles. And all three of us in the jeep wrapped up in blankets.

In spite of all that, we almost froze before the night was over.

*   *   *

We moved out of the barnlot, and half a mile away we swung onto the main road, at the direction of motorcyclists who stood there guiding the traffic.

Gradually our eyes grew accustomed to the half-darkness, and it wasn't hard to follow the road. We had orders to drive in very close formation, so we kept within 50 feet of each other.

*   *   *

After a few miles we had to cross over a mountain range. There were steep grades and switchback turns, and some of the trucks had to back and fill to make the sharper turns.

There was considerable delay on the mountain. French trucks and busses would pass and tie up traffic, swinging in and out. And right in the center of these tortuous mountains we met a huge American hospital unit, in dozens of trucks, moving up to the front. They were on the outside of the road, and at times their wheels seemed about to slide off into the chasm.

We had long waits while traffic jams ahead were cleared. We would shut off our motors and the night would be deathly silent except for a subdued undertone of grinding motors far ahead. At times we could hear great trucks groaning in low gear on steep grades far below, or the angry clanking of tanks as they took sharp turns behind us.

Finally the road straightened out on a high plateau. There we met a big contingent of French troops moving silently toward the front we had just vacated. The marching soldiers seemed like dark ghosts in the night. Hundreds of horses were carrying their artillery, ammunition and supplies.

I couldn't help feeling the immensity of the catastrophe that has put men all over the world, millions of us, to moving in machinelike precision throughout long foreign nights— men who should be comfortably asleep in their own warm beds at home.

War makes strange giant creatures out of us little routine men who inhabit the earth.

Scripps-Howard wire copy, February 16, 1943

"Only Slightly Above the Caveman Stage"

THE TUNISIAN FRONT—(by wireless)—It must be hard for you folks at home to conceive how our troops right at the front actually live. In fact it is hard to describe it to you even when I'm among them, living in somewhat the same way they are.

You can scarcely credit the fact that human beings—the same people you've known all your life—could adjust themselves so acceptingly to a type of living that is only slightly above the caveman stage.

*   *   *

Some of our troops came directly to the Tunisian front after the original occupation of North and West Africa, and have been here ever since. They have not slept in a bed for months. They've lived through this vicious winter sleeping outdoors on the ground. They haven't been paid in three months. They have been on British rations most of the time, and British rations, though good, get mighty tiresome.

They never take off their clothes at night, except their shoes. They don't get a bath oftener than once a month. One small detachment acquired lice and had to be fumigated, but all the rest have escaped so far. They move so frequently they don't attempt to put in many home touches, as the men do at the more permanent camps toward the rear. Very few of the front-line troops have ever had any leave. They never go to town for an evening's fun. They work all the time.

Nobody keeps track of the days or weeks. I'll wager that 90% of our frontline troops never know when Sunday comes.

Furthermore, the old traditional differences between day and night have almost ceased to exist. Nighttime no longer necessarily means rest, nor daytime work. Often it's just reversed. The bulk of our convoying of supplies and shifting of troops is done at night. The soldiers are accustomed to traveling all night, sometimes three or four nights in a row.

Irregularity of sleep becomes normal. One soldier told me he once went three days and nights without sleep.

You see men sleeping anywhere, anytime. The other day I saw a soldier asleep in blankets under an olive tree at 2 in the afternoon. A few feet away a full colonel was sleeping soundly on the ground. In battle you just go until you drop.

It isn't always possible to get enough food up to the fighting soldiers. I have just been with one artillery outfit in the mountains who were getting only one cold meal a day.

Nurses tell me that when the more seriously wounded reach the hospital they are often so exhausted they fall asleep without drugs, despite their pain.

*   *   *

The war coarsens most people. You live rough and talk rough, and if you didn't toughen up inside you simply wouldn't be able to take it. An officer friend of mine, Lieut. Lennie Bessman of Milwaukee, was telling me two incidents of a recent battle that touched him deeply.

One evening he and another officer came up to a tiny farmhouse, which was apparently empty. To be on the safe side he called out "Who's there?" before going in. The answer came back:

"Captain Blank, and who the hell wants to know?"

They went in and found the captain, his clothes covered with blood, heating a can of rations over a gasoline flame. They asked if they could stay all night with him. He said he didn't give a damn. They started to throw their blankets down, and the captain said:

"Look out for that man over there."

There was a dead soldier lying in a corner.

The captain was cooking his supper and preparing to stay all night alone in that same room. The flood and fury of death about him that day had left him utterly indifferent both to the companionship of the living and the presence of the dead.

The other incident was just the opposite. Another captain happened to be standing beside Bessman. It was just at dusk and they were on the desert. The night chill was coming down. The captain looked to the far horizon and said, sort of to himself:

"You fight all day here in the desert and what's the end of it all? Night just closes down over you and chokes you."

A little later Bessman got out a partly filled bottle of gin he had with him and asked this same sensitive captain if he'd like a drink. The captain didn't even reach out his hand. He simply answered:

"Have you got enough for my men too?"

He wouldn't take a drink himself unless the enlisted men under him could have some.

All officers are not like that, but the battlefield does produce a brotherhood. The common bond of death draws humans toward each other over the artificial barrier of rank.

Scripps-Howard wire copy, February 19, 1943

"Too Little to Work With, As Usual"

AT THE TUNISIAN FRONT—(by wireless)—You folks at home must be disappointed at what happened to our American troops in Tunisia. So are we over here.

Our predicament is damned humiliating, as Gen. Joe Stilwell said about our getting kicked out of Burma a year ago. We've lost a great deal of equipment, many American lives, and valuable time and territory—to say nothing of face. Yet no one over here has the slightest doubt that the Germans will be thrown out of Tunisia. It is simply in the cards.

It is even possible that our defeat may not even delay Rommel's exodus, for actually our troops formed only a small part of the total Allied forces in Tunisia. Estimates among men at the front run anywhere from two to six months for finishing the Tunisian campaign.

One thing you folks at home must realize is that this Tunisian business is mainly a British show. Our part in it is small. Consequently our defeat is not as disastrous to the whole picture as it would have been had we had been bearing the major portion of the task.

We Americans did the North African landings and got all the credit, although the British did help us. The British are doing the Tunisia job and will get the credit, though we are giving them a hand. That's the way it has been planned all the time. That's the way it will be carried out.

When the time comes the British 1st Army will squeeze on the north, the British 8th Army will squeeze on the south, and we will hold in the middle. And it will really be the British who will run Rommel out of Tunisia.

The fundamental cause of our trouble over here lies in two things: we had too little to work with, as usual, and we underestimated Rommel's strength and especially his audacity.

Both military men and correspondents knew we were too thinly spread in our sector to hold if the Germans were really to launch a big-scale attack. Where everybody was wrong was in believing they didn't have the stuff to do it with.

Correspondents are not now permitted to write anything critical concerning the Tunisian situation, or to tell what we think was wrong. The powers that be feel that this would be bad for "home morale." So you just have to trust that our forces are learning to do better next time.

Personally, I feel that some such setback as this—tragic though it is for many Americans, for whom it is now too late—is not entirely a bad thing for us. It is all right to have a good opinion of yourself, but we Americans are so smug with our cockiness. We somehow feel that just because we're Americans we can whip our weight in wildcats. And we have got it into our heads that production alone will win the war.

There are two things we must learn, and we may be learning them right now—we must spread ourselves thicker on the front lines, and we must streamline our commands for quick and positive action in emergencies.

*   *   *

As for our soldiers themselves, you need feel no shame nor concern about their ability. I have seen them in battle and afterwards and there is nothing wrong with the common American soldier. His fighting spirit is good. His morale is okay. The deeper he gets into a fight the more of a fighting man he becomes.

I've seen crews that have had two tanks shot out from under them but whose only thought was to get a third tank and "have another crack at them blankety-blanks."

It is true they are not such seasoned battle veterans as

the British and Germans. But they had had some battle experience before this last encounter, and I don't believe their so-called greenness was the cause of our defeat. One good man simply can't whip two good men. That's about the only way I know to put it. Everywhere on every front we simply have got to have more stuff before we start going forward instead of backward.

I happened to be in on the Battle of Sbeitla, where we fought the German break-through for four days before withdrawing. In the next few days I shall try to describe to you what it was like.

Scripps-Howard wire copy, February 23, 1943

"Overrun Before They Knew What Was Happening"

THE TUNISIAN FRONT, Feb. 24—(by wireless)—On the morning the big German push started against the American troops in Tunisia, our forward command post in that area was hidden in a patch of cactus about a mile from the town of Sidi bou Zid.

It had been there more than a week, and I had visited there myself only three days previously. I had spent a lot of time with our forward troops in the hills, and I knew most of the officers.

A command post is really the headquarters of a unit. In this case a brigadier general was in command. His staff included intelligence and planning officers, unit commanders, a medical detachment, kitchens and various odds and ends.

A command post of this size has several score vehicles and two or three hundred men. Its work is all done in trucks, half-tracks or tents. It is always prepared to move, when at the front. And it does move every few days, so the enemy won't spot it.

This special command post was about ten miles back from the nearest known enemy position. Our artillery and infantry and some tanks were between it and the enemy.

I am describing all this because I will use the men of this command post as characters in our story as I try to picture the tragedy of that first day's surprise push.

That Sunday morning hordes of German tanks and troops came swarming out from behind the mountains around Faid Pass. We didn't know so many tanks were back there, and didn't know so many Germans were either, for our patrols had been bringing in mostly Italian prisoners from their raids.

The attack was so sudden nobody could believe it was in full force. Our forward troops were overrun before they knew what was happening. The command post itself didn't start moving back till after lunch. By then it was too late—or almost too late.

Command cars, half tracks and jeeps started west across the fields of semi-cultivated desert, for by then the good road to the north was already cut off. The column had moved about eight miles when German tanks came charging in upon the helpless vehicles from both sides.

A headquarters command post is not heavily armed. It has little to fight back with. All that these men and cars could do was duck and dodge and run like hell. There was no such thing as a fighting line. Everything was mixed up over an area of ten miles or more.

It was a complete melee. Every jeep was on its own. The accompanying tanks fought till knocked out, and their crews then got out and moved along on foot. One tank commander whose whole crew escaped after the tank caught fire said that at least the Germans didn't machine-gun them when they jumped from the burning tank.

Practically every vehicle reported gasoline trouble that afternoon. Apparently there was water in the gas, yet nobody feels that it was sabotage. They say there had been similar trouble before, but never so bad.

A friend of mine, Maj. Ronald Elkins, of College Station, Tex., had his half-track hit three times by German shells. They were standing still, cleaning a carburetor filter, when the third shell hit. It set them afire. Some of the crew eventually got back safely, but others are still missing. Major Elkins said they could have got clear back with the car "if the damned engine had only kept running."

The Germans just overran our troops that afternoon. They used tanks, artillery, infantry, and planes divebombing our troops continuously. Our artillery was run over in the first rush. We were swamped, scattered, consumed, by the German surprise.

Twilight found our men and machines straggling over an area extending some ten miles back of Sidi bou Zid. Darkness saved those that were saved.

During the night the command post assembled what was left of itself in another cactus patch about 15 miles behind its first position. Throughout the night, and for days afterward, tired men came straggling in from the desert afoot.

That night the Germans withdrew from the area they'd taken, and next morning we sent trucks back to bury the dead and tow out what damaged vehicles they could. But by next afternoon the battle was on again.

Scripps-Howard wire copy, February 24, 1943

"Nothing To Do"

THE TUNISIAN FRONT, Feb. 26 — (by wireless) — On the morning of the Germans' surprise break-through out of Faid Pass, I was up in the Ousseltia Valley with another contingent of our troops.

Word came to us about noon that the Germans were advancing upon Sbeitla from Faid. So I packed into my jeep and started alone on the familiar 85-mile drive south to Sbeitla. It was a bright day and everything seemed peaceful. I expected to see German planes as I neared Sbeitla, but there were none, and I drove into my cactus-patch destination about an hour before sundown.

I hadn't been there 15 minutes when the dive-bombers came, but that's another story, which will come later.

I checked in at the intelligence tent to see what was going on, and found that things were dying down with the coming of dusk. So I pitched my tent and went to bed right after supper.

Next morning I got up before daylight and caught a ride, just after sunrise, with two officers going up to the new position of our forward command post. We drove very slowly, and all kept a keen eye on the sky. I didn't have a gun, as correspondents are not supposed to carry arms. Occasionally we stopped the jeep and got far off the road behind some cactus hedges, but the German dive bombers were interested only in our troop concentrations far ahead.

Finally we spotted a small cactus patch about half a mile off the road. We figured this was the new home of the forward command post, and it was. They had straggled in during the night and were still straggling in.

The cactus patch covered about two acres. In it were hidden half a dozen half-tracks, a couple of jeeps, three light tanks and a couple of motorcycles—all that was left of the impressive array of the traveling headquarters that had fled Sidi bou Zid 18 hours before.

The commanding general had already gone forward again, in a tank, to participate in the day's coming battle. The remainder of the command post were just sitting around on the ground. Half of their comrades were missing. There was nothing left for them to work with, nothing to do.

When I came into this cactus patch the officers that I knew, and had left only four days before, jumped up and shook hands as though we hadn't seen each other in years. Enlisted men did the same thing.

I thought this was odd, at first, but now I know how they felt. They had been away—far along on the road that doesn't come back—and now that they were still miraculously alive it was like returning from a voyage of many years, and naturally you shook hands.

During the next few hours there in the cactus patch I listened to dozens of personal escape stories. Every time I would get within earshot of another officer or enlisted man he'd begin telling what had happened to him the day before.

Talk about having to pull stories out of people—you couldn't keep these guys from talking. There was something pathetic and terribly touching about it. Not one of them had ever thought he'd see this dawn, and now that he had seen it his emotions had to pour out. And since I was the only newcomer to show up since their escape, I made a perfect sounding board.

The minute a man would start talking he'd begin drawing lines on the ground with his shoe or a stick, to show the roads and how he came. I'll bet I had that battleground scratched in the sand for me fifty times during the forenoon. It got so I could hardly keep from laughing at the consistency of their patterns.

That morning should have been by all rights a newspaper-man's dream. There were fantastic stories of escape, intimate recountings of fear and elation. Any one of them would have made a first-page feature story in any newspaper. Yet I was defeated by the flood of experiences. I listened until the stories finally became merged, overlapping and paralleling and contradicting until the whole adventure became a composite, and today it is in my mind as in theirs a sort of generalized blur.

The sun came out warmly as though to soothe their jagged feelings, and one by one the men in the cactus patch stretched on the ground and fell wearily asleep at mid-day. And I, satiated with the adventures of the day before, lay down and slept too, waiting for the day's new battle to begin.

Scripps-Howard wire copy, February 26, 1943

"What a Tank Battle Looks Like"

THE TUNISIAN FRONT, March 1 — (By wireless) — This and the next few columns will be an attempt to describe what a tank battle looks like.

Words will be poor instruments for it. Neither can isolated camera shots tell you the story. Probably only Hollywood with its machinery of many dimensions is capable of transferring to your senses a clear impression of a tank battle.

The fight in question was the American counter attack on the second day of the battle at Sidi Bou Zid which eventually resulted in our withdrawal.

It was the biggest tank battle fought so far in this part of the world. On that morning I had a talk with the commanding general some 10 miles behind the front lines before starting for the battle scene.

He took me into his tent and showed me just what the

battle plan was for the day. He picked out a point close to the expected battle area and said that would be a good place for me to watch from.

The only danger, he said, would be one of being encircled and cut off if the battle should go against us.

"But it won't," he said, "for we are going to kick hell out of them today and we've got the stuff to do it with."

Unfortunately, we didn't kick hell out of them. In fact the boot was on the other foot.

I spent the forenoon in the newly picked, badly shattered forward command post. All morning I tried to get on up where the tanks were but there was no transportation left around the post and their communications were cut off at noontime.

We sat on the ground and ate some British crackers with jam and drank some hot tea. The day was bright and mellow. Shortly after lunch a young Lieutenant dug up a spare jeep and said he'd take me on up to the front.

We drove a couple of miles east along a highway to a crossroads which was the very heart center of our troops' bivouacks. German airmen had been after this crossroads all morning. They had hit it again just a few minutes before we got there. In the road was a large crater and a few yards away a tank was off to one side, burning.

The roads at that point were high and we could see a long way. In every direction was a huge semi-irrigated desert valley. It looked very much like the valley at Phoenix, Ariz.—no trees but patches of wild growth, shoulder-high cactus of the prickly pear variety. In other parts of the valley were spotted cultivated fields and tiny square stucco houses of Arab farmers. The whole vast scene was treeless, with slightly rolling big mountains in the distance.

As far as you could see out across the rolling desert in all four sections of the "pie" formed by the intersecting roads was American equipment—tanks, half tracks, artillery, infantry—hundreds, yes, thousands of vehicles extending miles and miles and everything standing still. We were in time; the battle had not yet started.

We put our jeep in super low gear and drove out across the

sands among the tanks. Ten miles or so east and southeast were the Germans but there was no activity anywhere, no smoke on the horizon, no planes in the sky.

It all had the appearance of an after-lunch siesta but no one was asleep.

As we drove past tank after tank we found each one's crew at its post inside—the driver at his control, the commander standing with his head sticking out of the open turret door, standing there silent and motionless, just looking ahead like the Indian on the calendars.

We stopped and inquired of several what they were doing. They said they didn't know what the plan was—they were merely ready in place and waiting for orders. Somehow it seemed like the cars lined up at Indianapolis just before the race starts—their weeks of training over, everything mechanically perfect, just a few quiet minutes of immobility before the great struggle for which they had waited so long.

Suddenly out of this siesta-like doze the order came. We didn't hear it for it came to the tanks over their radios but we knew it quickly for all over the desert tanks began roaring and pouring out blue smoke from the cylinders. Then they started off, kicking up dust and clanking in that peculiar "tank sound" we have all come to know so well.

They poured around us, charging forward. They weren't close together—probably a couple of hundred yards apart. There weren't lines or any specific formation. They were just everywhere. They covered the desert to the right and left, ahead and behind as far as we could see, trailing their eager dust tails behind. It was almost as though some official starter had fired his blank pistol. The battle was on.

(Continued tomorrow)

Scripps-Howard wire copy, March 1, 1943

"The Fantastic Surge of Caterpillar Metal"

THE TUNISIAN FRONT, March 2. —(By Wireless)—We were in the midst of the forward rushing tanks, but didn't know what the score was. So I pulled the jeep to the side, gradually easing a way out.

We decided to get to a high spot and take a look at what was happening, before we got caught. So we bounced over gullies and ditches, up the side of a rocky hill.

There—in a hidden gully—we found the commanding colonel, standing beside a radio half-track. We stood close enough to the radio to hear the voice of the battalion commander, who was leading the tank attack. At the same time, through binoculars, we watched the fantastic surge of caterpillar metal move forward amidst its own dust.

Far across the desert, in front of us, lay the town of Sidi bou Zid. Through the glasses we could see it only as a great oasis whose green trees stood out against the bare brown of the desert. On beyond were high hills, where some of our troops were still trapped after the surprise attack of the day before.

Behind our tanks, leading the attack, other armored vehicles puffed blue smoke. New formations began to move forward swiftly. The artillery went first, followed by armored infantry in half-tracks and even in jeeps. Now the entire desert was surging in one gigantic movement.

Over the radio came the voice of the battalion commander:

"We're in the edge of Sidi bou Zid, and have struck no opposition yet." So our tanks were across the vast plain, which the Germans had abandoned during the night—after the chaos of the previous day.

This peaceful report from our tank charge brought no comment from any one around the command truck. Faces were grave: It wasn't right—this business of no opposition at all; there must be a trick in it somewhere . . .

Suddenly, brown geysers of earth and smoke began to spout. We watched through our glasses. Then, from far off, came the sound of explosions.

Again the voice from the radio:

"We're getting shelled, but can't make out where it's coming from." Then a long silence, while the geysers continued to burst . . .

"I'm not sure, but I think it's artillery along the road north of town . . . Now there is some from the south."

We looked, and could see through our glasses the enemy advancing. They were far away, perhaps 10 miles—narrow

little streaks of dust, like plumes, speeding down the low slop-
ing plain from the mountain base toward the oasis of Sidi bou
Zid.

We could not see the German tanks, only dust plumes extending and pushing forward.

Just then I realized we were standing on the very hill the
general had picked out for me on his map that morning. It
was not good enough. I said to the young lieutenant:

"Let's get on up there." He replied: "I'm ready."

So we got into the jeep, and went leaping and bounding up
toward what was—but we didn't know it then—the most
ghastly armored melee that has occurred so far in Tunisia.

(Continued tomorrow)

Scripps-Howard wire copy, March 2, 1943

"Into the Thick of Battle"

THE TUNISIAN FRONT, March 3—(By Wireless)—It was
odd, the way we went up into the thick of the battle in our
jeep. We didn't attach ourselves to anybody. We didn't ask
anybody if we could go. We just started the motor and
went.

Vehicles ahead of us had worn a sort of track across the
desert and through irrigated fields. We followed that awhile,
keeping our place in the forward-moving procession. We were
just a jeep with two brown-clad figures in it, indistinguishable
from anyone else.

The line was moving cautiously. Every now and then the
procession would stop. A few times we stopped too. We shut
off our motor to listen for planes. But, finally, we tired of the
slow progress. We dashed out across the sand and the Arabs'
plowed fields, skirting cactus fences and small farmyards.

As we did this, a sensation of anxiety—which had not
touched me before—came over me. It was fear of mines in
the freshly dug earth; the touch of the wheel—we could so
easily be blown into little bits. I spoke of this to the lieutenant, but he said he didn't think they had had time to plant
mines.

I thought to myself: "Hell, it doesn't take all night to plant a mine." We did not—it is obvious to report—hit any mines.

The battlefield was an incongruous thing. Always there is some ridiculous impingement of normalcy on a field of battle.

Here on this day were the Arabs. They were herding their camels, just as usual. Some of them continued to plow their fields. Children walked along, driving their little sack-ladden burros, as tanks and guns clanked past them. The sky was filled with planes and smoke bursts from screaming shells.

As we smashed along over a field of new grain, which pushed its small shoots just a few inches above earth, the asinine thought popped into my head: "I wonder if the Army got permission to use this land before starting the attack."

Both sides had crossed and recrossed these farms in the past 24 hours. The fields were riddled by deep ruts and by wide spooky tracks of the almost mythical Mark VI. tanks.

Evidence of the previous day's battle was still strewn across the desert. We passed charred half-tracks. We stopped to look into a burned-out tank, named Temes, from which a Lieut. Colonel friend of mine and his crew had demolished four German tanks before being put out of commission themselves.

We passed a trailer still full of American ammunition, which had been abandoned. The young lieutenant wanted to hook our own jeep to it as a tow when we returned, but I talked him out of it. I feared the Germans had booby-trapped it during the night.

We moved on closer to the actual tank battle ahead, but never went right into it—for in a jeep that would have been a fantastic form of suicide. We stopped, I should judge, about a mile behind the foremost tanks.

Behind us the desert was still alive with men and machines moving up. Later we learned that some German tanks had maneuvered in behind us, and were shooting up our half-tracks and jeeps. But, fortunately, we didn't know all this at the time.

Light American tanks came up from the rear and stopped near us. They were to be held there in reserve, in case they had to be called into the game in this league which was much too heavy and hot for them. Their crews jumped out the moment they stopped, and began digging foxholes against the inevitable arrival of the dive bombers.

Soon the dive bombers came. They set fires behind us. American and German tanks were burning ahead of us.

Our planes came over, too, strafing and bombing the enemy.

One of our half-tracks, full of ammunition, was livid red, with flames leaping and swaying. Every few seconds one of its shells would go off, and the projectile would tear into the sky with a weird whang-zing sort of noise.

Field artillery had stopped just on our right. They began shelling the German artillery beyond our tanks. It didn't take long for the Germans to answer.

The scream of an approaching shell is an appalling thing. We could hear them coming — (You sort of duck inside yourself, without actually ducking at all).

Then we could see the dust kick up a couple of hundred yards away. The shells hit the ground and ricocheted like armor-piercing shells, which do not explode but skip along the ground until they finally lose momentum or hit something.

War has its own peculiar sounds. They are not really very much different from sounds in the world of peace. But they clothe themselves in an unforgettable fierceness, just because born in danger and death.

The clank of a starting tank, the scream of a shell through the air, the ever-rising whine of fiendishness as a bomber dives — these sounds have their counterparts in normal life, and you would be hard put to distinguish them in a blindfold test. But, once heard in war, they remain with you forever.

Their nervous memories come back to you in a thousand ways — in the grind of a truck starting in low gear, in high wind around the eaves, in somebody merely whistling a tune. Even the sound of a shoe, dropped to the floor in a hotel room above you, becomes indistinguishable from the faint boom of a big gun far away. A mere rustling curtain can paralyze a man with memories.

Scripps-Howard wire copy, March 3, 1943

"Brave Men. Brave Men!"

NORTHERN TUNISIA—(by wireless)—I was away from the front lines for a while this spring, living with other troops, and considerable fighting took place while I was gone. When I got ready to return to my old friends at the front I wondered if I would sense any change in them.

I did, and definitely.

The most vivid change is the casual and workshop manner in which they now talk about killing. They have made the psychological transition from the normal belief that taking human life is sinful, over to a new professional outlook where killing is a craft. To them now there is nothing morally wrong about killing. In fact it is an admirable thing.

I think I am so impressed by this new attitude because it hasn't been necessary for me to make this change along with them. As a noncombatant, my own life is in danger only by occasional chance or circumstance. Consequently I need not think of killing in personal terms, and killing to me is still murder.

Even after a winter of living with wholesale death and vile destruction, it is only spasmodically that I seem capable of realizing how real and how awful this war is. My emotions seem dead and crusty when presented with the tangibles of war. I find I can look on rows of fresh graves without a lump in my throat. Somehow I can look on mutilated bodies without flinching or feeling deeply.

It is only when I sit alone away from it all, or lie at night in my bedroll re-creating with closed eyes what I have seen, thinking and thinking and thinking, that at last the enormity of all these newly dead strikes like a living nightmare. And there are times when I feel that I can't stand it and will have to leave.

* * *

But to the fighting soldier that phase of the war is behind. It was left behind after his first battle. His blood is up. He is fighting for his life, and killing now for him is as much a profession as writing is for me.

He wants to kill individually or in vast numbers. He wants to see the Germans overrun, mangled, butchered in the Tunisian trap. He speaks excitedly of seeing great heaps of dead, of our bombers sinking whole shiploads of fleeing men, of Germans by the thousands dying miserably in a final Tunisian holocaust of his own creation.

In this one respect the front-line soldier differs from all the rest of us. All the rest of us—you and me and even the thousands of soldiers behind the lines in Africa—we want terribly yet only academically for the war to get over. The front-line soldier wants it to be got over by the physical process of his destroying enough Germans to end it. He is truly at war. The rest of us, no matter how hard we work, are not.

*   *   *

Say what you will, nothing can make a complete soldier except battle experience.

In the semifinals of this campaign—the cleaning out of Central Tunisia—we had large units in battle for the first time. Frankly, they didn't all excel. Their own commanders admit it, and admirably they don't try to alibi. The British had to help us out a few times, but neither American nor British commanders are worried about that, for there was no lack of bravery. There was only lack of experience. They all know we will do better next time.

The First Infantry Division is an example of what our American units can be after they have gone through the mill of experience. Those boys did themselves proud in the semifinals. Everybody speaks about it. Our casualties included few taken prisoners. All the other casualties were wounded or died fighting.

"They never gave an inch," a general says. "They died right in their foxholes."

I heard of a high British officer who went over this battlefield just after the action was over. American boys were still lying dead in their foxholes, their rifles still grasped in firing position in their dead hands. And the veteran English soldier remarked time and again, in a sort of hushed eulogy spoken only to himself:

"Brave men. Brave men!"

Scripps-Howard wire copy, April 22, 1943

"Little Boys Again, Lost in the Dark"

NORTHERN TUNISIA—(By wireless)—We moved one afternoon to a new position just a few miles behind the invisible line of armor that separates us from the Germans in Northern Tunisia. Nothing happened that first night that was spectacular, yet somehow the whole night became obsessed with a spookiness that leaves it standing like a landmark in my memory.

We had been at the new camp about an hour and were still setting up our tents when German planes appeared overhead. We stopped work to watch them. It was the usual display of darting planes, with the conglomerate sounds of ack-ack on the ground and in the sky.

Suddenly we realized that one plane was diving straight at us, and we made a mad scramble for foxholes. Two officer friends of mine had dug a three-foot hole and set their tent over it. So they made for their tent, and I was tramping on their heels. The tent flap wouldn't come open, and we wound up in a silly heap. Finally it did open, and we all dived through the narrow opening all at once.

We lay there in the hole, face down, as the plane came smack overhead with a terrible roar. We were all drawn up inside, waiting for the blow. Explosions around us were shatteringly loud, and yet when it was all over we couldn't find any bomb holes or anybody hurt.

But you could find a lot of nervous people.

*   *   *

Dusk came on, and with dusk began the steady boom of big guns in the mountains ahead of us. They weren't near enough for the sound to be crashing. Rather it was like the lonely roll of an approaching thunderstorm—a sound which since childhood has always made me sad with a kind of portent of inevitable doom.

We went to bed in our tents. A nearby farmyard was full of dogs and they began a howling that lasted all night. The roll of artillery was constant. It never stopped once in 24 hours. Once in a while there were nearer shots which might have been German patrols or might not.

We lay uneasily in our cots. Sleep wouldn't come. We turned and turned. I snapped on a flashlight.

"What time is it?" asked Chris Cunningham from the next cot.

"Quarter to one," I answered. "Haven't you been asleep?"

He hadn't.

A plane droned faintly in the distance and came nearer and nearer until it was overhead.

"Is that a Jerry or a Beaufighter," Chris asked out of the darkness.

"It hasn't got that throb-throb to it," I said, "so it must be a Beaufighter. But hell, I never can tell really. Don't know what it is."

The plane passed on, out of hearing. The artillery rolled and rolled. A nearer shot went off uncannily somewhere in the darkness. Some guinea hens set up a terrific cackling.

I remembered that just before dusk a soldier had shot at a snake in our new camp, and they thought it was a cobra. We'd just heard our first stories of scorpions, too. I began to feel creepy and wondered if our tent flaps were tight.

Another plane throbbed in the sky, and we lay listening with an awful anticipation. One of the dogs suddenly broke into a frenzied barking and went tearing through our little camp as though chasing a demon.

My mind seemed to lose all sense of proportion, and I was jumpy and mad at myself.

Concussion ghosts, traveling in waves, touched our tent walls and made them quiver. Ghosts were shaking the ground ever so lightly. Ghosts were stirring the dogs to hysteria. Ghosts were wandering in the sky peering for us in our cringing hideout. Ghosts were everywhere, and their hordes were multiplying as every hour added its production of new battlefield dead.

You lie and think of the graveyards and the dirty men and the shocking blast of the big guns, and you can't sleep.

"What time is it?" comes out of darkness from the next cot. I snap on the flashlight.

"Half past 4, and for God's sake go to sleep!"

Finally just before dawn you do sleep, in spite of everything.

*   *   *

Next morning we spoke around among ourselves and found one by one that all us had tossed away all night. It was an unexplainable thing. For all of us had been through dangers greater than this. On another night the roll of the guns would have lulled us to sleep.

It's just that on some nights the air becomes sick and there is an unspoken contagion of spiritual dread, and you are little boys again, lost in the dark.

Scripps-Howard wire copy, April 27, 1943

"The Greatest Damage Is Psychological"

AT THE FRONT LINES IN TUNISIA—(by wireless)—When our infantry goes into a big push in northern Tunisia each man is issued three bars of D-ration chocolate, enough to last one day. He takes no other food.

He carries two canteens of water instead of the usual one. He carries no blankets. He leaves behind all extra clothes except his raincoat. In his pockets he may have a few toilet articles. Some men carry their money. Others give it to friends to keep.

In the days that follow they live in a way that is inconceivable to us at home. They walk and fight all night without sleep. Next day they lie flat in foxholes, or hide in fields of freshly green, kneehigh wheat.

If they're in the fields they dare not even move enough to dig foxholes, for that would bring the German artillery. They can't rise even for nature's calls. The German feels for them continually with his artillery.

*   *   *

The slow drag of these motionless daylight hours is nearly unendurable. Lieut. Mickey Miller of Morgantown, Ind., says this lifeless waiting in a wheatfield is almost the worst part of the whole battle.

The second evening after the attack begins, C-rations and five-gallon cans of water are brought up across country in jeeps, after dark. You eat in the dark, and you can't see the can you are eating from. You just eat by feel. You make cold coffee from cold water.

One night a German shell landed close and fragments punctured 15 cans of water.

Each night enough canned rations for three meals are brought up, but when the men move on after supper most of them either lose or leave behind the next day's rations, because they're too heavy to carry. But, as they say, when you're in battle and excited you sort of go on your nerve. You don't think much about being hungry.

The men fight at night and lie low by day, when the artillery takes over its blasting job. Weariness gradually creeps over them. What sleeping they do is in daytime. But, as they say, at night it's too cold and in daytime it's too hot. Also the fury of the artillery makes daytime sleeping next to impossible. So does the heat of the sun. Some men have passed out from heat prostration. Many of them get upset stomachs from the heat.

But as the third and fourth days roll on weariness overcomes all obstacles to sleep. Men who sit down for a moment's rest fall asleep in the grass. There are even men who say they can march while asleep.

Lieut. Col. Charlie Stone, of New Brunswick, N.J., actually went to sleep while standing up talking on a field telephone — not while listening, but in the middle of a spoken sentence.

When sometimes they do lie down at night the men have only their raincoats to lie on. It is cold, and the dew makes the grass as wet as rain. They don't dare start a fire to heat their food, even in daytime, for the smoke would attract enemy fire. At night they can't even light cigarets in the open, so after digging their foxholes they get down and make hoods over their heads with their raincoats, and light up under the coats.

They have plenty of cigarets. Those who run out during battle are supplied by others. Every night new supplies of water and C-rations are brought up in jeeps.

*　　*　　*

You can't conceive how hard it is to move and fight at night. The country is rugged, the ground rough. Everything is new and strange. The nights are pitch black. You grope with your feet. You step into holes, and fall sprawling in little gullies and creeks. You trudge over plowed ground and push through waist-high shrubs. You go as a man blindfolded, feeling unsure and off balance, but you keep on going.

Through it all there is the fear of mines. The Germans have mined the country behind them beyond anything ever known before. We simply can't take time to go over each inch of ground with mine detectors, so we have to discover the mine fields by stumbling into them or driving over them. Naturally there are casualties, but they are smaller than you might think—just a few men each day.

The greatest damage is psychological—the intense watchfulness our troops must maintain.

The Germans have been utterly profligate with their mines. We dug out 400 from one field. We've found so many fields and so many isolated mines that we have run out of white tape to mark them with. But still we go on.

Scripps-Howard wire copy, May 1, 1943

"The God-Damned Infantry"

IN THE FRONT LINES BEFORE MATEUR—(by wireless)— We're now with an infantry outfit that has battled ceaselessly for four days and nights.

This northern warfare has been in the mountains. You don't ride much any more. It is walking and climbing and crawling country. The mountains aren't big, but they are constant. They are largely treeless. They are easy to defend and bitter to take. But we are taking them.

The Germans lie on the back slope of every ridge, deeply dug into foxholes. In front of them the fields and pastures are hideous with thousands of hidden mines. The forward slopes are left open, untenanted, and if the Americans tried to scale these slopes they would be murdered wholesale in an inferno of machine-gun crossfire plus mortars and grenades.

Consequently we don't do it that way. We have fallen back to the old warfare of first pulverizing the enemy with artillery, then sweeping around the ends of the hill with infantry and taking them from the sides and behind.

* * *

I've written before how the big guns crack and roar almost constantly throughout the day and night. They lay a screen ahead of our troops. By magnificent shooting they drop shells on the back slopes. By means of shells timed to burst in the air a few feet from the ground, they get the Germans even in their foxholes. Our troops have found that the Germans dig foxholes down and then under, trying to get cover from the shell bursts that shower death from above.

Our artillery has really been sensational. For once we have enough of something and at the right time. Officers tell me they actually have more guns than they know what to do with.

All the guns in any one sector can be centered to shoot at one spot. And when we lay the whole business on a German hill the whole slope seems to erupt. It becomes an unbelievable cauldron of fire and smoke and dirt. Veteran German soldiers say they have never been through anything like it.

* * *

Now to the infantry—the God-damned infantry, as they like to call themselves.

I love the infantry because they are the underdogs. They are the mud-rain-frost-and-wind boys. They have no comforts, and they even learn to live without the necessities. And in the end they are they guys that wars can't be won without.

I wish you could see just one of the ineradicable pictures I have in my mind today. In this particular picture I am sitting among clumps of sword-grass on a steep and rocky hillside that we have just taken. We are looking out over a vast rolling country to the rear.

A narrow path comes like a ribbon over a hill miles away, down a long slope, across a creek, up a slope and over another hill.

All along the length of this ribbon there is now a thin line of men. For four days and nights they have fought hard, eaten little, washed none, and slept hardly at all. Their nights have been violent with attack, fright, butchery, and their days sleepless and miserable with the crash of artillery.

The men are walking. They are fifty feet apart, for dispersal. Their walk is slow, for they are dead weary, as you can tell even when looking at them from behind. Every line and sag of their bodies speaks their inhuman exhaustion.

On their shoulders and backs they carry heavy steel tripods, machine-gun barrels, leaden boxes of ammunition. Their feet seem to sink into the ground from the overload they are bearing.

They don't slouch. It is the terrible deliberation of each step that spells out their appalling tiredness. Their faces are black and unshaven. They are young men, but the grime and whiskers and exhaustion make them look middle-aged.

In their eyes as they pass is not hatred, not excitement, not despair, not the tonic of their victory—there is just the simple expression of being here as though they had been here doing this forever, and nothing else.

The line moves on, but it never ends. All afternoon men keep coming round the hill and vanishing eventually over the horizon. It is one long tired line of antlike men.

*   *   *

There is an agony in your heart and you almost feel ashamed to look at them. They are just guys from Broadway and Main Street, but you wouldn't remember them. They are too far away now. They are too tired. Their world can never be known to you, but if you could see them just once, just for an instant, you would know that no matter how hard people work back home they are not keeping pace with these infantrymen in Tunisia.

Scripps-Howard wire copy, May 2, 1943

"When a Unit Stops to Rest"

IN THE FRONT LINES BEFORE MATEUR—(by wireless)—After four days in battle the famous infantry outfit that I'm with sat on its newly won hill and took two days' rest while companion units on each side of it leap-frogged ahead.

The men dig in on the back slope of the hill before any rest begins. Everybody digs in. This is an inviolate rule of the commanding officers and nobody wants to disobey it. Every time you pause, even if you think you're dying of weariness, you dig yourself a hole before you sit down.

The startling thing to me about these rest periods is how quickly the human body can recuperate from critical exhaustion, how rapidly the human mind snaps back to the normal state of laughing, grousing, yarn-spinning, and yearning for home.

*   *   *

Here is what happens when a unit stops to rest.

My unit stops just after daybreak on Hill 394. Foxholes are dug, outposts placed, phone wires strung on the ground. Some patrol work goes on as usual. Then the men lie down and sleep till the blistering heat of the sun wakes them up.

After that you sit around in bunches recounting things. You don't do much of anything. The day just easily kills itself.

That first evening is when life begins to seem like Christmas Eve. The mail comes up in jeeps just before dark. Then comes the men's blanket rolls. At dark hot food arrives—the first hot food in four days.

This food is cooked in rolling kitchens several miles back and brought up by jeep, in big thermos containers, to the foot of the hill. Men carry the containers, slung on poles over their shoulders, up goat paths in the darkness to all parts of the mountain.

Hot food and hot coffee put life in a man, and then in a pathetic kind of contentment, you lie down and you sleep. The all-night crash of the artillery behind you is completely unheard through your weariness.

There are no mosquitoes so far in the mountains, and very few fleas, but there are lots of ants.

Hot food arrives again in the morning, before daylight. You eat breakfast at 4 a.m. Then begins a day of reassembling yourself.

Word is passed that mail will be collected that evening, so the boys sit on the ground and write letters. But writing is hard, for they can't tell in their letters what they've just been through.

The men put water in their steel helmets and wash and shave for the first time in days. A few men at a time are sent to the creek in the valley to take baths. The remainder sit in groups on the ground talking, or individually in foxholes cleaning their guns, reading, or just relaxing.

A two-months-old batch of copies of the magazine *Yank* arrives, and a two-weeks-old bunch of the *Stars and Stripes*. Others read detective magazines and comic books that have come up with their bedrolls.

At noon everybody opens cans of cold C-ration. Cold coffee in five-gallon water cans is put in the sun to warm.

Soldiers cut each other's hair. It doesn't matter how it looks, for they aren't going anywhere fancy, anyhow. Some of them strip nearly naked and lie on their blankets for a sunbath. By now their bodies are tanned as though they had been wintering at Miami Beach. They wear the inner part of their helmets, for the noonday sun is dangerous.

Their knees are skinned from crawling over rocks. They find little unimportant injuries that they didn't know they had. Some take off their shoes and socks and look over their feet, which are violently purple with athlete's-foot ointment.

*   *   *

I sit around with them, and they get to telling stories, both funny and serious, about their battle. They are all disappointed when they learn I am not permitted to name the outfit they're in, for they are all proud of it and would like the folks at home to know what they've done.

"We always get it the toughest," they say. "This is our third big battle now since coming to Africa. The Jerry is really afraid of us now. He knows what outfit we are, and he doesn't like us."

Thus they talk and boast and laugh and speak of fear. Evening draws down and the chill sets in once more. Hot chow arrives just after dusk.

And then the word is passed around. Orders have come by telephone.

There is no excitement, no grouching, no eagerness either. They had expected it.

Quietly they roll their packs, strap them on, lift their rifles and fall into line.

There is not a sound as they move like wraiths in single file down tortuous goat paths, walking slowly, feeling the ground with their toes, stumbling and hushfully cussing. They will walk all night and attack before dawn.

They move like ghosts. You don't hear or see them three

feet away. Now and then a light flashes lividly from a blast by our big guns, and then for just an instant you see a long slow line of dark-helmeted forms silhouetted in the flash.

Then darkness and silence consume them again, and somehow you are terribly moved.

Scripps-Howard wire copy, May 3, 1943

"This Is Our War"

The Tunisian campaign was ended. Our air forces moved on farther into Tunisia, to the very edge of the chasm of sea that separated them only so little from Sicily and Sardinia and then from Europe itself. We and the British leaped upon the demolished ports we had captured, cleared out enough wreckage for a foothold for ships, and as the ports grew and grew in usefulness they swarmed with thousands of men, and ships, and trucks. Our combat troops moved back—out of range of enemy strafers—to be cheered and acclaimed momentarily by the cities in the rear, to take a few days of wild and hellroaring rest, and then to go into an invasion practice that was in every respect, except the one of actually getting shot, as rigorous as a real invasion.

Surely before autumn we of Tunisia would be deep into something new. Most of us realized and admitted to ourselves that horrible days lay ahead. The holocaust that at times seemed so big to us in Tunisia would pale in our memories beside the things we would see and do before another year ran out.

Tunisia for us was not only an end in itself, but without the War of Tunisia we would have been ill-prepared to go on into the bigger wars ahead. Tunisia has been called a warm-up ground. That is a proper word for it, I suppose. We found through actual test which of our weapons and planes and vehicles were good, and which were bad, and which could be made good with a little changing. We seasoned our men in battle, and we found the defects that needed to be found in our communications systems, our supply lines, our methods of organization.

It is hard for you at home to realize what an immense,

complicated, sprawling institution a theater of war actually is. As it appears to you in the newspapers, war is a clear-cut matter of landing so many men overseas, moving them from the port to the battlefield, advancing them against the enemy with guns firing, and they win or lose.

To look at war that way is like seeing a trailer of a movie, and saying you've seen the whole picture. I actually don't know what percentage of our troops in Africa were in the battle lines, but I believe it safe to say that only comparatively few ever saw the enemy, ever shot at him, or were shot at by him. All the rest of those hundreds of thousands of men were churning the highways for two thousand miles behind the lines with their endless supply trucks, they were unloading the ships, cooking the meals, pounding the typewriters, fixing the roads, making the maps, repairing the engines, decoding the messages, training the reserves, pondering the plans.

To get all that colossal writhing chaos shaped into something that intermeshed and moved forward with efficiency was a task closely akin to weaving a cloth out of a tubful of spaghetti. It was all right to have wonderful plans ahead of time, but we really learn such things only by doing. Now, after our forces have had more than six months' experience in North Africa, I for one feel that we have washed out the bulk of our miscomprehensions, have abandoned most of our fallacies, and have hardened down into a work-weary and battle-dirtied machine of great effect, capable of assimilating and directing aright those greener men who are to follow by the hundreds of thousands and maybe millions.

What I have seen in North Africa has altered my own feelings in one respect. There were days when I sat in my tent alone and gloomed with the desperate belief that it was actually possible for us to lose this war. I don't feel that way any more. Despite our strikes and bickering and confusion back home, America is producing and no one can deny that. Even here at the far end of just one line the trickle has grown into an impressive stream. We are producing at home and we are hardening overseas. Apparently it takes a country like America about two years to become wholly at war. We had to go through that transition period of letting loose of life as it was, and then live the new war life so long that it finally became the normal life to us. It was a form of growth, and we couldn't press it. Only time can produce that change. We have survived that long passage of time, and if I am at all correct we have about changed our character and become a war nation. I can't yet see when we shall win, or over what route geographically, or by which of the many means of warfare. But no longer do I have any doubts at all that we shall win.

The men over here have changed too. They are too close to themselves to sense the change, perhaps. And I am too close to them to grasp it fully. But since I am older and a little apart, I have been able to notice it more.

For a year, everywhere I went, soldiers inevitably asked me two questions: "When do you think we'll get to go home?" and "When will the war be over?" The home-going desire was once so dominant that I believe our soldiers over here would have voted—if the question had been put—to go home immediately, even if it meant peace on terms of something less than unconditional surrender by the enemy.

That isn't true now. Sure, they all still want to go home. So do I. But there is something deeper than that, which didn't exist six months ago. I can't quite put it into words—it isn't any theatrical proclamation that the enemy must be destroyed in the name of freedom; it's just a vague but growing individual acceptance of the bitter fact that we must win the war or else, and that it can't be won by running excursion boats back and forth across the Atlantic carrying homesick vacationers.

A year is a long time to be away from home, especially if a person has never been away before, as was true of the bulk of our troops. At first homesickness can almost kill a man. But time takes care of that. It isn't normal to moon in the past forever. Home gradually grows less vivid; the separation from it less agonizing. There finally comes a day—not suddenly but gradually, as a sunset-touched cloud changes its color—when a man is living almost wholly wherever he is. His life has caught up with his body, and his days become full war days, instead of American days simply transplanted to Africa.

That's the stage our soldiers are in now—the ones who have been over since the beginning, I mean. It seems to take about that long. It's only in the last few weeks that I've begun to hear frequent remarks, said enthusiastically and sincerely, about the thrill it will be to see Paris and to march down the streets of Berlin. The immediate goal used to be the Statue of Liberty; more and more it is becoming Unter den Linden. When all of our army has bridged that gap we shall be in the home stretch.

Our men can't make this change from normal civilians into warriors and remain the same people. Even if they were away from you this long under normal circumstances, the mere process of maturing would change them, and they would not come home just as you knew them. Add to that the abnormal world they have been plunged into, the new philosophies they have had to assume or perish inwardly, the horrors and delights and strange wonderful things they have experienced, and they are bound to be different people from those you sent away.

They are rougher than when you knew them. Killing is a rough business. Their basic language has changed from mere profanity to obscenity. More than anything else, they miss women. Their expressed longings, their conversation, their whole conduct show their need for female companionship, and the gentling effect of femininity upon man is conspicuous here where it has been so long absent.

Our men have less regard for property than you raised them to have. Money value means nothing to them, either personally or in the aggregate; they are fundamentally generous, with strangers and with each other. They give or throw away their own money, and it is natural that they are even less thoughtful of bulk property than of their own hard-earned possessions. It is often necessary to abandon equipment they can't take with them; the urgency of war prohibits normal caution in the handling of vehicles and supplies. One of the most striking things to me about war is the appalling waste that is necessary. At the front there just isn't time to be economical. Also, in war areas where things are scarce and red tape still rears its delaying head, a man learns to get what he needs simply by "requisitioning." It isn't stealing, it's the only way to acquire certain things. The stress of war puts old virtues in a changed light. We shall have to relearn a simple fundamental or two when things get back to normal. But what's wrong with a small case of "requisitioning" when murder is the classic goal?

Our men, still thinking of home, are impatient with the strange peoples and customs of the countries they now inhabit. They say that if they ever get home they never want to see another foreign country. But I know how it will be. The day will come when they'll look back and brag about how they learned a little Arabic, and how swell the girls were in England, and how pretty the hills of Germany were. Every day their scope is broadening despite themselves, and once they all get back with their global yarns and their foreign-tinged views, I cannot conceive of our nation ever being isolationist again. The men don't feel very international right now, but the influences are at work and the time will come.

I couldn't say truthfully that they are very much interested in foreign affairs right now, outside of battle affairs. Awhile back a friend of mine in Washington wrote me an enthusiastic letter, telling of the Ball Resolution in the Senate calling for the formation of a United Nations organization to co-ordinate the prosecution of the war, administer reoccupied countries, feed and economically reestablish liberated nations, and to assemble a United Nations military force to suppress any future military aggression.

My friend told of the enthusiasm the bill had created at home, hailed it as the first definite step in winning the peace as well as the war, and asked me almost pleadingly to send back a report on what the men at the front thought of the bill.

I didn't send any report, because the men at the front thought very little about it one way or the other. I doubt that one out of ten of them remembered the thing two days, even though they may have read about it in *Stars and Stripes*. There wasn't anything specific to get their teeth into and argue about. It sounded too much like another Atlantic Charter or committee meeting.

Of course, by digging, a person could find plenty of politically and internationally minded men in our army—all the way from generals to privates—who do spend considerable time thinking of what is to come after the victory, and how we are to handle it. But what I'm trying to get over is that the bulk of our army in Africa, the run-of-the-mine mass of soldiers, didn't think twice about this bill if they heard of it at all. Their thoughts on the peace can be summed up, I believe, in a general statement that after this war is won they want it fixed so it can't happen again and they want a hand in fixing it, but our average guy has not more conception of how it should be done than to say he supposes some kind of world police force is the answer. There is a great deal more talk along the line of, "Those bluenoses back home better not try to put prohibition over on us while we're away this time," than you hear about bills and resolutions looking toward the post-war world.

Your men have been well cared for in this war. I suppose no soldiers in any other war in history have had such excellent attention as our men overseas. The food is good. Of course we're always yapping about how wonderful a steak would taste on Broadway, but when a soldier is pinned right down he'll admit ungrudgingly that it's Broadway he's thinking about more than the steak, and that he really can't kick on the food. Furthermore, cooking is good in this war. Last time good food was spoiled by lousy cooking, but that is the exception this time. Of course, there were times in battle when the men lived for days on nothing but those deadly cold C rations out of tin cans, and even went without food for a day or two, but those were the crises, the exceptions. On the whole, we figure by the letters from home that we're probably eating better than you are.

A good diet and excellent medical care have made our army a healthy one. Statistics show the men in the mass healthier today than they were in civil life back home.

Our men are well provided with clothing, transportation, mail, and army newspapers. Back of the lines they had Post Exchanges where they could buy cigarettes, candy, toilet articles, and all such things. If they were in the combat zone, all those things were issued to them free.

Our fighting equipment was the only thing that didn't stand head and shoulders above everything issued to soldiers of any other country, and that was only because we weren't ready for war at first, and for two years we have been learning what was good and what was bad. Already many of our weapons are unmatched by any other country. Give us another year and surely it can be said that our men are furnished better weapons, along with better food, health and clothing, than any other army.

Here it is June of 1943 and it seems a long time since we landed at Oran in November of 1942. Of course there were thousands of us even in those first days in Africa, and yet it seemed like a little family then. And specially so when we went on to Tunisia—in those bitter January days we were so small that I knew almost every officer on the staff of every unit, in addition to hundreds of the soldiers. Nothing was very official in our lives then; there was almost no red tape; we correspondents at the front were few and were considered by the army rather like partners in the firm. We made deep friendships that have endured.

During the winter I dropped in frequently at Corps Headquarters, buried deep in a gulch beyond Tebessa. They put up a little tent for me, and I tried to work and sleep in it, but was never very successful at either because of being constantly, paralyzingly cold throughout the twenty-four hours of the day. We ate in a tent with a crushed-stone floor and an iron-bellied stove in the center. It was the only warm place I knew, and so informal was the war in those first days that often I sat around the stove after supper and just gabbed country-storelike with Lieutenant General Lloyd Fredendall, then commander of our armies in Tunisia. I was very fond of General Fredendall, and I admired and respected him. For some unknown reason I always thought of him to myself as "Papa" Fredendall, although I don't think anybody else ever did. I still wear the Armored Corps combat jacket he gave me.

The first pioneering days of anything are always the best days. Everything is new and animating, and acquaintanceships are easy and everyone is knit closely together. In the latter part of the Tunisian war things were just as good for us correspondents—we had better facilities and the fighting army continued to be grand to us—and yet toward the end it became so big that I felt like a spectator instead of a participant.

Which is, of course, all that a correspondent is or ever should be. But the old intimacy was gone.

And then finally the Tunisian campaign was over, spectacularly collapsed after the bitterest fighting we had known in our theater. It was only in those last days that I came to know what war really is. I don't know how any of the men who went through the thick of that hill-by-hill butchery could ever be the same again. The end of the Tunisian war brought an exhilaration, then a letdown, and later a restlessness from anticlimax that I can see multiplied a thousand times when the last surrender comes. That transition back to normal days will be as difficult for many as was the change into war, and some will never be able to accomplish it.

Now we are in a lull and many of us are having a short rest period. I tried the city and couldn't stand it. Two days drove me back to the country, where everything seemed cleaner and more decent. I am in my tent, sitting on a newly acquired cot, writing on a German folding table we picked up the day of the big surrender. The days here are so peaceful and perfect they almost give us a sense of infidelity to those we left behind beneath the Tunisian crosses, those whose final awareness was a bedlam of fire and noise and uproar.

Here the Mediterranean surf caresses the sandy beach not a hundred yards away, and it is a lullaby for sleeping. The water is incredibly blue, just as we always heard it was. The sky is a cloudless blue infinity, and the only sounds are the birds singing in the scrub bushes that grow out of the sand and lean precisely away from the sea. Little land terrapins waddle around, and I snared one by the hind leg with a piece of string and tied it in Photographer Chuck Corte's tent while he was out, just for a joke. Then I found myself peeking in every few minutes to see how the captive was getting along, and he was straining so hard to get away that I got to feeling sorry for the poor little devil, so I turned him loose and ruined my joke.

An occasional black beetle strolls innocently across the sandy floor. For two hours I've been watching one of them struggling with a cigarette butt on the ground, trying to move it. Yesterday a sand snake crawled by just outside my tent door, and for the first time in my life I looked upon a snake not with a creeping phobia but with a sudden and surprising feeling of compassion. Somehow I pitied him, because he was a snake instead of a man. And I don't know why I felt that way, for I feel pity for all men too, because they are men.

It may be that the war has changed me, along with the rest. It is hard for anyone to analyze himself. I know that I find more and more that I wish to be alone, and yet contradictorily I believe I have a new patience with humanity that I've never had before. When you've lived with the unnatural mass cruelty that mankind is capable of inflicting upon itself, you find yourself dispossessed of the faculty for blaming one poor man for the triviality of his faults. I don't see how any survivor of war can ever be cruel to anything, ever again.

Yes, I want the war to be over, just as keenly as any soldier in North Africa wants it. This little interlude of passive contentment here on the Mediterranean shore is a mean temptation. It is a beckoning into somnolence. This is the kind of day I think I want my life to be composed of, endlessly. But pretty soon we shall strike our tents and traipse again after the clanking tanks, sleep again to the incessant lullaby of the big rolling guns. It has to be that way, and wishing doesn't change it.

It may be I have unconsciously made war seem more awful than it really is. It would be wrong to say that war is all grim; if it were, the human spirit could not survive two and three and four years of it. There is a good deal of gaiety in wartime. Some of us, even over here, are having the time of our lives. Humor and exuberance still exist. As some soldier once said, the army is good for one ridiculous laugh per minute. Our soldiers are still just as roughly good-humored as they always were, and they laugh easily, although there isn't as much to laugh about as there used to be.

And I don't attempt to deny that war is vastly exhilarating. The whole tempo of life steps up, both at home and on the front. There is an intoxication about battle, and ordinary men can sometimes soar clear out of themselves on the wine of danger-emotion. And yet it is false. When we leave here to go on into the next battleground, I know that I for one shall go with the greatest reluctance.

On the day of final peace, the last stroke of what we call the "Big Picture" will be drawn. I haven't written anything about the "Big Picture," because I don't know anything about it. I only know what we see from our worm's-eye view, and our segment of the picture consists only of tired and dirty soldiers who are alive and don't want to die; of long darkened convoys in the middle of the night; of shocked silent men wandering back down the hill from battle; of chow lines and atabrine tablets and foxholes and burning tanks and Arabs holding up eggs and the rustle of high-flown shells; of jeeps and petrol dumps and smelly bedding rolls and C rations and cactus patches and blown bridges and dead mules and hospital tents and shirt collars greasy-black from months of wearing; and of laughter too, and anger and wine and lovely flowers and constant cussing. All these it is composed of; and of graves and graves and graves.

That is our war, and we will carry it with us as we go on from one battleground to another until it is all over, leaving some of us behind on every beach, in every field. We are just beginning with the ones who lie back of us here in Tunisia. I don't know whether it was their good fortune or their misfortune to get out of it so early in the game. I guess it doesn't make any difference, once a man has gone. Medals and speeches and victories are nothing to them any more. They died and others lived and nobody knows why it is so. They died and thereby the rest of us can go on and on. When we leave here for the next shore, there is nothing we can do for the ones beneath the wooden crosses, except perhaps to pause and murmur, "Thanks, pal."

Here Is Your War, 1943

Quest for Mollie

by A. J. Liebling

MOLLIE is a part of the history of La Piste Forestière, and La Piste Forestière is perhaps the most important part of the history of Mollie. La Piste Forestière, or the Foresters' Track, is a dirt road that connects Cap Serrat, on the northern coast of western Tunisia, with Sedjenane, a town twenty miles inland. The country it runs through is covered with small hills, and almost all the hills are coated with a ten-foot growth of tall bushes and short trees, so close together that once you leave the road you can't see fifty feet in front of you. From the top of any hill you can see the top of another hill, but, because of the growth, you can't tell whether there are men on it. This made the country hard to fight in. The hillsides that have no trees are bright with wild flowers in the spring, and two years ago, when some other war correspondents and I travelled back and forth along the Foresters' Track in jeeps, we sometimes used to measure our slow progress by reference to the almost geometrical patterns of color on such slopes. There was, for example, the hill with a rough yellow triangle of buttercups against a reddish-purple background of other blooms; it indicated that you were five miles from the road's junction with the main highway at Sedjenane. With luck you might reach the junction in two hours, but this was extremely unlikely, for the road was just wide enough for one truck—not for a truck and a jeep or even for a truck and a motorcycle. Only a man on foot or on a horse could progress along the margin of the road when there was a vehicle on it, and the horse would often have to scramble by with two feet off the road, like the sidehill bear of eastern Tennessee. When a jeep met a convoy, it sometimes had to back up for hundreds of yards to where there was room to get off the road and wait. Then, when all the heavy vehicles had passed, the jeep would resume its journey, perhaps to meet another convoy before it had recovered the lost yardage. Even when you got in behind trucks going your way, they were packed so closely together that they advanced at a crawl, so you did too. Bits of the war were threaded along the Foresters' Track like beads on a string, and the opportunity to become familiar with them was forced upon you. Mollie, for me, was the gaudiest bead.

The reason the Foresters' Track is such a miserable excuse for a road is that in normal times there is little need for it. There is a lighthouse at Cap Serrat and a forest warden's house about halfway between that and Sedjenane. The few Berbers in the district, who live in brush shelters in the bush, have no vehicles or need of a road. But in late April and early May of 1943, La Piste Forestière was an important military thoroughfare. The Allied armies, facing east, lay in a great arc with their right flank at Sousse, on the Gulf of Tunis, and this little road was the only supply line for twenty miles of front; that is, the extreme left flank of the Allied line. The actual front line ran parallel to the road and only a few hundred yards east of it during the first days of the offensive that was to end the Allies' North African campaign, but because of the hills and the brush, people on the road couldn't see the fighting. However, American artillery placed just west of the road—it would have been an engineering feat to get it any considerable distance into the brush—constantly fired over our heads as our jeeps piddled along. The gunners hoped that some of their shells were falling on the Germans and Italians who were trying to halt our infantry's advance with fire from hidden mortars and machine guns. The Luftwaffe in Africa had predeceased the enemy ground forces; the budget of planes allotted it for the African adventure was exhausted, I suppose, and the German High Command sent no more. This was lucky for us, because one good strafing, at any hour, would have jammed the road with burned-out vehicles and Allied dead. By repeating the strafing once a day, the Germans could have kept the road permanently out of commission. The potential danger from the air did not worry us for long, however. You soon become accustomed to immunity, even when you cannot understand the reason for it.

Trucks left ammunition along the side of the road to be

carried up to the fighting lines on the backs of requisitioned mules and horses and little Arab donkeys, a strangely assorted herd conducted by an equally scratch lot of soldiers. The Washington army had decided years before that the war was now one-hundred-per-cent mechanized, so the field army, quite a different organization, had to improvise its animal transport as it went along. The wounded were carried down to the road by stretcher bearers. Ambulances, moving with the same disheartening slowness as everything else, picked up the casualties and took them out to a clearing station near the yellow-triangle hill I have mentioned, where some of the viable ones were patched up for the further slow haul out. Cruder surgical units, strung out along the road, took such cases as they were equipped to handle. These units were always right by the side of the road, since in that claustrophobe's nightmare of a country there was no other place for them to be. The advanced units were French and had women nurses with them. A French doctor I knew used to say that it helped the men bear pain if nurses were looking at them. "Since we have so little anesthesia," he said, "we rely upon vanity." Sometimes I would sit in my jeep and watch that doctor work. He had broken down a few saplings and bushes by the side of the road to clear a space for his ambulance, and next to the ambulance he had set up a camp stool and a folding table with some instruments on it. Once a traffic jam stopped my jeep near his post when he had a tanned giant perched on the camp stool, a second lieutenant in the Corps Franc d'Afrique. The man's breasts were hanging off his chest in a kind of bloody ruff. "A bit of courage now, my son, will save you a great deal of trouble later on," the doctor said as he prepared to do something or other. I assumed, perhaps pessimistically, that he was going to hack off the bits of flesh as you would trim the ragged edges of an ill-cut page. "Go easy, Doctor," the young man said. "I'm such a softie." Then the traffic started to move, so I don't know what the doctor did to him.

The Corps Franc d'Afrique was a unit that had a short and glorious history. Soon after the Allied landings in North Africa, in October, 1942, the Corps Franc organized itself, literally, out of the elements the Darlanists in control of the

North African government distrusted too much to incorpo-
rate into the regular French Army—Jews, anti-Nazis from
concentration camps, de Gaullists, and other Allied sympathizers. A French general named Joseph de Goislard de Montsabert, who had helped plan the landings, had been thrown
out by his collaborationist superiors, who, even after Darlan's
agreement to play ball with the forces of democracy, had remained his superiors. De Montsabert, because he had a red
face and snowy hair, was known to his troops as Strawberry in
Cream. There had been, among the French in North Africa, a
number of other professional officers and many reservists
who, like the General, were apparently left out of the war
because they were suspected of favoring de Gaulle or merely
of being hostile to Germany. The Darlan regime had refused
to mobilize the Jews because it clung to the Vichy thesis that
they were not full citizens, and it did not want them to establish a claim to future consideration, and it was holding
thousands of Spanish and German refugees and French Communists in concentration camps.

De Montsabert and a few of his officer friends, talking on
the street in Algiers one rainy November day of that year,
decided to start a "Free Corps" of men who wanted to fight
but whom the government would not allow to. They took
over a room in a schoolhouse on the Rue Mogador as headquarters and advertised in the *Echo d'Alger* for volunteers.
The ad appeared once and then the Darlanist censorship,
which was still operating under the Americans, like every
other element of Vichy rule, suppressed it. But scores of volunteers had already appeared at the schoolhouse and de
Montsabert sent them out with pieces of schoolroom chalk to
write "Join the Corps Franc" on walls all over the city. Hundreds of new volunteers came in. General Giraud, who had
arrived in Africa to command all the French but had subsequently accepted a rôle secondary to Darlan's, heard of the
movement and interceded for it. Giraud, whatever his limita-
tions, considered it natural that anybody in his right mind
should want to fight the Germans. Darlan and his Fascist
friends began to think of the Corps Franc as a means of getting undesirables out of the way, so the government recognized it but at the same time refused it any equipment. The

Corps began life with a miscellany of matériel begged from the British and Americans. Its men wore British battle dress and French insignia of rank, lived on American C rations, and carried any sort of weapons they could lay their hands on. The most characteristic feature of their appearance was a long beard, but even this was not universal, because some of the soldiers were too young to grow one. After the Corps Franc's arrival in Tunisia, it added to its heterogeneous equipment a great deal more stuff it captured from the enemy. The Corps went into the line in February of 1943, in the zone north of Sedjenane, and it remained there into the spring.

Late April in Tunisia is like late June in New York, and heat and dust were great nuisances to our men when they were attacking. In February and March, however, coastal Tunisia is drenched with a cold and constant downpour. The Foresters' Track was two feet deep in water when the Corps Franc began to fight along it. There were two battalions to start with— about twelve hundred men—to cover a sector twenty miles long. A third and fourth battalion had been added by the time the Americans began their offensive. The Corps, in the beginning, had only two ambulances, converted farm trucks owned by a Belgian colonist in Morocco. The Belgian and his son had driven the trucks across North Africa to join the Corps. But the trucks were unable to negotiate the flooded Track, so the men of the Corps carried their wounded out to Sedjenane on their shoulders. I once asked my doctor friend why they had not used mules. "The mules rolled over in the water and crushed the wounded men," he said. "We know. We tried it with wounded prisoners."

Now that the great attack was on, there were other troops along the Track with the Corps—the Sixtieth Infantry of the American Ninth Division, part of the American Ninth Division's artillery, an American tank-destroyer battalion, some Moroccan units, and some American motor-truck and medical outfits. The medics and the artillery made the French feel pampered and their morale got very high. One hot morning, I passed a lean, elderly soldier of the Corps Franc who was burying two of his comrades. He looked about sixty— there was no age limit in the Corps—and had a long, drooping mustache of a faded biscuit color. He had finished one

grave and was sitting down to rest and cool off before beginning the other. The two dead men lay with their feet to the
road. Blueflies had settled on their faces. I told my jeep driver
to stop and asked the gravedigger what men these were.
"One stiff was an Arab from Biskra," the old soldier said,
"and the other a Spaniard, a nihilist from Oran." I asked him
how his work was going. He wiped the sweat from his forehead and said happily, "Monsieur, like on roller skates."

A quarter of the men in the Corps Franc were Jews. A Jewish lieutenant named Rosenberg was its posthumous hero by
the time I arrived in the Foresters' Track country. He had
commanded a detachment of twenty men covering the retreat
of his battalion during a German counterattack in early
March. This was a sequel to the counterattack against the
Americans at Kasserine Pass in late February, and both assaults
were prototypes, on a small scale, of the counter-offensive the
Germans were to launch in Belgium at the end of 1944—the
last flurry of the hooked and dying fish. Rosenberg, holding
one of the innumerable little hills with his men, had decided
that it was not fitting for a Jew to retire, even when the Germans looked as though they had surrounded his position. He
and his men held on until the rest of the battalion had made
its escape. Then he rose, and, intoning the "Marseillaise," led
his men in an attack with hand grenades. He and most of his
men were, of course, killed.

Besides the Jews, the Corps had hundreds of political prisoners from labor camps in southern Algeria—Spanish Republicans who had fled to Africa in 1939, anti-Nazi Germans who
had come even before that, and French "Communists and de
Gaullists," to employ the usual Vichy designation for dissi-
dents. The political prisoners had been released upon agree-
ing to enter the Corps Franc, which they did not consider an
onerous condition. There were also hundreds of Frenchmen
who had joined because they distrusted the Vichy officers in
the regular Army, or because they were "hard heads" who
detested any species of regularity, or because they were too
old or ill for more conventional fighting units. In the Corps
Franc, they were at liberty to march and fight until they
dropped. There were also a fair number of Mohammedans,
good soldiers who had joined to earn the princely wage of

twenty-three francs a day, ten times what they would have got if they had waited to be mobilized in their regular units. Whenever I had a chance, I asked Corps Franc soldiers who they had been in civilian life and why they had enlisted. I remember a former *carabiñero* who had fought in the Spanish Loyalist Army, and a baker of Italian parentage from Bône, in Algeria, who said, "I am a Communist. Rich people are poison to me."

Other members of the Corps who made a special impression on me were a former admiral in the Spanish Republican Navy, who was now a company commander and would not allow junior officers to shout at soldiers; a Hungarian poet who had been studying medicine at the University of Algiers; a sixteen-year-old Alsatian from Strasbourg who had run away from home to avoid being forced to become a German citizen; and a French captain, a shipping broker in civil life, who proclaimed himself a Royalist. The captain's sixteen-year-old son was also in the Corps; the boy was a motorcycle dispatch rider. I also remember two tough Parisians who had not seen each other since one had escaped from jail in Dakar, where they had both been imprisoned for trying to join the Free French in Brazzaville. The other had escaped later. "Say, it's you, old pimp!" one of the men shouted joyously. "And how did you get out of the jug, old rottenness?" the second man shouted back. Once I shared a luncheon of C-ration vegetable hash, scallions, and medlars with a little fifty-three-year-old second lieutenant, one of those Frenchmen with a face like a parakeet, who until 1942 had been vice-president of the Paris Municipal Council, in which he represented the *arrondissement* of the Opéra. He had got out a clandestine paper and had helped Jewish friends smuggle millions of francs out of France. Betrayed to the Gestapo, he had been arrested and put in Cherche-Midi Prison; he had escaped with the aid of a jailer and come to Africa and the Corps Franc. The middle-aged soldier who waited on us spoke French with a farce-comedy Russian accent; he had been a waiter at the Scheherazade, a night club in Montmartre, and had often served the lieutenant when he was a civilian. A handsome young Viennese half-Jew, who had been on the Austrian track team in the last Olympic Games, once asked me for some sulfanilamide. He had been in a labor camp for six months without seeing a woman but had been allowed one night's leave in Oran before being sent on to the front. He wanted the sulfanilamide, he said, so that he could treat himself; he was afraid that a doctor might order him away from the firing line. And in a hospital tent at the clearing station I came across a man with a French flag wrapped around his waist; the medics discovered it when they cut his shirt away. He was a hard-looking, blondish chap with a mouthful of gold teeth and a face adorned by a cross-shaped knife scar—the *croix de vache* with which procurers sometimes mark business rivals. An interesting collection of obscene tattooing showed on the parts of him that the flag did not cover. Outwardly he was not a sentimental type.

"Where are you from?" I asked him.

"Belleville," he said. Belleville is a part of Paris not distinguished for its elegance.

"What did you do in civilian life?" I inquired.

That made him grin. "I lived on my income," he said.

"Why did you choose the Corps Franc?"

"Because I understood," he said.

The American soldiers interspersed with the men of the Corps Franc along the Foresters' Track found them a fantastic lot. Most of the men then in the Ninth Division came from New York, New Jersey, or New England, and their ideas of North Africa and Frenchmen had been acquired from films with Ronald Colman as Beau Geste or Charles Boyer as Charles Boyer. They thought the Frenchmen very reckless. The Ninth had had its first experience in battle on the road to Maknassy, in southern Tunisia, only a few weeks earlier, and it was not yet a polished division. The men of the Ninth in Germany recently took risks as nonchalantly as any Corps Franc soldier used to, but at the time I am speaking of they would sometimes call the Frenchmen "those crazy headhunters." This term reflected a tendency to confuse the Corps Franc with the Moroccans in the same zone; the Moroccans are not headhunters, either, but there is a popular American belief that they are paid according to how many enemy ears they bring in.

There were two tabors, or battalions, of Moroccans in the zone; a tabor consists of several goums, or companies, and each soldier who is a member of a company is called a goumier. For the sake of simplicity and euphony, Americans called the Moroccan soldiers themselves goums. The goums used to ride along the side of the road on bay mules or gray horses—sure-footed, mountain-bred animals—until they got near the place where they were going to fight. Then they would dismount and go off into the brush on bare feet, and return with their booty when they had finished their business. The goum's sole outer garment is the *djellabah*, which looks like a long brown bathrobe with a hood. It is made of cotton, wool, linen, goats' hair, or camels' hair and usually has vertical black stripes. It sheds water, insulates against heat and cold, is a substitute for a pup tent at night, and serves as a repository for everything the goum gloms, like the capacious garment of a professional shoplifter. In their Moroccan homeland the goums live with their wives and children in their own villages and are supposed to pay themselves with the spoils of tribes that resist the French government. In Tunisia the spoils were pretty well confined to soldiers' gear. As a goum killed or captured more and more enemies, he would put on layer after layer of tunics and trousers, always wearing the *djellabah* over everything. The girth of the goums increased as the campaign wore on. This swollen effect gave a goum an air of prosperity and importance, in his opinion; his standing as a warrior, he thought, was in direct ratio to his circumference. A goum who was doing well often wore, between sorties, one German and one Italian boot and carried a string of extra boots over his saddlebow. The funny part of it was that a goum wearing six men's clothing could slip noiselessly through a thicket that was impassable to a skinny American. The French officers commanding the goums assured me that their men were not paid by the ear; if a goum occasionally had a few dried ears concealed in a fold of his *djellabah*, one officer explained, it was because goums had discovered that such souvenirs had a trade value in G.I. cigarettes and chewing gum. "Far from paying for ears," this officer said, "we have recently been offering a small reward for live prisoners for interrogation. It is evident that a prisoner without ears is not a good subject for interrogation, because he does not hear the questions plainly." To hold the goums' respect, the officers had to be able to march, climb, and fight with them, and a goum is as inexhaustible as a mountain sheep and about as fastidious as a hyena. Most goums come from the Atlas Mountains and few of them speak Arabic, much less French, so the officers have to be fluent in the southern Berber dialects, which are all that the men know. The goums are trying companions in minefields, because, as one officer remarked, "They say, 'If it is the will of God, we go up,' and then they just push forward." Neither they nor the Corps Franc had mine detectors. An American captain named Yankauer, who was the surgeon at the clearing station near the yellow-triangle hill, was once digging scraps of steel out of a goum who had stepped on a mine. The man let out one short squeal—there was no anesthetic—and then began a steady chant. Yankauer asked a goum officer, who was waiting his turn on the table, what the goum was saying. The officer translated, "He chants, 'God forgive me, I am a woman. God forgive me, I am a woman,' because, you see, he has cried aloud, so he is ashamed." The goums' chief weapons were curved knives and long rifles of the vintage of 1871, and one of the supply problems of the campaign for the American G-4 was finding ammunition for these antediluvian small arms. Colonel Pierre Magnan, who had succeeded de Montsabert in command of the Corps Franc, was the senior French officer in the zone. I was with him one day when the commander of a newly arrived tabor presented himself for orders. "How are you fixed for automatic weapons, Major?" Magnan asked. "We have two old machine guns," the goum officer said. Then, when he saw Magnan's glum look, he added cheerily, "But don't worry, my Colonel, we use them only on maneuvers."

Magnan was a trim, rather elegant officer who, before the Allied landings, had commanded a crack infantry regiment in Morocco. On the morning of the American landings, he had arrested General Noguès, the Governor General of Morocco, and then asked him to prevent any fighting between the French and Americans by welcoming the invading forces. Noguès had telephoned to a tank regiment to come and arrest Magnan. Magnan, unwilling to shed French blood, had surrendered to the tankmen and become a prisoner in his turn. The liberated Noguès had then ordered a resistance which cost hundreds of French and American lives. Magnan was kept in prison for several days after Noguès, who was backed by our State Department, had consented to be agreeable to the Allies. Magnan had then been released, but he was deprived of his command and consigned to the Corps Franc. He now commands a division in France, and de Montsabert has a *corps d'armée*, so the scheme to keep them down has not been precisely a success.

The Axis forces north of Sedjenane must have been as hard put to it for supply routes as we were. I don't remember the roads the Intelligence maps showed behind the enemy's lines, but they could not have been numerous or elaborate. The Germans did not seem to have a great deal of artillery, but they occasionally landed shells on our road. Once, I remember, they shot up a couple of tank destroyers shortly after the jeep I was in had pulled out to let them pass. Throughout, it was a stubborn, nasty sort of fighting in the brush, and casualties arrived in a steady trickle rather than any great spurt, because large-scale attacks were impossible. Our men fought their way a few hundred yards further east each day, toward Ferryville and Bizerte. Eventually, when Rommel's forces crumpled, men of the Corps Franc, in trucks driven by American soldiers, got to Bizerte before any other Allied troops.

On Easter Sunday, which came late in April, I was out along the Track all day, riding in a jeep with Hal Boyle, a correspondent for the Associated Press. At the end of the afternoon we headed home, hoping to get back to the press camp before night so that we wouldn't have to buck a stream of two-and-a-half-ton trucks and armored vehicles in the blackout. Traffic seemed, if anything, heavier than usual along the Foresters' Track, as it always did when you were in a hurry. The jeep stopped for minutes at a time, which gave Boyle the opportunity to climb out and get the names and home addresses of American soldiers for his stories. Sometimes he would stay behind, talking, and catch up with the jeep the next time it was snagged. We could have walked

along the Track faster than we rode. Finally we came to a dip
in the road. Fifty yards below and to our right there was a
shallow stream, and there was almost no brush on the slope
from the road down to the water. This, for the Foresters'
Track country, was a considerable clearing, and it was being
used for a number of activities. Some goums were watering
their mounts in the stream, some French and American soldiers were heating rations over brush fires, a number of vehicles were parked there, and Colonel Magnan and some
officers were holding a staff meeting. As we approached the
clearing, we were stopped again for a moment by the traffic.
A dismal American soldier came out of the brush on our left,
tugging a gaunt, reluctant white horse. "Come along, Horrible," the soldier said in a tone of intensest loathing. "This
goddam horse got me lost three times today," he said to us,
looking over his shoulder at the sneering, wall-eyed beast. He
evidently thought the horse was supposed to guide him.

We moved downhill a bit and stopped again, this time behind an ambulance that was loading wounded. There was a
group of soldiers around the ambulance. Boyle and I got out
to look. There were four wounded men, all badly hit. They
were breathing hard and probably didn't know what was going on. Shock and heavy doses of morphia were making their
move easy, or at least quiet. The four men were all from the
Sixtieth Infantry of the Ninth Division. A soldier by the road
said that they had been on a patrol and had exchanged shots
with a couple of Germans; the Germans had popped up waving white handkerchiefs, the Americans had stood up to take
them prisoners, and another German, lying concealed, had
opened on them with a machine gun. It was the sort of thing
that had happened dozens of times to other units, and that
undoubtedly has happened hundreds of times since. Such casualties, a Polish officer once said to me, are an entry fee to
battle. That doesn't make them easy to take, however. The
soldiers had been told about this particular trick in their training courses, but they had probably thought it was a fable invented to make them hate the enemy. Now the men around
the ambulance had really begun to hate the enemy.

While Boyle was getting the names and addresses of the
men, I saw another American soldier by the side of the road.

This one was dead. A soldier nearby said that the dead man had been a private known as Mollie. A blanket covered his face, so I surmised that it had been shattered, but there was no blood on the ground, so I judged that he had been killed in the brush and carried down to the road to await transport. A big, wild-looking sergeant was standing alongside him—a hawk-nosed, red-necked man with a couple of front teeth missing—and I asked him if the dead man had been in the patrol with the four wounded ones. "Jeez, no!" the sergeant said, looking at me as if I ought to know about the man with the blanket over his face. "That's Mollie. Comrade Molotov. The Mayor of Broadway. Didn't you ever hear of him? Jeez, Mac, he once captured six hundred Eyetalians by himself and brought them all back along with him. Sniper got him, I guess. I don't know, because he went out with the French, and he was found dead up there in the hills. He always liked to do crazy things—go off by himself with a pair of big field glasses he had and watch the enemy put in minefields, or take off and be an artillery spotter for a while, or drive a tank. From the minute he seen those frogs, he was bound to go off with them."

"Was his name really Molotov?" I asked.

"No," said the sergeant, "he just called himself that. The boys mostly shortened it to Mollie. I don't even know what his real name was—Warren, I think. Carl Warren. He used to say he was a Broadway big shot. 'Just ask anybody around Forty-fourth Street,' he used to say. 'They all know me.' Me, I'm from White Plains—I never heard of him before he joined up."

"I had him with me on a patrol that was to contact the French when the regiment was moving into this zone last Thursday," a stocky blond corporal said. "The first French patrol we met, Mollie says to me, 'This is too far back for me. I'm going up in the hills with these frogs and get me some Lugers.' He was always collecting things he captured off Germans and Italians, but the one thing he didn't have yet was a Luger. I knew if I didn't let him go he would take off anyway and get into more trouble with the C.O. He was always in trouble. So I said, 'All right, but the frogs got to give me a receipt for you, so I can prove you didn't go A.W.O.L.' One of the soldiers with me could speak French, so he explained it and the frog noncom give me a receipt on a piece of toilet paper and Mollie went off with them." The corporal fished in one of the pockets of his field jacket and brought out a sheet of tissue. On it, the French noncom had written, in pencil, *"Pris avec moi le soldat américain Molotov, 23 avril, '43, Namin, caporal chef."*

"Mollie couldn't speak French," the American corporal went on, "but he always got on good with the frogs. It's funny where those big field glasses went, though. He used to always have them around his neck, but somebody must have figured they were no more good to him after he was dead, so they sucked them up. He used to always say that he was a big-shot gambler and that he used to watch the horse races with those glasses."

By now the four wounded men had been loaded into the ambulance. It moved off. Obviously, there was a good story in Mollie, but he was not available for an interview. The driver of the truck behind our jeep was giving us the horn, so I pulled Boyle toward the jeep. He got in, still looking back at Mollie, who said nothing to keep him, and we drove away. When we had gone a little way, at our customary slow pace, a tall lieutenant signalled to us from the roadside that he wanted a hitch and we stopped and indicated that he should hop aboard. He told us his name was Carl Ruff. He was from New York and thought I might know his wife, an advertising woman, but I didn't. Ruff was dog-tired from scrambling through the bush. I said something about Mollie, and Ruff said that he had not known him alive but had been the first American to see his body, on Good Friday morning. The French had led him to it. "He was on the slope of a hill," Ruff said, "and slugs from an automatic rifle had hit him in the right eye and chest. He must have been working his way up the hill, crouching, when the German opened on him and hit him in the chest, and then as he fell, the other bullet probably got him in the eye. He couldn't have lived a minute."

It was a month later, aboard the United States War Shipping Administration steamer Monterey, a luxury liner that had been converted to war service without any needless suppression of comfort, that I next heard of Molotov, the Mayor of Broadway. The Monterey was on her way from Casablanca to New York. On the passenger list were four correspondents besides myself, a thousand German prisoners, five hundred wounded Americans, all of whom would need long hospitalization, and a couple of hundred officers and men who were being transferred or were on various errands. It was one of the advantages of being a correspondent that one could go to America without being a German or wounded, or without being phenomenally lucky, which the unwounded soldiers on our boat considered that they were. The crossing had almost a holiday atmosphere. We were homeward bound after a great victory in the North African campaign, the first the Allies had scored over Germany in a war nearly four years old. The weather was perfect and the Monterey, which was not overcrowded and had wide decks and comfortable lounges, had the aspect and feeling of a cruise ship. The wounded were glad, in their sad way, to be going home. The prisoners were in good spirits, too; they seemed to regard the journey as a Nazi Strength through Joy excursion. They organized vaudeville shows, boxing matches, and art exhibitions, with the energetic coöperation of the ship's chaplain, who found much to admire in the Christian cheerfulness with which they endured their increased rations. A couple of anti-Nazi prisoners had announced themselves on the first day out, but the German noncoms had knocked them about and set them to cleaning latrines, so order had soon been restored. "That's an army where they really have some discipline!" one of the American officers on board told me enviously. The prisoners had to put up with some hardships, of course. They complained one evening when ice cream was served to the wounded but not to them, and another time they didn't think the transport surgeon, a Jew, was "sympathetic" enough to a German officer with a stomach ache.

The hospital orderlies would wheel the legless wounded out on the promenade deck in wheelchairs to see the German boxing bouts, and the other wounded would follow them, some swinging along on crutches or hopping on one foot, some with their arms in slings or casts, some with their broken necks held stiffly in casts and harnesses. They had mixed reactions to the bouts. An arm case named Sanderson, a private who wore the Ninth Division shoulder patch, told me one day that he wished he could be turned loose on the prisoners with a tommygun, because he didn't like to see them jumping about in front of his legless pals. Another arm case, named Shapiro, from the same division, always got a lot of amusement out of the show. Shapiro was a rugged-looking boy from the Brownsville part of Brooklyn. He explained how he felt one day after two Afrika Korps heavyweights had gone through a couple of rounds of grunting, posturing, and slapping. "Every time I see them box, I know we can't lose the war," he said. "The Master Race—phooey! Any kid off the street could of took the both of them."

Shapiro and Sanderson, I learned during one ringside conversation with them, had both been in the Sixtieth Infantry, Molotov's old regiment. They had been wounded in the fighting around Maknassy, in southern Tunisia, early in April, the first serious action the regiment had been in. Molotov had been killed late in April, during the drive on Bizerte, and until I told them, the boys hadn't heard he was dead. I asked them if they had known him.

"How could you help it?" Shapiro said. "There will never be anybody in the division as well known as him. In the first place, you couldn't help noticing him on account of his clothes. He looked like a soldier out of some other army, always wearing them twenty-dollar green tailor-made officers' shirts and sometimes riding boots, with a French berrit with a long rooster feather that he got off an Italian prisoner's hat, and a long black-and-red cape that he got off another prisoner for a can of C ration."

"And the officers let him get away with it?" I asked.

"Not in the rear areas, they didn't," Shapiro said. "But in combat, Mollie was an asset. Major Kauffman, his battalion commander, knew it, so he would kind of go along with him. But he would never have him made even a pfc. Mollie couldn't of stood the responsibility. He was the greatest natural-born foul-up in the Army," Shapiro added reverently. "He was court-martialled twenty or thirty times, but the Major always got him out of it. He had the biggest blanket roll in the Ninth Division, with a wall tent inside it and some

Arabian carpets and bronze lamps and a folding washstand and about five changes of uniform, none of them regulation, and he would always manage to get it on a truck when we moved. When he pitched his tent, it looked like a concession at Coney Island. I was with him when he got his first issue of clothing at Camp Dix in 1941. 'I've threw better stuff than this away,' he said. He never liked to wear issue. He was up for court-martial for deserting his post when he was on guard duty at Fort Bragg, but the regiment sailed for Morocco before they could try him, and he did so good in the landing at Port Lyautey that they kind of forgave him. Then he went over the hill again when he was guarding a dock at Oran in the winter, but they moved us up into the combat zone before they could try him then, so he beat that rap, too. He was a very lucky fellow. I can hardly think of him being dead."

"Well, what was so good about him?" I asked.

Sanderson, who was a thin, sharp-faced boy from Michigan, answered me with the embarrassed frankness of a modern mother explaining the facts of life to her offspring. "Sir," he said, "it may not sound nice to say it, and I do not want to knock anyone, but in battle almost everybody is frightened, especially the first couple of times. Once in a while you find a fellow who isn't frightened at all. He goes forward and the other fellows go along with him. So he is very important. Probably he is a popoff, and he kids the other guys, and they all feel better. Mostly those quiet, determined fellows crack up before the popoffs. Mollie was the biggest popoff and the biggest screwball and the biggest foul-up I ever saw, and he wasn't afraid of nothing. Some fellows get brave with experience, I guess, but Mollie never had any fear to begin with. Like one time on the road to Maknassy, the battalion was trying to take some hills and we were getting no place. They were just Italians in front of us, but they had plenty of stuff and they were in cover and we were in the open. Mollie stands right up, wearing the cape and the berrit with the feather, and he says, 'I bet those Italians would surrender if somebody asked them to. What the hell do they want to fight for?' he says. So he walks across the minefield and up the hill to the Italians, waving his arms and making funny motions, and they shoot at him for a while and then stop, thinking he is crazy. He goes up there yelling *'Veni qua!,'* which he says afterward is New York Italian for 'Come here!,' and *'Feeneesh la guerre!,'* which is French, and when he gets to the Italians he finds a soldier who was a barber in Astoria but went home on a visit and got drafted in the Italian Army, so the barber translates for him and the Italians say sure, they would like to surrender, and Mollie comes back to the lines with five hundred and sixty-eight prisoners. He had about ten Italian automatics strapped to his belt and fifteen field glasses hung over his shoulders. So instead of being stopped, we took the position and cleaned up on the enemy. That was good for the morale of the battalion. The next time we got in a fight, we said to ourselves, 'Those guys are just looking for an easy out,' so we got up and chased them the hell away from there. A disciplined soldier would never have did what Mollie done. He was a very unusual guy. He gave the battalion confidence and the battalion gave the regiment confidence, because the other battalions said, 'If the Second can take all those prisoners, we can, too.' And the Thirty-ninth and the Forty-seventh Regiments probably said to themselves, 'If the Sixtieth is winning all them fights, we can also.' So you might say that Mollie made the whole division." I found out afterward that Sanderson had oversimplified the story, but it was essentially true and the tradition endures in the Ninth Division.

"What kind of a looking fellow was Mollie?" I asked.

"He was a good-looking kid," Shapiro said. "Medium-sized, around a hundred and sixty pounds, with long, curly blond hair. They could almost never get him to have his hair cut. Once, when it got too bad, Major Kauffman took him by the hand and said, 'Come along with me. We'll get a haircut together.' So he sat him down and held onto him while the G.I. barber cut both their hair. And everything he wore had to be sharp. I remember that after the French surrendered to us at Port Lyautey, a lot of French officers gave a party and invited a couple of officers from the battalion to it, and when the officers got there they found Mollie was there, and the Frenchmen were all bowing to him and saluting him. He was dressed so sharp they thought he was an officer, too—maybe a colonel."

Another boy, a badly wounded one in a wheelchair, heard

us talking about Mollie and rolled his chair over to us. "It was the field glasses I'll always remember," he said. "From the first day we landed on the beach in Morocco, Mollie had those glasses. He told some fellows once he captured them from a French general, but he told some others he brought them all the way from New York. He told them he used to watch horse races with the glasses; he was fit to be tied when he got to Morocco and found there was no scratch sheets. 'Ain't there no way to telegraph a bet on a race?' he said, and then he let out a howl. 'Vot a schvindle!' That was his favorite saying—'Vot a schvindle!' He was always bitching about something. He used to go out scouting with the glasses, all alone, and find the enemy and tip Major Kauffman off where they were. He had a lot of curiosity. He always had plenty of money, but he would never tell where he got it from. He just let people understand he was a big shot—maybe in some racket. When we was down at Fort Bragg, he and another fellow, a sergeant, had a big Buick that he kept outside the camp, and they used to go riding all around the country. They used to get some swell stuff."

"He never shot crap for less than fifty dollars a roll when he had the dice," Shapiro said, "and he never slept with any woman under an actress." The way Shapiro said it, it was as if he had said, "He never saluted anybody under the rank of brigadier general."

During the rest of the voyage, I heard more about Mollie. I found nobody who was sure of his real name, but the majority opinion was that it was something like Carl Warren. "But he wasn't American stock or Irish," Sanderson said one day in a group discussion. "He seemed to me more German-American." Another boy in the conversation said that Mollie had told him he was of Russian descent. Sanderson was sure that Molotov wasn't Russian. "Somebody just called him that because he was a radical, I guess," he said. "He was always hollering he was framed." "He used to have a big map of the eastern front in his tent in Morocco," another soldier said, "and every time the Russians advanced he would mark it with pins and holler, 'Hey, Comrade, howdya like that!'" One boy remembered that Mollie had won fifteen hundred dollars in a crap game at Fort Bragg. "He had it for about three days," he said, "and then lost it to a civilian. When he got cleaned in a game, he would never borrow a buck to play on with. He would just leave. Then the next time he played, he would have a new roll. Right after we landed in Morocco, he was awful flush, even for him, and he told a couple of guys he'd climbed over the wall of an old fort the French had just surrendered and there, in some office, he found a briefcase with fifty thousand francs in it. The next thing he done was hire twelve Arabs to cook and clean and wash dishes for him."

"I was inducted the same time with him, at Grand Central Palace," an armless youngster said, "and him and me and the bunch was marched down to Penn Station to take the train. That was way back in January, 1941," he added, as if referring to a prehistoric event. "He was wearing a blue double-breasted jacket and a dark-blue sport shirt open at the neck and gray flannel trousers and a camel's-hair overcoat. They took us into a restaurant on Thirty-fourth Street to buy us a feed and Mollie started buying beers for the whole crowd. 'Come on, Comrades,' he says. 'Plenty more where this comes from.' Then he led the singing on the train all the way down to Dix. But as soon as he got down there and they took all his fancy clothes away from him, he was licked. 'Vot a schvindle!' he says. He drew K.P. a lot at Dix, but he always paid some other guy to do it for him. The only thing he could ever do good outside of combat was D.R.O. — that's dining-room orderly at the officers' mess. I've seen him carry three stacks of dishes on each arm."

When I told them how Mollie had been killed, Shapiro said that that was just what you'd have expected of Mollie. "He never liked to stay with his own unit," he said. "You could hardly even tell what battalion he was in."

I was not to see the Army's official version of what Mollie had done in the fight against the six hundred Italians until last summer, when I caught up with the Second Battalion of the Sixtieth Infantry near Marigny, in Normandy. Mollie's protector, Major Michael S. Kauffman, by then a lieutenant colonel, was still commanding officer. "Mollie didn't capture the lot by himself," Kauffman said, "but he was instrumental in getting them, and there were about six hundred of them all right. The battalion S-2 got out a mimeographed training pamphlet about that fight, because there were some points in it that we thought instructive. I'll get you a copy." The pamphlet he gave me bears the slightly ambitious title "The Battle of Sened, 23 March, '43, G Co. 60th Infantry Dawn Attack on Sened, Tunisia." The Sened of the title was the village of Sened, in the high *djebel* a couple of miles south of the Sened railroad station. It was country I remembered well: a bare plain with occasional bunch grass, with naked red-rock hills rising above it. The Americans had fought there several times; I had seen the taking of the railroad station by another regiment at the beginning of February, 1943, and it had been lost and retaken between then and March 23rd.

On the first page of the pamphlet there was a map showing the Italian position, on two hills separated by a narrow gorge, and the jump-off position of the Americans, two much smaller hills a couple of miles to the north. Then there was a list of "combat lessons to be learned," some of which were: "A small aggressive force can knock out a large group by determined action," "Individuals, soldiers with initiative, aggressiveness, and courage, can influence a large battle," and "Confusion is normal in combat." I have often since thought that this last would make a fine title for a book on war. The pamphlet told how an Italian force estimated at from thirty men to three thousand, according to the various persons interviewed in advance of the fight by S-2 ("Question civilians," the pamphlet said. "Don't rely on one estimate of enemy strength. Weigh all information in the light of its source."), had taken refuge in the village of Sened. G Company, about a hundred and fifty men, had been ordered to clean out the Italians. It had artillery support from some guns of the First Armored Division; in fact, a Lieutenant Colonel MacPherson, an artillery battalion commander, was actually the senior American officer in the action. This colonel, acting as his own forward observer, had looked over the situation and at four in the afternoon of March 22nd had ordered the first platoon of the company to attack. It was soon apparent, judging by the defenders' fire, that the lowest estimate of the enemy's strength was very wrong and that there were at least several hundred Italians on the two hills. Then, in the words of the pamphlet, "Private Molotov"—even his officers had long since forgotten his civilian name—"crawls to enemy position with Pfc. De Marco (both are volunteers) and arranges surrender conference. C.O. refuses to surrender and fire fight continues. Individual enemy riflemen begin to throw down their arms. First platoon returns to Sened Station at dark with 147 prisoners, including 3 officers."

"De Marco was a friend of Molotov's," Colonel Kauffman told me. "It was Mollie's idea to go up to the enemy position, and De Marco did the talking. It must have been pretty effective, because all those Italians came back with them."

"G Company," the pamphlet continued, "attacks again at dawn, first and third platoons attacking. Entrance to town is deep narrow gorge between two long ridges. Town lies in continuation of gorge, surrounded on all sides by 1,000–2,000 foot *djebels* as shown in sketch. (Possible enemy escape route was used by Ancient Romans as park for wild animals used in gladiatorial matches.) Approach to gorge entrance is terraced and well concealed by a large olive-tree grove; five (5) or six (6) field pieces in grove have been knocked out by previous day's artillery fire."

Although the pamphlet didn't say so, the olive groves had once covered all the plain. That plain is now given over to bunch grass, but it was carefully irrigated in the days of the Roman Empire. The "wild animals used in gladiatorial matches" were for the arena at the splendid stone city of Capsa, now the sprawling, dried-mud Arab town of Gafsa, fifteen miles from Sened.

"Company attacks as shown on sketch," the pamphlet continued, "third platoon making steep rocky climb around right, first platoon (Molotov's) around left. Light machine guns and mortars follow close behind by bounds, grenadiers move well to front with mission of flushing enemy out of numerous caves where he has taken up defensive positions. Left platoon, commanded by Sergeant Vernon Mugerditchian, moves slowly over ground devoid of concealment, and finally comes to rest. Molotov goes out alone, keeping abreast of faster moving platoon on right, and assists Lt. Col. MacPherson in artillery direction by shouting."

The combined artillery and infantry fire made the Italians quit. The pamphlet says, in closing, "Italian captain leads column of prisoners out of hills, bringing total of 537 (including officers). Total booty includes 2 large trucks, 3 small trucks, several personnel carrier motorcycles, 200 pistols, machine guns, rifles, and ammunition."

"Mollie liked to go out ahead and feel he was running the show," Colonel Kauffman said. "We put him in for a D.S.C. for what he did, but it was turned down. Then we put in for a Silver Star, and that was granted, but he was killed before he ever heard about it. He was a terrible soldier. He and another fellow were to be tried by a general court-martial for quitting their guard posts on the docks at Oran, but we had to go into action before court could be held. The other fellow had his court after the end of the campaign and got five years."

The officers of the battalion, and those at division headquarters, knew that I was going to write a story about Mollie sometime. Whenever I would encounter one of them, in a country tavern or at a corps or Army headquarters, or on a dusty road behind the lines, during our final campaign before Germany's surrender, he would ask me when I was going to "do Mollie." I am doing him now.

Even after I had been back in the States for a while that summer of 1943, I had an intermittent interest in Mollie, although La Piste Forestière assumed a curious unreality after I had been living on lower Fifth Avenue a couple of weeks. I asked a fellow I knew at the *Times* to check back through the casualty lists and see if the death of a soldier with a name like "Carl Warren" had been reported, since I knew the lists gave the addresses of the next of kin and I thought I might be able to find out more about Mollie. The *Times* man found out that there hadn't been any such name but that there was often a long interval between casualties and publication. I took to turning mechanically to the new lists as they came out and looking through the "W"s. One day I saw listed, among the Army dead, "Karl C. Warner, sister Mrs. Ulidjak, 230 E. Eightieth Street, Manhattan." The juxtaposition of "a name like Warren" with one that I took to be Russian or Ukrainian made me suspect that Warner was Molotov, and it turned out that I was right.

A couple of days later, I went uptown to look for Mrs. Ulidjak. No. 230 is between Second and Third Avenues, in a block overshadowed by the great, brute mass of the Manhattan Storage & Warehouse Company's building at the corner of Eightieth. Along the block there were a crumbling, red-brick elementary school of the type Fusion administrations like to keep going so that they can hold the tax rate down, a yellowish, old-fashioned Baptist church, some boys playing ball in the street, and a banner, bearing a number of service stars, hung on a line stretched across the street. As yet, it had no gold stars. No. 230 is what is still called a "new-law tenement," although the law governing this type of construction is fifty years old: a six-story walkup with the apartments built around air shafts. Ulidjak was one of the names on the mailboxes in the vestibule. I pushed the button beside it, and in a minute there was an answering buzz and I walked upstairs. A thin, pale woman with a long, bony face and straight blond hair pulled back into a bun came to the apartment door. She looked under thirty and wore silver-rimmed spectacles. This was Mrs. Ulidjak, Private Warner's sister. Her husband is in the Merchant Marine. She didn't seem startled when I said I was a correspondent; every American expects to be interviewed by a reporter sometime. Mrs. Ulidjak had been notified of her brother's death by the War Department over a week before, but she had no idea how it had happened or where. She said he had been in the Sixtieth Infantry, all right, so I was sure Warner had been Mollie. "Was he fighting the Japs?" she asked me. When I told her no, she seemed slightly disappointed. "And you were there?" she asked. I said I had been. Then, apparently trying to visualize me in the context of war, she asked, "Did you wear a helmet, like Ernie Pyle? Gee, they must be heavy to wear. Did it hurt your head much?" When I had reassured her on this point, she led me into a small sitting room with a window opening on a dark air shaft. A young man and a young woman, who Mrs. Ulidjak said were neighbors, were in the room, but they went into the adjoining kitchen, apparently so that they would not feel obliged to look solemn.

"Was your name Warner, too, before you were married?" I asked Mrs. Ulidjak.

"No," she said, "Karl and I were named Petuskia—that's Russian—but he changed to Warner when he came to New York because he thought it sounded sweller. We were from a little place called Cokesburg, in western Pennsylvania. He hardly ever came up here. He had his own friends."

"Did he go to high school in Cokesburg?" I asked.

The idea amused Mrs. Ulidjak. "No, just grammar school," she said. "He was a pit boy in the coal mines until we came to New York. But he always liked to dress nice. You can ask any of the cops around the Mall in Central Park about him. Curly, they used to call him, or Blondy. He was quite a lady's man."

Then I asked her the question that had puzzled Mollie's Army friends: "What did he do for a living before he went into the Army?"

"He was a bartender down to Jimmy Kelly's, the night club in the Village," Mrs. Ulidjak said.

She then told me that her brother's Christian name really was Karl and that he was twenty-six when he was killed, although he had looked several years younger. Both parents are dead. The parents had never told her, as far as she could remember, what part of Russia they came from. When I said that Mollie had been a hero, she was pleased, and said he had always had an awful crust. She called the young neighbors, who seemed to be of Italian descent, back into the sitting room and made me repeat the story of how Mollie captured the six hundred Italians (I hadn't seen the official version of his exploit yet and naturally I gave him full credit in mine). "Six hundred wops!" Mrs. Ulidjak exclaimed gaily. She got a lot of fun out of Mollie's "big shot" stories, too. She showed me a large, expensive-looking photograph of him "addressing" a golf ball. He was wearing light-colored plus-fours, white stockings, and brogues with tassels, and there was a big, happy grin on his face that made it plain that he was not going to hit the ball but was just posing. He had a wide, plump face with high cheekbones and square white teeth, and the hair about which I had so often heard looked at least six inches long. "He had a room at 456 West Forty-fourth Street, and a little Jewish tailor down in that neighborhood made all those nice things for him special," she said admiringly. She had never heard him called Molotov.

I went over to West Forty-fourth Street a few days later. The 400 block, between Ninth and Tenth Avenues, looks more depressing than the one the Ulidjaks live on. It is mostly shops dealing in the cheap merchandise that is used as premiums, and stores that sell waiters' supplies, and lodging houses favored by waiters and cooks. It was evident from the look of the house at No. 456 that though Mollie had spent a disproportionate share of his income on clothes, he had not wasted anything on his living quarters. No one at No. 456 remembered Mollie. The tenants and the janitor had all come there since his time. I couldn't find the little tailor. But on the north side of Forty-fourth Street, near Ninth Avenue, there is a building occupied by the Warner Brothers' Eastern offices, and I was sure that this had given Mollie the idea of calling himself Warner.

That evening I went down to Jimmy Kelly's, on Sullivan Street. Kelly's is the kind of club that never changes much but that you seldom remember anything specific about unless you have had a fight there. I had been there a few times before I had gone overseas, in 1941, but I couldn't even remember the bartender's face. Kelly's has a dance floor a little bigger than two tablecloths, and there is always a show with young, sometimes pretty girls imitating the specialties that more famous and experienced performers are doing at clubs uptown, and a master of ceremonies making cracks so old that they have been used in Hollywood musicals. The man behind the bar the night I showed up said he had been there several years and had known his predecessor, whose name was not Molotov. He had never heard of a bartender named Molotov or Warner or Mollie or Karl at Kelly's. After I had had a couple of Scotches and had told him the story, he said he wondered if the fellow I meant hadn't been a busboy. The description seemed to fit one who had worked there. "We all used to call this kid Curly," he said, "but Ray, the waiter who is the union delegate, might remember his real name."

Ray was a scholarly-looking man with a high, narrow fore-head and shell-rimmed spectacles. "Curly's name *was* Karl C. Warner," he said after he had been told what I wanted to know. "I remember it from his union card. He was a man who would always stand up for his fellow-worker. Waiters and Waitresses Local No. 1 sent him down here in the summer of 1940 and he worked until late the next fall. He was outspoken but a hard worker and strong—he could carry three stacks of dishes on each arm. A busboy has a lot to do in a place like this when there is a rush on—clearing away dishes, setting up for new parties, bringing the waiters their orders—and a stu-pid boy can spoil the waiters' lives for them. We had another boy here at the same time, an Irish boy, who kidded Curly about the fancy clothes he wore, so they went down in the basement and fought for a couple of hours one afternoon. Nobody won the fight. They just fought until they were tired and then stopped. Curly had wide interests for a busboy," Ray continued. "When there was no rush on, he would some-times stop by a customer's table, particularly if it was some man who looked important, and talk to him for ten minutes or so. The customers didn't seem to mind. He had a nice way about him. He had a kind of curiosity."

The Army stories about Mollie's wealth made Ray and the bartender laugh. "He used to come back here now and then during the first year he was in the Army," Ray said, "and always he would borrow ten or twenty dollars from one of us waiters. We would lend it to him because we liked him, with-out expecting to get it back." A busboy at Kelly's is paid only nominal wages, Ray told me—just about enough to cover his laundry bill—but the waiters chip in a percentage of their tips for the boys. "I guess Curly averaged about forty a week here," he said. "If he was anxious to get extra money, he might have had a lunch job someplace else at the same time, but I never heard about it. A tailor like he had probably made those suits for about twenty-five per. What else did he have to spend money on? His night life was here. He used to tell us he had worked at El Morocco, but we used to say, 'What's the difference? Dirty dishes are the same all over.'"

At the union headquarters, which are on the twelfth floor of a loft building on West Fortieth Street, Mollie was also remembered. The serious, chunky young woman in the union secretary's office said, "Warner was always a dissident. He would speak up at every meeting and object to everything. But we all liked him. He stopped paying dues a few months before he went into the Army, but at Christmastime in 1941 he came back here and said he heard that union members in the services were getting a present from the local, so he wanted one, too. So we gave it to him, of course. The secretary will be interested to know he is dead."

The young woman called the secretary, a plump, olive-complexioned man, from his desk in an inner room and said to him, "You remember Karl Warner, the blond boy with curly hair? He has been killed in Africa. He was a hero."

"Is that so?" the secretary said. "Well, get a man to put up a gold paper star on the flag in the members' hall right away and draw up a notice to put on the bulletin board. He is the first member of Local No. 1 to die in this war."

I thought how pleased Mollie would have been at being restored to good standing in the union, without even having paid up his dues. Then I thought of how much fun he would have had on the Mall in Central Park, in the summertime, if he could only have gone up there with his Silver Star ribbon on, and a lot of enemy souvenirs. I also thought of how far La Piste Forestière was from the kitchen in Jimmy Kelly's.

The New Yorker, May 26, June 2, 1945

"When American Citizens Murder U.S. Soldiers"

by George S. Schuyler

THE EXECUTION by Japanese militarists of three of the captured Army airmen who bombed Tokyo in accordance with
orders from superiors has horrified the country. These men
were just performing their duty in the uniform of the United
States and yet were murdered in cold blood for allegedly
bombing non-military targets. These executions were contrary to all international law and practice among white nations, although none of these nations has hesitated to execute
"natives" who were captured while fighting for freedom. In
1930 when several leaders of the Burma revolt were captured,
the British chopped off their heads and paraded them on a
plank through the countryside as a "lesson" to the natives.
International law also failed to save the shipwrecked Japanese
sailors hanging on to floats and debris after the American victory in the Bismarck Sea. These Japanese swimming for their
lives were all doing their duty as commanded by superiors.

Undoubtedly the United States will wreak vengeance on the
Japanese for executing these uniformed Army airmen who
were only doing their duty. In the meantime I wish the
United States would wreak vengeance on those people within
the confines of this country and easily arrested who have
killed American soldiers in uniform and gone unpunished to
date.

There is, for example, the case of Pvt. Raymond Carr, a
colored citizen of the United States. Private Carr while in the
uniform of the U.S.A., and while on duty as directed by his
superior officers, was killed in cold blood by an officer of the
State Police department of Louisiana in Alexandria, La., because he refused to leave his post of duty. The grand jury in
Louisiana refused to act, so Wendell Berge, Assistant Attorney

General of the United States has recommended to the Attorney General that no further action be taken concerning this murder of a uniformed American soldier on duty by a member of the Louisiana armed forces. The killing of Private Carr was contrary to the laws of the United States and Louisiana, and yet the Department of Justice is going to forget the whole matter!

On March 22, 1942, Sgt. Thomas B. Foster of the United States Army was shot to death at the doorstep of the Allison Presbyterian church in Little Rock, Ark., by a member of the armed forces of that city. The U.S. government halted prosecution of this white murderer because he was inducted into the U.S. Army! Would we excuse the murderers of the three Army aviators because the Japanese government transferred them to the ambulance corps!

On July 28, 1942, Pvt. Charles J. Rico of the United States Army was murdered in cold blood by a member of the armed forces of Beaumont, Texas. The local U.S. Attorney announced in January 1943, that the case against the murderer would not be prosecuted because "it is lacking in those elements promising a successful prosecution." When the NAACP legal department protested in February against this attitude, the Attorney General replied that the case "would not be opened or re-investigated."

Of course there have been almost countless cases of Negro soldiers in the uniform of the United States being beaten to a pulp by civilian police, sometimes resulting in death or permanent injury. There are few if any instances of the culprit or culprits being punished. Certainly none of the members of the armed forces of Arkansas nor any of the citizens who joined them in assaulting colored soldiers and their white officers have been prosecuted for this outrageous violation of U.S. laws. After elaborate investigation the Department of Justice told the NAACP that "the department's files in this matter have been closed."

In other words, when the Japanese murder captured U.S. soldiers in uniform and performing their duties, the United States seethes with indignation and horror, and the government vows to spare no expense in wreaking vengeance upon the yellow murderers who have flouted international law.

But when American citizens murder U.S. soldiers in uniform and in some instances performing their duties, the crimes get brief and often obscure notice in the daily press, and after a certain legal shadow-boxing, Uncle Sam throws up his hands and says "case closed." Meanwhile the murderers walk the streets and scoff at the law, knowing it will not be enforced when non-whites are involved.

Would you not think that the most powerful government on earth could more easily punish its citizens who murder men wearing its uniform than it could punish the nationals of a great military power 7,000 miles across the Pacific who were guilty of the same crime?

Is the statement of Justice Taney still true, that "a Negro has no rights that a white man is bound to respect"? If so, where is the "progress" in race relations to which orators and editorial writers are always referring?

Pittsburgh Courier, May 8, 1943

The Japanese Mind

by Robert Sherrod

THE JAPS' last mad rush on Attu against the weary but un-mercifully relentless American troops has been compared by Radio Tokyo to the Charge of the Light Brigade. Militarily, it was a wash-out. Between 800 and 1,000 furious, frustrated Japs, jabbering insanely, died as a result of their saber- and flag-waving rush. They killed less than one-fourth as many Americans, though they had all the advantage of surprise against troops who were chiefly untrained non-combatants. Not only that. Many a Jap—the number is estimated at more than 500—killed himself by pressing a grenade to his stomach and blowing his guts out, though he could have continued killing Americans. Instead of fulfilling their mission of killing as many of the enemy as possible, the Japanese seem to have been too intent upon screaming *"Banzai!"* and then dying. In this intention they were eminently successful, creating the most violent carnal scene ever laid upon a battlefield of comparable size. Literally, the Jap upon Attu was exposed. Looking upon the grotesque masses of exploded bodies, one young American officer remarked: "That just ain't good soldiering."

Some hint of the Japanese fixation upon dying can be found in various documents they left behind them. Such actual morbidity is difficult of understanding to men who love life and living. Reading translations of their writings, one can imagine cold, hungry little men in little black rubber boots and muddy khaki uniforms, waiting for death in their fox-holes, assuring themselves that it will be pleasant. One after another they write: "I await death with a smile," or "I shall smile when the enemy arrives." One superior private (the grade above first-class private) writes continuously, almost ravenously, of death throughout the record of his last few days: "The enemy finally landed so we sentries all swore to sacrifice our life for our country." Note that he did not say that he would die for Japan if necessary. He took an oath to die. Period. Four days later, still alive and doubtless fretting about it, he indicates smugly that he has not forgotten his oath: "My regards to all my acquaintances. Seiji will die with a smile."

Another Jap soldier pursues the same tack. He notes that the Kato position advanced about 30 meters, "but was caught in concentrated fire, and all fell. We sang the military song, *The Dream of Camping*, and shouted '*Banzai*'! Alas—" Later the same day he notes that Kato himself died, having done a good job of taking care of communications, a very dangerous mission. "He has become an incarnation of a hero, the best within the company." (Japs apparently qualify as heroes only in the post-mortem state.) To reassure the spirit of Kato, the writer adds: "Rest in peace, old man, we'll follow you."

Next day there was more song about death. "Sergeant Nakamura sang: 'Even though I die on the lonely fields of Attu, I must obey the customs of Samurai.'" Having listened to the lugubrious sergeant, the writer's contentedly morbid thoughts turn to his late sergeant major: "Kawoso's body will decay with the earth." Then the writer fairly wallows in his morbidity: "I feel just like the song that Sergeant Nakamura sang." Then the chronicler pinches himself to make sure that he is still on the spectral beam. "It is easy to die in this land, but how can I secure my honor?" Apparently he is wondering how the folks back home can be certain about the details of his demise. The next day presumably was his last, which caused him great happiness because "it is the anniversary of my father's death."

The little defenders of Attu reminded themselves frequently that, once dead, they would become deified. "I am writing this note under shell bursts dropping near our trench," wrote Superior Private Kikuchi. "However, it is still too early to despair, since we have arms and legs and can fight as human bullets until becoming deities of guardianship." On another leaf he states his creed: "If a warrior dies when he should, he becomes a god and suppresses the enemy." Several writers mention the shrine at Tokyo where rest the spirits of dead, deified soldiers. "Let's meet at the Yasukini Shrine after all have died gloriously in this battle," suggests Kikuchi happily. Said an incredulous American colonel upon reading this sentiment: "Do they really believe it's better to be a dead god than a live Jap?"

Death gets top billing in the Japs' pre-deification breeding, but worldly considerations sometimes creep into their thoughts. "It is very cold at night and my feet are frozen and numb, so I can't sleep due to the pain," one soldier notes. Says another: "Even in the midst of trench-mortar fire, I regain my self-possession when I smoke tobacco." And another: "The hours are long. Could do any type of work if I could only get two rice balls a day. I haven't slept for eight days."

While all of them looked to death with some degree of eagerness, not all the Jap chroniclers despaired of winning the Battle of Attu. Some even hoped for help, and the rumors that abounded in Attu's trenches were strangely reminiscent of the optimistic rumors that flitted endlessly around Bataan, where American troops looked forward to dying with no eagerness whatsoever. Early in the Attu campaign one Jap noted: "Our only hope is the arrival of a transport convoy and planes." Two days later he was confidently waiting for reinforcements, and by the fifth day he had seen two P-40 planes shot down (anyway, he thought so, though none was). Ten days after the battle's beginning he was nursing a whopper of a rumor: "We are now waiting for reinforcements by two battleships, two cruisers, two aircraft carriers, three destroyers and four transports." In his final entry, five days later, this Jap was still telling himself: "Heard the news that transport convoy would come in."

In all this human misery and disappointment, which might be expected to make a normal man fret, there is no complaining among the Japanese. The Jap does not say: "Why in hell don't they send reinforcements?" or "Snafu again. No food and no blankets up here in this freezing foxhole." He meekly observes that it is colder on Attu in May than it would be in northernmost Japan in January, and lets it go at that. He is not disposed to criticize, nor even to express a controversial opinion. He gives no evidence of being able to think for himself. He never lifts his voice against his officers, because this would be going against established authority. (Besides, won't his officers lead him to blissful death and subsequent god-hood?) Stern militarists might argue that this blind submission to authority makes for better soldiers. Most U.S. generals say they prefer a good, griping soldier to one who shows no tendency toward reasoning for himself.

The Jap is no easy soldier to conquer, because he does not give up. But he does crack on the anvil of his own desperation. In the face of defeat his frustration leads him to sub-human fanaticism, including self-destruction. As we learn more about the dark, unexplored crevasses of his thinking processes (or lack thereof), we perceive better means of fighting him. This is the value of the Battle of Attu.

The other side of the picture is the Japanese soldier whose will has been broken: the prisoner. As he is taught to anticipate death as the final reward, the Japanese soldier is taught that surrender is eternal disgrace, extending to his descendants, relatives and friends. Consequently, few surrender. Two weeks after the battle for Attu had ended, 25 Japs—roughly one per cent—had given themselves up. There probably will be a few others—hunger inspires hopelessness in the Jap quicker than bullets.

Most of these 25 have been amazed at not being killed by their captors, although some of them put enough faith in the U.S. to present surrender leaflets. (One was warned that he could expect no kind treatment unless he cooperated in questioning. He pointed to the leaflet assuring him of good treatment and, insisting on his rights, said: "Oh, yes, you said so right here.") Many prisoners are overjoyed upon learning that they will be fed and warmly clothed—they fairly burst with gratitude.

The prisoner interrogation is conducted by an Army captain of the Intelligence branch through a number of soldiers who have lived in Japan and know its language well. At the end of each questioning period the captain tells the prisoner: "You are a prisoner of the United States and, accordingly, you will be given the best of treatment as provided by international law." One stocky little Jap upon hearing these words jumped up, saluted, smiled broadly, then insisted on shaking hands with his captors. The captors grinned as they accepted the handshake.

Most prisoners volunteer to work for the United States, to do everything possible to help the U.S. win the war. They have become, in the eyes of Japan, not merely prisoners but traitors. It is not difficult to understand why few Japs surrender, nor why those who do surrender say they never want to return to Japan. Two of the 25 prisoners have admitted that they regretted surrendering. One asked that he be allowed to commit suicide. Another, asked why he surrendered, said: "The devil got into me." Most, however, are normal enough to be glad to be alive.

In their writings and in their interrogations the Japs express no hatred against their enemy, who to them is evidently quite impersonal. The severest thing one has written about us is a note: "I will be born seven times until I subdue the American troops, and even the grass steams up."

This is from a series of paragraphs entitled *Poems and Words of Sentiments*. These paragraphs provide a key to the simple-minded, single-minded little men we are fighting:

"Is war such a thing as this? Soon after firing ceases, birds are singing and flying around above the quiet and frozen ground.

"Even the gun firing which echoes in the sky above the frozen ground can't be heard while I am eating.

"My comrade, whose left lung was shot, stopped breathing before he finished repeating the word 'water' three times.

"I feel keenly dear to those who were killed in this battle.

"Voices of 'Banzai' spoken by dying soldiers who were hit by enemy shells would make a wild god weep.

"Water has all been used up. It has been eight days, and still no reinforcements. I will make this my dying place.

"I think of this severe battle over and over as I look at the rice balls covered with dirt.

"I will become a deity with a smile in this heavy fog. I am only waiting for the day of death, but how many days of trench-mortar fire I have survived!"

History in the Writing, 1945

The Sicilian Campaign

by Ernie Pyle

"The Dying Man Was Left Utterly Alone"

SOMEWHERE IN SICILY—(by wireless)—It was flabbergasting to lie among a tentful of wounded soldiers recently and hear them cuss and beg to be sent right back into the fight.

Of course not all of them do. It depends on the severity of their wounds, and on their individual personalities, just as it would in peacetime. But I will say that at least a third of the moderately wounded men ask if they can't be returned to duty immediately.

When I took sick I was with the 45th Division, made up largely of men from Oklahoma and West Texas. You don't realize how different certain parts of our country are from others until you see their men set off in a frame, as it were, in some strange faraway place like this.

The men of Oklahoma are drawling and soft-spoken. They are not smart-alecks. Something of the purity of the soil seems to be in them. Even their cussing is simpler and more profound than the torrential obscenities of Eastern city men. An Oklahoman of the plains is straight and direct. He is slow to criticize and hard to anger, but once he is convinced of the wrong of something, brother, watch out.

These wounded men of Oklahoma have got madder about the war than anybody I have seen on this side of the ocean. They weren't so mad before they got into action, but now to them the Germans across the hill are all "sonsabitches."

And these quiet men of the 45th, the newest division over here, have already fought so well they have drawn the high praise of the commanding general of the corps of which the division is a part.

*   *   *

It was these men from the farms, ranches and small towns of Oklahoma who poured through my tent with their wounds. I lay there and listened for what each one would say first.

One fellow, seeing a friend, called out, "I think I'm gonna make her." Meaning he was going to pull through.

Another said, "Have they got beds in the hospital? Lord how I want to go to bed."

Another said, "I'm hungry, but I can't eat anything. I keep getting sick at my stomach."

Another said, as he winced from their probing for a deeply buried piece of shrapnel in his leg, "Go head, you're the doc. I can stand it."

Another said, "I'll have to write the old lady tonight and tell her she missed out on that $10,000 again."

Another, who was put down beside me, said, "Hi, Pop, how you getting along? I call you Pop because you're gray-headed. You don't mind, do you?"

I told him I didn't care what he called me. He was friendly, but you could tell from his forward attitude that he was not from Oklahoma. When I asked him, it turned out he was from New Jersey.

One big blond Oklahoman had slight flesh wounds in the face and the back of his neck. He had a patch on his upper lip which prevented his moving it, and made him talk in a grave, straight-faced manner that was comical. I've never seen anybody so mad in my life. He went from one doctor to another trying to get somebody to sign his card returning him to duty.

The doctors explained patiently that if he returned to the front his wounds would get infected and he would be a burden on his company instead of a help. They tried to entice him by telling him there would be nurses back in the hospital. But he said, "To hell with the nurses, I want to get back to fightin'."

*   *   *

Dying men were brought into our tent, men whose death rattle silenced the conversation and made all the rest of us grave.

When a man was almost gone the surgeons would put a

piece of gauze over his face. He could breathe through it but we couldn't see his face well.

Twice within five minutes chaplains came running. One of these occasions haunted me for hours.

The man was still semi-conscious. The chaplain knelt down beside him and two ward boys squatted alongside. The chaplain said:

"John, I'm going to say a prayer for you."

Somehow this stark announcement hit me like a hammer. He didn't say, "I'm going to pray for you to get well," he just said he was going to say a prayer, and it was obvious he meant the final prayer. It was as though he had said, "Brother, you may not know it, but your goose is cooked."

He said a short prayer, and the weak, gasping man tried in vain to repeat the words after him. When he had finished the chaplain said, "John, you're doing fine, you're doing fine." Then he rose and dashed off on other business, and the ward boys went about their duties.

The dying man was left utterly alone, just lying there on his litter on the ground, lying in an aisle, because the tent was full. Of course it couldn't be otherwise, but the awful aloneness of that man as he went through the last few minutes of his life was what tormented me. I felt like going over and at least holding his hand while he died, but it would have been out of order and I didn't do it. I wish now I had.

Scripps-Howard wire copy, August 9, 1943

"Damn Sick of War—and Deadly Tired"

SOMEWHERE IN SICILY—(by wireless)—Outside of the occasional peaks of bitter fighting and heavy casualties that high light military operation, I believe the outstanding trait in any campaign is the terrible weariness that gradually comes over everybody.

Soldiers become exhausted in mind and in soul as well as physically. They acquire a weariness that is mixed up with boredom and lack of all gaiety. To lump them all together, you just get damn sick of it all.

The infantry reaches a stage of exhaustion that is incomprehensible to you folks back home. The men in the First Division, for instance, were in the lines 28 days—walking and fighting all that time, day and night.

After a few days of such activity, soldiers pass the point of known human weariness. From then on they go into a sort of second-wind daze. They keep going largely because the other fellow does and because you can't really do anything else.

Have you ever in your life worked so hard and so long that you didn't remember how many days it was since you ate last or didn't recognize your friends when you saw then? I never have either, but in the First Division, during that long, hard fight around Troina, a company runner one day came slogging up to a certain captain and said, excitedly, "I've got to find Captain Blank right away. Important message."

The Captain said, "But I am Captain Blank. Don't you recognize me?"

And the runner said, "I've got to find Capt. Blank right away." And he went dashing off. They had to run to catch him.

Men in battle reach that stage and still go on and on. As for the rest of the Army—supply troops, truck drivers, hospital men, engineers—they too become exhausted but not so inhumanly. With them and with us correspondents it's the ceaselessness, the endlessness of everything that finally worms its way through you and gradually starts to devour you.

It's the perpetual dust choking you, the hard ground wracking your muscles, the snatched food sitting ill on your stomach, the heat and the flies and dirty feet and the constant roar of engines and the perpetual moving and the never settling down and the go, go, go, night and day, and on through the night again. Eventually it all works itself into an emotional tapestry of one dull, dead pattern—yesterday is tomorrow and Troina is Randazzo and when will we ever stop and, God, I'm so tired.

I've noticed this feeling has begun to overtake the war correspondents themselves. It is true we don't fight on and on like the infantry, that we are usually under fire only briefly and that, indeed, we live better than the average soldier. Yet our lives are strangely consuming in that we do live primitively and at the same time must delve into ourselves and do creative writing.

That statement may lay me open to wise cracks, but however it may seem to you, writing is an exhausting and tearing thing. Most of the correspondents actually work like slaves. Especially is this true of the press-association men. A great part of the time they go from dawn till midnight or 2 a.m.

I'm sure they turn in as much toil in a week as any newspaperman at home does in two weeks. We travel continuously, move camp every few days, eat out, sleep out, write wherever we can and just never catch up on sleep, rest, cleanliness, or anything else normal.

The result is that all of us who have been with the thing for more than a year have finally grown befogged. We are grimy, mentally as well as physically. We've drained our emotions until they cringe from being called out from hiding. We look at bravery and death and battlefield waste and new countries almost as blind men, seeing only faintly and not really wanting to see at all.

Just in the past month the old-timers among the correspondents have been talking for the first time about wanting to go home for a while. They want a change, something to freshen their outlook. They feel they have lost their perspective by being too close for too long.

I am not writing this to make heroes of the correspondents, because only a few look upon themselves in any dramatic light whatever. I am writing it merely to let you know that correspondents too can get damn sick of war—and deadly tired.

Scripps-Howard wire copy, August 25, 1943

"A Hell of a Job"

SOMEWHERE IN SICILY—(by wireless)—When the 45th Division went into reserve along the north coast of Sicily after several weeks of hard fighting, I moved on with the Third Division which took up the ax and drove the enemy on to Messina.

I am still doing engineers and it was on my very first day with the Third that we hit the most difficult and spectacular engineering job of the Sicilian campaign.

You've doubtless noticed Point Calava on your maps. It is a great stub of rock that sticks out into the sea, forming a high ridge running back into the interior. The coast highway is tunneled through this big rock, and on either side of the tunnel the road sticks out of the sheer rock wall like a shelf.

Our engineers figured the Germans would blow the tunnel entrance to seal it up. But they didn't. They had an even better idea. They picked out a spot about 50 feet beyond the tunnel mouth and blew a hole 150 feet long in the road shelf. They blew it so deeply and thoroughly that if you dropped a rock into it the rock would never stop rolling until it bounced into the sea a couple of hundred feet below.

We were beautifully bottlenecked. You couldn't by-pass around the rock, for it dropped sheer into the sea. You couldn't by-pass up over the mountain, for it would take weeks. You couldn't fill the hole, for it would keep sliding off into the water.

All you could do was bridge it, and that was a hell of a job. But bridge it they did, and in only 24 hours.

*   *   *

When the first engineer officers went up to inspect the tunnel, I went with them. We had to leave the jeep at a blown bridge and walk the last four miles uphill. We went with an infantry battalion that was following the retreating Germans.

When we got there we found the tunnel floor mined. But each spot where they'd dug into the hard rock floor left its telltale mark, so it was no job for the engineers to uncover and unscrew the detonators of scores of mines. Then we went on through to the vast hole beyond, and the engineering officers began making their calculations.

As we did so, the regiment of infantry crawled across the chasm, one man at a time. You could just barely make it on foot by holding on to the rock juttings and practically crawling.

Another regiment went up over the ridge and took out after the evacuating enemy with only what weapons and provisions they could carry on their backs. Before another 24 hours, they'd be 20 miles ahead of us and in contact with the enemy, so getting this hole bridged and supplies and supporting guns to them was indeed a matter of life and death.

*   *   *

It was around 2 p.m. when we got there and in two hours the little platform of highway at the crater mouth resembled a littered street in front of a burning building. Air hoses covered the ground, serpentined over each other. Three big air compressors were parked side by side, their engines cutting off and on in that erratically deliberate manner of air compressors, and jack hammers clattered their nerve-shattering din.

Bulldozers came to clear off the stone-blocked highway at the crater edge. Trucks, with long trailers bearing railroad irons and huge timbers, came and unloaded. Steel cable was brought up. And kegs of spikes and all kinds of crowbars and sledges.

The thousands of vehicles of the division were halted some 10 miles back in order to keep the highway clear for the engineers. One platoon of men worked at a time in the hole. There was no use of throwing in the whole company, for there was room for only so many.

At suppertime, hot rations were brought up by truck. The Third Division engineers go on K ration at noon but morning and evening they get hot food up to them, regardless of the job.

If you could see how they toil, you would know how important this hot food is. By dusk the work was in full swing and half the men were stripped to the waist.

The night air of the Mediterranean was tropical. The moon came out at twilight and extended our light for a little while. The moon was new and pale, and transient high-flying night clouds brushed it and scattered shadows down on us.

Then its frail light went out, and the blinding nightlong darkness settled over the insidious abyss. But the work never slowed nor halted, throughout the night.

Scripps-Howard wire copy, September 3, 1943

"Miracle Bridge"

SOMEWHERE IN SICILY—(by wireless)—It was an hour after daylight when I returned to the German-blown highway crater which our Third Division engineers had been working on all night.

It really didn't look as though they'd accomplished much, but an engineer's eye would have seen that the groundwork was all laid. They had drilled and blasted two holes far down the jagged slope. These were to set upright timbers into so they wouldn't slide downhill when weight was applied.

The far side of the crater had been blasted out and leveled off so it formed a road across about one-third of the hole. Small ledges had been jack-hammered at each end of the crater and timbers bolted into them forming abutments of the bridge that was to come.

Steel hooks had been imbedded deep into the rock to hold wire cables. At the tunnel mouth lay great timbers, two feet square, and other long pieces of timber bolted together in the middle to make them long enough to span the hole.

*   *   *

At about 10 a.m., the huge uprights were slid down the bank, caught by a group of men clinging to the steep slope below, and their ends worked into the blasted holes. Then they were brought upright by men on the banks, pulling on ropes tied to them. Similar heavy timbers were slowly and cautiously worked out from the bank until their tops rested on the uprights.

A half-naked soldier doing practically a wire-walking act, edged out over the timber and bored a long hole down through two timbers with an air-driven bit. Then he hammered a steel rod into it, tying them together.

Others added more bracing, nailing them together with huge spikes driven in by sledge hammers. Then they slung steel cable from one end of the crater to the other, wrapped it around the upright stanchions and drew it tight with a winch mounted on a truck.

*   *   *

Now came the coolie scene as 20 shirtless, sweating soldiers to each of the long-spliced timbers carried and slid them out across the chasm, resting them on the two wooden spans just erected. They sagged in the middle, but still the cable beneath took most of the strain. They laid 10 of those across and the bridge began to take shape. Big stringers were bolted down, heavy flooring was carried on and nailed to the stringers. Men built up the approaches with stones. The bridge was almost ready.

Around 11 a.m., jeeps had begun to line up at the far end of the tunnel. They carried reconnaissance platoons, machine gunners and boxes of ammunition. They'd been given No. 1 priority to cross the bridge.

First, Maj. Gen. Truscott arrived again and sat on a log talking with the engineering officers, waiting patiently. Around dusk of the day before, the engineers had told me they'd have jeeps across the crater by noon of the next day. It didn't seem possible at the time, but they know whereof they spoke.

But even they will have to admit it was pure coincidence that the first jeep rolled cautiously across the miracle bridge at high noon, to the very second.

In that first jeep was Gen. Truscott and his driver, facing a 200-foot tumble into the sea if the bridge gave way. The engineers had insisted they send a test jeep across first. But when he saw it was ready, the General just got in and went. It wasn't done dramatically but it was a sort of dramatic thing. It showed that the "Old Man" had complete faith in his engineers. I heard soldiers speak of it appreciatively for an hour.

* * *

Jeeps snaked across the rickety bridge behind the General while the engineers kept stations beneath the bridge to watch and measure the sag under each load. The bridge squeaked and bent as the jeeps crept over. But it held, and nothing else matters. When the vital spearhead of the division got across, traffic was halted again and the engineers were given three hours to strengthen the bridge for heavier traffic by inserting a third heavy upright in the middle.

That, too, was a terrific job but at exactly 4 p.m. the first 3/4-ton truck rolled across, and they kept putting over heavier and heavier loads until before dark a giant bulldozer was sent across, and after that, everything could follow.

The tired men began to pack their tools into trucks. Engineer officers who hadn't been to sleep in 36 hours went back to their olive orchard to clean up. They had built a jerry bridge, a comical bridge, a proud bridge, but above all the kind of bridge that wins wars. And they had built it in one night and half a day. The General was mighty pleased.

Scripps-Howard wire copy, September 6, 1943

This Is Democracy

by John Hersey

ARMY DESK JOBS are famous for dullness. And yet one of the most exciting things you can do in Sicily right now is to sit for a day by the desk of the Major who runs the town of Licata in the name of the Allies.

For a long time we have taken pleasure in the difficulties met by Germany and Japan in organizing the conquered lands. Here at the Major's desk you see difficulties, hundreds of them, but you see shrewd action, American idealism and generosity bordering on sentimentality, the innate sympathy of common blood that so many Americans have to offer over here. You see incredible Italian poverty, you see the habits of Fascism, you see a little duplicity and a lot of simplicity and many things which are comic and tragic at one time. Above all you see a thing succeeding—and it looks like the future.

First look at the desk. It is no ordinary Army desk. It is oak and it is vast. Underneath it there is a little wooden scroll-work footstool. On each end of the desk are Fasces and the inscription "ANNO XV"—for the 15th year of Fascism, 1937, when the desk must have been made. It sits at the end of a huge marble-floored room in the Palazzo Dicitta or Town Hall—a room obviously copied from the famous room of the recent Number One boy. Sitting at the desk you see pictures of King Victor Emmanuel, his Queen, Prince Umberto and his Princess, and scenes of the King driving through town after it was bombed some time ago. Approaching the desk you see a huge and violent painting which the Major's fawning interpreter will tell you represents Columbus discovering America but actually is a scene from Sicilian Vespern, the bloody revolt against a previous invader.

The Major comes in at 7:45. His assistant, Cpl. Charles Nocerini of Franklin, Kansas, is already at his improvised table at the opposite end of the huge room from the Major's desk. The corporal goes to a closet against the wall, takes out a big tin of orange juice, pokes holes in it with a bayonet and pours out breakfast for the Major which he takes at his desk. He is already deep in his account book, balancing fines and incomes from sales of seized equipment against home relief payments and repair costs. Bent over his work the Major appears furiously energetic in a La Guardia kind of way. His skin is dark. He has a mustache which he says he grew "because it makes me look more fitted for the job." His dark brown eyes are clear and quick in spite of the fact that he didn't sleep very well last night because he had so many things to think about for today.

After balancing his books he writes a couple of brief reports and then the process begins which makes his day both killing and fascinating—a stream of visitors bring their problems to him. First come two women dressed in black. For some reason the women always come in pairs. The younger of these two has a baby in her arms. The Major sits them down. As the older one starts explaining trouble in fine circumlocutions the younger one pulls out a tit and starts nursing the baby which is pathetically thin. It seems the family had nine goats, eight of which were killed by the bombing. It seems that the roof leaks. The girl's husband is in the Italian Army. Her brother deserted but is in Palermo. The family has always been against Fascism. There is much malaria in Sicily . . . and so the tale of woe rambles on until the Major says sharply, "You wish?"

"We wish," says the old lady, "permission to go to Palermo to find the brother of my daughter here, my son who fought for his country but still does not work for his family."

The Major politely explains that there is a war going on, that trains are not now carrying civilians, that everything is being done to hurry the war but that one must have patience.

Next visitor is a lawyer, an unctuous man in a white suit and blue glasses who out of habit raises his hand in the Fascist salute and then, remembering, slides it over to his forehead. With gestures which beggar description he describes the unhappy lot of an old man who is a client of his and who owns a five-room house. Three of the rooms the old man has sold. He is dying. He wants permission to sell the other two rooms at once so that he will not die intestate still owning the rooms. Major grants permission.

An old fisherman comes in. His face is like the hills of Sicily and his hands are like good rope, though he is over 60. He is very sad. The Major brought it about that Licata was the first Sicilian town to send out civilian fishing boats, for in the first days after the invasion people almost starved. Yesterday one of the seven boats hits a stray mine and all but one of the crew were killed. The old man tells what is known of the accident. The Major asks if the others are willing to go out today. The old man straightens himself up and says, "Yes, Mr. Major, we will go because our people are hungry."

A prosperously dressed man comes in complaining that he has perfectly good draft notes on the Bank of Sicily but that no one will advance cash against them. The Major explains that the Allies had to close the banks for a few days because it was feared that a panic might develop which would break all the banks. Allied funds, he says, will soon be forwarded to the banks which will then be able to give out cash in controlled amounts. Meanwhile the man must get along as best he can.

An M.P. breaks into the room. He salutes snappily and says, "A problem for you, sir. We have here a diseased whore." The Major orders her brought in. A sorry procession comes in: a 45-year-old woman in a pink blouse and black polka-dotted skirt with the mouth of a mackerel, a scarecrow of a man in green slacks and white shirt, a soldier who caught the clap from this mockery of woman-kind, and a witness. The evidence is clear and frank. The sick and frightened boy says, "I seen a G.I. who says he had a piece off this whore in a pink shirt and I says to him, 'She's the one who dosed me, Mac.' We had her took in by the M.P.'s." The Major then asks the thin man if he is a pimp. He acts most offended and denies it. Major says, "I am a lover of truth. If you speak truly you will merely be a man in trouble but if you speak lies you will go to jail." The Major has somehow made the truth seem an admirable thing to this thin contemptible man and he tells it—he pimped for this girl and three others whose names were . . . "Never mind," says the Major, "this is a case for the Carabinieri," and he turns the pair over to the local police, all of whom the Major has continued in office.

A merchant comes in. His shirt is buttoned but he has no tie. He is a man who was recommended to the Major as honest. He says (as does everyone including the notorious Squadristi or Fascist thugs in Licata) that he has been against the Fascists for many years and if there is anything he can do to help he will be glad. The Major says that his men have found certain clothing and stuffs which had been impounded by the Fascists and which he wishes now to sell since the people have had no new clothes for a long time. Will the merchant please prepare him a list of really fair prices on the understanding that all the merchants in town will be allowed to sell the goods at a small commission, proceeds to go to the town government for home relief? The merchant waves his hand from habit and says he will gladly do so.

It is time for lunch. As the Major leaves his office and makes his way through the big crowd of waiting beseechers outside you can hear the whisper, "Kiss your hand . . . kiss your hand . . . kiss your hand . . ." This is a vestigial expression of respect left over from times when hands really were to be kissed. It embarrasses the Major and he says he is going to pass the word that the expression ought not to be used any more.

You lunch in a little restaurant where for breakfast, lunch and dinner the menu is *pasta* and eggplant, fried fish, red wine and grapes. During lunch the Major tells you his own story which is a thoroughly American history. His parents were peasants from Parma who went to the States when they were 16. His father has always worked in hotels and now is assistant steward in the Merchants Club in New York. Frank went to school through high school. When he was 14 he began working nights. When he was 16 he lied and said he was 18 so that he could get a driver's license and a truck driver's job. For two years he drove trucks and lifted terrible weights—until they ruptured him. When he was well a friend suggested a job with the city. He was afraid he hadn't enough education, but on his exams he came out 177th out of 1,100. They gave him a job as clerk in the Markets Department. When La Guardia was elected he was laid off. He married a daughter of one of the owners of a big trucking firm, borrowed money, bought a grocery store in the Bronx and made out all right for two years. Then he sold out and went back to the city where he worked up to be a second-class clerk in the Sanitation Department at $42 a week. Then he went into the Army.

He says, "I can't tell you how anxious I was to get on shore to see what this was all about. At first I looked around all the time at these people, their mannerisms, their expressions, their dress. I saw them barefooted and didn't believe white people could be in that state. I am the son of an immigrant. I have seen what I thought was poverty. But now I can just picture my father's family and how poor they were. I want to help these people out as much as possible, I don't want to see them suffer that way." Then he adds, "But we've got to go now. I'm holding trials this afternoon."

Back at the office the Major finds a note from Arturo Verdirami, 82-year-old eccentric who owns most of Licata's sulphur business and has for many years been agent there for Lloyds of London. He writes the Major many notes in an English for which he apologizes "because it is Shakespearean, I am sorry." The letter says:

"I beg to notify for the necessary steps: since four months the small people at Licata does not receive the Italian *rasione tesspata* of olive oil or other fats, but the officials both of commune civil and military staff have been largely provided for the families and personal friends.

"I am informed that the small population is therefore compelled to pay at the black market any price up to lira 80 per liter equal to 800 grammes. The price fixed by the Fascist government for the supply is lira 15½ per kilo of 1,000 grammes.

"You cannot allow any longer this tyranny against the poors. You should therefore stop this tyrannical sufferance for the poor inhabitants by giving dispositions on the subject of the Commissario at the municipality *dokt sapio*, inviting him to notify his guards that any preference for anyone in the distribution of ailments will be punished inexcrably and any official civil or communal is not allowed to take the quantity to which his family has a right before the poors have received their rations respectfully signed Arturo Verdirami."

The Major is acutely aware of the black market and he has

already taken the steps which the ancient Verdirami suggests. He called all the municipal employees together one day. Most of them were in the same jobs they had held under the Fascists. The Major said to them, "Now that the Americans are here, Licata is a democracy. Democracy is this—it is that the people in its government are no longer the masters of the people. How are the government people paid? They are paid out of taxes which come from the people. And so the people are really masters of the government, not the government of the people. You are now servants of the people of Licata." And he warned them about standing in line for rations among many other things.

Now the trials begin. The chief of the Carabinieri reads off the accusations and practically acts out the crime, so acute is his sense of drama. The culprits stand before the desk and all without exception give an absentminded Fascist salute, then the first is led in.

The first case is of a man who refused to take American dollars but, much worse, refused to sell bread on credit to the local people. His plea, supported by the unctuous lawyer in white suit and blue glasses, is ignorance. He says he never had time to read the proclamations. The Major is stern as he says that ignorance of the law is no defense and he fines the man a stiff penalty.

The second case also concerns bread. A loaf is produced in evidence to show that it was badly baked of inferior flour. Major points at the baker's hands and tells him that filth is as great a crime as cheating and he fines the man.

Next comes a pathetic old man who stole some clothing from an Italian military storehouse. He pleads guilty and says he can't read but hates Fascists. He is so patently poor that the Major sentences him to three months' suspended sentence and gives him a lecture on honesty.

Next, six peasants are brought forward. They are very slow of speech and mind and heartbreaking to look at. They are accused of having taken some hay from an abandoned warehouse. Again the Major gives only a warning.

The last case is both the funniest and saddest. The accused is an old cartman. He stands before the desk with his cloth cap clutched in his hand and as defiant as if his accusers are

Fascists whom he says he hates. The chief of the Carabinieri starts to read the accusation. It appears that the old cartman was driving through town when a train of American amphibious trucks approached. The old man was drowsing at his reins and blocked their way. Leaping about the room and roaring, the chief of Carabinieri describes how one of his men grasped at the reins of the horse and with towering strength got the cart aside and saved the honor of Licata. The old man stays silent.

The chief now describes how the old man jumped down from his cart and charged the Carabinieri and tried to fight with him. Finally the old man speaks.

He speaks slowly about the death of his wife and the number of his children and grandchildren with malaria. He describes in detail how the Fascists once took away a horse. Then he himself begins to act out the scene in question and it really turns out after much swooping and shouting and another near fight that the reason he charged the Carabinieri was that he who loved his horse could not bear to see this rider of motorcycles attack his old animal. The Major dismissed the case.

After the trials an embarrassment walks up to the desk in the person of Signor Guiseppe Santi, owner of the house at Number 29 Piazzi San Sebastiano. Signor Santi's house had been requisitioned for billets. This, he says, pleased him because he hated the Fascists. But it did not please him, he says, to go into the house and find drawers broken open, glasses broken and door panels split. The Major tells the man that the soldiers were not willfully destructive but that war had given them rough habits. The Major's explanation is a masterpiece of tact. He tells Signor Santi to file a claim for damages.

Now a girl comes in who is quite pretty but very frightened-looking. She says her sweetheart is in the Army and she has heard that he was captured by the Americans. The Major asks his name. He calls up the prisoner-of-war enclosure and asks if the man is there. He is able then to tell the girl that her man is indeed a prisoner. Tears come into her eyes. "Mr. Major, I thank you, I thank you and I kiss your hand," she says.

The Major says, "I think I'll go home. I like to end each

day on a happy note if I can because there are so many un-happy ones." But before he leaves, if you ask him, he will tell you the ways in which the people of Licata are already, after only a handful of days, better off than they were under the Fascists whom they say with varying degrees of honesty that they hated.

"Sure, they're better off," he says. "For one thing they can congregate in the streets any time they want and talk about whatever they want to. They can listen to the radios. They came to me and asked if they could keep their receiving sets. I said sure. They were surprised. They asked what stations they could listen to. I said any stations. They said, 'Can you mean it?' Now they prefer the English news to the Italian and today a crowd of them laughed and whistled at an Italian propa-ganda broadcast saying Sicilians were being oppressed by Americans. They can come to the City Hall and talk to the Mayor at any time they want. The Fascist Mayor had office hours from 12 to 1 each day and you had to apply for an interview weeks in advance. Their streets are clean for the first time in centuries. I have forty-five men with a water truck and eight wagons cleaning up the place. Oh, there are lots of ways and there will be lots more."

And then he adds, "We have a big job to do here. You see, I can't stop imagining what it must have been like for my father and his family."

History in the Writing, 1945

I Saw Regensburg Destroyed

by Beirne Lay, Jr.

IN the briefing room, the intelligence officer of the bombard-ment group pulled a cloth screen away from a huge wall map. Each of the 240 sleepy-eyed combat-crew members in the crowded room leaned forward. There were low whistles. I felt a sting of anticipation as I stared at the red string on the map that stretched from our base in England to a pin point deep in Southern Germany, then south across the Alps, through the Brenner Pass to the coast of Italy, then past Corsica and Sardinia and south over the Mediterranean to a desert air-drome in North Africa. You could have heard an oxygen mask drop.

"Your primary," said the intelligence officer, "is Regens-burg. Your aiming point is the center of the Messerschmitt One Hundred and Nine G aircraft-and-engine-assembly shops. This is the most vital target we've ever gone after. If you destroy it, you destroy thirty per cent of the Luftwaffe's single-engine-fighter production. You fellows know what that means to you personally."

There were a few hollow laughs.

After the briefing, I climbed aboard a jeep bound for the operations office to check up on my Fortress assignment. The stars were dimly visible through the chilly mist that covered our blacked-out bomber station, but the weather forecast for a deep penetration over the Continent was good. In the of-fice, I looked at the crew sheet, where the line-up of the lead, low and high squadrons of the group is plotted for each mis-sion. I was listed for a copilot's seat. While I stood there, and on the chance suggestion of one of the squadron command-ers who was looking over the list, the operations officer erased my name and shifted me to the high squadron as copilot in the crew of a steady Irishman named Lieutenant Murphy, with whom I had flown before. Neither of us knew it, but that operations officer saved my life right there with a piece of rubber on the end of a pencil.

At 5:30 A.M., fifteen minutes before taxi time, a jeep drove around the five-mile perimeter track in the semi-darkness, pausing at each dispersal point long enough to notify the waiting crews that poor local visibility would postpone the take-off for an hour and a half. I was sitting with Murphy and the rest of our crew near the Piccadilly Lily. She looked sinister and complacent, squatting on her fat tires with scarcely a hole in her skin to show for the twelve raids behind her. The postponement tightened, rather than relaxed, the tension. Once more I checked over my life vest, oxygen mask and parachute, not perfunctorily, but the way you check something you're going to have to use. I made sure my escape kit was pinned securely in the knee pocket of my flying suit, where it couldn't fall out in a scramble to abandon ship. I slid a hunting knife between my shoe and my flying boot as I looked again through my extra equipment for this mission: water canteen, mess kit, blankets and English pounds for use in the Algerian desert, where we would sleep on the ground and might be on our own from a forced landing.

Murphy restlessly gave the Piccadilly Lily another once-over, inspecting ammunition belts, bomb bay, tires and oxygen pressure at each crew station. Especially the oxygen. It's human fuel, as important as gasoline, up where we operate. Gunners field-stripped their .50-calibers again and oiled the bolts. Our top-turret gunner lay in the grass with his head on his parachute, feigning sleep, sweating out his thirteenth start.

We shared a common knowledge which grimly enhanced the normal excitement before a mission. Of the approximately 150 Fortresses who were hitting Regensburg, our group was the last and lowest, at a base altitude of 17,000 feet. That's well within the range of accuracy for heavy flak. Our course would take us over plenty of it. It was a cinch also that our group would be the softest touch for the enemy fighters, being last man through the gantlet. Furthermore, the Piccadilly Lily was leading the last three ships of the high squadron — the tip of the tail end of the whole shebang. We didn't relish it much. Who wants a Purple Heart?

The minute hand of my wrist watch dragged. I caught myself thinking about the day, exactly one year ago, on August 17, 1942, when I watched a pitifully small force of twelve B-17's take off on the first raid of the 8th Air Force to make a shallow penetration against Rouen, France. On that day it was our maximum effort. Today, on our first anniversary, we were putting thirty times that number of heavies into the air — half the force on Regensburg and half the force on Schweinfurt, both situated inside the interior of the German Reich. For a year and a half, as a staff officer, I had watched the 8th Air Force grow under Maj. Gen. Ira C. Eaker. That's a long time to watch from behind a desk. Only ten days ago I had asked for and received orders to combat duty. Those ten days had been full of the swift action of participating in four combat missions and checking out for the first time as a four-engine pilot.

Now I knew that it can be easier to be shot at than telephoned at. That staff officers at an Air Force headquarters are the unstrung heroes of this war. And yet I found myself reminiscing just a little affectionately about that desk, wondering if there wasn't a touch of suicide in store for our group. One thing was sure: Headquarters had dreamed up the biggest air operation to date to celebrate its birthday in the biggest league of aerial warfare.

At 7:30 we broke out of the cloud tops into the glare of the rising sun. Beneath our B-17 lay English fields, still blanketed in the thick mist from which we had just emerged. We continued to climb slowly, our broad wings shouldering a heavy load of incendiary bombs in the belly and a burden of fuel in the main and wing-tip Tokyo tanks that would keep the Fortress afloat in the thin upper altitudes eleven hours.

From my copilot's seat on the right-hand side, I watched the white surface of the overcast, where B-17's in clusters of six to the squadron were puncturing the cloud deck all about us, rising clear of the mist with their glass noses slanted upward for the long climb to base altitude. We tacked on to one of these clutches of six. Now the sky over England was heavy with the weight of thousands of tons of bombs, fuel and men being lifted four miles straight up on a giant aerial hoist to the western terminus of a 20,000-foot elevated highway that led east to Regensburg. At intervals I saw the arc of a sputtering red, green or yellow flare being fired from the cabin roof of a group leader's airplane to identify the lead squadron to the high and low squadrons of each group. Assembly takes longer when you come up through an overcast.

For nearly an hour, still over Southern England, we climbed, nursing the straining Cyclone engines in a 300-foot-per-minute ascent, forming three squadrons gradually into compact group stagger formations—low squadron down to the left and high squadron up to the right of the lead squadron—groups assembling into looser combat wings of two to three groups each along the combat-wing assembly line, homing over predetermined points with radio compass, and finally cruising along the air-division assembly line to allow the combat wings to fall into place in trail behind Col. Curtis E. Le May in the lead group of the air division.

Formed at last, each flanking group in position 1000 feet above or below its lead group, our fifteen-mile parade moved east toward Lowestoft, point of departure from the friendly coast, unwieldy, but dangerous to fool with. From my perch in the high squadron in the last element of the whole procession, the air division looked like huge anvil-shaped swarms of locusts—not on dress parade, like the bombers of the Luftwaffe that died like flies over Britain in 1940, but deployed to uncover every gun and permit maneuverability. Our formation was basically that worked out for the Air Corps by Brig. Gen. Hugh Knerr twenty years ago with eighty-five-mile-an-hour bombers, plus refinements devised by Colonel Le May from experience in the European theater.

The English Channel and the North Sea glittered bright in the clear visibility as we left the bulge of East Anglia behind us. Up ahead we knew that we were already registering on the German RDF screen, and that the sector controllers of the Luftwaffe's fighter belt in Western Europe were busy alerting their *Staffeln* of Focke-Wulfs and Messerschmitts. I stole a last look back at cloud-covered England, where I could see a dozen spare B-17's, who had accompanied us to fill in for any abortives from mechanical failure in the hard climb, gliding disappointedly home to base.

I fastened my oxygen mask a little tighter and looked at the little ball in a glass tube on the instrument panel that indicates proper oxygen flow. It was moving up and down, like a visual heartbeat, as I breathed, registering normal.

Already the gunners were searching. Occasionally the ship shivered as guns were tested with short bursts. I could see puffs of blue smoke from the group close ahead and 1000 feet above us, as each gunner satisfied himself that he had lead poisoning at his trigger tips. The coast of Holland appeared in sharp black outline. I drew in a deep breath of oxygen.

A few miles in front of us were German boys in single-seaters who were probably going to react to us in the same way our boys would react, emotionally, if German bombers were heading for the Pratt & Whitney engine factory at Hartford or the Liberator plant at Willow Run. In the making was a death struggle between the unstoppable object and the immovable defense, every possible defense at the disposal of the Reich, for this was a deadly penetration to a hitherto inaccessible and critically important arsenal of the *Vaterland*.

At 10:08 we crossed the coast of Holland, south of The Hague, with our group of Fortresses tucked in tightly and within handy supporting distance of the group above us, at 18,000 feet. But our long, loose-linked column looked too long, and the gaps between combat wings too wide. As I squinted into the sun, gauging the distance to the barely visible specks of the lead group, I had a recurrence of that sinking feeling before the take-off—the lonesome foreboding that might come to the last man about to run a gantlet lined with spiked clubs. The premonition was well founded.

At 10:17, near Woensdrecht, I saw the first flak blossom out in our vicinity, light and inaccurate. A few minutes later, at approximately 10:25, a gunner called, "Fighters at two o'clock low." I saw them, climbing above the horizon ahead of us to the right—a pair of them. For a moment I hoped they were P-47 Thunderbolts from the fighter escort that was supposed to be in our vicinity, but I didn't hope long. The two FW-190's turned and whizzed through the formation ahead of us in a frontal attack, nicking two B-17's in the wings and breaking away in half rolls right over our group. By craning my neck up and back, I glimpsed one of them through the roof glass in the cabin, flashing past at a 600-mile-an-hour rate of closure, his yellow nose smoking and small pieces flying off near the wing root. The guns of our group were in action. The pungent smell of burnt cordite filled the cockpit and the B-17 trembled to the recoil of nose and ball-turret guns. Smoke immediately trailed from the hit B-17's, but they held their stations.

Here was early fighter reaction. The members of the crew sensed trouble. There was something desperate about the way those two fighters came in fast right out of their climb, without any preliminaries. Apparently, our own fighters were busy somewhere farther up the procession. The interphone was active for a few seconds with brief admonitions: "Lead 'em more." . . . "Short bursts." . . . "Don't throw rounds away." . . . "Bombardier to left waist gunner, don't yell. Talk slow."

Three minutes later the gunners reported fighters climbing up from all around the clock, singly and in pairs, both FW-190's and Me-109-G's. The fighters I could see on my side looked like too many for sound health. No friendly Thunderbolts were visible. From now on we were in mortal danger. My mouth dried up and my buttocks pulled together. A co-ordinated attack began, with the head-on fighters coming in from slightly above, the nine and three o'clock attackers approaching from about level and the rear attackers from slightly below. The guns from every B-17 in our group and the group ahead were firing simultaneously, lashing the sky with ropes of orange tracers to match the chain-puff bursts squirting from the 20-mm. cannon muzzles in the wings of the jerry single-seaters.

I noted with alarm that a lot of our fire was falling astern of the target—particularly from our hand-held nose and waist guns. Nevertheless, both sides got hurt in this clash, with the entire second element of three B-17's from our low squadron and one B-17 from the group ahead falling out of formation on fire, with crews bailing out, and several fighters heading for the deck in flames or with their pilots lingering behind under the dirty yellow canopies that distinguished some of their parachutes from ours. Our twenty-four-year-old group leader, flying only his third combat mission, pulled us up even closer to the preceding group for mutual support.

As we swung slightly outside with our squadron, in mild

evasive action, I got a good look at that gap in the low squadron where three B-17's had been. Suddenly I bit my lip hard. The lead ship of that element had pulled out on fire and exploded before anyone bailed out. It was the ship to which I had been originally assigned.

I glanced over at Murphy. It was cold in the cockpit, but sweat was running from his forehead and over his oxygen mask from the exertion of holding his element in tight formation and the strain of the warnings that hummed over the interphone and what he could see out of the corners of his eyes. He caught my glance and turned the controls over to me for a while. It was an enormous relief to concentrate on flying instead of sitting there watching fighters aiming between your eyes. Somehow, the attacks from the rear, although I could see them through my ears via the interphone, didn't bother me. I guess it was because there was a slab of armor plate behind my back and I couldn't watch them, anyway.

I knew that we were in a lively fight. Every alarm bell in my brain and heart was ringing a high-pitched warning. But my nerves were steady and my brain working. The fear was unpleasant, but it was bearable. I knew that I was going to die, and so were a lot of others. What I didn't know was that the real fight, the *Anschluss* of Luftwaffe 20-mm. cannon shells, hadn't really begun. The largest and most savage fighter resistance of any war in history was rising to stop us at any cost, and our group was the most vulnerable target.

A few minutes later we absorbed the first wave of a hailstorm of individual fighter attacks that were to engulf us clear to the target in such a blizzard of bullets and shells that a chronological account is difficult. It was at 10:41, over Eupen, that I looked out the window after a minute's lull, and saw two whole squadrons, twelve Me-109's and eleven FW-190's climbing parallel to us as though they were on a steep escalator. The first squadron had reached our level and was pulling ahead to turn into us. The second was not far behind. Several thousand feet below us were many more fighters, their noses cocked up in a maximum climb. Over the interphone came reports of an equal number of enemy aircraft deploying on the other side of the formation.

For the first time I noticed an Me-110 sitting out of range on our level out to the right. He was to stay with us all the way to the target, apparently radioing our position and weak spots to fresh *Staffeln* waiting farther down the road.

At the sight of all these fighters, I had the distinct feeling of being trapped—that the Hun had been tipped off or at least had guessed our destination and was set for us. We were already through the German fighter belt. Obviously, they had moved a lot of squadrons back in a fluid defense in depth, and they must have been saving up some outfits for the inner defense that we didn't know about. The life expectancy of our group seemed definitely limited, since it had already appeared that the fighters, instead of wasting fuel trying to overhaul the preceding groups, were glad to take a cut at us.

Swinging their yellow noses around in a wide U turn, the twelve-ship squadron of Me-109's came in from twelve to two o'clock in pairs. The main event was on. I fought an impulse to close my eyes, and overcame it.

A shining silver rectangle of metal sailed past over our right wing. I recognized it as a main-exit door. Seconds later, a black lump came hurtling through the formation, barely missing several propellers. It was a man, clasping his knees to his head, revolving like a diver in a triple somersault, shooting by us so close that I saw a piece of paper blow out of his leather jacket. He was evidently making a delayed jump, for I didn't see his parachute open.

A B-17 turned gradually out of the formation to the right, maintaining altitude. In a split second it completely vanished in a brilliant explosion, from which the only remains were four balls of fire, the fuel tanks, which were quickly consumed as they fell earthward.

I saw blue, red, yellow and aluminum-colored fighters. Their tactics were running fairly true to form, with frontal attacks hitting the low squadron and rear attackers going for the lead and high squadrons. Some of the jerries shot at us with rockets, and an attempt at air-to-air bombing was made with little black time-fuse sticks, dropped from above, which exploded in small gray puffs off to one side of the formation. Several of the FW's did some nice deflection shooting on side attacks from 500 yards at the high group, then raked the low group on the breakaway at closer range with their noses cocked in a side slip, to keep the formation in their sights longer in the turn. External fuel tanks were visible under the bellies or wings of at least two squadrons, shedding uncomfortable light on the mystery of their ability to tail us so far from their bases.

The manner of the assaults indicated that the pilots knew where we were going and were inspired with a fanatical determination to stop us before we got there. Many pressed attacks home to 250 yards or less, or bolted right through the formation wide out, firing long twenty-second bursts, often presenting point-blank targets on the breakaway. Some committed the fatal error of pulling up instead of going down and out. More experienced pilots came in on frontal attacks with a noticeably slower rate of closure, apparently throttled back, obtaining greater accuracy. But no tactics could halt the close-knit juggernauts of our Fortresses, nor save the single-seaters from paying a terrible price.

Our airplane was endangered by various debris. Emergency hatches, exit doors, prematurely opened parachutes, bodies and assorted fragments of B-17's and Hun fighters breezed past us in the slip stream.

I watched two fighters explode not far beneath, disappear in sheets of orange flame; B-17's dropping out in every stage of distress, from engines on fire to controls shot away; friendly and enemy parachutes floating down, and, on the green carpet far below us, funeral pyres of smoke from fallen fighters, marking our trail.

On we flew through the cluttered wake of a desperate air battle, where disintegrating aircraft were commonplace and the white dots of sixty parachutes in the air at one time were hardly worth a second look. The spectacle registering on my eyes became so fantastic that my brain turned numb to the actuality of the death and destruction all around us. Had it not been for the squeezing in my stomach, which was trying to purge, I might easily have been watching an animated cartoon in a movie theater.

The minutes dragged on into an hour. And still the fighters came. Our gunners called coolly and briefly to one another, dividing up their targets, fighting for their lives with every round of ammunition—and our lives, and the formation. The tail gunner called that he was out of ammunition. We sent another belt back to him. Here was a new hazard. We might run out of .50-caliber slugs before we reached the target.

I looked to both sides of us. Our two wing men were gone. So was the element in front of us—all three ships. We moved up into position behind the lead element of the high squadron. I looked out again on my side and saw a cripple, with one prop feathered, struggle up behind our right wing with his bad engine funneling smoke into the slip stream. He dropped back. Now our tail gunner had a clear view. There were no more B-17's behind us. We were last man.

I took the controls for a while. The first thing I saw when Murphy resumed flying was a B-17 turning slowly out to the right, its cockpit a mass of flames. The copilot crawled out of his window, held on with one hand, reached back for his parachute, buckled it on, let go and was whisked back into the horizontal stabilizer of the tail. I believe the impact killed him. His parachute didn't open.

I looked forward and almost ducked as I watched the tail gunner of a B-17 ahead of us take a bead right on our windshield and cut loose with a stream of tracers that missed us by a few feet as he fired on a fighter attacking us from six o'clock low. I almost ducked again when our own top-turret gunner's twin muzzles pounded away a foot above my head in the full forward position, giving a realistic imitation of cannon shells exploding in the cockpit, while I gave an even better imitation of a man jumping six inches out of his seat.

Still no letup. The fighters queued up like a bread line and let us have it. Each second of time had a cannon shell in it. The strain of being a clay duck in the wrong end of that aerial shooting gallery became almost intolerable. Our Piccadilly Lily shook steadily with the fire of its .50's, and the air inside was wispy with smoke. I checked the engine instruments for the thousandth time. Normal. No injured crew members yet. Maybe we'd get to that target, even with our reduced fire power. Seven Fortresses from our group had already gone down and many of the rest of us were badly shot up and short-handed because of wounded crew members.

Almost disinterestedly I observed a B-17 pull out from the

group preceding us and drop back to a position about 200 feet from our right wing tip. His right Tokyo tanks were on fire, and had been for a half hour. Now the smoke was thicker. Flames were licking through the blackened skin of the wing. While the pilot held her steady, I saw four crew members drop out the bomb bay and execute delayed jumps. Another bailed from the nose, opened his parachute prematurely and nearly fouled the tail. Another went out the left-waist-gun opening, delaying his opening for a safe interval. The tail gunner dropped out of his hatch, apparently pulling the ripcord before he was clear of the ship. His parachute opened instantaneously, barely missing the tail, and jerked him so hard that both his shoes came off. He hung limp in the harness, whereas the others had shown immediate signs of life, shifting around in their harness. The Fortress then dropped back in a medium spiral and I did not see the pilots leave. I saw the ship, though, just before it trailed from view, belly to the sky, its wing a solid sheet of yellow flame.

Now that we had been under constant attack for more than an hour, it appeared certain that our group was faced with extinction. The sky was still mottled with rising fighters. Target time was thirty-five minutes away. I doubt if a man in the group visualized the possibility of our getting much farther without 100 per cent loss. Gunners were becoming exhausted and nerve-tortured from the nagging strain—the strain that sends gunners and pilots to the rest home. We had been aiming point for what looked like most of the Luftwaffe. It looked as though we might find the rest of it primed for us at the target.

At this hopeless point, a young squadron commander down in the low squadron was living through his finest hour. His squadron had lost its second element of three ships early in the fight, south of Antwerp, yet he had consistently maintained his vulnerable and exposed position in the formation rigidly in order to keep the guns of his three remaining ships well uncovered to protect the belly of the formation. Now, nearing the target, battle damage was catching up with him fast. A 20-mm. cannon shell penetrated the right side of his airplane and exploded beneath him, damaging the electrical system and cutting the top-turret gunner in the leg. A second

20-mm. entered the radio compartment, killing the radio operator, who bled to death with his legs severed above the
knees. A third 20-mm. shell entered the left side of the nose,
tearing out a section about two feet square, tore away the
right-hand-nose-gun installations and injured the bombardier
in the head and shoulder. A fourth 20-mm. shell penetrated
the right wing into the fuselage and shattered the hydraulic
system, releasing fluid all over the cockpit. A fifth 20-mm.
shell punctured the cabin roof and severed the rudder cables
to one side of the rudder. A sixth 20-mm. shell exploded in
the No. 3 engine, destroying all controls to the engine. The
engine caught fire and lost its power, but eventually I saw the
fire go out.

Confronted with structural damage, partial loss of control,
fire in the air and serious injuries to personnel, and faced with
fresh waves of fighters still rising to the attack, this commander was justified in abandoning ship. His crew, some of
them comparatively inexperienced youngsters, were preparing
to bail out. The copilot pleaded repeatedly with him to bail
out. His reply at this critical juncture was blunt. His words
were heard over the interphone and had a magical effect on
the crew. They stuck to their guns. The B-17 kept on.

Near the initial point, at 11:50, one hour and a half after the
first of at least 200 individual fighter attacks, the pressure
eased off, although hostiles were still in the vicinity. A curious
sensation came over me. I was still alive. It was possible to
think of the target. Of North Africa. Of returning to England.
Almost idly, I watched a crippled B-17 pull over to the curb
and drop its wheels and open its bomb bay, jettisoning its
bombs. Three Me-109's circled it closely, but held their fire
while the crew bailed out. I remembered now that a little
while back I had seen other Hun fighters hold their fire, even
when being shot at by a B-17 from which the crew were bailing. But I doubt if sportsmanship had anything to do with it.
They hoped to get a B-17 down fairly intact.

And then our weary, battered column, short twenty-four
bombers, but still holding the close formation that had
brought the remainder through by sheer air discipline and
gunnery, turned in to the target. I knew that our bombardiers
were grim as death while they synchronized their sights on

the great Me-109 shops lying below us in a curve of the winding blue Danube, close to the outskirts of Regensburg. Our B-17 gave a slight lift and a red light went out on the instrument panel. Our bombs were away. We turned from the target toward the snow-capped Alps. I looked back and saw a beautiful sight—a rectangular pillar of smoke rising from the Me-109 plant. Only one burst was over and into the town. Even from this great height I could see that we had smeared the objective. The price? Cheap. 200 airmen.

A few more fighters pecked at us on the way to the Alps and a couple of smoking B-17's glided down toward the safety of Switzerland, about forty miles distant. A town in the Brenner Pass tossed up a lone burst of futile flak. Flak? There had been lots of flak in the past two hours, but only now did I recall having seen it, a sort of side issue to the fighters. Colonel Le May, who had taken excellent care of us all the way, circled the air division over a large lake to give the cripples, some flying on three engines and many trailing smoke, a chance to rejoin the family. We approached the Mediterranean in a gradual descent, conserving fuel. Out over the water we flew at low altitude, unmolested by fighters from Sardinia or Corsica, waiting through the long hot afternoon hours for the first sight of the North African coast line. The prospect of ditching, out of gasoline and the sight of other B-17's falling into the drink seemed trivial matters after the vicious nightmare of the long trial across Southern Germany. We had walked through a high valley of the shadow of death, not expecting to see another sunset, and now I could fear no evil.

With red lights showing on all our fuel tanks, we landed at our designated base in the desert, after eleven hours in the air. I slept on the ground near the wing and, waking occasionally, stared up at the stars. My radio headset was back in the ship. And yet I could hear the deep chords of great music.

The Saturday Evening Post, November 6, 1943

Fear of Death as Green
Troops Sail to Invasion

by John Steinbeck

SOMEWHERE IN THE MEDITERRANEAN THEATER—On the iron floors of the L. C. I.'s, which stands for Landing Craft Infantry, the men sit about and for a time they talk and laugh and make jokes to cover the great occasion. They try to reduce this great occasion to something normal, something ordinary, something they are used to. They rag one another, accuse one another of being scared, they repeat experiences of recent days, and then gradually silence creeps over them and they sit silently because the hugeness of the experience has taken them over.

These are green troops. They have been trained to a fine point, hardened and instructed, and they lack only one thing to make them soldiers, enemy fire, and they will never be soldiers until they have it. No one, least of all themselves, knows what they will do when the terrible thing happens. No man there knows whether he can take it, knows whether he will run away or stick, or lose his nerve and go to pieces, or will be a good soldier. There is no way of knowing and probably that one thing bothers you more than anything else.

And that is the difference between green troops and soldiers. Tomorrow at this time these men, those who are living, will be different. They will know then what they can't know tonight. They will know how they face fire. Actually there is little danger. They are going to be good soldiers for they do not know that this is the night before the assault. There is no way for any man to know it.

In the moonlight on the iron deck they look at each other strangely. Men they have known well and soldiered with are strange and every man is cut off from every other one and in their minds they search the faces of their friends for the dead.

Who will be alive tomorrow night? I will, for one. No one ever gets killed in the war. Couldn't possibly. There would be no war if any one got killed. But each man, in this last night in the moonlight, looks strangely at the others and sees death there. This is the most terrible time of all. This night before the assault by the new green troops. They will never be like this again.

Every man builds in his mind what it will be like, but it is never what he thought it would be. When he designs the assault in his mind he is alone and cut off from every one. He is alone in the moonlight and the crowded men about him are strangers in this time. It will not be like this. The fire and the movement and the exertion will make him a part of these strangers sitting about him, and they will be a part of him, but he does not know that now. This is a bad time, never to be repeated.

Not one of these men is to be killed. That is impossible, and it is no contradiction that every one of them is to be killed. Every one is in a way dead already. And nearly every man has written his letter and left it somewhere to be posted if he is killed. The letters, some misspelled, some illiterate, some polished and full of attitudes, and some meager and tight, all say the same thing. They all say: "I wish I had told you, and I never did, I never could. Some obscure and impish thing kept me from ever telling you, and only now when it is too late, can I tell you. I've thought these things," the letters say, "but when I started to speak something cut me off. Now I can say it, but don't let it be a burden on you. I just know that it was always so, only I didn't say it." In every letter that is the message. The piled up reticences go down in the last letters. The letters to wives, and mothers, and sisters, and fathers, and such is the hunger to have been a part of some one, letters sometimes to comparative strangers.

The great ships move through the night though they are covered with silence. Radios are dead now, and the engines make no noise. Orders are given in soft voices and the conversation is quiet. Somewhere up ahead the enemy is waiting and he is silent too. Does he know we are coming, and does he know when and in what number? Is he lying low with his machine guns ready and his mortars set on the beaches, and his artillery in the hills? What is he thinking now? Is he afraid or confident?

The officers know H-hour now. The moon is going down. H-hour is 3:30, just after the moon has set and the shore is black. The convoy is to moonward of the shore. Perhaps with glasses the enemy can see the convoy against the setting moon, but ahead where we are going there is only a musty pearl-like grayness. The moon goes down into the ocean and ships that have been beside you and all around you disappear into the blackness and only the tiny shielded position-lights show where they are.

The men sitting on the deck disappear into the blackness and the silence, and one man begins to whistle softly just to be sure he is there.

New York *Herald Tribune*, October 3, 1943

Three Americans

by the Editors of *Life*
photo by George Strock

HERE lie three Americans.

What shall we say of them? Shall we say that this is a noble sight? Shall we say that this is a fine thing, that they should give their lives for their country?

Or shall we say that this is too horrible to look at?

Why print this picture, anyway, of three American boys dead upon an alien shore? Is it to hurt people? To be morbid?

Those are not the reasons.

The reason is that words are never enough. The eye sees. The mind knows. The heart feels. But the words do not exist to make us see, or know, or feel what it is like, what actually happens. The words are never right.

Last winter, in the issue of Feb. 22, we told about Bill, the Wisconsin boy; how he struggled through the dark and nervous jungle of New Guinea, stalking Japs like a cat; how he came at last to the blue sea at the rim of the jungle, and ran out onto the white beach, blazing mad; how the Japs got him there, suddenly, when the job was almost finished, so that he fell down on the sand, with his legs drawn up; and how the tide came in. . . .

And we said then that we thought we ought to be permitted to show a picture of Bill—not just the words, but the real thing. We said that if Bill had the guts to take it, then we ought to have the guts to look at it.

Well, this is the picture.

And the reason we print it now is that, last week, President Roosevelt and Elmer Davis and the War Department decided that the American people ought to be able to see their own boys as they fall in battle; to come directly and without words into the presence of their own dead.

And so here it is. This is the reality that lies behind the

names that come to rest at last on monuments in the leafy squares of busy American towns.

Here in this picture we meet upon a battlefield of the war.

It is true that we come late to the battlefield—much later than these boys, who were the first to arrive. The tide has already covered them at least once. The sand has almost buried the leg of one of them, and you can see the dark marking of high water on his helmet.

Even so, we are not too late to understand this battlefield. We can see roughly what happened.

They were shipped to Australia in 1942, thence to Port Moresby, New Guinea, thence by airplane over the Owen Stanley Mountains. They were set down in the heart of the jungle. Their objective was Buna.

They struggled through the nightmare—week after week of Japs lurking in trees and jungle pillboxes, week after week of foxholes and bugs and skin sores and sleepless nights. Then at last Sergeant Bottcher, with a dozen men, broke through to the sea. Bottcher's Corner, where he held out for days, lies just beyond the coconut palms in the background of this picture.

And meanwhile the Japs had been trying to bring up reinforcements in landing barges. Many barges were wrecked on the shore by American airmen, just as the one shown here. But when the Jap soldiers were finally driven back to the sea they hid in these half-sunken barges. And they also constructed hidden machine-gun nests all along the shore.

So when these three boys broke out of the jungle they ran down to the beach, chasing Japs in a kind of fury. They were running in from the left and they had just passed the barge. And then there was a sudden, murderous burst of fire—apparently not from the barge, but from a machine-gun nest located in the direction of where you, the reader, are sitting. The boy in front was riddled. The one in the center, who was apparently blasted over backward and has been rolled by the waves, was hit above his left hip; a bullet went into his left leg and his right leg was shattered. The third has fallen forward as if clutching a wound in his abdomen. It all must have happened in a split second.

George Strock, Life Magazine, © Time Warner Inc.

Yes, when LIFE's photographer, George Strock, arrived with his camera to take this picture, it was all over. And yet, miraculously, it is not too late; miraculously the battle still goes on, and we can still see, in every line of action, why it is that American boys win.

We can still sense the high optimism of men who have never known oppression—who, however scared, have never had to base their decisions upon fear. We are still aware of the relaxed self-confidence with which the leading boy ran into the sudden burst of fire—almost like a halfback carrying the ball down a football field.

We can share their impatience, their outrage at the evil of war. We can feel the fury of their attack, the hard muscles driving forward, the hot blood surging. Yes, we can tell even on this distant shore that these are our boys, born of our women, reared in our schools, bred to our horizons. . . .

Even though the tide has come in at least once to cover them. . . .

And it is not enough to say that words are not enough. There is something lying on this beach that the camera doesn't show.

It doesn't show a green meadow stretching down from a whitewashed barn to the brook that bubbles through an American valley. And it doesn't show an elderly man climbing up a ladder in a ripe American orchard; or a stout, gray-haired woman pulling out of the oven an American apple pie; or a red setter asleep on the sunny porch dreaming of American birds.

The camera doesn't show a road leading around the wood lot under the big harvest moon. It doesn't reproduce the sound of a girl's voice when she told him, or the feel of her waist, or the memory of her promise.

And it doesn't show the pool hall where the boys get the baseball scores, or the Congressman leaning back in his law office with his hands behind his head, or the banker scrutinizing old Sam Lawrence, or the minister in his pulpit pointing upward to where he thinks God is.

No, the camera doesn't show America, not any part of America, not even her mighty hills and rivers, not even the great gray cities or the freight trains tramping through the night loaded with the paraphernalia of war. Out there at Buna it couldn't show any of that.

And yet here on the beach is America, three parts of a hundred and thirty million parts, three fragments of that life we call American life: three units of freedom.

So that it is not just these boys who have fallen here, it is freedom that has fallen: the smell, the taste, the sound, the sight of freedom, the desire, the realization, the manifold, intoxicating experience that freedom is. All this has fallen upon the white New Guinea sand.

America is the symbol of freedom.

It is the symbol, not only here at Buna, and not only at Guadalcanal, where the crosses crowd the shore; and not only in half-starved Sicily, and not only in trembling Rome:

It is the symbol of freedom all over the earth, wherever men dream of freedom, or desire it;

In the bright green hills of China, and under the old roofs of Prague, and in the teeming alleys of Cairo, and along the jagged Scandinavian shore.

And all over the world, now, there are living fragments of this symbol, and all over the world they are being shot down, like these fragments.

And it is not an easy thing to understand why they are there, and why, if freedom is to live, they must be willing to die.

But this is because freedom is something more than a set of rules, or a set of principles. Freedom is a free man. It is a package. But it is God's package.

So when these living units of freedom are extinguished we cannot bring them back to life. All we can do is to give meaning to their death.

And this is to say that when freedom falls, as it has here on the beach at Buna, it is our task to cause it to rise again: not in living units, which we cannot make and to which we cannot give life, but in the mighty symbol, America, the beacon for all men, which is ours to have, to hold, and to increase.

Life, September 20, 1943

The American Radio Traitors

by William L. Shirer

WHEN last July a Federal grand jury returned indictments charging treason against eight American citizens who had been broadcasting Nazi and Fascist propaganda from Berlin and Rome, it set me to wondering again why they had sold out to the enemy. For I had known some of them, and another convert to Nazism who did not appear in the government list—Charles Flicksteger, alias Flick—during my fifteen-year assignment abroad.

These Americans,* most of them native born, did, in the stilted words of the indictments, "knowingly, intentionally, feloniously, traitorously and treasonably adhere to the enemies of the United States . . . giving to the said enemies aid and comfort" by repeated broadcasts of propaganda designed to "persuade citizens of the United States to decline to support the United States in the conduct of the war."

Why did they do it? For money? Most men turn traitors for money. But from what I know of these citizens, material gain was not the motive, or at least not the main one. To be sure, Bob Best, who spent most of his waking hours for twenty years glued to the corner table in the journalists' hangout at the Café Louvre in Vienna, was nearly always broke. But his financial state never seemed to worry him very much except possibly during one period when there arose what Dorothy Thompson called the other day "those doubtful affairs around Credit Anstalt Bank," the details of which I've forgotten. Constance Drexel, an insignificant, mixed-up, and ailing woman of forty-six who always had a bad cold, used to tell

*Frederick Wilhelm Kaltenbach, Dubuque, Iowa; Robert H. Best, Sumter, South Carolina; Ezra Pound, New York City; Douglas Chandler, Baltimore; Edward Leo Delaney, Olney, Illinois; Constance Drexel, Philadelphia; Jane Anderson, Atlanta; Max Otto Koischwitz, New York City. Flicksteger, who was brought up in Saylesville, Rhode Island, and attended Brown University, was not included in the indictment.

me during the first winter of the war in Berlin that she needed money—and wouldn't I hire her as a broadcaster? But she went over to the service of Dr. Goebbels mainly because she had always been pro-German and pan-German and since 1933 had been bitten by the Nazi bug. The money the Germans paid her no doubt was welcome, but she would have taken mine (which had an anti-Nazi taint) had I been fool enough to hire her.

Edward Leopold Delaney, alias E. D. Ward, who before the first war had once toured our republic in a road company playing "Get-Rich-Quick Wallingford," had undoubtedly never got rich at home even after a number of years of acting and writing. (He wrote two books, *The Lady by Degrees* and *The Charm Girl*, the latter advertised as the "scream-line correspondence of a radio charmer and her girl friend.") The Nazis paid him the standard traitor's salary of 1,000 marks a month ($400 at the official rate of exchange) and threw in a comfortable apartment off the Kurfuerstendamm out of which some unfortunate Jew had been thrown. But he probably could have done almost as well at home—except for the flat—since in terms of prices 1,000 marks really amounted to only $250. With a little luck, no doubt, he could have earned $62.50 a week right here.

It wasn't money, primarily, which turned these Americans into traitors. And it wasn't love, for which sometimes a man or a woman will betray his country. It was for love that Baille Stewart, a captain of the Seaforth Highlanders, betrayed England and served a sentence in the Tower before fleeing to Germany in search of his loved one. Stewart did not seem happy about his lot when I used to run into him at the German Broadcasting House, where for a short time he made broadcasts to his native land, but he was not strong enough to overcome his passion for a certain German woman.

Fred Kaltenbach and Douglas Chandler apparently were happily married, the former to a German girl, the latter to a descendant of John Jay, the first Chief Justice of the United States, whom he had married at Bar Harbor, Maine, in 1924. No Nazi siren seems to have influenced them. Best was engaged to an Austrian girl at the moment Germany declared war on the United States and she may have had some

influence on his decision not to return. During the internment of 138 American diplomats and journalists at Bad
Nauheim from December, 1941, until March, 1943, Best used
to hint to his colleagues that his fiancée had some property
in Austria which he did not feel they could abandon. A
Freudian might see a deeper meaning there. But I am sure
that it was not Best's feelings for his fiancée which primarily
moved him to remain in Germany and betray his country.

II

What was it then? Of all the American turncoats, I knew
Best the most intimately. I had met him first in January, 1929,
in Vienna, to which I had repaired for a long newspaper assignment. I saw him off and on during the next ten turbulent
years, the last time being in June, 1938, after the Anschluss,
when I left Vienna for good. Frankly, over the years, I liked
him as did all the other American correspondents whose fortunes took them to the baroque Austrian capital. Those were
great days in our little American newspaper world. Most of
the "stars" of a great generation of foreign correspondents
gathered there at one time or another: Dorothy Thompson,
Sinclair Lewis, H. R. Knickerbocker, John Gunther, Eric
Gedye, M. W. Fodor, Edgar Mowrer, Whit Burnett, George
Seldes, Edwin L. James, Walter Duranty, Jim Mills, and Vincent Sheean. Unless I greatly err, they all liked Best and were
often to be seen chewing the rag with him at the table in the
Café Louvre which served both as his home and his office, for
he wrote all his dispatches there. He never rated with his colleagues as a very brilliant or even able journalist, but he had a
mine of information and misinformation about Austria, Central Europe, and the Balkans, he knew everyone in town, including the most suspicious agents of the Comitadji, and he
shared his news with everyone. As the years went by he grew a
little strange. "Eccentric," we used to call it. But everyone
liked him for his generous heart. He would do the slightest
acquaintance any favor asked or hinted. He would lend you
his last Austrian schilling.
    Best had no deep political beliefs. He didn't like the Social-
ists, who controlled the city government of Vienna until Doll-

fuss massacred them in 1934, but this was because he thought they taxed him too much, and not for any ideological reasons. During the heyday of Prince Starhemberg's fascist Heimwehr, he was pretty much for the Prince. Later he was for Dollfuss and Schuschnigg and their clerical Fascism, with only occasional lapses into wondering whether there wasn't something in the Nazi business.

That fantastic night of the Anschluss when Austria perished, Best held out hopes to the last minute that Schuschnigg somehow would master the situation and keep the Nazis out. About ten o'clock that night I found him at his table in the Café Louvre scribbling dispatches. He was called away to the phone and when he returned he announced proudly to the half-hysterical newsmen that Schuschnigg had come back as chancellor and that the Nazis were out. This was typical of his reporting but there was no doubt that he was happy about his "tip." "Things are not over yet," he kept saying to me. At that time, he was not Nazi.

By his side that evening, I remember, was one Major Goldschmidt, a Legitimist follower of Otto and a Jew. About eleven o'clock the Major rose quietly and said, "I will go home and get my revolver." Best did his best to dissuade him. And Best's closest friend in Vienna, as everyone knew, was a Jew.

And yet this is the man who to-day out-Goebbelses the Propaganda Doktor in the very violence of his attacks on the Jews. He has become Berlin's star American Jew-baiter. When he skipped out from Bad Nauheim, he addressed an open letter to the American *chargé d'affaires* with such expressions as "Rascal-Roosevelt's Jewed-up Administration." Recently he ended his broadcast from Berlin: "Down with the Jew–United States campaign. Give the donkey [Roosevelt] the gate and give his kikes the kick they have so long deserved."

The trouble with Bob Best was that he stayed in Europe too long. Born in Sumter, South Carolina, April 16, 1896, the son of a Methodist minister, he had graduated from Wofford College in 1917, served as a lieutenant in the Coast Artillery during the war, and had then enrolled as a graduate student in the Columbia School of Journalism. In 1922 he went to Europe on a year's Pulitzer traveling fellowship. He never saw his native land again. Most American foreign correspondents came home every three or four years not only because it was pleasant to come home but because they knew how absolutely essential it was to retain their native roots and their contact with their own people and their own civilization. Best never came home. He settled down at his table in the Café Louvre, from which he was only budged twenty years later by Hitler's declaration of war on the United States and his own temporary internment as an enemy citizen.

Some years after his arrival in Vienna, I gathered from my talks with him, he became *afraid* to return. Life certainly was pleasant in Vienna, as all of us who lived and worked there could testify. It was a dying city, because it was no longer the capital of an empire, but it was dying with great dignity and even beauty, and a charm still hung over its inhabitants and its streets and its baroque and rococo buildings that captured us all and made us love it deeply. Yes, Vienna was pleasant, so why go home — even for a visit, Best used to say. Pretty soon he began to fear that life in America had passed him by, that probably he could never make a go of it here, that he would only be a misfit. A few other correspondents who had gone home for good had found the readjustment difficult. Bob heard of their difficulties. And not unnaturally, and perhaps at first quite unconsciously, he began to share the stirrings that were going on in the breasts of the not-very-well-paid middle class in Europe. Fascism of the clerical brand such as Austria first produced or of the Mussolini-Hitler brand began to attract them. Best, his native American roots decayed, was impressed. It was not difficult for him to drift toward Fascism. It was difficult for him to retain any sense of duty or even loyalty to his own country. America began to loom to him as a land which he no longer knew or belonged to and to which he would never return. Shortly before I left Berlin at the end of 1940 I had a letter from him. He was in Vienna and he wrote that he would stay on there "even if we get into the war." He was becoming ripe for what was to happen a year later.

Just how and why Best became so violently anti-Semitic remains a mystery to his former friends and acquaintances. As we have seen, his closest friend was a Jew and a good half of his European newspaper friends who gathered at the Café

Louvre were Jews. One of the last things he did before the war was to lend a month's salary to an Austrian editor who was a Jew and then help him escape over the Nazi frontier. This editor happened to be listening to the Berlin short-wave radio in the New York Listening Post of CBS one spring evening of 1942. Suddenly he dashed into my office, a few steps away. He was in tears. "There's someone talking from Berlin who calls himself 'Guess Who,'" he cried. "It sounds like Bob Best. Come and see." I did and there was no doubt that it was Best. He was thundering away at the Jews. The Jewish editor from Vienna could not believe his ears and cannot to this day explain how his friend, who helped him escape the Nazis, suddenly turned so hysterically on the Jewish people.

Perhaps one reason was that Best's never-too-fertile brain started to crack and give way. Psychologists may say that this is an absurd explanation. But are not people who we say are "cracked" on a subject fairly common phenomena? Is not an obsession one of the first signs of a cerebral weakening? Best certainly developed an obsession about the Jews. He developed another which was just as strange. In his twenty years behind the table in the Café Louvre, he had always struck his fellow correspondents as a most modest and even self-effacing fellow. But once among the crackpots of the Propaganda Ministry in Berlin, to which he repaired after skipping out of Bad Nauheim shortly before the Americans there were repatriated, he developed a most comical *illusion de grandeur*. He had deserted his colleagues, he told them, "in the interest of history." On his broadcasts from Berlin, he began to imagine himself as a savior of mankind, as a divine leader to "save the American people from the kikes," as he once put it.

"My pleasure is increased," he shouted in a broadcast from Berlin on May 21, 1942, "by the fresh hope which the scope of my activity gives me for the future of America, for Britain, and the world. Of the most divine sanctity of my crusade for the overthrow of kike rule in America and Britain I have no doubt whatever."

A year ago last fall he "announced" his "candidature" for Congress and implored his listeners, if any, to write in his name on their ballots. Recently he informed his American audience that he was running for President in the 1944 election, and in his broadcast reply last July 28 to his indictment he complained that our "Jewed-up Attorney General" launched the indictment only because he, Best, had stood for Congress, and obtained it only after he had stated he was running for President. The funniest thing in this ludicrous episode is that Best actually seems to have convinced Dr. Goebbels, whose ignorance of America is Gargantuan, that his "candidacy" for Congress and the Presidency threatened to throw a spoke into our elections and should therefore be taken seriously. Otherwise the Doktor would not have wasted so much valuable radio time on Best's "election" speeches.

III

Bob Best's case obviously is a special one but it has this in common with those of the other radio traitors: all of them had a sense of frustration about their role, however small, in the American scene. All of them had come to be conscious of being misfits in their native land. In another epoch they might have become minute and cheap imitations of Henry James, who also became estranged from the current of life of America and who—wrongly, as it later proved—thought he was not appreciated or understood by his own people.

But between the two wars Fascism and Nazism attracted human derelicts as a flame attracts a moth. Most of the Nazi hierarchy consisted of derelicts from the first war, men who could not find a place in the Germany of the Republic. Nazism offered them, as it offered our American traitors, a chance to become somebody. It offered them a career. And it gave them something ready-made on which to vent their hates.

I happen to know that some of these Americans who were to become traitors made half-hearted attempts in the thirties to "make good" in the land of their birth. Having failed, as they lazily thought, they returned to Europe and threw themselves into the arms of the two Axis nations. Already Goebbels must have been thinking in his mind that they would come in handy when the new weapon of radio was turned to the service of total war. Their American accents, especially, would be valuable when this new weapon was really put to use in the service of conquest.

Two Americans who had thus made a last attempt to adjust themselves at home told me about it when they came back to Europe. They were Charles Flicksteger, who wrote under the name of "Flick," and George Nelson Page, nephew of our former Ambassador in Rome. Neither of them was included in the July indictment, presumably because they had taken out German and Italian citizenship, respectively, as did Lord Haw-Haw, the British radio traitor, who now is technically a Nazi citizen.

To earn his living, Flicksteger had worked for an American press association in Berlin, but his chief interest lay in music. Married at that time to a retired Munich opera singer, he composed operas and naturally Germany, which had a state-subsidized opera house going full blast in every provincial city as well as two in Berlin, gave him more of an outlet than he could find in America, where there was little opera outside of New York and a half-dozen of our largest cities. I went to his house a couple of times in Berlin to listen to him pound out one of his new operas on the piano, and afterward he would complain of how little opportunity America offered to one of his musical talents.

Flicksteger, who had many friends in the Nazi party, including Goering, got into trouble with them during the June, 1934, purge and found it necessary to get himself transferred to Vienna, where he was promptly arrested as a Nazi agent. This seems to have soured him temporarily on the Nazis and shortly afterward he returned to America to see if he could make a go of it here. He got a good job as an editor on a Philadelphia paper but he did not last and some time before the war he returned to Berlin, bitter against his native country. "I guess they just don't want me over there," he complained to me.

When I saw him next, he had made his decision. It was June, 1940, and the Germans were in Paris. I came home one night sick in the stomach from the nauseating spectacle of Hitler prancing about the little clearing in Compiègne Forest where the Armistice was being signed. I slipped into a seat at a large table in the dining room of the Hotel Scribe. It was full of arrogant, half-drunk German officers. One of them, a first lieutenant, looked familiar. He was grinning at me. "Guess you didn't expect to see me here in this," he said sheepishly, pointing at his uniform. Flicksteger had been making frontline recordings which were being played to America on the German short-wave. To-day he manages the German-owned radio station XGRS, which pours out anti-American propaganda from Shanghai.

George Nelson Page was an introspective American youngster who had spent most of his life with his relatives in Italy. Unfortunately he elected to return home at the height of the depression and after going jobless for a few months and, according to him, being snubbed for his poverty, he returned to Rome, took out his citizenship papers, did his military service, and became an Italian citizen. One night in Rome he poured out to me his bitterness against America for treating him so badly. Through his friendship with Ciano, he got a high post in the Italian Propaganda Ministry (Ministry of Popular Culture, as it was called) but I imagine he has not fared so well since the departure of his friend and his friend's father-in-law.

I did not know Douglas Chandler, who broadcasts from Berlin as "Paul Revere." He was a bit of a mystery man among the American correspondents there, for though he was constantly being quoted in the German press as "an American correspondent," none of us had ever seen him in the flesh. In fact we thought for a time he was a fictional character.

In the end he proved to be real enough, and later on I learned something about the man. Life in this country proved a little too tough for him too, it seems. Born in Chicago May 26, 1889, he grew up in Baltimore where after the war, in which he served for a short time in the Navy, he worked as a reporter and columnist on the Sunday *American*. After his marriage in 1924—which I have mentioned—to a descendant of John Jay, he went into the brokerage business and, like a great many others who had chosen this particular line of business activity, he was wiped out in the crash of 1929.

Some recovered from that blow, but not Chandler. Soon he was complaining that the "miasma of Washington" was stifling chaps like himself and in 1930, asserting that his wife's income would provide a better living for him and his family in

Europe than at home, he set out for Europe. For a time he wrote travel articles for American magazines, but most of them dropped him when they learned some time after 1933 that he was in the pay of the Nazi government.

In the spring of 1941, as it happened, Dr. Goebbels was trying desperately to find an American radio personality who could build up in the United States a vast listening audience, if only by being amusing, as had Lord Haw-Haw in Britain. Kaltenbach, the former Iowa boy, had not been quite good enough and Delaney, alias Ward, had been a positive failure.

So if in April, 1941, you had listened to the German short-wave programs, you would have heard a tremendous build-up for a new American voice. On April 18, the 166th anniversary of Paul Revere's famous ride, that famous horseman and patriot, Berlin said, would gallop again. April 18 came and nothing happened, but a week later, preceded by the thumping of horses' hoofs and the tune of "Yankee Doodle," "Paul Revere" rode. "Paul Revere" also spoke, trying to incite his fellow Americans to throw off the terrible tyranny of "Roosevelt and his Jews." Before he had finished speaking he was the flop of the year. He was even worse on the air than the aging Delaney-Ward. A few weeks afterward, "Paul Revere" revealed that he was really Douglas Chandler. His standard beginning for his broadcasts is: "Misinformed, misgoverned friends and compatriots."

Jane Anderson, the Countess de Cienfuegos, born in Atlanta on January 6, 1893, turned traitor, I suppose, because she was bitten by the bug that has smitten a few other of our citizens. Like them she got it into her head that the "Bolshevist hordes" were about to engulf our world and she thought Hitler and men like Franco could save us. She had been sentenced to death as a spy by the Spanish Loyalists but the sentence was quelled at the request of the State Department and she was released. After that her tongue never ceased wagging—and always on the same tiresome subject. "I had not been twenty-four hours upon American soil," she reported in a Berlin broadcast, "before I had confirmed . . . that from the pulpits of the land of the Star-Spangled Banner, no word of the God-fearing had been lifted against the hordes from Moscow which had descended upon Madrid to unleash upon a Christian land rivers of blood as the first stride forward in world revolution. . . ."

Miss Anderson's "ranting, melodramatic voice," as one British official described it, ceased abruptly to come off the Berlin air waves in April, 1942. She had broadcast to America a tall tale about the wonderful food and champagne in the capital's night clubs. OWI transmitters rebroadcast her glowing account to the German people. She was never heard on the air from Berlin again.

IV

Of all this motley group of Americans, Fred Kaltenbach, of Dubuque, Iowa, probably was the most sincere in his conversion to Nazism. He really believed in it. Born in Dubuque in 1895 of German immigrant parents, he remained essentially German in outlook and like so many other Germans was early attracted to the mysticism—or whatever it was—of Nazism.

His American education was considerable. He studied at Grinnell College, took a B.A. from Iowa State Teachers College in 1920 (after serving a short time as a second lieutenant in the Coast Artillery during the war) and an M.A. in history at the University of Chicago. But by 1933, while teaching at the Dubuque High School, he was organizing a group of high school boys into a "hiking club" which he called the "Militant Order of Spartan Knights" and which he modeled on the pattern of the Hitler Youth, the members sporting brown-shirted uniforms. I am glad to report that Iowa, my own state, had more sense than Germany. The school authorities disbanded the "Knights" and fired Kaltenbach. He left shortly thereafter for Germany where, studious fellow that he is, he took a Ph.D. at the University of Berlin and zealously embraced Hitlerism and all its foul works. I will never forget him standing by my side outside the little railway carriage at Compiègne. Through the car windows you could see Hitler sitting proudly at a table while General Keitel read the French the armistice terms. Kaltenbach, as if in a trance, gazed longingly at his Fuehrer as other men might gaze toward their god. It was no surprise, then, when he elected to remain in Germany and betray his country. He was a born Nazi.

So was Max Otto Koischwitz, who did not come to this country until 1925, where he found employment on the faculties of Columbia University and Hunter College. He became a naturalized citizen in 1935, when he had already been converted to Nazism. A former pupil has described him as "thin, dark, Mephistophelean" and his lectures, in which he did not fail to get in his Nazi propaganda, especially on the racial issue, seem to have been very popular. At least his classrooms were always crowded. He turned out to be a versatile fellow on the air and in his broadcasts appears sometimes as "Dr. Anders," a scholarly rogue, sometimes as "Mr. O.K.," a glib talker in the American vernacular, and sometimes just as himself, Dr. Koischwitz. The only wonder about him is that his Nazi loyalties were not discovered before he departed for the Fatherland in 1939.

Ezra Pound, the only one of the traitors to sell out to Italy, was already obsessed by the "decadence of democracy" when as a youth just out of college I used to listen to him prattle on the terrace of the Café Sélect in Paris in the middle twenties. He was a talented poet but had no political sense and Mussolinism already at that time seemed to attract his flamboyant nature. I suspect also that he became embittered at what he thought was the lack of appreciation of his poetry in his native America. He used to lecture us, if I remember rightly, about "our cultural backwoods we left behind us." His broadcasts from Rome were curiously incoherent for a writer so much interested in language. But he loved the sound of his own words, as when he shouted hoarsely from Rome one day to his former compatriots: "You have been hugger-muggered and scarum-shouted into a war and you know nothing about it."

I heard his last broadcast. It was on the evening of July 25, about three hours after his radio station in Rome had announced the "resignation" of the Duce, whom he had always praised as a god. It was obvious that poor Pound knew nothing about it. But he was not heard from again.

V

Two of the traitors, Best and Kaltenbach, broadcast replies to their indictments. Best was truculent; Kaltenbach sounded as though he were hurt.

Said Best on the evening of July 28: "The decision not only to indict but to execute most of us was taken by Washington's Jews and Judocrats already in 1942. . . . When I packed my bags and walked out of the internment hotel at Bad Nauheim seventeen months ago, I knew quite well what I was doing. . . . I knew . . . that I was crossing a Rubicon and at the same time burning my bridges behind me. I knew, in other words, that it meant the beginning of a battle to the death between me and the clique of Jewish reptiles which are to-day running America. . . . In reality, America's Jews have all intended from the first to shoot or to hang every one of us who exposes their game of world enslavement. . . . The idea behind this Judocratic circus is to frighten you away from our broadcasts to you. Roosevelt and his Jewish bosses wish that you see always before you a life-sized picture of yourself standing under a gallows beside me if you dare pass my messages on to others, or even listen to them yourself. If you are a wishy-washy namby-pamby, therefore, please turn off your radio immediately. If you are a real man, however, pass on to others every day my warning appeal: To Arms! To Arms, you patriots! The red-coats of Katyn and Dimitrov are on their way to both America and Britain."

Kaltenbach, replying in his broadcast of July 30, was more wistful. Said he: "Technically I suppose I am guilty of treason—of treason to Roosevelt and his warmongers, but not to the American people. . . . To have deserted the German people would have been an act of treason against my conscience. On December 8, 1941, I was suddenly confronted with the choice of committing a possible act of treason against my native America, or of deserting the German people in their hour of need. I could have returned to the United States. . . . That would have been the easy way out. . . . Don't think the choice was easy. It was not easy to turn my back perhaps forever on my friends in the United States, never to see the land of my birth again. . . . Nevertheless I made then my choice, and I have never regretted that choice for an instant. . . . If that be treason, make the most of it."

Were the words of Patrick Henry ever turned to a more ironical use?

Harper's Magazine, October 1943

So Proudly We Fail

by James Agee

WE SUFFER—we vaguely realize—a unique and constantly intensifying schizophrenia which threatens no other nation involved in this war. Geography is the core of the disease. Those Americans who are doing the fighting are doing it in parts of the world which seem irrelevant to them; those who are not, remain untouched, virginal, prenatal, while every other considerable population on earth comes of age. In every bit of information you can gather about breakdowns of American troops in combat, overseas, even in the camps, a sense of unutterable dislocation, dereliction, absence of contact, trust, wholeness, and reference, in a kind and force which no other soldiers have to suffer, clearly works at the root of the disaster. Moreover, while this chasm widens and deepens daily between our fighting and civilian populations and within each mind, another—much deeper and wider than any which geography alone could impose—forms and increases between this nation and the other key nations of the world. Their experience of war is unprecedented in immediacy and unanimity. Ours, even in the fraction which has the experience at all, is essentially specialized, lonely, bitter, and sterile; our great majority will emerge from the war almost as if it had never taken place; and not all the lip-service in the world about internationalism will make that different. This, and more and worse, is all so obvious, so horrifying, and so apparently unalterable that, being a peculiarly neurotic people, we are the more liable to nod and pay it the least possible attention. That is unfortunate. Our predicament is bad enough as it stands; the civil and international prospect is unimaginably sinister.

Since it is beyond our power to involve ourselves as deeply in experience as the people of Russia, England, China, Germany, Japan, we have to make up the difference as well as we can at second hand. Granting that knowledge at second hand, taken at a comfortable distance, is of itself choked with new and terrible liabilities, I believe nevertheless that much could be done to combat and reduce those liabilities, and that second-hand knowledge is at least less dangerous than no knowledge at all. And I think it is obvious that in imparting it, moving pictures could be matchlessly useful. How we might use them, and how gruesomely we have failed to, I lack room to say; but a good bit is suggested by a few films I want to speak of now.

Even the Army Orientation films, through no fault intrinsic to them, carry their load of poison, of failure. You can hear from every sort of soldier from the simplest to the most intricate what a valuable job they are doing. But because they are doing it only for service men they serve inadvertently to widen the abyss between fighters and the civilians who need just as urgently to see them. Civilians, however, get very little chance to learn anything from moving pictures. We are not presumed to be brave enough. And the tragic thing is that after a couple of decades of Hollywood and radio, we are used to accepting such deprivations and insults quite docilely; often, indeed, we resent anyone who has the daring to try to treat us as if we were human beings.

Just now it is a fought question whether numbers four and five of the Orientation Series, "The Battle of Britain" and "The Battle of Russia," will get public distribution. Whether they do depends on what is laughingly called the Office of War Information and on what is uproariously called the War Activities Committee. The OWI's poor little pictures, blueborn with timidity from the start, have finally been sabotaged out of existence; and judging by the performance to date of the WAC, it is not very likely that we shall see these films. And if we do see them, it is more than likely that we shall see them with roast albatrosses like "The Keeper of the Flame" hung around their necks.

I can only urge you to write your Congressman, if he can read. For these films are responsible, irreplaceable pieces of teaching. "Britain," one hour's calculated hammering of the eye and ear, can tell you more about that battle than you are ever likely otherwise to suspect, short of having been there.

"Russia," though it is a lucid piece of exposition, is cut neither for fact nor for political needlepoint but purely, resource-
fully, and with immensely powerful effect, for emotion. It is
by no means an ultimate handling of its material, but it is
better than the Russian records from which it was drawn, and
next to the tearful magnificence of "The Birth of a Nation" is,
I believe, the best and most important war film ever assembled in this country.

Beside it Samuel Goldwyn's "The North Star" is something
to be seen more in sorrow than in anger and more in the
attitude of the diagnostician than in any emotion at all. It
represents to perfection some crucially symptomatic characteristics of Hollywood and of the American people in so far as
Hollywood reflects, or is accepted by, the people. Hollywood's noble, exciting, all but unprecedented intention here
is to show the conduct of the inhabitants of a Russian border
village during the first days of their war; to show real people,
involved in realities, encumbered by a minimum of star-
spotlighting or story. The carrying out of that intention im-
plies in every detail the hopeless mistrust in which Hollywood
holds its public. To call this "commercial" and to talk about
lack of intelligence and taste is, I think, wide of the main
mark. The attitude is more nearly that of the fatally misguided
parent toward the already all but fatally spoiled child. The
result is one long orgy of meeching, sugaring, propitiation,
which, as a matter of fact, enlists, develops, and infallibly cor-
rupts a good deal of intelligence, taste, courage, and disinter-
estedness. I am sorry not to talk at length and in detail about
this film. I can only urge you to watch what happens in it:
how every attempt to use a reality brings the romantic juice
and the annihilation of any possible reality pouring from every
gland. In its basic design Lillian Hellman's script could have
become a fine picture: but the characters are stock, their lines
are tinny-literary, their appearance and that of their village is
scrubbed behind the ears and "beautified"; the camera work
is nearly all glossy and overcomposed; the proudly complicated action sequences are stale from overtraining; even the
best of Aaron Copland's score has no business ornamenting a
film drowned in ornament: every resourcefulness appropriate
to some kinds of screen romance, in short, is used to make

palatable what is by no remote stretch of the mind romantic. I think the picture represents the utmost Hollywood can do, within its present decaying tradition, with a major theme. I am afraid the general public will swallow it whole. I insist, however, that that public must and can be trusted and reached with a kind of honesty difficult, in so mental-hospital a situation, to contrive; impossible, perhaps, among the complicated pressures and self-defensive virtuosities of the great studios.

The thing that so impresses me about the non-fiction films which keep coming over from England is the abounding evidence of just such a universal adulthood, intelligence, and trust as we lack. I lack space to mention them in detail (the new titles are "I Was a Fireman," "Before the Raid," and, even better, "ABCA" and the bleak, beautiful, and heart-rending "Psychiatry in Action"), but I urge you to see every one that comes your way. They are free, as not even our Orientation films are entirely, of salesmanship; they are utterly innocent of our rampant disease of masked contempt and propitiation. It comes about simply enough: everyone, on and off screen and in the audience, clearly trusts and respects himself and others.

There is a lot of talk here about the need for "escape" pictures. To those who want to spend a few minutes in a decently ventilated and healthful world, where, if only for the duration, human beings are worthy of themselves and of each other, I recommend these British films almost with reverence as the finest "escapes" available.

The Nation, October 30, 1943

Morale Sags at Camp Forrest as Jim Crow Rules

by Deton J. Brooks, Jr.

TALLAHOMA, Tenn.—This little town tacked on the map just a stone's throw from Camp Forrest is where General Sherman started his march to the sea during the Civil War.

And the whites both in town and in camp never seem to forget it. They seem determined to convince Negro troops here that war is just what General Sherman said it was.

Jim Crow rules the roost with an iron hand at Camp Forrest. Colored soldiers at this Tennessee army post bitterly complain at the treatment they get here.

War is what General Sherman called it—at least to the Negro soldiers.

In talking to hundreds of soldiers and officers during a recent tour of this maneuver area, they cited any number of humiliating incidents which they have suffered and which tend to eat away morale so necessary in developing an effective fighting force.

Here's a description one northern-born soldier gave me of Camp Forrest: "My unit as well as all colored units, with the exception of the WACs, are isolated in one section of the camp, as if by contact we'd give our white brothers-in-arms the 'black plague.'

"When we are fortunate enough to get into the camp theatre, we're segregated. Any time there's a good picture, they won't let us in. They tell us it's crowded.

"They bar us from the camp library. Why they even refused to let a captain of the 931st Field Artillery Battalion stay in there. Yet there's no library for us. Since they put the captain out, they're building a dinky addition to our recreation hall. But as yet that's not finished.

"The facilities that we do have, like our recreation hall, and

Post Exchange, are small and inadequate. While the white boys have large buildings with separate game room and reading rooms, ours are one-room affairs.

"The post command seems to spare no efforts to let us know that we are different, something apart from the other soldiers."

I visited in Tullahoma and found conditions equally as bad as the soldiers described within it. The colored USO center is located near the end of town in what is known as the Negro district. There is one medium-sized lounge room, a kitchen and a room which could pass for an office. This in contrast to four large, spacious buildings for white troops which are strategically located in various sections of the village.

The very location is depressing. All around the center are hovels and shacks, as bad as the worst to be found elsewhere in the South. The director of the USO club is a Chicagoan and former football player of Fenger high school by the name of Emmet Spurlock. Together with his wife and curly-headed little 10-year-old son, he is forced to live in a trailer because the whites won't rent him a decent house. He is striving manfully to carry on a real recreation program under the most impossible handicaps.

The railroad station is another rotten spot. Colored soldiers complain that they often miss their train when leaving on short precious furloughs because the clerks in the station won't sell them tickets until after all the whites have been waited on. Then it is too late to catch the train.

The soldiers say further that no matter how many men are travelling, they are allowed only one Jim-Crow car. If this is overcrowded they either have to ride in the baggage car or forfeit their travel privilege.

With the exception of the colored USO club, there is no decent place for a Negro soldier to go in town. Tullahoma is the typical southern village which is still fighting the Civil War. It will be remembered that it was from this town that a white soldier attached to the Illinois 33rd division had to be escorted back to camp by military police as a protective measure for asking to see where General Sherman started his march to the sea.

Investigation shows that all attempts to improve conditions

for Negro troops in this camp have been blocked by post commanders. It was during the administration of Col. Millard F. Waltz that the theatre incident involving officers of the 931st Field Artillery Battalion occurred. It was Col. Waltz who, backed by MP's carrying tommy guns, ordered these officers to leave the theatre for sitting in the non-segregated section. Col. Waltz, a southerner by birth, made no provision for Negro troops.

He has since been relieved by Col. Frank T. Addington, another southerner who boasts Virginia as his home. It is reported that he is an ardent believer in segregation although he is trying to make some provision for the recreation of colored troops. It is he who is building the "dinky" library addition. And he has given Negroes a couple of nights a month in the post dance hall.

The net effect of these conditions is extremely low morale among the troops. The northern boys and the more intelligent southern ones are bitterly and deeply resentful. They only go into Tullahoma when they have to. They spend most of their time in the camp areas.

The lower calibre southern boys, most of whom are in the engineering units, are not as resentful, but their appearance belies the state of their morale.

They are dirty, some of them look as if they haven't had a bath for a month. Their uniforms are untidy. They don't have the snap and zip which is a natural part of a fighting man.

Apparently, their white officers are doing nothing to inject into them the feeling that they are part of a proud fighting American army, which is destined to make a world safe for the democratic ideology.

Chicago Defender, November 6, 1943

Patton Struck Soldier in Hospital, Was Castigated by Eisenhower

by Edward Kennedy

ALLIED HEADQUARTERS, ALGIERS, Nov. 23 (AP).—It was disclosed officially today that Lt. Gen. George S. Patton Jr. had apologized to all officers and men of the Seventh Army for striking a soldier during the Sicilian campaign.

While Patton was not relieved of his command and was not given a formal reprimand, he received a castigation from Gen. Dwight D. Eisenhower such as has seldom been administered to a commander of an army.

Permission to write the story, which has been known to thousands of soldiers since last August, was given correspondents following a broadcast by Drew Pearson from Washington Sunday night. Pearson in his broadcast said that Patton had been "severely reprimanded" by Eisenhower and gave as his opinion that Patton would not "be used in combat any more."

Pearson's broadcast resulted in the formal statement from Allied headquarters last night, saying Patton still was in command of the Seventh Army and that he had not been reprimanded.

This statement was technically correct, though it did not give the full picture. There was no formal reprimand, as the term is known in the army. Correspondence on the subject is in Eisenhower's personal files and in Patton's personal files, and known to the War Department. But it is not on Patton's record.

The story is a strange one—the story of a General, whose excellence is admitted by all, who in the heat of battle lost his temper and later admitted he was wrong and made amends.

The incident consisted of this, according to eyewitnesses:

Gen. Patton slapped a shell-shocked soldier in a hospital

tent because he thought the soldier was shirking his duty. The incident occurred early in August when the Sicilian campaign was in one of its most critical periods.

Patton visited the evacuation hospital and went among the wounded, trying to cheer them. He patted some on the back, sympathizing with them. He then came upon a 24-year-old soldier sitting on a cot with his head buried in his hands, weeping.

"What's the matter with you?" Patton asked, according to persons who were in the hospital tent at the time.

The soldier mumbled a reply which was inaudible to the General. Patton repeated his question.

"It's my nerves. I guess I can't stand shelling," the soldier was quoted as replying.

Patton thereon burst into a rage. Employing much profanity, he called the soldier a "coward," "yellow belly," and numerous other epithets, according to those present. He ordered the soldier back to the front.

The scene attracted several persons, including the commanding officer of the hospital, the doctor who had admitted the soldier and a nurse.

In a fit of fury in which he expressed sympathy for men really wounded but made it plain that he did not believe that the soldier before him was in that class, the General struck the youth in the rear of the head with the back of his hand.

The soldier fell over slightly and the liner of his helmet which he was wearing fell off and rolled over the floor of the tent.

A nurse, intent on protecting the patient, made a dive toward Patton but was pulled back by a doctor. The commander of the hospital then intervened.

Patton then went before other patients, still in high temper, expressing his views. He returned to the shell-shocked soldier and berated him again. The soldier appeared dazed as the incident progressed but offered to return to the front and tried to rise from his cot.

Patton left the hospital without making further investigation of the case.

The facts concerning the soldier were later ascertained: He was a regular Army man who had enlisted before the war from his home town in the South. He had fought throughout the Tunisian and Sicilian campaigns and his record was excellent. He had been diagnosed as a medical case the week previously, but had refused to leave the front and continued on through the strain of battle. He finally was ordered to the hospital by his unit doctor.

After Patton left, the soldier demanded to return to the front. This request was refused at the time, but after a week of rest, he was in good shape and returned to his unit at the front.

Immediately after the incident the soldier was reported in a miserable state. As a regular Army man with pride in his record, he felt his whole world dashed to pieces.

"Don't tell my wife! Don't tell my wife!" he was quoted as saying by persons who talked to him later. The chaplain at the hospital however pointed out that the incident was the result of an outburst of temper due to the strain of battle and after several conversations with the soldier, persuaded him to accept it in that light.

The incident was reported to Eisenhower. The Commander-in-Chief immediately wrote Patton a letter in which he denounced his conduct and ordered him to make amends or be removed from his command.

"The Old Man certainly took the hide off him," an Allied headquarters spokesman said.

Patton's conduct then became as generous as it had been furious. He apologized to the soldier whom he had struck, to the commander of the hospital and to all those present at the time. He then went before as many officers and men as could be assembled from each division under his command and repeated his apology.

At the close of the campaign in talking to correspondents, Patton after recounting the history of the Sicilian drive, said:

"When these things are happening a commanding general is under great nervous tension. He may do things he may afterward regret. I know a great many people regard me as a ——

"But I have patted five soldiers on the back for every one I have spoken a harsh word to. I dealt harshly with a couple of soldiers and was wrong. I am going to apologize to them."

Soon after the hospital tent incident, this correspondent told Gen. Eisenhower that since it was known to thousands of persons, many of them returning to the United States, it was almost certain that it would eventually find its way into print. I expressed the view that it might be preferable for correspondents here to write the story.

Eisenhower agreed in principle and said he might arrange a press conference at which Patton himself would bring the matter up. This plan was never carried out.

Eisenhower described Patton's conduct as "despicable" and said Patton himself had admitted the incident and realized he was in error and was willing to apologize fully. The commander-in-chief, at the same time, expressed the greatest confidence in Patton as a general and said no one else could have achieved such results in Sicily.

Eisenhower indicated that after Patton's apology was accepted, his only other move would be to investigate and see whether there was animosity on the part of the troops toward Patton which would impair his value as a commander. Presumably, the investigation disclosed no such animosity because Patton was retained as Seventh Army commander.

Eisenhower imposed no censorship on correspondents in the matter. He said they were free to write the story if they chose, but made it clear that he believed its publication would be of value to the enemy as propaganda and might embarrass the command in this theater.

This placed correspondents in a difficult position. Because of the possibility that publication of the story might help the enemy, no correspondent in this theater sent the story.

Then followed the period in which the incident was known to thousands of soldiers here and continued to be a widespread subject of discussion and debate among them. This, however, was not published at home.

After the Pearson broadcast, censorship on the matter was applied temporarily and when the headquarters statement was issued last night, correspondents were told they might not send any information on the incident other than what was in the statement.

This morning, however, a high officer of headquarters appeared before correspondents telling them they might now send anything on the matter which they knew to be facts. This officer again stressed what all correspondents knew to be true—that Patton had made amends for his conduct.

The incident reflected the character of Patton—a general who drives both himself and his men to the very limit in battles, who is highly emotional at times and is given to outbursts when under strain. But he is regarded by many officers as the best field general in the American Army.

It is generally believed here by military men that Sicily would never have been conquered in 38 days had it not been for Patton's driving force. His value as a general was one reason why his case was dealt with as it was.

While many soldiers under Patton's command may not have much affection for him, they all respect him as a great general and have confidence in him as a commander. Patton himself doesn't care whether they like him or not—he regards his job as winning battles.

Patton is one of the most dynamic and colorful officers in the American Army and has been called the "General who never lost a battle." He also has been dubbed with various nicknames such as "Blood and Guts."

He commanded the Western task force which occupied the Atlantic coast of French Morocco in landings last November. His forces then occupied all Morocco and he remained in command there until the German breakthrough at Kasserine Gap in Tunisia in February, precipitating an American retreat.

After that reverse, Patton relieved Maj. Gen. Lloyd Fredendall as commander of the American Second Corps. He rallied this force and led it to victory at Maknassy, El Guettar and Gafsa. These victories led to a junction of Americans with the British Eighth Army between Gafsa and Gabes.

The Second Corps then was shifted to northern Tunisia for the final phase of that campaign. Patton's deputy commander, then Major General and now Lt. Gen. Omar Bradley, took command while Patton devoted himself to the final training of American soldiers who were to invade Sicily as the Seventh Army.

On arriving in Africa, Patton had a wartime rank of Major General. He was advanced to Lieutenant General when he took command in Tunisia. His permanent rank was Brigadier

General, higher than Eisenhower's permanent rank at the time. After the Sicilian campaign, both Eisenhower and Patton were given the permanent rank of Majors General.

Patton supervised the landing of the Seventh Army in Sicily from a headquarters ship, and then landed himself into that successful campaign with driving energy.

The Seventh Army swept over the western part of the island as Gen. Sir Bernard L. Montgomery's British Eighth Army took the eastern part. In a race between the two armies, the Americans drove along the north coastal road and were the first into Messina, final Sicilian city captured.

During the battle, Patton had driven the soldiers under him as hard as he had driven himself. Many times during the Sicilian campaign, he sent exhausted and almost collapsing troops into battle for the final blow which took enemy positions.

In the heat of battle Patton is contemptuous of his personal safety. He has been known to break into tears on occasion.

———————

In Washington, congressional sources showed a disposition to let the Army deal with the incident. The War Department declined to comment.

"This thing must be clarified for the people," declared Senator Kilgore (Dem.), West Virginia. "Army regulations cover the whole situation. Gen. Pershing wouldn't stand for any misfits in his army. A man who is emotionally unstable should be given a rest or sent back home."

Chairman Truman (Dem.), Missouri, of the Senate Special War Investigating Committee, who said prior to confirmation of the incident that the matter was not within the jurisdiction of his committee, commented today:

"Army regulations specifically forbid this sort of thing. I'm perfectly confident that Gen. Eisenhower is capable of handling the situation under those regulations—and I hope he will."

Chairman Reynolds (Dem.), North Carolina, of the Senate Military Affairs Committee said:

"It seems to be a matter for the consideration of the Chief of Staff and the President, the Commander-in-Chief."

Chairman May (Dem.), Kentucky, of the House Military

Committee: "It's unfortunate, but I don't think there is anything the Military Affairs Committee can do about it. It's a
matter of military discipline."

Representative Arends (Rep.), Illinois, military committee-
man: "If the stories are true, there should be some investigation."

Drew Pearson, commenting on yesterday's Army statement
from Algiers denying that Patton had been reprimanded, suggested that the Truman Committee investigate "if Gen.
Eisenhower has not acted."

St. Louis Post-Dispatch, November 23, 1943

"Then I Got It"

by Richard Tregaskis

November 22

This morning we could see how close the shells had landed. One fresh crater, no more than fifty feet away from the house, had come closest. Three others had landed within a radius of 100 feet.

Col. Yarborough, Capt. Tomasik and I started out in a jeep for Ranger headquarters, to check on the latest developments on Mount Corno. Maj. Saam said that the fighting had quieted down after last night's outburst, but that the Germans still held the cave on the far side of Mount Corno near the top.

"It's something to see," he said. "You can watch 'em sticking out their heads and throwing grenades. Our plan for today is to carry up bangalore torpedoes. The boys on Corno will try to lower 'em close to the cave and blow out the Krauts. We've already flopped with dynamite and grenades. This has got to work. There's only a squad of Germans in the cave itself, but on the far slope, two fresh battalions of enemy troops are moving up. If the squad in the cave can hold on long enough, the rest of the Krauts will creep up and grab the ridge."

Tomasik, Yarborough and I started up the steep, craggy slope of Mount Corno in our jeep.

"We might as well go as far as we can by jeep," said Yarborough. "It'll take us long enough to walk up the darn mountain after that."

So we chugged through a stony orchard, bouncing over the outcrops of rock, and came to a virtually insurmountable slope. We left the jeep and began to clamber up the rocks on foot.

Col. Yarborough said, "I know a place where you can

watch the fireworks, if you want to. You'd better leave that mackinaw behind." He indicated the heavy coat I was wearing. "We'll work up enough of a sweat if we go in shirtsleeves. It's only a couple of miles, but it'll take a couple of hours."

We were certainly perspiring as we passed beyond the fringe of scrub trees which covers the lower slopes of the mountain. Progress was slow up the stony mule track leading toward the bare summit.

There was no firing now. I kept my eyes on the rocks underfoot—and soon realized that we were following a literal trail of blood! Some of the stones were spattered with dark-red spots. This trail was the only negotiable route up the precipitous slope. Consequently, the wounded were bound to leave marks on the white rocks as they staggered or were carried down the winding path.

The track had a macabre fascination for me. I watched the variations in the trail of red spots; occasionally, the drops covered more rocks in one area, indicating, possibly, that a man had been wounded at that spot, or had stopped for a rest as he struggled to the aid station.

We walked in single file, at wide intervals, so that we would not all be killed or wounded by a single shell. This territory might be under heavy enemy fire at any moment, without warning. We halted several times and sat down in the trail, streaming sweat, but even when we rested, we remained scattered.

After another hour of climbing, we heard the sound of tumbling rocks from somewhere above us. Tomasik whipped out his .45; we halted and listened. "It might be an enemy patrol," Tomasik whispered. The sounds continued: falling stones, large objects brushing through the tall grass on the flank of the hill above.

We waited, frozen, and then saw an American helmet, then another, in the underbrush—one of our own patrols. We breathed more freely.

Farther up the trail, we spotted a single figure of a man, wearing an American uniform. When he came closer, we recognized Col. Darby. The Ranger leader was grimy and disheveled. A great rent had been torn in his trousers, exposing his long woolen underwear. Despite his ragged appearance, he spoke with his usual energy. "Rough up here last night," he said. "The damn Krauts were giving us hell." He pointed out a great knout of rock clinging to the flank of the ridge. At the top of the rock mass, we could see a sharp cleft through which the trail passed. "The sons of bitches were laying 'em right on there. Had to hang on so we wouldn't get blown off."

Yarborough, Tomasik and I stopped at the cleft in the rock, where twenty or thirty bedraggled and dirty Rangers sprawled. They had been up on the white rock at the top of Mount Corno, battling with the Germans who were trying to seize the peak. Other forces had relieved them.

They looked utterly exhausted, all the more unhappy because they reclined amidst a litter of ration cans, pasteboard boxes and empty shell cartons.

Gradually we progressed along the flank of the ridge running between the peaks of Mount Corno and Mount Croce. Near the top of this great massif, I realized, as always in mountainous terrain, the vastness of the hills in which we are fighting, and how puny our destructive efforts have been. We could wipe a town off the map with concentrated shelling, but we could not do more than scratch the hide of the earth. Up here, we were like fleas picking our way across the ribs of a mammoth animal.

We turned off the mule trail and started up the steepest part of the ridge. "You can get a good look at the fighting on Mount Corno from the top of this ridge," Yarborough offered.

He and Tomasik moved along toward Mount Croce, to inspect other positions. I stayed behind. At the top of the ridge, a few hundred yards from the crest of Mount Corno, I found an American observation post. The view of the peak and the large white rock on the German side was magnificent. With binoculars, I could make out occasional helmeted heads of Americans, barely distinguishable round spots, marking positions where Rangers were dug in on the summit of Mount Corno. While I watched, a squirt of black smoke dabbed the skyline. Then another, and another. They were German hand grenades, probably tossed from the base of the great white boulder. Somewhere at the foot of that boulder, I knew, the Germans were hiding in their cave. Presumably, the American helmets moving across the peak were the squad which had the job of lowering bangalore torpedoes over the rock and down into positions where they might blast the German strong point.

To the west of the peak of Mount Corno, the mountain mass, speckled with small trees, sloped steeply downward. Somewhere on that slope, the Germans were dug in. From the stubble of vegetation, a far-spreading cloud of smoke was rising. Large, rapidly springing bursts leaped from the woods as shells were striking. Our big 4.2-inch mortars were trying to keep back the tide of Germans inching up the grade.

From the ridge top where I was lying, there spread below me to the west the vast panorama of Italy. The brown scattering of roofless buildings in the next valley was the village of Concasale, where the cancerous pittings of shell craters disfigured the green face of the ground. Two ridges beyond, the town of Cassino sprawled up the mountainside. And beyond that, gray in the mist of distance, the mountain ridges were piled up, one on top of the other as far as we could see, like giant stony steps ascending gradually to Rome. Where, I wondered, was the "level, straight route" which is supposed to be ours once we conquer Cassino?

Near me, in a shallow, rocky foxhole, sat Maj. Bill Hutchinson, shouting corrections by phone to his 4.2 mortar batteries near Venafro. He cautioned me sharply against exposing myself in my movements across the ridge.

"We're within machine-gun range of Mount Corno," he said.

One of the group of men scattered over the ridge top was Capt. Shunstrom, the same wild man who had operated the mobile artillery so effectively with the Rangers back at Chiunzi Pass. Now he was fiddling with a 60-mm. mortar tube, preparing to add a few shells to the torrent of explosives falling on the German positions atop Mount Corno. "Here's the way to shoot one of these things," he announced. He braced the base-end of the tube against the ground and gave a demonstration, firing the powerful field weapon as if it were a pistol or rifle.

Usually, the 60-mm. mortar tube, which throws a projectile about two and a half inches in diameter and nearly a foot long, is attached to a heavy base plate when it is set up for firing, with a bipod supporting the tube at the proper angle. A mortar man drops the projectile down the mouth of the barrel and steps back to keep clear of the shell as it speeds from the muzzle. But Shunstrom had his own system. He wrapped the bare tube, without stand or bipod, in an old glove—which would insulate the heat of the barrel—seized the tube with his left hand, aimed it approximately, and dropped the mortar shell down the mouth with his right hand.

His marksmanship was surprisingly accurate. The first burst sprang up less than fifty feet from the top of the white rock at the peak of Mount Corno, and the second blew up on the rock itself. Shunstrom fired ten or eleven shells, three of them landing on the stone, and one close to the cave where the Germans must have been dug in. Shunstrom gave a grunt of satisfaction.

I watched the fireworks: the firing of the heavy mortars which were giving the Germans hell on the far slope of Corno, and had set fire to some of the trees there; Shunstrom's wildcat marksmanship with his mortar; the slender plume of smoke raised by a German hand grenade near the top of Corno. Finally, I saw a great explosion blossoming from the white rock itself—perhaps the detonation of the bangalore torpedoes, or a charge of dynamite. Maj. Hutchinson said, "Great fun, as long as we're dishing it out and not taking it."

Yarborough and Tomasik came back from their inspection tour, and we started down the tedious trail toward home. I felt a healthy fatigue. For the first time in several weeks, I had a bang-up eyewitness story of an action at a crucial sector of the front. But there was an even better story ahead of me.

We reached the cleft rock, the local C.P., and I stopped for a few minutes to talk to some of the Rangers, while Tomasik and Yarborough went on. I would catch up with them later. I got the notes I wanted and hurried after them. Past the curve in the trail where we had listened, tautly, to the approach of a patrol on our way up, I was making my way along the relatively straight stretch where the German mortar shells had been falling on the previous day. Then I got it.

I heard the scream of something coming, and I must have dived to the rocks instinctively. Months of conditioning on many battlefields resolved themselves in that instantaneous, life-saving reflex. Then a smothering explosion descended around me. It seemed to flood over me from above. In a fraction of a second of consciousness, I sensed that I had been hit. A curtain of fire rose, hesitated, hovered for an infinite second. In that measureless interval, an orange mist came up quickly over my horizon, like a tropical sunrise, and set again, leaving me in the dark. Then the curtain descended, gently.

I must have been unconscious for a few seconds. When a rudimentary awareness came back, I knew everything was all wrong. I realized I had been badly hit. I was still stretched on the rocks. A couple of feet from me lay my helmet which had been gashed in at least two places, one hole at the front and another ripping through the side.

Catastrophe had struck me down. My shocked perceptions groped for an understanding of what had happened. It was no use.

There was no pain. Everything seemed finished, quiet, as if time had stopped. I sat up and looked back at the path. Now I saw the motion of figures of men running up the trail at a half crouch, as a man would zigzag through shellfire. There must be danger. I was aware of that at least. I tried to shout at them, but only incoherent sounds tumbled from my mouth, and my voice rattled, as if it were coming from some place far off and beyond my control. It was like a broken, muted phonograph.

My mind formulated frantic questions. What's wrong? Why can't I talk? What am I going to do? And then I felt a slight easing of tension, a slight relaxation. I knew, then, that even though I could not utter the words, I could still think. I had lost my power of speech, not my power to understand or generate thought. It was clear to me what I wanted to say, but I couldn't say it.

By this time the men had gone, and it was evident that they were too concerned with something else to come back and pay attention to me.

A shell was coming. I knew that because I heard the sound of the approaching projectile. But the sound was just a tinny little echo of something which had once been terrifying and all-powerful. And the explosion, while it seemed to rattle my skull, was certainly not terrifying. I couldn't understand the fear written on the face of a soldier who had skidded into the ground near me as he sought to take cover from the bursting of the shell.

I tried, with my distant and almost uncontrollable voice, to talk intelligibly to the frightened soldier during the few seconds he was there. I was trying to say, "Can you help me?" And after a number of unconnected, stumbling syllables, I finally managed two words, "Can help?"

I heard the tinny sound of a little shell, and saw the soldier's face, hollowed by terror. He was saying, "I can't help you, I'm too scared." And then he was gone, running, up the trail.

I have no recollection how soon the first-aid man dropped to the ground beside me and bandaged my head. But it was done, in those few minutes, and I saw the needle of the hypo as he gave me a shot of morphine. I did not feel the prick of the needle. The first-aid man was gone. I was alone on the mountainside.

I knew, then, that if I wanted to get back to the field dressing station, I would have to go under my own power. I would have to get up and walk down the trail in the hope that I might still catch up with Col. Yarborough. Somehow, shock seemed to have allayed any pain I might otherwise have experienced. The quick administration of morphine within a few minutes of the time of injury dulled my concern about my wound.

My glasses were lying on the rocks a few inches away. Miraculously, they had been blown off without being broken. I tried to move my right hand to pick up the spectacles, and realized that the whole arm was as inert as a board. I grabbed the glasses with my left hand and put them on. They were not very secure because my head was bandaged, and they were askew on my nose. I picked up my helmet. It would be a fine souvenir, I thought illogically. That too sat precariously on my bandaged head. I grasped my right arm in my left hand.

Touching it was like touching a foreign body, and when I dropped it, it fell limply, beyond control, at my side.

I stood up and started down the trail. My helmet bobbed on the bulky bandages around my head, and finally it slid off and bounced on the ground. Determined to save it at all costs, I picked it up and put it back on my head.

Then a shell came. I heard the same ragged, distant whistling, and the rattling explosion, as I automatically fell to the rocks for protection. I waited for the rest of the group of shells to arrive, and they were close. I looked up and saw tall spouts of smoke and high explosive jumping up all around me—but it was all unreal, like a movie with a feeble sound track. Probably the concussion of the shell burst which had hit me had also deafened me. I was amazed, but not frightened, as one huge shell burst suddenly sprang into being, towered over me like a genie. It was so close that I could have reached out and touched it. Yet none of the flying fragments had brushed me.

When the burst of firing was over, I scrambled to my feet again. Dropping my helmet, I stubbornly picked it up and put it back on my head. My glasses slipped down on my nose again and again. A red drapery of blood ran down over the glasses and blurred my vision. Staggering down the trail, I dropped my helmet again, several times, and doggedly retrieved it. My right arm and hand dangled loosely. I muttered to myself, trying to talk straight, practicing—and still able to mouth only a sort of ape-chatter. If anyone had been there to see me, I would have been a grotesque apparition.

Shells were coming again. This time I headed for a shallow cave carved in the rock at the side of the trail, and took refuge in it. A feeling of simple contentment came over me because the shells were landing harmlessly outside, while I was secure in my hideaway. Here, in a shelter originally dug by a German, I smiled, sat and waited for the spell of firing to cease. I remembered that I must go on as soon as the firing stopped. My mind fixed on the idea that the only way to get out of this was by catching up with Yarborough and Tomasik. If I had to stay up on the mountain overnight, and wait for someone to find me, before I could be carried down, I might not be alive in the morning.

When the firing stopped, I staggered onto the path. I went as fast as I could, dropping my helmet occasionally and picking it up; I was determined to preserve it. I heard the rustle of the shells again, and automatically sprawled on the rocks. The muffled explosions seemed quite a distance away now. I got up. If only I could catch up with Yarborough. Nothing else seemed too important. After all, I had realized the odds and often speculated upon them. Already I had more than used up my chances. If I could get through this thing alive, I thought, I could start on a fresh bunch of chances.

I came around a bend of the trail, and felt a surge of pleasure as I saw Col. Yarborough and Capt. Tomasik, bending over a wounded man. Fortunately for me, they had stayed behind to care for him. Yarborough started to wave to me, then noticed the bandaged head, the bloody glasses and red-stained shirt.

More shells squeaked and rattled into the side of the ridge, and we ducked. When it was over, Bill Yarborough and I started together down the trail. My one usable arm was draped over his shoulder. He provided support for my staggering feet.

Once, we had to stop to shoo from the trail three wild-eyed pack mules, frightened by the shelling and deserted by their keeper. Once, we had to take shelter when the shells came again. Twice or three times, I lost my dubious balance and fell. Yarborough helped me to my feet. The trail seemed endlessly long—actually it was about a mile that we had to travel—and it would have seemed nightmarish had it not been for the shot of morphine, and the great shock of the wound. Still, there was not the faintest trace of pain.

And so we reached a command post, in a peasant house at the fringe of the woods. Two aid men sat me down, looked at my head and expertly slit the sleeve of my shirt to inspect my useless arm. There were no marks on the arm. Then I knew it had been paralyzed in some way. Yarborough gave me five or six sulfa tablets. The dashing parachutist doctor, Capt. Alden, looked at my head, said nothing. I tried to talk. The words were still unintelligible. I lay on the dirt floor and looked up at the line of soldiers staring at me, the Badly Wounded Man.

I must have stared just that way at many a wounded man whom I had seen. Now I was on the other side of the picture, for a change.

I had another shot of morphine, and dozed. I remember being sick. Then I was stretched out in the rear of a jeep. I asked again and again whether my notes, and especially my helmet, were aboard. They were. The air felt cool as we began to move down the steep mountain side. A faint light hovered in the sky. It was late afternoon. The time must have been about four-thirty, about two hours after I was hit.

Once we had begun to move, I lost consciousness. We must have stopped somewhere, for I remember being in a tent, and hearing voices that said something about "tetanus shot." I did not see or feel the needle.

Then I became aware that it was dark and cold, and that I was being carried on a stretcher. They put me down inside a tent, where a bright electric light glared. I heard gruff voices. The stretcher bearers picked me up again. We passed into the night, the stretcher bumping with the steps of the aid men. They carried me into another tent, less garishly lighted than the first. It was cold. I lay and shivered.

I was brought to still another tent, which seemed warmer. A voice asked me about my right arm, and, in general, how I felt. I tried to explain these matters, but my words would not come out right. They were as badly tangled as before. Instead of saying something like "The arm's been like that since I got hit up on the mountain," I said, "The sam—I mean farm—I mean tam—farm, sam—like that since I got bit—rot —rat—hut, on the rountain, I mean fountain—bounty— fountain."

I was feeling warmer. The stretcher bearers came in again and picked me up and carried me to still another tent, which, even in my present drugged condition, I recognized as an X-ray room. I knew that I had been set down on the floor, still on my stretcher, while loud voices could be heard talking. I was sensitive, as I suppose patients in general must be, to the tone of the voices. These were rough and grumbling.

Very different was the next voice I heard talking to me as I was carried back to the tent which I had just left. It was cheerful, very considerate. The man said that he was sorry but that he was going to have to shave my head. He did not want it to hurt.

Another man came in, looked down at me and informed me, "We're going to have to operate on you." This voice was very brusque. I wanted to ask him something. It was the question, "Am I going to die?" After several attempts, I conveyed the intended meaning, but the man, evidently the doctor, wouldn't commit himself.

Then there was another, pleasant man, sitting by my side. I realized that he must be a minister. His voice was very calm and soothing. He was saying a prayer. I thanked him; the mere sound of the words was comforting. Then I had another shot of morphine.

Invasion Diary, 1944

from *Tarawa: The Story of a Battle*

by Robert Sherrod

"I Didn't Know Whether We Had the Heart to Fight a War"

I spent a lot of time studying the Marines. They looked like any group of ordinary, healthy young Americans. The range of their background was as broad as America: farmers, truck drivers, college students, runaway kids, rich men's sons, orphans, lawyers, ex-soldiers. One day Lieutenant William B. Sommerville, the battalion supply officer, himself a Baltimore lawyer, was showing me around the ship. On deck we passed a Marine corporal with a bandaged thumb. Sommerville stopped and asked what happened.

"I let my air hose get away from me," grinned the corporal. We walked on. "That guy," said Sommerville, "was a county judge in Texas when he enlisted."

All these Marines were volunteers. Only now, several months after voluntary enlistments had been stopped—to the unconcealed disgust of old-line Marine sergeants who had from time immemorial been able to fall back on the final, scathing word, "Nobody asked you to be a Marine, bub"— were the first Marine draftees being sent overseas as replacements.

The Marines ate the same emergency rations that soldiers ate in battle. They used the same weapons. They came from the same places.* They went to the same schools. What, then, had gained the Marines a reputation as fighting men far ex-

---

*With some differences. A glance at the roster of men aboard the *Blue Fox* showed a preponderance of Midwesterners, Southerners, and Californians, and almost no New Englanders. Thus, of 1,618 Marines and attached naval units aboard, 115, or seven percent, were from Texas, whereas Texas holds just under five percent of the U.S. population. But I had seen no units overseas in this war, outside some National Guard outfits, to which Texas had not contributed more than her pro-rata share. Texans were sometimes immodest on this point, but their boast was well-founded.

celling any attributed to the average young U.S. citizen in a soldier's uniform?

I had been curious about this question for at least a year before the United States went to war. I recalled a White House press conference in June, 1940, when President Roosevelt said angrily that a year of military training would be good for the mollycoddled youth of the United States—at least, it would teach them to live with their fellow men. The weeks I spent on maneuvers with the Army in the swamps of Louisiana and in the Carolina hills did not serve to ease my fears that perhaps we had grown too soft to fight a war; at that time some low-moraled outfits were threatening to desert, rather than stay in the Army. Almost none of them deserted, but the threat was an unhealthy sign, and it could not be blamed entirely on poor leadership.

When I came back to the United States after half a year in Australia, in August, 1942, I went around Cassandra-fashion, crying, "We are losing the war—you don't realize it, but we are losing the war!" I talked to several men at the top of the Army and Navy. I went to the White House and sang my mournful tune to the President. To bear bad tidings is a very rocky road to popularity, but I felt that somebody had to do it.

What worried me was not our productive ability, although it was barely in evidence at the time. I knew we could make the machines of war. But I didn't know whether we had the heart to fight a war. Our men who had to do the fighting didn't want to fight. Their generation had been told in the all-important first ten years, in its teens, and at the voting age that it was not necessary to fight. Sometimes it almost seemed that they had been taught that peace was more important than honor. Our men just wanted to go home.

I could not forget my conversation one chilly August day in a room in Lennon's Hotel in Brisbane. My companion was an Army general, a friend of many years. I asked his opinion of the American soldier. He became very depressed. He said, "I'm afraid, Bob. I'm afraid the Americans of this generation are not the same kind of Americans who fought the last war."

In the spring of 1943 I went to the Aleutians. The Battle of Attu in its early stages was not well handled. Our equipment was poor. Nearly fifteen hundred men became casualties from exposure because of their poor equipment, and because their leaders allowed them to be pinned down for days in icy water on the floor of Massacre Valley. But the Battle of Attu did not make me feel any worse. In this primitive, man-against-man fighting enough of our men rose up to win. I thought I learned a lesson on Attu which probably applied to all armies: not all soldiers are heroes—far from it; the army that wins, other things being fairly equal, is the army which has enough men to rise above duty, thus inspiring others to do their duty. There were many such Americans on Attu—men received the fairly commonplace Silver Star for deeds that would have earned a Congressional Medal of Honor earlier in the war. I thought I learned another lesson on Attu: no man who dies in battle dies in vain. There is no time for mourning during a battle, but the after-effect a soldier's battlefield grave has on his comrades is sometimes overpowering. Five weeks after the Battle of Attu ended, a memorial service was held for the six hundred Americans who died there. No man of the 17th, 32nd, or 4th Regiments who attended this service is likely ever to forget that hundreds of men scaled Attu's summer-clad brown peaks to pick wild mountain flowers, with which they made wreaths for the graves of their brothers-in-arms. Could the living fail to gain from their own dead an inspiration which would sustain them in future battles? Can one American watch another die in his cause, by his side, without realizing that that cause must be worth while, and, therefore, must be pursued to a victorious end, whatever the cost?

This was the hard way of gaining an education, but, since we in America had made such an abominable job of educating a generation, we had no other method during the first two years of war. Therefore, our soldiers showed up poorly in their first battles. The number of "war neuroses" or "shell-shock" cases among them simply reflected the fact, in my opinion, that they were not mentally prepared to bridge the vast gap between the comforts of peace and the horrors of war. In other words, they had been brought up to believe that it was only necessary to wish for peace to have peace, and the best way to avoid war was to turn our heads the other way when war was mentioned. I had no words to describe the effect the first bombs and bullets had on many of the men educated in such fashion. Fortunately, most of them recovered their equilibrium after the initial shock. Fortunately, there were signs after two years of war that the oncoming generation of soldiers—those who had been conscious for two years of the nearness of war to them—would go into battle better prepared, better educated.

I thought Attu could be told in the story of the sergeant. On top of one of those snowy, marrow-chilling peaks in May, 1943, the platoon leader, a second lieutenant, ordered the sergeant to take a squad and go over there and knock out that Jap machine-gun nest. The sergeant just stared. His mouth was open. He was horrified. He had been in the Army two years; now, all of a sudden, he was told to go out and risk his life. He, like most Americans, had never thought of the war in terms of getting killed. In disgust, the second lieutenant said, "All right, sergeant, you just sit here. If any of you bastards," turning to the rest of his men, "have got the guts, follow me. We've got to get that machine gun. A lot of our men are getting killed by that machine gun."

Well, about ten men followed the second lieutenant. They killed the Japs and the machine gun didn't kill any more Americans.

That afternoon the sergeant went to the second lieutenant and said, "Sir, I am ashamed of myself. Give me another chance." By then there was another machine gun to be knocked out. So, the second lieutenant ordered the sergeant to take a squad and knock it out. The sergeant did just that. In fact, he knocked it out personally. The necessity of risking his life had finally been demonstrated to him.

Why didn't the sergeant on Attu do as he was told? Why did he volunteer to do the same thing the second time? I think men fight for two reasons: (1) ideals, (2) *esprit de corps*. The sergeant's education had not included any firm impression of the things that are worth fighting for, so he didn't see why he should risk his life the first time. But the second time he was willing to risk his life for his fellows, for the lieutenant and the ten men who had risked *their* lives, possibly for him, in the morning. The bonds of their common peril of the moment had gripped him as nothing in the past could.

In talking to the Marines aboard the *Blue Fox* I became convinced that they didn't know what to believe in, either—except the Marine Corps. The Marines fought almost solely on *esprit de corps*, I was certain. It was inconceivable to most Marines that they should let another Marine down, or that they could be responsible for dimming the bright reputation of their corps. The Marines simply assumed that they were the world's best fighting men. "Are you afraid?" Bill Hipple asked one of them. "Hell, no, mister," he answered, "I'm a Marine."

View of the Carnage

Betio had been declared "secured" at 1312 on the fourth day, seventy-five hours and forty-two minutes after the first Marines hit the beach. Occasional snipers would fire from holes and rubble-and-corpse-packed pillboxes for days afterward. Until the battle ended I had covered only a small part of the island—perhaps a total of four hundred yards along the beach, and no more than one hundred yards inland. To understand what had happened in each sector, it was necessary to walk over the island yard by yard. This I did for a day and a half before I flew out of the lagoon on a PB2Y on the afternoon of the sixth day.

What I saw on Betio was, I am certain, one of the greatest works of devastation wrought by man. Words are inadequate to describe what I saw on this island of less than a square mile. So are pictures—you can't smell pictures.

So that the reader may be able to place the scenes I describe in their approximate positions, I have inserted three drawings of the three trips I made over Betio. (See pp. 688, 698, 703.)

Here on the south beach the coconut-log and sand and concrete pillboxes are larger and more powerfully constructed than on the beach we invaded. Undoubtedly, the Japs, who had themselves landed on the north beach, expected us to land there, and not through the lagoon. In the water there are rows of land mines and double fences of barbed wire. There are fifteen dead Japs in and around the first pillbox next to the tank trap, all dressed in green uniforms, wrap-around leggings, and hobnailed shoes except one who wore a Navy flyer's blue uniform. Two of the fifteen have blown their guts out with hand grenades, as evidenced by their missing stomachs and right hands. Most of the bodies are already turning a sickly green, though they have been corpses only two days—as against five for most of the five thousand putrefying bodies on Betio.

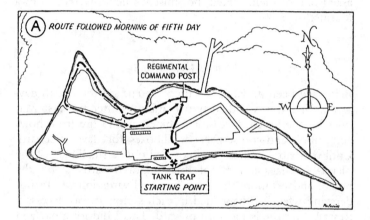

Down the beach, it is possible to see these mighty fortresses, one after another, as far as the eye can reach. There are twelve Japs inside the second pillbox—more than the smaller machine-gun boxes on the north shore could contain—and there are thirteen outside. Some of these wear only shorts, some only the G-string shorts which do not cover the flanks.

After a brief alert, caused by friendly planes, which we spend in a foxhole on the beach, Dick Johnston and I start across the airstrip toward the regimental command post near the northern shore. On the edge of the airstrip we find that the huge, fifteen-foot-high, box-like structures made of coconut logs are not blockhouses, but revetments to contain two planes. All the bombing and shelling have blown a few logs off these three-sided pens (the open side faces toward the runway), but generally they are surprisingly intact. There are perhaps a dozen Jap planes—Zeros and twin-engined bombers—along the runway, but only two inside the revetments which are fairly well riddled by shrapnel and bullets. The first light, maneuverable Zero we examine is in fairly good condition, however. The red ball of the Japanese is painted on both sides of the fuselage just back of the cockpit and on the top and bottom near each end of the wings.

A bullet-riddled, brown truck is on the edge of the runway. Inside the next big coconut-log revetment there are three identical trucks. Though they are Japanese-made, the dashboards of the trucks have their instruments labeled in English. Here is an example of the Japanese tendency to imitate: the "water" thermometer dial is in the centigrade of the French, as is the "kilos" of the speedometer; "oil" and "amperes" dials might have been taken from either the Americans or the British, but the fuel indicator is labeled "gasoline" instead of the British "petrol." The tires on this truck are four different brands: Dunlop, Bridgestone, Yokohama, and Firestone. An uncamouflaged black sedan nearby, also of Japanese make, had been hit and burned until there is less than half of it left. It has a license plate with the Navy anchor insignia on it, and the number 7/233. The blackout oilcloth over the headlights has no ordinary little hole through which a small beam of light might show; it has a Navy anchor, which gives the headlights the appearance of a Hallowe'en pumpkin.

Beside one of the revetments four naked Marines take a bath in a well of brackish water. The well, many years old, had been there before the Japs came. It had gone through the Battle of Betio unharmed.

At headquarters Captain J. L. Schwabe, one of the regimental staff officers, says we will find at the northwest tip of the island (the bird's beak) spots where our flamethrowers killed thirty and forty Japs at a time. He estimates that 250 Marines were killed in the water along the north beach between headquarters and the beak. Estimates of casualties in the Second Regiment are sickening: First Battalion 63 killed, 192 wounded, 41 missing; Second Battalion has 309 left out of 750 who landed; Third Battalion has 413 left, about the same as Major Crowe's Second Battalion of the Eighth. These figures were found later to be somewhat exaggerated, but they indicate how forcefully the first casualty compilations struck us. Five cemeteries have been started thus far—by 0800 of the fifth day—and less than one-fourth of our dead have been buried. The largest cemetery, next to the regimental command post, has 134 graves; the others 80, 53, 20, and 41 respectively.

A bandy-legged little Korean who wears white cotton pants and golf stockings is trying to talk to the M.P.'s who are taking him to an interpreter. He is trying to tell the M.P.'s how many were on the island. He says "Nippon" and draws "6000" in the sand; then he says "Korean" and draws "1000."

Going westward up the beach, beyond the farthest point I had yet reached, we see on the beach the bodies of Marines who have not yet been reached by the burial parties. The first is a husky boy who must have been three inches over six feet tall. He was killed ten feet in front of the seawall pillbox which was his objective. He is still hunched forward, his rifle in his right hand. That is the picture of the Marine Corps I shall always carry: charging forward. A bit further up the beach there are four dead Marines only a few feet apart; ten feet along, another; fifteen feet further another; then there are six bunched together. These men, we are told, are from I and K companies of the Third Battalion, Second Regiment.

Fifty feet further up the beach, ten Marines were killed on the barbed wire on the coral flats. One of them was evidently shot as he placed his foot on the top rung of the wire—his trouser leg was caught on the barbs and the leg still hangs in the air. There are eighty more dead Marines scattered in a twenty-foot square of the beach just beyond. Six more . . . two more . . . four more. Here four got to the very mouth of the coconut-log pillbox, but none of them made it, because there are no dead Japs inside. But in the next pillbox there are two Japs sprawled over their machine gun, and in the next, five yards further along the seawall, there are three. All appear to have been killed by hand grenades.

We detour inland a few yards. Here, perhaps thirty feet back of the seawall, four Marines lie dead outside a larger pillbox. There are six dead Japs inside. Still thirty feet further inland three dead Japs lie inside another pillbox, and there are three Marines lying around the pillbox. It is not difficult to see that the Marines were determined to keep on killing Japs while the breath of life remained in them, whether that last breath was drawn in the water, at the barricade, or at some undetermined point inland. What words can justify such bravery in the face of almost certain death? They died, but they came on. Those machine guns were killing other Marines out in the water, and who ever heard of one Marine letting another down?

Here Amphtrack Number 15—name: "Worried Mind"—is jammed against the seawall. Inside it are six dead Marines; next to it are three more. Two more lie impaled on the barbed wire next to the twenty-eight-seater Jap privy over the water. Their clothing ties them to the wire. They float at anchor. A half dozen Marines, members of the engineer regiment, are walking around the beach, examining the bodies. "Here's Larson," says one. "Here's Montague," says another. The bodies, as they are identified, are tenderly gathered up and taken fifteen or twenty yards inland, where other Marines are digging graves for them.

This is unusual, because most of the Marines are being gathered up by burial parties, which have not progressed this far. But these men are looking for the dead from their own particular company. Since they are leaving by transport in a few hours, I suppose they think: "Here is the last thing we can do for these boys we have known so long. We'll do it with our own hands."

When I passed that way again several hours later, the Eighteenth Marines had gone, had sailed away. But I noticed the fifteen graves this particular company had dug. A rude cross had been erected over each grave—undoubtedly replaced later by a neat white cross—and on the cross had been written the name of the Marine who lay underneath it, the designation that he was a Marine, and the date of his death, thus:

A. R. Mitlick
U.S.M.C.
20–11–43

In front of the fifteen graves, so that all would know which outfit they came from, and that they all came from D Company of the Eighteenth, the Marines had proudly erected a larger cross:

3 – 2 – 18

The names of these fifteen, right to left, were: R. C. Mc-Kinney, G. G. Seng,* R. C. Kountzman, R. L. Jarrett, Max J. Lynnton, C. Montague,* S. R. Parsons, M. W. Waltz, H. H. Watkins, H. B. Lanning, J. S. Castle, A. B. Roads, A. R. Mitlick, W. A. Larson, and R. W. Vincent, First Lieutenant.

Just behind the coconut-log wall where the men of D Company had died there is a pit containing a 77-mm. gun, whose ammunition supply had been half exhausted. A few yards further along the wall there is a 13-mm. machine gun. Inside the gun pit is a half-pint bottle of the only brand of whisky I have ever seen in Japanese possession. The label, like the labels of many Japanese commercial products, is in English:

Rare Old Island Whisky
SUNTORY
First Born in Nippon
Choicest Products
Kotobukiya Ltd.
Bottled at our own Yamazaki Distillery

A Marine near the gun pit had evidently been hit squarely by a 77-mm. shell (77 mm. is about three inches). There is a hole through his midsection, and he is badly burned—so badly that he could hardly be identified as a Marine but for the laced leggings under his trouser legs. A Marine who is standing nearby, Pfc. Glenn Gill of Oklahoma, explains that the remnants of the first and second waves of 3/2 rushed over the barricade, where they were pinned down as the third wave got all the machine-gun attention.

A hundred yards inland we find an air-raid sound detector, which is sandbagged all around, and a power plant, which was protected only by a tin roof that was smashed to a thousand pieces. There are wooden-compartmented boxes full of

---

*Gene Seng and Charlie Montague, aged twenty-one, had been childhood friends. They had gone to school together in Texas. On February 3, 1942, they had volunteered for the Marines together. On November 20, 1943, on Tarawa, they died together.

carpenter's tools and some more delicate instruments. Next to the power plant there is a thirty-six-inch searchlight, and in the middle of a group of buildings and pillboxes a hole ten feet deep, twenty feet in diameter. The sixteen-inch shell or one-thousand-pound bomb which made that hole could not have fallen anywhere else within a hundred yards without destroying something. Near the shellhole there are two Japs blown completely in two. Only the lower extremities of either are anywhere in sight—one was cut in two at the waist, the other at the hips. In a smaller shellhole there are six dead Japs around a 77-mm. gun—this had once been a Jap gun pit. On the rim of the gun pit lies a dead Marine, who looks as if he might have been killed while diving in. Another 77-mm. gun—they are very thick along this northwest beach—has been knocked out by shellfire. The barrel is splintered and twisted. In a bomb crater there are fourteen Japs, evidently tossed in there by Marines cleaning out pillboxes before inhabiting them. Another 77-mm. gun has not been touched by shellfire, but the eight Japs in the pit were killed by rifle fire.

Amphtrack Number 48 is jammed against the seawall barricade. Three waterlogged Marines lie beneath it. Four others are scattered nearby, and there is one hanging on the two-foot-high strand of barbed wire who does not touch the coral flat at all. Back of the 77-mm. guns there are many hundreds of rounds of 77-mm. ammunition.

At the tip of the Betio bird's beak, there is the first big Jap gun I have seen: 5.5 inches. It is set in a concrete cup, and the degrees of the compass are painted on the rim of the cup. Shells for the gun, which are about twenty inches long, are contained in six little compartments, six shells to a compartment, inside the walls of the cup. Outside the cup there are hundreds more shells. The gun turret has been hit by about fifty fifty-caliber strafing bullets which probably also killed the gun crew, who have been removed, but otherwise the gun is untouched.

Turning southward up the Betio bird's forehead, we find another 5.5-inch gun thirty yards away. Shells or bombs have nicked the inside of its cup at 170 degrees, 220 degrees, and 30 degrees. The four Japs inside the pit have been charred to sticks of carbon.

Outside the gun emplacement a dog, suffering from severe shell shock, wanders drunkenly. When some Marines whistle and call him he trembles and tries to run, but falls. Not far away there is a placid cat with a dirty red ribbon around his neck. A sergeant of an engineer platoon calls the roll of his outfit, which arrived late and had only one man wounded. But its flamethrowers killed dozens of the reeling Japs.

The pillboxes here along the west beach, spaced only ten feet apart, are connected by trenches. Near another 77-mm. gun there is another 36-inch searchlight. Like all seven searchlights on Betio, this one was a favorite target of strafing planes, and all were destroyed. Between this 77-mm. gun and another similar gun thirty yards up the beach the Japs have pointed a coconut log out to sea. To a pilot five hundred feet in the air it could very well be mistaken for a six-inch gun.

About halfway up the west beach we turn inland and start back through the center of the island, past the body of a bloated Jap officer lying next to more dull-brown trucks. A bit further toward the center, the Marines have thrown a few shovelfuls of sand over the ghastly, mangled bodies of a dozen Japs. Dead Japs are strewn liberally along the road that leads through the center, eight here, two there, thirty over there where they were caught by a flamethrower. Two lie beside a Jap light tank, which is camouflaged in the navy fashion of World War I. On the other side of the tank lies a Marine, whose body's site is marked for burial parties by the age-old method; his bayoneted rifle jabbed upright into the ground.

Here was a Jap warehouse, which burned to the ground at least three days ago. It was filled apparently with foodstuffs, mostly canned: salmon, shrimp, rice. Whoever dreams of starving out Japs should know that they always have enough food to last many months, not counting fish that they can catch, birds that they can kill, and coconuts they can pick. Near the warehouse there are the mangled remains of a dozen bicycles, of which the Japs must have had a thousand on Betio, in addition to perhaps a hundred cars and trucks, and great quantities of miniature rail equipment. Further on there are bales of sacks labeled in English: "Stores Government— Stores Department." Great stacks of cases of rifle ammunition have not been touched by the terrific bombardment. A Seabee walks out of a pillbox with a fencing costume that looks like a baseball catcher's equipment: a steel face mask and a "belly protector" made of laced bamboo and heavy blue cloth. Scattered along the road are several one-man sniper pits: gasoline drums sunk into the ground, with a lid for cover.

Between the road and the north beach, spaced some fifty yards apart, there are three big coconut-log bomb shelters, about twenty by fifty feet inside. Outside they are covered on the top and on the sides by three to ten feet of sand. None was touched either by aerial or naval bombardment. The occupants, cowering in their corners, had been killed by TNT and flamethrowers. A Marine intelligence officer tells his sergeant to tell his men to search the bodies for documents. "Sir, don't ask them to," pleads the sergeant. "They are puking already."

A tank trap has been constructed diagonally across the section of the island north of the runway that forms part of the air-strip triangles. It is a long, deep ditch whose sides are braced by upright coconut logs. Nearby there is another twenty-by-fifty bomb shelter, which is reinforced concrete inside, tiers of coconut logs in the middle and sand on the outside covered by palm fronds. I wonder: would the heaviest bomb ever made tear up this unbelievable fortification? Or if the bomb hit on the rounded sides of the blockhouse, would it not glance off and explode harmlessly alongside the blockhouse? Several bomb holes around the sides of the blockhouse indicate that "near misses" do no good.

Another burned warehouse contains hundreds of bottles of sake, most of them broken. Also stacks of uniforms, hundreds of pots and pans, several gross of little blue enamelware cereal bowls and cups with the Navy anchor stenciled on them, about eighty bicycles, and a number of pressure cookers. Like other navies, the Japanese Navy apparently is far more luxuriously equipped than the Army.

By 1030 the Seabees are working like a thousand beavers on the airfield, which must be prepared quickly in order that the Americans on Betio will have fighter protection. Actually, there is not a great deal for them to do before planes can land. The main runway, along the longitudinal center of the island, is concrete and it is in almost perfect condition. The shorter runways, of gravel, are almost as well preserved. The planes and ships had orders to lay off the runways. If their accuracy was such that they could lay off specified areas, then why could they not hit the targets assigned to them? The Seabees, many of them skilled workmen old enough to be the fathers of most of the Marines, are having a great time. Little, rubber-tired Jap carts provide much amusement for Seabees who wheel supplies up and down the runways with them. One Seabee boasts that his outfit has already killed two Jap snipers this morning.

More evidence of the care the Japs had used in building up Betio: an unharmed gasoline truck sunk into an underground revetment, a twelve-by-thirty concrete water storage tank, still three-quarters filled with water, another big warehouse — the battleships and bombers really tore up the unprotected warehouses, two black automobiles, three more destroyed buildings.

Two hundred yards west of the regimental command post there is an American graveyard which by now contains seventy Marines, and seven more bodies lie on the ground awaiting burial. The first grave is marked, on a crude piece of packing-case lumber, "Unidentified." Other names I note at random: Lieutenant Colonel David K. Claude,* J. F. Svoboda, Duffy, Jenkins, P. L. Olano, W. R. Jay, W. A. Carpenter, M. D. Dinnis, C. E. McGhee, W. C. Culp, F. R. Erislip, W. H. Soeters, "Unknown," L. N. Carney, Hicks, R. E. Bemis, E. R. Pero, C. J. Kubarski, H. Schempf.

Before I returned to regimental (now division) headquarters, the corps commander of the Gilbert Islands assaults (i.e., both Makin and Tarawa) had arrived: Major General Holland McTyeire Smith, one of the most colorful figures in the Marine Corps. Alabama-born Holland Smith is the father of amphibious training of U.S. armed forces. Many years ago he foresaw that one day it would be necessary for American soldiers and Marines to land on enemy beaches in the face of hostile fire. In awarding him the Distinguished Service Medal,

---

*Later that day someone remarked, "I wonder where Colonel Claude is. I haven't seen him in two days." Colonel Claude was an observer from another division, unattached to any particular outfit. He was killed up front with the Scout and Sniper Platoon.

Navy Secretary Frank Knox had said of him: "He laid the groundwork for amphibious training of practically all American units, including at various times the First and Third Marine Divisions, the First, Seventh, and Ninth Infantry Divisions of the Army and numerous other Marine Corps and Army personnel. His proficient leadership and tireless energy in the development of high combat efficiency among the forces under his supervision were in keeping with the highest traditions of the United States Naval Service."

Nonetheless, Holland Smith, beloved by the Marine Corps, had assumed the aspects of a barnacle, so far as much of the regular Navy was concerned. He spoke his mind whenever he saw something wrong, even if that something were a brain child of his own. And in the regular Navy the first rule is to speak softly, particularly if the speech contains something that might not reflect credit on everybody else. Holland Smith at sixty-one was a military liberal, which few men in the U.S. Navy dare to be after fifty.

I had known General Smith a long time, in San Diego where he was training amphibious forces, on Attu, on Kiska, aboard a transport, a battleship, and a couple of airplanes. Because he was an unusual major general, he was delightful, and I was glad to see him. Although his route over the western end of the island duplicated some of the territory I had covered in the morning, I looked forward to listening to his comments on an inspection during the afternoon, along with his Tarawa division commander, Julian Smith, his aide Major Clifton A. Woodrum, Jr., and two newsmen who had accompanied him by plane from Makin, Bernard McQuaid of the Chicago *Daily News* and Robert Trumbull of the New York *Times.* Said one of the newsmen—I forget which—"I guess we had a pretty tame show on Makin, compared to what the Marines had here." On Makin the 165th New York Infantry— the onetime "Fighting Sixty-Ninth"—had found about 250 Japs, plus some Korean laborers. In exterminating them, the 165th had had 65 killed, 121 wounded. "A lot of our casualties were caused by the wild firing of our men"—but that was not news; it always happens when green troops go into battle. The 165th had had the misfortune to lose its colonel, Gardiner Conroy, who was killed by a Jap sniper.

Before the tour started there was, at Julian Smith's suggestion, a double flag-raising near headquarters; U.S. and British flags went up on twin flagpoles. There had been a devil of a time finding a British flag. Finally, Major Frank Lewis George Holland, who had been schoolmaster of the Gilberts before he was forced to flee when the Japs came, produced a British flag about half the size of the Stars and Stripes. In the words of Henry Keys, the Australian correspondent representing the London *Daily Express*, "Major Holland looked in his bag. It contained one pair of drawers and the Union Jack."

The generals' tour of the island started from headquarters southward, then west on the south shore, down the western end, then eastward along the northern shore:

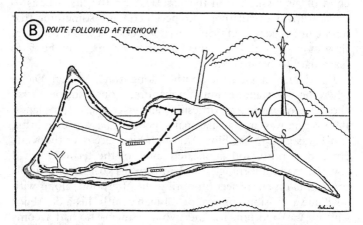

The first three dead men the generals see are Marines; one near a disabled Jap tank on the edge of the runway, two more in a shellhole not far away. Fifty yards before they reach the south shore, after crossing the runway, they find the hastily scooped graves of three more Marines. I note the casualty tag on one grave: "W. F. Blevins, Killed in Action, 11-22-43." Nearby there is the lone grave of "Pvt. J. M. Redman, Killed in Action, 11-23-43." His helmet hangs on the cross, a bullet hole through the center of it. A Marine near the south beach reports that some of his buddies killed Japs in a machine-gun nest over there only three hours ago. And there are still snipers scattered throughout the island that the Marines just can't find. "Uh-huh," uh-huhs Holland Smith, who carries a carbine slung from his shoulder.

"There was one thing that won this battle, Holland," says Julian Smith, "and that was the supreme courage of the Marines. The prisoners tell us that what broke their morale was not the bombing, not the naval gunfire, but the sight of Marines who kept coming ashore in spite of their machine-gun fire. The Jap machine-gun fire killed many Marines in the water and on the beach. But other Marines came behind those who died. They landed on the beaches, they climbed the seawall, and they went into those enemy defenses. The Japs never thought we would get to those defenses. They never thought they would lose this island. They told their men a million of us couldn't take it." Julian Smith tells Holland Smith about Lieutenant Hawkins, that he is going to name the airfield for Hawkins. "His will be my first recommendation for the Medal of Honor," says Julian Smith.

On the beach there is a twin-mount 5.5-inch seacoast gun, which obviously had been demounted from a ship for shore duty. Three dead Japs are inside the cup surrounding the gun, and there are two more in a cut-back which has been hit directly. In the area of this twin-mount naval gunfire has obviously been very effective. On a sand hill thirty yards behind the guns the Japs had mounted a fire director and range finder.

A hundred yards or so west of the first guns there is another twin-mount 5.5-inch set of guns. This is a grisly sight. There are two Japs under the gun barrels who have committed suicide with hand grenades. Four more are in a ditch leading from a nearby dugout. Only one of these is a suicide, but another's heart bulges out of his chest, which apparently has been rent open by a shell, and a third is only a stick of char.

The generals marvel at the strength of the machine-gun emplacements on this south shore—almost a solid wall of apparently impregnable defenses all the way up to the southwest tip of the island. They concede that one-six must have done a thoroughgoing job.

At the southwest tip of the island they see two of the four eight-inch guns which the Japs had on Betio. Both guns are pointed toward the direction from which our transports approached, but it is obvious that they were put out of action by some of the first salvos fired by our battleships. Hardly a round of eight-inch shells has been fired. It is easy to see what did the trick: a direct hit on the concrete powder chamber next to the guns. A gaping hole through the powder chamber indicates that a sixteen-inch shell perforated there. Inside the chamber there are about twenty-five charred Japs. Others are hanging on the jagged edge of the hole and for fifty yards beyond the hole Japs are spewed out over the sandy terrain. That must have been the terrific explosion we saw on the third battleship shot.

Next to the exploded powder chamber is the biggest hole on the pockmarked island of Betio—some sixty feet in diameter and much deeper than the sub-surface water level of the island. Scattered about the rim of the great hole are about two hundred rounds of eight-inch ammunition, evidence that the ammunition dump as well as the powder house blew up.

These two guns were served by a small mechanical trolley whose tracks circle the inside of the gun emplacements. The guns are labeled V. S. and M. (Vickers), indicating that they were captured from the British, or purchased from the British when Japan was an ally. Both eight-inch guns have been hit directly many times. The smaller guns, notably 77-mm. and machine guns, might escape hits from the terrific bombing and shelling which preceded our attack, but the larger ones were comparatively easy targets.

The generals and their inspecting party turn north and head back from the Betio bird's tufted head toward its beak. They see what had been a Japanese radar screen, mounted on a concrete pedestal. In front of a sign—"Danger: Mines"—battle-weary Marines are swimming nude, attempting to wash the crust, the scum, and the odors of Betio from their tanned bodies. There are no dead bodies on the western end of the island to impede the swimming. The generals note the lone grave of Captain Thomas Royster of the Second Amphibious Tractor Battalion. As they pass two of the deadly 77-mm. guns which are still in working condition, Julian Smith remarks, "These are the guns that kill our people; we can knock out the big guns."

Three pigs lie in a pen. One of them is dead from shrapnel hits. The other two act dazed, merely grunt.

The Generals Smith examine a 13-mm. machine gun at the northwest tip of Betio. Hundreds of empty shells show that it was fired many times before the nearby Jap had the top of his head blown off. "That gun killed a lot of Marines," says Julian Smith.

When we reach the northern shore—the bird's throat—we notice an amazing phenomenon: the full tide is now washing against the seawall to a depth of three feet, and the Marines who were lying on the beach this morning are now floating against the seawall. In other words, the tide during those first two critical days was exceptionally low, perhaps due to a wind from the south, or the Marines would have had no beachhead at all! This was truly an Act of Providence.

The Marines floating in the water are now pitiful figures. Many of them have had the hair washed off their heads by this time. Julian Smith orders an additional burial party formed to speed up the interment of the Americans. The eyes of the two veteran major generals are misty when they view the bodies of gallant Marines who were killed just before they reached the seawall. Says Holland Smith, "You must have three or four hundred here, Julian." But the most stirring sight is the Marine who is leaning in death against the seawall, one arm still supported upright by the weight of his body. On top of the seawall, just beyond his upraised hand, lies a blue and white flag, a beach marker to tell succeeding waves where to land. Says Holland Smith, "How can men like that ever be defeated? This Marine's duty was to plant that flag on top of the seawall. He did his duty, though it cost him his life. *Semper fidelis* meant more to him than just a catch phrase." We pass on down the seawall rather quickly, because it is impossible to look at such a sight, and realize its implications, without tears.

Three dead Japs lie in a pillbox behind the seawall. Near one of them there is a green-covered bound volume of the *National Geographic* for September–December, 1931, with markings in Japanese on the ends. The first article in the volume is about New Hampshire. Says New Hampshire–born

Barney McQuaid, sticking the volume under his arm, "I am not ordinarily a souvenir-hunter, but, gentlemen, this is my souvenir."

The generals are awestruck when they inspect the pillboxes the assault troops had to knock out. "By God," says Holland Smith, "those Marines just kept coming. Many of them were killed, but more came on. It looks beyond the realm of a human being that this place could have been taken. These Japanese were masters of defensive construction. I never saw anything like these defenses in the last war. The Germans never built anything like this in France. No wonder these bastards were sitting back here laughing at us! They never dreamed the Marines could take this island, and they were laughing at what would happen to us when we tried it."

Back at headquarters there is the first complete report on what happened on the other twenty-four islands of the Tarawa Atoll. The Second Battalion of the Sixth Infantry had landed on the next island, Bairiki, where a few Japs offered light resistance. But most of them fled to Abaokora, northernmost island of the atoll, with the Marines pursuing hotly. From there the Japs could go no further. The Marines killed the 150 to 200 Japs who fought to the last. Three officers and twenty-six men of the battalion were killed, and about six officers and sixty men were wounded. On Abemama, the other Gilbert atoll where there were Japs, about thirty Marine scouts had landed and hemmed in the Japs. One Marine was killed; the twenty-five Japs committed suicide.

By now the LST's have nosed up to the edge of the shelf that surrounds Betio. At low tide they discharge trucks by the dozen which carry supplies ashore over the coral flats, through the hole that has been cut into the seawall. Within a very few days Betio will be a strong American base—stronger offensively than the Japs had made it defensively.

Not until next day did we learn that three Marines had been killed on the western end of the island by Jap snipers, shortly after the generals had passed that point.

On the sixth day I walked over the eastern half of Betio—the half which got almost as much attention prior to the landing as the western half, plus an additional four days' pounding by every gun in the U.S. Navy, every gun up to 75 mm. in the

U.S. Marine Corps, and many hundreds of Navy bombers and fighters. If the western half was a shambles, the tail end was the acme of destruction and desolation. Shellholes and bomb craters, uprooted coconut trees, exploded ammunition dumps, some pulverized pillboxes, big guns broken and bent, and many hundreds of rotting Japanese bodies. This is the route I took in viewing the carnage on the tail end of Betio:

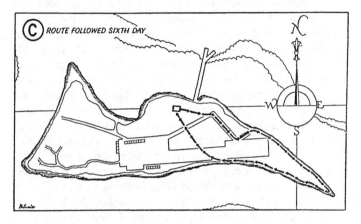

At the pillbox near Major Crowe's headquarters where I had seen the first Jap fried by a flamethrower, I note the details of the fortification, now that it has been stripped down by repeated charges of TNT. The three feet of sand that covered its rounded top has been blasted away. The top actually was a cone-shaped piece of armor, two layers of quarter-inch steel. Beneath that steel turret there were two layers of eight-inch coconut logs—the turret armor was used apparently to give the top a rounded shape which would deflect bombs. This pillbox was five-sided, each side about ten feet, with a buffer tier at the entrance for protection against shrapnel. Each side consisted of a double tier of coconut logs, hooked together by steel spikes with sand between the tiers. Over the whole, including the sides, there was a deep layer of sand, which gave the pillbox the appearance of a tropical igloo. There were two entrances to the pillbox—one to seaward and one to the east.

The machine-gun emplacements on the north side of the

island's tail are much the same as those on the west end. Beside them and back of them there are trenches, some containing twenty-five Jap dead. Inland thirty yards there is a fifteen-foot-high cement-and-coconut-log, sand-covered ammunition dump. There are gashes in the coconut logs where the sand has been blasted away, but no penetration by hundreds of rounds of high explosives.

A mess kitchen, with two-by-four walls and a tin roof, has been blasted to bits. It measures about twenty-five by one-hundred feet and there are many ten-gallon pots laid on the fire holes in the cement stoves. A hen sets calmly inside the debris. At the east end of the kitchen there are thousands upon thousands of cans of food and broken bottles. Nearby there are a dozen half-Japs whose life had been flicked away by a flamethrower. One of them is only a charred spinal cord and a lump of burnt flesh where his head had been. A little further on, there are fifty more dead Japs—they seem to be thicker on this end of the island. Scattered around a big blockhouse and what apparently had been a power plant there are at least 150 more who had been hit by a variety of weapons: some are charred, others have their heads blown off, others are only chests or trunks. Only one of them appears to be a suicide. In the midst of them there is a lone Marine, lying under two sprawling Japs. What had been this man's fate—this man whose pack containing two cans of C ration had been ripped by shrapnel? Had he been killed by a Jap bullet, or hit by some of our own high explosives? Or had he single-handed tried to attack 150 Japs? No reporter is ever likely to answer that question.

The march up the tail of the island is strewn with carnage. Now, on the sixth day, the smell of the dead is unbelievable. The ruptured and twisted bodies which expose their rotting inner organs are inexpressibly repelling. Betio would be more habitable if the Marines could leave for a few days and send a million buzzards in. The fire from a burning pile of rubble has reached six nearby Jap bodies, which sizzle and pop as the flame consumes flesh and gases. Fifteen more are scattered around a food dump, and two others are blown to a hundred pieces—a hand here, a head there, a hobnailed foot farther away.

There is a warehouse near the end of the Burns Philp pier, whose contents have been scattered over many hundreds of square feet. A small trolley leads from the end of the pier to the warehouse. Unlike the Jap Army on Attu, the Navy troops on Tarawa were well supplied with mechanized tools and vehicles. Next to the pier there is another armored turret that served atop a pillbox. This one is smashed in on two sides, and perforated a hundred times by strafing bullets. Two Japs are in a shellhole that was a coconut-log pillbox—here the additional four days of shelling proves that some of these pillboxes can be smashed by heavy gunfire. Under the Burns Philp pier lie a dozen Japs who machine-gunned the Americans as they waded ashore (a destroyer finally smashed the pier). Under a privy platform which is also smashed lie fourteen more Japs. At the end of this pier lies a pig, his hams shot off. Three wrecked barges are on the beach. Two of them have double-fuselaged bows, look something like P-38's.

Inland there is one of the biggest concrete blockhouses on the island—about sixty by forty, and twenty-five feet high. Four direct hits, probably from battleships, smashed through its walls, and a Marine souvenir-hunter says there are 300 charred Jap bodies inside. Steps lead to the roof of the blockhouse, where there are two 13-mm. machine guns. In one gun nest there are four dead Japs, in the other, two. Four others are scattered around the rooftop and two more are in a pen covered by sandbags. All apparently were killed by strafing planes, although some naval gun shrapnel nicked the extension of the walls which protect the roof-bound machine gunners. These nicks show that the entire thick concrete structure was laced with half-inch reinforcing steel. A Marine sits down on the roof, opens a can of C ration, and eats heartily.

Outside there are two burned Jap tanks, carrying license plates number 102 and 113 and the Navy anchor insignia. A black automobile in a nearby wooden garage has hardly been touched. None of the glass windows has been broken and there are only a few strafing bullets through the top of the car. An indifferent Marine gets in the car, steps on the starter. The engine runs like a sewing machine. Near the garage there is what was once a motor pool—the concrete blockhouse was undoubtedly a headquarters. A dozen motorcycles with side-cars are burned to steel skeletons, but one little motorcycle truck is in fairly good condition.

Another warehouse a hundred yards beyond is torn to pieces, but only one of the five coconut-log pillboxes surrounding it is not intact. Another warehouse was also the site of another motor pool. None of its trucks or motorcycles will run again!

Back on the north beach opposite the inland warehouses, there are three fifty-foot-long pillboxes and eight or ten smaller ones. One of the larger fortifications has its top blown completely off. The rest are untouched, but the mounted gun inside—37 mm. or 40 mm.—is twisted and broken, its wheels demolished. Further down the beach there are contiguous shellholes, and shellholes within shellholes, as far as the eye can see. A strong, small pillbox is smashed in, pinning a Jap machine gunner to the bottom of the dugout. The next pillbox also had an armored turret for a top, but it, too, is only a smashed steel cone.

Within a few hundred yards of the end of the island the Japs had used great bulbous roots of coconut trees for fortifications, back of layers of barbed wire and rows of mines on the beach. Back of the beach, where eight Japs lie in a blasted pillbox, there is a long tank trap fenced in on either side by barbed wire. A little Jap pack howitzer, about 75 mm., but having wheels only thirty inches in diameter, is the first of its kind I have seen on Betio. A 36-inch searchlight on the beach has been shattered. The coconut logs supporting it have been smashed to the ground and the machinery which operated the searchlight is good only for scrap iron.

Thirty yards inland from the searchlight there is another concrete blockhouse which was an ammunition dump serving the two nearby shattered twin-mount 5.5-inch guns. A direct hit on the ammunition dump had set off the shells inside, which blew the roof heaven knows where. There are hundreds of rounds of ammunition inside. The concrete walls are fairly well intact, however. These walls measure, by a twelve-inch shoe, just eight feet thick, which is a lot of concrete. There is evidence of only one Jap nearby: a leg and arms which probably matched. On the airfield to the west the first F6F lands on Betio.

Beside an unexploded five-hundred-pound bomb there is a hole caused by a bomb that was not a dud. Six Japs are in the hole, which is filled to a depth of two feet by seeping water. Inland there is another mess kitchen with a capacity for ten ten-gallon pots. Near it there had been a barracks building of which now only the floor remains. Scattered around the remains of the building are blankets, shoes, buttons, underwear, "writing pads"—so labeled in English, pans and cups carrying the Navy insignia, sake bottles. Much of the clothing is civilian—evidently there were quite a few Japanese civilians on Betio, or the Navy takes its civilian clothes with it. My souvenir of Betio is a fine, red-figured Japanese silk necktie.

Near the tail end of the island I cross the 150 yards to the southern shore. In the middle of the tail end of the island there are hundreds of tons of unrusted steel rail and at least a thousand wheels to fit those rails. Unmistakably, the Japs had big plans for Betio.

On the south shore, near the tail end, are the remains of two more eight-inch Vickers guns. One of the gun barrels is broken off about four feet from where it sticks out of the turret. The other gun is badly burned and strafing bullets had nicked the inside of the barrel so badly that it probably could not have been fired again. There are three searchlights within 300 yards, and numerous 13-mm. and 77-mm. anti-aircraft guns protect the big guns. Not far away there are twenty dead Japs in a shellhole. Perhaps they had worked at the mixer which had been pouring dozens of pyramidal concrete blocks for the defense of Betio against the expected American invasion.

By running most of the mile and a half back to the pier, past Seabees and trucks and graders and rollers working on the airfield, past several hundred more dead Japs and one well-hidden live Jap who pestered the Seabees, past hundreds of shellholes and bomb craters of varying depths, I made the plane for Funafuti. I was not sorry to leave the appalling wreckage of Betio and its 5,000 dead. I was thankful that I had lived through the toughest job ever assigned to the toughest outfit the U.S. has produced: the magnificent U.S. Marines.

That night as I gratefully soaped myself in an outdoor shower on Funafuti, Co-pilot Hugh Wilkinson said, "I hated to tell you this when you boarded the plane at Tarawa, but all of you smelled like dead Japs." Lieutenant Wilkinson gave me some of his clothing, for I had none except the dirty Marine dungarees I had worn for six days. "Can't I give you these in exchange?" I said. "Perhaps a native woman would wash them."

Said Wilkinson, "Thanks just the same, but I think we'll bury the dungarees. Let's go get a bottle of beer."

"The Hard Facts of War"

Just eight days after the first Marines hit the beach at Betio, I was again in Honolulu. Already there were rumblings about Tarawa. People on the U.S. mainland had gasped when they heard the dread phrase, "heavy casualties." They gasped again when it was announced that 1,026 Marines had been killed, 2,600 wounded.* "This must not happen again," thundered an editorial. "Our intelligence must have been faulty," guessed a member of Congress.

This attitude, following the finest victory U.S. troops had won in this war, was amazing. It was the clearest indication that the peacetime United States (i.e., the United States as of December, 1943) simply found it impossible to bridge the great chasm that separates the pleasures of peace from the horrors of war. Like the generation they educated, the people had not thought of war in terms of men being killed—war seemed so far away.

Tarawa, it seemed to me, marked the beginning of offensive thrusts in the Pacific. Tarawa appeared to be the opening key to offensive operations throughout the whole Pacific—as important in its way as Guadalcanal was important to the defense of the U.S.-Australian supply line. Tarawa required four

*This first estimate actually was somewhat higher than revised casualty figures: 685 killed, 77 died of wounds, 169 missing, about 2100 wounded.

days; Guadalcanal, six months. Total casualties among Marines alone, not even including malaria cases, were about twenty percent higher on Guadalcanal.

Tarawa was not perfectly planned or perfectly executed. Few military operations are, particularly when the enemy is alert. Said Julian Smith: "We made mistakes, but you can't know it all the first time. We learned a lot which will benefit us in the future. And we made fewer mistakes than the Japs did." Tarawa was the first frontal assault on a heavily defended atoll. By all the rules concerning amphibious assaults, the Marines should have suffered far heavier casualties than the defenders. Yet, for every Marine who was killed more than four Japs died—four of the best troops the Emperor had. Looking at the defenses of Betio, it was no wonder our colonels could say: "With two battalions of Marines I could have held this island until hell froze over."

Tarawa must have given the Japanese General Staff something to think about.

The lessons of Tarawa were many. It is a shame that some very fine Americans had to pay for those lessons with their lives, but they gave their lives that others on other enemy beaches might live. On Tarawa we learned what our best weapons were, what weapons needed improving, what tactics could best be applied to other operations. We learned a great deal about the most effective methods of applying Naval gunfire and bombs to atolls. Our capacity to learn, after two years of war, had improved beyond measure. The same blind refusal to learn, which had characterized many of our operations early in the war, had almost disappeared. We were learning, and learning how to learn faster.

The facts were cruel, but inescapable: Probably no amount of shelling and bombing could obviate the necessity of sending in foot soldiers to finish the job. The corollary was this: there is no easy way to win the war; there is no panacea which will prevent men from getting killed. To me it seemed that to deprecate the Tarawa victory was almost to defame the memory of the gallant men who lost their lives achieving it.

Why, then, did so many Americans throw up their hands at the heavy losses on Tarawa? Why did they not realize that there would be many other bigger and bloodier Tarawas in

the three or four years of Japanese war following the first
Tarawa? After two years of observing the Japanese I had become convinced that they had only one strategy: to burrow
into the ground as far and as securely as possible, waiting for
the Americans to dig them out; then to hope that the Americans would grow sick of their own losses before completing
the job. Result: a Japanese victory through negotiated peace.
It seemed to me that those Americans who were horrified
by Tarawa were playing into Japanese hands. It also seemed
that there was no way to defeat the Japanese except by extermination.

Then I reasoned that many Americans had never been led
to expect anything but an easy war. Through their own wishful thinking, bolstered by comfort-inspiring yarns from the
war theatres, they had really believed that this place or that
place could be "bombed out of the war." It seemed to many
that machines alone would win the war for us, perhaps with
the loss of only a few pilots, and close combat would not be
necessary. As a matter of fact, by the end of 1943 our airplanes, after a poor start, had far outdistanced anything the
Japanese could put in the air. We really did not worry particularly about Japanese airpower. If we could get close enough,
we could gain air supremacy wherever we chose. But did that
mean we could win the war by getting only a few pilots killed?
It did not. Certainly, air supremacy was necessary. But airpower could not win the war alone. Despite airplanes and the
best machines we could produce, the road to Tokyo would be
lined with the grave of many a foot soldier. This came as a
surprise to many people.

Our information services had failed to impress the people
with the hard facts of war. Early in the war our communiqués
gave the impression that we were bowling over the enemy
every time our handful of bombers dropped a few pitiful tons
from 30,000 feet. The stories accompanying the communiqués gave the impression that any American could lick any
twenty Japs. Later, the communiqués became more matter-
of-fact. But the communiqués, which made fairly dry reading,
were rewritten by press association reporters who waited for
them back at rear headquarters. The stories almost invariably
came out liberally sprinkled with "smash" and "pound" and

other "vivid" verbs. These "vivid" verbs impressed the head-line writers back in the home office. They impressed the read-ing public which saw them in tall type. But they sometimes did not impress the miserable, bloody soldiers in the front lines where the action had taken place. Gloomily observed a sergeant: "The war that is being written in the newspapers must be a different war from the one we see." Sometimes I thought I could see a whole generation losing its faith in the press. One night a censor showed me four different letters saying, in effect: "I wish we could give you the story of this battle without the sugar-coating you see in the newspapers."

Whose fault was this? Surely, there must have been some reason for tens of millions of people getting false impressions about the war. Mostly, it was not the correspondents' fault. The stories which gave false impressions were not usually the front-line stories. But the front-line stories had to be sent back from the front. They were printed somewhat later, usu-ally on an inside page. The stories which the soldiers thought deceived their people back home were the "flashes" of rewrit-ten communiqués, sent by reporters who were nowhere near the battle. These communiqué stories carrying "vivid" verbs were the stories that got the big headlines. And the press as-sociation system willy-nilly prevented these reporters from making any evaluation of the news, from saying: "Does this actually mean anything, and if it does, what does it mean in relation to the whole picture?" The speed with which the competing press associations had to send their dispatches did not contribute to the coolness of evaluation. By the time the radio announcers had read an additional lilt into the press association dispatches—it was no wonder that our soldiers spat in disgust.

Said a bomber pilot, after returning from the Pacific: "When I told my mother what the war was really like, and how long it was going to take, she sat down and cried. She didn't know we were just beginning to fight the Japs."

My third trip back to the United States since the war began was a let-down. I had imagined that everybody, after two years, would realize the seriousness of the war and the neces-sity of working as hard as possible toward ending it. But I found a nation wallowing in unprecedented prosperity. There was a steel strike going on, and a railroad strike was threatened. Men lobbying for special privilege swarmed around a Congress which appeared afraid to tax the people's newfound, inflationary wealth. Justice Byrnes cautioned a group of newsmen that we might expect a half million casualties within a few months—and got an editorial spanking for it. A "high military spokesman" generally identified as General Marshall said bitterly that labor strikes played into the hands of enemy propagandists. Labor leaders got furious at that. The truth was that many Americans were not prepared psychologically to accept the cruel facts of war.

The men on Tarawa would have known what the general and the justice meant. On Tarawa, late in 1943, there was a more realistic approach to the war than there was in the United States.

Tarawa: The Story of a Battle, 1944

"The Target Was To Be the Big City"

By Edward R. Murrow

YESTERDAY AFTERNOON, the waiting was over. The weather was right; the target was to be the big city. The crew captains walked into the briefing room, looked at the maps and charts and sat down with their big celluloid pads on their knees. The atmosphere was that of a school and a church. The weather-man gave us the weather. The pilots were reminded that Berlin is Germany's greatest center of war production. The intelligence officer told us how many heavy and light ack-ack guns, how many searchlights we might expect to encounter. Then Jock, the wing commander, explained the system of markings, the kind of flare that would be used by the Path-finders. He said that concentration was the secret of success in these raids, that as long as the aircraft stayed well bunched, they would protect each other. The captains of aircraft walked out.

I noticed that the big Canadian with the slow, easy grin had printed "Berlin" at the top of his pad and then embel-lished it with a scroll. The red-headed English boy with the two weeks' old moustache was the last to leave the room. Late in the afternoon we went to the locker room to draw parachutes, Mae Wests and all the rest. As we dressed, a couple of the Australians were whistling. Walking out to the bus that was to take us to the aircraft, I heard the station loud-speakers announcing that that evening all personnel would be able to see a film, *Star Spangled Rhythm*, free.

We went out and stood around a big, black, four-motored Lancaster *D for Dog*. A small station wagon delivered a ther-mos bottle of coffee, chewing gum, an orange and a bit of chocolate for each man. Up in that part of England the air hums and throbs with the sound of the aircraft motors all day. But for half an hour before take-off, the skies are dead, silent and expectant. A lone hawk hovered over the airfield, absolutely still as he faced into the wind. Jack, the tail gunner, said, "It would be nice if *we* could fly like that."

D for Dog eased around the perimeter track to the end of the runway. We sat there for a moment. The green light flashed and we were rolling—ten seconds ahead of schedule! The take-off was smooth as silk. The wheels came up, and *D-Dog* started the long climb. As we came up through the clouds, I looked right and left and counted fourteen black Lancasters climbing for the place where men must burn oxygen to live. The sun was going down, and its red glow made rivers and lakes of fire on tops of the clouds. Down to the southward, the clouds piled up to form castles, battlements and whole cities, all tinged with red.

Soon we were out over the North Sea. Dave, the navigator, asked Jock if he couldn't make a little more speed. We were nearly two minutes late. By this time we were all using oxygen. The talk on the intercom was brief and crisp. Everyone sounded relaxed. For a while the eight of us in our little world in exile moved over the sea. There was a quarter moon on the starboard beam. Jock's quiet voice came through the intercom, "That'll be flak ahead." We were approaching the enemy coast. The flak looked like a cigarette lighter in a dark room—one that won't light. Sparks but no flame. The sparks crackling just above the level of the cloud tops. We flew steady and straight, and soon the flak was directly below us.

D-Dog rocked a little from right to left, but that wasn't caused by the flak. We were in the slip stream of other Lancasters ahead, and we were over the enemy coast. And then a strange thing happened. The aircraft seemed to grow smaller. Jack in the rear turret, Wally, the mid-upper gunner; Titch, the wireless operator—all seemed somehow to draw closer to Jock in the cockpit. It was as though each man's shoulder was against the other's. The understanding was complete. The intercom came to life, and Jock said, "Two aircraft on the port beam." Jack in the tail said, "Okay, sir, they're Lancs." The whole crew was a unit and wasn't wasting words.

The cloud below was ten tenths. The blue-green jet of the exhausts licked back along the leading edge, and there were other aircraft all around us. The whole great aerial armada was hurtling towards Berlin. We flew so for twenty minutes, when Jock looked up at a vapor trail curling across above us, remarking in a conversational tone that from the look of it he thought there was a fighter up there. Occasionally the angry red of ack-ack burst through the clouds, but it was far away, and we took only an academic interest. We were flying in the third wave. Jock asked Wally in the mid-upper turret and Jack in the rear turret if they were cold. They said they were all right, and thanked him for asking. Even asked how I was, and I said, "All right so far." The cloud was beginning to thin out. Up to the north we could see light, and the flak began to liven up ahead of it.

Boz, the bomb aimer, crackled through on the intercom, "There's a battle going on on the starboard beam." We couldn't see the aircraft, but we could see the jets of red tracer being exchanged. Suddenly there was a burst of yellow flame, and Jock remarked, "That's a fighter going down. Note the position." The whole thing was interesting, but remote. Dave, the navigator, who was sitting back with his maps, charts and compasses, said, "The attack ought to begin in exactly two minutes." We were still over the clouds. But suddenly those dirty gray clouds turned white. We were over the outer searchlight defenses. The clouds below us were white, and we were black. *D-Dog* seemed like a black bug on a white sheet. The flak began coming up, but none of it close. We were still a long way from Berlin. I didn't realize just how far.

Jock observed, "There's a kite on fire dead ahead." It was a great golden, slow-moving meteor slanting toward the earth. By this time we were about thirty miles from our target area in Berlin. That thirty miles was the longest flight I have ever made. Dead on time, Boz, the bomb aimer, reported, "Target indicators going down." The same moment the sky ahead was lit up by bright yellow flares. Off to starboard, another kite went down in flames. The flares were sprouting all over the sky—reds and greens and yellows—and we were flying straight for the center of the fireworks. *D-Dog* seemed to be standing still, the four propellers thrashing the air. But we didn't seem to be closing in. The clouds had cleared, and off to the starboard a Lanc was caught by at least fourteen searchlight beams. We could see him twist and turn and finally break out. But still the whole thing had a quality of unreality about it. No one seemed to be shooting at us, but it was getting lighter all the time. Suddenly a tremendous big blob of yellow light appeared dead ahead, another to the right and another to the left. We were flying straight for them.

Jock pointed out to me the dummy fires and flares to right and left. But we kept going in. Dead ahead there was a whole chain of red flares looking like stop lights. Another Lanc was coned on our starboard beam. The lights seemed to be supporting it. Again we could see those little bubbles of colored lead driving at it from two sides. The German fighters were at him. And then, with no warning at all, *D-Dog* was filled with an unhealthy white light. I was standing just behind Jock and could see all the seams on the wings. His quiet Scots voice beat into my ears, "Steady, lads, we've been coned." His slender body lifted half out of his seat as he jammed the control column forward and to the left. We were going down.

Jock was wearing woolen gloves with the fingers cut off. I could see his fingernails turn white as he gripped the wheel. And then I was on my knees, flat on the deck, for he had whipped the *Dog* back into a climbing turn. The knees should have been strong enough to support me, but they weren't, and the stomach seemed in some danger of letting me down, too. I picked myself up and looked out again. It seemed that one big searchlight, instead of being twenty thousand feet below, was mounted right on our wing tip. *D-Dog* was corkscrewing. As we rolled down on the other side, I began to see what was happening to Berlin.

The clouds were gone, and the sticks of incendiaries from the preceding waves made the place look like a badly laid out city with the street lights on. The small incendiaries were going down like a fistful of white rice thrown on a piece of black velvet. As Jock hauled the *Dog* up again, I was thrown to the other side of the cockpit, and there below were more incendiaries, glowing white and then turning red. The cookies—the four-thousand-pound high explosives—were bursting below like great sunflowers gone mad. And then, as we started down again, still held in the lights, I remembered that the *Dog* still had one of those cookies and a whole basket of incendiaries in his belly, and the lights still held us. And I was very frightened.

While Jock was flinging him about in the air, he suddenly flung over the intercom, "Two aircraft on the port beam." I looked astern and saw Wally, the mid-upper, whip his turret around to port and then look up to see a single-engined fighter slide just above us. The other aircraft was one of ours. Finally, we were out of the cone, flying level. I looked down, and the white fires had turned red. They were beginning to merge and spread, just like butter does on a hot plate. Jock and Boz, the bomb aimer, began to discuss the target. The smoke was getting thick down below. Boz said he liked the two green flares on the ground almost dead ahead. He began calling his directions. And just then a new bunch of big flares went down on the far side of the sea of flame and flare that seemed to be directly below us. He thought that would be a better aiming point. Jock agreed, and we flew on. The bomb doors were open. Boz called his directions, "Five left, five left." And then there was a gentle, confident, upward thrust under my feet, and Boz said, "Cookie gone." A few seconds later, the incendiaries went, and *D-Dog* seemed lighter and easier to handle.

I thought I could make out the outline of streets below. But the bomb aimer didn't agree, and he ought to know. By this time all those patches of white on black had turned yellow and started to flow together. Another searchlight caught us but didn't hold us. Then through the intercom came the word, "One can of incendiaries didn't clear. We're still carrying it." And Jock replied, "Is it a big one or a little one?" The word came back, "Little one, I think, but I'm not sure. I'll check." More of those yellow flares came down and hung about us. I haven't seen so much light since the war began. Finally the intercom announced that it was only a small container of incendiaries left, and Jock remarked, "Well, it's hardly worth going back and doing another run-up for that." If there had been a good fat bundle left, he would have gone back through that stuff and done it all over again.

I began to breathe and to reflect again—that all men would be brave if only they could leave their stomachs at home. Then there was a tremendous whoomp, an unintelligible shout from the tail gunner, and *D-Dog* shivered and lost altitude. I looked at the port side, and there was a Lancaster that seemed close enough to touch. He had whipped straight under us, missed us by twenty-five, fifty feet, no one knew how much. The navigator sang out the new course, and we were heading for home. Jock was doing what I had heard him tell his pilots to do so often—flying dead on course. He flew straight into a huge green searchlight and, as he rammed the throttles home, remarked, "We'll have a little trouble getting away from this one." And again *D-Dog* dove, climbed and twisted and was finally free. We flew level then. I looked on the port beam at the target area. There was a sullen, obscene glare. The fires seemed to have found each other—and we were heading home.

For a little while it was smooth sailing. We saw more battles. Then another plane in flames, but no one could tell whether it was ours or theirs. We were still near the target. Dave, the navigator, said, "Hold her steady, skipper. I want to get an astral site." And Jock held her steady. And the flak began coming up at us. It seemed to be very close. It was winking off both wings. But the *Dog* was steady. Finally Dave said, "Okay, skipper, thank you very much." And a great orange blob of flak smacked up straight in front of us. And Jock said, "I think they're shooting at us." I'd thought so for some time.

And he began to throw *D for Dog* up, around and about again. And when we were clear of the barrage, I asked him how close the bursts were and he said, "Not very close. When they're really near, you can smell 'em." That proved nothing, for I'd been holding my breath. Jack sang out from the rear turret, said his oxygen was getting low, thought maybe the lead had frozen. Titch, the wireless operator, went scrambling back with a new mask and a bottle of oxygen. Dave, the navigator, said, "We're crossing the coast." My mind went back to the time I had crossed that coast in 1938, in a plane that had taken off from Prague. Just ahead of me sat two refugees from Vienna—an old man and his wife. The co-pilot came back and told them that we were outside German territory. The old man reached out and grasped his wife's hand. The work that was done last night was a massive blow of retribution for all those who have fled from the sound of shots and blows on the stricken Continent.

We began to lose height over the North Sea. We were over England's shore. The land was dark beneath us. Somewhere down there below American boys were probably bombing-up Fortresses and Liberators, getting ready for the day's work. We were over the home field. We called the control tower, and the calm, clear voice of an English girl replied, "Greetings, *D-Dog*. You are diverted to Mule Bag." We swung around, contacted Mule Bag, came in on the flare path, touched down very gently, ran along to the end of the runway and turned left. And Jock, the finest pilot in Bomber Command, said to the control tower, "*D-Dog* clear of runway."

When we went in for interrogation, I looked on the board and saw that the big, slow-smiling Canadian and the red-headed English boy with the two weeks' old moustache hadn't made it. They were missing. There were four reporters on this operation—two of them didn't come back. Two friends of mine—Norman Stockton, of Australian Associated Newspapers, and Lowell Bennett, an American representing International News Service. There is something of a tradition amongst reporters that those who are prevented by circumstances from filing their stories will be covered by their colleagues. This has been my effort to do so.

In the aircraft in which I flew, the men who flew and fought it poured into my ears their comments on fighters, flak and flares in the same tones they would have used in reporting a host of daffodils. I have no doubt that Bennett and Stockton would have given you a better report of last night's activities.

Berlin was a kind of orchestrated hell, a terrible symphony of light and flame. It isn't a pleasant kind of warfare—the men doing it speak of it as a job. Yesterday afternoon, when the tapes were stretched out on the big map all the way to Berlin and back again, a young pilot with old eyes said to me, "I see we're working again tonight." That's the frame of mind in which the job is being done. The job isn't pleasant; it's terribly tiring. Men die in the sky while others are roasted alive in their cellars. Berlin last night wasn't a pretty sight. In about thirty-five minutes it was hit with about three times the

amount of stuff that ever came down on London in a nightlong blitz. This is a calculated, remorseless campaign of destruction. Right now the mechanics are probably working on
D-Dog, getting him ready to fly again.

CBS Radio Broadcast, December 3, 1943

The Price of Fire

By Martha Gellhorn

THE WARD is a long, wide, cold room with bright green curtains at the windows. There are yellow and mauve potted chrysanthemums on the table down the center of the room, and a black iron coal stove at either end. Wicker chairs and a table covered with magazines stand in front of the far stove, and this is where the patients, wearing Royal Air Force uniforms, gather. Five or six men are lying in the white-painted beds.

The ward has the casual, cheerful, faintly bored feeling of any place where men are convalescing. But this ward is not like other wards, because no one here has a real face, and many of the patients have hands that are not much good, either. These men are members of the air crews who crashed in planes or were thrown clear or dragged from the burning wreckage—but not quite soon enough.

The men around the stove interrupted their conversation to talk to one of the patients in bed. The wagon that will carry him to the operating room is drawn up alongside the bed, and a nurse is helping him onto it.

"What's it to be today, Bill?"

"Eyebrows!"

"Won't he be pretty!"

Then there is a chorus of "Cheerios," and the operating-room trolley rolls away. There was no special feeling about this, because eyebrows aren't bad. The boy had been through so many operations and was so close to having a face again that this little extra pain did not worry him. Besides, men have been wheeled in and out of this ward all day long, day after day, and each man, alone, has learned how to wait for and endure these trips.

In a bed farther down, another boy is waiting. His turn will come after the eyebrows are made. He is going to get a nose. For weeks, he has been growing the skin for his nose in a narrow sausage-shaped pedicle attached to the unharmed skin of his shoulder. His face is incredible, and one hand is entirely gone.

There is no expression in these burned and scarred faces; all the expression is in the eyes and in the voice. You cannot tell age. Fire takes that away, too. The boy has light brown, tufty hair and good, laughing eyes and a good voice and a dreadful face that will soon, at least, have a nose. He was twenty-one, though you could only know this if you were told. He had been a chauffeur before the war, driving for the squire of his village.

The welfare officer had arranged to get him an industrial job when he would have enough of a face, but he did not want it. He wanted to go back with one hand and that face and be a chauffeur again in his village. Because the village is "home" and what he loves. His people are there. The village is a recognizable world.

In fact, they would all like to go back to what was before — before the war and before the flames got them.

Around the stove, there are now four boys gossiping together. One has just come from London, and they are asking him about his trip. He is going to be operated on tomorrow and, after that, he will return to flying and he is very happy. He is an American from Columbus, Ohio, and he crashed in a Hurricane.

His face, they say, was simply pushed back two inches inside his head. Now his nose is very flattened, and the skin around his eyes is odd, but by contrast with the others, he looks fine. He feels fine, too, because what he likes is to fly and he will be doing that again.

The others will not fly. They are talking easily and generously about his squadron, and neither you nor they nor anyone looks at the curled claws of hands of the 19-year-old Canadian or at the melted stump that the 21-year-old English boy has, or at the stiff, reddish, solidified fingers of a boy who always worked on a farm in Canada and who would like to again. Maybe some day his hands will bend just enough to let him do it.

The 19-year-old Canadian with the claw hands wants to be a boat builder. He is a darling with a lively brain, but one half of his face is hardened, twisted, reddish meat, and the other half is fairly okay, so that you can see what a nice-looking kid he was. He thought he'd lost his left eye after he was pulled out of the wrecked plane because he couldn't see out of that eye. He was a gunner, and his pal, the navigator, pulled him out, and he said to his pal, "Where's my eye? I have lost my eye somewhere here."

So his pal said: "Well, we'll look for it then." And they crawled around on the grass dazed and burned, looking for the eye.

This story, you may not instantly guess, produces roars of laughter from everyone, because it just goes to show how dopey a guy can be.

There is a wonderful man on the staff of this hospital, a former schoolteacher, now a flight sergeant, who lives with these wounded boys and whose job it is to see that they make the hard and lonely adjustment to their disfigurement that they must make if they are to live. He is their friend and confidant and he knows as much about them as one man can know about another. He treats them with a matter-of-factness which is essential and, in the beginning, startling to an outsider.

He said casually, "Pete, show your hand. He's got a real bad hand."

And there was the hand, or rather the non-hand, and there above it was the serious, hesitant face of the 21-year-old Englishman. We looked at his hand as if it belonged to someone else and we were only interested to see what fire could do to a hand. His face was fairly good, but the sides of his head had been burned flat and a head is strange without ears. This boy had been a talented pilot. He completed his operational tour, which means thirty separate missions against the enemy. Then, as a rest, he was sent to be an instructor. It happened that his student crashed the training plane when he was flying with him, and the pilot got these burns trying to pull the student out of the wreckage. But this is just bad luck, you see.

The saline baths, which are the essential basis of burn treatment, are in rooms alongside the ward. We went in to see the baths, and there was a boy sitting in the deep tub in the chilly white room. The attendants were keeping his face dampened and under the water. He was patiently flexing his purplish hands. He was being cheered on by a sergeant who is in charge of the baths and who loves the baths only less than he loves the boys he is saving.

"Come on!" the sergeant said. "You can bend them more than that." Then, not to be too hard on this child, who had been here only three days, he said, "You see yourself how good they are. Your face is fine, too. We'll have you out of here in no time."

The boy answered, but you could not understand what he said. His skin was burned so tight that he could scarcely move his mouth, and the words came out in a shy mumble. The face was absolutely expressionless, so set that it looked dead, and yet the shape of it was still intact. Two bright blue eyes stared out of the scarred face and watched the stiff hands that bent ever so slightly under water. The rest of him was the fragile tender body of a very young boy, for, after all, nineteen is a very young boy.

"Come, now," the sergeant said. "Come on. Bend them."

The boy had been opening and shutting his fingers the distance of a quarter of an inch for two hours and he would go on doing that for more days than one wanted to think about. But in the end, he would move his hands, and his face would be fixed, and then he would fly again.

They were having tea in the reception office. This is a wonderful hospital, in which the staff and patients call one another by their first names and nicknames, and the patients feel as at home as if they were guests at a summer camp and they have all been together so often or so long that they have permanent jokes, and they have all got such guts that there is no place for pity.

In the office, there was a pretty blond girl in khaki who is a chauffeur now and who drives these boys to the village pub or to a neighboring football field where the hospital team plays an army team or to the train or the movies or wherever they want to go. Another pretty girl, who wears a Saint John's black uniform, is the secretary, and there were a few interns getting a quick cup of tea during a lull in the operating room. There was also a girl wearing a blue silk bandanna handkerchief over her hair, and a polo coat. She was tiny and pink-cheeked and absurdly young-looking to be a married woman. But she was married, and her husband was sitting beside her, and he was very young, too, and tall. He was blind now. Beneath the bandage over his eyes, you could see the familiar drawn, burned face.

The girl had come to this hospital on the first day her husband arrived and she had not left him since. He was new to being blind and very awkward about it. She managed so that her husband should not feel his awkwardness. The blind soldier talked happily and easily, with the confidence his wife had given him. He was teasing the girl chauffeur about the football team that she lugged all over the countryside: What sort of football team was she sponsoring anyhow? They had been beaten everywhere since she started driving them.

This hospital is one of four Royal Air Force burn centers and it was planned as a wartime hospital. But there will be five or seven years' work after the war, not counting the men now prisoners in Germany who will need this sort of care. The average hospitalization is from six to eight weeks; but these bad burn cases take two years, at a minimum, to be repaired.

Not only R.A.F. cases are treated here. There are bomb wounds where the face has been torn apart, and sailors who have been burned and rescued from the sea, and men of all services who have been terribly damaged in accidents. But the largest group are the boys in Air Force blue, and the oldest among them is twenty-nine.

The hospital is a marvel. The men have unbounded confidence in the surgeons. This confidence is based on observation. They see with their own eyes the slow, patient miracles performed by Doctor Archibald McIndoe. He works with them tirelessly, operating three or five days a week, sometimes from ten in the morning until ten at night. But he does more than surgery, and that is why the hospital is a marvel. You would never see a more delicate and unpretentious job of life-saving than goes on here.

Mac believes that, with sufficient time, he can fix a man's face "so that it will not cause comment." This is what he tells them, promising nothing more and delivering nothing less. When these burned boys arrive, they see others like themselves, and the rubber in the human soul is so resilient that they always see someone who looks worse than they look. Mirrors are handy. The men are not allowed to become afraid of facing their present disfigurement.

Since they will be in and out of this hospital regularly for years, they do not wear hospital uniforms. As soon as they can walk, they are given their R.A.F. uniforms and shipped off to the village to mingle with people and get used to living in the daily world. The local people are accustomed to them. They are not stared at, and this first adjustment is fairly easy. After this, they are encouraged to go to London, mainly to see and be seen. They are apt to go in pairs and keep each other company, but the job of making them accept themselves without self-consciousness is so well done that this initial contact with strangers appears to come off successfully every time.

Mac has abandoned the basket-weaving school of occupational therapy. He feels it is silly. These are men vitally concerned in the war effort, and there is an industrial workshop at the hospital which makes small airplane parts. The work is voluntary, and they know that they are doing something useful. When Mac is through with a patient for a time, feeling that he has had all the operations he can take, the patient is sent away to work at a job or, if the disability is too serious, the patient is sent to a rest home which is also a limited factory and training school. The men are not permitted to become idle or to feel that they have lost all chance of fitting into an average life during the long years of treatment.

Mac says that the worst disability is blindness, but after that comes the loss of hands. Fortunately, total loss of both hands is rare, and it is amazing what these boys can learn to do with a hook for a hand or by using the stumps of fingers. And when they come back to the hospital—as they must—they build up an affection for the staff. They find old friends in the wards and, due to Mac, there is no hospital gloom, none of that excessive starched hospital discipline, and the men are really very cheerful about their return visits.

They have a club called the Guinea Pig Club, which gives a bang-up dinner in the village once a year, and all the old patients come as if they were attending a school reunion. It is a great enough achievement to repair these damaged faces, but to keep the minds behind the faces so sound and so self-reliant is a triumph.

There are some things which even Mac cannot handle, and they are not talked of especially. There is the heartbreak of parents when they first see their children come back like this. There is the tragedy of the wives who cannot take it. One doesn't talk of this, and the losses are cut, and life goes on.

There is something else, perhaps worse and deeper. It is the fear of these very young men that, after the war, they will never really be able to compete with whole men and that they will not find a decent job and will not be able to provide properly for themselves or their families. So they make a joke of disaster and form a beggars' union.

It is natural that these boys should not be thinking much about the peace and how to prevent the Germans from ever starting another war. They have done their share. They have paid for the safety of our world in advance.

Collier's, May 20, 1944

The Italian Campaign: "Slow Progress"

by Ernie Pyle

"The Land and the Weather Are Both Against Us"

AT THE FRONT LINE IN ITALY, Dec. 14—(by wireless)—The war in Italy is tough. The land and the weather are both against us.

It rains and it rains. Vehicles bog down and temporary bridges wash out. The country is shockingly beautiful, and just as shockingly hard to capture from the enemy. The hills rise to high ridges of almost solid rock. You can't go around them through the flat peaceful valleys, because the Germans look down upon you and would let you have it.

So you have to go up and over. A mere platoon of Germans, well dug in on a high, rock-spined hill, can hold out for a long time against tremendous onslaughts.

Having come from home so recently, I know you folks back there are disappointed and puzzled by the slow progress in Italy. You wonder why we move northward so imperceptibly. You are impatient for us to get to Rome.

Well, I can tell you this—our troops are just as impatient for Rome as you. But they all say such things as this: "It never was this bad in Tunisia." "We ran into a new brand of Krauts over here." "If it would only stop raining." "Every day we don't advance is one day longer before we get home."

*   *   *

Our troops are living in a way almost inconceivable to you in the States. The fertile black valleys are knee deep in mud. Thousands of the men have not been dry for weeks. Other thousands lie at night in the high mountains with the temperature below freezing and the thin snow sifting over them.

They dig into the stones and sleep in little chasms and behind rocks and in half caves. They live like men of prehistoric times, and a club would become them more than a machine

728

gun. How they survive the winter misery at all is beyond us who have the opportunity of drier beds in the warmer valleys.

It is not the fault of our troops, nor of their direction, that the northward path is a tedious one. It is the weather and the terrain and the weather.

If there were no German fighting troops in Italy, if there were merely German engineers to blow the bridges in the passes, if never a shot were fired at all, our northward march would still be slow.

The country over here is so difficult we've created a great deal of cavalry for use in the mountains. Each division has hundreds of horses and mules to carry it beyond the point where vehicles can go no farther. On beyond the mules' ability, mere men—American men—take it on their backs.

Here is a little clue to the war over here. I flew across the Mediterranean in a cargo plane weighted down with more than a thousand pounds beyond the normal load. The cabin was filled with big pasteboard boxes which had been given priority above all other freight.

In those boxes were packboards, hundreds of them, for husky men to pack—100, even 150, pounds of food and ammunition on their backs—to comrades high in the miserable mountains.

*   *   *

But we can take consolation from many things. The air is almost wholly ours. All day long Spitfires patrol above our fighting troops like a half dozen policemen running up and down the street watching for bandits. During my four days in the lines, just ended, I saw German planes only twice, then just two at a time, and they skedaddled in a hurry.

Further, our artillery prevails and how! We are prodigal with ammunition against these rocky crags, and well we should be, for a $50 shell can often save 10 lives in country like this. Little by little, the fiendish rain of explosives upon the hillsides softens the German. They've always been impressed by, and afraid of, our artillery and we have concentrations of it here that are demoralizing.

And lastly, no matter how cold the mountains, or how wet the snow, or how sticky the mud, it's just as miserable for the German soldier as for the American.

Our men will get to Rome all right. There's no question about that. But the way is cruel. Right this minute some of them are fighting hand-to-hand up there in fog and clouds so dense they can barely see each other—one man against another.

No one who has not seen this mud, these dark skies, these forbidding ridges and ghost-like clouds that unveil and then quickly hide your killer, should have the right to be impatient with the progress along the road to Rome.

Scripps-Howard wire copy, December 14, 1943

"One Demolished Town After Another"

IN ITALY, Dec. 28—(by wireless)—The little towns of Italy that have been in the path of this war from Salerno northward are nothing more than great rubble heaps. There is hardly enough left of most of them to form a framework for rebuilding.

When the Germans occupied the towns we rained artillery on them for days and weeks at a time. Then after we captured a town the Germans would shell it heavily. They got it from both sides.

Along the road for 20 or 30 miles behind the fighting front you pass through one demolished town after another. Most of the inhabitants take to the hills after the first shelling. At least they did up here. Some go to live in caves, some go to relatives in the country. A few in every town refuse to leave no matter what happens, and many of them have been killed by the shelling and bombing from both sides.

A countryside is harder to disfigure than a town. You have to look closely, and study in detail, to find the carnage wrought upon the green fields and the rocky hillside. It is there, but it is temporary—like a skinned finger—and time and the rains will heal it. Another year and the countryside will cover its own scars.

If you wander on foot and look closely you will see the signs—the limb of an olive tree broken off, six swollen dead horses in the corner of a field, a strawstack burned down, a chestnut tree blown clear out with its roots by a German bomb, little gray patches of powder burns on the hillside, snatches of broken and abandoned rifles and grenades in the bushes, grain fields patterned with a million crisscrossing ruts from the great trucks crawling frame-deep through the mud, empty gun pits, and countless foxholes, and rubbish-heap stacks of empty C-ration cans, and now and then the lone grave of a German soldier.

These are all there, clear across the country, and yet they are hard to see unless you look closely. A countryside is big, and nature helps fight for it.

*　　*　　*

The apple season is on now, and in the cities and those towns that still exist there are hundreds of little curbside stands selling apples, oranges, and hazelnuts. The apples are to us here what the tangerines were in North Africa a year ago, and the tomatoes and grapes in Sicily last summer.

I haven't been in Italy long enough really to know much about the people, but I do know that the average soldier likes Italy a great deal better than he did Africa. As one soldier said, "They seem more civilized."

Our soldiers are a little contemptuous of the Italians and don't fully trust them, and yet with the typical American tender-heartedness they feel sorry for them, and little by little they are becoming sort of fond of them. They seem to us a pathetic people, not very strong in character but fundamentally kind-hearted and friendly.

A lot of our American-Italian soldiers are taking to the land of their fathers like ducks to water, but not all of them. The other night I was riding in a jeep with an officer and an enlisted man of Italian extraction, both from New York. The officer was talking about the plenitude of girls in Naples, and he said most of the soldiers there had girls.

"Not me," said the driver. "I won't have anything to do with them. The minute they find out I speak Italian they start giving me a sob story about how poor and starved they are and why don't the Americans feed them faster.

"I look at it this way—they've been poor for a long time and it wasn't us that made them poor. They started this war and they've killed plenty of our soldiers, and now that they're whipped they expect us to take care of them. That kind of talk gives me a pain. I tell them to go to hell. I don't like 'em."

*   *   *

But our average soldier can't seem to hold an animosity very long. And you can't help liking a lot of the Italians. For instance, when I pull back to write for a few days, I stay in a bare, cold room of a huge empty house out in the country. My roommates are Reynolds Packard, of the United Press, and Clark Lee, of the International News Service.

We have an Italian boy 24 years old who takes care of the room. I don't know whether the Army hired him or whether he just walked in and went to work. At any rate, he's there all day and he can't do enough for us. He sweeps the room six times and mops it twice every day.

He boards up blown-out windows, does our washing, and even picks up the scraps of wood and builds a little fire to take the chill off. When he runs out of anything to do he just sits around, always in sight awaiting our pleasure.

His name is Angelo. He smiles every time you look at him. We talk to each other all the time without knowing what we're saying. He admires my two-fingered speed on the typewriter. He comes and looks over my shoulder while I'm writing, which drives me crazy, but he's so eager and kind I can't tell him to go away. It's hard to hate a guy like that.

Scripps-Howard wire copy, December 28, 1943

"Mule Packing Outfit"

AT THE FRONT LINES IN ITALY, Jan. 5—(by wireless)—You have been reading in the papers for weeks about the mountain fighting in Italy, and how some of the troops are so high and remote that they have to be supplied by pack mule.

Well, for the last few days I have been hanging around with one of these mule outfits.

There is an average of one mule packing outfit for every infantry battalion in the mountains. Some are run by Americans, some by Italian soldiers.

The pack outfit I was with supplied a battalion that was fighting on a bald, rocky ridge nearly 4,000 feet high. It fought constantly for ten days and nights, and when it finally came down less than a third of the original men were left.

All through those bitter days every ounce of their supplies had to go up to them on the backs of mules and men. Mules took it the first third of the way. Men took it the last bitter two-thirds, because the trail was too steep even for mules.

The mule skinners of my outfit were Italian soldiers. The human packers were mostly American soldiers.

The Italian mule skinners were from Sardinia. They belonged to a mountain artillery regiment, and thus were experienced in climbing and in handling mules. They were bivouacked in an olive grove alongside a highway at the foot of the mountain.

They made no trips in the daytime, except in emergencies, because most of the trail was exposed to artillery fire. Supplies were brought into the olive grove by truck during the day, and stacked under trees. Just before dusk they would start loading the stuff onto mules.

The Americans who actually managed the supply chain liked to get the mules loaded by dark, because if there was any shelling the Italians instantly disappeared and you never could find them.

There were 155 skinners in this outfit and usually about 80 mules were used each night. Every mule had a man to lead it, and about ten extra men went along to help get mules up if they fell, and to repack any loads that came loose, and to unpack at the top. They could be up and back in less than three hours.

Usually a skinner made just one trip a night, but sometimes in an emergency they made two.

*   *   *

On an average night the supplies would run something like this—85 cans of water, 100 cases of K ration, 10 cases of D ration, 10 miles of telephone wire, 25 cases of grenades and rifle and machine-gun ammunition, about 100 rounds of heavy mortar shells, one radio, two telephones, and four cases of first aid packets and sulfa drugs.

In addition, the packers would load their pockets with cigarets for the boys on top; also cans of Sterno, so they could heat some coffee once in a while.

Also, during that period, they took up more than 500 of the heavy combat suits we are issuing to the troops to help keep them warm. They carried up cellophane gas capes for some of the men to use as sleeping bags, and took extra socks for the boys too.

Mail was their most tragic cargo. Every night they would take up sacks of mail, and every night bring a large portion of it back down—the recipients would have been killed or wounded the day their letters came.

On the long man-killing climb above the end of the mule trail they used anywhere from 20 to 300 men a night. They rang in cooks, truck drivers, clerks, and anybody else they could lay their hands on.

A lot of stuff was packed up by the fighting soldiers themselves. On the biggest night, when they were building up supplies for an attack, another battalion which was in reserve sent 300 first-line combat troops to do the packing.

*   *   *

Back to the mules again—they would leave the olive grove in bunches of 20, starting just after dark. American soldiers were posted within shouting distance of each other all along the trail, to keep the Italians from getting lost in the dark.

Those guides form a little sidelight that I wish everybody in America who thinks he's having a tough time in this war could know about.

The guides were men who had fought all through a long and bitter battle at the top of the mountain. For more than a week they had been far up there, perched behind rocks in the rain and cold, eating cold K rations, sleeping without blankets, scouraged constantly with artillery and mortar shells, fighting and ducking and growing more and more weary, seeing their comrades wounded one by one and taken down the mountain.

Finally sickness and exhaustion overtook many of those who were left, so they were sent back down the mountain under their own power to report to the medics at the bottom and be sent back to a rest camp. It took most of them the better part of a day to get two-thirds of the way down, so sore were their feet and so weary their muscles.

And then—when actually in sight of their haven of rest and peace—they were stopped and pressed into this guide service, because there just wasn't anybody else to do it.

So there they stayed, right on the mountainside, for at least three additional days and nights that I know of, just lying miserably alongside the trail to shout in the darkness and guide the mules.

They still had no blankets to keep them warm, no beds but the rocks. And they did it without complaining. The human spirit is an astounding thing.

Scripps-Howard wire copy, January 5, 1944

"This One Is Captain Waskow"

AT THE FRONT LINES IN ITALY, Jan. 10—(by wireless)—In this war I have known a lot of officers who were loved and respected by the soldiers under them. But never have I crossed the trail of any man as beloved as Capt. Henry T. Waskow, of Belton, Tex.

Captain Waskow was a company commander in the 36th Division. He had been in this company since long before he left the States. He was very young, only in his middle 20s, but he carried in him a sincerity and gentleness that made people want to be guided by him.

"After my own father, he comes next," a sergeant told me.

"He always looked after us," a soldier said. "He'd go to bat for us every time."

"I've never known him to do anything unkind," another one said.

*   *   *

I was at the foot of the mule trail the night they brought Captain Waskow down. The moon was nearly full, and you could see far up the trail, and even part way across the valley. Soldiers made shadows as they walked.

Dead men had been coming down the mountain all evening, lashed onto the backs of mules. They came lying belly down across the wooden packsaddle, their heads hanging down on the left side of the mule, their stiffened legs sticking awkwardly from the other side, bobbing up and down as the mule walked.

The Italian mule skinners were afraid to walk beside dead men, so Americans had to lead the mules down that night. Even the Americans were reluctant to unlash and lift off the bodies, when they got to the bottom, so an officer had to do it himself and ask others to help.

The first one came early in the morning. They slid him down from the mule, and stood him on his feet for a moment. In the half light he might have been merely a sick man standing there leaning on the other. Then they laid him on the ground in the shadow of the stone wall alongside the road.

I don't know who that first one was. You feel small in the presence of dead men, and you don't ask silly questions.

We left him there beside the road, that first one, and we all went back into the cowshed and sat on watercans or lay on the straw, waiting for the next batch of mules.

Somebody said the dead soldier had been dead for four days, and then nobody said anything more about him. We talked for an hour or more; the dead man lay all alone, outside in the shadow of the wall.

                    *   *   *

Then a soldier came into the cowshed and said there were some more bodies outside. We went out into the road. Four mules stood there in the moonlight, in the road where the trail came down off the mountain. The soldiers who led them stood there waiting.

"This one is Captain Waskow," one of them said quickly.

Two men unlashed his body from the mule and lifted it off and laid it in the shadow beside the stone wall. Other men took the other bodies off. Finally, there were five lying end to end in a long row. You don't cover up dead men in the combat zones. They just lie there in the shadows until somebody else comes after them.

The uncertain mules moved off to their olive groves. The men in the road seemed reluctant to leave. They stood around, and gradually I could sense them moving, one by one, close to Captain Waskow's body. Not so much to look, I think, as to say something in finality to him and to themselves. I stood close by and I could hear.

One soldier came and looked down, and he said out loud: "God damn it!"

That's all he said, and then he walked away.

Another one came, and he said, "God damn it to hell anyway!" He looked down for a few last moments and then turned and left.

Another man came. I think he was an officer. It was hard to tell officers from men in the dim light, for everybody was grimy and dirty. The man looked down into the dead captain's face and then spoke directly to him, as though he were alive:

"I'm sorry, old man."

Then a soldier came and stood beside the officer and bent over, and he too spoke to his dead captain, not in a whisper but awfully tenderly, and he said:

"I sure am sorry, sir."

Then the first man squatted down, and he reached down and took the captain's hand, and he sat there for a full five minutes holding the dead hand in his own and looking intently into the dead face. And he never uttered a sound all the time he sat there.

Finally he put the hand down. He reached up and gently straightened the points of the captain's shirt collar, and then he sort of rearranged the tattered edges of his uniform around the wound, and then he got up and walked away down the road in the moonlight, all alone.

The rest of us went back into the cowshed, leaving the five dead men lying in a line end to end in the shadow of the low stone wall. We lay down on the straw in the cowshed, and pretty soon we were all asleep.

Scripps-Howard wire copy, January 10, 1944

San Pietro a Village of the Dead; Victory Cost Americans Dearly

by Homer Bigart

WITH THE 5TH ARMY, Dec. 18 (Via London) (Delayed).
—We crossed the valley to San Pietro through fields littered
with dead. The village, rising in terraces on the southern
hump of Monte Samucro, loomed out of the blue haze of
battle smoke like an ancient ruined castle, and even from the
creek bed we could see that not one house in that tight little
cluster of buildings had escaped ruin.

The Germans had cleared out—that much had been established late yesterday when patrols penetrated the outskirts
without drawing fire. But we heard that enemy snipers were
still clinging to their bunkers in the ravine north of the village
and, since San Pietro was likely to receive further pastings
from German artillery, no infantrymen ventured into the
death trap. Instead, a force led by Lieutenant James Epper-
man, of Hot Springs, Tex., skirted the town and took up positions on the high ground just beyond.

We followed a unit of medical-aid men into San Pietro. In
the wrecked buildings, sprawling on blood-drenched rubble,
were American as well as German wounded. Three times during Wednesday's initial attack American assault parties had
penetrated San Pietro. Each time they had been driven off
with severe casualties.

Early today litter bearers had cleared the lower buildings of
wounded. In darkness they groped through narrow alleys
choked with rubble, shouting into open doorways and listening intently for some response.

From the wine cellar of a house, sheered off nearly to the
ground by weeks of shelling, came a faint cry for help. On the
straw-covered earthen floor lay three wounded Americans
who had been there two days and nights, too weak to get

back to friendly lines. One had been wounded three times on successive days. In Wednesday's assault he received shell fragments in the right hip, and lay helpless in a dugout just outside the village. Next day the Germans renewed their shelling, and his right hip was subject to a near miss. Yesterday, while crawling toward a wine cellar, another fragment pierced his right hip.

He had used all his sulfa tablets. A comrade, less seriously hurt, gave him more. Without sulfa he would have died of shock. His condition is good, and he will receive the Purple Heart with Oak Leaf Cluster.

With him were two other privates mangled by shell fragments. One had sulfa and, despite grave injuries, will live. The third youth found the stuff too nauseous. He will lose a leg.

At noon, when we cleared the eastern base at Monte Rotunda and struck out across the valley, the battlefield was strangely still. A thick haze lay stagnant above the pass and a wan sun bathed the scene in sickly light. There was not a sound except our own cautious footsteps as we crossed the pasture, still uncleared of mines.

Near the forward aid station we met Captain Ralph Phelan, of Waurika, Okla, who had done such a heroic job evacuating wounded from within the range of snipers. Phelan warned us not to enter San Pietro. The town, he said, was full of booby traps and subject to intermittent shelling.

He showed us a path up the steep bank of the creek, where three days previously Major Milton Landry's men formed for their bloody, futile assault on San Pietro. We merged on the field, so thickly pocked with shell holes that there must have been a hundred bursts within an acre of bare rocky ground.

The assault waves had met an intense and deadly hail of artillery at the very line of departure. On the far side of the field sprawled some dead. One boy lay crumpled in a shallow slit trench beneath a rock. Another, still grasping his rifle, peered from behind a tree, staring with sightless eyes toward the Liri plain. A third lay prone where he had fallen. He had heard the warning scream of a German shell. He had dropped flat on his stomach but on level ground affording no cover. Evidently some fragment had killed him instantly, for there had been no struggle. Generally, there is no mistaking the

dead—their strange contorted posture leaves no room for
doubt. But this soldier, his steel helmet tilted over his face,
seemed merely resting in the field. We did not know until we
came within a few steps and saw a gray hand hanging limply
from a sleeve.

Somehow we became separated from the medical aid patrol. We crossed another field scattered with abandoned rifles,
cartridge belts, blood-stained bandages and other debris of
battle, and reached a pass curving along the walled terrace. It
was along this wall that American remnants which had survived a dash across the fields crept in a desperate effort to gain
the village.

We heard a sudden rushing noise that made us stop, involuntarily. It was only a brook that tumbled down a wall and
crossed our path beneath strands of enemy barbed wire. The
brook was kind to us. It had carried away the dirt which covered a German Teller mine.

The mine lay just to the left of the path. A thin strand of
trip wire ran from it directly across our trail. Don Whitehead,
Associated Press reporter, was scrambling over the barbed
wire. One of us saw that the trip wire was draped over the
bottom strand. We were very careful getting across that barrier.

[Mr. Whitehead in his dispatch credited Mr. Bigart with
noticing the trip wire and shouting a warning.]

Now the path widened and became a cobbled alley. We
passed the first house. A rifle was in position near the door
step. Looking within we saw an American man lying beneath
a heap of straw.

There were three other dead in the shallow gully house.
Every approach to San Pietro, every ravine and sunken path
offering shelter from machine-gun fire had been covered by
German snipers.

The cobbled lane wound steeply up the slope into the heart
of San Pietro. The village was a ghastly sight. Pounded for
three weeks by American guns and bombed many times from
the air, this village of 500 peasants was reduced to one great
pile of shattered stone. Whole blocks were obliterated. The
street pattern was almost unrecognizable, for the narrow lanes
were buried under five feet of rubble. A high wall, towering
above the lesser buildings, showed where the Church of St.

Michael and Archangel had stood. The choir loft hung crazily above an altar almost buried under masonry.

In alcoves against the wall stood the statues of St. Michael, and beneath the statue of St. Peter was the inscription: "By the devotion of Americans from San Pietro." A young woman who had followed us into the church explained that natives had emigrated to America and that her uncle Pietro Rossai had a farm near Syracuse.

She showed us a large iron crucifix which, she said, had "passed many miracles." In September the natives had prayed for peace and a few days later the armistice had come. The crucifix had survived the great earthquake of 1915, but the bombardment was 100 times worse than the earthquake. Now the figure of Christ was headless, the Madonna of the Waters had lost an arm.

The Germans had evacuated San Pietro last Thursday afternoon. The steep slopes on both sides of the village were honeycombed with bunkers strongly walled with sandbags and roofed with stone. With flanking heights the Germans could have held out for weeks. They had taken a terrific toll from units attacking frontally and down the valley from the east. But now the Italians held Monte Lungo, to the west, and repeated German counter-attacks had failed to budge the Americans from the crest of Monte Samucro above the town.

So the 15th Panzer Grenadiers became panicky and left six German wounded in the town. A medical-aid sergeant stayed with them. They begged for food and water when the Americans arrived.

The German wounded were evacuated early this morning. As a precaution against a counter-attack, Corporal John Ahrens, of Middle Village, Queens, set up a machine gun at the head of the main street, while medical-aid men went to work. Corporal Peter Vaglia, of 1740 Melville Street, the Bronx, said that one German with a shattered shoulder cursed his comrades for deserting him.

Since the dawn the German guns have been silent and now San Pietro's survivors have emerged from caves and gathered around the Americans. There were about a score of middle-aged men, a few women and children, all very dirty and unkempt, but showing no signs of hysteria. One old man ran behind the medical patrol, pointing toward a collapsed build-ing and mumbling, "Many dead, many dead." But the patrol was concerned with the living.

Near a ruined cathedral two German trucks lay buried be-neath a collapsed wall, and across the street were piles of enemy ammunition in cans. Great vats of water had been stored in one building and in an adjoining house we made a curious discovery. The floor was strewn with letters addressed to an American soldier and on a table was a baseball glove. Evidently the Germans had taken letters from an American prisoner. But the baseball glove was unexplained.

Above the village of Piazza the street narrowed and became nothing more than a steep lane between ghostly shells of houses. Occasionally we found a home with some of the lower rooms well intact. In one, Medical Aid Private Ben-jamin Selleck, of 10 Sunset Road, Bay Shore, L.I., and Private Albert Schempp, of Pittsburgh, were dressing some wounded Italians. One of the natives had retrieved a case of wine from the ruins and toasts were offered to the American victory.

In another house, strongly built and with the lower floor undamaged, we found what apparently had been the enemy's command post. A copy of the "Voelkischer Beobachter" dated Dec. 6 lay on the table. It was the edition published in Posen, indicating that one of the officers recently passed through eastern Germany, probably en route from the Rus-sian front.

Dead mules and pigs lay amid the debris in the eastern sec-tion of the village. Rounding a curve on the edge of the town we found two charred hulks of the only American tanks to reach San Pietro during Wednesday's abortive tank attack. They had been knocked out by German anti-tank guns before they could support the infantry advancing across the valley from the south. Farther up the road were other tanks, dis-abled by mines.

We went back across the fields, reaching the safety of Monte Rotunda, just as the German 88's began shelling San Pietro. At the command post Lieutenant Colonel Aaron Wyatt, of Tarrytown, N.Y., said the battle had been the grim-mest since the Volturno crossing.

The assault was led by Major Landry, of San Antonio, Tex.,

who told us how two sergeants, Nolan Peele, of Robstown, Tex., and Frauston, of El Paso, rounded up remnants of the company's cruelly mauled men in the initial attack and attached them to other companies preparing a new thrust.

"It is awfully hard to try to attack more than once in one night," Landry explained. "The men were desperately tired, and they suffered losses grim enough to demoralize any one.

"All officers were dead or wounded. The German outpost laid low until the Americans were well within the trap, then opened with automatic fire. In the company all officers were killed or wounded. Sergeant Frauston, assuming command, gathered thirty-two survivors and led them back.

"They could have melted into darkness, lying low until dark and then come straggling back to the regiment with the story of how they were cut off without officer leadership in no-man's-land. No one would have blamed them. They had been in the line twenty-seven days.

"Many had 'fox hole feet'—their arches were cracked and swollen from wearing wet shoes for days without a change. Yet such was their morale that they reported to the nearest officer and were ready when the attack was resumed a few hours later."

Wednesday's casualties were so heavy that Captain William Farley, of St. Louis, the regimental surgeon, ran out of litter squads. A call for volunteers brought twenty-five replacements from anti-aircraft and coast artillery units. They included several who had never been to the front.

That night they made two trips into no-man's-land, bringing back wounded, despite snipers and shell fire. Among the volunteers were Private Robert Guertin Manville, of Rhode Island, who had fought the Japanese in Java and the Vichy French in New Caledonia. "I figured some day I'd need the medics, so I joined," he said.

In attempting to cover their withdrawal from San Pietro the Germans threw a final vicious counter-attack against the Americans attacking on the east. Just after dark Thursday night enemy troops swarmed from pillboxes on Monte Samucro's southern slope and struck hard at the right flank of a battalion led by Lieutenant Colonel Howard K. Dodge, of Temple, Tex.

Back at the American command post the regimental commander heard the sudden clatter of small arms fire. Through the telephone he could hear the confused shouting of riflemen trying to stem the assault. He heard one infantryman groan: "My God, when are we going to get artillery support?"

"At first we thought it was merely the usual enemy patrol probing our position and we didn't dare to fire for fear of endangering our men," the colonel said. "But when the firing increased in intensity we ordered a barrage. It came within a few minutes and fell smack where we wanted it. It must have caught a lot of Germans, for we could hear them hollering and moaning in a draw just beyond our lines."

The attack lasted four hours. Three times the Germans tried to crack the American lines. Their last attempt nearly succeeded. Company I, commanded by Lieutenant David R. Fields, was badly chewed up by mortar and machine-gun fire and a break-through was prevented in the nick of time by the arrival of Company E, led by Lieutenant Eben C. Bergman, who quickly organized a stonewall defense. Not one inch of ground was abandoned.

Company K, which shared the brunt of the attack, fought valiantly under the cool leadership of Lieutenant Henry C. Bragaw, of Wilmington, N.C., whose name has been put up for battlefield promotion. Bragaw, a mild-mannered horticulturist with a strawberry-colored handlebar mustache, steadied his men when the weight of the attack shifted from the right to the center and fell furiously against his line.

On his right Bergman's men saw the German wave fall back in disorder. They were too tired to cheer. On the previous afternoon they had supported the abortive tank attack on San Pietro, and their casualties were sore. No sooner did the survivors of the tank attack return than they were pressed back into action to save Company I.

Dawn saw a noticeable lessening of enemy artillery fire. The Americans who had tried to attack San Pietro across an open valley from the south were able to recover their dead and wounded, cut down by machine guns and snipers' bullets Thursday.

A force atop Monte Samucro, commanded by Major David Frazior, of Houston, Tex., advanced and seized the extreme northwestern rim of the crest. Frazior's battalion had beaten off a dozen desperate counter-attacks in five days, leaving the slopes littered with at least 500 dead and wounded Germans. His battalion took forty prisoners.

Outstanding among Frazior's men was Lieutenant Rufus J. Cleghorn, of Waco, Tex., a barrel-chested football player from Baylor University. Exulting in battle, Cleghorn clambered to the highest rock of Samurco's pinnacle and howled insults at the Germans, pausing now and then to toss grenades. For variety, Cleghorn occasionally put his weight against a huge bowlder and sent it rolling down the slope. He roared with laughter as Germans attempted to dodge the hurtling bowlders.

The supply problem was terrific. Every available rifleman was needed in the line, so cooks and clerks donned pack-boards and carried food, clothing and ammunition up the mountain. Each man carried a forty-two-pound can of water, plus two bandoliers of ammunition, mail and Sterno cans. They filled their pockets with hand grenades. Ahead of them was a grueling three-hour climb of an 1,000-foot slope, so steep that the men had to crawl hand over hand up the guide ropes.

Captain William R. Lynch, of Huntsville, Tex., estimated that Frazior's battalion had thrown 2,000 hand grenades—more than a division would expend in a normal combat. They used more than three times the normal amount of mortar shells.

It is very cold these December nights on Samurco's peak, and the uniforms and overcoats issued to the men were none too warm. Yesterday Army cooks carried war combat suits to the troops and a can of Sterno to each man.

New York *Herald Tribune*, December 20, 1943

Over the Lines

by Margaret Bourke-White

"THIS STRIP is really a nerve jerker," Lieutenant Mike Strok called to me over his shoulder.

We were circling above the tiniest airfield I had ever seen. The landing strip was so pocked with shell craters that I did not see how my Grasshopper pilot was going to slip in among them. It was nothing more than the beaten edge of a plowed field, but for the Air OP's, the "Eyes of the Artillery" as they are called in heavy-gun circles, this strip was their most forward operating base.

Lieutenant Strok had to divide his attention between the shell pits below and the sky above. This was because we were landing in the region airmen called Messerschmitt Alley. If an unarmed, unarmored observation plane such as our Cub is attacked, the pilot's means of escape is to outmaneuver the enemy.

"Good idea to make sure there's no Jerry fighter hanging about," said Lieutenant Strok. "If you can see him first, then he doesn't get the chance to blast the daylights out of you."

A final inspection confirmed that the sky was clear, and he brought our tiny Cub to a standstill on a piece of earth as big as a back yard in Brooklyn.

The commanding officer of the field and his ground crew of one ran up to greet us.

The ground crew spoke first. "If that ain't an American girl, then I'm seeing things!" he exclaimed.

The young officer laughed. "Sorry we're out of red carpet," he said. "We live like gypsies up here."

The CO of the Grasshoppers was twenty-six-year-old Captain Jack Marinelli of Ottumwa, Iowa. He was chief pilot and supervisor for a group of artillery liaison pilots who hedge-hopped along the front lines in their Cubs, acting as flying

Margaret Bourke-White, Life Magazine, © Time Warner Inc.

Below us lay the Volturno and ahead stood the mountain barrier, heavy with the menace of German guns. The Cub's job was to hunt them out, and direct with accuracy the fire of our artillery.

observation posts to spot enemy targets and adjust fire for Fifth Army artillery. I had seldom seen a flier who bore less resemblance to Hollywood's idea of a pilot than Captain Marinelli. He looked more like the tractor and hay-machine demonstrator which I learned he had been back in Iowa before the war. He was plump, pleasant, and easygoing. This last characteristic, I was to find, faded as soon as the enemy was in sight. He had the reputation of being the coolest and most resourceful artillery pilot on the Fifth Army front.

Mike Strok explained that I wanted to take airplane pictures of the front, and Captain Marinelli said, "Well, I've just had a call to go out on a mission. There's a *Nebelwerfer* holding up an infantry division and they asked me to go out and try to spot it. She can come along if she wants to."

"Jees, you don't want to take a girl on a mission," said the ground crew of one.

"She'll go if you'll take her," stated Lieutenant Strok.

"What's a *Nebelwerfer*?" I inquired.

"You've heard of a screaming meemie, haven't you? Wicked weapon! It's a multiple mortar: eight-barreled rocket gun."

By the time the screaming meemie was explained to me, I had been strapped into the observer's seat, and the ground crew was adjusting a parachute to my back and shoulders.

Knowing that one of the functions of observer is to watch all quadrants of the sky for enemy planes, I said to the Captain, "I'm not going to make a very good observer for you. Most of the time I'll have my face buried in my camera, and even when I haven't, I'm not sure I'll know the difference between an enemy fighter and one of ours."

"Don't worry about that," Captain Marinelli said. "If you see anything that looks like an airplane, you tell me and I'll decide whether it's a bandit or an angel."

I placed my airplane camera on my knees and arranged additional equipment and a couple of spare cameras, telephoto lenses, and some aerial filters on the low shelf behind my shoulders. The space was so cramped, and any extra movement so pinched, with the parachute crowded on my back, that I wanted to be sure I had everything near at hand where I could reach it in a hurry. There was no room in the Cub to

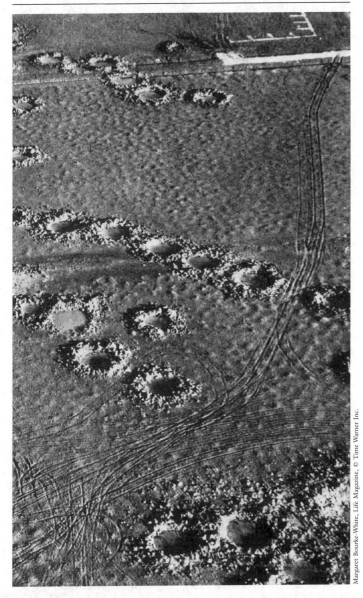

Wherever we flew we found the face of Italy scarred like the face of the moon. This airfield shows the pattern.

wear helmets, as our heads touched the roof. Someone had lent me one of the fur caps used by our Alaska troops, and I tucked my hair back under it and tied it firmly around my chin. When you lean out into the slipstream with an airplane camera, any escaping strand of hair will lash into your eyes and sometimes blind you during just that vital second when you are trying to catch a picture. The Captain lowered the whole right side of the airplane, folding it completely out of the way so I would have an unobstructed area in which to lean out and work. Then he spoke into his microphone. "Mike-Uncle-Charlie! This is Mike-Uncle-Charlie five-zero. I'm taking off on a mission. Stand by!"

"Who is Mike-Uncle-Charlie?" I asked.

"That's our brigade HQ's code word for today," replied the Captain. "Just our phonetic alphabet for MUC—today's call letters. When I find something that radio guy will be sitting up there with his ear phones on, listening."

The ground crew spun the props. "We'll be back in time for lunch," shouted Captain Marinelli to Lieutenant Strok as we started to taxi between the shell craters. I glanced at my watch, which registered quarter after eleven, and couldn't help wondering if we really would be back for lunch. I was trying hard not to wonder whether we would be back at all.

As we headed toward the front I was impressed with how regular the pattern of war, seemingly so chaotic from the ground, appears from the air. The tracks of pattern bombing on an airfield were as regular as though drawn with a ruler and compass. In some olive groves the traffic patterns made by trucks and jeeps which had parked there looked as if a school child had drawn circles in a penmanship exercise, his pen filled not with ink but with a silvery mud-and-water mixture which held the light of the sun. Each bridge had been demolished with a Teutonic precision. The delicate arches of the small bridges were broken through the crest; larger bridges were buckled like giant accordions. Paralleling these were bypasses and emergency bridges which our engineers had thrown up. Most regular of all was German railroad demolition. Between the rails an endless succession of V's marched into the distance, an effect produced by the giant plow which the retreating Germans had dragged from their

Margaret Bourke-White, Life Magazine, © Time Warner Inc.

Below us, always, the tracks of war. Moving in mud, tanks, heavy trucks, artillery could not conceal their footprints.

last railroad train, cracking each tie in two so neatly that it seemed as if someone had unrolled a narrow length of English tweed, flinging this herringbone strip over the hills and valleys of Italy.

The irregularities were furnished by the smashed towns, so wrecked that seldom did two walls stand together, and never was a roof intact. Flying low, sometimes we could see Italian civilians picking through the sickening rubble that once had been their homes.

As we flew over the ghastly wreckage of Mignano and headed toward the still more thoroughly wrecked town of San Pietro, suddenly our plane was jarred so violently that it bounced over on its side, and we heard what sounded like a thunderclap just below.

"That's a shell leaving one of our big hows," Marinelli said as he righted the plane.

"Sounded close," I said.

"I'd hate to tell you how close," Captain Marinelli replied.

"How are you going to know when you get to the front?" I asked.

"Oh, that's easy," he explained. "When you stop seeing stars on things you know you've left your own side behind."

I looked down and saw our jeeps, trucks, and half-trucks crawling along Highway Six below us, each plainly marked with its white star.

"But the best way to tell is by the bridges," he continued. "As long as you see trestle bridges below you know we're over friendly territory, because those are bridges our engineers have built. When you begin spotting blown-out bridges you know we're approaching no man's land. The last thing the Germans do when they pull out is to blow up their bridges, and if they haven't been repaired it's because it's been too hot for our men to get in and mend them.

"When you see a stretch of road with no traffic at all, that's no man's land. And when you see the first bridge intact on the other side, you know you're crossing into Jerry territory."

We were flying over the crest of hills which surrounded Cassino valley like the rim of a cup. Highway Six wound between bald, rocky mountains here, and we almost scraped their razorback edges as we flew over. I could look down and see entrenchments and gun emplacements set in layers of rock. Then the land dropped away sharply, and all at once we were high over Cassino corridor.

As I looked down, the earth seemed to be covered with glistening polka dots—almost as though someone had taken a bolt of gray coin-spotted satin and unrolled it over the landscape. I knew these were shell holes, thousands of them, and made by the guns of both sides, first when we shelled the Germans here, and now by their guns shelling us. As we rose higher I could look down and see hundreds of thousands of these holes filled with rain and glistening in the sun.

"It's been so rough down there," said Captain Marinelli, "that the boys are calling it Purple Heart Valley."

I could hardly believe that so many shells could have fallen in a single valley. It was cruelly contradictory that with all this evidence of bloodshed and destruction, the valley seemed to clothe itself in a sequin-dotted gown.

As we flew on, we glanced back toward our own territory and could see the muzzle flashes from our guns winking on and off as though people were lighting matches over the hillsides. Each gun flash left a smoke trail until our Allied-held hills appeared to be covered with the smoke of countless campfires.

"The worst of that smoke is from our howitzers," Marinelli said.

And then he added, "Usually we don't fly across the lines unless the mission absolutely requires it. But it looks to me as though we're going to have to today, to find that *Nebelwerfer*. O.K. with you?"

"I'm right with you, Captain."

We circled lower over a loop of Highway Six where wrecked tanks were tumbled around the curve of road. "First day they've brought tanks out into the open," said Marinelli. "I want to radio back a report." The tanks seemed to have been picked off one by one as they tried to round the bend, but I could see one tank charging bravely ahead. Then as we bobbed over it, I could see a giant retriever coming in with a derrick to evacuate one of the blasted tanks.

Just beyond we began seeing demolished bridges, and we circled above these also, because the Captain's secondary

Italian villages which died in Purple Heart Valley.

mission was to report on any bridges that had been blown up. He was just phoning back his observations, and I was taking pictures, when suddenly our plane was rocked sharply back and forth and we heard a sound like freight trains rumbling under us.

"Jerry shells," said Marinelli. "High explosives! You know, they've been missing that road junction by a hundred yards every day this week."

We were tossing around violently now, and dark whorls and spirals of greasy smoke were blanketing the ground beneath.

"We've got infantry troops down there," the Captain said. The realization was almost more than I could bear—that our own boys were trying to slog through that fatal square of earth being chewed up by high-explosive shells.

An instant later we were flying over a desolate stretch of road with no traffic at all. This, then, was no man's land. At the farther end we saw a beautifully arched ancient bridge, its masonry quite intact.

"Jerry territory," said the Captain, and took the plane sharply upward.

Over our own side the Cubs make a practice of flying low, because this makes an attack by enemy fighters more difficult, as they cannot come in under; but when the observation planes cross the lines, they must increase altitude, for without armor they are very vulnerable to small-arms fire.

In search of the German rocket gun, we flew four miles over enemy territory and Captain Marinelli began hunting for the *Nebelwerfer* in the region of San Angelo.

"That's the 'Gargling River,'" he pointed out. "GI for Garigliano. And there's the Rapido." The road to Rome stretched forward into the distance, with a railroad running parallel some distance to the left. A hairpin turn branched upward toward the Benedictine monastery, at that time still intact. The ruins of Cassino lay in white smudges at the foot of snowcapped Mt. Cairo.

Cassino corridor presented an extraordinary appearance, with white plumes rising up at intervals from the valley floor. These were phosphorus shells from our own Long Toms, falling on the enemy. Whenever one landed close below us we could see it opening out into a pointed splash of fire, which quickly became transformed into a rising chunk of smoke.

Suddenly I spotted a tiny silhouette in the sky, behind us. "There's a plane," I yelled.

"Just another Cub out on a mission," said Marinelli. "But you did the right thing. Tell me anything you see."

Just then he picked up the flash of the German *Nebel-werfer*—too quick for my untrained eye—and caught sight of the shrubbery blowing back on the ground from the gun blast.

"Mike-Uncle-Charlie," he spoke into his microphone. "This is Mike-Uncle-Charlie five-zero. Enemy gun battery located at co-ordinate 86-16-2. I can observe. Over."

Then to me, over his shoulder, "It's going to take them a little time now, because they've got to compute their data and consult their fire-direction chart to see which guns can reach the target. They'll let me know when they've assigned a battery. We'll be hanging right around here, so speak up if you want to be put into position for anything special."

There were many things that I wanted to be put into position for. Below us it looked as though someone were shaking an enormous popcorn shaker with white grains of popcorn bursting all over the valley floor. These were thickest in front of Cassino. The Captain maneuvered the plane so that I was practically lying on my side over the valley, and—strapped in safely—I could get an unobstructed view of the battleground below.

In a few minutes a message came through that Xray-King-Item would fire. While I took pictures of the popcorn-sprinkled valley, Marinelli carried on his radio conversation with Xray-King-Item, the battery assigned to knock out the *Nebelwerfer*.

I was overwhelmed to learn that it would be my pilot, up in our little Cub, who would actually give the command to fire. The next message he received was, "Mike-Uncle-Charlie five-zero, this is Xray-King-Item. Will fire on your command. Over."

"Fire," said Marinelli, and the reply came back, "Seventy-two seconds. On the way."

It seemed amazing that the shell traveling from the Long Tom battery several miles back of us would take almost a minute and a quarter to reach the enemy gun target below. The Captain was checking with his watch. "Don't want to sense the wrong round," he explained.

He had to make this precise time check because with other guns peppering the valley it was easy to make an error, and it would have caused great confusion had he started correcting the aim of some other gun.

On the seventy-second second, a white geyser began rising toward us from below, and we knew that this was Xray-King-Item's smoke shell. Marinelli spoke into his microphone: "Xray-King-Item; this is Mike-Uncle-Charlie five-zero; five hundred yards right, one hundred yards short. Over."

Then he explained, "We've got to give them a little time again to make their correction. They're laying number-one gun on it now. When they get it adjusted they'll tie in the whole battery."

Soon another message came from Xray-King-Item: seventy-two seconds on the way. Again at the end of seventy-two seconds a feather of smoke rose from below. The aim was closer now: "Five-zero right; seven-zero short," Captain Marinelli radioed.

I realized that the Captain was handling a great many tasks at once. Not only was he checking his watch during each seventy-two-second interval, radioing his sensings in terms of deflection and elevation data, but he was keeping an eye on the sky for enemy planes. And taking care of me, too! Every time I saw a fresh shell burst I would yell to be put in position, and he would maneuver the Cub so that I could photograph while he observed.

Suddenly he exclaimed, "We're being shot at." We could hear faint sounds as though twigs were snapping against the plane—a little like hot grease spitting in a frying pan just beyond us. "It's a Spandau," said Marinelli, and he knew exactly what to do. Since the Spandau, a German machine gun, has an effective range up to 2400 feet, he simply circled up to 3200 feet, where he went on making his observations and I went on taking photographs.

"Hands cold?" he called.

They were almost numb. At our higher altitude the air was colder and I had been leaning out into the windstream with the camera. The Captain, more protected by the nose of the Cub, stripped off his gloves and gave them to me.

The whole process of adjusting fire had gone on for about fourteen minutes when Captain Marinelli finally radioed, "Deflection correct, range correct. Fire for effect."

"They're bringing in several batteries this time," said the Captain. "And this time it will be HE shells."

At the end of seventy-two seconds we could see that whole area being blanketed, not with white smoke bursts as before, but with the deadlier high-explosive shells. Curls and twists of black smoke spurted over the ground and billowed upward, and we knew that the *Nebelwerfer* was being chewed to bits.

"This is Mike-Uncle-Charlie five-zero," called Captain Marinelli. "Target area completely covered. Fire effective. Enemy battery neutralized."

Less than a minute later he exclaimed, "I see a fighter." Then, "I see two fighters."

Coming around Mt. Cevaro I could see them too: a black speck growing larger and behind it another smaller speck. In less time than it takes to tell, they had taken on the size and shape of airplanes.

We were in such a steep dive by that time that I was practically standing on my head, when I heard Marinelli say, "I see four fighters."

Sure enough, there were four shapes coming toward us, looking unmistakably like Focke-Wulf 190's.

This was the steepest dive I had ever been in in my life. I tried to take a picture, a plan I very quickly had to abandon because, with the whole side of the plane completely open, and the shelf behind me full of cameras and lenses, it was all I could do to hold back my equipment with my elbows and shoulders, to keep it from sailing into space.

I was bracing myself with the back of my neck when Captain Marinelli exclaimed, "I've lost my mike. Can you find my mike for me?" I knew he needed his microphone so he could report the fighters as a warning to all the other Cubs in the air. Groping with my left hand, and holding back my cameras with my right elbow, I retrieved his mike and handed it to him. We were still gliding down at a terrific angle when he reported, "Four enemy fighters sighted."

We were within fifteen feet of the ground when he pulled out of that dive. I have never seen such flying. He ducked into a gully and began snaking along a stream bed. Soon we were behind a small hill and over our own territory, where the fighters could not follow us in so low. In another instant we were behind a mountain and blocked from sight of the enemy planes.

We flew back to our field in time for mess, and when we rolled into the tiny landing strip, the ground crew came running up, bursting with news. To Captain Marinelli this news was much more exciting than being chased by four Focke-Wulfs: there was steak for lunch.

They Call It "Purple Heart Valley," 1944

Christmas on New Guinea

by Vincent Tubbs

SOMEWHERE IN NEW GUINEA—(By Cable, Censored)—
The singing was as crude as a child's copy of Whistler's
"Mother" because work-toughened GI's found it hard to get
into the right frame of mind for carols.

But it was sincere—as sincere as the unexpressed wish in
each man's heart that this thing will soon be over.

Women on the scene served to temper the usual boisterous
New Guinea atmosphere. Their arrival earlier in the week was
the best collective gift anyone could have given these men.

Perspiration poured off everyone in little rivulets. The room
was stuffy. Outside, the screened windows were crowded with
men, peering through like scolded children not allowed to go
and play.

"Joy to the World, the Lord Is Come," they sang, and
when they had finished, Sgt. Clyde Montgomery of Selma,
Ala., read the Christmas story from a tiny Bible sent him
through this correspondent by a church group in Ohio.

Cpl. Andrew Burleigh, Carnegie, Pa., played a saxophone
solo; Hubert Jackson, club head, made a talk; a soldiers' chorus sang "O Come All Ye Faithful."

There was the hanging of the green, the singing of "Silent
Night," prayer by the base chaplain and the boys went home.
That was Christmas at the Club Papuan.

In the area of an engineer regiment, at 1 minute past twelve
on Christmas morning, hundreds of colored and white Yanks
and even more Aussies filed into an outdoor theatre. Each
man held a tiny white lighted candle in his hand.

As one approached, the scene was the sort that makes cold
chills dance up your spine, your flesh tingle, and your heart
glad, for here, under a Blue Pacific Sky, was true Christian
Democracy in action.

All sang "Joy to the World." Pvt. Joseph Bickers of Atlanta sang "The Lord's Prayer," Chaplain Jason Cowan read the scripture—the second time in twenty-four hours that the words ending the Christmas, "Peace on Earth, Good Will to All Men."

Pvt. William Jones of Atlanta, director of the chorus, sang "Ave Maria." In the middle of his song we were reminded that there is still a war going on.

A horn tooted three times. Six soldiers snuffed their candles and moved stealthily away from the gathering. They had other duties to perform more urgent at the time than the supplication they sought to offer their God.

The orchestra moved into seats. A soldier on the front row said, "Come on, give us 'Tuxedo Junction'." The chaplain eyed him into ignoble submission.

Orchestra, chorus and Clara Wells rendered "O Holy Night," someone pronounced the benediction, reminded us it was now Christmas Day, and asked that we try just for the day to feel peaceful toward all men, for then we should be approaching the Kingdom of God.

By signal the candles were doused. Only the moon cast a ray into the pitch black night in this place which for the past hour had been our Cathedral.

In the day room of a port outfit, later in the day, rain played a faint tattoo on the roof as T/Sgt. Jacob Austin spoke the call to worship.

In order the packed room heard selections by Squire Graham, S/Sgt. Steven Taylor, T/4th Leonard Howell, Cpl. William Madden, Pvts. Sampson Pruitt, Chester Gates, James E. Brown; a sermon by Chaplain Darneal Johnson of Washington, a song by the American Red Cross Ensemble and Nola Cox, Norma Manly, Rosa Spears, Laura Anderson and Clara Wells, with Harvey Shaw as pianist.

That is how your soldiers in one part of New Guinea worshipped.

The day itself began with a mist on it and the thermometer at 103 degrees. Then the mist condensed into torrents of rain that washed away a part of one of the main roads.

Some soldiers worked through the day; other soldiers and

officers who had hung socks the night before found them containing the world's greatest variety of things next morning.

There was no lunch, but at 4 p.m. there was turkey, surrounded with accessories fit for a king. Later the enlisted men sought out their favorite officers and laid before them the spirits of the yule.

With inhibitions gone, reminiscenses set in. A showman recalled how he used to take his girl gifts in ankle-deep snow. Before he had finished he had to be rolled into bed. Someone played a clarinet and made the room hospital quiet with "I've Got It Bad and that Ain't Good."

Far into the night and the early morning this went on in some sectors; in others men just talked, some prayed, some sang.

This correspondent was nearly drowned visiting different outfits, where he found many hearts full and many burly men on the verge of tears, but nobody really cried. They, like everyone else in New Guinea, made the best of a bad situation.

In the chorus and orchestra appearing on one of the programs were:

Sgts. Harry Murray, 149 S Street, Northwest, Washington; Charles Ackers, Bessemer, N.C.; Leonard Reese, Meridian, Miss.; John Harris, Birmingham; Clinton Woodard, Detroit; Maurice Reynolds, Pittsburgh; Wilbur Wilson, 2127 E. Williams Street, Philadelphia;

Cpls. Charles Elmo, Alexanderia, La.; Willie Reynolds, Brooklyn, N.Y.; Otis Johnson, Atlanta; William Hubbard, New Orleans; Arthur Thompson, Birmingham;

Pfcs. Fred Jons, Troy, Ala.; Steve Smith, Newport, Tenn.; John Shafer, New Orleans; Pvts. John Quarrels, Nashville; Square Wilbourne, Memphis; Joe Barton, Monessen, Pa.; Arthur Dubose, Birmingham; Jesse Tarrent, NYC; George Lowry, Alton, Ill.; Oliver Evans, NYC.

Baltimore Afro-American, January 1, 1944

"Tired of Winter Tired of War"

by Gertrude Stein

THE OWNER of the local drugstore is what they call a collabo, that is one who wanted to collaborate with the Germans, there were quite a few of them and they are getting less and less but there still are some and he is one. A German said a nice thing about that. It was in Paris and it was over a year ago it was in the beginning of '42 and he was talking to a group of French people who had met about some question of protecting French works of art, and he said the French are a pleasant people and I like them but they none of them have three qualities they only have two. They are either honest and intelligent, they are either collabo and intelligent or they are collabo and honest but I have never met one who was collabo honest and intelligent, everybody laughed and it is true there is no such thing as being collabo honest and intelligent. Well the drug store man was collabo and honest but certainly not intelligent. He had already been sent a coffin and other attentions and the other day the Germans went to his house to make a search. Of course he was terribly upset. Apparently some one to tease him sent an anonymous accusation against him to the German authorities giving the detail of explosives that he had concealed in his premises. As they always investigate these accusations and as naturally they do not know the local political opinions they examine which is natural enough. The unfortunate man went to complain to the gendarmerie, and of course they told everybody and everybody roared with laughter finding it an exceedingly good joke, on all of them.

Around here it is getting to be just like Robin Hood. The young men in the mountains come down, they they took two tons of butter from a dairy and the other day to the delight of everybody they took a pig weighing one hundred and fifty kilos, he had two small ones and they told him to fatten them up and they would take one and leave the other, they took this from the local aristocrat who had been highly unpopular because of his political opinions and because having been a poor man and been put at the head of the local food distribution, he had only given supplies to those who had his political opinions, and they took his automobile from him, saying that he could go to mass on foot the way the rest of the world did and as he had no more food to distribute he did not need it, they also took eight hundred litres of eau de vie, which he had on hand, and as everybody says as they always pay the government prices for everything they take nobody has any cause for complaint. Everybody is excited and pleased, the young men are so young so gay so disciplined and they have so much money, presumably English and American gold and everybody is pleased, naturally enough, as nobody can stop them everybody takes it to mean that it is the beginning of the end of course all except the collabo who say they are gangsters and what will happen after the war. Everybody says the war will go on forever but in spite of that everybody does think that the war is closing in which it is the end of January forty-four.

Everybody wanders and it is interesting to know how much they wandered even before.

I was talking to two young workmen, they had gone twenty kilometers for provisions and I had gone twelve and they walked along quickly and I walked with them and they told me their own and their families' history, at least one did, the other only came along.

He was all alone he said, and he did his own cooking. He was a good cook he said, he had even cooked in a restaurant, he had been in the army in Algeria and he had had leave to come back to France to see his family and the day he was to go back the Americans arrived in Africa and so here he was all alone. To be sure his father had been born in Italy in Bergamo and so had he, his father had come to France to earn a living and then had brought his family with him, and he this boy was six years old then and so he too had been born in Italy. He had seen while he was doing his military service the lovely cathedral of Albi he knew it was beautiful although he had never been inside it and now he was all alone. And have you no brothers and sisters, I don't know where my brothers are and I have a sister married in Italy, to an Italian I asked, no he said to an American, South American I said, this I do not know he said and I have never heard from her since my mother died and I am all alone, and not married I said, no he said I am only twenty-eight and one should not marry before one is thirty, a cousin of my father he said, made a fortune in America, where I said, ah that I do not know, he said, and then we said good-bye and parted.

Workmen have always wandered, just as they did in the middle ages, they wander until they marry and then some of them begin to wander again. In the last war we had a Negro wounded man whose name was Hannibal and he said that he had been a great wanderer he had wandered all over Staten Island, well here in Europe they are just wanderers, they wander all over Europe, and very often they end up all alone very often. And now there is war, and they wander so much that they seem to be not moving at all, not anywhere at all.

I was talking to a woman the other day we were both walking carrying our baskets and intending to bring home something, and she told me of her two brothers and her husband who had all three escaped before the prisoners were taken to Germany, she said some families suffered so much and some not at all, she said it was fate. She herself had five children four of them girls. That too does happen very frequently in this country we both agreed. And then we got talking about the strange thing, that so many of the comparatively few Frenchmen killed in this war were only sons of widows whose husbands had fallen in the last war. Why I said. Well she said, it is probably because they went into the war more worried than those whose fathers had not been killed in the last war. It could be that. And she said might it not be that being raised by a widow they would naturally be more spoilt and not so active as those raised by father and mother. Naturally she said, a mother can never really dominate a son, a mother is bound to spoil children because she is with them all the time and she cannot always be saying no so she ends up by not saying no at all. And besides she said, if a mother had lost her husband in the war her little boy had been impressed by her crying so much and that would make him nervous, when he too had gone to war. It certainly is true that a very considerable percentage of the relatively few Frenchmen killed in this war were the only sons of widowed mothers who had had their husbands killed in the last war.

To-night Francis Malherbe who had been sent to Germany to work came to see us just back and very interesting, January nineteenth forty-four. One of the things he said was that in Paris he had come home that way they all said that there would be a landing on the twentieth of January. Of course everybody supposed it was going to be in France, and at the same time we had word that the man who always knows what the Germans expect to happen said that there was to be a landing between the sixteenth and the twentieth of January forty-four and he always knows what they know and so we were quite excited and there was a landing only it was in Italy instead of in France. Pretty good deception that, because and that must never be forgotten people do know what is going to happen and so far the Americans have been pretty good at it, twice we have known it was going to happen and the right date and everything but not the right place. We are very pleased with our countrymen, it is a good poker game. Very good indeed and we like them to play poker well. It pleases us.

However that was not all that Francis Malherbe told us. He described Germany the way it is now and the way the French who are compulsorily working there are. He gave such a good description, he said of course there was no food no fat, and the cooking of vegetables always in water, the German work-men were given fats but not the Frenchmen, but I said is there no black market no way of getting any, oh yes he said plenty of that among all the foreign workmen but never with the Germans, but I said where do the foreign workmen get it, how do they get it, they steal it, he said, each one who can steals a certain quantity of something and sells it or trades it with others for something else, and that is all the black market there is but and he laughed it is considerable, and we said how do they the Germans feel, still convinced of victory espe-cially the young, he said but why should they not the world is made for the young, the fifteen year old boys have older men get up in the street cars to give them seats, naturally they are convinced that they will win, if you have such a position in the world as that at fifteen of course you are bound to win. And really we said really he said they certainly can hold out six months longer, certainly. My brother he said he is a military prisoner a lieutenant, and as I was what they call the man of trust, that is to say I had to judge and patch up the incessant quarrels between French and German workers they gave me leave to go and see my brother. He had been a prisoner for four years and of course I had not seen him and now I saw him. He came in with two soldiers with guns and fixed bayonets at his back and it upset me so I began to cry but he said to me sternly control yourself do not show emotion, and we sat down at a table together and we talked and we compared photographs those he had of the family and those I had with me, and the adjutant who was there to listen to us said suddenly he is giving you photographs, how dare you said my brother accuse me of such a thing, apologise I insist that you apologise, first examine these photographs and then apologise, and the man said but it is all right, no said my brother look, look at them count them and examine them and then apologise, which the adjutant had to do. I was proud of my brother. When he told us this we were of course much moved, it was so real so normal, like a piece out of Dumas and yet happening, happening to a boy we knew very well and are very fond of, and then he went on describing, and telling about the different nationalities with which he was working and making it all real and the Russians he said, they are the most interesting, we Frenchmen get along better with them than with any others except Frenchmen, and they do impress us with their courage and their tenacity and the simple way they say naturally we expect to occupy this country and when we do and we think we will, we will make them very unhappy. And so he talked on and then he had to leave and he has to go back and he has to go back because he has two officer brothers as prisoners and something might happen to them if he did not and so he will go back. We hope to have him back again we are very very fond of him. He is a nice neighbor.

These days everybody hears from their sons or their nephews who are working there, one who really was too small and too weak to go but go he did, his father had been in the navy and then had been in a garage as electrician and we had liked

him and when the French were defeated the shock killed him
he could not believe it and this only son writes to his mother
dear mother I am hungry, I was never hungry before but I am
hungry now always hungry so hungry. And then there is a
nephew of some one here we know he is an intelligent fellow
a designer of machines, and he writes that he is in the capital
and that the sky is sad, it is a cold sad sky, and he plays the
violin and draws a little and hopes not very much but a little
as most of his compatriots have been killed in a bombardment, and so every day is another day which passes in that
way.

Yesterday I went my usual twelve kilometers to get some
bread and cake and I met three or four who were on a farm
wagon being drawn by a mule and they said come and sit, and
I said can the mule stand one more, why not they said and I
sat it was very comfortable. Basket the white poodle was completely upset but finally he decided to follow along and we
jogged along and it was a pleasant day although it was January and I said you know you French people you can make a
pleasant thing out of anything, but we are not rich like the
Americans no I said but you can go on working the kind of
working you do until you are ninety or a hundred and you
complain but any day is a pleasant enough day which it is not
in every other country, and they said perhaps but they would
like to be rich like the Americans and then we were on the
top of the hill and I went to get my bread and cake and they
went on to get their flour and it was a pleasant day.

The young ones who come back from Germany on leave
are puzzled by one thing, any Frenchman would be why are
the Germans so sentimental, when they are what they are why
are they so sentimental. No Frenchman can understand that.

Yesterday I was out walking and I met a man I used to
know, a casual country acquaintance, that is to say he and his
family were cousins of some very old friends of ours, and they
own a place around here, they used to be here for only a few
weeks in the summer but now, things being as they are, they
live here altogether. The father is a big gay man about town,
who has lots of property is a good business man and used to
spend all his life between here and other places and the Cote
d'Azur. His wife was born in Washington U.S.A. her father

having been in the French embassy and he is an amusing man, of course he says we live here now, the country is lovely in winter, I never saw it before but it is, it is like English pastels such a delicate color, and besides we all get all we want to eat, dont you, and I agreed that we did, as much of everything that we want, butter eggs meat cake and cheese, and I had to agree that we all did because we all do. Just why we do now when the years before we did not nobody seems to be able to explain but we do, is it because the army of occupation is getting smaller and smaller or is it, that everybody knows how now better and better, anyway it is undoubtedly true every- where in France now, everywhere and nobody seems to know quite why. Well anyway, the other day I met him M. Labadie, he saw Basket and he waited for us he was on his bicycle and I was on foot, and we stopped to talk together. I thought he had very funny clothes on and when I came nearer I said to him these are funny clothes that you are wearing what are they. Ah he said you would never guess look at the buttons and I did, they were large American army buttons with the eagle and the shield, nice brass buttons on a khaki coat and I said when in the name of wonder did you get that. Ah he said I bought it after the other war from the American stocks and I kept it here in the country and now it is very handy, and it was, some German soldiers on patrol had just passed but M. Labadie did not mind that, you know he said everybody wants to buy one off me, look he said counting them there are twelve of them, quite a little fortune, just to-day again they offered me forty francs for one, but not I, I keep them and wear them. Well we went on talking and I said your boy who is twenty-one, has he gone, oh dear no, he said, you see I keep him traveling, that is the way you do you either go off to some little bit of a place and stay there quietly and nobody bothers you or you keep moving, now I keep my boy moving, I have lots of business to attend to, and I send him around to attend to it, and if you keep on traveling for business your papers all always have to be in order which of course they are so no one bothers, that is the way he said, and of course he is right that is the way. And then we went on talking. We talked about the war, why not since there is this war. He said of course the Germans cannot win, which is natural enough because their country is so poor they know nothing about cooking and eating, people who know nothing about cooking and eating naturally cannot win. He went on reflectively, France always seems to be beaten but really a country that can see and shut one eye and then shut the other eye opening the first eye, is bound to come out of any mess not too badly, you see he went on meditatively, one must take care of oneself and be brave and be excited and at the same time must take care of one's business must not be poor. War said he is inevitably connected with money and naturally when two people want the same money or more money they must fight, and he said reflectively nowadays when one wants to spend so much money when everybody wants automobiles and electrical installations and everything else well naturally the more money everybody wants to spend the more men have to be killed when it comes to a war. People who spend little money when they make war kill few people, but the more money you want to spend, the more men you have to kill when you begin to go to war. And there is another thing if you can really spend the most money then you have less of your own men killed than the other side who wants to spend more money but has not got it to spend. And so America has less men killed and Germany more and that he said is natural enough. And just then another man whom we both knew was coming along, now said M. Labadie he is a poor thing an unfortunate man, he has a wife but one never sees her she is always away and a forsaken man and he shrugged his shoulders and we each of us went on our way.

To-day was another day, as usual in France feeling gets more and more complicated, and now when those who have taken to the hills come down and take food off the railways, well will it get them in the habit of stealing and should it, and they all worry, and there was one woman who was visiting and she quarreled with every one in Culoz, and when she left she said they needed the Germans to come to whip them into subjugation, and some one said and she an idler who has money what does she think will happen to her. Well anyway one thing is certain every day brings the war nearer and nearer to an ending but does any one around here believe that, certainly not, so little do they believe it that although we know it we do not really believe it ourselves. As one woman said well now as we have all made all our arrangements to live in a state of war I suppose the war will go on. We all suppose it will and it does this the first day of February in nineteen forty-four.

I have just been listening to a description of how the mountain boys captured two Germans and took them to the mountains as hostages and now the Germans even when they want to buy a piece of bread in a store they are all armed and always at least six of them and one standing outside as a guard for them. It makes everybody laugh. Every tenth birthday makes a man afraid and a woman too and even children every tenth birthday does that. Be careful everybody.

Everybody is feeling a little more cheerful about everything to-day even though it is a dark and gloomy day.

Breathes there a man with soul so dead who never to him-self has said, this is my own my native land.

Well yes, yesterday when the Swiss radio announced that the Americans had landed on the Marshall Islands and that these islands had belonged to Japan before the war I was so pleased. It was midnight and I was so pleased. As an Ameri-can and as a Californian I was so pleased. I went up stairs and woke up Alice Toklas who was asleep, and I said we have landed the Americans have landed on the Marshall Islands, which before the war belonged to Japan and Alice Toklas opened one eye slightly and said, well then they are invaded, and slept gently again. Of course that is what every one wants them to be that they are invaded, when that does come to pass it will be a comfort to every one, yes every one but them and they do not want at least their feelings are of no account no account. So that made this day a nice day. Otherwise not such a nice day because they are trying to take younger and younger men away to work but mostly they do not go this is undoubtedly so.

And then to-day when they said, that is to say the announc-ers said that the Marshall Islands were on the way to the Phil-ippines, it did make all one's youth come back the days when we saw the American soldiers preparing in San Francisco to go that way. They were more unformed than they are now, their character is more affirmed it was more so in the world

war than in the Spanish-American war and now we have not
seen them but we hear them they are as simply direct as they
were then but not so unbaked, the national security is undoubtedly stronger, we are hoping to see them soon, yes we
are. To-day we were in Belley my birthday the third of February and of course everybody was upset most horribly because
there is preparing an effort to round up the mountain boys
and as everybody's boys are there it is rather horrible. One of
the Bilignin women cried to me what can I do, my boy was
always so fond of you what can I do, and what can she do
with a nineteen year old boy, go or not go, stay or not stay,
go away or not go away, who can say. Who can. I said the
only thing I can advise is to do nothing, just now it is the
only thing to do and mostly it does succeed, do nothing but
he wont eat, and he got up at four in the morning to work
because he says if I have to leave I will have as much work
done for you as possible dear me. Our Swiss grocer he is a
nice man, he has three sons but as he says they just did not
give him his naturalisation papers before this war and now
they are all Swiss and so comparatively safe and all the same
he said to me, they must come the Americans must come and
they must come soon to save the boys to save the boys, oh yes
to save the boys. Everybody is unhappy and ashamed,
ashamed because French are arresting Frenchmen, the taxi-
man said the other day, three of the guard mobile who are
going up to the mountains missed their train and they asked
him to drive them. For you personally he said or by order, no
they said there is no order, well he said if I take you, you who
are going to shoot up our boys, if I take you you will have to
pay for it, and they asked me how much, and I said double
the ordinary fare, and pay they did, the pigs who are going to
shoot up our boys. Everybody is ashamed, everybody is crying, everybody is listening to everything and the trains go on,
with Germans who are not Germans and French who are not
French, oh dear me, there is no nineteenth century about
this, hardly the twentieth century, it is terribly the middle
ages, and in the meantime Alice Toklas came along with six
lemons, that seems nothing but for years there have been no
lemons, and there were a few while the Italians were here, and

since these have gone none. Where said I did you get them. From the grocer she said, and where did he get them, he said he had them because there had been a wedding in Tunis.

What that meant nobody can know, of course there has been no communication of any kind with Tunis since the Americans landed there, so what did he mean. Of course one never asks anybody what he means.

We get more and more excited about the Marshall Islands and being on the way to the Philippines, we cannot help wondering how the American commentator can speak so quietly about all that, shows he is no Californian, for us all of it is passionately interesting, Alice Toklas remembers the man who was second in command with Leahy who took possession of Guam coming back from Manila. They liked that island so they thought they would take possession, and as they had never taken possession of anything before they did not know how, and two of the native girls fell in love with Leahy and as he was reading the preamble to the constitution which he thought was the right way to take possession the two girls right in front began biting each other and as Leahy finished the constitution his second in command Spear hit him on the shoulder and pointing to the girls said you're it. Well anyway it is all real to us here in a little town in France and everybody fighting. And then there was the young boy Ned Hanford that Alice Toklas knew then and he had volunteered and had become an orderly to General King who afterward wrote novels about it and in one he said and I threw my bridle to my orderly Ned Hanford, well everybody was a hero then and everybody is a hero now only none of it was sad then and it all is pretty sad now and just here, just here now. It is sad when at nineteen and twenty you have to decide for yourself, shall you betake yourself to the mountains, shall you stay at home and risk it, shall you go to Germany and hate it and perhaps be bombed working for your country's enemies and shall you what shall you what can you do, what will you do, it is hard at eighteen or nineteen to have to decide all these things for yourself, each one for himself, in a war it is comparatively easy, you are drafted you go you are with a crowd and you are all more or less of an age and you are all together and even if it hurts it is not so bad, but now these French boys have to decide each one all alone by himself which has he strength for, has he people to whom he can go, will he get there, can he be fed, and all the rest, and the winter and the mountains and will he find any one, and if he has not gone what will happen, it is hard at nineteen and twenty for each one to decide things like that for himself. Very hard.

We are in the very thick of it now, rumors and rumors but some of them are true, they have suppressed the use of the telephone all through the region, nobody can go anywhere without very special leave and just to-night we have heard that the captain of the gendarmerie and our very good friend and the father of the most charming little girl, who has a charming curl in the middle of her forehead and a very sweet and attractive wife has just been carried off, whether by the mountain boys whether by the Germans nobody seems to know and we are most awfully upset, everybody is trembling lest anybody is taken as hostage and if they are dear me if they are. Whether it is to put down the mountain boys whether it is because a German colonel has been killed whether it is because they are afraid of a landing whether it is because they expect to retreat into this country out of Italy whether it is because they do not know what to do, whether it is because it is coming to an end and an end has to be like the end at the theatre when the piece comes to an end a state of confusion, whatever it is our good and gentle friend has been taken and we are very sad.

In the nineteenth century we all became accustomed to permanence. Permanence was natural and necessary and continuous. Permanence and progress were synonymous, that seems strange but of course it is natural enough. If things are permanent you can believe in progress if things are not permanent progress is not possible and so the nineteenth century believed in progress and permanence, permanence and progress. And now. Well now there is neither the one or the other. England and Germany who strangely enough are more nineteenth century even yet than any other part of the globe do still hope to believe in permanence and progress, progress and permanency, but nobody else does and nobody else is interested in their believing in progress and in permanency, nobody else.

In these days January forty-four, here where we are, we are once more as we were in nineteen forty—we have the terror of the Germans all about us, we have no telephone, we hear stories and do not know whether they are true, we do not know what is happening to our friends in Belley, except for the life of this village of Culoz we seem separated from everything, we have our dog, we have the radio, we have electricity, we have plenty to eat, and we are comfortable but we are completely isolated and rumor follows rumor, and on the road for the first time now in two years we meet automobiles with German officers, motor bicycles with Germans on them going by quickly quickly, and at the station are long trains of railroad trucks marked Italy, and Munich and Breslau, and we none of us know why, why this little corner of France which is so very peaceable should be harassed. In the newspapers they say it is Savoy but actually it is not, in Savoy they can telephone they are peacefully left alone and here one little town and another little town is surrounded and the principal inhabitants are taken away and nobody knows why, nobody can think of any reason for it, what is the reason for it, nobody knows, and those who do it, naturally do not say so that makes it that nobody knows. Why. Nobody knows. The young men are getting restless, they stand around and laugh and their fathers and their mothers are very nervous, but the young men just stand around and watch them go by, and they laugh, they laugh at them, and it does seem as if it were not they that are being sought, but others and older and why. Nobody does know why. Nobody can go in and out of Belley, such an innocent town, and for so long there has been a German garrison there, learning its military lessons, and nobody interfered with them and they did not interfere with any one and now they came and surrounded the town and took fifty men away and nobody knows why, nobody knows.

As I say everybody feels as if it was like the beginning of the invasion in forty, but then it was a beginning a long beginning and a very long middle and now everybody feels that it is an ending and the French have always felt that a wounded beast is always worst when it is cornered, and the winter has been pleasant and long and now it is snowing and dreary and everybody feels it so except the young boys who are up and down on their bicycles on their feet all day long and they stand and laugh as the others go past. Everybody else feels like crying but not they, and so it is to-day.

And so it is to-day. Yesterday I went to see the mayor and the mayoress of our little town and we talked about everything. Naturally she is very nervous. These days, nobody knows why the Germans surround a town take the mayor prisoner and sometimes they let him go and sometimes they do not. So naturally the mayor's wife is nervous, the mayor too a little but he does not say so. The mayor's wife does. And they have been doing all this to the towns around here and about and will they do so here.

Here they are. Our neighbor a nice old maid who lives alone in a little house and has plenty of land and has plenty of everything and is sometimes double faced and can be called a viper by our cook but mostly is very kind and nice. She came in to say that they had come. They knocked at her door, she was not dressed yet and she called out what is it and they said it was the German army so in fear and trembling she opened the door and they said are there any men here and she said no, and they said honestly and she said yes honestly there are no men here, and they said pointing to our house are there any men there, and she said no two ladies and two servants all women, and they said honestly and she said yes honestly there are only four women there and then they went away. Later in the day naturally we did not go out but later in the day I saw her going out to look every time any soldier went up or down the steep mountain road, and I said what's the news, and she said I am so scared, well why said Alice Toklas if you are so scared do you go out to look. I go out to look she said because I am so scared.

Then later the boy that carries our wood up-stairs three times a week came in. He was very sad, his father who is an Italian has been taken and is being sent to Germany, but said I he is more than forty-five, yes I know said he sadly but although he has always lived in France he is an Italian and they have taken him. They are still here the Germans and Basket our dog has gone out for the evening it worries us but we expect he will come back again. Although you never can tell with soldiers, they like dogs and he is a very pretty one.

And nobody knows why they are here nor how long they will
stay, and no one can come in to the town and no one can go
out not even the priest, and nobody knows why, all this country is so peaceful. Of course there are a great many young
men who have not gone to Germany who have been called
but that is all yes dear me that is all. To be sure those who go
up into the mountain and do behave a good deal like Robin
Hood, they carry off a doctor and his wife and all their possessions, so that the doctor can take care of them and his wife
take care of him, and his possessions so that nobody takes
them away to punish him. They are careful to choose a doctor
who has no children. Everybody says and that too does sound
so like the middle ages, we are between two armed forces, the
mountain boys shoot if you do not do what they say, and the
Germans shoot if you do not do what they say, and what can
you do, each side blames us if we do what the other side tells
us to do but what can we do. And indeed what can they do.
Anyway it goes on and it goes on just like that. And how
many have been caught, here and in Belley, oh dear we do
not know, everybody says something but nobody knows.

It is funny why do the Germans wear camouflaged raincoats but not camouflaged uniforms now why do they. The
first I saw was the other day, they went by on bicycles, and
they reminded me of the chorus of the Tivoli Opera House in
San Francisco, it used to cost twenty-five cents and the men
in mediaeval costume looked so like these camouflaged coats,
with sort of keys and crosses on them in contrasted colors.
Oh dear. It would all be so funny if it were not so terrifying
and so sad, this in January forty-four.

Ma foi it's long is what they say. Everybody in the country
in France says ma foi, a nice mediaeval expression, you say
anything to them and they say ma foi, that can mean yes or
oh hell, or no, or just nothing. At present any of them can
say, it's long, and the answer is ma foi, which also means to
be sure. In this particular part of the world they have another
thing, they say taisez-vous, or shut up, or shut it, and they say
it as they are talking, they are talking along about something
and they say, oh shut it, and it is not to themselves, nor to
you, it is of the facts of which they are speaking, sometimes
they say taisez-vous, taisez-vous, and the sentence goes on, it

is rather delightful, I do not quite know why, they may say and the war is long and the Germans might be coming this way again oh shut up oh shut up and do you think it is possible that they will. This is a kind of a sentence it makes, and it is enjoyable. Ma foi.

And now once more the telephone is working and we can see people and the roads are open and the Germans are gone from the village and everybody is breathing a little more freely not entirely so but a little so, although some few unpleasant things did happen, oh dear me. Everybody looks at their neighbors and says oh dear me or ma foi, and anyway everybody is relieved. Nobody knows what it is all about excepting that it is to find out who is supplying the mountain boys with food. So many strange things the curfew at seven o'clock instead of ten o'clock, two young fellows who had sling shots and had themselves taken away, one young fellow who tried to run away was shot, and one old man who was drunk and out at ten o'clock was killed, and as it was very bad weather, snow and sleet and wind the rest of them stayed at home, it is so difficult to make a French population realise that it is dangerous not to do as they are told, they like to do what they like, and they do. As one Frenchman said to me in France a civilian is always more important than a policeman unless he happens to be a criminal, but just any civilian is always more important than just any policeman. This is ingrained in every Frenchman and so it is almost impossible to make them do what they are told. Such strange things happen, a funny little man who was known as being a collaborator and had even gotten a coffin, the kind they send to them, had all his things taken by the Germans, it seems that his father in days long gone was a receiver of stolen goods, naturally enough as this town has always been an important railroad junction a small town but an important railroad junction, and his son, well perhaps he did not receive stolen goods, but he had stores of forbidden provisions here there and anywhere, and among them some very ancient fire-arms from the revolution, or Napoleon collected by his father and somebody mentioned them and the Germans went to look for them and they found them and so naturally they took away all the soap and iron and wine and spirits that were there too naturally enough, and he the little man was away and they have given him three days to give himself up, but where is he and does he know, and how can he or anybody else know why they went to him. There are also an elderly man and his sister, here, and it has just been told us that their father who had been a railroad worker, once stole precious jewels and tried to sell them in Geneva and was given five years prison and the son and daughter now quite old were never married and they live together, and the son for all that was employed by the railroad, he still is as a night guard, and she after a long life of domestic service has stomach ulcers, and anyway these stories did distract our minds from anxiety and the distresses of one of our neighbors whose son was finally killed in trying to run away. To-day now that it is all over everybody went to the funerals of every one who had been killed, and now to-day it was Sunday and the sun shone and the snow was on the ground and the whole population were out skiing and sledding and the mayor was tired and so was his wife, and with reason, it is no fun being a mayor these days. The mayor finally persuaded the Germans that there were no mountain boys in the mountain back of us because as he explained there is no water there. In the days when he used to go hunting we always had to carry a flask of water to refresh the dogs with because the dog could not find any water there so how could men stay there. No it is not possible, and finally the Germans were convinced and they left. They left. And the telephone goes again, and the people can move around the streets again, and I can let the dog out again the dog Basket and we can go walking again and the snow is beginning to melt, and to-day is Monday in February nineteen forty-four.

Tired of winter tired of war but anyway they do hope and pray that it will end some day.

Wars I Have Seen, 1945

I Love Mountain Warfare

by Walter Bernstein

THERE is a nice sound to the phrase "mountain warfare." It has a ring of daring; it sounds cleaner than trench warfare and lighter than tank warfare. The only thing that can match it is war in the air, and that has become too deadly to be nice any more. It has also become too familiar, while war in the mountains is still strange enough to sound romantic. Except, of course, to the men who have to fight it.

I spent some time last winter on temporary duty with an infantry battalion operating in the Italian mountains against the Germans. When I got my orders I tried to find out where the battalion was, but no one seemed to know. Everyone agreed, however, that information could be obtained at a certain village on top of a mountain. It was not quite clear who held that mountain, but everyone said I could find out there one way or another. So I got my bedding roll and hitched along the front until I came to the base of this mountain. There was a crossroads here, with one dirt road running along a valley up to the contact line and another road winding out of sight up the mountain. A worried M.P. stood at the crossroads, directing traffic. He had reason to be worried; German artillery had been shelling the crossroads all day. Nothing had hit closer than a hundred yards from the M.P., but that was close enough for him. While we were standing there another shell came over and hit an already bombed-out house about fifty yards down the road. We hit the ground and stayed there while rocks flew all over the place. When we got up the M.P. was shaking with rage. "The dirty bastards," he kept saying. I figured he meant the Germans and added a few words of my own, but then he added, "Those dirty bastards who keep telling me how soft I got it in the M.P.s."

There was not much traffic, and that kept along the valley. The sun was on the way down, but still held warmth. I sat on a rock by the road and waited. A few more shells came over, but not anywhere near. Finally a jeep with a trailer full of rations came up from the rear and turned onto the mountain road. I flagged it down and hopped in beside the driver. He said he was going up to the battalion supply dump. The road wound dizzily up the mountain; the windshield was down so it wouldn't reflect the sun to planes, and the cold wind cut my face. In the valley below were puffs of white smoke from one of our artillery batteries. Then the road climbed over the top of the mountain and dipped into a plateau. Everything else was immediately shut out; there was only the sky and the cupped plateau, with a tiny village in the center. We stopped at a house on the outskirts. Six mules stood patiently in front of the house, and some officers and men lounged around. I got out and the driver continued into the village. I went up to a tall, blond captain sitting on the porch and asked how to get to the battalion. He said the battalion was on another mountain, but these mules were soon to be packed and taken there and I could go along. The captain said the enlisted men were going up with the mules. The officers were staying behind. They were specialists in mountain climbing, skiing and mule packing, but so far they had only packed mules. The captain's name was Mueller and he was fresh from a well-known ski division in the States. I had a friend named Smith in this division and asked Mueller if he knew him. "Sure I know him," Mueller said amiably. "The son of a bitch owes me ten dollars."

There were four enlisted men waiting to go back with the mules, but only three had come down from the battalion. The fourth was rejoining the outfit from a hospital. He was a short, red-haired boy named Kramer; this was not his real name, but he was A.W.O.L. from the hospital and afraid they would send him back. He had been wounded in the shoulder and was not yet fully recovered, but he said the hospital had been too GI; he felt he would recover better in a more relaxed atmosphere. When the sun was almost down, one of the men suggested to Mueller that they get the mules packed. Mueller nodded and three lieutenants went over to the mules and started to work. They worked slowly and very methodically; in the Air Force they would have been called "eager." It

was apparent that they were very new at the front, not because they were so thorough, but because of a certain air of
seriousness about them; they were like officers I remembered
from training in the States, who would show you how to
make a bed with the same intensity as how to shoot a rifle. At
last they stood back and eyed the mules carefully. It was hard
to see the mules for the ration boxes. "I think that will hold
for a while," one of the lieutenants said modestly. The three
enlisted men each took the halters of two mules and started
off without saying a word. I said good-by to Mueller and fell
in behind with Kramer. We followed the dirt road the way I
had come, then cut off on a little trail that wound across the
plateau and down the other side of the mountain. As soon as
we got out of sight of the house, the soldiers stopped and
readjusted the packs. Then we started off again.

It was dark when we got to the foot of the mountain. I
couldn't feel any trail underneath, but they seemed to know
where they were going. We crossed a little valley and started
up another mountain. We had to stop several times for
breath. When we reached the top we walked along the crest.
It was very dark and cold. Kramer and I talked for a while,
mostly about food, then shut up and just walked. Artillery
flashed in the sky ahead of us, like heat lightning. My watch
said five minutes after twelve when we stopped. Kramer said,
"Guess we're here." It didn't look as if we were anywhere,
but the others were already unloading the mules. Kramer and
I helped, dropping the ration boxes where we stood. One of
the soldiers said we could sleep here until morning; the battalion was all around us, but there was no sense looking for
them now. I unrolled my blanket and shelter half, then rolled
up again in them. I fell asleep right away.

There was light mist on the ground when I awoke. Kramer
was beside me, wrapped in a German blanket. He stirred
when I got up and said, "I should have stood in the hospital."
The mist rose as I made my roll; we were on another plateau,
spotted with clumps of trees. I could see other mountain tops
surrounding us through the mist. There was the sound of
talking near by and Kramer said, "Let's get some breakfast."
We walked over a little rise; in a hollow were four soldiers
seated around a fire.

"Why, you gold-bricking son of a gun," one of them said to Kramer. "I bet it took six M.P.s to bring you back."

Kramer told him pleasantly where he could go, then we sat down with them. They all looked equally dirty, unshaven, and worn out. One was evidently a lieutenant, since a helmet on the ground had a gold bar painted on it, but I couldn't tell which one. They were eating K rations and heating canteen cups of coffee over the fire. I got a breakfast ration from one of the men, slit it open, ate the fruit bar, made the coffee, and opened the chopped ham and eggs and placed it near the fire. I put the biscuits in my pocket, in case I was some day reduced to absolute starvation. While we ate, Kramer told them where he had been. They all told him he was a fool for leaving the hospital. "Stinky's got us marchin' over every damned mountain in Italy," a tall boy with a Southern accent said. I asked who Stinky was. "Colonel Williams," Kramer said, "Battalion C.O." I asked how he was and the Southern boy said with considerable affection, "Stinky's a fightin' bastard. He's goin' to get us all killed dead one of these days."

After breakfast I asked the way to battalion C.P. and they pointed across a clearing. "It's in a little house across there," the Southern boy said, "but you'd better watch it goin' across. There's been kraut planes around." I said I'd be careful. "See you later," Kramer said. I got up and ran across the clearing. The house was just on the other side, hidden by trees. It was made of stone and looked like an outhouse. Outside was a staff sergeant, tying up a bedding roll. I asked where the colonel was and he said the colonel was meeting with the company commanders. The sergeant's name was Kinsey and he was battalion sergeant major. He said the colonel was briefing the other officers, because we were moving out this afternoon. I asked him what our position was and he said he didn't know and didn't think anyone else knew either. He said the battalion had been out of contact with the Germans for two days now and were just moving ahead until they made contact. He said I could go up ahead to the edge of the mountain and take a look.

I left Kinsey and walked along a path until it forked, then followed the right fork up the side of the mountain. At the top were a captain and a sergeant, lying on their stomachs and looking through field glasses. I said hello and slid down beside them. I wondered how many views there were like this in Italy: mountain, valley, little village and more mountain. It had been beautiful once, but now you could not look at it any more as a scene. You looked at trees for 88s and at houses for observation posts. Too many men had died trying to get a view like this; it was not as innocent as it looked.

The captain wore artillery insignia and I asked him where his artillery was. "Oh, we left that behind two days ago," he said cheerfully. "They couldn't get over the mountains. We're just looking to see what targets we'd have if we had artillery." The captain was named Llewellyn; the sergeant, who was large and blond, was just called Moose. They were target spotters and liaison for the battalion's artillery, when it was close enough to function. The targets they were hopefully picking out were in the valley town. I asked who had the town and Moose said the British were in it now. "We had patrols in there first," he said, "but it's in the British sector, so we had to pull out and let the Limeys take it officially."

"They can have it," Llewellyn said. "The wine was no good anyhow."

After a while I went back to the C.P. Kinsey was still out in front, talking to a private named D'Crenzo, who turned out to be the battalion draftsman. "Any time you want a golf lesson, just see D'Crenzo," Kinsey said. "He used to be a pro." D'Crenzo and I talked golf the rest of the morning, while Kinsey made up the battalion roster. He would shake his head every time he added up a company total and say, "If the krauts only knew what we had." The battalion was considerably under strength, due more to the Italian winter than to enemy action. No one had bothered sending replacements for these casualties, probably because it was too difficult finding the battalion. Colonel Williams returned later in the afternoon: a short, dark, balding man with a mustache. He looked at least forty, but D'Crenzo said he was closer to thirty. "You should have seen him back in the States," D'Crenzo said. "He looked like a kid." The colonel told Kinsey to get ready, we were leaving in a few minutes.

"Where are we going?" Kinsey asked.

"To another god-damned mountain," the colonel said.

When the battalion staff section was assembled, the colonel led us down the path to the edge of the mountain. We passed the other companies waiting along the path. The men looked tired and bowed down under their equipment. The colonel started over the edge without pause, picking his way among the rocks. "Oh, well," said a voice in back of me. "Here we go again."

The night was like all other nights. We stumbled down one mountain and crawled up another. We crossed a stream with the water up to our knees. No one talked; no one sang. We didn't know where we were going or what we would find when we got there. Some of the officers might have known, but they probably weren't very sure. We didn't know where the enemy was. We didn't even know where we were. We just walked. There was nothing at all nice about the walk. It was dirty, tiring, dangerous and without immediate compensation, and it was exactly what this war was like to most of the men in it. No matter how they felt about the war, this was how it was fought. And there were no Purple Hearts for either trench foot or jaundice.

We finally came to a village on top of another mountain and marched quietly through, the noise of our feet like sand on the cobblestones. The village was dark and asleep. The colonel stopped on the other side of town and went off to disperse the companies along the mountain in case of attack. "Another delightful place to spend the night," Kinsey said. I looked around and found a space hollowed out between two rocks. I unrolled my pack there and crawled in. It was very cold. I drew my knees up to my neck and pulled the blanket over my head, but couldn't sleep. I just lay there and shivered most of the night, and finally fell asleep toward morning. When I got up, we were in the clouds. They were all around us, between our mountain and the others. It gave you the feeling of being so far above the world that even airplane flight went on below. Kinsey and D'Crenzo were a few yards away, trying to start a fire. I joined them and they said the colonel was in town, trying to set up a C.P. We got the fire started, but none of us had any rations. Kinsey had a couple of bouillon packages and I had the biscuits from the day before, so we had them. The biscuits were edible if you heated them first. The colonel returned while we were eating. "We're moving into the mayor's house," he told Kinsey.

"Where's the mayor going to stay?" Kinsey asked.

"He's dead," the colonel said. "The krauts strung him up just before they left."

The three of us got our equipment and walked back up the road into the village. The houses were old and close together. It was like all the other Italian villages we had come through, except that this one had not been shelled. We came to a house with some civilians standing outside and D'Crenzo asked in Italian if this was the mayor's house. They nodded vigorously, so we went in. The door opened into a little hall. To the right was a large kitchen with a fireplace and to the left was a dining room. A flight of stairs probably led to bedrooms. We went into the kitchen. A pretty, black-haired girl, a middle-aged lady, an old man, and a young man in knickers stood by the fireplace. They smiled at us. "Welcome," the girl said.

"Get a load of that," Kinsey said.

We dropped our stuff in a corner and the people made room for us by the fireplace. D'Crenzo spoke to them in Italian, while Kinsey and I concentrated on getting warm and eying the girl.

"This is the mayor's family," D'Crenzo said to us. "Wife, daughter, and father. This other character is a cousin."

"I am medical student," the young man in knickers said in English. "I am continuing to Napoli for my studies."

"What's the name of the tomato?" Kinsey said.

D'Crenzo said, "Inez," and the girl smiled at us.

"That's for me," Kinsey said.

Just then a little boy ran into the kitchen and stopped by the door, looking at us with wide eyes. The girl said *"Americano"* and Kinsey took out a piece of C-ration candy and tossed it to the kid. The boy caught and unwrapped it in one motion, and popped it into his mouth. Then he smiled. The outside door opened and Colonel Williams walked into the kitchen, followed by Captain Llewellyn and Moose. Llewellyn was rubbing his hands. "Don't tell me we're going to be warm," he said. "You'd better not let Division hear about this."

The colonel told Kinsey that the enlisted men of the staff section would sleep on the floor of the kitchen and the officers on the floor of the dining room. The colonel sat down on a bench by the fireplace and took out a map. "This is the situation," he said. The Italians all moved into a corner and kept very quiet as the colonel talked. The colonel explained that we were some ten miles ahead of the rest of the Fifth Army. On our right flank were Germans, on our left flank were Germans, and there were probably Germans ahead of us. For all the colonel knew there might very well be Germans behind us. To our right were just more mountains, but directly across the mountain on our left was a road running north. South of us on this road was another town, which was still being battled for by the Americans and Germans. If we were to cross the mountain and cut that road, we could trap all the Germans still fighting in that town. This, said the colonel, was not quite possible at the moment, since we had no communications, no artillery, no supply and very few men.

"So what are we going to do?" Kinsey asked.

"Well, we can send out patrols," the colonel said.

"We can sit," D'Crenzo said. "I could use a little sitting."

"That's about all we can do," the colonel said. He sat back on the bench and shook his head sadly. "What a fine opportunity."

"Imagine being warm for a whole day," Llewellyn said.

The colonel went out again to see about the patrols. Kinsey whispered to D'Crenzo, who asked the girl something in Italian. The girl laughed and pointed upstairs. Kinsey left the room. There was a loud knock on the door and Inez went to answer. She came back with two old men. They spoke rapidly to D'Crenzo, making large and fierce gestures as they spoke. D'Crenzo said to me, "They want to see the colonel and report the big Fascist here. They say he's been helping the *Tedeschi*." One of the old men nodded at this last word and pulled his hand ferociously across his throat. "He says this bird was head of the local Blackshirts," D'Crenzo said. He spoke politely to the old men, then ushered them to the door. Kinsey came down, looking very pleased. "They got a real one here," he said. "You can even sit down on it."

"You don't say?" Moose said. He left the room and I heard his feet on the stairs.

"They even got sheets on the beds," Kinsey said. "What do you think of that?"

We spent the rest of the morning just sitting around, relishing the unaccustomed warmth. Lieutenant Jones, the battalion intelligence officer, wandered in and D'Crenzo told him what the two old men had reported. Jones nodded wearily and said he'd take a look. I sat on the bench with Llewellyn and Kinsey, while D'Crenzo talked with the Italians. We had our shoes off and were toasting our feet. Llewellyn talked about his college days at the University of Florida and what a fine bunch the Phi Eps were. Kinsey didn't say much; he seemed overwhelmed at being in a house that had both a sit-down toilet and sheets on the bed. After a while D'Crenzo came over and sat with us. He said the Germans had taken fifteen hostages before they left, because an Italian had killed a German soldier for looting. They had kept the hostages two weeks and then hanged six of them. One of the six was the mayor and they had left him hanging for several days as a lesson to the town.

In the afternoon I took a walk around the edge of the mountain and found Kramer and the Southern boy in a foxhole. The Southern boy had a harmonica and was playing while Kramer sang to the tune of *I Love Mountain Music*:

> *"I love mountain warfare*
> *I love mountain warfare*
> *Warred by a real hillbilly band."*

They had just come back from patrol. "The krauts are evacuating the hell out of that town back there," Kramer said. "If we had anything at all we could cream them." The clouds were still so heavy that you could not see the surrounding mountains. The clouds had changed color from white to black, and it looked as if it would rain. Most of the men had tried to dig their holes into the side of the mountain, since the ground was too rocky to dig well. They huddled there now, some with shelter halves over their holes and some with rocks piled around the entrance to keep out the wind. Kramer asked where I was sleeping that night and shook his head when I told him. "The lap of luxury," he said. "The goddamned lap of luxury."

We slept that night on the kitchen floor. It was stone, but it was dry. We kept the fire going all night. I lay on my side and stared into the fire until I couldn't keep my eyes open. The last thing I remember was Kinsey heaving a deep sigh and saying, "All we need now is a box of marshmallows."

It was raining when we awoke. Inez and her mother came down and heated water for coffee. Kinsey made a couple of tentative passes at Inez, but she wouldn't play. "I'm probably too tired to do anything, anyway," Kinsey said. It rained the whole day, and all we did was sit by the fire and talk. Every so often a company runner would come to report to the colonel; he would stand in the doorway, rain pouring off his helmet, eying the fire. The mayor's father came down in the afternoon, and of course it turned out that he had lived in the States. "I was a big a bootlegger in Rochester, New York," he kept saying. He was very proud that he had survived three gang wars and returned to Italy with a lot of money. He kept giving us hints on how to tell bathtub gin from the real stuff, until D'Crenzo took him aside and told him that prohibition was a thing of the past in the U.S.

The medics set up an aid station in a stable across the way, and there was a steady stream of men on sick call. Kinsey was busy altering his roster all day, muttering, "If the krauts only knew. If they only knew." The colonel kept sending out patrols, but they never met anything. The colonel's temper got shorter as the day wore on. The patrols would come back with reports of Germans evacuating up the road and the colonel would roar, "Where the hell are my god-damned communications?" It rained all night, too, but stopped by morning. The sick call was even longer this day. Lieutenant Jones came in early, followed by the two old Italians who had reported the Fascist. Jones said he had just searched the man's house, but hadn't found any evidence that he had helped the Germans.

"Well, was he a Fascist?" D'Crenzo asked.

"Yeah, I guess so," Jones said. "There were some papers that said he was the boss Blackshirt in this district."

I asked Jones if that weren't enough and he said he didn't think so. "Hell," he said. "Just being a Fascist doesn't prove anything. If we're going to make this a democratic country we got to let them be anything they want."

D'Crenzo tried to explain this to the old men, but they didn't seem to understand. They kept shaking their heads and trying to butt in. Finally D'Crenzo shouted very loudly and they shut up. D'Crenzo then spoke to them in a low and polite tone, took their arms and ushered them out. He came back wiping his forehead. "They think we're crazy," he said.

Later that afternoon a patrol returned with the news that the Germans were no longer evacuating up the road. "Well, I guess we'll just have to chase them some more," Kinsey said.

"We could have trapped them," the colonel said. "We could have trapped them like rats in a trap." He seemed very unhappy at the thought of letting the Germans get away. He took out his map and was showing us how we could have trapped them when there was a knock on the door and a lieutenant and two enlisted men walked in. They were soaked to the skin and dripping with mud.

"Who the hell are you?" the colonel said.

"Regimental wire team, sir," the lieutenant said. "We've got you a wire to regiment if you want it."

"Want it!" the colonel said. "What the hell took you so long?"

"Well, these mountains," the lieutenant said.

"Oh, nuts," the colonel said. "If you got over them today, you could have got over them yesterday." He shook his head disgustedly. "Well, where is the god-damned wire?"

The wire team strung the wire into the dining room and the colonel finally got in touch with Regiment. We sat in the kitchen, eating a *pizza* that Inez and her mother had made. There wasn't much on it, but it tasted good. We talked about how terrible it was to be away from home for two or even three years. We were well into the subject when one of the outposts brought in a British captain and a Tommy. They were also soaked; the captain went into the dining room to talk to the colonel and the soldier sat around the fire with us. He seemed very young and didn't talk at all, just listened to us. Finally Kinsey asked him how long he had been overseas and the Tommy said quietly, "Six years." After that we talked about cities we had visited.

The British captain was with the colonel about fifteen minutes; then they both came out and shook hands and said "Cheerio" and the Englishmen left. The colonel came into the kitchen and said, "Well, our flanks are protected now. We can move out tomorrow." He said the British had moved up on our right and the Americans up that road to our left.

"Where are we going?" Kinsey asked.

"Are you kidding?" the colonel said.

We got up very early the next morning and rolled our packs. Inez and her mother came out and waved to us when we left. "You know," Kinsey said, "two more days and I would have had that broad eating out of my hand." We walked out to the edge of the village, where the battalion had assembled. The men were standing silently. There seemed to be fewer than before. I looked for Kramer, but couldn't find him. As we were lining up, we heard the low, rising sound of a shell. Everyone ducked, and the shell hit behind and to the right of the village. "Oh, Jesus," somebody said, and then another shell came over and hit in the same place.

"Well, they know we're here," Kinsey said.

The colonel came up from the village and moved out immediately. The rest of the battalion followed, straggling over the edge of the mountain and down the cloudy slope. Another shell came over and somebody screamed back in the village.

"You mean we *were* here," D'Crenzo said.

—*January 1944.*

Keep Your Head Down, 1945

Chronology, 1933–1945

1933   Adolf Hitler, leader since 1921 of the National Socialist German Workers' (Nazi) Party, is named chancellor of Germany by President Paul von Hindenburg on January 30, heading cabinet with only two other Nazi members. (Appointment is result of agreement between Hitler and small group of right-wing politicians and military leaders, who hope that Nazis will provide popular support for an authoritarian government dominated by traditional conservatives and the army.) Hitler dissolves Reichstag (parliament), in which Nazis hold almost 34 percent of the seats, and calls for new election. Using emergency decree powers of the 1919 Weimar constitution and exploiting their control of the Prussian state police, Nazis begin campaign of violence and intimidation directed against Communists and Social Democrats. Following destruction of Reichstag chamber by arson on February 27, emergency decree is issued suspending all civil liberties and allowing indefinite detention without trial. In election on March 5, Nazis win 44 percent of Reichstag seats. On March 23 Reichstag approves, 441–94, enabling act that allows Hitler unilaterally to alter the constitution and enact legislation (dissenting votes are from Social Democrats; all of the Communist deputies have been arrested). Nazis begin purging civil service and educational institutions of Jews and political opponents and take control of trade unions, civil organizations, and local and state governments throughout Germany. Decree issued July 14 makes Nazis only legal party in Germany. Germany withdraws from League of Nations and Geneva Disarmament Conference on October 14. Hitler continues policy, begun by military in early 1920s, of clandestinely circumventing 1919 Versailles Peace Treaty, which limited German army to 100,000 men and prohibited it from possessing tanks or aircraft.

1934   Tensions increase between Hitler and leadership of the SA ("Storm Detachment," Nazi party paramilitary force), who seek greater share of power and more radical social and economic change. With support from the army, Hitler has SA leaders and several other political opponents shot without trial, June 30–July 2. Hindenburg dies on August 1 and Hitler is proclaimed Führer ("Leader") of Germany; military and civil service personnel swear personal oath of allegiance to him on August 2. Purge of SA makes the SS ("Protection Detachment," originally Hitler's Nazi party bodyguard) the main instrument of terror in Germany (in 1936 SS is given control of all German police).

795

1935   Hitler reintroduces military conscription on March 16 and
              announces that Germany will no longer honor military restric-
              tions of Versailles Treaty. Britain and Germany conclude naval
              pact on June 18 that allows Germany to contravene Versailles
              Treaty by building surface ships over 10,000 tons and U-boats
              (submarines). "Nuremberg laws" enacted in September deprive
              German Jews of their remaining citizenship rights and make
              marriages between Jews and non-Jews a criminal offense.

                   Italy, ruled by Fascist dictator Benito Mussolini since 1922, in-
              vades Ethiopia on October 3. League of Nations votes limited
              economic sanctions against Italy in October but does not impose
              oil embargo.

1936   Ultranationalist Japanese army officers stage coup attempt in
              Tokyo, February 26, that is quickly suppressed by army high
              command. Incident weakens civilian government in Japan and
              strengthens influence of generals favoring further expansion
              in China (Japanese had seized Manchuria in 1931 and part of
              northeast China in 1933).

                   Hitler reoccupies German Rhineland, an area demilitarized
              under the Versailles Treaty, on March 7; France and Britain take
              no action.

                   Italian army completes conquest of Ethiopia on May 6. League
              of Nations votes July 4 to lift sanctions against Italy.

                   Civil war begins in Spain on July 17 with army rebellion against
              elected left-wing Republican government. Italy and Germany
              move quickly to support insurgents with arms, transport, and
              troops (at their peak Italian forces in Spain number 50,000; Ger-
              man forces reach 10,000, including strong air force contingent
              that gains valuable experience). Soviet Union begins supplying
              arms and military specialists to the Republican government in
              autumn, and directs Communist parties to organize Interna-
              tional Brigades of foreign volunteers. Britain, France, and the
              United States adopt policy of nonintervention.

1937   Eight prominent generals are executed in Moscow on June 12 on
              false charges of treason as Josef Stalin, general secretary of the
              Soviet Communist party since 1922, begins purge of Soviet mili-
              tary (by late 1938 over 80 percent of the senior commanders
              in the Soviet army will have been shot or imprisoned; victims
              include many key proponents of modern mechanized warfare).

                   Fighting breaks out near Peking on July 7 between Chinese
              troops and Japanese legation garrison, and by the end of July
              Japanese troops control the Peking-Tientsin region. Chinese Na-
              tionalist leader Chiang Kai-shek orders attack on Japanese zone in
              Shanghai on August 14, leading to full-scale Sino-Japanese war.

Japanese army breaks through Chinese lines at Shanghai in November and enters Nanking, Chinese Nationalist capital, on December 13; its capture is followed by weeks of widespread killing, rape, and looting in which at least 40,000 Chinese die.

1938   German army occupies Austria without opposition on March 12, and on March 13 Germany annexes Austria in violation of the Versailles Treaty. Britain and France take no action. Hitler begins planning invasion of Czechoslovakia and launches propaganda campaign protesting alleged persecution of Germans in the Sudetenland (border regions of Bohemia and Moravia, which contain frontier fortifications essential to Czech defense). Neville Chamberlain, Conservative prime minister of Great Britain since May 1937 and leading proponent of conciliatory "appeasement" policy toward Germany, presses Czech government to make concessions to Sudeten Germans while declaring that Britain and France will fight Germany if it attacks Czechoslovakia (France has treaty of alliance with Czechoslovakia; Soviet Union is committed to assisting Czechoslovakia once France takes military action). Hitler escalates threats against Czechoslovakia in September. Chamberlain goes to Germany twice to negotiate with Hitler, while French and Soviet governments are unable to agree on response to crisis. French army and British navy begin partial mobilization, September 24–27, as German military prepares to attack Czechoslovakia on September 30. Chamberlain, French premier Édouard Daladier, Mussolini, and Hitler meet in Munich, September 29–30, and agree that Czechoslovakia will cede Sudetenland to Germany; Hitler and Chamberlain also sign declaration of Anglo-German friendship. Chamberlain returns to England and declares that agreement will bring "peace in our time." German army enters Sudetenland on October 1. Britain and Germany accelerate rearmament efforts, and Hitler plans invasion of remainder of Czechoslovakia.

After five-month battle, Japanese capture Wuhan in central China on October 25; by end of year Sino-Japanese war approaches stalemate as Japanese consolidate their conquests.

Nazi party carries out pogrom throughout Germany, November 9–10, in which 91 German Jews are killed; in its aftermath, 26,000 Jews are sent to concentration camps, and expropriation of Jewish property is intensified (pogrom becomes known as "Kristallnacht," from the broken glass of Jewish-owned shop windows).

1939   German army occupies Czechoslovakia on March 15 in violation of Munich Pact. Bohemia and Moravia become German protectorate, Slovakia a German satellite state; Hungary annexes

Ruthenia. Under threat of attack, Lithuania cedes city of Memel to Germany on March 23. Spanish civil war ends March 29 with victory of insurgent Nationalist regime led by General Francisco Franco. Chamberlain abandons appeasement policy after seizure of Czechoslovakia, and on March 31 declares that Britain and France will defend Poland against aggression.

Apr.–May   Hitler orders preparations for attack on Poland completed by September 1. Italy occupies Albania on April 7. Germany and Italy sign military alliance on May 22. Soviet and Japanese troops clash in disputed Khalkhin Gol region along Mongolian-Manchurian border in late May; both sides send reinforcements, and fighting continues for three months.

June–Aug.   Britain, France, and the Soviet Union are unable to agree on terms for an alliance. Soviet offensive in late August drives Japanese from Khalkhin Gol region (cease-fire is declared September 16; Soviet victory will contribute to Japanese decision not to attack Soviet Union in summer 1941). Germany and Soviet Union sign nonaggression pact on August 23 containing secret protocol partitioning Poland and establishing spheres of influence in eastern Europe.

Sept.   Germany invades Poland September 1. Italy declares neutrality despite alliance with Germany. Britain, Australia, New Zealand, and France declare war on Germany September 3 (South Africa and Canada declare war by September 10). Winston Churchill, severest critic of Chamberlain appeasement policy, joins British cabinet as First Lord of the Admiralty. Britain begins naval blockade of Germany. President Franklin D. Roosevelt signs American neutrality proclamation on September 5 after expressing sympathy for Allied cause in radio address. Luftwaffe (German air force) achieves air superiority over Poland, and German army advances rapidly despite determined Polish resistance. Soviets invade eastern Poland on September 17. Warsaw falls to Germans September 27, and fighting in Poland ends October 6. (New Polish government is formed in exile; its air, land, and naval forces will fight with Allies until end of the war.) SS units in Poland begin committing widespread atrocities. Allies do not attack into western Germany, fearing that assault against frontier fortifications would be repulsed with heavy losses and hoping that blockade will eventually cause German economic collapse. Numerically weaker German navy does not attempt to break blockade, but begins attacking British commerce (although Germans begin war with less than 30 U-boats capable of operating in the Atlantic, Allies will lose over 2 million tons of merchant shipping to U-boats, surface ships, mines, and aircraft by end of June 1940; Germans lose 24 U-boats in first ten months of war). Hitler orders planning for attack in western Europe.

General George C. Marshall, new U.S. Army Chief of Staff, begins planning expansion and modernization of the army, which has less than 200,000 men on active service (German army has mobilized over 2,700,000).

Oct.   Hitler orders killing of mentally and physically handicapped Germans (over 100,000 such persons will be systematically murdered before killings are suspended in August 1941). Soviets press Finnish government to make territorial concessions. British code-breakers continue work begun by Poles in 1930s on Enigma machine used by German armed forces to cipher radio messages (by late May 1940 British are able to break some Luftwaffe Enigma ciphers on daily basis).

Nov.–Dec.   U.S. neutrality law is modified on November 4 to allow Britain and France to purchase munitions and transport them in their own shipping. Soviet Union invades Finland November 30. Initial Soviet attacks are unsuccessful due to poor training, tactics, and leadership, and Finnish superiority at winter warfare.

1940   Reinforced and reorganized Soviet forces launch successful offensive against Finns in February. Finland signs armistice, March 13, yielding border territory to Soviets. Paul Reynaud succeeds Daladier as premier of France on March 21.

April   Germans invade Denmark and Norway (both neutral countries) April 9, beginning campaign designed to obtain northern naval bases and safeguard shipments of Swedish iron ore along Norwegian coast. Denmark is occupied without resistance. Attacks by sea and air against Norwegian ports and airfields achieve surprise, but despite initial confusion and loss of Oslo, Norwegian forces resist. British navy and air force attack German ships, and British troops begin landing in Norway April 14 (later joined by French and Polish forces). Germans win air superiority and Allies are unable to prevent German capture of key objectives.

Germans begin confining Polish Jews in ghettos.

May   British and French troops are evacuated from central Norway in early May; fighting continues in the north. After bitter parliamentary debate over Norwegian campaign, Chamberlain resigns May 10 and is replaced as prime minister by Churchill, who forms coalition government with opposition Labour party. Germans invade Holland, Belgium, and Luxembourg (all neutral countries) on May 10 and launch heavy air attacks against France. British and French send strong forces into Belgium and Holland, where they take up defensive positions. Allies fail to detect movement of concentrated German armor through the Ardennes, and Germans break through French positions along the Meuse River at Sedan on May 13. Dutch army capitulates,

May 15, after heavy German bombing of Rotterdam. German armored formations rapidly advance across northeastern France with close support from the Luftwaffe, which has achieved air superiority. French army, which has dispersed most of its tanks along the front in small units, is unable to mount effective counterattacks. Germans reach English Channel near Abbeville on May 20, completing encirclement of British and French armies in Belgium. After attempts to break encirclement fail, British begin evacuating troops from Dunkirk on May 27. Belgian army capitulates May 28 as Germans continue attacks on trapped Allied forces (Belgian and Dutch governments have gone into exile in Britain).

June

Dunkirk evacuation ends June 4 after approximately 225,000 British and 110,000 French troops are rescued; all of their heavy weapons and equipment are abandoned. Germans launch new offensive June 5 and break through French defensive line along Somme and Aisne rivers. Allies evacuate remaining troops from northern Norway June 8, and Norwegian government-in-exile orders its army to cease fighting on June 9. Italy declares war on France and Britain June 10. German army enters Paris on June 14. New French government headed by Marshal Philippe Pétain asks for armistice on June 17. Brigadier General Charles de Gaulle flies to England and organizes Free French movement. Armistice between France and Germany is signed June 22. Germans occupy northern France and Atlantic coast; Pétain establishes collaborationist regime (known as "Vichy," after its capital) with authority over unoccupied southern zone, North Africa, and other French colonies overseas.

Soviets occupy Lithuania on June 15 and force Romania to cede Bessarabia and northern Bukovina on June 27 (Soviet annexation of Lithuania, Latvia, and Estonia is completed by August 3, 1940).

Churchill government moves toward full mobilization of British society and economy for prolonged war and maximum military production, while Hitler directs that German economy continue to give high priority to production of goods for civilian consumption; German war production also suffers from confused planning and expectation that war will not be prolonged. (In 1940–41 Britain produces 6,200 tanks and self-propelled guns and 35,000 military aircraft, while Germany manufactures 5,400 tanks and self-propelled guns and 22,000 military aircraft.)

U.S. Congress approves major expansion of armed forces in response to German victories, but public opinion remains divided over extent to which U.S. should aid Britain. American arms production increases rapidly to fill orders from Britain and U.S. military.

July   British demand on July 3 that French fleet based at Mers-el-
               Kebir in Algeria take immediate action to ensure that its ships
               will not fall under German control. When French commander
               obeys order from Vichy to reject ultimatum, British ships open
               fire, destroying or damaging three battleships and killing over
               1,200 French sailors. British and Italians begin prolonged naval
               struggle for control of Mediterranean.

               Heavy air fighting begins between Luftwaffe and Royal Air
               Force (RAF) in early July as Germans attack Channel ports
               and convoys. Germans begin planning invasion of England;
               weakness of German navy, increased by serious losses in Nor-
               wegian campaign, makes achievement of air superiority over
               southern England essential. RAF and Luftwaffe fighter planes
               are roughly equal in number and performance, and British
               fighter production is higher; although Luftwaffe has more
               trained pilots, their fighters have limited range that allows
               them to escort bombers only over southern England. Revolu-
               tionary RAF air defense system allows commanders to control
               interception of enemy formations using information from radar
               (invented in Britain in 1935 and still secret in 1940) and ground
               observers.

               Germans use naval and air bases along French coast to renew
               offensive against British commerce in the Atlantic, sinking over 5
               million tons between July 1940 and June 1941 while losing only
               20 U-boats. Loss of merchant shipping poses serious threat to
               British ability to wage war.

               British form commando units for conducting coastal raids and
               begin working with exile governments to organize and supply
               resistance movements in occupied Europe (resistance movements
               will engage in espionage, sabotage, propaganda, and occasionally
               partisan warfare; Germans respond with indiscriminate reprisals).

               In late July Hitler directs planning to begin for invasion of
               Soviet Union in 1941, intending to deprive Britain of possible
               ally and fulfill long-standing ambition of conquering "living
               space" (*Lebensraum*) for Germany in the east. Soviets continue
               supplying large amounts of raw materials to Germany while
               consolidating control over newly acquired territory.

               Konoye Fumimaro becomes prime minister of Japan on July
               17. New cabinet, which includes General Tojo Hideki as war min-
               ister, decides to seek alliance with Germany and Italy, isolate
               Nationalist China from foreign supplies, and pursue aggressive
               policy against vulnerable French and Dutch colonies in Southeast
               Asia in order to secure sources of oil, rubber, tin, and other raw
               materials.

Aug.   Luftwaffe begins offensive against RAF fighter airfields and
               air defense headquarters on August 13. Although German air-

craft losses are higher than British, by end of August damage to airfields and attrition of fighter pilots places severe strain on RAF.

Sept.   In attempt to damage British morale and draw out remaining RAF fighters, Luftwaffe begins heavy bombing of London on September 7; switch in targets gives respite to RAF airfields. Battle of Britain reaches climax on September 15, when British destroy 60 aircraft while losing 26. Hitler indefinitely postpones invasion on September 17.

Under executive agreement concluded September 2, U.S. sends 50 old destroyers to Britain in return for bases in British territories in the Western Hemisphere (British are in severe need of escort vessels for convoys). Roosevelt signs act on September 16 establishing first peacetime draft in American history; law requires draftees to serve for only one year.

Italian army in Libya invades Egypt on September 13 and advances 60 miles before halting.

Under Japanese pressure, Vichy French agree on September 22 to allow Japan to station troops and aircraft in northern Indochina. U.S. responds with embargo of iron and steel scrap exports to Japan. Germany, Italy, and Japan sign Tripartite Pact, designed to deter the U.S. from entering the war in Europe or Asia, on September 27.

Oct.–Nov.   Germans gradually end daylight raids and begin intensive night bombing of London and other cities in campaign ("The Blitz") that continues into May 1941. Luftwaffe loses over 1,700 aircraft in Battle of Britain, July 10–October 31, 1940, the RAF over 900. RAF engages in limited night bombing of Germany. Hitler and Franco meet on October 23 and are unable to agree on terms for Spain to enter the war against Britain. Italy invades Greece October 28. Greek army repels attack and advances into Albania by the end of 1940. British carrier aircraft destroy or damage three Italian battleships in night raid on Taranto harbor, November 11–12.

Roosevelt is reelected for unprecedented third term on November 5.

Dec.   British and Indian troops in Egypt begin successful offensive against Italians on December 9 (Indian, Australian, New Zealand, South African, and Canadian troops comprise major portion of forces under British command throughout campaigns in the Mediterranean).

Hitler issues directive on December 18 for German invasion of Soviet Union in late spring 1941, with objective of capturing Leningrad, Moscow, and Kiev by early autumn. Encouraged by Stalin's 1937–38 purge of the army and poor Soviet performance in Finnish war, German high command expects to destroy

Soviet army during summer in series of encirclement battles near frontier.

1941   British begin series of offensives against Italians in Ethiopia and Somalia on January 19 (last Italian garrison in Ethiopia surrenders November 28, 1941).

British advance in North Africa stops at El Agheila in Libya on February 9 after capturing 130,000 Italian prisoners in two months; British, Indian, and Australian troops in campaign never total more than about 30,000. German forces land in Libya as British send troops and aircraft from North Africa to Greece.

In response to worsening British financial crisis, Roosevelt administration proposes Lend-Lease bill, which authorizes U.S. government to purchase war materials and then "lend" or "lease" them to Allied nations. House of Representatives passes bill by 260–165 vote on February 8.

March   After Senate passes Lend-Lease by 60–31, Roosevelt signs bill into law on March 11 (most Lend-Lease aid is never repaid in any form).

British sink three Italian cruisers and two destroyers off Greece in Battle of Cape Matapan, March 28–29, and achieve ascendancy over Italian navy in the Mediterranean. Germans and Italians (Axis) launch offensive in Libya on March 31 and drive British back to Egyptian border.

April   Coup in Iraq brings pro-German government to power (new regime is ousted by Allied military intervention, May 30, as British act to protect Persian Gulf oil fields). Germans invade Yugoslavia and Greece April 6. Yugoslavia surrenders April 17 and is partitioned into German, Italian, Hungarian, and Bulgarian zones; Germans also establish Serbian and Croatian puppet regimes. (Two rival resistance movements, the Serbian nationalist Chetniks and the Partisans, formed by Communist leader Tito, begin fighting Axis forces and each other in 1941.) Germans achieve air superiority in Greece and advance rapidly. British begin evacuating troops April 24. Germans capture Athens April 27, and country is occupied by Germans, Italians, and Bulgarians.

Stalin receives warnings of impending German attack from Soviet, British, and American sources, but dismisses them as British "provocations" designed to involve Soviets in war with Germany.

Roosevelt orders U.S. navy on April 10 to patrol into mid-Atlantic and report sightings of German ships to Allies.

U.S. and Japanese diplomats begin informal talks in Washington. Japan and Soviet Union sign neutrality pact on April 13. Roosevelt signs executive order on April 15 permitting pilots to resign from the U.S. armed forces and volunteer for combat service in China (American Volunteer Group, later known as the

"Flying Tigers," begins operations in late December 1941 and becomes part of U.S. army air forces in summer 1942).

May   Intensive bombing of Britain ends as Luftwaffe redeploys to the eastern front; British civilian deaths from bombing exceed 40,000.

Germans begin airborne invasion of Crete on May 20 and win battle for island June 1 after intense fighting. British are able to evacuate most of their troops despite heavy German air attacks. (German aircraft and U-boats inflict serious losses on British navy in Mediterranean in 1941–42.)

Sinking of German battleship *Bismarck* by the Royal Navy on May 27 ends Atlantic commerce raiding by large surface ships (in 1942 all large German warships are withdrawn to Germany or Norway, where they operate against convoys to Soviet Union with little success; limited raiding by armed merchant ships continues until autumn 1943).

U.S. begins sending Lend-Lease supplies to Nationalist China.

June   British invade Vichy-controlled Syria and Lebanon on June 8 (Vichy forces surrender July 11).

Germans invade Soviet Union on June 22, attacking with 3 million men (Soviet army has about 5 million men overall, with 3 million serving in western districts). Attack achieves complete surprise. Britain and United States pledge aid to Soviets. Romania, Italy, Hungary, Slovakia, and Finland declare war on Soviet Union. Luftwaffe destroys 4,000 Soviet aircraft in first week of fighting and wins control of air. German armor advances rapidly and Soviets suffer huge losses of men and matériel in series of encirclements.

Special SS and police units (*Einsatzgruppen*) begin systematically murdering Jewish population in conquered Soviet territory with assistance of German army and local collaborators; over 500,000 Jews are killed by December 1941. (Although no written orders survive, evidence strongly indicates that by spring 1941 Hitler had directed SS leaders to plan and carry out extermination of European Jews.) Hitler also orders mass murder of Roma and Sinti (Gypsies), which results in at least 250,000 deaths by 1945, and merciless treatment of Soviet prisoners; by early 1942 over two-thirds of the 3 million Soviet soldiers captured in 1941 have been shot, or have died from hunger, disease, and exposure.

British break Enigma machine cipher used by German navy and begin reading U-boat radio signals. Tracking of U-boat movements allows Royal Navy to engage in evasive convoy routing, and U-boat sinkings, July–December 1941, fall to about 700,000 tons, while U-boat losses in this period rise to 23 as number and effectiveness of British and Canadian escort vessels increase.

Japanese government debates whether to join attack on Soviet Union.

July–Aug.   Germans capture Smolensk, 400 miles east of frontier and 250 miles west of Moscow, on July 16. Supply difficulties, mechanical wear on vehicles, heavy casualties, and fierce Soviet resistance begin to slow German advance. Hitler orders halt in attack on Moscow in August and shifts armored forces from central front to offensives against Leningrad and the Ukraine. Soviets begin organizing partisan warfare behind German lines.

U.S. troops land in Iceland in July, relieving British forces for use elsewhere (British occupied island in May 1940). Churchill and Roosevelt meet off Newfoundland, August 9–12, to discuss strategy (first of their 12 wartime conferences). U.S. House of Representatives votes 203–202 to extend required service of draftees beyond one year; vote allows expansion of armed forces to continue.

British and Soviets occupy Iran on August 25 and begin opening overland supply route into Soviet Union; British also send convoys to Russian Arctic ports of Murmansk and Archangel, despite increasingly heavy losses to U-boat and aircraft attack. (U.S. later opens major shipping route across North Pacific to Siberia, and supplies most of the aid sent to Soviets, including extremely valuable railroad and telephone equipment, large amounts of food, and over 400,000 trucks.)

Japanese government formally decides on July 2 to remain neutral in German-Soviet war unless the Soviet Union collapses, to occupy southern Indochina, and to prepare for war with Britain and the United States. Vichy French sign agreement on July 21 giving Japanese military control of southern Indochina, including air and naval bases that can be used to attack Malaya, the Dutch East Indies, and the Philippines. Roosevelt responds on July 26 by freezing Japanese assets in the U.S. (implementation of policy results in total embargo of oil exports to Japan, although Roosevelt intended only to sharply reduce them; U.S. is the source of 80 percent of Japanese oil imports).

Sept.   Germans begin siege of Leningrad (some supplies continue to reach city across Lake Lagoda). Kiev falls to Germans, September 19, during encirclement battle in which they capture over 500,000 prisoners.

Following U-boat attack on U.S. destroyer, September 4, Roosevelt orders navy to escort convoys between the U.S. and Iceland and to destroy Axis naval vessels operating in this zone.

As negotiations in Washington continue, Japanese leadership decides on September 3 to go to war with the United States unless the U.S. accepts Japanese domination of China and Southeast Asia.

Oct.   Germans begin attack on Moscow October 2 and capture over
                    600,000 prisoners before advance is halted October 30 by au-
                    tumn rain and mud. Soviet defense is strengthened by increasing
                    production of T-34 tanks (until 1943 T-34 is superior to all Ger-
                    man tanks, and is equal to new German models introduced in
                    1943). Relocation of factories to Urals region allows Soviet arms
                    production to increase in 1942 despite German occupation of
                    many key industrial centers.

                    Roosevelt orders intensification of U.S. research into atomic
                    weapons on October 9 after receiving British report concluding
                    that atomic bomb could be built within three years.

                    U-boat sinks U.S. destroyer on convoy duty in Atlantic,
                    October 31, killing 115 men.

                    Konoye resigns as Japanese prime minister on October 16 and
                    is succeeded by Tojo. Navy staff approves, October 20, proposal
                    by fleet commander Admiral Yamamoto Isoroku to begin war
                    with surprise air attack against U.S. naval base at Pearl Harbor in
                    Hawaii (Yamamoto had begun planning for attack in December
                    1940).

Nov.   Attack on Moscow resumes November 15 after ground freezes.
                    Germans continue offensive in blizzards and subzero tempera-
                    tures despite lack of winter clothing and equipment and reach
                    within 15 miles of Moscow by end of November.

                    British begin successful offensive into Libya on November 18.

                    Japanese government formally decides on November 5 to
                    begin war in early December. War plan calls for conquering the
                    Philippines, Malaya, Dutch East Indies, Burma, and the Ameri-
                    can islands in the western Pacific within six months, creating an
                    extended defensive perimeter; Japanese hope that the U.S. will
                    negotiate peace rather than fight a long and costly war. Task
                    force of six aircraft carriers and 24 supporting ships sails from
                    northern Japan on November 26 and begins crossing Pacific,
                    avoiding normal shipping routes and maintaining complete radio
                    silence.

Dec.   Soviets surprise Germans by launching major counteroffen-
                    sive around Moscow on December 5, using recently mobilized
                    reservists and troops brought from Siberia during autumn. Ger-
                    mans are driven back and their central front is threatened with
                    disintegration.

                    Deciphered Japanese diplomatic messages alert Roosevelt and
                    his senior advisers that Japanese have decided to go to war, but
                    do not indicate that Pearl Harbor will be attacked. Administra-
                    tion anticipates that hostilities will begin in Malaya and East
                    Indies, and army and navy commanders in Hawaii fail to act on
                    general warnings of war and do not detect approaching task
                    force. Japanese carriers approach to within 200 miles of Oahu on

morning of December 7 and launch 350 aircraft in two waves. At 7:55 A.M. (Honolulu time) attack on Pearl Harbor and nearby airfields begins, achieving complete surprise. Attack sinks or damages eight battleships, three cruisers, three destroyers, and four auxiliary vessels, destroys 188 aircraft, and kills 2,335 servicemen. (Two battleships and one auxiliary vessel are permanently lost; all of the other ships are eventually repaired and see service during the war.) Japanese lose only 29 aircraft, but fail to launch second strike against oil storage tanks and repair facilities, allowing Pearl Harbor to continue serving as fleet base. All three U.S. carriers in the Pacific are at sea and escape damage (Japan has total of 10 carriers, the U.S. seven).

Japanese begin offensive across Southeast Asia, attacking Hong Kong, occupying Thailand, landing in northern Malaya, and bombing the Philippines on December 8 (December 7 in U.S.). In the Philippines more than 100 U.S. aircraft are destroyed on the ground nine hours after General Douglas MacArthur and other commanders learn of Pearl Harbor attack. United States, Britain, and Commonwealth nations declare war on Japan on December 8. Japanese capture Guam and land advance forces on main Philippine island of Luzon on December 10. Sinking of British battleship and battle cruiser by aircraft off Malaya on December 10 gives Japanese control of South China Sea, and long range and superior performance of their Zero fighters give Japanese control of the air in Malaya and over Luzon. Attempted landing on Wake Island is repulsed by U.S. marines on December 11.

Germany and Italy declare war on the United States on December 11 and the U.S. immediately responds with its own declarations. Hitler assumes direct operational control of German army, dismisses many senior commanders, and forbids general retreat on eastern front.

Roosevelt and Churchill begin conference in Washington, December 22, which confirms strategy, agreed upon in earlier Anglo-American consultations, of defeating Germany before Japan (Germany is considered by both American and British leaders to be the more dangerous enemy).

Main Japanese force of 43,000 men lands on Luzon in the Philippines on December 22. Japanese capture Wake Island on December 23. About 15,000 American and 65,000 Filipino troops on Luzon retreat to Bataan peninsula, where they suffer from severe shortages of food and medicine. British garrison surrenders at Hong Kong on December 25. U.S. submarines begin operations in Pacific, but achieve little success at first due to poor tactics, inexperienced leadership, defective torpedoes, and doctrine that emphasizes attacks on well-defended warships.

1942   Japanese forces begin offensive on Bataan, January 9, land in Dutch East Indies, January 11, advance into southern Burma, January 15, and seize Rabaul on New Britain on January 23. British, Indian, and Australian forces retreat from southern Malaya to Singapore on January 31, ending campaign in which 35,000 Japanese with superior training, equipment, and leadership defeat 60,000 Allied troops.

Stalin orders general offensive along entire front against advice of senior army commanders, who favor concentrating Soviet forces to achieve destruction of Germans outside of Moscow. Resulting dispersion of reserves, heavy losses since June 1941, and strength of German defensive positions prevent Soviets from winning decisive victory (Soviets will drive Germans back 80 miles from Moscow but fail to relieve Leningrad or regain major ground on southern front before thaw in April brings reduction in fighting).

Germans and Italians end their retreat in Libya at El Algheila. Reinforcement of Luftwaffe in Mediterranean allows more Axis supply ships to reach North Africa. Axis counterattack on January 21 reaches Gazala on February 7 before halting.

U-boats open offensive along U.S. Atlantic coast in January (later extended to Gulf of Mexico and Caribbean). Refusal of U.S. navy to organize coastal convoys until late spring and delay in instituting coastal blackout results in heavy losses, especially of tankers.

SS leaders meet with other German officials in Berlin district of Wannsee on January 20 to coordinate plans for deportation and murder of European Jews. *Einsatzgruppen* continue mass killings in eastern Europe in 1942, while from December 1941 to November 1942 SS establishes killing centers in Poland at Chelmno, Belzec, Auschwitz-Birkenau, Sobibor, Treblinka, and Majdanek, where Jews are brought by train from throughout Europe to be gassed. Genocide campaign eventually involves thousands of German officials and European collaborators and continues until the end of the war.

Feb.–Mar.   New Enigma cipher, introduced February 1, ends British reading of U-boat signals, while German navy begins breaking British code used to control convoy movements. Germans sink over 3 million tons of shipping, January–June 1942, while losing only 21 U-boats.

RAF abandons attempts to bomb precise targets at night and begins "area bombing" offensive designed to break morale of German industrial workers by destroying their housing (British will not have sufficient aircraft to begin sustained bombing offensive until 1943).

Germans begin economic mobilization for prolonged war and,

despite Allied bombing, are able to increase weapons production in 1942–44 by reducing civilian production, improving their economic planning and administration, and exploiting slave labor from occupied countries. (In 1942–44 Germany produces 37,000 tanks and self-propelled guns, while Britain manufactures 20,000; the Soviet Union, 77,000; and the U.S., 72,000. Germany produces 80,000 military aircraft in 1942–44, while Japan manufactures 53,500; Britain, 76,000; the Soviet Union, 100,000; and the U.S., 230,000.)

Japanese halt offensive on Bataan, February 8, and wait for reinforcements after suffering heavy losses in combat and from disease. Strength of Japanese air and naval forces in Pacific prevents any U.S. attempt to relieve or evacuate Philippines. Japanese attack Singapore on February 8. Singapore garrison surrenders on February 15 in worst British defeat of the war (Japanese capture 130,000 prisoners in Malaya and Singapore). Dutch, British, Australian, and U.S. navies lose five cruisers and six destroyers in surface actions in East Indies, February 27–March 1. Japanese capture Rangoon on March 8 and continue their advance into Burma, severing Allied supply route into China. MacArthur leaves the Philippines. Last Allied forces on Java surrender, March 12, completing Japanese conquest of Dutch East Indies.

Roosevelt signs executive order on February 19 that results by September 1942 in internment without trial or hearing of over 120,000 Japanese-Americans and Japanese resident aliens living on the West Coast. (Japanese-Americans are eventually permitted to join the military, and over 17,000 serve in the infantry in Europe and in front-line intelligence units in Asia and the Pacific.)

April Japanese launch new offensive on Bataan on April 3. Campaign ends April 9 with surrender of 12,000 U.S. and 63,000 Filipino troops, who are forced to make 65-mile "Death March" on which thousands are murdered or die from disease. (Less than 60 percent of the 20,000 Americans captured in the Philippines survive the war.) Japanese carriers raid into the Indian Ocean in early April, bombing Ceylon and sinking a British light carrier and two cruisers. In raid designed to raise American morale, 16 twin-engine B-25 bombers take off from aircraft carrier 650 miles from Japan on April 18 and bomb Tokyo and four other cities before flying on to China. Raid causes very little damage, but shames Japanese commanders and results in final approval of proposal by Yamamoto to capture Midway Island and draw U.S. carriers into decisive battle. U.S. navy learns from Japanese radio signals of planned landing at Port Moresby in southeastern New Guinea, first in series of operations designed to sever

U.S.–Australia supply routes. Admiral Chester Nimitz, commander of U.S. Pacific fleet, sends two carriers to Coral Sea to block invasion.

May   Japanese capture of Corregidor on May 6 ends major resistance in the Philippines (Filipino guerrillas will fight throughout Japanese occupation). In Battle of the Coral Sea, May 7–8, U.S. navy turns back Port Moresby invasion force, losing one carrier and two smaller ships while sinking a Japanese light carrier and inflicting damage and aircraft losses that prevent two other Japanese carriers from participating in subsequent Midway operation. Battle is first in naval history fought between opposing carrier forces, and in which opposing ships never come into sight of one another. Japanese complete conquest of Burma in mid-May. U.S. navy codebreakers provide detailed information concerning Midway operation and simultaneous diversionary attack on Aleutian Islands. Nimitz commits the three remaining carriers in Pacific fleet to battle in hopes of taking Japanese by surprise (Yamamoto anticipates that U.S. carriers will be in harbor when Midway invasion begins).

British invade Vichy-controlled island of Madagascar on May 5 to prevent its possible use as naval base by Axis (campaign continues until Vichy forces surrender on November 5, 1942).

Soviet offensive against Kharkov in eastern Ukraine is defeated, May 12–29, with loss of over 200,000 prisoners.

Axis begins new offensive in Libya on May 26.

June   In Battle of Midway, June 3–6, U.S. carrier aircraft sink four Japanese carriers and one cruiser, while the U.S. loses one carrier and one destroyer to air and submarine attack. Japanese navy also loses many of its most experienced pilots, and abandons planned invasion of Midway. Victory allows U.S. to take the initiative in the Pacific war.

Japanese occupy Kiska and Attu, uninhabited islands at western end of the Aleutians, June 6–7.

Roosevelt authorizes full-scale U.S. effort to build atomic weapons on June 17.

Germans capture 30,000 Allied prisoners in Libyan port of Tobruk on June 21 and then advance into Egypt.

Germans launch general offensive in southern Russia and eastern Ukraine on June 28 with objective of capturing Caucasian oil fields (Germans no longer have enough men, vehicles, or draft horses to attack along entire front as in 1941; though heavy fighting will occur on central and northern fronts in 1942, neither side will gain or lose much territory).

July   British halt Axis advance in Egypt near El Alamein, only 60 miles from Alexandria, in heavy fighting July 1–22. Defense is aided by recent breaking of German army Enigma ciphers. (Allies will intermittently gain valuable intelligence from German army signals for remainder of war.)

German attack in southern Russia rapidly gains ground, but Soviets are generally able to retreat and avoid major encirclements. Hitler issues directive on July 23 calling for simultaneous advances southward into the Caucasus and eastward toward Stalingrad, industrial and transportation center on Volga River; order results in serious overextension of German forces.

U-boats end American coastal offensive and return in strength to Atlantic convoy routes, sinking over 3 million tons of shipping, July–December 1942; although Germans lose 65 U-boats in this period, increased production replaces these losses and allows Germany to begin 1943 with over 200 operational U-boats. Allied convoys lose most heavily in "air gap," mid-Atlantic region beyond the range of land-based air patrols (U-boats have limited underwater speed and endurance; to effectively pursue convoys, they must cruise on the surface and risk air attack). Although new American construction promises to eventually replace losses, rate of sinking threatens ability of Allies to move men and supplies overseas and launch offensives against the Axis.

U.S. transport aircraft based in northeastern India begin flying supplies across mountains ("The Hump") into China.

Japanese land at Buna on northern coast of eastern New Guinea (Papua), July 21, and begin overland advance toward Port Moresby. Americans prepare for landing on Guadalcanal, first stage of planned counteroffensive in the Solomon Islands and New Guinea with ultimate objective of capturing Rabaul, key Japanese naval and air base in the southwest Pacific.

Aug.   Marines land on Guadalcanal and nearby islands of Tulagi and Gavutu, August 7, and capture partially constructed airfield on northern Guadalcanal; surviving Japanese retreat inland. Night attack by Japanese cruiser force early on August 9 sinks one Australian and three U.S. cruisers in Battle of Savo Island. (For most of Guadalcanal campaign superior training, tactics, equipment, and torpedoes give Japanese navy advantage in night surface engagements.) Allied transport ships are withdrawn on August 9 before they are fully unloaded, leaving 17,000 marines onshore short of supplies and equipment. Marines establish defensive perimeter around airfield (Henderson Field) and complete its construction. Japanese begin landing reinforcements on Guadalcanal. First aircraft land at Henderson Field on August 20. U.S. achieves control of air during day, but Japanese navy is able to land supplies and troops and bombard American positions at night. Japanese lose one light carrier in Battle of the Eastern Solomons on August 24. In Papua Japanese continue advance across Owen Stanley mountains toward Port Moresby, and on

August 25 land troops at Milne Bay on eastern end of New Guinea.

Germans advance into northern Caucasus. Allied raid against French port of Dieppe on August 19 is repulsed with loss of over 3,000 men killed or captured, almost all of them Canadian; disaster causes Allied planners to avoid direct assaults on well-defended ports in future amphibious landings.

Renewed Axis offensive in Egypt is defeated in battle of Alam Halfa, August 30–September 5. British receive emergency shipment of American tanks and prepare for major counteroffensive in Egypt.

Sept.   Germans reach outskirts of Stalingrad in early September. Stalin agrees to proposal by generals Georgi Zhukov and Alexander Vasilevsky to hold city with minimum of forces possible while building large reserves of men, tanks, and artillery for counteroffensive against German flanks in open country outside Stalingrad. House-to-house fighting begins in city.

Australian defenders repulse Milne Bay landing in New Guinea, and surviving Japanese are evacuated on September 7. Major Japanese attack on Henderson Field on Guadalcanal is defeated in heavy fighting, September 12–14. Air and sea engagements in Solomons continue as both sides struggle to send men and supplies to Guadalcanal. Australians halt Japanese advance 30 miles from Port Moresby, September 16, then take the offensive (both sides in Papua fighting suffer from extreme terrain and climate conditions).

Oct.–Nov.   British offensive at El Alamein begins October 23 and achieves decisive victory. Axis forces begin retreating toward Libya on November 4. U.S. and British forces land in Morocco and Algeria on November 8. Fighting between Allied and Vichy French troops ends November 11. Germans occupy southern France and begin moving troops and aircraft into Tunisia. British troops enter Tunisia November 16 and encounter strong German resistance. Vichy French navy scuttles remainder of its Mediterranean fleet to prevent its falling under German control.

Soviet positions in Stalingrad are reduced by mid-November to series of strongholds in ruins along Volga. Soviet counteroffensive outside Stalingrad begins November 19, and on November 23 Soviets complete encirclement of 250,000 German troops. Hitler forbids trapped German forces from attempting to break out of encirclement.

Two Japanese battleships bombard Henderson Field early on October 14, destroying about half the aircraft on Guadalcanal. Japanese land several thousand reinforcements and attack Henderson Field perimeter, October 23–26, but are repulsed in intense fighting and lose over 2,000 dead. U.S. loses aircraft carrier in Battle of Santa Cruz Islands, October 26; Japanese have two carriers damaged, and suffer severe aircraft losses (U.S. now has only two carriers in Pacific, both of which are undergoing repair for battle damage). Australians advance over Owen Stanley mountains in Papua.

In series of air attacks, submarine attacks, and two night surface engagements fought November 13–15 and later known as Naval Battle of Guadalcanal, U.S. loses two cruisers and seven destroyers while sinking two Japanese battleships, one cruiser, and three destroyers, and destroying large convoy carrying reinforcements and supplies. Increasing numbers of Japanese troops on Guadalcanal die from hunger and disease as U.S. gains control of waters around island.

Australians force Japanese in Papua to retreat into fortified Buna-Gona coastal area. American troops are flown into improvised landing strips and join attack on Buna-Gona position.

Dec.   German offensive designed to break into Stalingrad encirclement fails. Soviets launch new offensive on December 16 that threatens to reach Rostov-on-Don and cut off German forces in the Caucasus.

Tunisian fighting stalemates as winter rains make road movement extremely difficult. Axis forces continue retreat across Libya.

British break U-boat Enigma cipher system introduced in February 1942 and begin intermittently reading U-boat signals (Enigma cipher keys change daily; some keys are never broken, while others are broken only after considerable delay).

First self-sustaining nuclear chain reaction is achieved on December 2 at University of Chicago.

U.S. forces on Guadalcanal begin series of attacks against Japanese positions on jungle-covered ridges overlooking Henderson Field. Allies suffer high casualties in offensive against Buna-Gona in Papua, but use air attacks to keep supplies from reaching Japanese defenders. Concerned by Allied gains in Papua, Japanese command decides on December 26 to evacuate Guadalcanal.

British and Indian troops begin limited offensive in Burma in Arakan region along coast.

1943   Germans begin retreating from Caucasus. Soviets continue offensives in southern Russia and, in northwestern Russia, open narrow land corridor into Leningrad on January 18.

Roosevelt announces and Churchill endorses demand for "unconditional surrender" of Germany, Italy, and Japan at close of their conference in Casablanca, January 24. American bombers based in England attack Germany for first time on January 27. (American air strategy calls for daylight precision bombing of key industrial targets by aircraft flying beyond the range of fighter escort; U.S. commanders believe that close-formation flying and heavy defensive armament will sufficiently protect bombers against fighter attack.)

Americans begin major offensive on Guadalcanal. Allies complete capture of Buna-Gona position on January 22, ending six-month campaign in Papua costing about 3,000 U.S. and Australian and 7,000 Japanese lives.

Feb. – Mar.   Last German troops in Stalingrad surrender on February 2. Soviets capture Kharkov February 16 as their advance threatens destruction of entire German southern front. Germans open counteroffensive against overextended Soviet forces on February 20, and recapture Kharkov March 14. Front stabilizes as thaw in late March brings lull in fighting.

British forces advance from Libya into southeastern Tunisia. Germans begin counteroffensive against U.S. troops in Tunisia, February 14, and capture Kasserine Pass before being halted by British and American forces on February 22. British drive Axis forces from Mareth Line, defensive position in southeastern Tunisia, March 20–28.

RAF begins sustained night area bombing offensive against Germany on March 5, repeatedly attacking cities in the Ruhr and elsewhere with hundreds of bombers; by July 1943 campaign exceeds intensity of 1940–41 "Blitz" of Britain.

U-boats sink nearly 1.2 million tons of shipping, January–March 1943; Allies sink 40 U-boats, but grow increasingly concerned about safety of North Atlantic convoy routes.

Japanese complete evacuation of Guadalcanal on February 8, ending air, sea, and land campaign in which 7,000 Americans and 30,000 Japanese die (over 4,700 U.S. deaths are at sea). Allies begin logistical preparations for further operations in New Guinea and the Solomons with eventual objective of capturing Rabaul. (All Allied plans for amphibious operations are constrained by worldwide shortages of shipping and landing craft, and operations in the Pacific are generally given lower priority than those in Europe in accordance with "Germany First" strategy.) Losses at Midway, Guadalcanal, and Papua force Japanese to go on defensive throughout Pacific. In Battle of the Bismarck Sea, March 2–4, U.S. and Australian aircraft destroy convoy bringing reinforcements to Lae in eastern New Guinea, killing over 3,000 Japanese troops at sea. American air strength in Southwest Pacific increases as U.S. begins to produce land-based fighter aircraft equal in performance to the Japanese Zero.

Japanese begin series of counterattacks in Burma against Allied advance in the Arakan.

April   Germans begin planning offensive to destroy Soviet forces in
               large salient around Kursk. Soviets anticipate attack and begin
               building anti-tank defenses and accumulating armored reserves.

               Axis forces retreat into northern Tunisia as Allied air attacks
               sharply reduce supplies reaching them from across the Medi-
               terranean.

               Jewish resistance organizations in Warsaw ghetto begin upris-
               ing on April 19 as SS prepares to send remaining inhabitants to
               Treblinka extermination camp.

               Secret scientific laboratory at Los Alamos, New Mexico, begins
               work on design and manufacture of fission atomic weapons (con-
               struction of industrial facility for separating uranium-235 from
               uranium ore began in November 1942 at Oak Ridge, Tennessee;
               in August 1943 construction begins at Hanford, Washington, for
               reactor and processing plant for production of plutonium-239).

May–June   Allies break through Axis lines in northern Tunisia after heavy
               fighting, May 6–7. North African campaign ends May 13 with
               capture of 125,000 German and 115,000 Italian troops.

               Fighting in Warsaw ends May 15. Ghetto is destroyed by SS,
               and 56,000 Jews are killed either in Warsaw or at Treblinka; sev-
               eral thousand survivors hide among Polish population.

               Allies gain decisive advantage in Battle of the Atlantic as in-
               creasing numbers of long-range land-based aircraft and small es-
               cort aircraft carriers close mid-Atlantic "air gap." Improved
               airborne and ship radar, growing number of escort vessels with
               high-frequency direction-finding equipment (used to locate
               U-boats making radio transmissions), improved tactics and weap-
               ons, and increasing success in reading U-boat ciphers also con-
               tribute to sinking of 15 U-boats in April 1943 and 41 in May. On
               May 24 German navy orders U-boats to withdraw from main
               North Atlantic convoy routes. Allies adopt secure cipher for con-
               voy signals in June.

               Roosevelt, Churchill, and their staffs meet in Washington in
               May and set May 1, 1944, as date (D-Day) for cross-Channel
               invasion of France and opening of major land campaign against
               Germans in northwest Europe.

               U.S. forces land on Attu in Aleutians on May 11 and kill last
               defenders on May 30 as Japanese garrison fights until it is annihi-
               lated; over 2,300 Japanese and 600 Americans die in battle
               (Japanese will evacuate Kiska in July).

               British and Indian troops in Burma retreat from Arakan.

               Allies launch major offensive in Southwest Pacific on June 30,
               with U.S. and Australian troops attacking in New Guinea and
               U.S. forces landing on New Georgia in the Solomons.

July   Germans launch offensive against Kursk salient July 5, begin-
               ning largest tank battle of the war. British and Americans invade

Sicily July 10. Germans are unable to break through Soviet defenses and suffer heavy tank losses. Concerned about possible Italian collapse, Hitler orders Kursk offensive abandoned on July 13 and begins shifting troops to Italy. Mussolini is overthrown by coup in Rome, July 25, and new Italian government begins secret talks with Allies on surrender. (New regime imprisons Mussolini, but he is freed by Germans on September 12 and establishes a fascist government in northern Italy.)

RAF night raid on Hamburg on July 28 kills 40,000 civilians when unusually dense concentration of incendiary bombs create intense fires.

Aug.   Soviets begin series of major offensives on southern and central fronts on August 3 and capture Kharkov on August 23.

Allies enter Messina August 17, ending Sicilian campaign; most German troops escape to southern Italy.

American bombers attack Regensburg and Schweinfurt, August 17, in their deepest raid yet into Germany, losing 60 out of 376 aircraft. RAF continues area offensive against German cities.

Anglo-American chiefs of staff approve choice of Caen-Bayeux area of Normandy for invasion (landing area is later extended westward onto shore of Cotentin peninsula).

Americans capture Munda airfield, key objective on New Georgia, on August 5 after heavy fighting. U.S. destroyers sink three Japanese destroyers bringing reinforcements to New Georgia on August 6 as effective use of radar gives U.S. navy increasing advantage in night surface engagements. Japanese resistance on New Georgia ends in late August.

Sept.   British troops cross Straits of Messina on September 3 and land in southern Italy. Italian surrender is announced September 8. U.S. and British forces land at Salerno on September 9. Germans occupy Italy and launch counterattacks at Salerno, September 12–16, that threaten beachhead before they are repulsed with aid of heavy naval gunfire. Allied advance northward is slowed by mountainous terrain, poor roads, and extensive German demolitions.

Soviets capture Smolensk September 25 and begin establishing bridgeheads along western bank of Dnieper River. Recovery of agricultural and industrial resources of eastern Ukraine eases strain on Soviet economy.

U-boats return to North Atlantic convoy routes, hoping to regain initiative by using new acoustic homing torpedoes against escorts, but Allies quickly adopt effective countermeasures. Sinkings by U-boats, April–December 1943, total 1.4 million tons, while Allies sink 197 U-boats in this period.

U.S. and Australian forces land in New Guinea near Lae, September 4, and capture village on September 16. Allies continue offensive westward along northern New Guinea coast in series of overland advances and amphibious landings. U.S. submarine operations become increasingly effective as reliability of American torpedoes improves and more submarines are equipped with search radar. Submarine campaign now concentrates on destruction of merchant ships transporting oil and raw materials from Southeast Asia to Japan, and is aided by intelligence derived from decoded Japanese signals. Japanese lose 2.8 million tons of shipping from December 1941 to December 1943, almost 80 percent sunk by submarines; in this period 22 U.S. submarines are lost on Pacific patrols. (Japanese use their submarines for attacks on warships and for transporting supplies to isolated island garrisons, and lose 130 during the war.)

Oct.   Allies enter Naples October 1 and attack across Volturno River in mid-October. New Italian government declares war on Germany October 13.

Soviets attack across Dnieper into western Ukraine, preventing the Germans from using the river as winter defensive line. (Summer and autumn Soviet offensives in 1943 are aided by growing strength of their air force in close support of ground operations, and by increasing mobility given to their army by American trucks; most of German army still relies upon horse-drawn transport.)

U.S. loses 148 bombers over Germany in seven days, including 60 out of 291 sent October 14 on second raid against Schweinfurt ball-bearing plants. Losses force suspension of raids beyond range of fighter escort, which extends only over northwestern Germany.

Allies begin series of intensive air attacks on Rabaul; new plan calls for Rabaul to be heavily bombed and blockaded, but rejects land assault as unnecessary and highly costly.

Nov.–Dec.   Germans reinforce troops in France and begin strengthening coastal fortifications in anticipation of Allied invasion in 1944 (majority of German army will continue to fight Soviets for remainder of war).

Soviets capture Kiev November 6. Series of Soviet offensives in south during winter result in heavy German casualties and recovery by early 1944 of almost all Ukrainian territory lost in 1941.

In Italy, Allies attack across Sangro River in late November and reach Garigliano River in December. Heavy infantry casualties, difficult terrain, bad weather, and skillful defense slow Allied advance as Germans fight to hold southern Italy for as long as possible. (Hitler fears that Allies will use central and northern Italy to invade the Balkans, depriving Germany of important raw materials.)

RAF attacks Berlin November 18, beginning unsuccessful attempt to repeat devastation caused in Hamburg; British lose over 500 bombers in 16 raids through late March 1944.

Roosevelt, Churchill, and Stalin meet in Teheran, November 28–December 1. Stalin promises to enter war against Japan after defeat of Germany, and Roosevelt and Churchill agree in principle to major shifts in Polish borders (Poland eventually loses 70,000 square miles of its pre-war territory to the Soviet Union and is compensated with 40,000 square miles of eastern Germany, from which several million Germans are expelled in 1945–46). General Dwight Eisenhower is appointed as supreme allied commander for invasion of France with orders to "undertake operations aimed at the heart of Germany" and the destruction of its armed forces.

U.S. troops land on November 1 on Bougainville in the Solomons, where they establish defensive perimeter and begin constructing airfield. Japanese concentrate aircraft and warships at Rabaul to oppose Bougainville landing, but abandon counteroffensive after damaging raids by U.S. carrier aircraft in early November (in early 1944 Japanese withdraw remaining aircraft from Rabaul).

Growing number of U.S. aircraft carriers and support ships allows launching of series of offensives against Japanese-held Gilbert, Marshall, and Caroline island chains in central Pacific. (In 1942–45, Japanese bring into service 14 carriers of all sizes, many of them inadequate conversions of existing ships, while the U.S. commissions 17 large fleet carriers, nine light carriers, and 77 small escort carriers.) American forces land on Tarawa and Makin atolls in the Gilberts on November 20. Battle on Tarawa ends on November 23 after 1,000 Americans and 4,800 Japanese are killed. Fighting on Makin ends on November 23 with destruction of smaller Japanese garrison. U.S. marines land on Cape Gloucester at western end of New Britain on December 26.

1944   Soviet offensive, January 14–27, drives Germans away from Leningrad and brings final end to siege in which 800,000–1,000,000 Soviet civilians died of starvation and disease.

Allies launch major offensive against Gustav Line, main German defensive position south of Rome, on January 17. British and American troops land at Anzio, 30 miles south of Rome and 60 miles behind Gustav Line, on January 22. Germans send troops to contain beachhead as Allied forces consolidate their position near the coast. Heavy fighting continues along Gustav Line, especially in mountains around Cassino, town commanding main highway to Rome.

Marines capture airfield on Cape Gloucester and repulse Japanese counterattacks. After preliminary carrier raids and shore bombardment, U.S. forces begin landing on Kwajalein atoll in the Marshalls on January 31.

Feb.–Mar.   Attacks by British, Indian, and New Zealand troops, February 15–18 and March 15–23, fail to drive Germans from Cassino. German counteroffensive at Anzio is repulsed in intense fighting, February 16–18, but Allies are unable to subsequently advance from beachhead.

Increasing numbers of P-51B long-range fighter aircraft allow U.S. to resume daylight raids deep into Germany in series of raids against aircraft factories, February 20–25 ("Big Week"). Escorted U.S. bombers attack Berlin on March 6 as daylight air battle continues over Germany with heavy losses on both sides. RAF suspends deep raids into Germany and begins major bombing campaign against French and Belgian railway system in preparation for invasion.

Using dummy landing craft, false radio signals, and their complete control of the German espionage network in Britain, Allies begin successful deception operation designed to lead Germans to suspect invasion will occur not in Normandy but in the Pas de Calais, northeastern region of France that is closer to Germany.

Fighting on Kwajalein ends February 4. U.S. launches highly successful carrier raid against Truk, major Japanese air and naval base in the Carolines (after further raids against Truk in April, Carolines are bypassed for remainder of war). Landings begin on Eniwetok atoll in the Marshalls, February 17, and fighting continues until February 23. U.S. casualties in Marshalls are lower than on Tarawa; Japanese garrisons are almost completely annihilated.

British and Indian troops advance in Burma in renewed offensive in the Arakan. Japanese counterattack and succeed in encircling several Allied positions, but surrounded troops receive supplies by parachute drop and hold their positions (in previous jungle battles in Southeast Asia, Allied troops usually retreated when the Japanese launched infiltration attacks against their supply lines). Small American infantry force joins U.S.-trained and -equipped Chinese troops in offensive in northern Burma intended to increase flow of supplies into China.

U.S. troops land in Admiralty Islands north of New Britain on February 29, and Japanese resistance on islands ends March 18. Japanese counteroffensive on Bougainville in March is defeated in heavy fighting. Securing of bases on Bougainville, New Britain, and Admiralties completes the containment of Japanese at Rabaul. (Australian troops relieve U.S. forces on New Britain and Bougainville in autumn 1944, and fighting continues on both islands until the end of the war, when over 90,000 Japanese troops surrender.)

Japanese launch major offensive into northeastern India on March 8 with objective of capturing Allied bases at Imphal and Kohima. British and Indian troops withdraw into perimeter around Imphal airfields as siege begins on March 29.

April

Soviets approach Hungarian border and cross into northern Romania before end of their spring offensive.

British garrison at Kohima is besieged, April 5–18, but is supplied by parachute drops during intense close-range battle. Heavy fighting continues at Kohima, Imphal, and in Arakan throughout spring.

Japanese begin series of major offensives in central and southern China on April 17 that continue into autumn and inflict severe losses on Nationalist Chinese forces.

U.S. forces land at Aitape and Hollandia in northern New Guinea on April 22, bypassing Japanese position at Wewak in westward advance designed to secure bases for invasion of the Philippines.

May

Allies launch major offensive in Italy against Gustav Line on May 11. French and North African troops break through and force German withdrawal. Polish troops capture monastery at Cassino, May 18. Allies break out of Anzio beachhead, May 23, but are unable to trap retreating Germans, who begin pulling back in stages to Gothic Line, defensive position extending across northern Italy from Pisa to Rimini.

Allies win air superiority over western Europe as Luftwaffe is crippled by heavy losses in battles with U.S. fighters over Germany and increasing shortages of fuel and adequately trained pilots. U.S. begins bombing synthetic oil plants.

Heavy fighting continues in northwestern New Guinea as U.S. forces begin offensive in Wakde-Sarmi area, May 17, and land on Biak island, May 27, where they meet strong resistance from Japanese dug into hillside caves and bunkers (fighting continues on Biak until end of July).

U.S. and Chinese troops capture Myitkyina airfield in northern Burma on May 17 and begin battle for nearby town.

June

Allies enter Rome June 4. Eisenhower postpones D-Day, which had been rescheduled for June 5, because of adverse weather forecast, then decides to invade on June 6. British and American parachute and glider troops begin airborne assault on Normandy during night of June 5–6 and secure key positions on western and eastern flanks of invasion area. American, British, and Canadian troops begin landing on five Normandy beaches on morning of June 6 in largest amphibious operation in history. Resistance is heaviest on Omaha Beach, where U.S. infantry suffers heavy casualties before capturing high ground overlooking shore. German commanders are surprised by timing and location of invasion and respond slowly. By night of June 6 Allies have landed over 150,000 men at cost of about 10,000 men killed, wounded, or captured. Initial German counterattacks fail, and individual beachheads are joined into single continuous front by June 12. Allied control of air and sea allows rapid buildup of men and matériel in Normandy, while German reinforcements are delayed by Allied air attack, sabotage and ambushes by the French resistance, and belief by German commanders that Allies will launch second invasion in the Pas de Calais. Germans concentrate majority of their armored forces at eastern end of front to defend Caen from British and Canadian attacks. (Open country southeast of Caen is suitable for rapid armored advance; Germans hope to keep Allies confined in hedgerow country near coast, well-suited to their defensive tactics.)

Germans begin attacking London with V-1 unmanned jet aircraft on June 13.

Soviets concentrate massive numbers of men, tanks, artillery, and aircraft in Belorussia and on June 22 launch offensive that destroys center of German eastern front (Soviet deception plan has led Germans to send their reserves to northern Ukraine in anticipation of a renewed attack there).

British and Canadians continue attacks in Caen sector. Americans capture port of Cherbourg June 27.

U.S. troops invade Saipan in the Marianas on June 15, beginning campaign designed to secure bases for long-range bombing of Japan. Japanese navy responds in hopes of winning decisive victory, leading to first carrier engagement in Pacific since October 1942. In Battle of the Philippine Sea, June 19–20, Japanese lose three carriers (two of which are sunk by U.S. submarines) and over 400 aircraft; U.S. loses about 50 aircraft in combat. (U.S. navy fighter pilots are now better trained than Japanese, and fly new Hellcat fighters superior to the Zero; effectiveness of anti-aircraft fire from U.S. ships is significantly increased by use of radar proximity fuses. Increasing shortage of fuel prevents Japanese from adequately training pilots to replace those lost in Philippine Sea.) Heavy fighting continues on Saipan, where Japanese defenders make extensive use of caves in jungle-covered hills.

U.S. begins bombing Japan from Chinese airfields on June 15, but is unable to mount major attacks due to supply difficulties in China.

Allied forces in India end siege of Imphal on June 22.

July   Soviets capture Minsk in Belorussia on July 3 and begin offensive into the Baltic states. By mid-July German losses in Belorussia total 350,000 men, mostly killed or captured. Soviets launch offensive in northern Ukraine and advance into Poland.

Americans capture key crossroads at St. Lô in western Normandy on July 18 after weeks of costly fighting. British offensive southeast of Caen, July 18–20, fails to break through but causes further attrition of German armor.

Hitler is slightly wounded when bomb planted by anti-Nazi military officers explodes at his East Prussian headquarters on July 20. Coup attempt in Berlin fails when his survival becomes known (over 200 people are executed for involvement in the plot). Americans launch major offensive west of St. Lô on July 25 that breaks through German lines and allows U.S. armor to reach open country.

Soviets establish bridgeheads across Vistula River and begin fighting in eastern suburbs of Warsaw.

Fighting ends on Saipan on July 9. Over 8,000 Japanese civilians living on the island commit suicide rather than surrender. Tojo resigns on July 18 and is replaced as prime minister by General Koiso Kuniaki. Marianas campaign continues with landings on Guam, July 21, and Tinian, July 24.

Japanese abandon Imphal offensive on July 9 and retreat through mountains into Burma; 30,000–50,000 Japanese die in Imphal-Kohima battles, many from hunger and disease. British prepare for offensive into Burma at end of monsoon season.

U.S. forces reach northwestern end of New Guinea on July 30. (Fighting continues in New Guinea until end of war, especially between Australians and Japanese in Aitape-Wewak area.)

Aug.   Polish Home Army, anti-communist resistance movement, begins uprising against Germans in Warsaw on August 1. Soviets obstruct Western attempts to parachute aid to insurgents. Soviet offensive in Poland is slowed by shortage of supplies and increasing German resistance.

U.S. forces advance rapidly into Brittany and northeastern France as British and Canadians attack south from Caen. German counteroffensive intended to cut off American advance is defeated, August 7–10. U.S. and French troops land in southern France west of Cannes on August 15. Refusal of Hitler to authorize retreat in Normandy results in severe German losses of men and equipment in "pocket" near Falaise, closed by U.S., Canadian, and Polish troops, August 19–21. Paris is liberated by French troops on August 25 as Germans retreat across France. Losses in Normandy campaign in men killed, wounded, or captured are 450,000 for Germans and over 200,000 for Allies.

Soviets launch offensive into Romania August 20. New Romanian government signs armistice with Soviets August 23, then declares war on Hungary and Germany. Germans lose almost 200,000 men killed or captured in collapse of Romanian front.

Allies begin offensive along Adriatic coast of Italy against Gothic Line on August 25.

U-boats are forced to leave French Atlantic ports and retreat to Norwegian and German bases. Use of *Schnorchel* underwater breathing apparatus allows increasing number of U-boats to re- charge their batteries without surfacing, but their effectiveness is severely limited by slow underwater speed. German development of new class of U-boats capable of high underwater speeds worries Allies, but production difficulties and Allied bombing prevents them from becoming operational before the end of the war. U-boats sink 1 million tons of shipping, January 1944–May 1945; Allies sink 393 U-boats (27,500 U-boat crewmen are killed, 1939–45).

Effective Japanese resistance ends on Tinian and Guam in early August; over 5,000 Americans and about 50,000 Japanese are killed in Marianas campaign, mostly on Saipan.

Allied forces capture town of Myitkyina on August 3 as engi- neers work on Ledo Road, new overland route from India through north Burma into China.

Sept.　　　Finland signs armistice with Soviet Union on September 4. Bul- garia declares war on Germany September 8 as Soviet army enters the country.

British troops liberate Brussels, September 3, and Antwerp on September 4. Germans begin attacking London with V-2 ballistic missiles on September 8. U.S. forces advancing from northern and southern France meet near Dijon and American patrols cross Ger- man frontier near Aachen, September 11. Allied advance is slowed by difficulty in bringing gasoline and other supplies forward from Normandy and the Mediterranean coast (Germans still control Scheldt estuary leading to Antwerp and have left garrisons in many Channel and Brittany ports). Hitler begins planning late autumn counteroffensive in the Ardennes designed to split the Allied front and recapture Antwerp. American and British airborne troops land near Dutch towns of Eindhoven, Nijmegen, and Arnhem on Sep- tember 17 as British armored forces attack northward in operation designed to seize bridges across Waal, Maas, and lower Rhine rivers. Attack is halted south of Rhine, and on September 26 surviving British airborne troops at Arnhem are either evacuated across river or taken prisoner; total Allied casualties in operation are over 17,000 men killed, wounded, or captured.

Attacks on Gothic Line continue on both Adriatic and Mediterranean sides of the Apennines.

Loss of Romanian oil fields and continued U.S. bombing of synthetic oil plants causes fuel shortage that cripples Luftwaffe training and operations and severely affects motorized forces of German army.

Soviets attack into Hungary in late September.

Americans begin campaign in Palau Islands with landings on

Peleliu, September 15, and Anguar, September 17. Resistance on Peleliu is unexpectedly intense, and U.S. troops begin protracted struggle to kill Japanese defenders fighting from fortified caves in steep coral ridges.

Oct.   Warsaw uprising ends October 2; over 200,000 Poles are killed during revolt and the city is almost completely destroyed. Soviet advance into Romania and Bulgaria forces Germans to begin evacuating Greece, Albania, and southern Yugoslavia.

Canadian troops begin offensive to clear Scheldt estuary on October 6. Germans begin bombarding Antwerp with V-1s and V-2s on October 13 (attacks are extended to other Belgian cities during winter; V-weapons kill over 12,000 people in England and Belgium by spring 1945 and cause considerable destruction, but are too inaccurate to be militarily effective).

Luftwaffe begins limited operational use of Me-262 jet fighter, with top speed 100 miles per hour faster than American P-51B, but is unable to regain control of the air because of difficulty of mass-producing jet engines, crippling lack of fuel, severe shortage of trained pilots, and overwhelming Allied numerical superiority. German war production begins to decline as intensive bombing of transportation system disrupts the movement of coal and other industrial materials.

Soviets reach Baltic coast of Lithuania on October 9. German coup installs fascist puppet regime in Hungary on October 16, preventing Hungarian armistice with Soviets. Soviet troops and Titoist Partisans capture Belgrade on October 20. U.S. troops capture Aachen, first German city to fall to Allies, on October 21. Continuing Allied attacks in Holland, Aachen region, Lorraine, and Alsace gain ground slowly in face of determined German resistance, bad weather, difficult terrain, and shortages of supplies and infantry replacements. Germans build armored reserves for Ardennes counteroffensive. Heavy rain and flooded rivers make Allied operations in Italy increasingly difficult.

U.S. troops begin invasion of Philippines with landing on island of Leyte on October 20. Japanese navy commits most of its remaining ships to battle in attempt to destroy supply ships for invasion force. In the Battle of Leyte Gulf, complex series of air, submarine, and night and day surface engagements fought around northern and central Philippine islands, October 23–27, Japanese lose four carriers, three battleships, nine cruisers, and nine destroyers; U.S. losses are one light carrier, two escort carriers, and three destroyers (battle is largest naval engagement in history). Defeat leaves Japanese incapable of mounting major naval operations. An escort carrier sunk on October 25 is victim of first mass suicide attack ("kamikaze") by Japanese aircraft. Suicide attacks against ships continue as Japanese attempt to break American morale; kamikaze tactics also allow minimally trained pilots to cause greater damage than they would in conventional attacks.

Nov.   Roosevelt is reelected for fourth term on November 6. Scheldt estuary is cleared of German troops on November 8 (minesweeping delays arrival of first supply ships in Antwerp until November 28). Major American offensive launched near Aachen on November 16 reaches Roer River by end of November but is unable to advance further.

Heavy fighting continues on Leyte as Japanese reinforce island with troops from Luzon. Japanese resistance ends on Peleliu in late November; over 1,200 Americans and 11,000 Japanese are killed in Palaus, mostly on Peleliu. U.S. begins bombing Japan from bases in the Marianas on November 24, attacking industrial targets in daylight from high altitude, although high winds and dense clouds over targets make accurate bombing extremely difficult.

Japanese begin consolidating gains from 1944 offensives in southern China (in 1945 some conquered territory is abandoned in order to free troops for use elsewhere).

Dec.   Winter halts major Allied offensive operations in Italy. Germans attack thinly held American front in the Ardennes on December 16. After initial surprise and confusion, U.S. commanders begin sending reinforcements and planning counterattacks. Bad weather prevents air attacks on advancing Germans. Outnumbered American troops delay or prevent German capture of key road junctions, and offensive quickly falls behind schedule. German advance is halted east of the Meuse River on December 24 and U.S. counteroffensive against southern flank of German salient ("the Bulge") begins December 25. Allied fighter-bombers attack as weather improves.

British, Indian, and African troops begin advancing across Chindwin River in northern Burma. U.S. troops in Philippines land on island of Mindoro on December 15. Major Japanese resistance on Leyte ends on December 31.

Japanese merchant fleet is crippled by loss of 3.9 million tons of shipping in 1944 (U.S. submarines sink 70 percent of total tonnage, with carrier aircraft destroying most of remainder). Land-based aircraft begin using bases on Mindoro for attacks on shipping in South China Sea.

1945   Germans launch counteroffensive against Americans in Alsace on January 1 that threatens Strasbourg before it is halted in late January. By January 16 heavy fighting has regained Allies almost all ground lost in December; Ardennes battle costs U.S. 19,000 men killed, 47,000 wounded, and 15,000 captured; Germans lose 80,000–100,000 men killed, wounded, or captured.

Soviets launch offensive in Poland January 12, attacking out of Vistula bridgeheads with overwhelming superiority in men and weapons, and capture Warsaw January 17 (German forces in Poland have been weakened by priority given by Hitler to Ardennes offensive and defense of Hungarian oil fields). German front disintegrates, and millions of refugees flee as Soviet troops advance into eastern Germany, where they commit widespread murder and rape against civilian population. Soviets reach Oder River, 50 miles east of Berlin, on January 31.

U.S. invasion force sailing from Leyte to Luzon comes under heavy kamikaze attack. Troops begin landing at Lingayen Gulf on January 9. Japanese do not defend invasion beaches and withdraw into Luzon mountains. American forces encounter increasing resistance as they advance inland.

British forces in Burma begin series of crossings of Irrawaddy River. U.S. and Chinese troops open Ledo Road into China.

Feb.   Roosevelt, Churchill, and Stalin meet at Yalta in the Crimea, February 4–11, and reach agreements on occupation of Germany, organization of the United Nations, terms for Soviet entry into war against Japan, and holding of free elections in Poland (Soviets will fail to honor agreement on Poland).

Allies begin series of attacks into the German Rhineland on February 8. Soviet advance on Berlin is halted along Oder by supply difficulties and concern about remaining German forces in East Prussia and Silesia; Soviets shift forces to complete conquest of both regions. German resistance in Budapest ends February 13 after seven-week battle in city (intense fighting continues in Hungary until early April). RAF bombing of Dresden on February 13–14 kills approximately 60,000 civilians and destroys much of city. Allies advance toward Rhine in heavy fighting.

U.S. troops reach northern suburbs of Manila on February 3, then begin house-to-house battle for city. American carrier aircraft attack Japan on February 16 in first in series of raids. U.S. troops land on Palawan as operations begin to free central and southern Philippines from Japanese.

Marines land on Iwo Jima, volcanic island 760 miles south of Tokyo, on February 19 in attack aimed at capturing airfields for use as refueling and emergency landing strips by bombers based in the Marianas. Island is defended by over 21,000 Japanese fighting from extensive network of tunnels, bunkers, and caves. Marines capture summit of Mount Suribachi at southern end of Iwo Jima on February 23 (photograph of second flag raising on Suribachi becomes famous). Intense fighting continues as marines slowly advance northward.

British and Indian troops in Burma continue offensive across

Irrawaddy, receiving supplies by air and successfully using tanks in open country east of the river.

March   Americans capture bridge across Rhine at Remagen on March 7. Allies make series of assault crossings of the Rhine, March 22–24. Heavy losses in Ardennes and Rhineland battles leave Germans incapable of mounting continuous defense east of the Rhine, and U.S. troops begin rapid advance across northern Germany.

Battle for Manila ends on March 3 after most of the city is destroyed; about 1,000 Americans and 20,000 Japanese die in the fighting, while as many as 100,000 Filipino civilians are killed by artillery fire or are massacred by Japanese troops. Fighting continues in Luzon mountains.

U.S. abandons high-altitude daylight precision bombing of Japan and begins low-altitude night area attacks. In first major raid using new tactics, 334 B-29 bombers attack Tokyo with napalm on night of March 9–10, killing at least 84,000 civilians. (Incendiary bombing of Japanese cities continues until end of war, killing over 180,000 people and causing immense devastation.)

Major fighting on Iwo Jima ends on March 26 as marines overrun Japanese positions on northern end of the island. Battle costs lives of over 6,800 Americans and 20,000 Japanese.

Allies capture Meiktila, key Burmese transportation center, March 3, and successfully defend it against counterattacks.

April   U.S. forces encircle over 300,000 German troops in the Ruhr on April 1 and advance rapidly across northern Germany toward the Elbe River. Allies open spring offensive in Italy on April 9. American troops reach the Elbe near Magdeburg, about 60 miles west of Berlin, on April 11. Roosevelt dies of cerebral hemorrhage on April 12, and Vice-President Harry S. Truman becomes president. Eisenhower halts advance toward Berlin and directs Allied commanders to concentrate instead on destruction of remaining German forces west of the Elbe, an objective he considers to be of greater military importance. Soviets launch massive offensive across Oder and Neisse rivers toward Berlin on April 16. U.S. and Soviet troops meet on Elbe at Torgau, east of Leipzig, on April 25, cutting Germany in half. Soviets begin assault on center of Berlin on April 26. Mussolini is summarily shot by Italian partisans near Milan on April 28 as Allies advance rapidly northward. Hitler appoints Admiral Karl Dönitz, commander of the German navy, as his successor, then commits suicide in his Berlin bunker on April 30, with attacking Soviet troops only a quarter of a mile away.

U.S. forces invade Okinawa, densely populated island 350 miles southwest of Japan, on April 1 in largest amphibious operation of Pacific war. Japanese do not defend landing beaches, concentrating troops instead in caves, bunkers, and tunnels dug into series of steep ridges on southern end of island. U.S. troops quickly capture airfields in center of island and begin advancing north and south. Prime Minister Koiso resigns on April 5 and is succeeded by retired admiral Suzuki Kantaro. Japanese begin series of mass air attacks against Okinawa invasion fleet, using both conventional and kamikaze tactics. Major Japanese resistance in northern Okinawa ends in late April, but intense fighting continues in south.

Allied forces in central Burma begin mechanized advance southward toward Rangoon.

May   German forces in Italy surrender, May 2. (Losses of men killed, wounded, or captured in Italian campaign are 312,000 for the Allies, 435,000 for the Germans.) Berlin garrison surrenders on May 2. British troops reach the Baltic and U.S. forces advance into Bavaria and Austria as organized German resistance on the western front collapses. U.S. troops reach Mauthausen, last in series of concentration camps liberated by Americans in spring 1945, on May 5. After their offer to surrender only in the west is summarily rejected, representatives of German high command sign unconditional surrender on all fronts at Reims, France, on May 7, effective May 8; at Soviet insistence, surrender is again signed in Berlin on May 9.

Australian troops land in Borneo on May 1, beginning campaign that continues until the end of the war. Indian troops occupy Rangoon on May 3 before monsoon brings halt to major Allied operations in Southeast Asia.

Intense kamikaze raids continue on U.S. and British ships off Okinawa, with especially heavy attacks directed at destroyers and other escort vessels serving as radar pickets. U.S. army troops and marines attack Shuri Line, main defensive position in southern Okinawa, despite heavy rain, thick mud, and most intense Japanese artillery fire of Pacific war. Loss of key hill positions forces Japanese withdrawal from Shuri Line in late May.

June   Major fighting on Okinawa ends on June 21 after final Japanese defensive line is overrun. Americans lose 7,600 dead in land fighting; 4,900 men are killed in Okinawa naval campaign, mostly by kamikazes. Over 100,000 Japanese and Okinawan soldiers and between 70,000 and 150,000 Okinawan civilians are killed. U.S. invasion of Kyushu, southernmost of Japanese home islands, is scheduled for November 1, 1945.

July   Blockade of Japan intensifies as U.S. bombers lay thousands of mines in ports and straits of Japanese home islands, drastically reducing coastal shipping essential to Japanese economy. Continued U.S. air and submarine attacks reduce Japanese merchant fleet to one-sixth of its 1941 size and effectively end importation of oil, food, and raw materials into Japan. (During Pacific war U.S. submarines also sink eight Japanese carriers and one battle-ship; 52 boats and 3,500 men are lost in wartime submarine operations.)

Liberation of Philippines is proclaimed on July 5, but U.S. and Filipino troops continue fighting on Luzon and Mindanao until end of war, when over 110,000 surviving Japanese surrender. U.S. loses 14,000 men killed in Philippines land fighting, October 1944–August 1945, while over 300,000 Japanese either are killed or die from starvation and disease. (Philippines campaign engages more U.S. troops than any other operation in Pacific war.)

Japanese begin diplomatic effort to enlist Soviets in medi-ating end to the Pacific war. U.S. learns from reading coded messages between Tokyo and Japanese ambassador in Moscow that Japanese government considers unconditional surrender unacceptable, but is unable to agree on acceptable peace terms.

Los Alamos scientists test implosion design for atomic bomb using plutonium in desert 60 miles northwest of Alamogordo, New Mexico, on July 16, detonating device with explosive force equivalent to 18,000 tons of TNT. (Design for "gun assembly" bomb using uranium-235 is judged not to require explosive test-ing.) At conference in Potsdam, Germany, Stalin promises Tru-man that Soviet Union will enter war against Japan on August 15. Truman and senior advisers agree to use atomic bombs if Japa-nese reject ultimatum demanding their surrender, and order is transmitted on July 25. United States, Britain, and China issue Potsdam Declaration on July 26, calling for unconditional surren-der of Japanese armed forces and warning that the "alternative for Japan is prompt and utter destruction." Declaration does not mention Japanese emperor, but promises eventual establishment of a "peacefully inclined and responsible" Japanese government "in accordance with the freely expressed will of the Japanese people." Japanese government rejects Potsdam ultimatum on July 28.

Aug.   B-29 flying from Tinian drops uranium bomb over Hiroshima on August 6. Weapon explodes 1,900 feet above city at 8:16 A.M. with force equivalent to about 13,000 tons of TNT, killing at least 80,000 people. Soviet Union declares war on Japan on Au-gust 8 and launches massive invasion of Manchuria on August 9. Plutonium bomb is dropped by B-29 over Nagasaki on August 9, and explodes 1,650 feet above city at 11:02 A.M. with force equiva-lent to 22,000 tons of TNT, killing at least 35,000 people (hills shield part of Nagasaki from blast and heat of bomb). Japanese supreme council divides over issue of surrender, with prime min-ister, foreign minister, and navy minister favoring immediate ac-ceptance of Potsdam Declaration on condition that the Allies preserve the sovereignty of the emperor; army minister and army and navy chiefs of staff advocate continuing the war in hopes of obtaining better terms. Emperor Hirohito makes unprecedented intervention on August 10 by expressing support for immediate conditional acceptance of Potsdam Declaration. Conditional surrender offer is communicated to Allies on August 10 as U.S. continues large-scale conventional air attacks on Japan. American reply on August 11 states that the authority of the Emperor "to rule the state" after the surrender "shall be subject" to the decisions of the Allied occupation commander. Hirohito decides on August 14 to accept terms of U.S. reply. Truman announces Japanese surrender on August 14. Coup attempt by army officers in Tokyo fails to prevent unprecedented radio broadcast by Emperor on August 15 announcing surrender to Japanese people.

Sept.   Surrender is formally signed onboard American battleship in Tokyo Bay on September 2.

Over 293,000 Americans died in battle, from battle wounds, or as prisoners of war from 1941 to 1945, while another 115,000 Americans died from non-combat causes while serving in the armed forces during World War II. Over 107,000 died in battle in the war against Japan, and over 185,000 were killed in the war against Italy and Germany, mostly in the 1944–45 campaign in northwest Europe. Battle deaths by service were approximately 180,000 in the army, 55,000 in the army air forces, 38,000 in the navy, and 20,000 in the marines.

Britain lost 400,000 dead in the war, including over 60,000 civilians killed by air attacks and over 30,000 merchant seamen killed by enemy action. Canada lost over 39,000 military dead; India, 36,000; Australia, 27,000; and New Zealand, over 11,000. France lost about 200,000 military and at least 400,000 civilian dead, and there were more than 300,000 military and civilian dead in Italy. Over 1 million people died in Yugoslavia. Japan lost at least 1,500,000 military and 400,000 civilian dead in 1941–45, as well as 185,000 soldiers killed in China, 1937–41. Germany lost at least 3,300,000 military dead; over 500,000 German civilians were killed in air raids and another 1 million civilians died during the Soviet conquest of eastern Germany in 1945. At least 5,400,000 people died in Poland, almost all of them as the result of German atrocities. About 3 million of the Polish dead were Jews, and throughout Europe at least 5,750,000 Jews were murdered. Chinese deaths from 1937 to 1945 are estimated at between 10 and 15 million, mostly from famine. The Soviet Union lost at least 20 million military and civilian dead, and perhaps as many as 27 million. It is estimated that between 50 and 60 million people died in World War II.

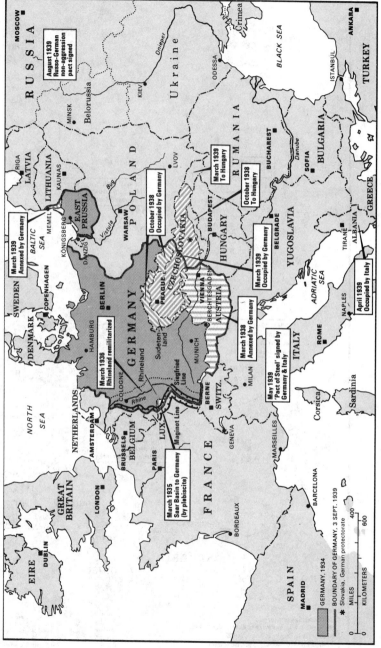

Europe, 1934–39

MOSCOW

RUSSIA

August 1939 Russo-German non-aggression pact signed

Crimea

BLACK SEA

ANKARA

TURKEY

ISTANBUL

Dnieper

Ukraine

ODESSA

MINSK

Belorussia

KIEV

RIGA

LATVIA

LITHUANIA

KAUNAS

RUMANIA

BUCHAREST

BULGARIA

SOFIA

Danube

March 1939 Annexed by Germany

EAST PRUSSIA

Baltic SEA

MEMEL

KÖNIGSBERG

SWEDEN

POLAND

Bug

LVOV

October 1938 Occupied by Germany

March 1939 To Hungary

October 1938 To Hungary

BUDAPEST

HUNGARY

GREECE

ALBANIA

TIRANE

YUGOSLAVIA

BELGRADE

COPENHAGEN

DANZIG

WARSAW

Vistula

DENMARK

HAMBURG

BERLIN

GERMANY

CZECHOSLOVAKIA

PRAGUE

March 1939 Occupied by Germany

VIENNA

BERCHTESGADEN

AUSTRIA

NAPLES

ADRIATIC SEA

NORTH SEA

COLOGNE

Rhineland

Rhine

Sudetenland

MUNICH

March 1938 Annexed by Germany

ROME

ITALY

NETHERLANDS

AMSTERDAM

March 1936 Rhineland remilitarized

Siegfried Line

SWITZ.

BERNE

May 1939 'Pact of Steel' signed by Germany & Italy

Sardinia

BRUSSELS

BELGIUM

LUX.

Maginot Line

PARIS

GENEVA

MILAN

Corsica

GREAT BRITAIN

LONDON

FRANCE

MARSEILLES

March 1935 Saar Basin to Germany (by plebiscite)

EIRE

DUBLIN

SPAIN

MADRID

BARCELONA

BORDEAUX

April 1939 Occupied by Italy

GERMANY, 1934

BOUNDARY OF GERMANY, 3 SEPT. 1939

* Slovakia, German protectorate

MILES

0   400   600

KILOMETERS

ARCTIC OCEAN

REYKJAVIK ICELAND

NARVIK

TRONDHEIM

BERGEN ● OSLO

3 Sept 1939 Britain & France declare war on Germany

STOCKHOLM

9 April 1940 Germany invades Norway & Denmark

Baltic Sea

ATLANTIC

NORTH SEA

EDINBURGH

GREAT

EIRE
DUBLIN ● LIVERPOOL

OCEAN

BRITAIN

AMSTERDAM

LONDON

DUNKIRK
BRUSSELS BELG.

DENMARK
COPENHAGEN

1 Sept 1939 Germany invades Poland

DANZIG E.PRU.

HAMBURG

BERLIN

COLOGNE

Vistula

GERMANY

4 June 1940

PARIS LUX.

Rhine

● PRAGUE

10 May 1940 Germany invades the Low Countries and France

Danube

SLOVAKI

Bay of
Biscay

FRANCE

VICHY ●

BERNE ● SWITZ.

MUNICH

VIENNA

BUD

HUNGAR

25 June 1940
BORDEAUX
(Vichy France)

MARSEILLES

MILAN

TURIN VENICE

FLORENCE ●

Adriatic Sea

BELGRADE

YUGOSLA

LISBON

MADRID

10 June 1940 Italy declares war on Britain and France

ROME ●

NAPLES

ALBANI

PORTUGAL

SPAIN

Sardinia

M E D

GIBRALTAR (Br)
SP.MOR.

CASABLANCA

ORAN

ALGIERS

TUNIS

PALERMO

Sicily

28 Oct 194 Italy invad Greece

MALTA (Br)

MOROCCO
(Fr)

ALGERIA
(Fr)

TUNISIA
(Fr)

TRIPOLI

SIRTE

L I B
(Italian)

Ceded Rumanian territories:
1. Bessarabia & N. Bukovina to Russia, June 1940
2. S. Dobruja to Bulgaria, August 1940
3. Transylvania to Hungary, September 1940

The War in Europe,
1939-40

Barents Sea

MURMANSK

White Sea

ARCHANGEL

Ceded to Russia,
1940

30 Nov 1939-1 March 1940
Russo-Finnish War

VIIPURI *L.Ladoga*

LENINGRAD

June 1940
Annexed by Russia

RIGA

MOSCOW

R U S S I A

SMOLENSK

VORONEZH

Volga

MINSK

17 Sept 1939
Russia invades
Poland

STALINGRAD

KHARKOV

KIEV *Dnieper*

LVOV

ROSTOV *Don*

*Caspian
Sea*

ODESSA

RUMANIA

BUCHAREST

Danube

SEVASTOPOL

TIFLIS

BULGARIA

SOFIA

BLACK SEA

IRAN

ISTANBUL

ANKARA

T U R K E Y

GREECE

ATHENS

IRAQ
(Br)

SYRIA
(Fr)

*Dodecanese
(Italian)*

Cyprus
(Br)

DAMASCUS

Crete

PALESTINE
(Br)

JERUSALEM

AMMAN

TRANSJORDAN
(Br)

TOBRUK

ALEXANDRIA

*Suez
Canal*

SAUDI
ARABIA

ENGHAZI

CAIRO

Nile

E G Y P T
(Br protectorate)

AXIS PARTNERS : 1939

GERMANY   ITALY

GERMAN SATELLITE

GERMAN OCCUPIED, 27 SEPT 1939

GERMAN OCCUPIED, 23 JUNE 1940

GERMAN FRONT LINES AT
DATES SHOWN

MILES   0   500

KILOMETERS   0   800

ARCTIC OCEAN

REYKJAVIK ICELAND

ATLANTIC

OCEAN

NORTH
SEA

GREAT
BRITAIN

EIRE
DUBLIN

EDINBURGH

LIVERPOOL

LONDON

AMSTERDAM

NETH.

BRUSSELS BELG.

PARIS LUX.

FRANCE

Bay of
Biscay

VICHY

BORDEAUX

MARSEILLES

Corsica

Sardinia

PORTUGAL

LISBON

MADRID

SPAIN

PORT
LYAUTEY

GIBRALTAR
(Br)

SP.MOR.

CASABLANCA

ORAN

ALGIERS

BÔNE

TUNIS

SAFI

ALGERIA
(Vichy French)

MOROCCO
(Vichy French)

TUNISIA
(Vichy French)

TRIPOLI

SIRTE

NORWAY

PETS

NARVIK

TRONDHEIM

BERGEN

OSLO

SWEDEN

STOCKHOLM

FIN

HELS

TALLIN

Baltic Sea

22 June 1941
("Barbarossa")
Germany invades
Russia

DENMARK COPENHAGEN

HAMBURG

BERLIN

KÖNI

DANZIG

E.PRUSS

Vistula

W

POLA

COLOGNE

GERMANY

Rhine

6-17 April 1941
Germany invades
Yugoslavia

SLOVAKIA

MUNICH

VIENNA

BUDAP

BERNE

SWITZ.

MILAN

TURIN

VENICE

HUNGARY

BELGRADE

YUGOSLAV

FLORENCE

Adriatic Sea

11 November 1942
Germans occupy
Vichy France

ROME

ITALY

ALBANIA

NAPLES

8 Nov 1942
US/British forces land
in Morocco & Algeria

MEDITER

9 Nov 1942
German forces
land in Tunisia

6-28 April 1941
Germany invades
Greece

RANE

AN

MALTA (Br)

20-2
Crete

1941-194
Axis forc
engaged

BENGHAZI

EL A

LIB
Y

(Italian)

The War in Europe
and North Africa,
1941-42

Barents Sea

MURMANSK

ARCHANGEL

White Sea

PETROZAVODSK

L. Ladoga

**15 Sept 1941
Siege of Leningrad
begins**

LENINGRAD

DEMYANSK

**5/6 Dec 1941–end April 1942
Russian counteroffensive
on Moscow axis**

SKOV

MOSCOW

R U S S I A

GA

AUNAS

SMOLENSK

TULA

Volga

MINSK

VORONEZH

**19 Nov 1942
High-tide of German expansion.
Russian counteroffensive begins**

STALINGRAD

KIEV

KHARKOV

Dnieper

Don

LVOV

ZAPOROZHYE

ROSTOV

Caspian
Sea

ODESSA

GROZNY

NOVOROSSIISK

SEVASTOPOL

TIFLIS

UMANIA

CHAREST

BLACK SEA

Danube

BULGARIA

SOFIA

IRAN

ISTANBUL

ANKARA

T U R K E Y

ECE

ATHENS

SYRIA
(Free French)

IRAQ
(Br)

Dodecanese
(Italian)

Cyprus
(Br)

DAMASCUS

941

Crete

PALESTINE
(Br)
JERUSALEM

AMMAN
TRANSJORDAN
(Br)

S E A

it Eighth Army
es across the desert

ALEXANDRIA

Suez
Canal

SAUDI
ARABIA

TRIPOLI

EL ALAMEIN

CAIRO

Nile

**23 Oct–4 Nov 1942
Battle of El Alamein**

E G Y P T

A

Map legend:

GERMAN OCCUPIED, 1 JAN 1941
ALLIED WITH AXIS
GERMAN OCCUPIED,
1 JAN – 29 MAY 1941
22 JUNE 1941 – 19 NOV 1942

GERMAN FRONT LINES
16 JULY 1941
5 DECEMBER 1941
END-APRIL 1942
19 NOVEMBER 1942

| 0 | MILES | 500 |
| 0 | KILOMETERS | 800 |

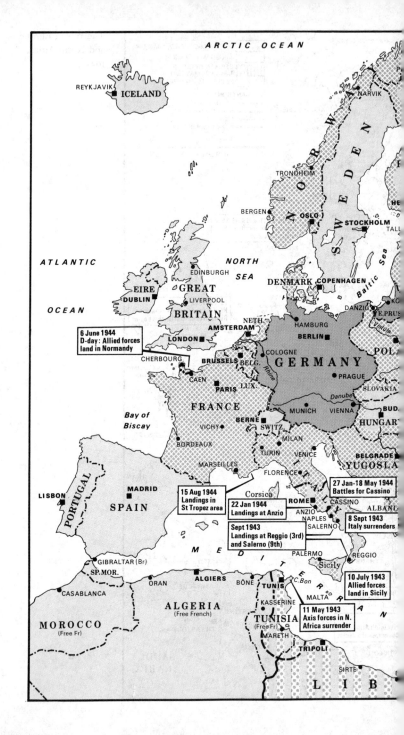

ARCTIC OCEAN

REYKJAVIK ICELAND

NARVIK

NORWAY

TRONDHEIM

BERGEN OSLO STOCKHOLM

SWEDEN

ATLANTIC

NORTH SEA

Baltic Sea

EDINBURGH

GREAT BRITAIN

EIRE DUBLIN

LIVERPOOL

DENMARK COPENHAGEN

HAMBURG

DANZIG

E.PRUS

OCEAN

AMSTERDAM

NETH.

Vistula

6 June 1944 D-day: Allied forces land in Normandy

LONDON

BERLIN

POL

CHERBOURG

BRUSSELS BELG.

COLOGNE

GERMANY

CAEN

PARIS LUX.

PRAGUE

SLOVAKIA

FRANCE

Rhine

MUNICH

VIENNA

Danube

BUD.

Bay of Biscay

BERNE

SWITZ.

VICHY

MILAN

HUNGAR

BORDEAUX

TURIN

VENICE

BELGRADE

MARSEILLES

YUGOSLA

FLORENCE

Corsica

27 Jan-18 May 1944 Battles for Cassino

LISBON

MADRID

15 Aug 1944 Landings in St Tropez area

22 Jan 1944 Landings at Anzio

CASSINO

ROME

ANZIO

NAPLES

ALBAN

PORTUGAL

SPAIN

Sept 1943 Landings at Reggio and Salerno (9th)

SALERNO

8 Sept 1943 Italy surrenders

PALERMO

REGGIO

GIBRALTAR (Br)

SP.MOR.

Sicily

10 July 1943 Allied forces land in Sicily

CASABLANCA

ORAN

ALGIERS

BÔNE

TUNIS

C.Bon

MALTA

MOROCCO (Free Fr)

ALGERIA (Free French)

KASSERINE

TUNISIA (Free Fr)

11 May 1943 Axis forces in N. Africa surrender

N

MARETH

TRIPOLI

SIRTE

L I B

LIBERATED BY ALLIES
19 NOVEMBER 1942 – 4 JULY 1943
4 JULY 1943 – 23 JUNE 1944

ALLIED FRONT LINES
——— 2 FEBRUARY 1943
········· 4 JULY 1943
–·–·– 14 JANUARY 1944
–··–··– 23 JUNE 1944

MILES
0   500
0   800
KILOMETERS

Barents Sea

MURMANSK

White Sea

ARCHANGEL

AND

PETROZAVODSK

IIPURI
L. Ladoga

Jan 1943
Leningrad relieved

LENINGRAD

RIGA
PSKOV

MOSCOW

R U S S I A

KAUNAS
ERG

SMOLENSK
TULA

MINSK

KURSK
VORONEZH

Volga

AW

4-23 July 1943
Battle of Kursk

KIEV
Dnieper

KHARKOV

STALINGRAD

LVOV

ZAPOROZHYE

Don

ROSTOV

Caspian
Sea

ODESSA

NOVOROSSISK

GROZNY

UMANIA
BUCHAREST

SEVASTOPOL

TIFLIS

Danube

BLACK SEA

BULGARIA
SOFIA

IRAN

ISTANBUL
ANKARA

T U R K E Y

REECE

ATHENS

Dodecanese

Cyprus
(Br)

SYRIA
(Free Fr)

IRAQ
(Br)

DAMASCUS

Crete

N   E   A

PALESTINE
(Br)
JERUSALEM

AMMAN
TRANSJORDAN
(Br)

TOBRUK
ALEXANDRIA

GHAZI
EL ALAMEIN

Suez
Canal
Nile

CAIRO

SAUDI
ARABIA

ILA

A

E G Y P T
(Br prot.)

The Defeat of
Germany,
1944-45

Barents Sea

MURMANSK

White Sea

ARCHANGEL

AND

L. Ladoga

LENINGRAD

PSKOV

MOSCOW

R U S S I A

KAUNAS
ERG

SMOLENSK

MINSK

VORONEZH

Volga

STALINGRAD

AW

KIEV

Dnieper

KHARKOV

Don

ROSTOV

*Caspian
Sea*

LVOV

ODESSA

SEVASTOPOL

TIFLIS

UMANIA

BUCHAREST

25 Aug 1944
Rumania and
8 Dec 1944
Bulgaria declare
war on Germany

BLACK SEA

Danube

BULGARIA

SOFIA

IRAN

ISTANBUL

ANKARA

T U R K E Y

REECE

ATHENS

SYRIA
(Free Fr)

IRAQ
(Br)

Dodecanese

Cyprus
(Br)

DAMASCUS

Crete

A N   S E A

PALESTINE
(Br)

JERUSALEM

AMMAN

TRANSJORDAN
(Br)

TOBRUK

ALEXANDRIA

*Suez
Canal*

SAUDI
ARABIA

GHAZI

EL ALAMEIN

Nile

CAIRO

A

E G Y P T
(Br prot)

Japanese Expansion, 1931-41

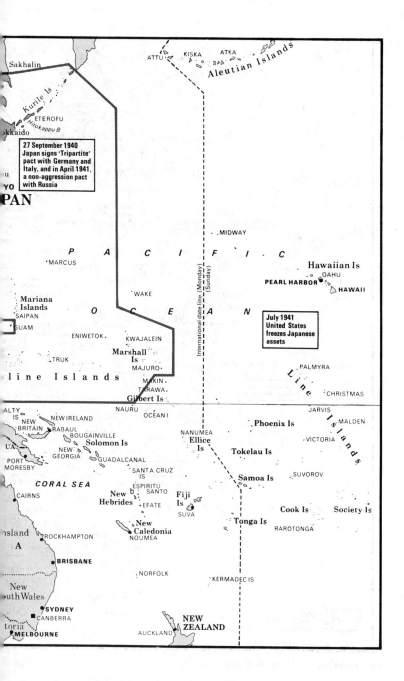

Sakhalin

Kurile Is
ETEROFU
Hitokappu B
okkaido

YO

PAN

27 September 1940
Japan signs 'Tripartite'
pact with Germany and
Italy, and in April 1941,
a non-aggression pact
with Russia

ATTU · KISKA · ATKA
Aleutian Islands

· MIDWAY

P   A   C   I   F   I   C
· MARCUS

Hawaiian Is
· OAHU
PEARL HARBOR · · HAWAII

· WAKE

O   C   E   A   N

July 1941
United States
freezes Japanese
assets

Mariana
Islands
SAIPAN
GUAM

ENIWETOK ·   · KWAJALEIN
· TRUK   Marshall
                Is
                · MAJURO

line Islands

· PALMYRA

Line

· CHRISTMAS

MAKIN ·
TARAWA ·
Gilbert Is

NAURU

OCEAN I

JARVIS

Islands

ALTY
IS   NEW
     NEW IRELAND
BRITAIN RABAUL
     BOUGAINVILLE
NEW Solomon Is
UA   GEORGIA · GUADALCANAL
PORT
MORESBY

NANUMEA
Ellice
Is

Phoenix Is

· MALDEN

· VICTORIA

Tokelau Is

SANTA CRUZ
IS

CORAL SEA

· CAIRNS

New
Hebrides

ESPIRITU
SANTO
· EFATE

Fiji
Is
SUVA

· Samoa Is

· SUVOROV

Cook Is   Society Is

nsland
A
· ROCKHAMPTON

· New
Caledonia
NOUMEA

· Tonga Is

RAROTONGA

· BRISBANE

· NORFOLK

· KERMADEC IS

New
uth Wales
· SYDNEY
· CANBERRA
toria
· MELBOURNE

AUCKLAND

NEW
ZEALAND

International date line (Monday)
(Sunday)

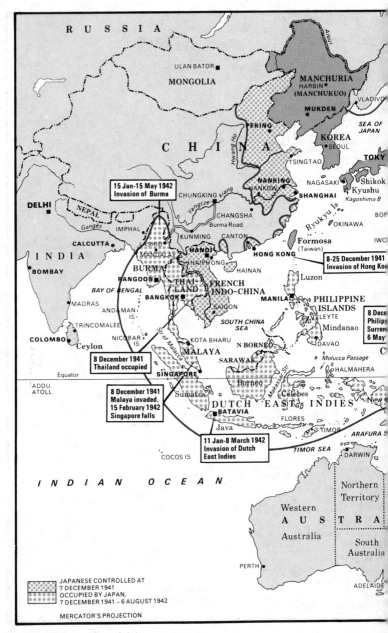

The War in the Pacific and Asia, 1941-42

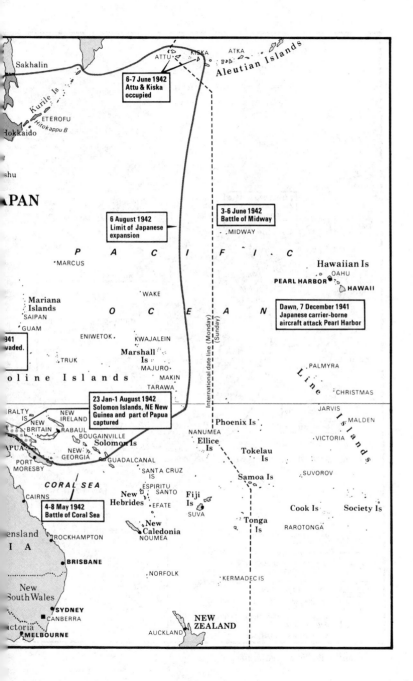

Sakhalin

Kurile Is

ETEROFU
Hitokappu B

Hokkaido

shu

JAPAN

6-7 June 1942
Attu & Kiska
occupied

ATTU   KISKA   ATKA   Aleutian Islands

6 August 1942
Limit of Japanese
expansion

3-6 June 1942
Battle of Midway

· MIDWAY

P   A   C   I   F   I   C

·MARCUS

Hawaiian Is
OAHU
PEARL HARBOR   HAWAII

·WAKE

Dawn, 7 December 1941
Japanese carrier-borne
aircraft attack Pearl Harbor

Mariana
Islands
SAIPAN
GUAM

O   C   E   A   N

941
vaded.

ENIWETOK·

·TRUK

KWAJALEIN

Marshall
Is
MAJURO·
·MAKIN
TARAWA

·oline Islands

·PALMYRA

·CHRISTMAS

International date line (Monday)
(Sunday)

·JARVIS

·MALDEN

·VICTORIA

23 Jan-1 August 1942
Solomon Islands, NE New
Guinea and part of Papua
captured

·Phoenix Is

NANUMEA

·Ellice
Is

Tokelau
Is

Line   Islands

·SUVOROV

RALTY
IS   NEW
IRELAND
NEW
BRITAIN   RABAUL
BOUGAINVILLE
APUA   NEW
GEORGIA   **Solomon Is**
PORT
MORESBY   ·GUADALCANAL

·SANTA CRUZ
IS

ESPIRITU
SANTO

New
Hebrides   ·EFATE

Fiji
Is
·SUVA

Samoa Is

Cook Is   Society Is

·RAROTONGA

CORAL SEA

CAIRNS

4-8 May 1942
Battle of Coral Sea

ensland
I A   ·ROCKHAMPTON

·BRISBANE

New
South Wales

·SYDNEY
·CANBERRA

ctoria
·MELBOURNE

New
Caledonia
NOUMEA

·Tonga
Is

·NORFOLK

·KERMADEC IS

NEW
ZEALAND

AUCKLAND

The War in the Pacific and Asia, 1942-44

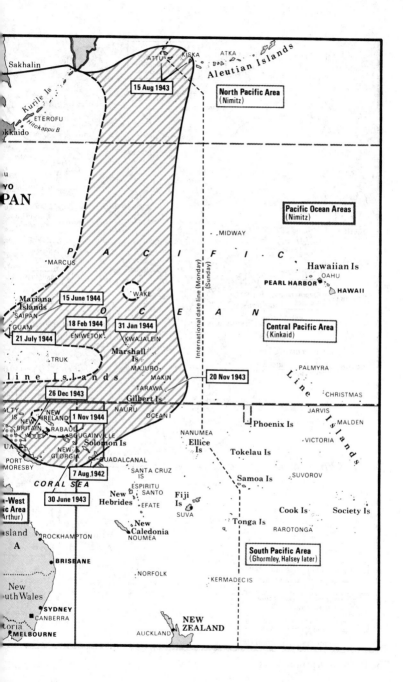

Sakhalin

Kurile Is

ETEROFU
Hitokappu B
okkaido

u

YO
PAN

ATTU   KISKA   ATKA
15 Aug 1943   Aleutian Islands

North Pacific Area
(Nimitz)

Pacific Ocean Areas
(Nimitz)

· MIDWAY

P   A   C   I   F   I   C

·MARCUS

International date line (Monday)
(Sunday)

Hawaiian Is
OAHU
PEARL HARBOR·   ·HAWAII

**Mariana
Islands**   **15 June 1944**   WAKE
SAIPAN·
○GUAM   **18 Feb 1944**   **31 Jan 1944**
21 July 1944   ENIWETOK·   KWAJALEIN

O   C   E   A   N

Central Pacific Area
(Kinkaid)

·TRUK   **Marshall
Is**·
MAJURO·
line Islands   MAKIN   PALMYRA
TARAWA   **20 Nov 1943**   L
26 Dec 1943   **Gilbert Is**·   i   CHRISTMAS
NAURU·   OCEAN I   n   JARVIS
·LTY   ·NEW   **1 Nov 1944**   Phoenix Is   MALDEN   e
Is   IRELAND   NANUMEA·   ·VICTORIA
·NEW   RABAUL   Is
BRITAIN   ·BOUGAINVILLE   Ellice   Tokelau Is   l   SUVOROV
UA·   NEW   Solomon Is   Is·   ·   a
GEORGIA   ·GUADALCANAL   Samoa Is   n
PORT
MORESBY   **7 Aug 1942**   SANTA CRUZ   d
IS·   ESPIRITU   Fiji   s
CORAL SEA   SANTO   Is   Cook Is   Society Is
30 June 1943   New   ·EFATE   ○   RAROTONGA
·West   Hebrides   SUVA   ·Tonga Is
ic Area   ·New
·rthur)   Caledonia
sland   ·ROCKHAMPTON   NOUMEA
A
·NORFOLK   ·KERMADEC IS
·BRISBANE

New
uth Wales
·SYDNEY
·CANBERRA
oria   NEW
·MELBOURNE   AUCKLAND   ZEALAND

South Pacific Area
(Ghormley, Halsey later)

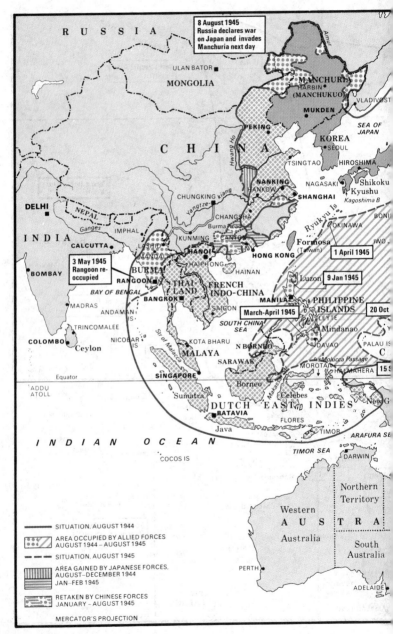

The Defeat of Japan, 1944-45

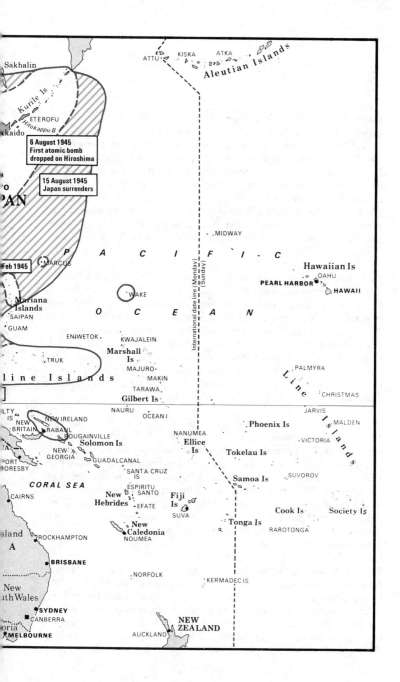

Sakhalin

Kurile Is

ETEROFU
Hitokappu B.
kaido

6 August 1945
First atomic bomb
dropped on Hiroshima

15 August 1945
Japan surrenders

JAPAN

Feb 1945

MARCUS

P A C I F I C

Mariana
Islands
SAIPAN

GUAM

WAKE

O C E A N

. MIDWAY

Hawaiian Is
OAHU
PEARL HARBOR
HAWAII

ENIWETOK.

KWAJALEIN

Marshall
Is
MAJURO.

MAKIN

TARAWA.

Gilbert Is

line Islands

TRUK

PALMYRA

Line

CHRISTMAS

International date line (Monday)
(Sunday)

NAURU

OCEAN I

JARVIS

MALDEN

Phoenix Is

VICTORIA

Islands

LTY
IS
NEW
BRITAIN

NEW IRELAND
RABAUL

BOUGAINVILLE
Solomon Is

NANUMEA
Ellice
Is

Tokelau Is

NEW
GEORGIA

GUADALCANAL

SANTA CRUZ
IS

Samoa Is

SUVOROV

CORAL SEA

CAIRNS

ESPIRITU
New SANTO
Hebrides
.EFATE

Fiji
Is

SUVA

Cook Is

Society Is

PORT
MORESBY

New
Caledonia
NOUMEA

Tonga Is

RAROTONGA

sland
A

ROCKHAMPTON

BRISBANE

. NORFOLK

KERMADEC IS

New
uth Wales

oria
MELBOURNE

SYDNEY
CANBERRA

AUCKLAND

NEW
ZEALAND

ATTU

KISKA

ATKA

Aleutian Islands

Biographical Notes

JAMES AGEE (November 27, 1909–May 15, 1955) Born in Knoxville, Tennessee. Educated at Harvard. Staff writer for *Fortune*, 1932–37. Published *Permit Me Voyage* (1934), a poetry collection, and *Let Us Now Praise Famous Men* (1941), report on Alabama sharecroppers with photographs by Walker Evans. Wrote book and film reviews and feature articles for *Time* and film reviews for *The Nation*. Wrote screenplays for *The Quiet One* (1949), *The African Queen* (1951), and *The Night of the Hunter* (1955); published novella *The Morning Watch* (1951). His novel *A Death in the Family*, published posthumously in 1957, won the Pulitzer Prize. Film reviews and screenplays collected in *Agee on Film* (1958–60), and correspondence in *The Letters of James Agee to Father Flye* (1962).

JACK BELDEN (1910–89) Born in Brooklyn, New York. Educated at Adelphi Academy and Colgate University. Following graduation lived in China for ten years, eventually becoming correspondent for United Press, International News Service, and *Time*; published *New Fourth Army* (1938). Accompanied General Joseph Stilwell on retreat from Burma in May 1942, described in *Retreat with Stilwell* (1942). Wounded at Salerno, Italy, in September 1943; after months of rehabilitation, returned to Europe to cover the final phases of the war. *Still Time to Die*, a collection of war pieces, published in 1944. Returned to China in 1946 to cover civil war; published *China Shakes the World* (1949). Spent last decades of his life in Paris.

WALTER BERNSTEIN (August 20, 1919–) Born in Brooklyn, New York. Educated at Dartmouth. Wrote for *The New Yorker* and *Yank*, publishing accounts of army training camps and later covering the war in Italy; in Yugoslavia in early 1944 met and interviewed Tito. In Hollywood, worked on screenplay of *Kiss the Blood Off My Hands* (1948); active in writing scripts for live television; blacklisted during 1950s. Later screenwriting credits include *That Kind of Woman* (1959), *Heller in Pink Tights* (1960), *Paris Blues* (1961), *Fail Safe* (1964), *The Train* (1964), *The Money Trap* (1966), *The Molly Maguires* (1970), *The Front* (1976), *Semi-Tough* (1977), *Yanks* (1978), and *The House on Carroll Street* (1988).

HOMER BIGART (October 25, 1907–April 16, 1991) Born in Hawley, Pennsylvania. Educated Carnegie Institute of Technology and New York University. Began to work for New York *Herald Tribune* as copyboy in 1929; became reporter in 1933. Traveled to Europe as war correspondent in 1942, moving to Pacific theater in autumn 1944. Won Pulitzer Prize in 1950 for coverage of Korean War (in Korea, intense professional rivalry with fellow *Tribune* correspondent Marguerite Higgins became famous among journalists). Left *Tribune* for *The New York Times* in 1955. In later years covered the Middle East, the trial of Nazi war criminal Adolf Eichmann, and the Vietnam War. Writings collected posthumously in *Forward Positions: The War Correspondence of Homer Bigart* (1992).

MARGARET BOURKE-WHITE (June 14, 1904–August 27, 1971) Born in the Bronx, New York. Educated at Columbia, where she studied photography with Clarence H. White, University of Michigan, and Cornell. Acquired reputation as industrial photographer and in 1929 went to work for *Fortune*. Traveled often to Soviet Union in early 1930s and made documentary films there. Became staff photographer for *Life* from its inception in 1936. With novelist Erskine Caldwell, produced collaborative works about southern sharecroppers (*You Have Seen Their Faces*, 1937), Central Europe (*North of the Danube*, 1939), and everyday life in America (*Say, is this the U.S.A.*, 1941); married to Caldwell 1939–42. Traveled in Soviet Union with Caldwell in 1941 and the following year published *Russia at War* (text by Caldwell) and *Shooting the Russian War* (text by Bourke-White). Covered war in North Africa and Italy; Italian experiences described in *They Called It "Purple Heart Valley"* (1944). In Germany in spring 1945 covered advance of American army; photographed Buchenwald concentration camp immediately after its liberation; published book on Germany, *"Dear Fatherland, Rest Quietly."* In later years, traveled in India (about which she wrote *Halfway to Freedom*, 1949), South Africa, and Korea. Career as photographer cut short by Parkinson's disease. An autobiography, *Portrait of Myself*, appeared in 1963.

DETON J. BROOKS, JR. (1909–75) Born in Chicago, Illinois. Educated at University of Chicago and Columbia University. Reporter for *Chicago Defender*, covering war in Burma. Editorial director of New York *People's Voice* in the late 1940s. Research director of Cook County Welfare Department, 1958–64; executive director of Chicago Committee on Urban Opportunity, 1964–69; and commissioner of Chicago Department of Human Resources, 1969–75.

CECIL BROWN (September 14, 1907–October 25, 1987) Born in New Brighton, Pennsylvania. Educated Western Reserve University and Ohio State University. Worked as reporter for United Press, Los Angeles, 1931–32; edited Prescott (Arizona) *Journal-Miner*, 1933; on staff of *Pittsburgh Press*, 1934–36, and *Newark Ledger*, 1936–37. In late 1930s freelanced in Europe and North Africa and worked for International News Service. Broadcaster for CBS in Rome (1940–41), until expelled by Mussolini government for "continuing hostile attitude," and in Yugoslavia, Cairo, and Singapore (1941–42); resigned from CBS in 1942, charging network with censorship of controversial opinion. Published *Suez to Singapore* in 1942. News commentator for NBC (1944–57) and ABC (1957–58) and Tokyo bureau chief for NBC from 1958 to 1962. He was later a television and radio news commentator in Los Angeles and taught at California State Polytechnic University.

RAYMOND CLAPPER (May 30, 1892–February 1944) Born on a farm in La Cygne, Kansas. Educated at University of Kansas. While a student, began to write for *Kansas City Star*; in 1916 joined United Press, serving as Washington correspondent, 1917–33. Published *Racketeering in Washington* (1933). Washington bureau chief for *Washington Post*, 1934–36. In 1936 became columnist for Scripps-Howard (column later also carried by United Features Syndicate). Toured Europe in 1937. From 1942, broadcaster for Mutual Broadcasting System. Killed in airplane crash in Marshall Islands in Central Pacific. Writings collected in *Watching the World* (1944).

VIRGINIA COWLES (August 24, 1910–September 17, 1983) Born in Brattleboro, Vermont. Traveled with family to England in 1917; educated privately. Contributed column to the Boston *Breeze* in the early 1930s. Foreign correspondent for *Sunday Times* (London), *London Daily Telegraph*, and Hearst newspapers. Covered Spanish Civil War; later reported from Russia, Germany, Czechoslovakia, Finland, and France; returned to England in 1940 after fall of France. Published *Looking for Trouble* in 1941. Special assistant to American ambassador to London, 1942–43; reported from Italy and France in 1944. Remained in London after the war; married Aidan Crawley (later British cabinet official and member of Parliament) in 1945. *No Cause for Alarm*, study of British society, published in 1949. Published many biographies and popular histories, including *Winston Churchill: The Era and the Man* (1953), *Edward VII and His Circle* (1956), *The Phantom Major: The Story of David Stirling and His Desert Command* (1958), *1913: The Defiant Swan Song* (1967), *The Russian Dagger: Cold War in the Days of the Czars* (1969), *The Romanovs* (1971), *The Rothschilds* (1973), *The Astors* (1979), and *The Great Marlborough and His Duchess* (1983).

WES GALLAGHER (October 6, 1911–   ) Born James Wesley Gallagher in Santa Cruz, California. As a stringer for International News Service in Louisiana, covered assassination of Huey Long in 1935; worked for Rochester (New York) *Democrat and Chronicle* as reporter-photographer. Joined staff of Associated Press in 1937. Went to Europe in 1940; in April witnessed German invasion of Norway. Worked out of Stockholm and Budapest, and covered war in Balkans and Greece; detained in Athens for several months by German authorities; in 1941 reported from Lisbon on refugees. Accompanied U.S. troops to North Africa in November 1942 and was severely injured in a jeep accident in Tunisia; published *Back Door to Berlin: The Full Story of the American Coup in North Africa* (1943). Oversaw AP reporting of D-Day invasion and directed its postwar European coverage (1945–51). Worked in managerial capacity at AP (1951–61), and from 1962 until his retirement in 1976 was its chief executive.

MARTHA GELLHORN (November 1908–   ) Born in St. Louis, Missouri. Educated at Bryn Mawr. Worked in New York for *The New Republic* and in Albany as a reporter for *Times Union*. Traveled in Europe and around the U.S. in early 1930s, often with French writer Bertrand de Jouvenel.

First novel, *What Mad Pursuit*, published 1934. Worked as field investigator for Federal Emergency Relief Administration; dined at White House with the Roosevelts, forming lifelong friendship with Eleanor Roosevelt. *The Trouble I've Seen*, collection of short stories based on relief work, published 1936. On trip to Key West in December 1936 met Ernest Hemingway and traveled with him in Spain, March–May 1937; worked in field hospitals and visited Loyalist fronts; account of fighting published in *Collier's*, to which she became a regular contributor. Returned three more times to Spain in 1938, and also reported from England and Czechoslovakia. Lived with Hemingway in Cuba for much of 1939–40, writing novel *A Stricken Field* (1940) and story collection *The Heart of Another* (1941). Covered Soviet-Finnish War, November–December 1939. Married Hemingway in November 1940, and traveled to Asia in February 1941, spending several months in China with him and traveling on alone to Java and Singapore. Covered war in Europe, October 1943–February 1944 and May 1944–May 1945. Published novel *Liana* (1944). Marriage to Hemingway ended in 1945. Collaborated with Virginia Cowles on play *Love Goes to Press* (1946), comedy about war correspondents. Reported on Indonesian rebellion against the Dutch and on Nuremberg war crimes trials. In 1947 launched attack on House Un-American Activities Committee. Published novels *The Wine of Astonishment* (1948; republished as *Point of No Return*), *His Own Man* (1961), and *The Lowest Trees Have Tops* (1967), story collections *The Honeyed Peace* (1953), *Two by Two* (1958), *Pretty Tales for Tired People* (1965), and *The Weather in Africa* (1981), and memoir *Travels with Myself and Another* (1978). Married to T. S. Matthews, 1954–63. Settled in England. War reporting collected in *The Face of War* (1959; revised edition, 1987). Reported on Eastern Europe and the Middle East; traveled to Vietnam as correspondent for *The Guardian* in 1966, and to Israel in 1967 during Six-Day War; reported on El Salvador and Nicaragua during 1980s.

BRENDAN GILL (October 4, 1914–   ) Born in Hartford, Connecticut. Educated at Yale. Contributor to *The New Yorker* since 1936, writing frequently on film and theater. During World War II wrote on aspects of the American home front. In later years active in campaign to preserve urban landmarks in New York City. Books include *The Trouble of One House* (1950), *The Day the Money Stopped* (1957), *Tallulah* (1972), *Ways of Loving* (1974), *Here at The New Yorker* (1978), *A Fair Land to Build In* (1984), *Many Masks: A Life of Frank Lloyd Wright* (1987), and *A New York Life* (1990).

WALTER GRAEBNER (December 16, 1909–November 9, 1976) Born in Columbus, Ohio. Educated at University of Wisconsin. Joined staff of *Time* in 1931, and served as Chicago bureau chief 1935–37; head of London bureau, 1937–46, and European area director, 1946–53. Traveled to Russia in 1942. With Allan Michie, co-edited *Their Finest Hour* (1941) and *Lights of Freedom* (1941). Author of *Conversations in London* (with Stephen Laird, 1942) and

Round Trip to Russia (1942). Later worked as advertising and public relations executive. Published *My Dear Mister Churchill* in 1965.

FOSTER HAILEY   (August 13, 1899–August 13, 1966)   Born in Meredosia, Illinois. Educated University of Missouri. Served in navy for two years during World War I. After the war worked as reporter for *New Orleans Item-Tribune*, *Miami Daily Tab*, *Tampa Sun*, and *Des Moines Tribune*. Staff member of Associated Press, 1927–37; joined *The New York Times* in 1937. Spent two years in the Pacific during World War II before being invalided home with malaria in September 1943; *Pacific Battle Line*, a memoir, published 1944. Continued to work for the *Times* on a variety of assignments, traveling extensively in Asia and Latin America. Published *Half of One World*, study of Asian nationalism, in 1947. After five years as member of the *Times* editorial board, resigned in 1948 because of dispute over the paper's coverage of Indonesia; continued to work for the *Times* as reporter and editorial writer until 1965. Co-author with Milton Lancelot of *Clear for Action: The Photographic Story of Modern Naval Combat, 1898–1964*.

JOHN HERSEY   (June 17, 1914–March 24, 1993)   Born in Tientsin, China, son of American missionaries; spent first ten years of life in China. Educated at Yale and Cambridge. Worked for Sinclair Lewis as secretary in 1937. Began to work for *Time* in 1937; traveled to Asia as correspondent in 1939; went to England in 1942 to cover war. Reported from Southwest Pacific and Italy for *Time* and *Life*, and published three nonfiction books about the war: *Men on Bataan* (1942), *Into the Valley* (1943), and *Hiroshima* (1946). His novel *A Bell for Adano*, about American occupation of Sicily, won Pulitzer Prize for 1944. Master of Pierson College at Yale, 1965–70. Later novels include *The Wall* (1950), *The Marmot Drive* (1953), *A Single Pebble* (1956), *The War Lover* (1959), *The Child Buyer* (1960), *Too Far to Walk* (1966), *Under the Eye of the Storm* (1967), and *The Call* (1985); also published nonfiction including *The Algiers Motel Incident* (1968), *Letter to the Alumni* (1970), and *The President* (1975).

MAX HILL   (1904–49) Born in Colorado Springs, Colorado. Educated at University of Colorado. Joined staff of *Denver Post*. Worked for Associated Press in New York and Washington for six years; became Tokyo bureau chief in 1940. Interned by Japanese authorities following Pearl Harbor attack; repatriated aboard *Gripsholm* in June 1942; experience recounted in *Exchange Ship* (1942). Subsequently joined NBC and covered war in North Africa, Italy, Turkey, and Greece. After the war, became a radio commentator, then worked with Wade Advertising Agency of Chicago.

ANNALEE JACOBY   (May 27, 1916–   )   Born Annalee Whitmore in Price, Utah; grew up in California. Educated at Stanford. Screenwriter for MGM. Worked in Chungking for United China Relief, 1941; married Melville Jacoby in Manila two weeks before Japanese invasion. With husband, escaped to

Australia in March 1942. Co-author, with Theodore H. White, of *Thunder Out of China* (1946). Later married Clifton Fadiman in 1950.

MELVILLE JACOBY (1916–42) Born in Los Angeles, California. Educated at Stanford; spent junior year in China as exchange student; returned to Asia after completing master's degree. Worked for Chinese government information bureau in Chungking, then worked in Indochina as United Press correspondent for six months. Became head of *Time*'s Far East bureau in Manila in 1941; married Annalee Whitmore on November 24th of that year. Escaped from Philippines in March 1942 to Australia, where he was killed in airplane accident a month later.

EDWARD KENNEDY (1905–63) Born in Brooklyn, New York. Studied architecture at Carnegie Tech. Worked for Cannonsburg (Pennsylvania) *Daily Notes* and on newspapers in New York, New Jersey, and Washington, D.C. Became staff member of Paris edition of *Herald Tribune* in 1931. Subsequently returned to U.S. and worked for *Newark Ledger*. Joined Associated Press in 1932; assigned to Paris bureau, 1934. Covered Spanish Civil War and developments in Balkans and Middle East. Accompanied General Archibald Wavell to Crete in 1940; was only American to cover British capture of Tobruk; subsequently reported on Italian campaign, including Anzio. After breaking a pledge to delay reporting the German surrender for 24 hours, stripped of credentials as war correspondent and dismissed by Associated Press. Became managing editor of Santa Barbara (California) *Press* in 1946, and in 1949 joined *Monterey Peninsula Herald*.

HELEN LAWRENSON (1907–82) Born Helen Brown in LaFargeville, New York. Educated at Vassar. Worked for *Syracuse Herald*, 1926–30; editor at *Vanity Fair*, 1932–35; later wrote frequently for *Esquire*. Early journalism collected in *The Hussy's Handbook, Including Latins Are Lousy Lovers and Others* (1937). Married to Jack Lawrenson, leading figure in National Maritime Union, 1939–57. Published two volumes of memoirs, *Stranger at the Party* (1975) and *Whistling Girl* (1978), as well as *Latins Are Still Lousy Lovers* (1968) and a novel, *Dance of the Scorpions*, which appeared posthumously in 1982.

BEIRNE LAY, JR. (September 1, 1909–May 26, 1982) Born in Berkeley Springs, West Virginia. Educated at Yale. Entered Army Air Corps in 1932. Published *I Wanted Wings* in 1937 (collaborated on screenplay of 1941 film version). As lieutenant colonel, commanded a B-24 bomber group in the 8th Air Force during World War II. Shot down over France in May 1944, he evaded capture with the aid of members of the French resistance; experience recounted in *I've Had It: The Survival of a Bomb Group Commander* (1945). With Sy Bartlett, wrote novel *Twelve O'Clock High* (1947) and was nominated for Academy Award for screenplay of 1949 film based on the book. Later screenwriting credits include *Above and Beyond* (1952), *Strategic Air*

Command (1955), *Toward the Unknown* (1956), and *The Gallant Hours* (1960). Published *Earthbound Astronauts* in 1971.

CLARK LEE (January 31, 1907–February 15, 1953)   Born in Oakland, California. His father, Clayton Lee, was a founder and first president of United Press. Educated Rutgers. After graduation joined Associated Press, becoming a foreign correspondent in 1933. While in charge of Honolulu bureau, married Liliuokalani Kawananakoa, descendant of Queen Liliuokalani. Stationed in Tokyo (1938–39), in Shanghai, and with Japanese forces in China. While traveling to U.S. for vacation in December 1941, caught in the Philippines by outbreak of war. Remained there until March 1942, when he was evacuated along with Melville and Annalee Jacoby. Published war memoir *They Call It Pacific* in 1943. Joined International News Service in 1943. Published *One Last Look Around* (1947) and *Douglas MacArthur* (1952).

LARRY LESUEUR (June 10, 1909–   )   Born in New York City. Educated at New York University. Worked as reporter for *Women's Wear Daily*; joined United Press 1931. Radio commentator for CBS in Europe from 1939; after French surrender became assistant to Edward R. Murrow in London. Went to Soviet Union in fall of 1941; published *Twelve Months That Changed the World* (1943) and broadcast weekly radio series "An American in Russia." Later traveled in Middle East and Africa. From 1963, worked for United States Information Agency as a writer, correspondent, and information specialist.

A. J. LIEBLING (October 18, 1904–December 21, 1963)   Born Abbott Joseph Liebling in New York City. Educated at Dartmouth and Columbia School of Journalism. Worked for *The New York Times* as copyreader, 1925–26, and briefly for Providence (R.I.) *Journal* as reporter. Sailed to Europe in summer 1926; studied French medieval literature at Sorbonne. Returned to Providence in autumn 1927, continuing to write for *Journal*. Moved to New York and wrote for New York *World*, 1930–31, and *World-Telegram*, 1931–35. Married Ann Quinn in 1934, despite knowing that she was schizophrenic (in the course of their marriage she was hospitalized many times). Joined staff of *The New Yorker* in 1935; early pieces collected in *Back Where I Came From* (1938) and *The Telephone Booth Indian* (1942). Flew to Europe in October 1939 to cover war; remained in Paris until June 10, 1940; returned to U.S. by way of Lisbon. Flew to Britain in July 1941 to cover war; after briefly returning to U.S. in early 1942, sailed to Algeria in November. Followed war on Tunisian front, January–May 1943. Early war pieces collected in *The Road Back to Paris* (1944). Covered D-Day invasion and afterwards spent two months in Normandy and Brittany, June–August, before returning to U.S. Began writing column "The Wayward Press" in 1945. Collected material from French resistance newspapers for *La République du Silence* (1946). Criticized House Un-American Activities Committee and became friend of Alger Hiss. Divorced from Ann Quinn; married Lucille

Spectorsky in 1949; following dissolution of second marriage, married novelist Jean Stafford in 1959. Later books include *The Wayward Pressman* (1947), *Mink and Red Herring: The Wayward Pressman's Casebook* (1949), *Chicago: The Second City* (1952), *The Honest Rainmaker: The Life and Times of Colonel John R. Stingo* (1953), *The Sweet Science* (1956), *Normandy Revisited* (1958), *The Press* (1961), *The Earl of Louisiana* (1961), and *Between Meals: An Appetite for Paris* (1962). Wartime articles collected posthumously in *Mollie and Other War Pieces* (1964).

EDWARD R. MURROW (April 25, 1908–April 27, 1965) Born Egbert Roscoe Murrow in Greensboro, North Carolina. Educated at Washington State College. President of National Student Federation of America (1930–31); as assistant director of Institute of International Education, 1932–34, participated in resettlement of German scholars fleeing Nazism. Became director of talks and educational programs for CBS in 1935, and in 1937 became head of CBS European bureau in London; assembled staff that eventually included William L. Shirer, Howard K. Smith, Charles Collingwood, Larry Lesueur, Richard C. Hottelet, and Cecil Brown. Became well known for broadcasts during London Blitz; broadcasts collected in *This Is London* (1941). Continued to report on war from Europe and North Africa. Became CBS vice-president for news programs in 1946. Produced radio program *Hear It Now*, which moved to television as *See It Now* (1951–58); also developed interview program *Person-to-Person* (1953–59). Critical television report on Senator Joseph McCarthy in 1954 played significant role in undermining McCarthy's influence. Became head of U.S. Information Agency in 1961, resigning in 1964 due to illness.

TED NAKASHIMA (August 19, 1911–September 14, 1980) Born Seattle. Degree in architecture from University of Washington. While interned as Japanese-American during the war, employed by federal government as architect in defense housing program. After a period as a chicken farmer in Spokane, worked in later years as director of facilities planning at school districts in Kirkland and Silverdale, Washington.

ROI OTTLEY (August 2, 1906–October 1, 1960) Born in New York City. Educated at St. Bonaventure College (Olean, New York), University of Michigan, and St. John's Law School (Brooklyn, New York). Worked for *New York Amsterdam News* as reporter, columnist, and editor, 1931–37. Joined New York City Writers' Project as editor in 1937. Published *New World A-Coming: Inside Black America* in 1943; it became a bestseller and was adapted into a series of radio programs. Worked as war correspondent for *PM*, *Pittsburgh Courier*, and *Liberty*; publicity director of National CIO War Relief Committee in 1943. Other books include *Black Odyssey: The Story of the Negro in America* (1948), *No Green Pastures* (1951), *The Lonely Warrior: The Life and Times of Robert S. Abbott* (1955), *White Marble Lady* (1965), a novel, and *The Negro in New York: An Informal Social History, 1626–1940* (1967, with William J. Weatherby).

ERNEST R. POPE (March 17, 1910–   ) Born in New York City. Educated at Cornell University; later studied in Germany. Went to Munich as freelance correspondent, working for major American newspapers and press associations there; correspondent for Reuter's. Published *Munich Playground* in 1941. After the war, worked for State Department as writer and translator.

ERNIE PYLE (August 3, 1900–April 18, 1945) Born Ernest Taylor Pyle on farm near Dana, Indiana. Attended Indiana University but did not complete journalism degree. Worked briefly in early 1923 as reporter for a local paper, *The La Porte Herald*, then joined the Scripps-Howard *Washington Daily News*. In 1926, with wife, Geraldine Siebolds, traveled around the U.S.; worked for a short time in New York for the *Evening World* before returning to *Washington Daily News* in 1927 as telegraph editor. Wrote aviation column and became aviation editor for Scripps-Howard chain, 1928–32. Managing editor of *Daily News*, 1932–35. In 1935 began six-day-a-week human interest column based on regular travels across U.S. and to Alaska, Hawaii, and Central and South America (prewar columns collected posthumously in *Home Country*, 1947). Went to England in November 1940 for three-month stay; English columns collected in *Ernie Pyle in England* (1941). Divorced in July 1942; Geraldine committed to sanitarium shortly afterward for six-month stay. Flew to England in June 1942 to cover training of American troops. Accompanied Allied troops to Algeria in November 1942; went to Tunisian front in January 1943. Remarried to Geraldine by proxy in March 1943. Covered Tunisian war with 1st Infantry Division until campaign's end in mid-May; Tunisian dispatches collected in *Here Is Your War* (1943). Covered Sicilian campaign (July–August 1943) and returned to U.S. in September; Geraldine hospitalized again at end of visit. Returned to Italy in November; at Anzio in March 1944, narrowly escaped death from a German bomb. Won Pulitzer Prize in 1943. Went to France immediately after D-Day invasion. Featured in *Time* cover story in July. Caught in accidental bombing of U.S. troops by American aircraft in Normandy on July 25. *Brave Men*, another compilation of columns, published 1944. Returned to U.S. in September and was hailed by press and public. Geraldine made suicide attempt during visit. Involved in discussions with makers of *The Story of G.I. Joe*, film based on his columns. In January 1945 sailed to Hawaii to cover Pacific theater; boarded aircraft carrier U.S.S. *Cabot*, sailing to Marianas and then proceeding to Okinawa with 1st Marine Division. Killed by Japanese sniper on Ie Shima, small island near Okinawa. Final columns collected in *Last Chapter* (1946).

J. SAUNDERS REDDING (October 13, 1906–March 2, 1988) Born Jay Saunders Redding in Wilmington, Delaware. Educated at Lincoln (Pennsylvania), Brown, and Columbia universities. Taught at various colleges and universities, including Morehouse College (1928–31), Southern University (1936–38), Hampton Institute (1943–66), and Cornell University (1970–75). As visiting professor at Brown in 1949, was first African-American to serve on faculty of an Ivy League university. Served intermittently on editorial board of *The American Scholar*, 1954–73. Director of research and publication division, National Endowment for the Humanities (1966–70). Member in 1970s of intellectual circle The Haverford Group, whose members also included Kenneth B. Clark and John Hope Franklin. Books include *To Make a Poet Black* (1938), *No Day of Triumph* (1942), *Stranger and Alone* (1950), *They Came in Chains* (1950), *On Being Negro in America* (1951), *An American in India* (1954), *The Lonesome Road* (1958), and *The Negro* (1967); co-editor with A.P. Davis of *Cavalcade* (1970), anthology of African-American literature.

ROBERT ST. JOHN (March 9, 1902–) Born in Chicago, Illinois. Studied at Trinity College (Connecticut). Reporter for *Hartford Courant, Chicago American*, and *Chicago Daily News*, 1922–23. With brother owned and operated *Cicero Tribune, Berwyn Tribune, and Riverside Times* in Illinois, 1923–35; was badly beaten by members of the Capone mob after writing an expose about one of its brothels. Editor, 1927–31, at Rutland (Vermont) *News, Rutland Herald*, Camden (New Jersey) *Courier*, and *Philadelphia Record*. Balkan correspondent for Associated Press, 1939–41; experiences in Yugoslavia and Greece recounted in *The Land of Silent People* (1942). NBC news commentator from London, Washington, and New York, 1942–46; subsequently correspondent for NBC-Monitor (1959–60) and Syndicated Broadcast Features (1960–70). Later books include *It's Always Tomorrow* (1944), *The Silent People Speak* (1948), *Shalom Means Peace* (1949), *Tongue of the Prophets* (1952), *This Was My World* (1953), *Through Malan's Africa* (1954), *Foreign Correspondent* (1957), *Ben-Gurion* (1959), *The Boss: The Biography of Nasser* (1960), *Builder of Israel* (1961), *They Came From Everywhere* (1962), *Roll Jordan Roll: The Story of a River and Its People* (1965), *Encyclopedia of Broadcasting* (1967), *Jews, Justice, and Judaism* (1969), *South America More or Less* (1970), and *Eban* (1972).

SIGRID SCHULTZ (January 5, 1893–May 14, 1980) Born in Chicago, Illinois, of Norwegian parents; raised in Europe, where her father worked as a portrait painter. Educated at the Sorbonne in Paris. Present in Germany at outbreak of World War I and was forced to remain there for duration of conflict because parents were too ill to travel; studied history and international law at Berlin University. Began working for *Chicago Tribune* in 1919, initially as interpreter for correspondent Richard Henry Little; reported on revolutionary violence in Berlin. Became Berlin bureau chief in 1926; as member of Foreign Press Association had close contact with leading Nazi political figures; published series of highly critical reports on Germany under pseudonym John Dickson, 1938–39; in July 1939 report predicted impending Nazi-Soviet pact. After the anti-Nazi tone of her reporting cut her off from news sources, left Germany in February 1941. Attempted to return to Germany in August 1941, but was denied a visa. Published *Germany Will Try It Again* (1944). Returned to Europe in 1945 as correspondent for *Chicago Tribune* and *McCall's*; in postwar period reported frequently on Europe for *Collier's* and Mutual Broadcasting. Edited *The Overseas Press Club Cookbook* (1962).

GEORGE S. SCHUYLER (February 25, 1895–August 31, 1977) Born in Providence, Rhode Island. Attended Syracuse public schools. Served in U.S. Army with 25th Infantry, 1912–19, attaining rank of first lieutenant. Moved to New York City in 1922; contributed column "Views and Reviews" to *Pittsburgh Courier* (1924–64), and became an editor and writer for A. Philip Randolph's *The Messenger*, 1926–28. Contributed widely to magazines including *The Nation* and *American Mercury*. Published satirical novel, *Black No More*, in 1931; a second novel, *Slaves Today* (1931), was based on investigation undertaken for New York *Evening Post* into Liberian rubber plantations. Ran unsuccessfully for Congress in 1966 against Adam Clayton Powell, Jr. Became associated with increasingly conservative views in the 1960s, supporting U.S. policy in Vietnam, opposing civil rights movement, and defending Portuguese colonialism in Africa; from 1966 contributed to *Manchester Union Leader*; published *Black and Conservative* in 1966.

VINCENT SHEEAN (December 5, 1899–March 15, 1975) Born James Vincent Sheean in Pana, Illinois. Educated at University of Chicago. Worked for *Chicago Daily News* and *New York Daily News*. Went to Paris in 1922 and became correspondent for *Chicago Tribune*. Covered Riff rebellion in Morocco in 1925, publishing *An American Among the Riffs* (1926). Worked thereafter as freelancer; during coverage of Chinese revolution in 1927, met American Communist Rayna Prohme, whom he credited with steering him toward an activist approach to journalism. Covered Jerusalem riots of 1929, Italian invasion of Ethiopia, and German reoccupation of the Rhineland. Memoir *Personal History* (1935) became bestseller. Covered Spanish Civil War for New York *Herald Tribune*. During World War II, joined U.S. Army Air Force and participated in invasion of Italy. Traveled to India to interview Mahatma Gandhi and witnessed Gandhi's assassination in 1948. Other books include *The New Persia* (1927); *Not Peace But a Sword* (1939); *Between the Thunder and the Sun* (1943); *This House Against This House* (1946); *Lead Kindly, Light* (1949), study of Gandhi; *The Indigo Bunting* (1950), memoir of Edna St. Vincent Millay; *Mahatma Gandhi* (1955); *Oscar Hammerstein I* (1956); *Orpheus at Eighty* (1958), biography of Verdi; *Nehru: Ten Years of Power* (1959); *Dorothy and Red* (1963), memoir of Dorothy Thompson and Sinclair Lewis; and *Faisal: The King and His Kingdom* (1975). Also published eight novels. Died at his home in Arolo, Italy.

ROBERT SHERROD (February 8, 1909–February 14, 1994) Born Thomas County, Georgia. Educated University of Georgia. Worked as reporter for *Atlanta Constitution*, Palm Beach (Fla.) *Daily News*, and other newspapers (1929–35). Correspondent and editor for *Time* and *Life* (1935–52). Began covering U.S. military in mid-1941; traveled with first convoys to Australia in February 1942, and covered Marine landings on Tarawa, Saipan, and Iwo Jima. Far East correspondent (1952–55) and editor (1955–64) at *The Saturday Evening Post*; vice-president of Curtis Publishing (1965–66). Author of

Tarawa: The Story of a Battle (1944), *On to Westward: War in the Central Pacific* (1945), and *History of Marine Corps Aviation in World War II* (1952); contributed to *Life's Picture History of World War II* (1950) and *Apollo Expeditions to the Moon* (1975).

WILLIAM L. SHIRER (February 23, 1904–December 28, 1993) Born in Chicago, Illinois; from age of nine grew up in Cedar Rapids, Iowa. Educated at Coe College. Worked for Paris edition of *Chicago Tribune*, 1925–27; foreign correspondent for *Tribune*, 1927–30, reporting from Paris, London, Rome, and Vienna; traveled to Afghanistan, India, and Middle East, 1930–31. Worked on Paris edition of New York *Herald*, 1934; went to Berlin in August 1934 as correspondent for Universal News Service. Joined CBS in 1937, broadcasting from Vienna, London, Prague, Berlin, and Paris. Witnessed French surrender at Compiègne in June 1940. Left Berlin in December 1940 after being warned that he might soon be arrested on charges of espionage; after return to U.S. published *Berlin Diary* (1941), which became bestseller. Left CBS in 1947 following public dispute with management, whom he accused of forcing him out because of his liberal views, a charge denied by Edward R. Murrow as network spokesman. Columnist for New York *Herald Tribune* (1942–48); news broadcaster for Mutual Broadcasting System (1947–49); after being cited in anti-Communist publication *Red Channels*, blacklisted from broadcasting during 1950s. Awarded National Book Award for *The Rise and Fall of the Third Reich* (1960). Other books include *End of a Berlin Diary* (1947), *Midcentury Journey* (1952), *The Sinking of the Bismarck* (1962), *The Collapse of the Third Republic* (1969), *20th Century Journey* (1976), *Gandhi: A Memoir* (1979), *The Nightmare Years* (1984), and *A Native's Return* (1990). Also published novels *The Traitor* (1950), *Stranger Come Home* (1954), and *The Consul's Wife* (1956).

HOWARD K. SMITH (May 12, 1914–) Born in Ferriday, Louisiana. Educated at Tulane University. Traveled to Europe in 1936 following graduation. Worked for *New Orleans Item-Tribune* before attending Oxford as Rhodes scholar. In 1939 served as London and Copenhagen correspondent for United Press; subsequently stationed in Germany. In 1941 worked as assistant to Harry Flannery, CBS radio correspondent, and became sole Berlin correspondent for CBS following Flannery's return to U.S. Left Berlin on December 7, 1941, and continued to broadcast from Berne, Switzerland. Published *Last Train from Berlin* (1942). Succeeded Edward R. Murrow in 1946, reporting on European and Middle Eastern affairs from London. After returning to the U.S., was a reporter and commentator for television shows including *CBS Reports*, *Face the Nation*, and *Eyewitness to History*. Later books include *The State of Europe* (1949) and *The Story of Our Nation's Capital* (1967). Became CBS Washington correspondent in 1957, resigning in 1961 because of policy disagreements; joined ABC as anchorman and commentator for the *ABC Evening News*.

GERTRUDE STEIN   (February 3, 1874–July 27, 1946)   Born in Allegheny,
Pennsylvania. Educated at Harvard Annex (now Radcliffe), where she studied
philosophy and psychology with William James, and attended Johns Hopkins
Medical School. Settled in Paris in 1903, at 27 rue de Fleurus, living with Alice
B. Toklas from 1907; as art patron supported the work of Picasso, Matisse,
Braque, Gris, and others. Wrote voluminously in a range of experimental
forms; her notable works include *Three Lives* (1909), *Tender Buttons* (1914),
Geography and Plays (1922), *The Making of Americans* (1925), *How to Write*
(1931), *The Autobiography of Alice B. Toklas* (1933), *Lectures in America* (1935),
The Geographical History of America (1936), *Paris France* (1940), and *Ida, a
Novel* (1941). Remained in France throughout the German occupation, living
in the country at Bilignin and later at Culoz; wartime experiences recounted
in *Wars I Have Seen* (1945); her final work, *Brewsie and Willie* (1946), was
based on conversations with American soldiers.

JOHN STEINBECK   (February 27, 1902–December 20, 1968)   Born in Sali-
nas, California. Studied at Stanford University. Published fiction including
The Pastures of Heaven (1932) and *To a God Unknown* (1933) before achieving
wider readership with *Tortilla Flat* (1935), *In Dubious Battle* (1936), and *Of
Mice and Men* (1937). *The Grapes of Wrath* (1939) became a bestseller.
Worked as writer for Foreign Information Service under Robert E. Sher-
wood, 1941–42. *The Moon Is Down*, novel about the Nazi occupation of Nor-
way, published in 1942. Visited air bases across U.S. to write *Bombs Away:
The Story of a Bomber Team* (1942) for army air force. Served as war correspondent in England, North Africa, and Italy for New York *Herald Tribune*,
June–October 1943, participating in naval commando raids as part of special
operations unit in Mediterranean. Later novels included *Cannery Row* (1945),
The Wayward Bus (1947), *The Pearl* (1947), *East of Eden* (1952), and *The
Winter of Our Discontent* (1961). Traveled to Vietnam as war correspondent
for New York *Newsday*, 1966–67.

C. L. SULZBERGER   (October 27, 1912–September 20, 1993)   Born Cyrus
Leo Sulzberger in New York City. Educated at Harvard. Worked briefly for
Pittsburgh Press and United Press. Visited Austria, Czechoslovakia, and the
Balkans in 1938 as correspondent for London *Evening Standard*; stationed
in Balkans, 1938–41. Reporter and columnist for *The New York Times*,
1939–78; chief foreign correspondent, 1944–54. Fled Yugoslavia following
German invasion in April 1941; stationed in Moscow, June–December 1941,
and in Cairo, 1943–45. Books include *Sit-Down* (with John L. Lewis, 1938),
The Big Thaw (1956), *What's Wrong with U.S. Foreign Policy* (1958), *My
Brother Death* (1959), *The Test: De Gaulle and Algeria* (1962), *Unfinished
Revolution* (1965), *History of World War II* (1966), *A Long Row of Candles*
(1969), *The Last of the Giants* (1970), *The Tooth Merchant* (1973), *Uncon-
quered Souls* (1973), *An Age of Mediocrity* (1973), *The Coldest War* (1974),
The Fall of Eagles (1977), and *Seven Continents and Forty Years* (1977). Died
in Paris.

DOROTHY THOMPSON (July 9, 1893–January 30, 1961) Born in Lancaster, New York. Educated at Syracuse University. Active in suffragist movement in upstate New York in 1917; worked in Cincinnati, 1918–19, as publicity director for The Social Unit, political reform organization. Settling in New York City, began to publish articles in newspapers and magazines around 1919. Traveled to Europe in 1920; reported for International News Service; worked as publicist for American Red Cross in Paris and, after 1921, in Vienna. Became Vienna correspondent for *Philadelphia Ledger*, reported on food riots in December 1921. Married Austrian writer Josef Bard in 1922. Moved to *Ledger* Berlin bureau in 1922, becoming bureau chief of *Ledger* and New York *Evening Post* (both Curtis newspapers) two years later. Met Sinclair Lewis in 1927 and married him the following year (marriage ended in divorce in 1942); resigned from *Ledger*. Returned with Lewis to America. Published *The New Russia* (1928), account of trip to Soviet Union the previous year. Traveled to Europe in 1930 and 1931; on second trip interviewed Adolf Hitler, declaring herself convinced of his "startling insignificance"; published *"I Saw Hitler!"* (1932). Continued to spend most of her time in Central Europe, with or without Lewis; reported on rise of Nazism in Germany and Austria; expelled from Germany, August 1934. Regular columnist for New York *Herald Tribune*, 1936–41. In 1937 began regular radio broadcasts and long-running column in *Ladies' Home Journal*; published *Dorothy Thompson's Political Guide* (1938), *Refugees: Anarchy or Organization?* (1938), and *Let the Record Speak* (1939). Traveled to Europe in March 1940, returning to U.S. just before fall of France. After break with *Tribune*, her column appeared in New York *Post* and other papers. *Listen, Hans!*, collection of radio talks broadcast to Germany and aimed at anti-Nazi aristocrat Helmuth von Moltke, published in 1942. Married Austrian painter Maxim Kopf in 1943. Column dropped from *Post* in 1947 following controversy over her defense of Palestinian Arabs; in 1950s, increasingly involved in Middle East as proponent of Arab interests. Columns for *Ladies' Home Journal* collected in *The Courage To Be Happy* (1957). Following husband's death suspended column in 1958.

OTTO D. TOLISCHUS (November 20, 1890–February 24, 1967) Born in Germany near Memel (now part of Lithuania). Renounced German citizenship in 1907 and went to U.S.; worked in factories in Syracuse, New York, and Trenton, New Jersey. Studied at Columbia School of Journalism. Joined staff of *Cleveland Press* in 1916. Returning to Europe in 1923, worked for Hearst's Universal Service in Berlin, 1923–31, and for International News Service in London, 1931–32. Returned to Berlin as correspondent for *The New York Times* in 1933; expelled by Nazis in 1940, receiving Pulitzer Prize the same year. Went to Tokyo in January 1941 to replace Hugh Byas as bureau chief. Imprisoned by Japanese following Pearl Harbor; subjected to harsh conditions including torture; repatriated on *Gripsholm* in July 1942. Author of *They Wanted War* (1940), *Tokyo Record* (1943), and *Through Japanese Eyes* (1945). After the war, member of the editorial board of the *Times*.

SONIA TOMARA (1897–1982)   Born in St. Petersburg, Russia. Educated at
University of Moscow. Father disappeared during Russian Revolution; with
mother and two sisters fled to Constantinople. Worked for British High
Commission in Turkey before going to Paris. Worked for *Le Matin*; became
staff writer for *Herald Tribune* in 1928. Except for brief stint (1937–39) in
New York, remained in Europe covering foreign affairs, including German
invasion of Poland, until the fall of France; fled from Paris through Portugal
to New York. Subsequently worked as war correspondent in India, Burma,
China, Egypt, and Iran. Returned to Europe in 1944; covered Normandy
campaign, liberation of Paris, and the Seventh Army's advance through
Alsace. Returned to New York in 1945 and retired from journalism after
marrying federal judge William Clark.

RICHARD TREGASKIS (November 28, 1916–August 15, 1973)   Born in
Elizabeth, New Jersey. Educated at Harvard; an editor of *Harvard Crimson*.
While still at Harvard began to write for *Boston American* where he subsequently joined editorial staff. Later joined cable department of International
News Service. Accompanied Marines on invasion of Guadalcanal; *Guadalcanal Diary* (1943) became bestseller. Severely wounded in Italy in November
1943; Italian experiences recounted in *Invasion Diary* (1944). After intensive
rehabilitation accompanied U.S. First Army from Normandy to Aachen. Flew
five missions with B-29 crew in Pacific and with torpedo squadron. Published
Stronger Than Fear, a war novel, in 1945. After the war, wrote for *The Saturday Evening Post* and other periodicals. Later books include *Seven Leagues to
Paradise* (1951), *X-15 Diary* (1961), *John F. Kennedy and PT 109* (1962), *Vietnam Diary* (1963), and *China Bomb* (1967).

VINCENT TUBBS (September 25, 1915–February 1989)   Born in Dallas,
Texas. Educated at Morehouse College and Atlanta University. Editor and
publisher of *Macon Broadcast*, 1940–41; news editor, *Norfolk Journal and
Guide*, 1942–43. From 1943 to 1947 he was foreign and war correspondent
for *Baltimore Afro-American*, and was an editor of the paper until 1954. Subsequently worked as editor for *Ebony* (1954–55) and *Jet* (1955–59), before establishing successful career in Hollywood as film publicist. Elected president
of Hollywood Publicists' Guild in 1967; press director for community relations at Warner Brothers, 1971–80.

MARY HEATON VORSE (October 9, 1874–June 14, 1966)   Born Mary
Heaton in New York City. Married writer and explorer Albert White Vorse in
1898 (he died in 1910). Lived in Provincetown, Massachusetts, from 1907;
associated there with writers including Eugene O'Neill, Edna St. Vincent
Millay, Susan Glaspell, and Max Eastman; involved in founding of Provincetown Players. Following husband's death, turned to writing to support family; early books included *The Very Little Person*, *The Heart's Country*, *The
Ninth Man*, *The Prestons*, *I've Come to Stay*, and *Growing Up: The Autobiography of an Elderly Woman*, about her mother's life, published in 1911. As

journalist, covered Lawrence, Massachusetts, textile strike of 1912; married radical journalist Joseph O'Brien in the spring of that year (he died in 1915). Reported on famine in Soviet Union, 1921–22, for Hearst papers. As labor activist, addressed striking textile workers in Passaic, New Jersey, in 1926, and textile union rally in Gastonia, North Carolina, in 1930 at which violence broke out. Wounded in 1937 by vigilante gunfire during steel strike in Youngstown, Ohio. Went to Europe in 1939 and covered German occupation of Czechoslovakia, invasion of Poland, and French preparations for war. Author of *Men and Steel* (1920), *Passaic* (1926), *Second Cabin* (1928), *Strike!: A Novel of Gastonia* (1930), *Footnote to Folly* (1935), *Labor's New Millions* (1938), and *Time and the Town* (1942). Traveled in Europe on behalf of United Nations Relief and Rehabilitation Administration, 1945–47.

E. B. WHITE (July 11, 1899–October 1, 1985) Born Elwyn Brooks White in Mount Vernon, New York. Educated at Cornell University. Worked from 1921 as reporter and editor for the *Cornell Sun*, the United Press, and the *Seattle Times*; also worked as advertising copywriter. Became contributor and editor at *The New Yorker*, largely responsible for "The Talk of the Town." Wrote monthly column "One Man's Meat" for *Harper's Magazine*, 1938–43. Lived with his wife Katharine on farm in Maine from 1938. Books include *Is Sex Necessary?* (with James Thurber, 1929), *Every Day Is Saturday* (1934), *The Fox of Peapack* (1938), *Quo Vadimus?* (1939), *One Man's Meat* (1942), *Stuart Little* (1945), *The Wild Flag* (1946), *Here Is New York* (1949), *Charlotte's Web* (1952), *The Second Tree from the Corner* (1953), *The Points of My Compass* (1962), and *The Trumpet of the Swan* (1970); co-edited *A Subtreasury of American Humor* (1941). Awarded Presidential Medal of Freedom in 1963 and Pulitzer Prize special citation in 1978.

Note on the Texts

This volume collects newspaper and magazine articles, transcripts of radio broadcasts, and excerpts from books by American writers and reporters written between 1938 and 1945, and dealing with events connected with World War II in the period between October 1938 and January 1944. The texts chosen are the first published versions.

The following is a list of the sources of the texts included in this volume, listed alphabetically by author. For untitled pieces and book excerpts, a phrase selected from the text has been enclosed in quotation marks and used as a title. (In the case of some newspaper articles, variant versions may exist in different editions.)

James Agee. So Proudly We Fail: *The Nation*, October 30, 1943.

Jack Belden. The Fever of Defeat: *Time*, May 11, 1942. Flight Through the Jungle: Belden, *Retreat with Stilwell* (New York: Alfred A. Knopf, 1943), pp. 289–304.

Walter Bernstein. Juke Joint: Bernstein, *Keep Your Head Down* (New York: The Viking Press, 1945), pp. 32–43. I Love Mountain Warfare: Bernstein, *Keep Your Head Down*, pp. 120–137.

Homer Bigart. San Pietro a Village of the Dead; Victory Cost Americans Dearly: New York *Herald Tribune*, December 20, 1943.

Margaret Bourke-White. Death and Life on the Battlefields: Bourke-White, *Shooting the Russian War* (New York: Simon & Schuster, 1942), pp. 257–270. Women in Lifeboats: *Life*, February 22, 1943. Over the Lines: Bourke-White, *They Called It "Purple Heart Valley": A Combat Chronicle of the War in Italy* (New York: Simon & Schuster, 1944), pp. 3–11.

Deton J. Brooks, Jr. Morale Sags at Camp Forrest As Jim Crow Rules: *Chicago Defender*, November 6, 1943.

Cecil Brown. "Prepare to Abandon Ship": Columbia Broadcasting System, *From Pearl Harbor Into Tokyo: The Story as Told by War Correspondents on the Air* (New York: Columbia Broadcasting System, 1945). Malay Jungle War: *Life*, January 12, 1942.

Raymond Clapper. "The Unexpected Couldn't Happen": Clapper, *Watching the World* (London and New York: McGraw-Hill Book Company, 1944), pp. 288–290.

Virginia Cowles. The Beginning of the End: Cowles, *Looking for Trouble* (New York and London: Harper & Brothers, 1941), pp. 375–383.

John Fisher. I First Saw the Ruins of Dunkerque: *Life*, June 24, 1940.

Wes Gallagher. "See You in Lisbon": Oliver Gramling (ed.), *Free Men Are Fighting: The Story of World War II* (New York and Toronto: Farrar and Rinehart, 1942), pp. 240–242.

Martha Gellhorn. The Price of Fire: "Men Made Over," *Collier's*, May 20, 1944.

Brendan Gill. X, B, and Chiefly A: *The New Yorker*, June 13, 1942.

Walter Graebner. The Battle for Scoops: Gordon Carroll (ed.), *History in the Writing* (New York: Duell, Sloan and Pearce, 1945), pp. 162–166.

Robert Hagy. "The Worst News That I Have Encountered in the Last 20 Years": *Time-Life-Fortune* News Bureau, *War Comes to the U.S.—Dec. 7th, 1941: The First 30 Hours* (New York: Time-Life-Fortune, 1942).

Foster Hailey. The Battle of Midway: Hailey, *Pacific Battle Line* (New York: The Macmillan Company, 1944), pp. 170–178.

John Hersey. The Battle of the River: *Life*, November 23, 1942. This Is Democracy: Gordon Carroll (ed.), *History in the Writing* (New York: Duell, Sloan and Pearce, 1945), pp. 238–244.

Max Hill. "This Is For Keeps": Hill, *Exchange Ship* (New York and Toronto: Farrar & Rinehart, 1942), pp. 36–46.

Annalee Jacoby. Bataan Nurses: *Life*, June 15, 1942.

Melville Jacoby. War Hits Manila: Gordon Carroll (ed.), *History in the Writing* (New York: Duell, Sloan and Pearce, 1945), pp. 45–50.

Edward Kennedy. Patton Struck Soldier in Hospital, Was Castigated by Eisenhower: St. Louis *Post-Dispatch*, November 23, 1943.

Helen Lawrenson. "Damn the Torpedoes!": *Harper's Magazine*, July 1942.

Beirne Lay, Jr. I Saw Regensburg Destroyed: *The Saturday Evening Post*, November 6, 1943.

Clark Lee. "Everybody Knew When the Planes Were Coming": Lee, *They Call It Pacific: An Eye-Witness Story of Our War Against Japan From Bataan to the Solomons* (New York: The Viking Press, 1943), pp. 166–171.

Larry Lesueur. "Tanks and Cannons Standing Starkly in the Snow": Lesueur, *Twelve Months That Changed the World* (New York: Alfred A. Knopf, 1943), pp. 85–99.

A. J. Liebling. Paris Postscript: *The New Yorker*, August 3 and 10, 1940. "Remoteness From the War Affected Everybody": Liebling, *The Road Back to Paris* (New York: Doubleday, Doran and Co., 1944), pp. 111–120. The Foamy Fields: *The New Yorker*, March 20, April 3, April 10, and April 17, 1943. Quest for Mollie: *The New Yorker*, May 26 and June 2, 1945.

Life. Three Americans: *Life*, September 20, 1943. Photograph by George Strock.

Edward R. Murrow. Can They Take It?: Murrow, *This Is London* (New York: Simon & Schuster, 1941), pp. 157–191. "A Horror Beyond What Imagination Can Grasp": Edward Bliss, Jr. (ed.), *In Search of Light: The Broadcasts of Edward R. Murrow, 1938–1961* (New York: Alfred A. Knopf, 1967), pp. 56–57. "The Target Was To Be the Big City": *In Search of Light*, pp. 70–76.

Ted Nakashima. Concentration Camp, U.S. Style: *The New Republic*, June 15, 1942.

New York *Herald Tribune*. President's War Message: New York *Herald Tribune*, December 9, 1941.

The New York Times. 1,000,000 Jews Slain by Nazis, Report Says: *The New York Times*, June 30, 1942. Allies Are Urged to Execute Nazis: *The New York Times*, July 2, 1942.

Roi Ottley. Negroes Are Saying . . . : Ottley, *'New World A-Coming'* (Boston: Houghton Mifflin Company, 1943), pp. 306–326.

Ernest R. Pope. Blitzkrieg Reporting: *Current History*, September 1940.

Ernie Pyle. "This Dreadful Masterpiece": Scripps-Howard wire copy, December 30, 1940. "Life Without Redemption": Scripps-Howard, January 29, 1941. "Our Policy Is Still Appeasement": Scripps-Howard, January 4, 1943. "I Gather a New Respect for Americans": Scripps-Howard, January 5, 1943. "Now It Is Killing That Animates Them": Scripps-Howard, February 9, 1943. "Moving At Night in Total Blackness": Scripps-Howard, February 16, 1943. "Only Slightly Above the Caveman Stage": Scripps-Howard, February 19, 1943. "Too Little to Work With, As Usual": Scripps-Howard, February 23, 1943. "Overrun Before They Knew What Was Happening": Scripps-Howard, February 24, 1943. "Nothing To Do": Scripps-Howard, February 26, 1943. "What a Tank Battle Looks Like": Scripps-Howard, March 1, 1943. "The Fantastic Surge of Caterpillar Metal": Scripps-Howard, March 2, 1943. "Into the Thick of the Battle": Scripps-Howard, March 3, 1943. "Brave Men. Brave Men!": Scripps-Howard, April 22, 1943. "Little Boys Again, Lost in the Dark": Scripps-Howard, April 27, 1943. "The Greatest Damage Is Psychological": Scripps-Howard, May 1, 1943. "The God-Damned Infantry": Scripps-Howard, May 2, 1943. "When a Unit Stops to Rest": Scripps-Howard, May 3, 1943. "This Is Our War": Pyle, *Here Is Your War* (New York: Henry Holt and Company, 1943), pp. 295–304. "The Dying Man Was Left Utterly Alone": Scripps-Howard, August 9, 1943. "Damn Sick of War—And Deadly Tired": Scripps-Howard, August 25, 1943. "A Hell of a Job": Scripps-Howard, September 3, 1943. "Miracle Bridge": Scripps-Howard, September 6, 1943. "The Land and the Weather Are Both Against Us": Scripps-Howard, December 14, 1943. "One Demolished Town After Another": Scripps-Howard, December 28, 1943. "Mule Packing Outfit": Scripps-Howard, January 5, 1944. "This One Is Captain Waskow": Scripps-Howard, January 10, 1944.

J. Saunders Redding. A Negro Looks at This War: *American Mercury*, November 1942.

Robert St. John. Under Fire: St. John, *From the Land of Silent People* (New York: Doubleday, Doran and Co., 1942), pp. 242–258.

Sigrid Schultz. Hitler Seizes 20,000 Jews: *Chicago Tribune*, November 10, 1938.

George S. Schuyler. "When American Citizens Murder U.S. Soldiers": "Views and Reviews," *Pittsburgh Courier*, May 8, 1943.

Vincent Sheean. Aufenthalt in Rosenheim: *The New Republic*, December 7, 1938.

Robert Sherrod. The Japanese Mind: Gordon Carroll (ed.), *History in the Writing* (New York: Duell, Sloan and Pearce, 1945), pp. 194–197. "I Didn't

Know Whether We Had the Heart to Fight a War": Sherrod, *Tarawa: The Story of a Battle* (New York: Duell, Sloan and Pearce, 1944), pp. 30–35. View of the Carnage: *Tarawa*, pp. 123–146. "The Hard Facts of War": *Tarawa*, pp. 147–151.

William L. Shirer. "It's All Over": Shirer, *Berlin Diary* (New York: Alfred A. Knopf, 1941), pp. 144–147. "At Dawn This Morning Hitler Moved Against Poland": *Berlin Diary*, pp. 198–202. "Revengeful, Triumphant Hate": *Berlin Diary*, pp. 419–425. "The Hour Will Come When One of Us Will Break": *Berlin Diary*, pp. 493–537. The American Radio Traitors: *Harper's Magazine*, October 1943.

Howard K. Smith. Valhalla in Transition: Smith, *Last Train from Berlin* (New York: Alfred A. Knopf, 1942), pp. 143–174.

Gertrude Stein. "Tired of Winter Tired of War": Stein, *Wars I Have Seen* (New York: Random House, 1945), pp. 132–150.

John Steinbeck. Fear of Death as Green Troops Sail to Invasion: New York *Herald Tribune*, October 3, 1943.

C. L. Sulzberger. Retreat of Serbs Related by Writer: *The New York Times*, April 14, 1941.

Dorothy Thompson. "Peace"—And the Crisis Begins: Thompson, *Let the Record Speak* (Boston: Houghton Mifflin, 1939), pp. 223–227.

Otto D. Tolischus. Last Warsaw Fort Yields to Germans: *The New York Times*, September 29, 1939. The Way of Subjects: Tolischus, *Tokyo Record* (New York: Reynald and Hitchcock, 1942), pp. 186–191. Tokyo Army Aide Bids Japan Fight If Parleys Fail: *The New York Times*, September 3, 1941.

Sonia Tomara. Nazi-Red Animosity Described Along Tense Frontier in Poland: New York *Herald Tribune*, November 20, 1939. French Conceal Despair; Move as Automatons: New York *Herald Tribune*, June 19, 1940.

Richard Tregaskis. Battle of the Ridge: Tregaskis, *Guadalcanal Diary* (New York: Random House, 1943), pp. 204–251. "Then I Got It": *Invasion Diary* (New York: Random House, 1944), pp. 203–214.

Vincent Tubbs. Christmas on New Guinea: *Baltimore Afro-American*, January 1, 1944.

Mary Heaton Vorse. The Girls of Elkton, Maryland: *Harper's Magazine*, March 1943.

E. B. White. "The Newspaper Reader Finds It Very Difficult to Get at the Truth": "One Man's Meat," *Harper's Magazine*, April 1942. Bond Rally: "One Man's Meat," *Harper's Magazine*, December 1942.

This volume presents the texts listed here without change except for the correction of typographical errors, but it does not attempt to reproduce features of their typographic design. The following is a list of typographical errors corrected, cited by page and line number: 17.25, at midnight; 27.5, for the a; 53.24, traddling; 54.5, agonied; 58.2, he; 71.19, more ten; 87.37, guards; 97.35, it's; 148.19, terrifically; 193.10, Hayto; 236.10, talk; 236.11, from hall-wide; 238.23, a.m.;

250.35, townstairs; 262.10, moters; 308.9, were had; 352.15, Massa-
chustts; 403.20, Sim's; 403.38, Sim's; 519.8, Phillip; 532.7, road;
540.19, Ouselltia; 549.25, multilated; 552.11, so; 557.25, infantryment;
598.20, Bismark; 599.5, Louiana; 599.29, Certeainly; 613.23, road;
640.34, on; 646.3, 1940; 668.37, that; 668.39, The; 716.32, was going;
731.2, granades; 733.37, cagarets; 740.4, step; 761.6, Whisler's; 762.17,
reminded,; 762.25, tatto.

ACKNOWLEDGMENTS

Great care has been taken to trace all owners of copyright material included in this book. If any have been inadvertently omitted or overlooked, acknowledgment will gladly be made in future printings.

James Agee. So Proudly We Fail: Reprinted with permission from *The Nation* magazine; © The Nation Company, Inc.

Jack Belden. The Fever of Defeat: © 1942 Time, Inc.; reprinted by permission.

Walter Bernstein. Juke Joint; I Love Mountain Warfare: From *Keep Your Head Down* by Walter Bernstein. Copyright © 1945; used by permission of Viking-Penguin, a division of Penguin Books USA, Inc.

Homer Bigart. San Pietro a Village of the Dead; Victory Cost Americans Dearly: From New York *Herald Tribune*, December 20, 1943. © 1943, New York Herald Tribune Inc.; all rights reserved, reprinted by permission.

Margaret Bourke-White. Death and Life on the Battlefields: Reprinted by permission of the Estate of Margaret Bourke-White. Women in Lifeboats: Life Magazine, Copyright Time, Inc.; reprinted with permission. Over the Lines: Reprinted by permission of the Estate of Margaret Bourke-White.

Virginia Cowles. The Beginning of the End: From *Looking for Trouble* by Virginia Cowles. Copyright 1941 by Virginia Cowles, copyright renewed 1969 by Virginia Cowles. Reprinted by permission of HarperCollins Publishers, Inc.

Wes Gallagher. "See You in Lisbon": Reprinted by permission of Associated Press.

Martha Gellhorn. The Price of Fire: First published in *The Face of War* (1959). Reprinted by permission of Martha Gellhorn.

Brendan Gill. X, B, and Chiefly A: Reprinted by permission; © 1942, The New Yorker Magazine, Inc. All rights reserved.

Foster Hailey. The Battle of Midway: Reprinted by permission of Curtis Brown, Ltd. Copyright © 1944 by Foster Hailey, renewed.

John Hersey. The Battle of the River: Life Magazine, Copyright 1942 Time, Inc.; reprinted with permission. This Is Democracy: Published by arrangement with the estate of John Hersey.

Max Hill. "This Is For Keeps": From *Exchange Ship* by Max Hill. Copyright 1942, © 1970 by Max Hill. Reprinted by permission of Henry Holt and Company, Inc.

Annalee Jacoby. Bataan Nurses: Reprinted by permission of the author.

Edward Kennedy. Patton Struck Soldier in Hospital, Was Castigated by Eisenhower: Reprinted by permission of Associated Press.

Beirne Lay, Jr. I Saw Regensburg Destroyed: Reprinted from *The Saturday Evening Post*; © 1943.

Clark Lee. "Everybody Knew When the Planes Were Coming": Reprinted by permission of Virginia Lee.

Larry Lesueur. "Tanks and Cannons Standing Starkly in the Snow": From *Twelve Months That Changed the World* by Larry Lesueur. Copyright 1943 by Larry Lesueur; reprinted by permission of Alfred A. Knopf.

A. J. Liebling. Paris Postscript: *New Yorker*, August 3 and 10, 1940. © 1940 by A. J. Liebling, copyrights renewed 1968 by Jean Stafford. "Remoteness From the War Affected Everybody": As appeared originally in A. J. Liebling, *The Road Back to Paris* (New York: Doubleday, Doran and Co., 1944), pp. 111–120. © 1944 by A. J. Liebling, copyright renewed in 1972 by Jean Stafford. The Foamy Fields: *New Yorker*, March 20, April 3, April 10, and April 17, 1943. © 1964 by Jean Stafford, renewed in 1992 by Norma Stonehill. Quest for Mollie: *New Yorker*, May 26 and June 2, 1945. © 1964 by Jean Stafford, renewed in 1992 by Norma Stonehill.

Edward R. Murrow. Can They Take It?: © 1941 by Edward R. Murrow; copyright re-
newed 1969 by Janet H. B. Murrow and Charles Casey Murrow. "A Horror Beyond
What Imagination Can Grasp": © 1942 by Edward R. Murrow; copyright renewed
1969 by Janet H. B. Murrow and Charles Casey Murrow. "The Target Was To Be the
Big City": © 1943 by Edward R. Murrow; copyright renewed 1969 by Janet H. B.
Murrow and Charles Casey Murrow.

Ted Nakashima. Concentration Camp, U.S. Style: Originally in *The New Republic.*

New York *Herald Tribune.* President's War Message: From New York *Herald Tribune,*
December 9, 1941. © 1941, New York Herald Tribune Inc.; all rights reserved; reprinted by permission.

The New York Times. 1,000,000 Jews Slain by Nazis, Report Says: Copyright © 1942 by
The New York Times Company; reprinted by permission. Allies Are Urged to Execute
Nazis: Copyright © 1942 by The New York Times Company; reprinted by permission.

Roi Ottley. Negroes Are Saying . . . : Reprinted with permission of Lynne Ottley Ware.

Ernest R. Pope. Blitzkrieg Reporting: Reprinted by permission of Current History, Inc.

Ernie Pyle. All Ernie Pyle pieces reprinted by permission of the Scripps-Howard Fund
with the exception of "This Is Our War," which is reprinted from *Here Is Your War*
by Ernie Pyle, copyright 1943 © 1971 by Henry Holt and Co., Inc. Reprinted by
permission of Henry Holt and Co., Inc. The assistance of Weil Journalism Library,
Indiana University, is gratefully acknowledged.

J. Saunders Redding. A Negro Looks at This War: Reprinted with permission of Mrs. J.
Saunders Redding.

Robert St. John. Under Fire: Copyright © 1942, © renewed 1969 by Robert St. John.
Reprinted by permission of Harold Matson Co., Inc.

Sigrid Schultz. Hitler Seizes 20,000 Jews: Reprinted by permission of the Chicago Tribune.

George S. Schuyler. "When American Citizens Murder U.S. Soldiers": Reprinted by
permission of GRM Associates, Inc., agents for The New Pittsburgh Courier. Copyright © 1943 by The Pittsburgh Courier; copyright renewed 1971 by The New Pittsburgh Courier.

Vincent Sheean. Aufenthalt in Rosenheim: Originally appeared in *The New Republic.*

Robert Sherrod. "I Didn't Know Whether We Had the Heart to Fight a War"; View of
the Carnage; "The Hard Facts of War": Reprinted by permission of The Admiral
Nimitz Foundation.

William L. Shirer. "It's All Over"; "At Dawn This Morning Hitler Moved Against Poland"; "Revengeful, Triumphant Hate"; "The Hour Will Come When One of Us Will
Break"; The American Radio Traitors: Reprinted by permission of Don Congdon Associates.

Howard K. Smith. Valhalla in Transition: From *Last Train from Berlin* by Howard K.
Smith. Copyright © 1942 and renewed 1970 by Howard K. Smith; reprinted by permission of Alfred A. Knopf, Inc.

Gertrude Stein. "Tired of Winter Tired of War": From *Wars I Have Seen* by Gertrude
Stein. Copyright © 1945 by Random House, Inc.; reprinted by permission of Random
House, Inc.

John Steinbeck. Fear of Death as Green Troops Sail to Invasion: From *Once There Was a
War* by John Steinbeck. Copyright 1943, 1958 by John Steinbeck; renewed © 1971 by
Elaine Steinbeck, John Steinbeck IV, and Thomas Steinbeck. Used by permission of
Viking-Penguin, a division of Penguin Books, USA, Inc.

C. L. Sulzberger. Retreat of Serbs Related by Writer: Copyright © 1942 by The New
York Times Company; reprinted by permission.

Dorothy Thompson. "Peace"—And the Crisis Begins: From *Let the Record Speak* by
Dorothy Thompson. Copyright © 1939 by Dorothy Thompson Lewis, renewed 1967
by Michael Lewis. Reprinted by permission of Houghton Mifflin Co.; all rights reserved.

Otto D. Tolischus. Last Warsaw Fort Yields to Germans: Copyright © 1939 by The New York Times Company; reprinted by permission. Tokyo Army Aide Bids Japan Fight If Parleys Fail: Copyright © 1941 by The New York Times Company; reprinted by permission.

Sonia Tomara. Nazi-Red Animosity Described Along Tense Frontier in Poland: New York *Herald Tribune*, November 20, 1939. © 1939, New York Herald Tribune Inc.; reprinted by permission. French Conceal Despair; Move as Automatons: New York *Herald Tribune*, June 19, 1940. © 1940, New York Herald Tribune Inc.; reprinted by permission.

Richard Tregaskis. Battle of the Ridge: From *Guadalcanal Diary* by Richard Tregaskis. Copyright © 1943 by Random House, Inc., and renewed 1971 by Richard Tregaskis; copyright 1955 by Richard Tregaskis; reprinted by permission of Random House, Inc. "Then I Got It": From *Invasion Diary* by Richard Tregaskis. Copyright © 1944 by Random House, Inc.; reprinted by permission of Random House, Inc.

Vincent Tubbs. Christmas on New Guinea: Reprinted by permission of the Afro-American Newspapers Archive and Research Center.

Mary Heaton Vorse. The Girls of Elkton, Maryland: Copyright © 1943 by Harper's Magazine; all rights reserved; reprinted from the March number by special permission.

E. B. White. "The Newspaper Reader Finds It Very Difficult to Get at the Truth": Copyright © 1942 by Harper's Magazine; all rights reserved; reproduced from the April number by special permission. Bond Rally: Copyright © 1942 by Harper's Magazine; all rights reserved; reproduced from the December number by special permission.

Notes

In the notes below, the reference numbers denote page and line of this volume (the line count includes headings). No note is made for information that can be found in common desk-reference books such as *Webster's Collegiate* and *Webster's Biographical* dictionaries. Footnotes and bracketed editorial notes within the text were in the originals. For historical background see Chronology in this volume. For weapons and military terms not identified in the notes, see Glossary in this volume. For further historical background and references to other studies, see Gerhard L. Weinberg, *A World at Arms: A Global History of World War II* (Cambridge: Cambridge University Press, 1994). For further background on wartime journalists and journalism, see Frederick S. Voss, *Reporting the War: The Journalistic Coverage of World War II* (Washington, D.C.: Smithsonian Institution Press for the National Portrait Gallery, 1994), and *Ernie's War: The Best of Ernie Pyle's World War II Dispatches*, ed. David Nichols (New York: Touchstone, 1987). For more detailed maps, see *The Times Atlas of the Second World War*, ed. John Keegan (New York: Harper & Row, 1989), and Richard Natkiel, *Atlas of World War II* (New York: Military Press, 1985).

1.7   Sudetenland] German-speaking border regions of Bohemia and Moravia that were included in Czechoslovakia under the terms of the 1919 Versailles Treaty. Under the Munich Pact Czechoslovakia ceded to Germany almost 11,000 square miles of land and 3,600,000 people, of whom 2,800,000 were German-speaking. The ceded territory included frontier fortifications vital to the defense of the remainder of Czechoslovakia. After the war almost the entire German-speaking population of Czechoslovakia was expelled into Germany.

1.10–11   Sportpalast boast] Hitler made his speech in the Berlin Sportpalast on September 26, 1938.

1.29–30   Dr. Masaryk] Hubert Masarik.

2.28   Wiegand] Karl H. von Wiegand, foreign correspondent for the Hearst papers.

2.29–30   Sir Horace Wilson] Neville Chamberlain's confidential adviser; Wilson previously accompanied the prime minister in negotiations with Hitler on the Sudetenland, September 16–17 and 22–23, 1938, and served as his special emissary in further negotiations, September 26–27.

2.37   Demaree Bess] Associate editor of *The Saturday Evening Post*.

3.25–26   Halfeld . . . *Nachtausgabe*]   Adolf Halfeld and Kriegk were editors of the respective newspapers.

6.18   Lord Runciman's Report]   Walter Viscount Runciman, former head of the British Board of Trade, was sent to Czechoslovakia by Chamberlain in early August 1938 to act as a mediator in the ongoing negotiations between the Nazi-controlled Sudeten German Party and the Czechoslovak government. His report to Chamberlain on his mission, dated September 21, was published on September 28, 1938.

7.19   "Peace . . . spirit."]   Cf. *Theological-Political Treatise* (1670): "Peace is not an absence of war, it is a virtue, a state of mind, a disposition for benevolence, confidence, justice."

11.16–18   Prince Bülow . . . memoirs]   Bernhard Furst von Bülow (1849–1929), German imperial chancellor under Kaiser Wilhelm II, 1900–9. His memoirs were published posthumously in 1930.

12.5   Reichswehr]   Name for the German armed forces, 1919–35; from 1935 to 1945 they were known as the Wehrmacht.

12.6   "third zone"]   The Munich Pact divided the ceded territory of the Sudetenland into four zones and established a timetable for their occupation by German troops between October 1 and October 10, 1938.

12.29–31   Goethe's . . . *versöhnt.*]   "Prelude in the Theater," *Faust*, Part I (1808), line 43.

13.9   the Red revolution]   Period of revolutionary agitation and insurrection in Germany following the collapse of the imperial regime in November 1918. By May 1919 Communist attempts to seize power in Berlin, Munich, and several other cities had been violently repressed by *Freikorps*, ad hoc military units formed by right-wing officers, whose assistance the moderate socialist government had sought to restore order.

13.21–22   Ernst von Rath . . . Grynszpan]   Third Secretary of Legation Ernst vom Rath (b. 1909) was shot on November 7, 1938, and died on November 9. Grynszpan (b. March 28, 1921), the son of Polish Jews who had moved to Hanover in 1911, bought a revolver and went to the embassy after learning that his family was among the 17,000 Polish Jews living in Germany who had been expelled without warning at the end of October 1938. Arrested by the French police, Grynszpan was imprisoned but not brought to trial before the German invasion in 1940. The Gestapo brought Grynszpan to Germany in July 1940 for the purpose of staging a show trial "revealing" an international Jewish conspiracy against Germany, but the trial was never held. Although no record of his death survives, Grynszpan almost certainly died in prison, or was killed, sometime between late 1942 and the end of the war in May 1945.

17.9   Jewish "reich representatives"]   The *Reichsvertretung der Juden in Deutschland* (Reich Representation of Jews in Germany), an association of

Jewish organizations, was founded by Jewish community leaders in 1933. In the aftermath of *Kristallnacht* it was reconstituted under Gestapo control as the *Reichsvereinigung* (Reich Association) *der Juden in Deutschland.*

17.16   GSP] *Geheime Staatspolizei* (Secret State Police), the Gestapo. Founded by Hermann Göring in 1933 as part of the Prussian state police, the Gestapo came under control of the SS in 1934.

19.11   *Rundfunk*] *Reichs Rundfunk Gesellschaft* (RRG), the Reich Broadcasting Company.

19.12   Adlon] Berlin hotel at the intersection of Wilhelmstrasse and Unter den Linden, a base for American journalists.

19.13   I. G. Farben] Popular name for Interessen Gemeinschaft Farbenindustrie Aktiengesellschaft, a leading industrial cartel; its production of synthetic materials made it crucial to the German war economy.

19.29–30   Axis . . . alliance] The German-Italian military pact signed on May 22, 1939. In 1936 Mussolini had boasted that the political affairs of Europe revolved around the "Rome-Berlin axis."

19.34   Nazi-Soviet accord] The nonaggression treaty between Germany and the Soviet Union was signed in Moscow on August 23, 1939. It included a secret clause providing for the partition of Poland between the two signing powers.

21.15   Wilhelmstrasse] Location of the German Foreign Ministry.

21.18   *D.A.Z.*] *Deutsche Allgemeine Zeitung.*

22.33   *Schupo*] A member of the *Schutzpolizei* (Protection Police), the regular uniformed urban police force; it came under SS control in 1936.

22.38   Coulondre's] French Ambassador Robert Coulondre.

25.6   General Werner von Fritsch] Werner Freiherr von Fritsch (1880–1939) became commander of the German army in February 1934. At a secret conference with Hitler on November 5, 1937, Fritsch opposed pursuing an aggressive policy against Czechoslovakia and warned that Germany was unprepared for a general European war. In January 1938 Fritsch was removed from his post by Hitler after being falsely accused of homosexual conduct by Heinrich Himmler, head of the SS. Fritsch was cleared by an honor court of officers and allowed to serve as commander of an artillery regiment. In a letter to a friend in August 1939, Fritsch wrote that he would accompany his regiment in the Polish campaign "only as a target."

27.20–21   Russian occupation . . . Poland] Soviet troops invaded Poland on September 17, 1939, and quickly overran the eastern area of the country.

27.38   General Rommel] Polish Major General Juliusz Rommel.

33.10   Albert Canal]   Canal in northern Belgium running from Liège to Antwerp. Eben Emael, the strongest fortress in Belgium, was built north of Liège to guard the canal. German combat engineers landed in gliders on Eben Emael on May 10, 1940, and destroyed its gun turrets with explosive charges while other glider troops captured two nearby bridges over the canal. On May 11 the garrison surrendered as German troops advanced in strength across the canal.

33.14   Maginot Line]   Series of underground fortresses built 1929–34 along the eastern border of France from the Swiss frontier to Longwy. For financial and diplomatic reasons the Maginot Line stopped short of the Belgian border.

33.17   "They . . . pass"]   Although often attributed to Pétain, the first recorded use of the phrase during the Battle of Verdun is in French General Robert Nivelle's Order of the Day to his troops, June 23, 1916: "You will not let them pass!"

33.23   break-through at Sedan]   See Chronology for May 1940.

35.21–22   deep incision . . . Allied armies.]   See Chronology for May 1940.

45.12   Paul Faure]   Faure (1838–1969) was co-editor with Léon Blum of *Le Populaire de Paris,* a minister in the Blum government, 1936–38, and secretary-general of the SFIO (French section of the Workers' International).

46.18–20   Skoda tanks . . . good tanks]   The Germans attacked France and the Low Countries in 1940 with 1,478 light and 961 medium tanks; 334 of the medium tanks were Czech. All four of the German tank models in service in 1940 had been introduced into service before the occupation of Czechoslovakia in 1939.

51.6–7   like Madrid]   The Spanish Loyalists had successfully defended Madrid from November 1936 until the final defeat of the Republic in March 1939.

51.29–30   Napoleon the Little's]   Name used by Victor Hugo in a speech before the Chamber of Deputies, July 17, 1851, to refer to Louis Napoléon (1808–73; emperor as Napoléon III, 1852–71).

51.30   Stavisky's]   Serge Alexandre Stavisky (1886?–1934), a Russian-born French underworld figure, engineered a series of major financial swindles involving the sale of worthless bonds to workers. His disappearance when the fraud was disclosed in December 1933 and his death, supposedly from suicide, in January 1934 were rumored to have been arranged by the police in collusion with Premier Camille Chautemps in an attempt to conceal the involvement of police, politicians, members of the judiciary, and prominent businessmen in Stavisky's crimes. Outrage over the scandal contributed to demonstrations and riots in Paris in January and February 1934 that led to the fall of the ministries of Chautemps and his successor, Édouard Daladier, and helped undermine public trust in the Third Republic. See also note 179.22–23.

53.25   Tom] Tom Healy, correspondent for London *Daily Mirror.*

57.36–37   *"Ne dites . . . espèrer."*] "Don't talk like that. One must hope."

58.29   Knickerbocker] H. R. (Hubert Renfro) Knickerbocker was chief foreign correspondent for the New York *Post* and Philadelphia *Public Ledger* and traveling correspondent for the International News Service.

59.37   Harold King] Foreign correspondent for Reuters News Service.

60.30   *"Nous . . . Boches!"*] "We've seen the *Boches!*" *Boches* is a pejorative term for Germans.

64.8   Maginot Line] The fortifications around Maubeuge were not part of the Maginot Line; see note 33.14

64.30   Lancasters] British soldiers from a Lancastershire regiment.

72.30   Kerker] William Kerker was foreign correspondent for NBC.

76.31   *Horst Wessel* song] Nazi party song that became the second national anthem of the Third Reich. Wessel (1907–30) was a Berlin SA (Storm Detachment) leader who, while living with a prostitute, was tracked down by a pimp and several Communist militants and fatally shot. Propaganda chief Joseph Goebbels made Wessel into a Nazi martyr and his poem "Up With The Flag" was set to the melody of a German sailors' song.

78.25   *PM*] Left-wing New York City tabloid newspaper (1940–48).

84.8   *The Damnation of Faust*] Dramatic cantata (1846) by Hector Berlioz.

97.32–33   children . . . last week.] A German U-boat sank the *City of Benares* on September 17, 1940, killing 217 adults and 73 children who were being evacuated to Canada by the British government.

98.7   disastrous retreat from Norway] The last Allied troops in Norway were forced to evacuate from Narvik June 8–9, 1940; the Norwegian government ordered cessation of hostilities on June 9. The aircraft carrier *Glorious* and the destroyers *Acasta* and *Ardent* were sunk during the evacuation, with the loss of more than 1,400 men.

100.21   Burma Road] The 717-mile road that ran from Lashio in Burma to Kunming in Yunnan province, China. Opened in December 1938 after the Japanese captured the major ports in southern China, it was used to transport military supplies to the Nationalist Chinese government based at Chungking. Under Japanese pressure, the British government closed the road on July 17, 1940, but reopened it three months later after receiving assurances of American support against further Japanese demands. The Japanese conquest of Burma in spring 1942 closed the road for the remainder of the war.

102.27   Lorna Doone] Title of a novel (1869) set in Exmoor by R. D. Blackmore.

105.37   *Volkswagen*] A new automobile promised to the masses; it was not manufactured until after the war.

107.31   RRG] See note 19.11.

112.1   Potsdamer Bahnhof] Potsdamer Railroad Station near the Brandenburg Gate.

112.28   Chargé d'Affaires Kirk] Alexander Kirk was the senior American diplomat in Germany; the United States withdrew its ambassador following the *Kristallnacht* pogrom in November 1938.

113.6–7   John Winant] Winant (1889–1947) was assistant director, 1938–39, and director, 1939–41, of the International Labor Office. In 1941 he replaced Joseph Kennedy as American ambassador to Great Britain and served until 1946. A progressive Republican, he was governor of New Hampshire, 1925–26 and 1931–34, first chairman of the U.S. Social Security Board, 1935–37, and U.S. representative to the United Nations, 1946–47.

113.7   International Labour Office] Headquarters of the International Labor Organization, created in 1919 by the Versailles Treaty as an arm of the League of Nations; the United States joined the organization in 1934. The ILO was commissioned to research and propose legislation to improve the conditions of workers in member countries. It became a United Nations agency in 1946.

113.30   *"Flieger-Alarm!"*] "Air-raid warning!"

114.19   wireless-directed torpedo] This weapon did not exist.

114.26–28   offensive . . . Sidi-el-Barrani] See Chronology, September 1940.

114.39–40   Serrano Suñer] Falangist leader and leading exponent of Spain's alignment with the Axis powers in the war, Ramón Serrano Suñer was minister of the interior (1937–40) and minister of propaganda and censorship (1939–40) in the government of his brother-in-law Francisco Franco; he became foreign minister in October 1940.

115.26   Joe Harsch] Joseph C. Harsch, foreign correspondent for *The Christian Science Monitor*.

118.18–19   Dr. Kurt Sell] Washington bureau chief for Deutsches Nachrichtenbüro (DNB), an agency established soon after Hitler became chancellor to regulate publication of news.

119.3   Pastor Bodelschwingh] Friedrich von Bodelschwingh (1877–1946), German Evangelical theologian and director of Bethel Institution for the Handicapped, was among those whose continued resistance to the "euthanasia" murder program (see Chronology for October 1939) led to its suspension in August 1941.

119.19   "Bund of Germans Abroad"] *Volksbund für das Deutschtum im Ausland* (Volk League for Germans Abroad) was founded 1881 to assist Germans living abroad; in the Third Reich it played a role in promoting the ideal of a "racially pure" nation.

122.18   Göring . . . London] A propaganda communiqué issued on September 16, 1940, falsely claimed that Hermann Göring, commander of the Luftwaffe, had flown over London in a Junkers 88 bomber.

125.3   opened fire . . . British] From September 23 to 25, 1940, British and Free French forces tried unsuccessfully to seize control of Dakar, then capital of French West Africa, from the Vichy government.

128.21–22   Carl Crow's . . . *Customers*] American author Crow's memoir (1937) recounts his experiences as an advertising and merchandising agent in China.

130.1   Munich *Putsch*] On November 9, 1923, Hitler led the Nazi party in a failed attempt to overthrow the government of Germany. The *putsch* collapsed after the police opened fire on a Nazi march in Munich, killing 14 people. Hitler was tried and convicted of treason but served less than one year of a five-year prison sentence.

131.22–24   three Americans . . . radio.] See also Shirer's "The American Radio Traitors," pp. 644–57 in this volume, and note 644.31-34.

132.24–25   *Gauleiter* Terboven] Josef Terboven was Nazi party area commander (*Gauleiter*) of Essen and from 1940 Reich Commissioner of Norway. He committed suicide with an explosive charge in Oslo on May 11, 1945.

137.7   Herr Stahmer] Heinrich Stahmer negotiated the Tripartite Pact in Tokyo.

137.13   Wheelers, . . . Lindberghs] U.S. senators Burton Wheeler, Democrat of Montana, and Gerald P. Nye, Republican of North Dakota, were leading isolationists, as was Charles Lindbergh.

137.39   Dr. Schmidt] Probably Paul Karl Schmidt (b. 1911), acting director of the news service and press department in the Reich Foreign Office. After the war he wrote popular World War II histories under the pseudonym Paul Carell.

139.35   Boemer] Karl Boehmer of the Propaganda Ministry.

140.2–4   Prien . . . *Royal Oak*] Günther Prien, commander of the *U-47*, sank the battleship *Royal Oak* inside the main British fleet anchorage at Scapa Flow on October 14, 1939, killing 833 men. After becoming a leading commander in the U-boat war against British merchant shipping, Prien was killed along with his entire crew on March 8, 1941, when the *U-47* was sunk in the North Atlantic by the British destroyer *Wolverine*.

140.17   Pete Huss] Pierre J. Huss, head of the International News Service Berlin bureau.

142.30   Max Schmeling] German world heavyweight boxing champion, 1930–32, whose defeat of Joe Louis in the 12th round at Yankee Stadium, June 19, 1936, was acclaimed by the Nazis as a triumph of the Nordic race. Louis's victory over Schmeling by a first-round knockout in a title rematch in New York City, June 22, 1938, was ascribed by Nazi propagandists to Jewish "trickery."

143.33   Mutual] Mutual Broadcasting System.

145.8   Doctor Sauerbruch] Leading German surgeon Ferdinand Sauerbruch (1875–1951); in 1940 he removed a growth from Hitler's throat.

147.18   * * *] These asterisks, and all others in pieces by Pyle printed in this volume, appear in the copy originally submitted to Scripps-Howard.

159.13   Shorty's] Engineer of the schooner *Spiradon Piraeus*, Greek army supply ship on which St. John had just sailed from Corfu to Patras.

159.25   *Etat Major*] Military Staff.

161.13–14   Mike and White and Atherton] Milan "Mike" Francisikovicz was a Yugoslav who navigated the fishing boat *Makedonka* on which St. John and his companions had escaped to Corfu. Leigh White of the New York *Post*, Terence Atherton of London *Daily Mail*, and Francisikovicz continued on from Corfu aboard the fishing boat.

172.9–10   King Peter's] Peter II (1923–70), king of Yugoslavia.

176.34–35   *New Masses*] Weekly magazine (1927–48) devoted to politics, literature, and art; it was affiliated with the American Communist Party.

179.21–22   De la Rocque] Retired army lieutenant colonel François de La Rocque was leader of the Croix de Feu, a right-wing paramilitary anti-parliamentary league, and founder (1936) of the pro-fascist Parti Social Français.

179.22–23   Chiappe . . . February 1934] Jean Chiappe, popular right-wing prefect of police in Paris, was removed from office by Premier Édouard Daladier on February 3, 1934, in an attempt to calm public outrage over the Stavisky affair (see note 51.30). On February 5 members of the Croix de Feu tried to storm the Ministry of Interior and on February 6 both rightists and Communists called for demonstrations in an attempt to bring down the new Republican Daladier government. More than 1,600 police and guards and 600 demonstrators were injured in the rioting, and 16 demonstrators were killed. Daladier resigned on February 7.

179.26–27   Front Populaire . . . 1936] The Popular Front, an anti-fascist coalition of Socialists, Communists, and Radical Socialists, came to power in France in June 1936 and governed until October 1938.

180.37   America First] The Emergency Committee to Defend America First was formed in the summer of 1940 and became the leading isolationist organization in the U.S.

180.38   article . . . *McCall's Magazine*] "Propaganda," *McCall's*, May 1941.

181.1–2   debate on the Lease-Lend Bill] The Lend-Lease bill was introduced in Congress on January 10, 1941, and passed in its final form on March 11, 1941. It authorized the President to lease or lend war matériel to any nation "whose defense the President deems vital to the defense of the United States." The bill was bitterly opposed by American isolationists.

181.6   president . . . First] Retired army officer Robert Wood, chairman of the board of Sears, Roebuck and Company, was acting chairman of America First.

181.27   connection . . . Oats] Liebling had written that R. Douglas Stuart Jr., national coordinator and a founder of America First (and later Quaker Oats president), was the son of the first vice-president of Quaker Oats.

184.9   *The Way of Subjects*] In Japanese, *Shinmin no Michi*; it was published by the Ministry of Education in August 1941.

184.28–30   Sun . . . Jimmu] Jimmu (711–585 B.C.E.), legendary first emperor of Japan and founder of its dynasty, is considered the direct descendant of sun goddess Amaterasu Omikami.

184.31   Hakko Ichiu] "The eight directions under one roof"; "Eight corners of the world under one roof."

185.2   Imperial Rescript] Issued on the occasion of the signing of the Tripartite Alliance on September 27, 1940.

185.14   "Manchurian Affair,"] On September 18, 1931, Japanese army officers in Manchuria provoked a clash between Japanese and Chinese troops by blowing up a stretch of railway line near Mukden. By the end of 1931 the Japanese had gained complete control of Manchuria, and in March 1932 they established a puppet Manchurian government under the former Manchu emperor Puyi.

185.31   Yamato] Name of the Japanese state founded by Jimmu.

185.32   Tanaka memorial] Document published in China in 1931 that presented a plan for Japanese world conquest allegedly left by emperor Meiji and submitted to Hirohito in 1927 by Prime Minister Tanaka Giichi (1863–1929). Its authenticity was disputed at the time of its publication, and most scholars consider it an anti-Japanese hoax.

186.29   "Showa] "Enlightened Peace," the reign name of Hirohito (1901–89; regent, 1921–26; emperor from 1926).

186.31   Meiji's hapless grandson]   Meiji ("Enlightened Rule") was the reign name of Mutsuhito (1852–1912; emperor from 1867), grandfather of Hirohito.

187.5–6   Imperial . . . Education]   Edict issued in 1890, the year after the constitution was completed, to ensure that Japan's educational system would promote loyalty and obedience to the emperor.

187.25–26   "turning . . . world,"]   Tolischus had written earlier in *Tokyo Record* that Japanese militarists were hailing the "Manchuria Incident" as the start of the creation of a new order in the world.

188.32   Joseph Warren Teets Mason]   United Press foreign correspondent, columnist, and author J.W.T. Mason (1879–1941); among his books are *The Creative East* (1928), *The Meaning of Shinto* (1935), and *The Spirit of Shinto Mythology* (1939).

188.38–39   Sakaki . . . *Nichi Nichi*]   The Sakaki tree (*Cleyera japonica*) is an ornamental Japanese evergreen shrub. *Nichi Nichi* was a leading pro-militarist Tokyo newspaper.

193.19–21   Washington negotiations . . . message]   In his message of August 28, 1941, Konoye offered to meet with Roosevelt to discuss resolving the Sino-Japanese War and stated that the Japanese government had no intention of using military force "without provocation" against neighboring nations. The message led to a resumption of talks in Washington between Roosevelt and Secretary of State Cordell Hull and the Japanese ambassador, Nomura Kichisaburo.

193.29–30   America, . . . assets]   Following the Japanese occupation of southern Indochina in July 1941, Japanese assets were frozen by the U.S., Britain and its Dominions, and the Netherlands.

194.33–35   Britain's infringement . . . occupation of Iceland."]   Britain and the Soviet Union sent troops into Iran on August 25, 1941, to protect oil fields against Axis sabotage and to open a land route for aid to the Soviets. On September 16, 1941, the pro-German ruler of Iran, Reza Shah Pahlavi, abdicated in favor of his son, Mohammed Reza Pahlavi, who ruled until the revolution in 1979. U.S. marines landed in Iceland in early July 1941 with the permission of the Icelandic government.

195.24   oil . . . Vladivostok]   On August 26, 1941, the Japanese government protested the shipment of American oil to the Soviet Far East at a time when the U.S. had embargoed oil exports to Japan. Both the U.S. and Soviet governments refused to halt the shipment, but did explain that the oil was intended primarily for use by Soviet forces fighting the Germans.

198.17   Smolensk]   The city was captured by the Germans on July 16, 1941.

202.18   battlefields of Yelnya] Yelnya, a town about 50 miles southeast of Smolensk, was captured by the Germans on July 19, 1941, and retaken by the Soviets on September 6, 1941. The Germans recaptured the town in early October 1941 at the beginning of their offensive toward Moscow. It was finally liberated by the Soviet army in late August 1943.

204.4   Erskine] Bourke-White's husband, the novelist Erskine Caldwell.

211.16   Alois . . . restaurant] Adolf Hitler's half-brother ran the Alois restaurant on Wittenberg Platz.

214.28   Jack Fleischer's] United Press correspondent who shared an apartment with Smith in Berlin.

214.31–36   Udet . . . Todt] Colonel General Ernst Udet (1896–1941), director of the Luftwaffe ordnance department and a leading World War I fighter ace, shot himself on November 17, 1941. For morale reasons, his death was falsely announced as having occurred while testing a new type of aircraft. Udet's poor management of aircraft production caused the Luftwaffe severe difficulty in replacing losses suffered during the Battle of Britain and the campaign in the Soviet Union, and by late 1941 he had lost the confidence of Hitler and Hermann Göring and become despondent. Fighter pilot Colonel Werner Mölders (1913–41) shot down 14 aircraft during the Spanish Civil War and 101 during World War II, and developed the four-plane Luftwaffe tactical fighter formation later adopted by Allied pilots. Mölders was killed in an airplane crash in Germany on November 22, 1941, while flying as a passenger to Berlin in order to serve as a pallbearer at Udet's state funeral. At the time of his death, he had more aerial victories than any other fighter pilot in the war. Field Marshal Walter von Reichenau (1884–1942), an ardent Nazi, died from a stroke in Russia on January 17, 1942, while commanding Army Group South. Fritz Todt (1891–1942) directed autobahn construction in the 1930s and became minister of armaments and munitions in March 1940. He was killed in an airplane crash on February 7, 1942, and was succeeded as armaments minister by Albert Speer.

215.27   Rostov] German troops captured Rostov-on-Don on November 20, 1941, but were driven out of the city by a Soviet counteroffensive on November 29 in one of the earliest German defeats of the Russian campaign. The Soviets again lost Rostov to the Germans on July 23, 1942, but regained the city on February 14, 1943, following their victory at Stalingrad.

215.28   *Attrapen.*] Dummies.

215.40   *buergerliche*] Bourgeois; plain.

217.3   *elegante Viertel*] Elegant, or smart, quarter.

221.18   P. G. Wodehouse] English humorist Wodehouse (1881–1975) had been captured by the Germans at his home in France in May 1940 and was eventually coerced into making several broadcasts from Berlin, in which he spoke humorously about his arrest and internment. He was released in October 1941 but not allowed to leave Germany. In 1955 he became a U.S. citizen.

221.30   Hess . . . Scotland] Rudolph Hess (1894–1987), the deputy leader of the Nazi party, flew alone to Scotland on May 10, 1941, in an unauthorized personal attempt to negotiate Britain's surrender. Hess was imprisoned in Britain during the war and sentenced to life imprisonment by the international war crimes tribunal at Nuremberg in 1946. He committed suicide in Spandau prison, Berlin, on August 17, 1987.

224.2   big "ear"] A large radar antenna.

236.20–22   Irene . . . dancer killed] Ballroom dancers Irene (1893–1969) and Vernon (1887–1918) Castle introduced dances including the turkey trot, one-step, and Castle walk, and initiated a "dancing craze" in the United States; Vernon, an Englishman, joined the Royal Flying Corps in 1916 and was killed in a training accident. Irene's third husband was Frederick McLaughlin. *The Story of Vernon and Irene Castle*, a film based on her memoirs and starring Fred Astaire and Ginger Rogers, was released in 1939.

236.29   *Greer* incident] On September 4, 1941, the U.S. destroyer *Greer* was carrying mail to American troops in Iceland when a British patrol aircraft alerted it that a submerged German U-boat lay 10 miles ahead. Following orders then in effect, the *Greer* used sonar to track the U-boat and reported its position to the British airplane, but did not attempt to attack the submarine. After the British plane dropped several depth bombs, the U-boat fired a torpedo at the *Greer*, apparently without knowing the nationality of its target. The torpedo missed, and the *Greer* then depth-bombed the U-boat, which fired a second torpedo that also missed; the *Greer* then lost sonar contact and proceeded to Iceland. In a national radio address on September 11, President Roosevelt did not mention the role of the British aircraft in the incident, accused the Germans of having "fired first . . . without warning," and described the attack as "piracy legally and morally." On September 13 Roosevelt ordered the navy to escort Allied convoys to Iceland and to destroy any Axis submarines or surface raiders it encountered between the U.S. and Iceland. By October 1, 1941, a full account of the *Greer* incident had been made public as the result of congressional inquiries.

238.20   50 ships] In September 1940 Roosevelt sent 50 destroyers to Britain in exchange for the right to use British bases in the Western Hemisphere.

241.15–16   Japanese Ambassador . . . colleague] Ambassador Nomura Kichisaburo (1887–1964) and special envoy Kurusu Saburo (1888–1954).

241.17–18   recent American message] On November 26, 1941, Secretary of State Hull presented a note to Nomura and Kurusu outlining the basis for an agreement between Japan and the United States. The document called for Japan to withdraw its troops from China and Indochina and to recognize the Chinese Nationalist government in return for the lifting of the embargo on U.S. exports to Japan.

241.30–31   American ships . . . Honolulu]   These reports were incorrect.

244.30–31   "Joe!" . . . Dynan]   Joseph Dynan was foreign correspondent for the *Honolulu Star-Bulletin*.

245.19   Bellaire . . . Stewart]   Dynan, Bellaire, and Stewart were interned until they were repatriated in the summer of 1942 aboard the Swedish ship *Gripsholm*.

252.29   Davao bombing]   Davao, on the Philippine island of Mindanao, was raided by Japanese carrier aircraft on December 8, 1941.

260.1–2   REPULSE. . . WALES]   The British battle cruiser *Repulse* and battleship *Prince of Wales* sailed from Singapore on December 8 in an attempt to intercept Japanese troop convoys headed for Malaya.

260.5   DECEMBER 11, 5:00:16 a.m.]   The text printed here is of a dispatch that Brown wrote and cabled to CBS as soon as he returned to Singapore.

264.29–30   Captain Leech]   John C. Leach.

265.3   Phillips and Leech]   Rear Admiral Phillips and Captain Leach were lost; Captain Tennant of the *Repulse* was rescued.

265.21–23   Wales. . . ratings.]   There were 1,285 survivors from the crew of 1,612 men on the *Prince of Wales*, and 796 survivors from the crew of 1,306 men on the *Repulse*.

267.9   Battle of Moscow]   See Chronology, October–December 1941.

269.25   Solnetchnogorsk]   The town, about 25 miles north of Moscow, was captured by the Germans on November 24, 1941, and recaptured by the Soviets on December 12.

273.14–15   Japanese border war]   See Chronology, May–August 1939.

274.25   General Vlasov]   Andrei A. Vlasov (1900–46) successfully commanded the 20th Army in the fighting around Moscow, November 1941–March 1942, and was promoted to lieutenant general in January 1942. On March 21, 1942, he assumed command of the 2nd Shock Army, which had been encircled in northern Russia during a failed attempt to break the German siege of Leningrad. After months of fighting, the trapped 2nd Shock Army disintegrated and Vlasov was captured on July 12, 1942. Disillusioned with Stalin and the Communist regime, in September 1942 Vlasov became the most prominent Soviet officer to collaborate with the German military in propaganda efforts aimed at enlisting Soviet prisoners-of-war in the German army. Although Vlasov hoped to form an independent anti-Communist "Russian Liberation Army" under Russian leadership, Hitler refused to authorize such a force. In January 1945 Vlasov was finally permitted to become commander of approximately 20,000–30,000 troops. He was captured by the Soviet army in Czechoslovakia on May 12, 1945, and hanged for treason in Moscow on August 1, 1946.

277.36   capture Volokolomsk] The Soviets recaptured the city on December 20, 1941.

277.37   Von Strauss] Colonel General Adolf Strauss, commander of the German Ninth Army.

280.28   stengahs] Drinks made with spirits and soda (e.g., whiskey stengahs).

280.34–35   Brooke-Popham . . . Layton] Air Chief Marshall Sir Robert Brooke-Popham was commander-in-chief in the Far East. Vice Admiral Sir Geoffrey Layton commanded the Far East fleet until December 8, 1941, when he was succeeded by Rear Admiral Sir Tom Phillips.

281.28   Kota Bharu] Malay city on the South China Sea near the Thai border.

283.39   Western Desert] British term for western Egypt and eastern Libya.

285.27–28   Lieutenant General Percival] Arthur Ernest Percival (1887–1966); he surrendered Singapore to the Japanese on February 15, 1942, and was imprisoned until August 1945.

298.4   Roberts report] Report of a commission established by executive order, December 18, 1941, to investigate responsibility for American losses at Pearl Harbor. Headed by U.S. Supreme Court Justice Owen J. Roberts (1875–1955), its ranking members included senior officers from the navy, army, and army air forces. It began hearings on December 22, 1941, and issued its report on January 23, 1942 (the full testimony of witnesses before the commission was not released until February 17, 1946). Controversy over responsibility for the American failure to anticipate the Pearl Harbor attack continued and led to congressional hearings in November 1945.

298.24   Shenandoah dirigible disaster] The U.S. navy dirigible *Shenandoah*, completed in 1923, was wrecked over Noble County, Ohio, in a thunderstorm, September 3, 1925, resulting in the deaths of 14 of its 43 crew members.

300.9   Vitalis] Brand of hair cream.

312.11   Lashio] Captured by the Japanese April 29, 1942; see also note 100.21.

313.15   dacoits] Bandits.

317.6   Gloucesters] British infantrymen from the 1st Battalion of the Gloucestershire Regiment.

318.33   Seagrave nurses] Burmese nurses working with Dr. Gordon Seagrave, an American medical missionary.

336.5–6   striking force . . . Hiryu]   The aircraft carrier *Hiryu* was part of
the Midway striking force, along with the carriers *Akagi*, *Kaga*, and *Soryu*.
All four ships had participated in the attack on Pearl Harbor.

340.2   Akagi]   The *Yorktown* dive bombers attacked the *Soryu*; *Akagi* and
Kaga were hit by dive bombers from the *Enterprise*. The three carriers
were fatally damaged between 10:25 and 10:30 A.M. on June 4, 1942, as they
were launching an air strike against the U.S. fleet.

341.5–6   Hiryu . . . Enterprise]   Dive bombers from the *Enterprise*
fatally damaged the *Hiryu* late on the afternoon of June 4.

342.17   die . . . Solomons]   The cruiser *Astoria* was sunk on August 9,
1942, in the Battle of Savo Island; 235 of her crew were killed.

343.14–15   Yorktown]   Despite its battle damage, the *Yorktown* remained
afloat until the morning of June 7, 1942, when it was torpedoed and sunk by
a Japanese submarine.

350.5   OPA]   Office of Price Administration.

352.33   "Camp Harmony."]   A holding center for internees from the
Seattle area, located in Puyallup, Washington, on the site of fairgrounds;
those held there were later relocated to Idaho.

355.4   *1,000,000 . . . Says*]   This story and the one printed on pp. 356–58 in
this volume originally ran on inside pages of *The New York Times*.

355.8   spokesmen . . . Congress]   Ignacy Schwartzbart, member of the
Polish National Council in London, Sidney Silverman, Labour member of
Parliament, and Ernst Frischer, member of the Czechoslovak State Council in
London, appeared at a press conference sponsored by the World Jewish Con-
gress, an international association of Jewish organizations formed in 1936.

355.21   Polish Government in London]   The Polish government-in-exile
was formed in Paris upon the resignation of President Ignacy Mościcki, September 30, 1939, and moved to London in 1940. Wladislaw Raczkiewicz
(1885–1947) served as president and General Wladislaw Sikorski (1881–1943)
as prime minister.

356.23–24   Szmul Zygelbojm]   Zygielbojm was representative of the
Jewish Labour *Bund* on the Polish National Council in exile; he committed
suicide on May 12, 1943, to protest world indifference to the fate of Polish
Jews.

357.31–32   Gouvernement General]   In 1939 approximately half of
German-occupied Poland was annexed into the Reich, while the General-
Government of Poland was established in Cracow to rule the remainder.

358.2   Hitler's threat]   In a speech to the Reichstag on January 30, 1939,
Hitler said that if "international finance Jewry within Europe and abroad
should succeed once more in plunging the peoples into a world war, then the

consequence will be not the Bolshevization of the world and therewith a victory of Jewry, but on the contrary, the destruction of the Jewish race in Europe."

359.1   DOROTHY LAMOUR]   Hollywood actress (b. 1914) whose films included *Her Jungle Love* (1938), *Tropic Holiday* (1938), *Moon Over Burma* (1940), *The Road to Singapore* (1940), *Aloma of the South Seas* (1941), and *Star Spangled Rhythm* (1942).

365.5   Col. Edson]   Merritt A. Edson, commanding officer of the First Raider Battalion.

365.11   Col. Griffith]   Lieutenant Colonel Samuel B. Griffith, executive officer of the First Raider Battalion.

367.24   Pursuits]   Single-engine, single-seat P-39 Airacobra fighter planes.

372.31   cross the Tenaru]   More than 750 Japanese soldiers were killed on August 21, 1942, in an unsuccessful attack against Marine positions west of the Tenaru River on Guadalcanal.

373.7   Tulagi]   Small island about 20 miles north of Guadalcanal, captured by the Marines, August 7–9, 1942.

375.19   Commissioner, Martin Clemens]   British district officer on Guadalcanal and coast watcher for the Australian navy. After the Marines landed, Clemens organized several companies of Melanesian scouts who served as jungle guides and provided intelligence on Japanese troop movements.

377.17   Gizo]   Island in the New Georgia group of the Solomons, about 240 miles northwest of Guadalcanal.

386.29   "Banzai"]   Japanese war cry, from *Tenno heika banzai*: "May the Son of Heaven live ten thousand years!" (The emperor was called "Son of Heaven.")

396.25   *Wasp*]   The aircraft carrier was sunk on September 15, 1942.

397.24   battle of Savo Island]   See Chronology, August 1942.

401.25   Maj. Bailey]   Major Bailey was posthumously awarded the Congressional Medal of Honor for his actions on the night of September 13–14, 1942. Edson also received the Medal of Honor for his leadership in the "Battle of the Ridge"; he survived the war.

402.2   *The Battle . . . River*]   An expanded version of this article was published as *Into the Valley: A Skirmish of the Marines* (1943).

402.7   Stalingrad . . . El Alamein]   See Chronology, September–November 1942 for Stalingrad and October–November 1942 for El Alamein. Japanese troops attacking Changsha, the capital of Hunan province, were repulsed by the Nationalist Chinese, December 1941–January 1942.

404.16–17   Lee . . . Chickahominy]   Robert E. Lee attacked the Army
of the Potomac along the Chickahominy River near Richmond, Virginia, on
June 26, 1862, during the Seven Days' Battles.

422.29   Churchill's visit to Moscow]   Churchill was in Moscow from August 12 to August 16, 1942. The secret purpose of his visit was to inform Stalin
that while Britain and the U.S. would not invade northwest Europe in 1942,
there would be an Anglo-American landing in French North Africa in the
autumn.

423.7   Willkie was in town]   Wendell Willkie was in Moscow during his
tour of Egypt, the Middle East, Russia, and China, September–October
1942; he wrote about his trip in *One World* (1943).

425.11   Leland Stowe]   Stowe was foreign correspondent for *The Chicago
Daily News.*

425.12   "Second Front"]   Term for the anticipated Anglo-American
invasion of northwest Europe.

427.13   sinking . . . *Lusitania*]   The unarmed British Cunard passenger
liner was torpedoed without warning by a German U-boat off the coast of
Ireland on May 7, 1915; 1,153 persons, including 114 U.S. citizens, were killed.
The incident turned American public opinion against Germany, and there
were calls for an immediate declaration of war.

434.13   Pittsburgh *Courier*]   African-American newspaper founded in
1910 and edited and published by Robert L. Vann (1879–1940); in 1940 his
widow, Jesse Matthews Vann, became publisher and P. L. Prattis, executive
editor. It was later called the *New Courier.*

435.6   Harlem's *People's Voice*]   Weekly New York tabloid (1942–47)
founded and edited by Adam Clayton Powell Jr. (1908–72).

435.32   Joe Louis bought!]   The heavyweight champion had donated his
share of the purse from a January 1942 title defense to the Navy Relief Fund,
and later helped raise contributions for the Fund.

441.29–30   Hastie . . . War]   William Hastie (1904–76) in 1940 took a
leave from his position as dean of the School of Law at Howard University to
serve as civilian aide to Secretary of War Henry L. Stimson; he resigned in
1943 to protest continued segregation in the armed services. He was judge of
the U.S. District Court for the Virgin Islands, 1937–39, and of the U.S. Circuit Court of Appeals, Third Circuit, 1949–71.

442.3–6   DuBois . . . statement]   In an editorial in *The Crisis,* July
1918.

442.35   *The Crisis*]   Magazine founded in 1910 by W.E.B. Du Bois, its first
editor, and published by the National Association for the Advancement of
Colored People; Roy Wilkins was editor, 1935–50.

445.36–38   battle . . . Homes] On February 28, 1942, local police stood by as a white mob prevented black families from moving into the Sojourner Truth Homes. Under National Guard and state police protection, several black families moved into the project on April 30, 1942.

447.32   Marcus Garvey's Black Star Line] Garvey (1887–1940) was a Jamaican-born leader whose United Negro Improvement Association advocated the resettlement of African-Americans in Africa and attracted widespread support from blacks in the 1920s. The Black Star Line, a steamship company, was established by the UNIA in 1919 to facilitate resettlement.

447.36–37   Anderson . . . 'Rochester'] Comedian Eddie (Edmund Lincoln) Anderson (1906–77), famous for his portrayal of "Rochester" on the Jack Benny radio and television shows, was also featured in films, including *Star Spangled Rhythm*, *Cabin in the Sky*, and *The Green Pastures*.

447.40   Andy Razaf] Razaf (1895–1973) wrote the lyrics for more than 1,000 songs by composers including Eubie Blake (1883–1983), J. C. Johnson (1896–1981), and Fats Waller (1904–43); his librettos included *Keep Shufflin'* (1928), *Hot Chocolates* (1929), and the 1930 *Blackbirds*. After retiring as a lyricist he became a newspaper reporter.

451.12   Vito Marcantonio] Marcantonio (1902–54) was a left-wing congressman from New York City, 1934–36 and 1938–50.

454.11–12   official report . . . Polish government] The report was issued in London on December 9, 1942.

454.24   German dictator] See note 132.24–25.

456.7   transport] The British liner *Strathallan*.

457.40   K2] A camera lens filter.

460.30–31   Kay Summersby] Summersby (1908–75), then a member of the British Transport Service, became Eisenhower's driver after his arrival in London in 1942 and was later his secretary, confidant, and companion; her books include *Eisenhower Was My Boss* (1948) and *Past Forgetting: My Love Affair with Dwight D. Eisenhower* (1975).

466.16   Oran] Oran, Algeria, was captured by American troops on November 8, 1942. See Chronology, November–December 1942.

476.18   Paul McNutt] Former governor of Indiana and chairman of the War Manpower Commission.

487.21–23   B-26 . . . there?"] When Liebling prepared "The Foamy Fields" for publication in his collection *Mollie & Other War Pieces* (1964), he added the footnote: "The B-26 was Lieutenant-General James Doolittle's personal plane. He was on a tour of inspection, and the three soldiers were members of his crew."

490.36   landscape . . . Technicolor.] Liebling noted in *Mollie*: "This use of the familiar false as touchstone of the unfamiliar real recurred often both in writing and conversation during World War II. 'Just like a movie!' was a standard reaction. It assured the speaker of the authenticity of what he had just experienced."

492.24   Larry Adler . . . player] American harmonica virtuoso.

496.22–24   ground fire . . . killed."] Liebling noted in *Mollie*: "Normal confusion."

497.13   an airfield] Liebling noted in *Mollie*: "This time it was Thélepte, in Tunisia."

498.10–11   Sam Spewack . . . Bella] The Spewacks were collaborative dramatists whose numerous Broadway plays and musicals included *Clear All Wires* (1932), *Boy Meets Girl* (1935), *Leave It to Me!* (1938), and later *Kiss Me Kate* (1948). Both were originally journalists.

499.23   Luna Park!"] An amusement park at Coney Island, Brooklyn, that featured nightly fireworks.

499.36   Major ———] In *Mollie* Liebling noted: "We were not allowed by the censor to mention names of casualties until they had appeared in the lists published at home. Now I cannot fill in this blank, because I forget the poor gentleman's name."

500.23–27   "I guess . . . for home.] In a footnote in *Mollie* Liebling cited this passage as another example of "confusion."

501.16   'Journey's End.'] Play (1929) by R. C. Sherriff about the British army fighting in the trenches in World War I; it was made into a film in 1930.

501.22   Léon] Liebling noted in *Mollie* that he had suppressed Léon Caplan's last name in case he had relatives living in France, and that after the war Caplan became the "number two man in the French Shell Oil Company—a *potentat petrolier.*"

501.31   Norgaard] In *Mollie & Other War Pieces*, Liebling dedicated "The Foamy Fields" and "Gafsa," another article describing his travels in Tunisia with Norgaard, to "Boots Norgaard."

502.38–39   Kostia Rozanoff] Liebling included "P.S. on Rozanoff in 1954" in *Mollie*; in it he wrote that Constantin Rozanoff became a leading French test pilot after the war and was killed in 1954, aged 49, while flying the new Mystère IV jet fighter.

502.39   Lafayette Escadrille] Free French unit named after the squadron of American pilots who flew in the French service before the United States entered World War I.

516.2–6   C-rations . . . P-40.] Liebling noted in *Mollie*: "I was back in 1956, but even the C-ration cans are gone. The natives of those parts are extremely poor, and may have thought even tin cans worth salvaging."

523.33–36   Horse . . . dead.] Liebling noted in *Mollie*: "Horse's square name was Alton B. Watkins, but hardly anybody at Thélepte knew. Father McCreedy buried him under a metal plate marked 'Horace.'"

524.40–525.1   radio . . . detectors] Radar.

526.5–7   Boone . . . planes."] Liebling noted in *Mollie*: "His luck did not last. He was killed a couple of weeks later."

527.34–35   Freddie Bartholomew] Child actor who starred in films including *David Copperfield* (1935), *Little Lord Fauntleroy* (1936), and *Captains Courageous* (1937).

538.8–9   Sbeitla . . . four days] Sbeitla is a town in central Tunisia about 100 miles west of Sfax and 120 miles southwest of Tunis. The German offensive in Tunisia began on February 14, 1943, with an attack through the Faïd Pass at the town of Sidi Bou Zid, about 25 miles southeast of Sbeitla. U.S. troops evacuated Sbeitla on February 17, and the Germans entered it the next day. The German offensive was halted on February 22, 1943.

557.30   famous infantry outfit] The 1st Infantry Division.

559.1–2   *Yank . . . Stars and Stripes*] Publications by and for U.S. armed forces enlistees. *Yank* (1942–45) was a weekly magazine featuring stories about the war, pinups, cartoons including George Baker's "Sad Sack," and letters from soldiers. *Stars and Stripes*, a daily newspaper begun in 1942 and published in most theaters in which U.S. troops were stationed, featured combat stories, the work of Bill Mauldin, a "Foxhole Who's Who," news of families from home, and a "G.I. gripes" column. It continued to be published for occupation forces after the war.

564.19   Ball Resolution] Introduced by Joseph Ball, Republican of Minnesota.

564.35   Atlantic Charter] A declaration of principles issued August 14, 1941, by President Roosevelt and Prime Minister Churchill following their shipboard conference off Newfoundland. It outlined in eight points policies that they hoped would shape the postwar world.

566.26–27   Lloyd Fredendall . . . Tunisia] Fredendall, commander of U.S. II Corps, was relieved of his command by Eisenhower in early March 1943 and replaced by Major General George S. Patton Jr.

572.39   October, 1942] The Allies landed on November 8, 1942.

575.15   Kasserine Pass] See Chronology, February 1943.

580.5–7   Noguès . . . Allies] Auguste Noguès (1876–1971) served as deputy high commissioner for North Africa from December 1942 until June

1943, when the Committee of National Liberation, led by De Gaulle and Giraud, took control of French North Africa.

583.6–7   *"Pris. . . chef."*]   "Took with me the American soldier Molotov, 23 April, '43, Namin, lance-sergeant."

584.20   Strength through Joy]   *Kraft durch Freude* (KdF), Nazi party organization that administered recreational activities for workers.

590.2   S-2]   Intelligence officer.

593.8   Fusion administrations]   Fiorello LaGuardia, mayor of New York 1934–45, was elected on Fusion tickets.

597.12   Karl Warner]   In a dispatch printed in the anthology *History in the Writing* (1945), correspondent Jack Belden wrote about his encounter with Company G of the 60th Infantry Regiment in Tunisia in April 1943. Belden described one soldier, "Karl Warriner of East 46th Street, New York," as a "sloppy, profane," long-haired "gremlin" who wore carnations stuck behind his ears and asked to be called "Molotov." Other soldiers from Company G told Belden that "Molotov" served as the regimental scout, did not "give a damn" about enemy fire, and had been twice recommended for the Silver Star.

598.6–8   EXECUTION. . . country.]   In October 1942 the Japanese army shot three of the airmen who had bombed Japan on April 18, 1942 (see Chronology). The airmen were condemned under a law adopted in August 1942 and applied retroactively. News of their execution first reached the American public through a White House statement on April 23, 1943.

598.20   Bismarck Sea]   In March 1943 U.S. and Australian aircraft sank four Japanese destroyers and eight troop transports in the Bismarck Sea off New Guinea, then searched out and strafed survivors in their lifeboats and rafts.

600.13   statement . . . Taney]   In his opinion in *Dred Scott* v. *Sandford* (1857).

601.4   JAPS' . . . Attu]   U.S. forces invaded Attu on May 11, 1943. The Japanese garrison made its final counterattack on May 29.

609.11   Troina]   American troops attacked Troina, about 60 miles southwest of Messina, on August 1, 1943, and captured the town on August 6.

609.32   Randazzo]   Town about 20 miles northeast of Troina, captured by British and American troops on August 13, 1943.

610.37   Point Calava]   The point is about 35 miles west of Messina.

614.4   Maj. Gen. Truscott]   Lucian K. Truscott Jr. (1895–1965), commander of the 3rd Infantry Division during the Sicilian campaign.

615.32   Sicilian Vespers]   Massacre of French soldiers and settlers in Sicily, so-called because it began with a riot in Palermo at the hour of vespers on Easter Monday, March 30, 1282.

625.29   Tokyo tanks]   So-called because it was hoped that they would eventually be used by B-17s bombing Tokyo.

626.14–15   Col. Curtis E. Le May]   In March 1945 LeMay, then a major general commanding the B-29 force based in the Marianas, began low-level incendiary raids against Japan (see Chronology). He later commanded the Strategic Air Command, 1948–57, and was Chief of Staff of the U.S. Air Force, 1961–65.

626.32   RDF]   Radio direction finding; radar.

630.4   *Staffeln*]   A *Staffel* was a Luftwaffe unit of 10 to 12 aircraft.

640.14   Buna]   See Chronology, July 1942 and November 1942–January 1943.

644.4   Federal . . . indictments]   The eight were indicted in absentia on July 26, 1943.

644.31–34   Kaltenbach . . . Koischwitz]   In July 1945, Frederick Kaltenbach (1895–?1945) was arrested in Berlin by the Soviets and imprisoned at a detention camp near Frankfurt an der Oder where he is believed to have died in October 1945. Robert Best (1896–1952) was apprehended in Austria in February 1946 and returned to the United States in January 1947. After a sanity hearing, he was convicted of treason in April 1948 and sentenced to life imprisonment. Best died in prison on December 16, 1952. Ezra Pound (1885–1972) was seized by Italian partisans on May 2, 1945, and turned over to the U.S. army, which imprisoned him in Italy until he was returned to the United States in November 1945. In February 1946 he was found unfit to plead by reason of insanity and remanded to St. Elizabeth's, a federal hospital in Washington, D.C. The indictment against him was dismissed in April 1958 and Pound returned to Italy after his release from St. Elizabeth's the following month. Douglas Chandler (1889–?) was taken into custody in Bavaria in February 1946 and returned to the United States with Robert Best. After a sanity hearing, he was convicted of treason in June 1947 and sentenced to life imprisonment. He returned to Germany after his sentence was commuted by President John F. Kennedy in August 1963. Edward Delaney (1885–1972) returned to the United States in 1947 and claimed that he was being persecuted for his anti-Soviet writings. The indictment against him was dismissed in August 1947, and Delaney became an anti-communist lecturer, radio broadcaster, and newspaper columnist. He was working for a California radio station when he was killed in a car accident on July 1, 1972. Constance Drexel (1894–1956), a naturalized American of German birth, was taken into custody by American soldiers in August 1945. In October 1946 she returned to the United States aboard the transport *Ernie Pyle*, and in April 1948 the indictment against her was dismissed for lack of evidence. Jane Anderson was arrested in Austria in April 1947, but in October 1947 the indictment against her was dropped and she returned to her home in Spain. Max Otto Koischwitz died in Berlin in August 1944, apparently from tuberculosis.

647.3   Heimwehr] "Home Guard."

647.20   Otto] Austrian archduke, until 1961 pretender to the Hapsburg throne.

653.31–32   sentenced . . . spy] Anderson was a World War I correspondent, journalist, and a figure in international literary circles before moving to Spain to marry Marquis Alvarez de Cienfuegos around 1933. At the outbreak of the Spanish Civil War she renewed her association with the London *Daily Mail* and traveled as a war correspondent with Franco's forces; she was captured by the Loyalists in September 1936 and imprisoned under extremely harsh conditions until her release the following month.

654.7   OWI] Office of War Information.

656.25   Katyn] In April 1943 the Germans announced the discovery of a mass grave in the Katyn Forest near Smolensk, Russia, containing the bodies of more than 4,000 Polish officers captured by the Soviets in 1939; they accused the Soviet Union of executing the officers in 1940. The Soviets responded by claiming that the Polish prisoners had been killed by the Nazis after the German army captured Smolensk in the summer of 1941. In 1989 the Gorbachev government acknowledged that 15,000 Polish officers, including the victims of the Katyn Forest massacre, were shot by the Soviet secret police in 1940.

659.25–26   "The Battle . . . Russia,"] The documentaries, released in 1943, were in the *Why We Fight* series produced by Frank Capra.

659.34   Keeper of the Flame"] Film (1943) directed by George Cukor, starring Katharine Hepburn and Spencer Tracy, about a famous American revealed after his death to have been a fascist sympathizer.

660.9   "The North Star"] Film (1943) directed by Lewis Milestone and written by Lillian Hellman, starring Dana Andrews, Walter Huston, Erich von Stroheim, and Anne Baxter. The film came under attack in the postwar period for its pro-Russian sentiments and was reedited for television distribution as *Armored Attack.*

661.14   "I Was a Fireman,"] A depiction (1943), using real firefighters, of a National Fire Service unit during the London Blitz; its alternate title was *Fires Were Started.* Written and directed by Humphrey Jennings, it was originally intended as a training film, but was shown to general audiences to boost morale.

673.39   Col. Darby . . . Ranger] William O. Darby was commander of the Ranger Force, made up of three Ranger battalions. The Rangers were elite troops, formed in 1942 as the American counterpart of the British

Commandos. Darby was killed April 30, 1945, just before the German surrender in Italy, and was posthumously promoted to the rank of brigadier general.

687.1   *Blue Fox*]   Pseudonym given by Sherrod to the transport *Zeilin* for security reasons.

687.12   Betio . . . fourth day]   Betio is the main island of Tarawa atoll. The Marines landed on November 20, 1943, and the island was declared secure on November 23.

688.16   Dick Johnston]   Richard Johnston, a United Press correspondent.

692.28   3/2]   Third Battalion, Second Marine Regiment.

697.32–36   Makin . . . killed]   See Chronology, November 1943.

699.15–17   Hawkins . . . Honor]   First Lieutenant William D. Hawkins, commander of the Scout and Sniper platoon of the Second Marine Regiment, was mortally wounded on November 21. He was posthumously awarded the Medal of Honor.

705.1   Burns Philp]   Burns Philp & Co., a South Seas trading firm.

708.19–20   1,026 . . . wounded]   Sherrod wrote in his preface to the 1954 edition of *Tarawa* that the final Marine Corps compilation for casualties in the battle showed 990 men killed and 2,296 wounded.

713.14   Jock . . . commander]   Wing Commander William Abercromby, commanding officer of 619 Squadron (wing commander is an RAF rank equivalent to lieutenant colonel). Abercromby was shot down and killed on January 2, 1944, while flying to Berlin with a different squadron.

713.15–16   Pathfinders]   Pathfinder aircraft used radio and radar navigational aids to locate targets, then marked them with colored parachute flares and slow-burning incendiary bombs known as "target indicators."

713.29   *Star Spangled Rhythm*]   Film (1942) written by Harry Turgend and directed by George Marshall; its all-star cast included Betty Hutton, Eddie Bracken, Victor Moore, and Walter Abel.

715.28   kite]   RAF slang for an airplane.

715.32–33   "Target indicators]   See note 713.15–16.

719.9   Mule Bag]   Radio code for an airfield.

719.19–20   Stockton . . . Bennett]   Stockton was killed; Bennett safely parachuted and was a prisoner of war until May 1945.

719.39–720.2   Berlin . . . blitz]   RAF Bomber Command sent 458 aircraft to Berlin on the night of December 2–3, 1943. Strong winds and mistakes in identifying navigational landmarks by radar resulted in the Pathfinders marking a point 15 miles south of the intended target area inside

Berlin. About three-quarters of the bombs dropped fell in open country outside the city, and those that fell on Berlin were widely scattered. Between 100 and 150 people were killed by the bombing, while the RAF lost 40 aircraft and 228 men killed; another 60 aircrew were captured.

732.34   Italian soldiers] Italy surrendered to the Allies on September 8, 1943, then declared war on Germany on October 13.

741.25   15th Panzer Grenadiers] German motorized infantry division.

742.22   "Voelkischer Beobachter"] The official newspaper of the Nazi party after 1920. Its name may be translated "National Observer" or "Racialist Observer."

742.39   Volturno crossing] U.S. troops crossed the Volturno River, October 12–13, 1943.

752.15   hows] Howitzers.

756.33–34   Benedictine . . . intact] The monastery was destroyed by Allied bombing on February 15, 1944.

772.18   Americans . . . Marshall Islands] See Chronology, January–February, 1944.

788.34   *Tedeschi.*"] Germans.

Glossary of Military Terms

Notes on U.S. Army organization appear at the end of the Glossary

Amphtrack] U.S. amphibious tractor that used specially shaped tracks to travel through water and over land. It could carry up to 20 men or two tons of cargo.

A-20] Twin-engine U.S. bomber. The "Havoc" had a three-man crew and a top speed of over 300 mph and was armed with at least seven machine guns; different versions carried between 2,000 and 4,000 pounds of bombs.

Baugeki '97] Japanese single-engine dive bomber commonly known in the U.S. by its American code name "Val." It had a two-man crew, a top speed of 240 mph, and was armed with three machine guns and a 550-pound bomb.

Beaufighter] Two-engine radar-equipped British night-fighter, with a two-man crew, top speed of 320 mph, and main armament of four rapid-firing 20 mm. cannon (i.e., cannon firing shells 20 mm. in diameter).

Bofors gun] Rapid-firing 40 mm. anti-aircraft gun, effective against airplanes flying below 11,000 feet.

Browning automatic rifle] American rifle capable of full automatic fire, used as a light machine gun by army and marine infantry. It fired a .30 caliber bullet (i.e., a bullet 30/100 of an inch in diameter), was fed from a 20-round magazine, had an effective range of over 600 yards, and weighed 19 pounds.

B-17] Four-engine U.S. heavy bomber. The "Flying Fortress" had a ten-man crew, a cruising speed of about 215 mph, was armed with 12 machine guns, and normally carried 4,000–6,000 pounds of bombs.

B-24] Four-engine U.S. heavy bomber. The "Liberator" had a crew of ten, a top speed of 290 mph, normally carried 5,000 pounds of bombs, and was armed with ten machine guns.

B-25] Twin-engine U.S. medium bomber. The "Mitchell" had a six-man crew, a top speed of about 275 mph, carried 3,000 pounds of bombs, and was armed with at least seven machine guns.

B-26] Twin-engine U.S. medium bomber. The "Marauder" had a six-man crew, a top speed of about 280 mph, carried 4,000 pounds of bombs, and was armed with up to 12 machine guns.

Dornier] Twin-engine German bomber. The Dornier 17, in service from 1939 to 1942, had a four-man crew, a top speed of 255 mph, and was armed with six machine guns and 2,200 pounds of bombs.

Douglas transport] Twin-engine C-47 transport, the military version of the DC-3 passenger plane.

88] German artillery gun firing shells or armor-piercing solid shot 88 mm. in diameter. Originally produced as an anti-aircraft gun, its high velocity and flat trajectory made it an extremely effective anti-tank gun, and it was also used as field artillery, often firing shells fused to burst in the air above Allied troops. As an anti-tank gun, it was effective at ranges up to 2,000 yards; as artillery, it could fire a 20-pound shell almost ten miles (17,500 yards).

F6F] Single-engine, single-seat U.S. naval fighter. Developed in response to the Japanese Zero, it entered carrier service in September 1943. The "Hellcat" had a top speed of 375 mph and was armed with six machine guns.

Focke-Wulf 190] Single-engine, single-seat German fighter that entered service in late 1941. The FW-190 had a top speed of 395 mph (increased to 408 mph in some 1943 models) and was armed with four 20 mm. rapid-fire cannon and two machine guns.

Fortresses] See B-17.

4.2 inch mortar] U.S. mortar that fired a 24-pound shell 4.2 inches in diameter, with a maximum range of over 2.5 miles (4,500 yards).

Grumman] See Wildcat.

Hurricane] Single-engine, single-seat British fighter; the main RAF fighter during the Battle of Britain. The Hurricane had a maximum speed of 320 mph and was armed with eight machine guns. After 1941 it was increasingly used for the close support of ground troops; later models were generally armed with rockets and rapid-firing 20 mm. cannon.

Junkers 52] Three-engine German transport plane.

Junkers 86] Twin-engine German aircraft, capable of flying at altitudes of over 39,000 feet and used mostly for photo-reconnaissance missions.

Junkers 88] Twin-engine German bomber. It had a four-man crew, a top speed of 286 mph, carried 4,000 pounds of bombs, and was armed with several machine guns.

Kogekiki '97] Japanese single-engine torpedo bomber commonly known in the U.S. by its American code name "Kate." It had a three-man crew, a top speed of 235 mph, and was armed with a single torpedo and one machine gun.

Lancaster] Four-engine British bomber, in service 1942–45. The Lancaster had a seven-man crew, a cruising speed of 216 mph, and was armed with eight machine guns. It carried between 8,000 and 14,000 pounds of bombs.

Liberator] See B-24.

Long Tom] American artillery gun with a maximum range of over 14.5 miles (25,700 yards). It fired a 95-pound shell 155 mm. in diameter.

LST] Landing Ship Tank, sea-going landing craft capable of unloading 18 tanks or 500 tons of cargo directly onto a beach.

Luger] German semiautomatic pistol.

Macchi C. 202] Single-engine, single-seat Italian fighter. It had a top speed of 369 mph and was armed with four machine guns.

Mark VI tank] German heavy tank that entered service in late 1942 and was first encountered by U.S. troops in Tunisia in 1943. The "Tiger" weighed 56 tons, had a five-man crew, very thick (100 mm.) frontal and turret armor, and was armed with a high-velocity 88 mm. gun. Highly effective in defensive fighting, the Tiger lacked mobility and mechanical reliability. Only 1,350 were made.

Me-109] Messerschmitt Bf 109, single-engine, single-seat German fighter. The Bf 109E, in service 1939–40, had a maximum speed of 354 mph and was armed with two 20 mm. cannon and two machine guns; the Bf 109G, the main Luftwaffe fighter from 1942 to 1945, had a top speed of 403 mph and was armed with one (sometimes three) cannon and two machine guns.

Me-110] Messerschmitt Bf 110, twin-engine German fighter with two-man crew. It had a top speed of 340 mph and was armed with two 20 mm. cannon and five machine guns.

Mitsubishi 97] Twin-engine Japanese bomber commonly known in the U.S. by its American code name "Betty." It had a seven-man crew, a top speed of about 270 mph, was armed with one 20 mm. cannon and three machine guns, and could carry up to 2,200 pounds of bombs.

105] Standard American field artillery gun of World War II. It fired a 33-pound shell 105 mm. in diameter and had a maximum range of almost seven miles (12,200 yards).

109] See Me-109

190] See Focke-Wulf 190

PB2Y] Four-engine flying boat used by U.S. navy as transport, and for air-sea rescue and ocean patrol missions.

P-38] Twin-engine, single-seat U.S. fighter with distinctive twin-boomed airframe. The "Lightning" entered service in late 1942, had a top speed of 395 mph, and was armed with a 20 mm. cannon and four machine guns. P-38s achieved their greatest success in aerial combat against the Japanese, and were also used as photo-reconnaissance and fighter-bomber aircraft.

P-39] Single-engine, single-seat U.S. fighter. The "Airacobra" had a maximum speed of 355 mph and was armed with a 37 mm. cannon and four machines guns. It proved unsatisfactory as a fighter and saw limited service as a ground-attack aircraft.

P-40] Single-engine, single-seat U.S. fighter. Various models of the "Warhawk" had top speeds of 345 to 364 mph, and were armed with six machine guns.

P-47] Single-engine, single-seat U.S. fighter. Introduced into service in 1943, the "Thunderbolt" had a maximum speed of 406 mph and was armed with eight machine guns.

75] Artillery gun firing a shell 75 mm. in diameter.

60 mm. mortar] U.S. mortar firing 60 mm. shell weighing 3.1 pounds, with a maximum range of over one mile (1,985 yards).

Spitfire] Single-engine, single-seat British fighter aircraft. The Spitfire I, in service 1939–40, had a maximum speed of 355 mph and was armed with eight machine guns; the Spitfire IX (1942) had a maximum speed of 415 mph and was armed with two 20 mm. cannon and four machine guns.

Springfield] U.S. bolt-action rifle. It fired a .30 caliber bullet, held five rounds in its clip, weighed nine pounds, and had an effective range of over 600 yards.

Stuka] Junkers 87, single-engine German dive bomber designed to give close support to ground troops. The "Stuka" (from *Sturzkampfflugzueg*— "dive bomber") had a two-man crew, a top speed of 242 mph, and was usually armed with three machine guns and a single 1,100 pound bomb carried under the fuselage. Stukas proved highly effective in the land campaigns of 1939–40, but suffered severe losses in the Battle of Britain. They remained in service until 1945, but their effectiveness declined as Allied fighter strength increased.

Tank destroyer] American armored vehicle, built on a tank chassis but with an open turret and thin armor. The M10 tank destroyer, introduced in 1942, was armed with a high-velocity anti-tank gun that fired 15-pound armor-piercing solid shot 76.2 mm. in diameter.

TBF] Single-engine U.S. torpedo bomber that entered carrier service in 1942. The "Avenger" had a crew of three, a top speed of 257 mph, and was armed with up to five machine guns and either one torpedo or 2,000 pounds of bombs.

Teller mine] German anti-tank mine containing 9–12 pounds of high explosives.

Thunderbolt] See P-47.

25-pounder] Standard British field artillery gun of World War II. It fired a 25-pound shell 87 mm. in diameter and had a maximum range of 13,400 yards.

Wildcat] Name for the F4F, American single-engine, single-seat naval fighter (also referred to as a "Grumman," after its manufacturer). The "Wildcat" had a maximum speed of 318 mph and was armed with six machine guns. It was replaced as the standard carrier-based fighter by the F6F in 1943.

Zero] Single-engine, single-seat Japanese naval fighter whose superior performance took the Allies by surprise in 1941. Highly maneuverable, it had a maximum speed of 316 mph (increased to 336 mph in 1942 models) and was armed with two 20 mm. cannon and two machine guns.

U.S. ARMY ORGANIZATION

Unit and formation strengths given below are those established by the U.S. Army for its infantry in 1943; equivalent units and formations in the U.S. Marines were similar in size.

Platoon] Unit of about 40 men, commanded by a second lieutenant.

Company] Unit made up of three rifle platoons, one weapons platoon, and other troops, with 193 men at full strength; usually commanded by a captain.

Battalion] Unit made up of three rifle companies, one weapons company, and a headquarters company, with 871 men at full strength; usually commanded by a lieutenant colonel.

Regiment] Formation made up of three battalions plus supporting troops, including artillery. It had 3,118 men at full strength and was commanded by a colonel.

Division] Formation made up of three regiments plus supporting troops, including artillery and combat engineers. It had 14,253 men at full strength and was commanded by a major general. The U.S. Army raised 89 divisions during World War II (67 infantry, 16 armored, five airborne, and one cavalry), and the Marine Corps raised six.

Index

CATALOGING INFORMATION

Reporting World War II.
       p.   cm. — (The library of America ; 77–78)
    Contents: 1. American journalism, 1938–1944 — 2. American
journalism, 1944–1946.
    1. Journalism—United States—History—20th century.   2. World
War, 1939–1945—Press coverage—United States.   I. Title: Reporting
World War Two.   II. Title: Reporting World War 2.   III. Series.

PN4867.R47   1995   94–45463
071'.3—dc20
ISBN 1–883011–04–3 (V. I)

*This book is set in 10 point Linotron Galliard,
a face designed for photocomposition by Matthew Carter
and based on the sixteenth-century face Granjon. The paper is
acid-free Ecusta Nyalite and meets the requirements for permanence
of the American National Standards Institute. The binding
material is Brillianta, a woven rayon cloth made by
Van Heek-Scholco Textielfabrieken, Holland.
The composition is by The Clarinda
Company. Printing and binding by
R. R. Donnelley & Sons Company.
Designed by Bruce Campbell.*

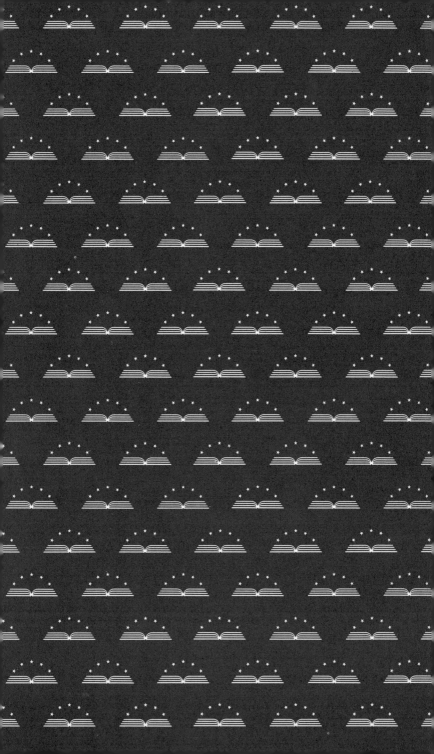